The New Law and Practice
of
Parish Administration

Second Edition

To
the Knowledgeable Amateurs
without whom democracy is
impossible

CA

THE NEW LAW
AND PRACTICE
OF
PARISH
ADMINISTRATION

being a treatise on the civil administration
of parishes in rural districts

by

CHARLES ARNOLD-BAKER, O.B.E.

of the Inner Temple, Barrister-at-Law
Secretary of the National Association of Parish Councils

Second Edition

LONGCROSS PRESS
1970

By the Same Author:
"*The 5000 and the Power Tangle*" (*John Murray*)

Printed in Great Britain at
the St Ann's Press, Park Road, Altrincham

Contents

A*

Appendix

Introduction

The author owes debts of gratitude in many places but especially to Miss Ann Rowen who typed a difficult manuscript with accuracy and speed, and who helped to check it, to Henry Brandon, Esq., M.C., Q.C. (now Sir Henry Brandon), for the use of his library, and to the author's wife who held the ring while the work was being done.

The author acknowledges with thanks the permission granted by the Controller of Her Majesty's Stationery Office to include extracts from statutes and orders and by the Council of the National Association of Parish Councils to include extensive quotations from documents published by the Association. Mistakes and inaccuracies are, of course, the author's.

Preface

This is the second edition of the successor to another book, published in 1958, which is now out of print. Much water from two different streams has flowed under the bridges since then. Some of the law has changed a great deal, and an intervening twelve years of correspondence with parish councils has convinced the author that the contents of a book of this kind should not be exclusively legal.

In any book intended for use by clerks and councillors, the legal subject matter, however arranged, falls into three recognisable heaps: the constitutional, the administrative and the functional. These have all changed somewhat since 1958, but on functions the legal changes have been important and far reaching. But practice has changed as well and parish councils have become more enterprising. It has become necessary to recount not only what they can do but how, very often, they do it. This book therefore represents an attempt to pool experience, and this explains why it is so different from its predecessor.

The Law is stated as at 1st March 1970 but it has been possible to print the text of the Parish Councils and Burial Authorities (Misc. Prov.) Act, 1970.

Anything stated in this book about a parish council should be taken to apply to a rural borough council unless otherwise specified.

History

The origin of most English parishes is the same as that of the manors which commonly formed their nucleus and with which they were often conterminous; in an era when money was seldom used and trade an abnormal activity, when agriculture was primitive, when the countryside was nearly empty of inhabitants and largely virgin, and when no effective central authority existed to enforce daily order, the manor was simultaneously a collective farm, a unit of local administration and police and a defensive organisation. Its inhabitants were the Lord, his retainers, and the free and unfree tenants, and they were bound to each other by a network of obligations and services. Naturally these varied from place to place but the way in which they were regulated was determined by committees or assemblies known as courts and held by the Lord or his steward. The most important of these were the Court Baron for the free tenants and the Court Customary for the unfree. The Lord was under an obligation to hold them regularly and the tenants were bound to attend. Their principal, and in a moneyless society, their all-important business was the management of the land, the rotation of agriculture and the regulation of agricultural jobs.

The commonest agricultural organisation consisted of an open field in which the tenants had their holdings, a waste or common in which each tenant was entitled to certain rights (such as pasture) and a demesne or 'home farm' belonging to the Lord and upon which some tenants were bound to do a certain amount of work in each year. A tenant's holding was not consolidated but was divided into strips scattered about the open field and intermingled with the holdings of the other tenants. After the harvest all the cattle were pastured upon the open field indiscriminately so that the holdings would benefit

equally. Obviously such a system was likely to keep the Courts
Baron and Customary well occupied settling disputes and
services and equally it was a system which required a simple
administrative apparatus and a local criminal jurisdiction for its
enforcement. Since officials could not be paid, officialdom was a
duty rather than a profession: the constable, the hayward, the
pinder and other officials were elected annually and laid down
their offices with a sigh of relief. The criminal jurisdiction was
vested in the Court Leet. Some manors had their own Leets but
in many cases towards the later middle ages a Leet was held for
a group of manors under one lordship. In some manors the
functions of the Courts Leet and Baron were exercised by the
same body.

Sometimes the priest came with the first settlers. More usually
he arrived after the manor was established. Initially he came as
the representative of his bishop and often as a missionary, but he
could not live upon the manor unless he was given a holding and
he could not have a church unless the manor provided the
labour and the materials with which to build it. At the
beginning the Lord was in a strong position and so the right to
appoint the priest often passed into his hands but the priest
nevertheless kept a certain independence because he had the
(sometimes very distant) support of the Church which soon
became more powerful than the greatest noble in the realm.

The Lord's power rested originally on force restrained by
local opinion which hardened first into custom and then into a
local law which the King's new circuit courts would enforce.
A custom is by definition inflexible and immovable but
agriculture moved steadily forward leaving the customs and the
manor courts which enforced them behind. This process was
accelerated by the improvement in communications, by increased trade in manufactured goods, by the circulation of
money and the consequent commutation of labour services for
cash, by evre-increasing external interference in manorial and
parochial affairs, and by the Black Death and the social
upheavals which followed it. When the first Tudor ascended the
throne the manor courts had already ceased to be important
though they survived (mainly for conveyancing purposes) well
into the twentieth century.

As the manor courts declined, the influence, wealth and
responsibility of the Church increased. The chancel of the parish

church was sacred but the body of the building was the parish hall and the only sheltered public meeting place of the inhabitants. The Church as an organisation had recognised rights and also obligations of Christian charity. The parson was paid by means of the tithe, which was a local income tax levied in kind on the produce of land. He combined in his person the offices of schoolmaster, registrar and religious adviser. Attendance at church was normal and enforceable. At Easter everybody went.

It is, therefore, not surprising that the inhabitants began to meet together under the parson's direction for the social and administrative purposes of their religious life. Such meetings were often held in the Vestry after which they came to be named. The old civil obligation of the Lord of the Manor to maintain his starving tenants was matched by the religious obligations of charity. Here again facts outran institutions. The Church and especially the monasteries came to administer the only generally recognised system of unemployment relief and it was the parson's duty to enjoin almsgiving and the succour of the poor upon his flock. Charity, however, remained a virtue and its organisation local. It was essential that the burden should be evenly spread and as early as the fourteenth century attempts were made to make vagrancy a crime. The dissolution of the monasteries and the improvement in communications made the voluntary system unworkable. It was accordingly quite natural for the legislators of 1601 to confer upon the vestries the power of levying a poor rate: in so doing they were merely strengthening machinery which existed already and which was in their mind proper to the relief of poverty and the exercise of charity.

But meetings of inhabitants in an expanding population have an inherent disadvantage; they become unwieldily large and so, especially but by no means exclusively, in urban areas authority tended to slip into the hands of smaller committees called Select Vestries which claimed a separate existence by immemorial custom and which often were self-perpetuating. These bodies could be administratively more efficient than the open vestries and so their number was increased by public and private legislation but in the absence of a powerful and impartial auditing system they became notoriously corrupt. By the Napoleonic Wars this latter characteristic had become important because the vestries were beginning to administer huge sums of money. By 1819 they were levying rates which in the aggregate exceeded £10 millions a year;[1] a reform was demanded and attempted: the Sturges Bourne Act enabled an open vestry by adopting the Act to create an annually elected committee (also called a Select Vestry) to administer poor relief.

Meanwhile the countryside was being transformed by inclosures. The manors had resembled islands of cultivation in a sea of common or unenclosed waste[2] which was subject to public or quasi-public rights; the modernisation of agriculture ended the older collective methods of farming. Private ownership spread across the wastes and the commoners of the manor were compensated for their extinguished rights with smallholdings and allotments for food, fuel, stone and recreation. Such allotments existed mainly for the relief of poverty and it was as natural to place them under the control of the vestry as it had been to enable that same vestry to raise poor rates. The inclosure awards in redistributing property made extensive redistributions of public obligations and usually committed their supervision to the vestries. As a result the awards became, and in many places still are the fundamental documents of parish administration.

Now the vestry was in origin an ecclesiastical institution and depended for its efficacy upon religious unity. The damage done to the reputation of the ancient parochial system by its amateurishness and occasional corruption was completed by the Methodist revival. In hundreds of parishes the representative of the established church had to preside over an assembly composed mainly or wholly of people who were actively hostile to that church. Over extensive areas the church rate ceased to be levied[3] and parish administration was reduced to the barest legal minimum. The critics who prized efficiency above democracy found unexpected allies in the democratic assemblies themselves and the glaring injustices inherent in the working of the Poor Law cried out for reform. From the third decade of the nineteenth century onwards public opinion turned, on the whole, against the parish. The Poor Law Act of 1834 withdrew much of the poor law administraton from the parochial

---

[1] In 1963–64 parish councils precepted for about £2,500,000.

[2] This simile is no mere figure of speech. In some districts lighthouses were erected to guide straying wayfarers.   [3] It was eventually abolished in 1868.

authorities and as new administrative services were created to meet the increasing elaboration of society they were committed as a rule to specialised bodies. The technique of organising these services on a comprehensive basis had not been learned. Local Government, notorious in the 1820s for inefficiency and corruption, became notorious half a century later for inefficiency and complication. The confusion was spectacular[4] and required twenty years of legislation and experiment to straighten out. The present system is based upon that legislation and the coping stone of the new edifice was the Local Government Act, 1894. This took a year to pass and excited much controversy both in Parliament and outside; Gladstone's government had to deal with over eight hundred amendments; it was the proposal to create parish councils which caused the uproar.

In relation to parish affairs the Act of 1894 was based upon two apparently simple principles. Firstly it created institutions having a civil origin, status and affiliations—the *Parish Meeting* and the *Parish Council*. Secondly it transferred the civil functions of the older parish authorities to the new institutions. As a result the church was excluded from formal participation in Local Government and the traditional functions of the parish, which had always had a 'Christian' complexion, were to be administered by laymen. This caused perturbation and acrimony at the time and it was expected that the new parish councils would embark upon a stormy career. Events, however, belied expectations. Parish councils fell rapidly into an undeserved obscurity from which they began to emerge only sixty years later.

In 1894 the squire, the parson and sometimes the schoolmaster were the leaders of the village. Their influence depended upon their traditional prestige, their superior education and their relative wealth, and, in a hierarchical society, upon their social standing. The vestries had followed their lead, taken their advice or bowed to their power. The parish councils were regarded as an intrusion. Most of them began without the co-operation of the influential and had even to face their active opposition. This, in an age when higher education was the privilege of a class, was a serious matter.

But their difficulties had only begun. In the 'seventies agriculture entered upon the long decline which only ended

[4] See Sir Henry Fowler's speech in the House of Commons on the second reading of the Local Government Bill in 1893.

with the Second World War. The squire maintained his state on industrial investments. The revenues of parish councils came mainly from rates on agricultural land. Within eighteen months of their creation agricultural land was derated by 50 per cent. without compensation. Until 1914 parish councils were locally opposed, often derided and poor. Nevertheless Parliament from time to time saw fit to increase their functions and it was in this period that they acquired their modern powers in relation to allotments, postal facilities and open spaces. The inconsistent currents of government policy (of which these early events are examples) are mainly responsible for the peculiar history of twentieth-century parish administration: the tendency (it can scarcely be called a policy) to give new functions to parish councils whilst reducing their financial assets was exaggerated during the period of the wars. Their spending powers, already attenuated by inflation, were again reduced (as usual without compensation) by still further derating and by the new administrative methods introduced for collecting rates from nationalised industries. Twentieth-century financial legislation has mostly been passed without regard to the interests of parish government.

In the meantime their position in English social life had altered. The sons of the Big House went away to the wars and were killed. Taxation uprooted the squires and impoverished the clergy, and educational policy began to drive the schoolmasters away from the villages. On the other hand the general standard both of living and of education rose and the commuter appeared. The old internal quarrels have died a natural death and new problems have had to be faced.

The characteristics of modern government are determined largely by the enormous growth and movement of population and by the nature of the equipment proper to an industrial organisation. Facts have again outrun institutions and the powers which are needed for the administration of the new society have for the most part been conferred upon new *ad hoc* authorities or upon authorities exercising their functions over substantial areas. From a strictly administrative standpoint the parish councils have remained the repositories of powers appropriate to an earlier stage in the development of society. This does not, of course, mean that parish councils are obsolete since these powers are still necessary now, but it does mean that

parish councils, in common with all other types of local
authority, must consider how they as institutions can be squared
with the requirements of the new age.

In local government perhaps the most significant single
modern development is the creation of Local Authority Associations whose principal function is to consider, formulate and
represent policies on national administration from the standpoint of a particular class of authority. These associations are a
characteristically modern reaction to the modern situation;[5]
individuals and individual bodies in the modern mass democracy
have little chance of defending their peculiar interest unless
they combine with others of like mind. It is largely due to the
associations that local government has retained its local
character, and it is largely due to the fact that parish councils
formed their own half a century later than the others that parish
administration is still comparatively primitive. Until an
organisation existed for the purpose it was not possible to
rethink the relationship between the small community and
modern society or to convert into effective action any conclusions which might have been reached. In its annual report
for 1964–1965 the National Association of Parish Councils
published a list of over sixty changes in the law which had been
made through its influence since 1947.

[5] The County Councils Association was formed in 1890
The Association of Municipal Corporations in 1873
The Urban District Councils Association before 1895
The Rural District Councils Association in 1895
The National Association of Parish Councils in 1947

General Description of the System

The Rural Districts of England (other than Scilly) and Wales include about 10,900 *rural parishes* which are independent administrative areas having their own administrative authority and may include a few urban parishes in the form of *rural boroughs*. A rural parish is also a *civil parish* but the latter exists also in urban areas where it has no independent authority of its own; a rural parish may decreasingly be conterminous with an *ecclesiastical parish*.

Rural parishes vary widely in their characteristics. Populations vary from nil to over 34,000 and areas from a few acres to nearly one hundred square miles; their financial resources are equally uneven: a penny rate in Elstree or Fawley produces thousands of pounds but in more than 3,000 parishes it produces less than £50.

Every rural parish must have a parish meeting consisting of all the registered electors of the parish. The number of parish meetings is somewhat less than the number of rural parishes because in a few parishes it is impossible to muster a quorum. In practice many parish meetings seldom meet because of the smallness or scattered nature of the populations[1] whilst in some parishes full meetings are impracticable because no place could be made available to hold all the electors entitled to attend.

Of the 10,900 rural parishes about 7,600 have, in addition to their parish meeting, an elected council called a parish council which is a corporation and whose powers are considerably greater than those of a parish meeting. The number of parish councils is again slightly less than the number of parishes in which the full powers of parish councils are exercised, for parish councils are of three distinguishable types, viz: *separate parish*

[1] For the legal obligation to meet see Chapter 10. The author has encountered a case where there was no meeting for 23 years.

councils each administering a single parish, *group or joint parish councils* each administering more than one parish and *rural district councils having parish council powers* because their district is co-extensive with a single parish. As a class the separate parish councils exceed the rest by a majority of over 100 to 1.

There are believed to be about 65,000 parish councillors, of whom, in 1969, roughly 20 per cent. were women. A large minority of these were members of other councils as well.

The power of creating and dissolving parish councils and groups of parishes is vested in the county council but it is controlled by statute so that in most cases the county council's discretion is limited to matters of detail.

The Local Government Acts make provision for administrative as well as geographical flexibility. County councils may on application confer on a parish meeting (where there is no parish council) any function of a parish council and rural district councils may delegate their powers (except those of raising a loan or levying a rate) either to a parochial committee or directly to a parish council. Applications by parish meetings are not common and delegations of either kind are rare.

Where there is a parish council it is the administrative authority but the giving of certain consents (mainly but not exclusively of a financial nature) is reserved to the parish meeting which alone has the power of adopting the Adoptive Acts. By its influence on finance the parish meeting has a certain measure of control over the parish council but for reasons connected with the size of populations and of penny rate products this control is more stringent in the poorer and less populous parishes than in those with numerous inhabitants and substantial resources.

In a number of parishes there exist some special bodies charged with administering particular parish services. These bodies include committees of parish meetings, burial boards and joint burial boards, and allotment trustees. In all parishes where there is no separate parish council there is a 'representative body' which acts as trustee of the parish property.

The Minister has power to create parish councils or other local authorities in the Isles of Scilly.[2]

[2] L.G.A. 1933 s. 292.

Creation, Alteration and Dissolution of the Parish Organisation

There is, except on review, a clear distinction between the processes which create, alter and extinguish a geographical parish and those which lead to the formation, constitution and dissolution of a parish council, whether it be a separate parish council or a joint parish council for a group of parishes. Orders relating to both classes are (with minor exceptions[1]) made by the county council but whereas orders for the creation and dissolution of parish councils and groups of parishes do not require the intervention or consent of the Minister, orders to alter local government boundaries cannot become effective without his confirmation and (in some cases) without his active intervention in the order making process.

Where a county review is being held the situation is different. The pattern of local government over a large area is under scrutiny by the county council whose conclusions are embodied in a Report to the Minister[2]; the proposals based on these conclusions (with or without amendments) are turned into facts by means of an order which, because of its far-reaching nature is made by the Minister and submitted to Parliament.[2] Such an order can alter the area of a parish, or create or abolish one, or group several parishes under a common parish council.[3]

A. THE DEFINITION OF A PARISH

Originally parishes were ecclesiastical areas coinciding with manors. Neither parishes nor manors covered the whole of the country and because many of them were very large, subdivisions were recognised from the earliest times. It thus

---

[1] See pages 14 and 15.   [2] L.G.A. 1958 s. 29.   [3] ibid., s. 28.

becomes necessary to notice, in addition to the parish, the sub-divisions known as *chapelries* and *townships* as well as the *extra parochial place*. Civil administration made use of the boundaries which the church had drawn[4] but as the population increased or shifted it tended on the one hand to ignore the distinction between parishes and extra parochial places, and on the other to erect into civil parishes areas which from the church's point of view were only sub-divisions. The details of this ancient organisation can still be of great local importance since most inclosure awards and parochial charity deeds were drawn in relation to them.

The Poor Relief Act of 1601 (which is the foundation of modern local authority finance) enjoined the appointment of overseers and the levying of a poor rate in parishes and Foulness only.[5] As the word 'parish' was not defined the Act was extended by judicial interpretation to a few areas which were reputed parishes at the passing of the Act; these were sometimes sub-divisions[6] and sometimes combinations[7] of ecclesiastical areas. In the following sixty years, however, it was realized that the Act was unworkable in the large parishes which were found everywhere but especially in the North of England,[8] and in 1662 it became lawful for such appointments and levies to be made for townships and villages within the parishes.[9] A township was a place for which a constable was appointed;[10] a village was a group of more than two dwelling houses which had a common name by reputation and in which it was inconvenient to execute the Act of 1601 without special provision.[11] The Act of 1662 made possible the creation of a class of civil parish which was visibly distinct from the ecclesiastical parish and which owed its existence solely to administrative convenience; and the process of sub-division which it initiated continued sporadically until

---

[4] Sometimes there was no known boundary and sometimes parishes shared (and still share) lands in common. In undisputed cases the boundaries could, after 1849, be settled by an inclosure award. (Inclosure Act, 1849 s. 1.)

[5] Poor Relief Act, 1601 ss. 1 and 18.   [6] Nicholas v. Walter Cro. Car. 394.

[7] Sharpley v. Mablethorpe 3 E. & B. 906.

[8] The Poor Relief Act, 1662 s. 21 singles out Lancashire, Cheshire, Derbyshire, Yorkshire, Northumberland, the Bishopric of Durham, Cumberland and Westmorland. There were only 70 parishes in Lancashire in 1834. See V. D. Lipman, *Local Government areas 1934–1945*.

[9] Poor Relief Act, 1662 s. 21.

[10] Per Buller J. in R. v. Horton 1 T.R. 374.

[11] R. v. Denham, Burr S.C. 37, and R. v. Leigh 3 T.R. 746.

1844, when new appointments for townships and villages were forbidden.[12] Meanwhile extra-parochial places had been left largely outside the system[13] but after 1857 it became possible either to appoint overseers and levy rates in them separately or to annex them to neighbouring parishes.[14]

It had thus taken over two and a half centuries for the civil parochial system to be extended effectively over the whole country, but the ancient framework of boundaries had (save for the provisions relating to annexation) remained virtually untouched. These boundaries were sometimes inconvenient because the territories of many parishes were intermingled,[15] and so power to make adjustments was given to the proper government department[16] and the appointment of overseers for any new parishes so created was legalised notwithstanding the prohibition of 1844.[17] In 1882 isolated parts of parishes were amalgamated with the parish surrounding them.[18]

Although these powers of boundary reorganisation were created over three-quarters of a century ago and have since devolved upon county councils the responsible authorities have been dilatory in exercising them. A number of intermingled parishes in Northumberland were not abolished until 1955.

In 1889 the word 'parish' in every act passed after 1866 was statutorily defined as 'a place for which a separate poor rate is or can be made or for which a separate overseer is or can be appointed'[19] and this remains the ruling definition even though overseer and poor rate were alike abolished in 1925,[20] for it was then substantially re-enacted subject, however, to any alteration of area made on or after the 1st April, 1927.[21]

---

[12] P.L.A.A. 1844 s. 22.

[13] In 1851 there were 598 of these—Lipman, op. cit.

[14] Extra Parochial Places Act, 1857 ss. I and IV.

[15] In 1873 the number of ancient ecclesiastical parishes divided into two or more parts was 1296, but the number of poor law parishes so divided was far greater—Lipman, op. cit.

[16] P.L.A.A. 1867 s. 2 (Poor Law Board). Divided Parishes and P.L.A.A. 1876 ss. 1 and 2 (Local Government Board).

[17] Divided Parishes and P.L.A.A. 1876 s. 6.

[18] Divided Parishes and P.L.A.A. 1882.

[19] Interpretation Act, 1889 s. 5.

[20] R.V.A. 1925 s. 69(1) and Eighth Schedule.

[21] R.V.A. 1925 s. 68 sub-sections 1 and 4.

B. ALTERATIONS OF PARISH STATUS

Parishes are either urban or rural. A rural parish is an effective unit of local government but an urban parish is not unless it happens to be a rural borough. If an urban parish is transferred to a rural district, it gains rural status unless it is in a rural borough, and conversely, if a rural parish is transferred to an urban area or is erected into an urban district or borough, it loses its rural status. The transfer of a parish from one rural district to another or its conversion into an independent rural district will not affect its status as a rural parish.

It follows that where a boundary between an urban and a rural area is altered so as to enclose within the urban area part of a parish which was hitherto rural, that part ceases to have any connection with the rural parish to which it belonged. On the other hand the division of a rural parish by a boundary between two rural districts, even if that boundary is a county boundary as well, will not automatically sever the parish. In practice such severance is now invariably ordered.

C. ALTERATIONS OF PARISH BOUNDARIES

The extent of a parish may now be altered in any of six different ways of which two are automatic and four administrative. The automatic methods are:—

1. Natural or artificial changes in the coast-line.
2. *Gradual* natural alteration of a river or water course.

The administrative methods are:—

3. Declaration after artificial change of a water course.
4. Adjustment.
5. Proposal.
6. Review.

The last two are the most important.

Effective reviews should eventually make proposals rare, but they were suspended in 1965-66 for the review of local government as a whole set up for Wales by the Welsh Office and for England by the Royal Commission.

Need for Vigilance

The method of bringing ordinary proposals to the notice of a parish affected by them is reasonably efficient, but the provisions relating to notices of the other procedures are, so far as parish councils are concerned, sometimes defective and have created a certain need for vigilance. Early information of intended changes is usually best obtained from the rural district council or through the county association of parish councils.

The Sea Coast

The foreshore to low water mark and all natural and artificial accretions form part of a coastal parish.[22] On the other hand parts of the sea bed may form part of a parish[23] and therefore the extent of a parish is not necessarily diminished by inroads of the sea.

Water Courses

Where a boundary runs along a river or water course, imperceptible natural changes in the position of the bed will produce changes in the boundary[24] even though the position of the old boundary is ascertainable. In the case of a sudden or artificial change, however, the boundary will remain as it was,[25] but if a river or water course is altered under powers conferred by the Land Drainage Act, 1930, the Minister may declare the new course to be the new boundary.[26]

Adjustment

The Minister may, on a joint representation by a county council and the council of a county borough, alter the boundary between them. An adjustment order of this kind must be preceded by a local public inquiry unless the Minister is satisfied that an inquiry is unnecessary.[27]

The general review of county boundaries was carried out by the Local Government Commissions[28] which have since been dissolved. The new inquiries substituted for this type of review were carried out by bodies (The Welsh office and the Royal Commission on Local Government in England) which could only make recommendations requiring legislation to become effective.

[22] L.G.A. 1933 s. 144.
[23] See re Hull and Selby Railway Co. (1839) 5 M. & W. 327.
[24] Brighton and Hove Gas Co. v. Hove Bungalows Ltd. [1924] 1 Ch. 372.
[25] Carlisle Corporation v. Graham (1869) L.R. 4 Exch. 361.
[26] L.G.A. 1933 s. 145.   [27] ibid., s. 143.
[28] See L.G.A. 1958 ss. 17–27. The Welsh Commission's review was abortive.

Proposals on County Boundaries

Where proposals are made for the alteration of the boundaries of a county or county borough, for the union of a county with another county or county borough, or for the inclusion in a borough of a rural district, the Minister (unless for special reasons he thinks that the proposals ought not to be entertained) must hold a public local inquiry and may either refuse to make an order or may make an order giving effect to the proposals with or without alteration. Such an order is subject to special parliamentary procedure.[29]

General and Local Alterations of areas

Different procedures exist for a general reorganisation of the local government areas in a county and for detailed local alterations of areas. These procedures are mutually exclusive, the general reorganisation being achieved by the method (temporarily in cold storage) of *review*, the particular routine alterations by the method of *proposal*. Both involve the holding of local inquiries but whereas the review is a frankly administrative procedure, the routine alterations are effected by means which are of a more judicial character, and include arrangements for a species of appeal.

Proposal

Where a county council considers either on receipt of proposals from a local authority (including a parish meeting where there is no parish council[30]) *or otherwise* that a *prima facie* case exists for altering the status or extent of a rural parish or urban or rural district[31] the county council must hold a public local inquiry. Usually such inquiries are held upon proposals made by local authorities but proposals may equally well be made by other bodies or individuals and an inquiry may be held even though no formal proposal has been made at all.

At least ten days before the inquiry the county council must give notice of its time and place and of the changes for which a *prima facie* case is considered to exist. This notice must be given by advertisement in local newspapers, by exhibition on or near the principal door of the parish church or chapel and, in addition by posting printed copies in conspicuous places in the area affected.[32] Copies must also be sent to the local authorities appearing for the county council to be concerned.[33]

If after holding the inquiry the county council is satisfied that a change is desirable, it makes an order giving effect to the change and submits it to the Minister for confirmation.[34] If, however, it is intended to include in the order a change which was not considered at the inquiry, the county council must for twenty-one days before the order is made make the details of the proposal available for inspection by any elector and must give public notice of the nature of the proposal and of the time and place where the details may be inspected. This notice is given in the same manner as the notice of the inquiry, and similarly particulars of the proposed change must be sent to the local authorities appearing to be concerned.[35]

Having made the order the county council sends copies of it to the Minister and must then publish in the local newspapers (only) a notice that the order has been made, that a copy of it is available for inspection at a specified place in the locality and that petitions with respect to it may be made to the Minister within six weeks of the publication of the notice.[36] If within that period a local authority (including as before a parish meeting) or either one-third or one hundred of the electors of a parish (whichever is the less) petition the Minister to disallow or modify the order, the Minister must cause a further local inquiry to be held before taking any action. The county council or the proposing local authority may also insist upon the holding of such an inquiry if the Minister informs one or other of them that he intends to refuse confirmation of the order.[37] Other authorities and persons have no such right of insistence.

If a county council refuses or neglects to hold an inquiry or to make an order, then if the refusal or neglect relates to a proposal made by a local authority (including as before a parish meeting) the latter may apply to the Minister. After he has given the county council and all other local authorities and persons concerned an opportunity to make representations, he may make

---

[32] L.G.A. 1933 s. 141(2) and L.G. (Alteration of Areas) (Notices) Regs. 1934, S.R. & O. 567 Art. 3.
[33] ibid., Art. 4. [34] L.G.A. 1933 s. 141(3).
[35] L.G.A. 1933 s. 141(3) proviso and S.R. & O. 1934 No. 567 Art. 5.
[36] L.G.A. 1933 s. 141(4). [37] L.G.A. 1933 s. 141(5).

B

any order which the county council could have made.[38] This right of appeal cannot be claimed by other authorities or persons.

The Minister may confirm an order with or without modifications or may refuse to confirm even though no petition has been presented against it, but before making a modification he must give notice to and be ready to hear all local authorities concerned and if no local inquiry has been held, he must hold one if so requested by the county council or the proposing local authority.[39]

Review before 1st August 1966

When a review of county and county borough boundaries had been carried to a point where it is practicable in the case of a particular administrative county for its county council to review the local government areas within the county, the county council was obliged to carry out such a review. This obligation ceased as from 31 August 1966[40] but the following description is relevant to counties which had already presented their report.

The county council had to consult the councils of non-county boroughs and districts and no doubt consulted other bodies concerned. As a result of its investigations it was entitled to propose any alteration in the area or status of any local government unit within its administrative area including the formation and abolition of parishes, the creation of groups of parishes under a common parish council and the reduction of a municipal borough to the status of a rural borough, but not including the creation of an entirely new borough or the reduction, without its own consent, of a borough to the status of a parish.

The report of the review was sent to the Minister and the proposals—which had to be advertised—to the councils of the boroughs and districts. The Minister could give effect to the proposals by order (which needed parliamentary agreement) but if any local authority, including a parish meeting, objected to them he had to hold a public inquiry before making the order. He could vary the county council's proposals but such a variation was subject, similarly, to consultation, advertisement and public inquiry upon objection.

[38] L.G.A. 1933 s. 141(6).   [39] L.G.A. 1933 s. 142(1).
[40] L.G.A. (Termination of Reviews) Act 1967.

D. FORMATION AND DISSOLUTION OF GROUPS

It is possible to alter the area administered by a parish council without altering the status or extent of a parish. This is done by grouping rural parishes together under a joint parish council or by dissolving such a group. Urban and rural parishes cannot, however, be grouped together and rural boroughs are therefore outside the grouping system. The reorganisation of parish government by means of grouping orders has several advantages, for the parishes concerned retain their identity and parish meeting and such orders, if made 'voluntarily' upon the application of the parish meeting do not require the Minister's confirmation. If a parish meeting refuses to apply, a grouping order can only be made as part of a review and with the consent of the Minister.[41]

Voluntary Formation

If a parish meeting applies to the county council for a voluntary grouping order, the county council may, by order, group the parish with a neighbouring parish under a common parish council. The parishes of the group may not, except for special reason, be in different rural districts. No parish can be included in an order against the will of its parish meeting,[42] and the order may provide for the consent of the parish meeting of a parish to be required for any particular act of the parish council in the parish concerned. Small parishes with some special interest to protect are therefore in a strong bargaining position when negotiating for the formation of a group.

In addition the order *must* provide for the naming of the group, for a separate parish meeting for each parish, for the election of separate representatives on the parish council for each parish, for the application of the Local Government Act, 1894, with respect to the appointment of trustees and beneficiaries of parochial charities[43] and for the application of any provisions of the Local Government Act, 1933, with respect to the custody of parish documents so[44] as to preserve the separate rights of each parish.

[41] L.G.A. 1958 s. 28(3)(f).
[42] For notice required see page 89.
[43] Especially s. 14(4), see pages 125–126.
[44] Especially ss. 280(4) and 281–284.

Finally a grouping order may make necessary adaptations of the Local Government Act, 1933, to the group of parishes or to the parish meetings of the parishes in the group.[45]

Dissolution

On application by the council of a group of parishes or by a parish meeting in the group, the county council may by order dissolve the group, and such an order must make necessary provisions for the election of a council or councils for any of the parishes formerly in the group.[45] A group cannot be dissolved compulsorily even on a review.

E. EXISTENCE, CREATION AND DISSOLUTION OF PARISH COUNCILS

Subject to later alterations parish councils which existed immediately before the 1st June, 1934, continue to exist[46] and to administer their parishes as geographically defined on the 17th November, 1933.[47] In addition, if a rural parish has no parish council, the county council must, by order, create one if the population at the last census[48] exceeds 299 or if in the case of a parish with over 199 inhabitants but less than 300 the parish meeting so resolves. Where the population is less than 200, it may create a parish council if the parish meeting requests it.[49]

Where the population is less than 200 the parish meeting[50] may petition the county council for the dissolution of the parish council and thereupon the county council may in its discretion dissolve it by order. If the petition is rejected, no petition for the same purpose may be presented for two years.[51]

F. CONSEQUENTIAL REARRANGEMENTS

Minor Matters

When alterations are made in the parish organisation it is

---

[45] L.G.A. 1933 s. 45.
[47] L.G.A. 1933 s. 1(2)(f).
[49] L.G.A. 1933 s. 43.
[51] L.G.A. 1933 s. 44.

[46] L.G.A. 1933 s. 43(1) and s. 308(1).
[48] L.G.A. 1933 s. 296.
[50] For notice required see page 89.

usually necessary to deal with a number of secondary matters which arise for settlement as a result. These may involve questions of nomenclature,[52] separate representation,[53] trusteeship,[54] and custody of parochial documents.[55] Orders for the creation and dissolution of groups and of parish councils may, in addition, contain such 'incidental, consequential and supplemental provisions' as may appear necessary for bringing them into operation and for giving them full effect.[56] Similar provisions exist in relation to orders involving alterations of boundaries and status.

Property and Liabilities. Agreements

Public bodies[57] affected by an alteration of areas or authorities may make agreements for adjusting any property, income, debts, liabilities and expenses (so far as they are affected by the alteration) of and any financial relations between the parties to the agreement.[58] Such an agreement may provide for the transfer or retention of property debts and liabilities with or without conditions and for the joint use of property, and for the transfer of functions and for the payment by either party in respect of such transfer, retention or joint use or in respect of any remuneration or compensation payable to any person. Such remuneration or compensation may consist of a capital sum or a terminable annuity for a period not exceeding that allowed by the Minister.[59]

Arbitration

In default of agreement all the matters upon which the parties could have agreed may be determined by the award[60] of an arbitrator agreed between them or appointed in the absence of such agreement by the Minister.[60] Such an arbitration must be held in accordance with the Arbitration Act, 1950.[61]

Derivation and Application of payments

A sum payable under an agreement or an award may be paid out of such fund or rate as is therein provided and in default of

---

[52] See page 23.   [53] See page 23. For division into wards see page 21.
[54] See page 125 et seq.   [55] See Chapter 11.   [56] L.G.A. 1933 s. 46.
[57] As defined in L.G.A. 1933 s. 305.   [58] L.G.A. 1933 s. 151(1).
[59] L.G.A. 1933 s. 151(2).   [60] L.G.A. 1933 s. 151(3).
[61] Arbitration Act, 1950 s. 31.

such provision it may be paid out of the general rate fund or from such other fund as the public body shall, with the Minister's approval, determine.[62] For the purpose of adjustments money may be borrowed without the consent of the Minister, but any such loan must be repaid within such period as the parish council shall, with the Minister's consent, determine; other public bodies may borrow under their enabling acts and public bodies without borrowing powers may be empowered to borrow by and in accordance with the order.[63]

Capital money received by way of adjustment must be applied as the Minister approves towards the repayment of debts or for any purpose for which capital may be employed.[64]

Transfer and Compensation of officers

Where an order contains provisions for the transfer of officers and employees they must be so framed as to protect the interests of existing officers[65]; but provision for the payment of compensation for loss caused by termination of office or by reduction of emoluments is regulated by a minister appropriate to the type of officer concerned. If an existing officer resigns within five years after the order because he is required to perform duties which are not analogous to or which are an unreasonable addition to his previous duties, he is deemed to have suffered a loss unless the contrary is shown,[66] and an officer who within the same period is dismissed as redundant (and not for misconduct) is subject to the same rule.[67] A parish council may borrow money in order to raise a lump sum for payment of such compensation.[68]

G. PARISH WARDS

A county council may by order divide a parish into wards for the election of parish councillors and may vary or revoke such an order. These orders can only be made upon application by the parish council or by not less than one-tenth of the electors of the parish; the county council before making the division must be satisfied either that a single election is likely to be impracticable or inconvenient or that certain parts of the parish ought to

---

[62] L.G.A. 1933 s. 151(4).
[64] ibid., s. 151(6).
[66] ibid., s. 150(2).
[68] ibid., s. 150(6).

[63] ibid., s. 151(5).
[65] ibid., s. 150(1).
[67] ibid., s. 150(3).

be separately represented, and special regard must be paid to the latest census population, evidence of population changes since the last census, the area of the parish, the distribution and pursuits of the population as well as all the other circumstances of the case.[69] A rural district ward must coincide with a parish ward or combination of parish wards.[70] In certain circumstances a parish meeting may be held for a ward.[71]

H. CHANGES OF NAME

A county council may at the request of the parish council or of the parish meeting change the name of the parish.[72] The change must be published and must be notified to the Minister, the Home Secretary and the Minister of Agriculture.[73]

Where there is any doubt about the name of a parish, the parish council must use the name which the county council, after consulting the parish meeting, directs.[74]

I. CONSEQUENTIAL TRANSFERS OF STOCK

Change of Name

If the name of a parish council, burial board or representative body is changed, a statutory declaration from the clerk (or chairman of the parish meeting) specifying the stock, and verifying the change of name and the identity of the parish authority, is sufficient authority to any person keeping books in which stock is inscribed to make the necessary alteration.

Change of Ownership

If by virtue of anything done under the Local Government Act, 1933, any other local authority has become entitled to stock standing in the name of a parish authority (or vice versa) a certificate from the clerk of the county council or the scheme, order or award causing the change of ownership is sufficient authority. In other cases a vesting order may be made by the High Court or the Chancery Courts of Durham and Lancaster or by a County Court where those courts respectively have jurisdiction, and the procedure of the Trustee Act, 1925, applies.[75]

---

[69] L.G.A. 1933 s. 52.   [70] L.G. Elections Act, 1956 s. 3.
[71] L.G.A. 1933 s. 78, see also page 83.   [72] L.G.A. 1933 s. 147(4).
[73] L.G.A. 1933 s. 147(5).   [74] L.G.A. 1933 s. 48(2).
[75] L.G.A. 1933 s. 275 and Trustee Act, 1925 ss 51 and 67.

J. RURAL BOROUGHS

Small boroughs may now be included in rural districts[76] and may be given the status of a 'rural borough'. The constitution and powers of their councils are with a few important exceptions to be the same as those of a parish council,[77] and much of this book may be read as applying to rural boroughs equally with parish councils. The exceptions will be noted in their proper places and the following is a brief summary of them.

The corporation retains its charter and therefore its surviving common law powers (which usually relate to such matters as markets and harbours) and its common seal; there is no parish meeting and the powers of the parish meeting are exercised by the Council; the order including the borough in the rural district may vary the application of the rate limits in the borough; the mayor retains his title and may be paid an allowance; the deputy mayor is appointed by the mayor; there are no aldermen; the clerk is styled Town Clerk; and if there is a sheriff or a court of petty or quarter sessions they remain unaffected and continue to function as before.

The charter powers of acquiring land cease but the corporation retains its power of providing a court house and of dealing with its corporate land.

A rural borough may not petition for an amendment to its charter or for a supplementary charter, but if it petitions to surrender its charter the minister may by order convert the borough into a rural parish.

[76] L.G.A. 1958 s. 28(3).
[77] See L.G.A. 1958 7th Schedule.

4

The People of a Parish

A. INHABITANTS AND PARISHIONERS

Inhabitants', 'residents', 'parishioners' and 'the public' figure in many documents such as charitable trust instruments, tithe and inclosure awards, grants and in claims involving proof of customs. The exact meaning of these words has to be established in each case by reference to the facts and law at the time and place to which they relate. The following summary must therefore be read with caution because in any particular case the evidence may establish an interpretation which differs from the normal.

Custom

If a right is given to or an obligation imposed upon all the Queen's subjects, it must be established by authority of the general law. A local custom can therefore never be general and a customary claim in the name of the general public will fail. Similarly a custom must be capable of definition and so the courts will not uphold a claim on behalf of a class whose membership cannot be ascertained.

The Public

Except in relation to highways the words 'the public' or 'the general public' are probably legally meaningless unless it is clear from the circumstances or wording of the document that the inhabitants of a definable locality is meant.

Inhabitants

The right to create corporations is vested in the sovereign

25

B*

(who may delegate it[1]) and to such other persons as Parliament appoints.[2] A crown grant to the inhabitants of a place might therefore be upheld on the ground that the crown had intended the inhabitants to be incorporated for the purposes of the grant, but such a grant by a subject would fail for want of a grantee unless it were charitable. Practical difficulties of this kind are usually overcome by vesting property in trustees or the parish council upon trust for the inhabitants of the parish, and such a trust will not fail for uncertainty because the beneficiaries can at any moment be ascertained.

Residents

The words 'inhabitant' and 'resident' are generally held to mean the same thing. It is not necessary for a person to reside for any particular period in a parish to become an inhabitant[3] nor need the residence be exclusive.[4] The residence ought, however, to be of such a kind that the person in question may fairly be described as having some root or stake in the parish. The court would take into account not only whether he habitually or occasionally sleeps[5] in the parish, but whether his family come there,[6] whether he occupies property there[7] or is employed there and any other matters which may be relevant.

Occupation

Residence is not the same as occupation for a man may occupy a house in which he does not reside.[8]

Parishioners and Burgesses

The word 'parishioners' is of wider import than the word 'inhabitants'[9] and includes people who merely own property in the parish.

The inhabitants of a rural borough are called 'burgesses'.

[1] e.g. to the Bishops of Durham until 1834 within the ancient palatinate of Durham, which included not only the county but the shires of Bedlington, Norham and Islandshire in Northumberland and Craik in Yorkshire.

[2] e.g. county councils can create parish councils.

[3] Though residence for a certain period is in practice necessary in most cases to become an elector.

[4] A.G. v. Coote (1817) 4 Price 183 and Bond v. the Overseers of St Georges, Hanover Square, (1870) L.R. 6 C.P. 312.

[5] R. v. The Mayor of Exeter, Dipstales Case (1868) L.R. 4 Q.B. 114.

[6] Whithorn v. Thomas (1844) 14 L.J.C.P. 38.

[7] Donne v. Martyr (1828) 8 B. & C. 62.

[8] Barlow v. Smith (1892) 9 T.L.R. 57 (D.C.).

[9] A.G. v. Parker (1747) 3 Atk. 576 (the Report is corrupt).

B. THE ELECTORS

In a rural parish every elector may exercise direct authority by speaking and voting at parish meetings.[10] In addition, where it has, or is represented upon, a parish council, he may vote in elections of parish councillors. No one is entitled to exercise either of these rights unless his name appears in the appropriate electoral register[11] currently in force but a properly qualified person has an enforceable right to have his name placed upon the register if it has been omitted therefrom.[12]

The Register

The register must be published annually by 15th February.[13] Every resident in the parish who is a British subject or citizen of the Republic of Ireland and not subject to any legal incapacity to vote[14] is entitled to be registered if he is of voting age or will attain it before the end of the twelve months following that 15th February; but if he is not of voting age on 16th February he cannot vote until he has actually attained that age.[15]

Voting Age

A person now reaches voting age on[16] his 18th[17] birthday.

British Subject

A person has in Great Britain the status of a British subject if he is a citizen of the United Kingdom and Colonies, or if he is a citizen of any other Commonwealth country (whether a Kingdom or a republic),[18] or if he falls within certain special classes of Irishmen for whom it has been necessary to make statutory provision.[19] The most numerous persons falling within these latter classes are persons born anywhere in Ireland before 6th December, 1922, and domiciled in Northern Ireland on that day, and Irish citizens who claim to remain British subjects by reason of service under the Crown or of association with the

[10] L.G.A. 1933 s. 47 and Third Schedule Part VI.
[11] R.P.A. 1949 s. 2 proviso and L.G.A. 1933 ss. 47(1) and 305.
[12] R.P.A. 1949 s. 8.   [13] E.R.A. 1949 and 1953 s. 1(1).
[14] R.P.A. 1949 s. 2(1)(b) and s. 8.   [15] R.P.A. 1969 s. 1(2).
[16] R.P.A. 1969 s. 1 (5).   [17] R.P.A. 1969 s. 1(1)
[18] British Nationality Act, 1948 s. 1 and legislation conferring independence upon various countries.
[19] See British Nationality Act, 1948 s. 2 and Ireland Act, 1949 s. 5.

United Kingdom. Citizenship in the other countries of the Commonwealth is determined by the law of the country concerned.[20, 21]

Lunacy

At Common Law idiots are subject to a permanent legal incapacity to vote[22] but persons of unsound mind may vote during lucid intervals.[23]

Crime

A convict detained in a penal institution in pursuance of his sentence is legally incapable of voting.[24]

Corruption

Incapacity may arise from conviction or report for corrupt or illegal election practices or for corruption of public officials.

If a person is convicted on indictment or by an election court[25] or is reported by an election court[26] for a corrupt practice[27] he becomes incapable for five years of being registered as an elector or voting at any election in Great Britain to any public office. If he is similarly convicted or reported for any illegal practice[27] he suffers during five years from a similar incapacity in respect only of any area which coincides with or partly overlaps or is contained in the area in respect of which the offence was committed.[28]

A person who is convicted for the second time of bribery or corruption of or by members, officers or servants of corporations, boards, commissions or other public bodies may, at the court's discretion, be adjudged incapable of being registered as an elector or voting for five years.[29]

The electoral registration officer must annually publish a list of those who, though otherwise qualified, suffer from a legal

[20] British Nationality Act, 1948 s. 1.
[21] The details of this subject are beyond the scope of this work. The purpose of these paragraphs on nationality is to indicate that the subject is full of pitfalls.
[22] Burgess' Case (1785) 2 Lud. E.C.   [23] Robin's Case (1791) 1 Fras.
[24] R.P.A. 1969 s. 4.   [25] R.P.A. 1949 s. 151.
[26] R.P.A. 1949 s. 140(3).
[27] For corrupt and illegal election practices see pages 39–40.
[28] R.P.A. 1949 s. 140(4).
[29] Public Bodies (Corrupt Practices Act, 1889, s. 2, as amended by R.P.A. 1948 s. 52(7).

incapacity to vote by reason of a conviction or report for a corrupt or illegal practice. This list must specify the offence for which each person in it was convicted.[39]

Residence

There is no qualifying period to establish residence and an elector may have more than one residence.[31]

Non-resident Qualification

The non-resident qualification for voting is abolished as from 15th February 1970 in respect of elections held after that date.[32]

Proxies

Postal voting is not allowed, and though the law permits arrangements for voting by proxy[33] no such arrangements have in fact been made. A proxy would have to be of voting age, not subject to any legal incapacity, to vote at the election in question and either a British subject or a citizen of the Republic of Ireland.[34]

---

[30] R.P.A. 1949 s. 40.
[31] See R. v. Mayor of Exeter (1868) 4 Q.B. 110 per Blackburn J.
[32] R.P.A. 1969 ss. 15 and 27.
[33] R.P.A. 1949 s. 23.   [34] R.P.A. 1949 s. 25(3).

5

The Parish Council and its Members

A. THE NATURE OF A PARISH COUNCIL

A parish council is a body corporate with perpetual succession, a name, and authority to hold land for the purposes of its constitution.[1] It is composed of a chairman and parish councillors.[2] The number of councillors is fixed by the county council but must be not less than five nor more than twenty-one.[3] One of the councillors may be elected vice-chairman by the council.[4]

In a rural borough the chairman is called the mayor and the deputy mayor, if any, is appointed by him.[5]

As a body corporate the parish council is a person[6] and is distinct from its members (either as individuals or collectively) for the time being.[7] Its lawful acts, assets and liabilities are its own and not those of its members. A newly created parish council comes into existence on the day named in the order which establishes it; it is immaterial that its members are not elected until some later day,[8] and therefore a gift of property to it made after its establishment will not be void for want of a grantee if made before the first election. Similarly it remains in uninterrupted existence from the moment of its creation until its lawful dissolution, even if all its members vacate office, or if its membership falls so low that it is unable to act for want of a quorum.

---

[1] L.G.A. 1933 s. 48(2).   [2] L.G.A. 1933 s. 48(1).
[3] L.G.A. 1933 s. 50(1) as amended by P.C.A. 1957 s. 12.
[4] L.G.A. 1933 s. 49(5).   [5] L.G.A. 1958 7th Schedule para. 5.
[6] Interpretation Act, 1889, s. 19.
[7] Society for the Illustration of Practical Knowledge v. Abbott and others (1840), 2 Beav. 559.
[8] The case of Sutton's Hospital (1612) 10 Co. Rep. la at 31a.

Where a parish council becomes unable to act the county council may by order authorise a person to act temporarily in the place of the parish council or of its chairman.[9] The exact status of such a person is not clear; he is probably a separate official body existing side by side with the dormant parish council but able to exercise its powers and deal with its property.[10]

B. ELIGIBILITY FOR OFFICE

Roughly speaking electors over 21 years of age may become members of parish councils, but certain additional qualifications and disqualifications have the effect of extending this class of eligible persons in one direction whilst restricting it in another.

Qualifications

Subject therefore to the rules on disqualification[11] a person is qualified if he is a British subject,[12] is over 21, and is an elector.[13] In addition a British subject will be qualified if he has either during the whole of the twelve months before the day on which he is nominated as a candidate or since the 25th March in the year before the year of the election resided in the parish or within three miles of it.[13]

One effect of these rules is that it is possible to be a member of more than one parish council.

The non-resident qualification for voting as an elector and the property qualification for membership of a parish council are abolished as from 15th February 1970 but any sitting member of a parish council qualified to be a member by reason only of the non-resident electors qualification or the property qualification may continue in office until the end of his current term.[14]

Six Disqualifications

A person may be disqualified from being elected or being a member in six ways.

[9] L.G.A. 1933 s. 55(2).
[10] Compare the wording of L.G.A. 1933 s. 55(2) with that of the analogous enactment relating to district councils in s. 72(3). The point does not appear to have been judicially considered.
[11] See below.
[12] L.G.A. 1933 s. 57. Note Irish citizens may vote but not take office.
[13] L.G.A. 1933 s. 57.
[14] R.P.A. 1967 s. 15 proviso and s. 27.

A disqualification arises if he holds a *paid office or other place of profit* in the gift or disposal of the council or any committee thereof;[15] an office includes any employment as a servant of the council[16] and in the case of an office of profit it is immaterial that no profits were actually received;[17] where a paid officer is employed under the direction of a committee any of whose members are appointed by some other local authority, the disqualification extends to the other authority as well;[18] an appointment which can be vetoed by some other body or person does not seem to be caught by this rule.

Bankruptcy is a disqualification which dates from the day of the judgment and ceases on the day of annulment if the bankruptcy is annulled because the bankrupt should not have been so adjudged or because his debts have been paid in full; it ceases also on the day of discharge if the discharge is given with a certificate that the bankruptcy was caused by misfortune without any misconduct. In any other case it ceases on the expiration of five years from the date of discharge.[19]

A person is disqualified if he makes a *composition or arrangement* with his creditors. This disqualification ceases when he pays his debts in full or on the expiration of five years from the date on which the terms of the deed of composition or arrangement are fulfilled.[20]

A person is disqualified if he has within five years before the election or since the election been *surcharged for more than £500* by a district auditor.[21] This disqualification is not restricted to the behaviour of the person in relation to the parish council for which he is standing or of which he is a member, but relates to any body whose accounts are subject to district audit.

The disqualification begins when the six weeks usually allowed for an appeal[22] or application for relief[23] has expired.[24] If, however, the aggrieved person avails himself of either or both of these rights, the disqualification will begin when the appeal or application is finally dismissed or abandoned or fails for want of prosecution.[25]

The disqualification does not take effect if the auditor's

---

[15] L.G.A. 1933 s. 59(1).
[16] See L.G.A. 1933 s. 305. [17] Delane v. Hillcoat (1829) 9 B & C. 310.
[18] L.G.A. 1933 s. 59(2). [19] L.G.A. 1933 s. 59(1).
[20] L.G.A. 1933 s. 59(1)(d). [21] Under L.G.A. 1933 s. 229.
[22] Under L.G.A. 1933 s. 230. [23] See pages 185–7.
[24] L.G.A. 1933 s. 59(1) proviso (v). [25] L.G.A. 1933 s. 229(2).

decision is quashed nor if it is varied so as to reduce the amount of the surcharge to £500 or less,[26] nor if on an application for relief, a declaration is made that the aggrieved person acted reasonably or in the belief that his action was lawful.[26]

A person is disqualified if he has within five years before the election or since his election been *convicted* in the United Kingdom, the Channel Islands or the Isle of Man of any offence and ordered to be imprisoned for not less than three months without the option of a fine.[27] Imprisonment includes preventive detention and probably also corrective training[28] and detention in a detention centre.[29] As in the case of disqualification by surcharge this disqualification begins when the ordinary period for making an appeal has expired or when the appeal is finally dismissed or abandoned or fails for want of prosecution.[30]

If the convict receives a free pardon, the disqualification ceases because the conviction upon which it depends is thereby expunged.[31]

Finally a person may be disqualified under any enactment relating to *corrupt or illegal practices*.[32] The name of any such person will be found in a special list which must be published with the electoral register.[33]

C. HOW TO ATTAIN OFFICE

A suitably qualified person may become a member of a parish council in seven different ways. These are:—

(1) Ordinary election.

(2) Bye-election.

(3) Return after a successful election petition.

(4) 'Constructive election'.

(5) Appointment by the county council.

(6) Co-option to a casual vacancy.

(7) Co-option as chairman.

---

[26] L.G.A. 1933 s. 230(2).
[27] L.G.A. 1933 s. 59(1)(c).   [28] See page 28, note 29.
[29] See C.J.A. 1948 s. 18.   [30] L.G.A. 1933 s. 59(1).
[31] See Hay v. Justices of the Tower of London Division (1890) 24 Q.B.D. 561 and the authorities quoted therein.
[32] L.G.A. 1933 s. 59(1)(f). See pages 39–40.   [33] See page 29.

In addition the county council under its 'reserve powers' may

(8) Appoint a person to act temporarily in the place of the parish council.

(9) Appoint a person to act temporarily in place of the chairman.

1. Ordinary Election

Date

Ordinary elections coincide with the election year of the rural district councillor representing the parish and must be held on the same day.[34] The interval between elections is ordinarily three years but in a few cases it may transitionally be extended to four or five years on occasions when a rural district council obtains a change in its method of election,[35] or reduced to two or even one if the county council is satisfied that it is not reasonably practicable on such an occasion to achieve its object by any other means.[36]

The election day must fall in the week beginning with the Sunday before 9th May or if the 9th May is a Sunday then the week beginning on that day, but if this week happens to be immediately before Whit Sunday, the week ending the Thursday before Whitsun must be substituted. Within these limits the county council may fix the day but must do so not later than the end of February, failing which the election must be held on the Tuesday.[37]

Election Rules

The election is conducted in accordance with the Representation of the People Act, 1949, and rules[38] made by the Home Secretary under it. These rules must provide for the appointment of a returning officer and for fixing or enabling the county council to fix the hours of poll.[39]

Officials

The returning officer is the clerk of the rural district council

[34] L.G. Elections Act, 1956 s. 1.   [35] See L.G.A. 1933 s. 35A.
[36] L.G. Elections Act, 1956 Second Schedule para. 5.
[37] R.P.A. 1948 s. 57.
[38] The following sections are a summary of the main points. For details the reader should refer to the rules themselves. They now provide for forms in Welsh for use in Wales and Monmouthshire.
[39] R.P.A. 1949 s. 29(1).

or if his office is vacant or he is unable to act, then some person appointed by the chairman of the rural district council.

The returning officer may appoint deputies who may act as returning officers within the parish to which they are appointed. He must also appoint and may pay a presiding officer for each polling station: it is convenient for one presiding officer in each parish to be appointed deputy returning officer so that the results of the poll may be declared quickly. The returning officer must also appoint and may pay such clerks as may be necessary at each polling station but must not appoint anyone employed by or on behalf of a candidate in connection with the election.

Time

Proceedings during the twenty-two days before the election must be conducted in accordance with a set time-table, and in computing the correct number of days Sundays, Christmas Day, Good Friday, any Bank Holiday, the Saturday before and the Tuesday after Easter and Whitsun and any day of public Thanksgiving or Mourning must be disregarded.

The hours of poll commence at the time fixed by the county council or if not so fixed, at noon. They end at 8 p.m. but may be extended to 9 p.m. if demanded in writing by at least as many candidates as there are vacancies.

The returning officer must give notice of the election in a prescribed form and publish it in the same manner as notices of parish council meetings are published.[40]

Nomination

Each candidate must be nominated on a separate nomination paper stating his full names, place of residence and description, but a misnomer or inaccurate description does not invalidate the paper in any case where the description is such as to be commonly understood.[41] The returning officer must supply nomination papers and prepare them for signature on request. Each nomination paper must be signed by a proposer and seconder ('subscribers') who must be electors for the area (i.e. parish or ward) for which the candidate is nominated. A nomination is void unless the candidate consents in writing,

[40] See page 48.   [41] R.P.A. 1949 s. 39(5).

which must be attested by a witness and must contain a statement that the candidate is qualified and the particulars of the qualification.

Nomination papers must be delivered at the place fixed by the returning officer. It is desirable that this place should be easily accessible to the electors, but it need not be in the parish.

Adjudication

As soon as practicable after the latest time for delivery of nomination papers the returning officer must adjudicate upon them. He may hold them invalid only on the ground that the particulars of the candidate or subscribers are not as required by law or that the paper is not properly signed. His decision on these points is final. It is therefore desirable in any doubtful case for him to be required to prepare the papers for signature himself.

Publication of Names

Having adjudicated, the returning officer must publish a list of candidates standing nominated and of persons who were nominated but who no longer stand nominated.

Withdrawal

A candidate may withdraw by notice in writing attested by one witness. If a candidate is validly nominated for more than one ward he must duly withdraw from all those wards except one; if he does not do so, he is deemed to have withdrawn altogether.

Method of Election

If the number of candidates remaining validly nominated after any withdrawals is equal to or less than the number of vacancies the returning officer must, not later than 11 o'clock on the day of the election, declare them elected.

If the number exceeds the number of vacancies, a poll must be held by the method of secret ballot. The rules contain lengthy provisions for the conduct of contested elections including provisions for the use of schools, notices of poll, proxies, appointment by candidates of polling and counting agents, challenge of voters, and counting and recounting of votes.

If there is a tie and an additional vote is needed to enable one or more candidates to be declared elected, the returning officer must decide between them by lot.[42]

Agents

A candidate at a parish council election may, but need not, appoint an election agent.[43]

Expenses

A candidate's expenditure is limited to £30 plus 1s. 0d. for every six entries in the electoral register and for any less number of entries above a multiple of six,[44] but in the case of a joint candidature the total figure is reduced by one-fourth each and if more than two candidates stand jointly, by one-third each.[45] Persons are deemed to be joint candidates where they appoint the same election agent, or employ the same polling agents, clerks or messengers, or use the same committee rooms or publish a joint address or circular.[46]

Claims for election expenses are barred *and may not be paid* if not made to the candidate (or his election agent) within fourteen days of the election; claims lawfully made must be paid within twenty-one days of the election[47] but both these time limits may in particular cases be extended by an order of the High Court, or an Election Court or the County Court.[48]

Within twenty-eight days of the election the candidate must send a declaration of his expenses supported by all the bills and receipts to the returning officer,[49] who must preserve them for a year and make them available for inspection by any person on payment of a fee of 1s. 0d.[50] A candidate is liable to a fine of £50 for every day on which he sits or votes as a member of the parish council without having made this declaration.

Use of Premises

A candidate may at all reasonable times and on reasonable notice use free of charge any suitable room in a county or voluntary school in the parish[51], but schools in any way maintained by

---

[42] Parish Council Election Rules 1952 Art. 44.   [43] R.P.A. 1949 s. 59.
[44] R.P.A. 1969 s. 8.   [45] R.P.A. 1949 s. 65(1).
[46] R.P.A. 1949 s. 65(2).   [47] R.P.A. 1949 s. 78 and Sixth Schedule Art. 1.
[48] R.P.A. 1949 s. 78 and Sixth Schedule Art. 6.
[49] R.P.A. 1949 s. 78 and Sixth Schedule Art. 3 amended by S.I. 1952 No. 368.
[50] R.P.A. 1949 s. 78 and Sixth Schedule Art. 8.
[51] R.P.A. 1949 s. 83.

a local education authority or aided from public funds may not be used as committee rooms[52] and neither may licensed premises, refreshment houses or clubs, other than permanent political clubs, where intoxicating liquor is sold to members.[53]

Election Offences

Election offences are classified into corrupt practices and illegal practices. The law regards corrupt practice as more serious than illegal practice,[54] but there is, in addition, an important difference in the nature of the two types of offences, for a person cannot be convicted of a corrupt practice unless he is proved to have had a corrupt intention when he committed the act for which he is prosecuted, whereas illegal practices are peremptorily forbidden and intention is consequently irrelevant.

The following are *corrupt* practices:—[55]

Treating.[56]

Undue influence.[57]

Bribery.[58]

Personation.[59]

False declaration of election expenses.[60]

Incurring or aiding and abetting the incurring of certain election expenses without written authority from an election agent.[61]

The following are *illegal* practices:—[62]

Illegal Payments:[63] that is payments for the conveyance of electors to the poll,[64] and payments to an elector for exhibiting bills and notices.[65] Corruptly inducing a candidate to withdraw in consideration of payment or withdrawnig in pursuance of such an inducement is also deemed an illegal payment.[66]

Providing money or knowingly allowing money to be provided for making illegal payments.[67]

---

[52] R.P.A. 1949 s. 93(3)(a). [53] R.P.A. 1949 s. 92(2).
[54] See pages 28–9 for the civil consequences. Offenders may in addition be fined or imprisoned or both.
[55] See page 28. [56] R.P.A. 1949 s. 100.
[57] ibid., s. 101. [58] ibid., s. 99.
[59] jbid., s. 28. [60] ibid., s. 70(4) and s. 63(5).
[61] ibid., s. 63. [62] See page 28-9.
[63] ibid., s. 97.(1) [64] ibid., s. 89(3).
[65] R.P.A. 1949 s. 94. [66] ibid., s. 92.
[67] ibid., s. 98 and 153.

Illegal Employment: that is employing paid canvassers.[68]

Illegal Hiring (by candidates or agents) of conveyances for electors,[69] or of prohibited premises[70] such as licensed premises.[71]

Improper Conduct: that is the publication of false statements about the character or conduct of a candidate, or concerning the withdrawal of a candidate.[72]

Illegal Broadcasting.[72A]

2. Bye-Elections

Bye-elections are exceedingly rare but can occur in any one of four different circumstances.

A bye-election of the *whole council* can occur when a parish council comes into existence in some year other than the year in which the rural district councillor for the parish is elected, and when an entire election is declared void on the trial of an election petition and lastly when a new election is ordered by the county council under its 'reserve power' as a result of a parish council becoming unable to act.[73]

A bye-election to a *particular vacancy* can only occur where the membership of a parish council has been increased[74] during the term of office of the existing members. The vacancies in such newly created offices are not 'casual'[75] and must therefore be filled in any of the ways in which vacancies are filled at or immediately after the ordinary elections.

Bye-elections are conducted in the same way as ordinary elections.

3. Constructive Election

If no candidates are validly nominated at an ordinary or bye-election or if their number is less than the number of vacancies, the resulting gaps must be filled by retiring councillors. In selecting who is to fill the vacancies the following rule must be observed:—

If there was a poll at the last ordinary election the vacancies

---

[68] ibid., s. 96 and 153.   [69] ibid., s. 89 and 153.
[70] ibid., s. 93 and 153.   [71] See page 47.
[72] R.P.A. 1949 s. 91.   [72A] R.P.A 1969 s. 9.   [73] L.G.A. 1933 s. 55.
[74] For the county council's power to regulate the size of membership see page 31.
[75] See page 42 and L.G.A. 1933 ss. 65–68. The phrase 'casual vacancy' though not explicitly defined is implicitly defined by enumeration so as to exclude newly created offices.

must be filled by the councillors who received the highest vote at that poll, but if the poll was equal or if there was no poll, the vacancies must be filled by lot.[76]

If there are no retiring councillors available it may be necessary to resort to the county council's reserve powers. In such a case a bye-election can be ordered[77] or appointments made.

If, as occasionally happens, a retiring councillor is unwilling to be dragged back to office, he should refuse to execute his declaration of acceptance of office[78] and thereupon a casual vacancy arises which may be filled by co-option.[79]

4. Appointment

If at any ordinary or bye-election the real and constructive methods fail to fill the required number of vacancies, the county council must as a last resort fill the remainder by appointment.[80] The duly elected councillors have no power to fill these vacancies by co-option not only because the vacancies are not casual but because the parish council is not properly constituted and can do nothing until it is.

The procedure by appointment may with the co-operation of the county council be assimilated to the procedures of co-option or election (as the case may be). Thus where a small number of vacancies only remain to be filled the regularly elected councillors may apply for the appointment of a named individual on the ground that they would co-opt him if they could; and where all or a majority of vacancies need to be filled, a similar request could be forwarded by the parish meeting.

5. Return after a Successful Election Petition

An election court may either declare a particular place vacant (in which case a casual vacancy occurs)[81] or it may scrutinize the votes given and strike off any which ought not to be counted. A vote is struck off where the voter has been personated or treated or bribed or unduly influenced. Where votes have been given for a candidate who is disqualified they will be struck off if the voters knew or can be or ought to be presumed to have known of the disqualification.

[76] Parish Council Election Rules 1952 Art. 13.   [77] See page 45.
[78] See page 43.   [79] See page 42.
[80] L.G.A. 1933 s. 55.   [81] L.G.A. 1933 s. 65(e).

When the scrutiny is complete the court may declare which of the candidates has been elected.

6. Co-option to a Casual Vacancy

A casual vacancy is filled by co-option.[82]

A casual vacancy is deemed to have occurred when a parish councillor fails to make his declaration of acceptance of office within the proper time; or when his notice of resignation is received; or on the day of his death; or in the case of a disqualification by surcharge or conviction on the day when either the time for appeal or application for relief expires, or such appeal or application is dismissed or abandoned; or in the case of an election being declared void upon the date of the report or certificate of the election court; or where a person ceases to be qualified, or becomes disqualified for any reason other than a surcharge or conviction, or is persistently absent from meetings[83] upon the date when his office is declared vacant by the High Court or parish council as the case may be.[84]

Procedure

Except where the vacancy arises from *the three cases* namely failure to accept office, resignation, or death an interval of days must elapse. The office must be declared vacant by an authority competent to make such a declaration or its equivalent; for instance the High Court may do so in appropriate cases (for instance on conviction) and a surcharge for more than £500 is equivalent to a declaration. There remain, however, a large residue of cases where the parish council must make the declaration itself; these occur where a member of a parish council ceases to be qualified or becomes disqualified for any reason other than a conviction, surcharge or breach of an enactment relating to corrupt or illegal election practices or where he ceases to be a member through persistent absence.[85]

The parish council must make the declaration within a reasonable time after the occurrence of the vacancy and must signify the vacancy by a public notice signed by the clerk.[85]

After the vacancy has (by whatever means) been declared,

---

[82] L.G.A. 1933 s. 67(6).   [83] See page 52.
[84] L.G.A. 1933 s. 65.   [85] See page 52 and L.G.A. 1933 s. 64.

the parish council must be convened within a reasonable time and the vacancy must then be filled.[86]

On the other hand in the three cases mentioned a vacancy may be filled at once without special notice.

Voting on Casual Vacancies

A successful candidate must have received an absolute majority vote of those present and voting.[87] It follows that if there are more than two candidates for one vacancy and no one of them at the first count receives a majority over the aggregate votes given to the rest, steps must be taken to strike off the candidate with the least number of votes and the remainder must then be put to the vote again; this process must, if necessary, be repeated until an absolute majority is obtained.

If there is more than one vacancy and the number of candidates equals the number of vacancies, all the vacancies may be filled by a single composite resolution, but if the number of candidates exceeds the number of vacancies, each vacancy must be filled by a separate vote or series of votes.

The parish council is not obliged to consider the claims of candidates who were unsuccessful at a previous election.

As in all other matters voting must be by show of hands.[88]

7. Co-option as Chairman

A parish council may co-opt a person who is not a parish councillor as chairman provided that he is qualified to be a parish councillor.[89] This is often done.

D. DECLARATION OF ACCEPTANCE OF OFFICE

The chairman and councillors may not (save for the purpose of taking declarations) act until each has executed a declaration of acceptance of office in a prescribed form.[90] The vice-chairman (if any) is not required by statute to make such a declaration.

The chairman must make his declaration at the meeting at

---

[86] L.G.A. 1933 s. 67(6).
[87] L.G.A. 1933 Third Schedule Part V para. 1(1).
[88] L.G.A. 1933 Third Schedule Part IV para. 5.
[89] L.G.A. 1933 s. 49(1).   [90] L.G.A. 1933 s. 61.

which he is elected and each councillor must make his declaration at the first meeting after he is elected unless in either case the council *at that meeting* permits the declaration to be made at a later meeting fixed by the council.[90] The declaration must be made in the presence of a member of the council and delivered to the council.[90]

If, therefore, a council meeting occurs between the ordinary elections and the 20th May, the declarations of the newly elected councillors must be made at that meeting in the presence of a member of the outgoing council. If, on the other hand, the first meeting occurs after the 20th May, the new councillors may execute their declarations in each other's presence.

Since the term of office of outgoing members is brought to an end by statute re-elected councillors must execute new declarations as well as the others.

If the declaration is not executed at the proper time, a casual vacancy automatically arises,[91] but the council may then lawfully co-opt the person whose failure to execute the declaration caused the vacancy, unless for any lawful reason, he is prevented from holding office.

E. TERM OF OFFICE

Councillors

Apart from the chairman and vice-chairman, parish councillors retire together on the 20th May[92] in the year when the rural district councillor representing their parish is to be elected;[93] therefore, the ordinary term of office of an elected parish councillor will be three years; but occasionally there may be exceptions of two kinds. Where a parish bye-election has to be held[94] the term of office of the bye-elected parish councillors will be shortened by the period which has elapsed since the rural district councillor was elected, and where a rural district council changes its method of election, the term of office of the parish councillors in some of the parishes in the rural district will usually be extended to four or a maximum of five years;[95]

---

[90] L.G.A. 1933 s. 61.   [91] L.G.A. 1933 s. 65(a).
[92] L.G.A. 1933 s. 50(2) amended by R.P.A. 1948 s. 57 and Sixth Schedule para. 3.
[93] L.G. Elections Act, 1956 s. 1.   [94] See page 40.

or where no other course is reasonably practicable the term of office may be reduced.[95]

Co-opted and appointed parish councillors hold office until the end of the current term of office of the other parish councillors.[96]

Chairman

The chairman is elected annually at the annual meeting where his election must be the first business, and he holds office (unless he resigns or is persistently absent or ceases to be qualified or becomes disqualified) until his successor is elected;[97] his term of office is not affected by the time limit on the term of office of parish councillors even where there has been a supervening election in which he, as a candidate, has failed to secure re-election.[98, 99]

Vice-Chairman

The vice-chairman may be appointed at any time and holds office until immediately after the appointment of the *chairman* at the next annual meeting.[100]

F. THE 'RESERVE POWER' OF THE COUNTY COUNCIL

A county council has far-reaching powers designed to prevent such breakdowns in parish administration as may result from a parish council being improperly constituted in the first instance or from its becoming unable to act at a later stage.

Firstly if any difficulty arises with respect to any election or to the first meeting after an ordinary election or if for any reason a parish council is not properly constituted, the county council may make such appointment or do anything necessary or expedient for the proper holding of the election or meeting and properly constituting the council, and it may also direct and fix the dates for the holding of such an election or meeting.[101] An application under this power can be made, for instance, for the appointment of a councillor where the ordinary machinery

[95] L.G. Elections Act, 1956. Second Schedule Part II Art. 5.
[96] L.G.A. 1933 s. 68.   [97] L.G.A. 1933 s. 49.
[98] L.G.A. 1933 s. 49(4).   [99] R. v. Jackson *ex parte* Pick 1913 3 K.B. 436.
[100] L.G.A. 1933 s. 49(6).   [101] L.G.A. 1933 s. 55(1).

for election has failed, or for leave to hold a first meeting out of time.

Secondly where a parish council becomes unable to act (whether from failure to elect or otherwise) the county council may order a new election and may authorise any person to act temporarily in the place of the parish council and its chairman.[102] This would include a single person or the remaining members of a council which has lost its quorum.[103]

In making orders of this kind the county council may modify the provisions of the Local Government Act, 1933, so far as may appear necessary for carrying the order into effect.[104]

[102] L.G.A. 1933 s. 55(2).
[103] Interpretation Act, 1889 s. 19.
[104] L.G.A. 1933 s. 55(3) amended by R.P.A. 1949.

6

Meetings and Procedure of a Parish Council

A. NUMBER, DATE AND TIME

A parish council must meet annually on 20th May or within fourteen days thereafter,[1] but if the last day of the period is a Sunday or Bank Holiday or day of public Thanksgiving or Mourning, the period is extended to include the next ordinary day.[2] Meetings may lawfully be held on such days.

In addition a parish council must meet on at least three other occasions during the year[3] (even if there is no business to transact) and may hold as many further meetings as it pleases. Such meetings may be held by virtue of a standing order, or they may be specially convened.

A parish council may meet at any time of day.

B. PLACE OF MEETING

Meetings may not take place in licensed premises unless no other room is available free of charge or at reasonable cost.[3] This prohibition extends not only to public houses but to hotels, breweries, licensed restaurants and licensed groceries.

If the parish council owns a suitable room in the parish which it can use free of charge, meetings must be held there; if not then at all reasonable times and after reasonable notice, the parish council may use free of charge a room in a 'public elementary school' or any room *maintainable out of any rate*, but a

---

[1] L.G.A. 1933 Third Schedule Part IV para. 1(2) Amended by R.P.A. 1948.   [2] L.G.A. 1933 s. 295.
[3] L.G.A. 1933, Third Schedule Part IV para. 1.

room in a dwelling house cannot be required for the purpose nor may a meeting be held so as to interfere with the hours in which a room is needed for education, justice or police.[4]

Before 1894 the vestry was entitled to meet in the church or vestry as the case might be unless an order had been made applying the Vestries Act, 1850, to the parish. Parish councils (or where there is no parish council the parish meeting) inherited the rights of their respective vestries as they stood in 1894.[5]

C. RIGHT TO CONVENE

The chairman may convene a meeting of the parish council at any time,[6] and unless the parish council, by standing order, otherwise directs, the vice-chairman may do so in the absence of the chairman.[7] In addition if two members sign a requisition that the council be convened and the chairman (or vice-chairman as the case may be) either refuses or neglects to convene a meeting for seven days, then any two members may convene a meeting.[6] The two convening members need not be the same as the requisitioning members.

Where a casual vacancy occurs in the office of chairman the clerk may, on his own authority, convene a meeting to fill the vacancy.[8] Strictly speaking, this is the only occasion when the clerk may convene a meeting, but in practice most meetings are convened by him either on instructions from the chairman as the occasion arises, or by virtue of a standing order. There does not appear to be any good reason for departing from these practices.[9]

D. PUBLIC NOTICES AND AGENDA

Notice

At least three clear days (not including the days of issue and meeting[10]) before a meeting of the parish council a notice of the

---

[4] L.G.A. 1933 s. 128.
[5] See Vestries Act, 1850 s. 2, **L.G.A.** 1888 s. 100, **L.G.A.** 1894 ss. 6(1), 19, and 75(1).
[6] L.G.A. 1933 Third Schedule Part IV para. 2.
[7] L.G.A. 1933 s. 49(7).   [8] L.G.A. 1933 s. 66(2).
[9] For the evidential effect of signed minutes in this context see page 62.
[10] Liffin v. Pitcher (1842) 1 Dowl. NS. 767.

time and place of the meeting must be affixed in some conspicuous place in the parish.[11] If the meeting is called by members of the council, they must sign it and it must specify the business to be transacted at the meeting;[12] if the business includes a statutory resolution under the Local Government Superannuation Acts the terms of the resolution and the fact that it will be moved must be set out in the notice, which must be exhibited *twenty-eight* clear days before the meeting.[13]

Agenda

A similar period before the meeting a summons signed by the clerk must be left at or sent by post to the usual residence of every member of the council[14] (including the retiring chairman and vice-chairman after an ordinary election even if they have failed to secure re-election). This summons must specify the business which it is proposed to transact[14] in such a way that the member who receives it can identify the matters which he will be expected to discuss. A parish council cannot lawfully decide any matter which is not specified in the summons.[15]

It is a common practice for the agenda to conclude with the item 'Any Other Business'. Since this conceals rather than specifies the business, if any, to which it relates no decisions may lawfully be made on business brought up for discussion under it unless the council has at a previous meeting passed a standing order which permits business left over from a previous meeting to be discussed under this head. There is, however, no objection to matters being discussed under the heading of 'Any Other Business' which involve no more than an exchange of information.

E. CONFIDENCE AND ADMISSION OF STRANGERS

A meeting of a parish council must be open to the public and the press. They can be excluded only by a resolution if publicity would prejudice the public interest by reason of the

---

[11] Apparently this notice need not be affixed at the church door—see L.G.A. 1933 s. 287.
[12] L.G.A. 1933 Third Schedule Part IV para. 2(3).
[13] L.G. Sup. Act, 1937 s. 40.
[14] L.G.A. 1933 Third Schedule Part IV para. 2(3).
[15] Lingfield Parish Council v. Wright (1918) 88 L.J. Ch. 119.

confidential nature of the business or for some other reason *stated in the resolution* and arising out of the business to be transacted. The power to exclude[16] is not exercisable generally but only for a particular occasion.

The press has the same right to be present as the public and in addition is entitled, on payment, to copies of the agenda. The parish council must also give the press facilities for taking their reports and (unless the meeting place is not owned by the parish council) for telephoning them.

These rules apply equally where a council resolves itself into committee.

There is no authority for the commonly-held belief that proceedings of committees are confidential, but neither the press nor the public are entitled to be present at committees as of right. In few cases is there any good reason for excluding the press or the public from committee meetings and in still fewer is it necessary to impose secrecy upon the members.

As a rule, however, it is desirable to treat the discussion of the following types of business as confidential:—

(a) Engagement, terms of service, conduct and dismissal of employees;

(b) Terms of tenders, and proposals and counter-proposals in negotiation for contracts;

(c) Preparation of cases in legal proceedings;

(d) The early stages of any dispute.

Public Participation

Some councils set aside a period when the public can ask questions or even make statements. This is an excellent practice as long as the period is defined and it is clearly understood that the public has no right to take part at any other time.

F. QUORUM

The quorum of a parish council is three or one-third of the total membership, whichever is the greater,[17] but where more than one-third of the members are disqualified at the same time

[16] Public Bodies (Admission to Meetings) Act, 1960.
[17] L.G.A. 1933 Third Schedule Part IV para. 4.

the quorum is either three or one-third of the qualified members whichever is the greater, until such time as the membership has been increased to not less than two-thirds of the total.[18]

If the council is no longer able to act because its membership has fallen so low that a quorum is unobtainable the County Council may authorise the remaining members to act temporarily in the place of the parish council.[19] It is doubtful whether such an authorisation would enable them to fill casual vacancies by co-option, thereby recreating the quorum, because they may only act 'in the place of' and not 'as' the parish council.[20]

G. INTERESTS

A member who has a direct or indirect pecuniary interest in a contract, proposed contract *or other matter* must declare his interest at the meeting where the contract or matter is to be discussed and must—as a general rule—take no further part in the proceedings. A general notice of such an interest to the clerk is a sufficient disclosure. The member may, by standing order, be excluded from the meeting and it is often as much in his interest as in that of the public that this should be done.

The type of interest to which these rules relate is a relationship between the member and the subject matter which is of such a kind that he may receive a business advantage (such as enrichment or publicity) if the council makes a particular decision, but he is not to be treated as having a pecuniary interest if it is so remote or insignificant that it cannot reasonably be regarded as likely to influence his conduct.[21] If, therefore, he or any nominee of his is a member of a company or other body with which a contract is to be made or if he is a partner or employed by a person with whom the contract is to be made, he has an interest.[22] On the other hand, if the body is a public body (such as another local authority) or if the member has no beneficial interest in a shareholding which would otherwise disqualify him (for instance because he is a bare trustee or executor) then he has no sufficient interest. Where married persons are living

[18] ibid., para. 6. [19] L.G.A. 1933 s. 55(2).
[20] Compare the wording of L.G.A. 1933 s. 55(2) with that of s. 72(3) relating to district councils.
[21] L.G. (Pecuniary Interests) Act, 1964 s. 1(1).
[22] L.G.A. 1933 s. 76.

together the interest of one is deemed, if known to the other, to be the interest of the other.[23] A salaried managing director who is not a shareholder would not be held to have an interest[24] but it would be otherwise if he received fees or commission on the contract.[25]

Where an interest is indirect and consists only in having a nominal shareholding of £500 or one per cent. of the issued capital or one per cent. of any class of issued capital (whichever is the less) the obligation of disclosure remains but the member may take part in the proceedings and vote.[26]

Interest Book

The clerk must keep a special interest book and must enter in it all disclosures of interest made at meetings and all general notices of interest. This book must be open to inspection at all reasonable hours by any member of the council.[27]

A member who fails to disclose an interest or who takes part in proceedings in which he should not have taken part, exposes himself to a fine of £200 on summary conviction unless he can prove that he did not know that the matter in which he was interested was being considered at the meeting. Prosecutions for these offences may, however, only be launched at the instance of the Director of Public Prosecutions.[27]

Removal of Disqualification

If so many members are disqualified by interest as to impede business, or where it appears to be in the interest of the inhabitants, the county council may remove the disqualification.[27]

H. PERSISTENT ABSENCE

If a member fails throughout six consecutive months to attend any meetings of the council or of its committees or sub-committees of which he is a member, or of a joint committee, joint board or other body to which any of the parish council's

---

[23] L.G.A. 1933 s. 76. [24] See Lapish v. Braithwaite 1926 A.C. 275.
[25] ibid. per Viscount Cave L.C. at page 278.
[26] L.G.A. 1933 s. 76(2A). This sub-section was inserted by L.G.A. 1948 s. 131 and amended by L.G.(M.P.)A. 1953 s. 15.
[27] L.G.A. 1933 s. 76.

powers have been transferred or delegated, he ceases automatically to be a member of the council[28] unless either he has a 'statutory excuse' or his failure is due to a reason approved by the parish council. The period begins with the first meeting missed.[29]

Excuses

Membership of the armed forces in time of war is a statutory excuse and so is such employment in the service of the Crown in connection with a war or emergency as in the Minister's opinion entitles the member to relief.[30]

Apologies need not necessarily be conveyed in writing but reasons for absence known to the council should be minuted.

Where a council is considering a reason for absence it is clear that some reason or explanation must be known to it and this must be approved by affirmative resolution at the earliest possible moment after the end of the six months. If at that moment the council fails to consider the question, the office falls vacant without further ado, and the vacancy must be declared and filled in the proper manner.

In practice if a parish council accidentally fails to approve a reason for absence, it may usually repair the omission by co-opting the absentee. It is, however, necessary to ensure that he is still qualified before doing so for though mere absence from the parish does not of itself lead to vacation of office it may produce a disqualification which did not exist when the vacancy arose.

There is nothing to prevent a parish council from approving a reason for absence in advance.

I. DISQUALIFICATION AND CESSATION OF QUALIFICATION

When a member ceases to be qualified or becomes disqualified he must at once cease to act and risks legal proceedings if he continues to do so.[31] The prohibition is absolute, though for the purpose of filling the vacancy his office is not deemed vacant

[28] L.G.A. 1933 s. 63.
[29] See Kershaw v. Shoreditch Borough Council (1906) 95 L.T. 55 which was decided on the wording of L.G.A. 1894 s. 46(6) now repealed.
[30] L.G.A. 1933 s. 63.   [31] See L.G.A. 1933 s. 84.

until so declared. The person concerned must not only not attend meetings (save as a member of the public) but must not sign documents.[32]

A member always ceases to be a member when he ceases to be a British subject, but apart from this some may be more effectively entrenched than others; thus one who resided in the parish or within three miles of it during the whole twelve months before the election day, or since the 25th March in the year before the election year, will remain a member for the whole of his term even though he leaves the qualifying area permanently on the day after he enters office, but another who is qualified only as an elector or property owner will cease to be eligible or to be a member when his name no longer appears on the electoral roll[33] or when his interest in the property comes to an end.

A disqualification is a consequence of a positive event[34] whereas a cessation of qualification is negative; disqualifications are therefore usually attended with greater publicity and are easier to ascertain.

J. ATTENDANCE REGISTER AND APOLOGIES

The names of members present at a meeting must be recorded[35] and this record should form part of the minutes of each meeting. It is unnecessary as a rule to record a late arrival, but it is very desirable to record briefly the grounds upon which apologies for absence are tendered in case they have to be approved to prevent a casual vacancy arising.[36] If a member withdraws on grounds of interest, his withdrawal should be recorded.

K. ANNUAL AND FIRST MEETINGS

First Meetings

Parish councillors are, of course, entitled to be present at all meetings but in addition certain others may, for a short time take part at certain first or annual meetings; these additional

---

[32] For the evidential effect of signed minutes in this context see page 62.
[33] For the right to be on the electoral roll and the date upon which it comes into force see pages 27–9.   [34] See pages 32–34.
[35] L.G.A. 1933 Third Schedule Part V para. 2.   [36] See pages 42–43.

persons are, in the case of the first meeting after the creation of the parish council, the person appointed by the county council to act in place of the chairman;[37] in the case of the first annual meeting after an election the chairman and vice-chairman who are about to retire; and in the case of any other annual meeting the retiring chairman.[38]

Who May Preside

The chairman, or in his absence the vice-chairman (if any), *must* preside.[39] Only if these are both absent may the council appoint some other person to preside and that person must be a councillor.[39] The once common practice whereby proceedings at first annual meetings after the elections were opened with the paid clerk in the chair is illegal.

First Business

The first business of the meeting must be the election of the chairman.[40] He may be either a parish councillor or a person qualified to be one.[41] The retiring chairman may vote and as chairman give a casting vote at this election[42] even though he is not a parish councillor, and he may vote for himself.[43] In his absence the retiring vice-chairman has the same voting rights as the chairman,[44] but if the chairman is present, the vice-chairman may only vote if he is a parish councillor. The possibility of the vice-chairman not being a parish councillor can only occur immediately after an election.

At the moment when the new chairman accepts office the previous chairman and vice-chairman automatically retire[45] and if they are not parish councillors they at the same moment cease to be members.

Removal of Difficulties

If any difficulty arises on the first meeting of the parish council the county council under its reserve power may by order make

---

[37] Under L.G.A. 1933 s. 55.   [38] L.G.A. 1933 s. 49. See page 79.
[39] L.G.A. 1933 Third Schedule Part IV para. 3.
[40] L.G.A. 1933 s. 49(2).   [41] L.G.A. 1933 s. 49(1).
[42] R. v. Jackson *ex parte* Pick. 1913 3 K.B. 436.
[43] See Halsbury, *Laws of England* (Hailsham Edition), Volume XII, page 333, where it is stated that a Mayor of a Borough may vote for himself.
[44] L.G.A. 1933 Third Schedule Part IV para. 3(2) and Part V para. 1(2).
[45] L.G.A. 1933 s. 49(3) and (6).

any appointment or do anything necessary or expedient for holding the meeting and may fix its date; such an order may modify the provisions of the Local Government Act, 1933.[46] The appointment of a person to preside at the opening is a common example of the use of this power.[47]

Routine Business at Annual Meetings

Apart from the appointment of the chairman the law does not require any particular business to be transacted at the annual meeting, but it is desirable to establish a routine list of matters which should always appear on its agenda. Such a list may conveniently be incorporated in a standing order and may include the checking of inventories of parish documents, the appointment of representatives to the parish councils association and other bodies and the hearing of reports from such representatives.

L. TIMING OF MEETINGS AND PRECEPTS

In fixing the dates of its meetings the parish council should have regard both to the timing of its precepts and the proposed date of the annual assembly of the parish meeting. There is no legal time-table for the issue of precepts by parish councils nor are rating authorities bound to send them estimates of penny rate products by any given date,[48] but on the other hand these estimates have to be calculated for county purposes by the beginning of February and county council precepts must be issued to the rating authorities at least twenty-one days before the beginning of the financial year and half year.[49]

Estimates should be considered after the penny rate figures are available but before the financial year begins, and it is desirable that the parish council should have decided its provisional programme before the annual assembly. In practice, therefore, the main financial meeting of the council should take place between the first week in February and the end of the first week in March.

[46] L.G.A. 1933 s. 55 as amended by R.P.A. 1949 ss. 175, 176 and Ninth Schedule.
[47] For the reserve power generally see page 45.
[48] Unless a scheme is in force under R.V.A. 1925 s. 9(3).
[49] i.e. on or before the 10th March and 9th September.

M. STANDING ORDERS ON BUSINESS[50]

A parish council may make standing orders to regulate its business and proceedings and may vary or revoke them.[51] Models are published by H.M. Stationery Office and by the National Association of Parish Councils. It is usually not necessary for very small councils to have standing orders, but it is always desirable for every parish council to possess a copy of one of the recognised models so that in a difficulty the chairman can give a decision based upon an established precedent.

N. SUBJECTS FOR CONSIDERATION

A parish council may obviously consider any matter in which it has statutory power to act, and the scope of this proposition has been widened by the power conferred in 1963 to spend a small amount of money for any purpose which in the parish council's opinion is for the benefit of the parish or its inhabitants.[52] In addition it seems clear that a parish council has the same power to discuss parish affairs as the parish meeting[53] because it has power to convene that body and therefore to discuss the reason for doing so. In any event it is usually cheaper and better to discuss parish affairs in the parish council than constantly to summon the electors to do so.

Moving

A parish council may by standing order require that a resolution shall be seconded as well as moved (and many do) but a seconder is not required by any rule of law and in the absence of such a standing order the chairman should permit resolutions and amendments to be discussed after they have been moved only.

Form

In all but the very simplest cases the mover of a resolution or amendment should be required to reduce it to writing.

A resolution should be specific and wherever possible vagueness should be avoided. If it is not possible to be specific a person

---

[50] For the compulsory standing orders on contracts see page 190.
[51] L.G.A. 1933 Third Schedule Part V para. 4.
[52] See pages 213-217.   [53] See page 90.

or committee should be instructed to fill in the details, or the matter should be adjourned pending inquiries.

A resolution should not deal with more than one subject and where a resolution combining more than one subject is moved, the chairman should require the mover to separate the component parts and move them one by one. Disregard of this rule usually leads to confused discussion and may lead to confused action if different parts of a resolution affect different interests or require consents from other and different bodies. In considering whether a resolution is duplex or not regard must be had to its substantial effect and not only to its wording which may be deceptively simple. A resolution 'that the parish field be sold' may turn out to be duplex if half the area happens to be held upon charitable trusts.

When the chairman has severed the resolution which he suspects of duplicity it may be convenient (if the subjects are in some way interdependent) to allow both resolutions to be moved together but to require that the discussion upon them shall proceed separately.

Discussion

In larger authorities it is common to limit the length of speeches and not to permit members other than the mover to speak more than once on any one resolution. In any but the largest parish councils these rules seem unduly restrictive. On the other hand the chairman ought not to allow members to introduce into their speeches matters which do not relate to the issue before council. A decision on relevance is often hard to make and no doubt a chairman should allow some latitude rather than incur the suspicion that he is trying to gag debate, but the duty should not be shirked and when matter is ruled out of order as irrelevant the ruling should be firmly enforced.

The Direct Negative

It is never necessary to move the rejection of a resolution because every decision must be reached by an affirmative vote of a majority present and voting and if this is not secured the resolution is rejected in any case.[54]

[54] See below.

Amendment

Amendments should be moved in the form of motions either to insert or to alter or to omit words in the resolution under discussion. A direct negative is not an amendment, and an amendment whose practical effect is to negative the resolution should not be permitted because its sponsor can achieve his object by persuading the council to vote against the resolution.

In putting resolutions and amendments to the vote the chairman *must put the amendment first*. The fact that an amendment is rejected does not mean that the main resolution is accepted, nor does acceptance of the amendment mean that the resolution as amended is accepted. In every case voting on an amendment must be followed by a decision on the main resolution. For instance, on a motion, 'that a motor mower be purchased' an amendment might be moved to insert the words 'second-hand' before 'motor'. If the amendment is passed the motion under discussion will read 'that a second-hand motor mower be purchased' and it will still be open to move a further amendment (for instance to substitute 'hand' for 'motor'). After all amendments have been disposed of it will still be necessary to decide if a mower shall be purchased at all, and this is done by voting upon the resolution in its final form as amended or not amended.

Enforcing Decisions

A decision on a topic ends discussion upon it. The council should proceed to the next business and the chairman must rule out of order (as irrelevant) any attempt at that meeting to re-open the previous topic.

O. VOTING

Every decision must be made by a majority of the members present and voting.[55] Provided that a quorum is present it is immaterial that a quorum of members take part in the voting. A motion may therefore be carried by a single voter if nobody votes against him.[56]

The person presiding may vote even if by so doing he creates

[55] L.G.A. 1933 Third Schedule Part V para. 1.
[56] For voting on co-options see page 43.

an equality of votes, and if there is an equality of votes he has a second or casting vote.[57, 58, 59]

Members *must* vote by show of hands. If any member so requires the manner in which each member voted on any particular question must be recorded in the minutes;[60] and a member who wishes the voting to be recorded may make his demand either before or after the vote.

P. DEFAMATION

[61]'A man disparages the good name of another when he publishes to some third person words or matter which are false and which injure his reputation . . . such disparagement, if embodied in some permanent form . . . is called *libel*: if expressed in some fugitive form . . . it is called *slander*.'[62]

It is presumed that libel causes injury and a similar presumption arises in slanders imputing crime, or infectious disease, or unchastity in a woman,[63] or which disparage a person in his office, profession, calling, trade, or business;[64] in other cases of slander the person alleging injury must prove it.[64]

Privilege

A person who has made a defamatory statement may claim privilege for it if he can show that he made it without malice and in pursuit of a public duty. For instance if a member has a *good* reason to believe that the parish council's funds are being misappropriated he is under a public duty to inform the parish council. If, on investigation, the statement is found to be true, it is not defamatory at all, but if it is found to be untrue he may claim privilege if he acted without malice.

Fair Comment

Fair comment on a matter of public interest is not actionable.

[57] L.G.A. 1933 Third Schedule Part V para. 1.
[58] See the facts in R. v. Jackson *ex parte* Pick 1913 3 K.B. 426.
[59] For casting vote at a parish meeting see page 89.
[60] L.G.A. 1933 Third Schedule Part IV para. 5.
[61] The subject matter of possible defamation is infinitely various and the law correspondingly complicated. The following paragraphs give only the barest outline of that part of the law which most commonly affects parish council proceedings.
[62] Gatley on *Libel and Slander*, Fifth Edn. (1960), p. 3.
[63] Slander of Women Act, 1891.
[64] Defamation Act, 1952, s. 2.

The acts and proceedings of a parish council are matters of public interest and a parish council or other local authority as such cannot maintain an action for defamation if it is criticised[65] even if such criticism is intemperately expressed.[66] Criticism must, however, be fair and if it is so worded that it can reasonably be held to impute unworthy or corrupt motives to particular members they would, as individuals, be entitled to take action.

Q. MINUTES

Minutes of proceedings of a parish council and of its committees must be kept.[67] They are intended to be formal records of official acts and decisions, not reports, still less as verbatim reports, of the speeches made by councillors. Minutes should, therefore, be as short as is consistent with clarity and accuracy, and the arguments used in the discussion need only be recorded if the decision cannot be clearly expressed in any other way.

Minute Book

The minutes must be entered in a book kept for the purpose[67] and the leaves of the book must not be in such a condition that they can without detection be detached.[68]

Signature

The minutes must be signed at the meeting which they record or at the next meeting, by the person presiding thereat. A council before allowing the chairman to sign should satisfy itself of their accuracy, but discussion of the words should not be allowed to stray into the merits of the decision which they express.

The practice of signing minutes at the next meeting should not be regarded as invariable. In a difficult or complicated matter, and especially when an interval of some months or a change of membership is expected, it is preferable to adjourn

---

[65] Purcell v. Sowler (1887) 2 C.P.D. 215.
[66] McQuire v. Western Morning News 1903 2 K.B. 100 C.A.
[67] L.G.A. 1933 Third Schedule Part V para. 3(1).
[68] See the decision of Bennett J. in Hearts of Oak Assurance Company v. James Flower and Sons 1936 1 Ch. 76 on the very similar wording of Companies Act, 1929 s. 120.

while the minutes are drawn up and to approve and sign them then and there. Minutes of an annual meeting, if not signed on the same day, should be signed at the next ordinary meeting and not held over for a year.

It is not necessary to record the majority by which a decision is made unless a member requires the voting to be recorded,[69] and though a member cannot be prevented from insisting upon this requirement, there are cases where it is undesirable or invidious to insist. Such cases arise mainly in relation to the appointment of employees and especially of the clerk.

Minutes as Evidence

Minutes purporting to be properly signed may be received in evidence without further proof. Until the contrary is proved, where the minutes relate to a meeting of the parish council, the meeting is deemed to have been duly convened and held and all members present are deemed to have been qualified; and where they relate to a meeting of a committee, the committee is deemed to have been properly constituted and to have had power to deal with the matter set out in the minutes.[70]

Minutes which are not drawn up or signed in accordance with the law are not receivable in evidence.

R. WELSH

Proceedings may be (and frequently are) in Welsh and where this is the common language of ordinary communication it is advisable for the minutes to be available in the language best understood by the members. It is, however, desirable for the accounts to be kept in English in case they become the subject of an appeal, because the making of an official translation will increase the cost of the proceedings.

S. SIGNING AND SEALING DOCUMENTS

A parish council signifies its acts under the hands, or if necessary, under the hands and seals of two of its members.[71] Naturally such signification must not take place without the

[69] See L.G.A. 1933 Third Schedule Part IV para. 6.
[70] L.G.A. 1933 Third Schedule Part V para. 3.
[71] L.G.A. 1933 s. 48(3).

authority of a resolution, but the law neither requires that the resolution shall name the members concerned nor that the formalities shall be performed in the presence of the council, but the sealing of the documents must be witnessed and in practice the best witness is the clerk.

As a chartered corporation a rural borough has a common seal which is affixed at meetings of the council. It is usual to make special arrangements for custody of the common seal and these are normally laid down in a standing order.

T. BRIBERY AND CORRUPTION

It is a misdemeanour at common law to bribe or attempt to bribe a public official and for such an official to accept a bribe,[72] and an officer of a local authority who under colour of his office exacts or accepts any fee or reward other than his proper remuneration is liable on summary conviction to a fine of £50.[73]

It is a statutory misdemeanour for a person to solicit, receive or agree to receive for himself or anyone else any gift, fee, loan, reward or advantage as an inducement to or reward for or otherwise on account of any member, officer or servant of a public body doing or forbearing to do anything in respect of any matter or transaction actual or proposed in which the public body is concerned[74] and it is similarly a misdemeanour for any one by himself or in conjunction with any other person to give, promise or offer such things for such purposes.[75] An offender cannot be prosecuted without the consent of the Attorney-General,[74] but he is liable to two years imprisonment, a fine of £500, and may in addition be required to pay to the council the value of the bribe, to forfeit his office and pension and he may also be disqualified for office and as an elector.[76, 77]

U. DISTURBANCES AT MEETINGS

Anyone (whether a member of the parish council or the public) who disturbs the proceedings may be required by

[72] See R. v. Whitaker 1914 3 K.B. 1283. See R. v. Lancaster and Worrall 16 Cox 727. See R. v. Beale (1797 K.B.) Crown Roll 384 Rot. 22.
[73] L.G.A. 1933 s. 123(2)(3).
[74] Public Bodies Corrupt Practices Act, 1889 s. 1.
[75] ibid. s. 4.   [76] ibid. s. 2.
[77] For disqualification from office see page 32, and for disqualification as an elector see page 28.

resolution to withdraw. It is not desirable for such a resolution to be moved until the chairman has at least once requested the offender to desist and the request has been ignored. Where the chairman's request has been disregarded the resolution should be moved automatically and without comment by the senior councillor able to do so, though legally any councillor or the chairman may move it. Mere heat or anger in discussion is not of itself a ground for excluding a member but almost any interruption by the public is technically a disturbance.

An offender who refuses to obey the resolution may be removed by force, but care should be taken to use no more force than is necessary. It is usually desirable (but not legally necessary) to secure the help of the police.

A resolution of exclusion ought not to extend to future meetings.[78]

[78] Barton v. Taylor (1886) 11 A.C. 197.

7

Committees and Delegation

A. GENERAL

A committee[1] is a temporary body which derives its powers from delegation by one or more authorities who may terminate both its functions[2] and its existence.[3] It is not a corporate body and though it may be given the widest discretion and the fullest membership allowed by law yet it can never act other than as agent for the delegating authority.

Statutory Authority

The general power to appoint and order committees is given by the Local Government Act, 1933, but if a particular type of committee is required to be set up by any other enactment, then the provisions of the latter apply to the exclusion of the Act of 1933,[4] which, however, applies in all but a minority of cases.

Membership

Committees may include all the members of the council and the council may appoint non-members to any committee other than a finance committee provided that at least two-thirds of the committee are members. In the administration of certain types of parish property such as the parish hall and the playing fields, this 'two-thirds rule' is sometimes inconvenient because

---

[1] For committees appointed by parish meetings and for advisory committees see pages 69-70.

[2] Huth v. Clarke (1890) 25 Q.B.D. 391.

[3] This definition is subject to some exceptions which are not important in parish administration, but which assume great importance in other spheres of local government. Most other kinds of local authority are required to appoint (and so to keep in existence) committees of various kinds.

[4] L.G.A, 1933 s, 85(5) and 91(4).

it may be impossible to secure that all the voluntary bodies using the property are represented upon it. This inconvenience can sometimes be circumvented by a lease[5] or by appointing advisory committees.

A member who is appointed to a committee by his authority, ceases to be a member of the committee if he ceases to belong to the authority,[6] but for this purpose he is not considered to have ceased to be a member of his authority if he has been re-elected not later than the day on which he was due to retire.[6]

Disqualifications

A person disqualified for being a member of a particular local authority (including a parish council) is disqualified for any of its committees or for representing it upon a joint committee.[7]

Interests

The rules on pecuniary interests apply as much to committees as they do to the authorities which appoint them, but a committeeman's right to inspect the interest book is limited to entries relating to members of his own committee.[8]

Procedure

The chairman has a second or casting vote.[9]

The authority or authorities which appoint a committee may make, vary or revoke standing orders regulating its quorum, proceedings and place of meeting, but if no such orders are made the committee may regulate these matters itself.[10]

Powers

A committee may not borrow money or levy or issue a precept for a rate,[11] but it may otherwise be allowed to do anything which the delegating authority can do itself. The latter has an absolute discretion to lay down restrictions or conditions upon the exercise of the committee's functions.[11]

Without the leave of the delegating authority a committee

---

[5] Allotments managers seem to be a genuine but unavowed exception to the two-thirds rule.
[6] L.G.A. 1933 ss. 85(4) and 91(3).   [7] L.G.A. 1933 s. 94.
[8] L.G.A. 1933 s. 95. See page 51.   [9] L.G.A. 1933 s. 96(2).
[10] L.G.A. 1933 s. 96(1).
[11] L.G.A. 1933 ss. 85(1), 87(2), 88(1), 91(1).

(except a committee dealing with records)[12] cannot appoint sub-committees nor can it delegate its functions further.[13]

B. PARISH COUNCIL COMMITTEES

Compulsory

If a parish council has functions which are discharged in only part of a parish or in relation to a recreation ground, building or property held for the benefit of a part and if that part has a defined boundary, the council must if required by a parish meeting for that part appoint annually a committee consisting both of members and of persons representing the part to discharge such functions.[14] It is not required, however, to appoint to the committee the persons proposed by the parish meeting, though in most cases it will no doubt be wise to do so.

Discretionary

The parish council may appoint a committee for any purpose which in its opinion would be better regulated by a committee and it may fix the membership and the area within which the committee is to exercise its authority.[15]

C. JOINT COMMITTEES

Compulsory

Where the circumstances of the appointment of a joint committee are such that a parish council could be required to appoint a committee for part of the parish,[16] the parish councils concerned must comply with the requirement that the joint committee must consist partly of non-members.[17]

If before the 5th March, 1894, the area of administration of an adoptive act was not comprised in one rural parish, the powers of the authority administering it were transferred to the parish councils (or parish meetings) of the parishes concerned and also to the council of any urban district concerned, and these authorities were then required to appoint a joint committee and administer the act through it.[18]

---

[12] Cook v. Ward (1877) L.R. 2 C.P.D. 255.
[13] L.G. (Records) Act, 1962 s. 3.   [14] L.G.A. 1933 s. 89.
[15] L.G.A. 1933 s. 85.   [16] See previous section.
[17] L.G.A. 1933 s. 92.   [18] L.G.A. 1894 s. 53(2).

Certain special rules apply where such a joint committee was appointed for the purposes of the Burial Acts.[19]

Discretionary

A parish council may concur with any other local authority[16] in appointing a joint committee for any purpose in which it may be jointly interested with the other authority. Unless the circumstances are such that the parish council could be required to appoint a committee for part of the parish all the representatives of the parish council must be members of it.[20]

Finance

The expenses of joint committees are defrayed in such proportions as the local authorities appointing them agree, and in default of agreement in the proportions settled by the county council. If, however, the appointing authorities include a county council, county borough council or the councils of county districts in different counties, the proportions are settled by the Minister.

D. PAROCHIAL ADMINISTRATION OF DISTRICT FUNCTIONS

Parochial Committees

A rural district council may at a meeting specially convened for the purpose appoint a parochial committee for a 'contributory place' consisting either wholly of members of the rural district council or partly of such members and partly of other persons. If the contributory place is a parish with a separate parish council the other persons must be members of that parish council.[21] The rural district council is not required to accept the members nominated by the parish council.

A parish council or parish meeting may request a rural district council to appoint a parochial committee, and if the request is refused, it may apply to the Minister who may order the rural district council to do so.[22]

Delegation by Rural District Council

A rural district council may delegate to a parish council any

[19] L.G. (Joint Committees) Act, 1897.   [20] L.G.A. 1933 s. 91(1).
[21] L.G.A. 1933 s. 87(1).   [22] L.G.A. 1933 s. 87(3).

function which it may delegate to a parochial committee,[23] and the parish council thereupon performs those functions as agent for the rural district council.[24] A parish council may request such delegation but there is no right of appeal.

Finance

The cost of administering the functions of a rural district council in a parish is normally borne as a part of the general expenses of the rural district council, but the Minister may, by order, made on application of the rural district council, declare any expenses incurred by the rural district council to be separately chargeable upon the parish. Where such an order has been made, the rural district council may nevertheless make a contribution from its general rate fund.[25] A parish council which asks for delegation, will strengthen its case if it is willing to support an application for such a special charging order.

Clerk

Where a parish council is administering a function delegated to it by the rural district council it may, whilst so acting, employ the services of the clerk of the rural district council unless his council otherwise directs.[26]

E. COMMITTEES OF PARISH MEETINGS

Where there is no separate parish council the parish meeting may, subject to the provisions of any grouping order, appoint a committee of parish electors for any purpose which it considers would be better regulated or managed by a committee. All acts of such a committee must be submitted to the parish meeting for approval.[27]

Apparently a parish meeting cannot appoint members of a joint committee unless it obtains an order from the county council enabling it to do so.[28]

---

[23] See General Rules, page 66. [24] L.G.A. 1933 s. 88.
[25] L.G.A. 1933 s. 190. [26] L.G.A. 1933 s. 114(3).
[27] L.G.A. 1933 s. 90.
[28] See L.G.A. 1933 s. 91. The order would have to be made under s. 273.

F. ADVISORY COMMITTEES

An advisory committee has no power to decide anything but only power to tender an opinion, and the body to whom the opinion is tendered remains free to accept or reject the opinion as it pleases. Any local authority (including a parish meeting) must carry out its work in a businesslike manner and ought to seek proper advice when necessary. There is no reason why a parish council or a parish meeting should not form permanent committees to tender advice on particular subjects,[29] just as it can retain a solicitor; such committees need not conform to the 'two-thirds' or any rule on membership. They are simply a method of discovering facts, and can sometimes be very convenient if the interests of large numbers of voluntary organisations have to be considered, for instance, in the management of a village hall or community centre.

[29] The Local Government (Records) Act, 1962, s. 3, enables a sub-committee dealing with records to ignore the two-thirds rule but at the expense of becoming advisory only. It is submitted that this enactment is unnecessary.

8

Co-operation

A. GENERAL

A Local Authority can act only within its own boundaries unless statutory means are available for the extension of its administrative activity beyond them. As has already been stated[1] the universal method whereby parish councils may co-operate with other local authorities in the administration of a joint service is by means of a joint committee. Fortunately, however, the statute book contains a considerable number of instances where other and less inconvenient means of co-operation between parish authorities, or between parish and other local authorities or even in some cases between parish authorities or other persons are available. Apart from the special case of the union of burial boards[2] the most important of the formal methods are contribution, combination and the appointment of representatives to other bodies.

More important, perhaps, than any of these purely technical arrangements are the informal methods of co-operation between parish councils and voluntary organisations which are becoming increasingly important in the administration of villages. The advisory committee[3] is one useful instrument for ensuring that the views of voluntary organisations are known; another is the grant to a managing body of a long lease in which the constitution of the managing body is laid down.[4] Moreover the parish council is entitled to see the accounts of parochial charities[5] and this gives it an annual opportunity to consider the ways in which the work of these charities (especially village hall and playing field charities) can be assisted.

[1] See page 66. [2] See pages 283–4. [3] See page 70.
[4] See page 115. [5] See page 127.

Finally in many parishes the electors may find it convenient to ensure that the members of the parish council represent their local voluntary bodies, and similarly in using its power of co-option to a casual vacancy a parish council can reasonably consider how its relationship with voluntary organisations can be strengthened.

B. CONTRIBUTION

Contribution consists in the payment of money by one local authority to a second or to some other person to defray expenses incurred by the latter which will benefit the inhabitants of the area of the first authority. In all cases of contribution the receiving body remains in control even though it may give and abide by undertakings as to the manner in which that control is to be exercised as a condition of receiving the contribution.

Parish Councils may contribute towards the expenses incurred by other parish councils in providing and laying out recreation grounds and public walks, in providing, laying out and embellishing village greens, in providing pleasure boats or in acquiring local rights of way.[6] They may contribute towards expenses incurred by any other parish council or person in providing a parish hall[7] or public seats and shelters,[8] clocks,[9] 'adoptive lighting',[10] cycle parks[11] and burial grounds;[12] they may contribute to the expenses of other local authorities, or voluntary bodies in operating the provisions of the Physical Training and Recreation Act, 1937;[13] they may contribute towards the rural district council's expenses in making a scheme for a common[14] and with the Minister's consent they may contribute to certain expenses of the National Trust.[15]

The free fifth has also very considerably extended the scope of a parish council's powers of contribution.[16]

C. COMBINATION

Combination is a much closer form of association than contribution: and for that reason it is only possible between parish

[6] L.G.A. 1894 s. 8(1).
[7] L.G.A. 1933 s. 127.
[8] P.C.A. 1957 s. 1(1) and s. 6.
[9] P.C.A. 1957 s. 2 and s. 6.
[10] P.C.A. 1957 s. 3 and s. 6.
[11] P.C.A., 1957 s. 4 and s. 6.
[12] P.C.A. 1957 s. 10.
[13] See pages 137 and 230.
[14] Commons Act, 1899 s. 7.
[15] National Trust Act, 1937 s. 7(2).
[16] See pages 213-217.

authorities having similar powers. Where parish authorities combine they agree to administer a service or part of a service in common and this community of administration implies that one is in some sort exercising authority within the area or over the property of the other; this administrative infringement of the parochial principle does not extend to rating, and therefore with the possible exception of adoptive lighting[17] differential rating does not occur as a result of combination.

Where combination is legally possible the parish authorities concerned may agree to combine for a certain purpose and may then agree how that purpose shall be carried out. Such an agreement is a form of contract and the parties to it have the same liberties and are subject to the same restrictions as in other cases of contract; thus adjacent lighting authorities may combine to light a street which happens to be the parish boundary and they might, for instance, agree that one of them shall manage all the lights in the street while the other contributes its proportionate share of the cost. A combination agreement may (but need not) include provision for the setting up of a joint committee or for joint meetings of the authorities concerned.

A parish meeting or parish council may combine with any other parish council or parish meeting with like powers to provide seats, shelters, clocks, adoptive lighting and cycle parks,[18] and parish councils could combine to spend funds for some common purpose which is in the interests of their parishes or their inhabitants provided that they restricted their expenditure to the amount of the free fifth.[19]

D. REPRESENTATION ON OTHER BODIES

There are many bodies which draw their power from legal sources which are independent of the source of power of the authorities which appoint their members. These bodies may be independent statutory corporations such as the Harbour Commissioners at Yarmouth (Isle of Wight), or statutory committees such as the Boards of Management of primary schools, or they may be charitable or non-charitable trustees deriving power and administering property under instruments enforceable in the courts under the general law, or again they may be voluntary committees set up for some local purpose. Some, and

[17] See page 249.   [18] P.C.A. 1957 s. 6(3).   [19] See page 213.

occasionally all, of the members of these bodies are appointed by a parish council, and there are very few parish councils which cannot make such appointments.

Disqualifications

Bodies of this sort differ fundamentally from local authority committees for since their power is not delegated to them by the appointing authorities, the latter cannot withdraw or influence the exercise of the powers unless the right to do so is specifically given by the 'Charter'[20] of the body concerned. Moreover they are not committees within the meaning of the Local Government Act, 1933, and therefore the rules on disqualification for membership or employment in the Act[21] do not apply.

Interests

It is not always easy to decide if a parish councillor who is also a member of such a body has a pecuniary interest sufficient to compel him to withdraw from a discussion by the parish council of the affairs of the body. In most cases there will be no such interest but in the residue of doubtful cases it is wise to take advice.

Duty of Representatives

The powers of representatives appointed by a parish council to these bodies are not in any sense delegated to them and unless the parish council has a right of removal[22] it has no control over their actions. When acting in their offices their primary duty is to the body to which they have been appointed; they may, of course, advocate the interests of the parish council which appointed them and may vote conscientiously in favour of those interests, but unless the 'Charter' endows the parish council with such a power it may not require them to vote in a particular way, nor if it issues instructions on voting can it challenge a vote given contrary to those instructions. Where there is a power of removal the 'disobedient' representative may be removed but his vote will stand.

A contract to vote only in accordance with instructions issued by the parish council is, at least in relation to a public body, void

---

[20] This word is not used here in a technical sense, but embraces the acts, instruments and laws which empower the body to perform its functions.
[21] See pages 66 and 86.   [22] e.g. under the Education Act, 1944.

as being against public policy and unconstitutional,[23] but there is no legal objection to a parish council representative undertaking to render reports to the parish council.

E. SCHOOLS

The Minor Authority

Where it appears to the local education authority that any school maintained by it serves a single parish, the parish council or if none, the parish meeting is the minor authority. If the school appears to serve more than one parish, the minor authorities of the parishes concerned acting jointly are the minor authority.[24]

Rights of Appointment

In a *county primary school* the local education authority appoints two-thirds of the managers and the minor authority one-third.[25] In a *controlled primary school* one-third of the managers are foundation managers and of the remainder not less than one-third are appointed by the minor authority and the rest by the local education authority.[25] In a *special agreement* or *aided primary school* two-thirds of the managers are foundation managers and the remainder are appointed in the same proportions as for controlled schools.[26]

Unless a *secondary school* forms part of a group a minor authority has no right to appoint any governors of secondary schools, but it is a common and increasing practice for a local education authority to ask the minor authorities concerned to propose persons for appointment, and it also has power in the case of county schools so to draft the instrument of government as to allow the minor authorities to make appointments direct.[27]

The constitution of the governing body of a *group of schools* varies. If all the schools in the group are county schools it consists of such number of persons appointed in such manner as the local education authority may determine.[28] If any of the

---

[23] See the speech of Lord Shaw of Dunfermline in Amalgamated Society of Railway Servants v. Osborne 1910 A.C. 87 at pp. 106 to 116.
[24] Education Act, 1944 s. 114.   [25] ibid. s. 18.
[26] Education Act, 1944 s. 18.
[27] ibid. s. 19. This has long been the case in Cambridgeshire.
[28] ibid. s. 20.

schools are voluntary schools the constitution must be settled by agreement between the local education authority and the managers or governors of those schools.[28] In either case the minor authority must be adequately represented if there is a primary school in the group.[28] This clearly means that the minor authority must in all circumstances be entitled to appoint at least one representative; and where its interest is substantial, representation should be based upon the proportions appropriate to the particular classes of schools involved if they had not been grouped.

Right of Removal

The minor authority may remove any manager which it has appointed.[29]

F. PARISH TRUSTS

Parish councils and parish meetings have extensive rights in connection with the appointment of parochial charity trustees.[30] Parish trusts are constantly being created especially in connection with village halls, and parish councils usually figure in the negotiations leading to the setting up of such trusts. Sometimes the parish council acts as the holding trustee of the assets of a trust; sometimes the deeds (such as the Model Trust Deed of the National Council of Social Service) empower the parish council, with others, to appoint members of the managing committee.

[28] ibid. s. 20.   [29] ibid. s. 21.   [30] See page 125.

9

Officers and Employees

A. CHAIRMAN OR MAYOR

A parish, or rural borough council is not properly constituted until it has appointed its chairman (or, as the case may be, mayor)[1] and therefore his appointment must be the first business of the council at its annual meeting.[2] He must be either a parish councillor or qualified to be one[3] and he remains in office until his successor is elected unless he resigns, ceases to be qualified or becomes disqualified.

Precedence

As the presiding officer of a local authority the chairman ought not within his parish to yield precedence to the representative of any unofficial body, but his status is not fixed by any rule. A mayor has precedence within the borough before all others except the sovereign.

Duties

If he is present at a parish council he must preside,[4] and he has a certain control of its procedure for the purpose of enforcing the law. Accordingly he must prevent decisions being taken on matters which are not on the agenda, and he may prevent irrelevance, but he has no right to stop discussion of subjects properly brought up nor, if matters on the agenda remain to be settled, will his departure of itself bring the meeting to an end.

[1] L.G.A. 1933 s. 48(1). [2] L.G.A. 1933 s. 49(2).
[3] L.G.A. 1933 s. 49(1).
[4] L.G.A. 1933 Third Schedule Part IV para. 3(1).

Casting Vote

The person presiding at a parish council meeting (whether he is the chairman or not) has a second or casting vote.[5]

Convening Meetings

The chairman may, on three days notice,[6] convene the parish council at any time[7] and on seven[8] (or in certain cases fourteen[9]) days notice he may convene the parish meeting at any time.[10] He presides at the parish meeting[11] but if he is not an elector for that parish he only has a casting vote.[12]

Minutes

Minutes must be signed by the person presiding at a meeting.[13]

Miscellaneous Duties

The chairman of the parish council is as such required to receive and preserve certain public documents; he must act as returning officer if a poll is held consequent upon a parish meeting; he is the proper person to whom notice of resignation must be given; and he is personally responsible for the public exhibition of notices mobilizing the Territorial Army.

Mayor's Allowance

The mayor of a rural borough may be paid an allowance to meet the expenses of his office.[14]

B. VICE-CHAIRMAN OR DEPUTY MAYOR

A parish council may,[15] but need not, appoint a vice-chairman. In a rural borough the deputy mayor is appointed by

[5] ibid. Part V para. 1(2).
[6] L.G.A. 1933 Third Schedule Part V para. 2(3).
[7] L.G.A. 1933 Third Schedule Part V para. 2(1).
[8] L.G.A. 1933 Third Schedule Part VI para. 2(2).
[9] See page 88.   [10] L.G.A. 1933 Third Schedule Part VI para. 2(1).
[11] L.G.A. 1933 Third Schedule Part VI para. 3(1).
[12] L.G.A. 1933 s. 77(2).   [13] See page 61.
[14] L.G.A. 1958 Seventh Schedule para. 5(5).
[15] L.G.A. 1933 s. 49(5).

the mayor.[16] He may[17] but is not required to execute a declaration of acceptance of office and he holds office until immediately after the election of the *chairman* at the next annual meeting unless he resigns or ceases to be qualified or becomes disqualified.[18]

Parish Meetings

Subject to any standing orders made by the parish council anything authorised or required to be done by, to or before the chairman, may be done by, to or before the vice-chairman.[19] This comprehensive rule certainly applies to the meetings of the parish council and the duties of the chairman as an individual; unfortunately in relation to parish meetings it is contradicted in the same act by a provision that in the absence of the chairman, a parish meeting may elect some other person to preside.[20] As the parish council may make standing orders for the parish meeting the result appears to be that in the absence of such standing orders the vice-chairman presides at the parish meeting unless the parish meeting decides otherwise, and if he presides he has exactly the same voting rights as the chairman.

Rotation

Some parish councils appoint a new vice-chairman every year and make him responsible for inspecting the council's property. This custom ensures that a reasonable number of members are personally familiar with the parish property.[21]

C. TREASURER

A parish council may appoint one of its members or some other fit person to be treasurer but it cannot pay him.[22] He need not be an individual[23] but may be, for instance, a bank.

Security

The parish council must be protected in the manner directed by the county council against the treasurer's possible default and

[16] L.G.A. 1958 Seventh Schedule para. 5(7).
[17] L.G.A. 1933 s. 49(7).   [18] L.G.A. 1933 s. 49(6).
[19] L.G.A. 1933 s. 49(7).   [20] L.G.A. 1933 Third Schedule Part VI para. 3.
[21] See page 173.
[22] L.G.A. 1933 s. 114(4).   [23] Interpretation Act, 1889 s. 19.

for this purpose it may either require him to give or may itself take the necessary security.[24] If he is employed by the parish council, the council may defray the cost of the security. If he is not so employed (but is, for instance, an independent person such as a bank) it is bound to defray the cost. The security must be produced to the auditors at the annual audit.[25]

If a treasurer keeps a regular banking account for the parish council's money, he will not be held personally liable if the bank fails unless he is personally guilty of some negligence or default.[26]

D. CLERK OR TOWN CLERK

A parish council may appoint one of its members or some other fit person to be its clerk. In a rural borough he bears the title of Town Clerk. If he is a member he may not be paid but if he is not a member he may receive reasonable remuneration.[27, 28] Where the parish council is exercising functions delegated to it by the rural district council, it may, unless the latter otherwise directs, make use of the services of the clerk of the rural district council.[29]

Duties

The extent to which the clerk's duties are defined by the general law is now obscure though the existence of certain particular duties can be asserted with some confidence; for this reason his duties and remuneration[30] should be specified in a written contract which should, amongst other matters, require him to attend at and keep the minutes of parish meetings; the parish council has, however, power to pay special remuneration for such attendances[31] if they are not included in the contract.

In the absence of specification in any contract the duties of the clerk in any given parish will be those which his predecessors have hitherto been accustomed to perform. There is no general authority for the belief that he need not attend parish meetings: indeed where the parish meeting is exercising powers which

---

[24] L.G.A. 1933 s. 119(3).   [25] L.G.A. 1933 s. 119(4).
[26] Colchester Guardians v. Moy (1893) 68 L.T. 564.
[27] L.G.A. 1933 s. 114.
[28] See also L.G.A. 1933 s. 122; for disqualification for employment see page 86.   [29] L.G.A. 1933 s. 114(3).
[30] See page 84 (Superannuation).   [31] L.G.A. 1933 s. 193(2).

were formerly exercisable by the vestry, the clerk, as successor to the vestry clerk, is probably bound to attend.

Subject to the direction of the parish council the clerk must keep the parish documents and records in his custody, and he is required to sign certain notices[32] and summonses.

Allotments

It is not the duty of the clerk as such to collect rents for allotments unless it has always been the custom of the parish for him to do so, but as separate allotment accounts must be kept[33] that part of his pay which is referable to his activities in connection with allotments should be charged to the allotments account; it will usually be most convenient for the council to fix this amount by entering into a separate contract with him and dealing specifically with his allotments duties in that contract.

Pay

Save that the clerk's remuneration must be reasonable[34] there are no rules for fixing its amount and parish councils vary widely in the amounts paid and in the methods by which they are calculated. Sometimes he is paid a salary or fee which may vary from the substantial to the nominal; in other cases he may be paid a fee for each meeting attended; and in some instances he is paid a sum which is the equivalent of a fixed percentage of the council's expenditure in each year. Combinations of these methods are not unknown, and many clerks are not paid at all.

The National Association of Parish Councils has attempted to introduce some order into the payment of clerks. Since 1958 this has taken the shape of a formula which is not binding on the member parish councils but which any council can use as a starting point for a rational consideration of the subject.

The Association thought that four specific matters should be taken into consideration: these are the population, the rate resources of the parish, the amount of work to be done and the clerk's own qualifications, but that it must always be borne in mind that parish council clerks are with rare exceptions part-time workers and that nothing must be done to discourage the principle of voluntary service.

[32] See page 83 (Accountability); page 42 (Casual Vacancy) and page 49 (Summons).
[33] See page 262.   [34] L.G.A. 1933 s. 114.

D

The result was a formula which is applicable to most parishes (other than those with extremes of population or rateable value) and to part-time clerks only. It is based upon the assumptions that in rural areas population and rateable value tend to go hand in hand, and that the amount of work is very roughly related to the population; but that since most parish council powers are discretionary a piecework element is desirable.

In 1965 the formula was as follows: a middle figure is reached by taking one quarter of the product of the penny rate of the parish and adding to it a sum (in pounds) represented by multiplying the number of parish councillors by the number of meetings of all kinds which the clerk must attend and dividing the result by eight. The salary payable is then a figure beginning 10 per cent. below and ending at 10 per cent. above this middle figure. This can be represented as follows: where $P =$ Penny Rate Product, $C =$ the number of Councillors and $M =$ the number of Meetings, the sum payable is between 90 per cent. and 110 per cent. of £ $\frac{P}{4} + \frac{C \times M}{8}$

E. STANDING AND TEMPORARY DEPUTIES

A parish council may appoint a standing deputy to the clerk or treasurer,[35] and if the deputy clerk is not a member, it may pay him; a deputy treasurer and a deputy clerk who is a member may not be paid.[36] Similarly the council may appoint temporary deputies during vacancies or if the principal officers or their standing deputies are unable to act.[37] Standing deputies hold office during pleasure[38] but apparently temporary deputies do not,[39] but the council may in either case include in the contract of service provisions for notice and for regular retirement.[40]

F. SECURITY AND ACCOUNTABILITY OF OFFICERS

The purpose of security is to ensure that if money or property is lost there will be a fund in existence from which it can be

[35] L.G.A. 1933 s. 115(1).   [36] ibid. 115(2).
[37] ibid. 116(1).   [38] ibid. 115(3).
[39] ibid. 116.   [40] ibid. 121.

replaced. The purpose of accountability is to provide a quick and simple method for settling accounts between a parish council and its officers and for recovering any outstanding debts owed by an officer to the council.

Safe Keeping

A parish council can give or take security only[41] for its treasurer, and therefore it is as a rule unwise to allow substantial sums to remain for any length of time in the hands of any other officer unless he is willing to give security himself and at his own expense. Money collected on behalf of the council (for instance the rents of allotments) should if possible be banked the same day and in particular all money should be safely lodged before a weekend. An unsecured officer may suffer great hardship if he loses (perhaps through burglary) money belonging to the council, and the method of safekeeping should be supervised as much in his interest as in the interest of the public.

Frankness

Where security involves entering into a contract of suretyship, there must be the utmost frankness and good faith between the parties. The sureties will be discharged if they have been misled by the parish council into a reasonable (but false) sense of security which put them off from making inquiries, or if the nature of the office or its duties changes materially so as to affect their risk. The release of one surety automatically discharges the others, but death is not necessarily a release.

Before cancelling a bond the parish council should be satisfied that no occasion to enforce it has actually arisen and that the public funds will be protected by other security from the time of cancellation.

Paying-in Book

Every officer who pays money into a bank must be provided by the parish council with a duplicate paying-in book.[42]

Accountability

Every officer may be required whilst in office or within three months afterwards to account for money and property committed to his charge and for receipts and payments due to or

[41] This limitation does not apply to rural boroughs.
[42] The Accounts (Payment into Bank) Order, 1922 S.R. & O. No. 1404.

from any person and must produce all the supporting vouchers and documents, and if he owes any money he must pay it in. If he refuses or wilfully neglects to pay, or if after three days written notice he refuses or wilfully neglects to deliver the necessary accounts or vouchers or fails to give proper satisfaction, he may be ordered to do so by the Court of Summary Jurisdiction where he is or where he resides. The written notice must be signed by the clerk or by three members and it must be given to him or left at his usual or last known address.[43]

Summary proceedings of this kind do not prejudice the council's right to sue the officer or his surety except that the officer must not be sued by action and proceeded against summarily for the same cause.[43]

G. SUPERANNUATION

Employees of parish councils and parish meetings are not automatically entitled to rights or subject to liabilities under the Local Government Superannuation Scheme[44] but (subject to certain exceptions and conditions) a parish council may by 'statutory resolution' specify that any of its employees is a contributory employee[45] and thereupon he and the parish council must make proper periodical contributions to the appropriate superannuation fund (which is usually the fund administered by the county council[46]) and the employee becomes entitled to such benefits as are specified by statutory instrument made under the Local Government Superannuation Acts.[47]

Statutory Resolution

The terms of a statutory resolution and the fact that it will be moved must at least twenty-eight days before the meeting be publicly notified in the usual manner for giving notices of meetings.[48] It is desirable to consult the administering authority before settling the terms of the resolution.

[43] L.G.A. 1933 s. 120.
[44] See L.G. Superannuation Acts 1937 and 1953 and the relevant statutory instruments.
[45] L.G. Superannuation Act, 1937 s. 3(2)(c) and s. 40.
[46] ibid. s. 4(2).
[47] There are many of these; the subject is not appropriate for detailed treatment here.
[48] L.G. Superannuation Act, 1937 s. 40.

The resolution cannot apply to any person under 18[49] nor to an employee who has attained the age of 55 and has not completed and cannot complete ten years' service before the age of 65.[50] A person legally attains a specified age on the day *before* his appropriate birthday.[51]

Grave Misconduct

A contributory employee who is dismissed or resigns or otherwise ceases to hold his employment as a result of a fraudulent offence or of grave misconduct forfeits his rights in respect of his previous service.[52] Misconduct here means conduct of a kind which would bring a moral stigma in any walk of life and is not confined to conduct in the employment, but the misconduct must be 'grave', and this seems to imply at least such conduct as would justify instant dismissal or the insertion in a bankrupt's certificate of discharge that he had been guilty of misconduct.

H. GRATUITIES

Where an employee is not entitled to a 'superannuation allowance'[53] a parish council or parish meeting may pay a gratuity not exceeding twice the amount of his annual salary to an employee on his ceasing to be employed by it. The gratuity may be paid in a lump sum or in instalments or by an annuity.[54]

Injury

Where a contributory employee under 65 ceases to be employed as a result of permanent incapacity caused by the employment, he may be paid a gratuity either in a lump sum or by periodical payments. The lump sum must be reasonable having regard to all the circumstances including any statutory right to compensation or superannuation allowance; the periodical payments must be limited to the difference between the statutory compensation or superannuation allowance to which he is entitled and the amount to which he would have

---

[49] ibid. s. 3(4)(b)   [50] ibid. s. 3(4)(b) and s. 7.
[51] See In re Shurey 1918 1 Ch. 263 where the authorities are collected.
[52] L.G. Superannuation Act, 1937 s. 24.
[53] This is the jargon phrase for 'pension' under these acts, see **L.G.** Superannuation Act, 1937 s. 8.
[54] L.G. Superannuation Act, 1953 s. 18.

been entitled if he had reached the age of 65 at the salary which he was receiving immediately before the injury.[54]

Gratuities are not paid from the superannuation fund but by the parish council or meeting itself.[54] No statutory resolution is therefore necessary and the provision for giving twenty-eight days notice does not apply.

I. BRIBERY AND CORRUPTION

It is an offence to offer or give bribes to public officers and for such officers to accept or solicit them.[55]

J. DISQUALIFICATION FOR EMPLOYMENT

A parish council may not appoint to a paid office under it any person during the period that he is a member or for twelve months after he ceases to be a member.[56]

[54] L.G. Superannuation Act, 1937 s. 11.
[55] For these offences see page 63. [56] L.G.A. 1933 s. 122.

The Parish Meeting and the Representative Body

Every rural parish must have a parish meeting[1] and meetings may also be held for a parish ward,[2] for a part of a parish where the parish has a defined boundary[3] and for part of a parish for lighting purposes.[4] A rural borough does not have a parish meeting.

Parish meetings are therefore of four main types, namely:—a parish meeting for the whole of a parish which has a separate parish council; for a parish which is grouped with other parishes under a common parish council; for a parish which is not represented upon a parish council at all; and finally for a part of a parish.

A. MEMBERSHIP AND RIGHT TO PRESIDE

A parish meeting consists of the local government electors registered for the area for which it is held[5] and in addition if there is a parish council the chairman of the parish council may attend (whether he is an elector or not[6]) and if he is present he must preside.[7] The vice-chairman of a parish council is allowed to preside in the chairman's absence, unless the parish council has made a standing order to the contrary,[8] but if the parish meeting wishes to appoint some other person to preside in the

---

[1] L.G.A. 1933 s. 43(1).   [2] L.G.A. 1933 s. 78.
[3] L.G.A. 1933 s. 89.   [4] P.C.A. 1957 s. 3.
[5] L.G.A. 1933 s. 47(1) and 78(1). [6] L.G.A. 1933 s. 77(2) and 78(2).
[7] L.G.A. 1933 Third Schedule Part VI para. 3(1).
[8] L.G.A. 1933 s. 49(7).

chairman's place it is entitled to do so[9] and the making of such an appointment supersedes the vice-chairman's rights.[10]

B. NUMBER, DATE AND TIME OF MEETINGS

The parish meeting must assemble annually between the 1st March and 1st April (both inclusive);[11] and where there is no separate parish council it must (subject to the provisions of any grouping order) meet on at least one other occasion in the year.[12] In addition it must meet when convened by the parish council or if there is no parish council by the chairman of the parish meeting,[13] and it may be convened as often as may be required.

There is no effective method of enforcing these rules.

Proceedings must not begin before six o'clock in the evening.[14]

C. RIGHT TO CONVENE

A parish meeting may be convened by the chairman of the parish council or any two parish councillors[15] or in a parish without a parish council by the chairman of the parish meeting or by any representative of the parish upon the rural district council[16] or in either case by six electors for the area for which it is to be held.[17] The parish council may also convene it[18] but is under no obligation to do so unless its consent is required before the parish council does certain acts.[19]

D. NOTICE

Notices specifying the time and place and business of an intended meeting and signed by the conveners[20] must be affixed

[9] L.G.A. 1933 Third Schedule Part VI para. 3(3).
[10] See page 74 (footnote).
[11] L.G.A. 1933 Third Schedule Part VI para. 1(1).
[12] ibid. para. 1(2) proviso.
[13] ibid. para. 1(2).
[14] ibid. para. 1(3).
[15] ibid. para. 2.
[16] ibid. para. 2(c).
[17] ibid. para. 2(d) and s. 78(b).
[18] ibid. para. 1(2).   [19] See page 91.
[20] L.G.A. 1933 Third Schedule Part VI para. 2(2).

at or near the door of each Anglican[21] church or chapel and in some conspicuous place or places in the parish and, in addition, the conveners may give such publicity to the notice as seems desirable.[22]

In ordinary cases a minimum of seven days' notice is required[23] but if any of the business relates to the establishment or dissolution of a parish council, to the grouping of the parish with another parish or to the adoption of an adoptive power, at least fourteen days' notice is required,[24] and if it is intended to move a statutory resolution relating to superannuation twenty-eight days' notice is required.[25]

E. QUORUM

The quorum of a parish meeting is two[26] unless a document has to be executed in which case it is three.[27]

F. DECISIONS

Decisions are taken in the first instance by a majority of those present and voting. If the chairman is an elector he has an original as well as a casting vote;[28] if he is not an elector he only has a casting vote.[29] Unless a poll is demanded before the end of the meeting, the chairman's declaration of the result is final.[30]

Voting

Unlike a parish council a parish meeting is not required to vote in any particular way and so the chairman may ascertain the effect of the voting from any evidence which may in the circumstances lead to an accurate result: thus a voice vote may in the case of an overwhelming majority be sufficient, but where the opposing opinions are represented with approximate equality, a count, whether of persons or voting papers must be taken.

[21] Ormerod v. Chadwick 16 L.J. MC 143.
[22] L.G.A. 1933 Third Schedule Part VI para. 2(3)(a). See also page 189.
[23] ibid. para. 2(2).   [24] ibid. para. 2(2) proviso.
[25] L.G. Superannuation Act, 1937 s. 3(2)(c) and s. 40. See also page 84.
[26] See Loughlin v. Guiness (1904) 23 N.Z.L.R. 748 per Denniston J. at page 754.   [27] L.G.A. 1933 s. 47(1).
[28] ibid. Third Schedule Part VI para. 5(3).
[29] ibid. s. 77(2) and 78(2).
[30] ibid. Third Schedule Part VI para. 5(2) and (3).

D*

Poll

A poll may be demanded not later than the end of the meeting on any question arising at it. Such a poll must be held only if five or one-third of the electors present (whichever is the less) insist or if the person presiding at the meeting consents.[31] It is not clear what happens if the chairman alone calls for a poll but the outcome probably depends on whether he is an elector or not.

The poll is held in accordance with rules made by the Home Secretary[32] and the procedure is generally similar to the procedure for electing a parish councillor[33] save that the returning officer is the chairman of the parish meeting[34] instead of the clerk of the rural district council. If, however, the chairman will not or cannot act or the poll concerns the appointment to an office for which he is a candidate, he must appoint someone else and must send him such particulars as will enable him to give the necessary notices.[35] If the chairman dies before appointing a returning officer, the latter is appointed by the chairman of the rural district council.[36]

The returning officer must appoint an office for the purpose of the poll.[37]

G. PLACES OF MEETING AND POLLING

In a parish where there is no separate parish council, the parish meeting is entitled and not entitled to meet in the same places as a parish council.[38] Where there is a separate parish council, the parish meeting has the same rights save that it is not entitled to meet in the church or vestry.[39]

Similar rules apply to polls.

H. RELATIONSHIP BETWEEN PARISH MEETING AND PARISH COUNCIL

Though a parish meeting may discuss parish affairs and pass resolutions thereon[40] its resolutions differ considerably in their

---

[31] L.G.A. 1933 Third Schedule Part VI para. 5.
[32] See R.P.A. 1949 s. 29.
[33] See Parish Meetings (Polls Rules) 1950 S.Is. 1950 Nos. 984 and 1272.
[34] S.I. 1950 No. 984 Art. 1(1).   [35] S.I. 1950 No. 984 Art. 1(2).
[36] S.I. 1950 No. 984 Art. 1(3).   [37] S.I. 1950 No. 984 Art. 1(4).
[38] See pages 47–8.   [39] See page 48.
[40] L.G.A. 1933 Third Schedule Part VI para. 4(1).

legal consequences. In a few cases a resolution is legally binding and in a few more the refusal to give a required consent will make a line of conduct intended by the parish council unlawful. In all other cases a resolution of the parish meeting is persuasive only; the parish council may legally disregard it and leave the electors to their remedy at the next election.

Binding Resolutions

A resolution by a well-attended parish meeting that the parish council ought to provide allotments, legally obliges the parish council to provide them.[41]

A resolution that a burial ground should be provided for the parish, has the same effect as the formal adoption of the Burial Acts,[42] and imposes upon the parish council a legal obligation to provide a burial ground.[43]

Sometimes a trust instrument will make certain resolutions binding upon a parish council acting as trustee.

Necessary Consents

The parish council must obtain the consent of the parish meeting to expenditure (other than expenditure mentioned in the First Schedule to the Parish Councils Act, 1957)[44] exceeding the product of a 4d. rate, or such higher amount as the Minister may by order in a particular case allow,[45, 46] and to any expense or liability which will involve a loan,[47] and it cannot sell, reappropriate[48] or exchange land without such consent,[49] nor can it exercise adoptive powers until the parish meeting has adopted them.[50] Certain consents are sometimes required by trust instruments.

Other Resolutions

The right of the parish meeting to discuss parish affairs extends to any public matter of a parochial nature and is not confined to the exercise of the statutory functions of the parish council or of any other parish authority. The parish meeting may accordingly pass resolutions on the public activities or

---

[41] See page 252.
[43] B.A. 1852 s. 25; see Chapter 29.
[44] P.C.A. 1957 s. 15.
[46] See page 133 for details.
[48] T. & C.P.A. 1959 s. 28.
[50] L.G.A. 1894 s. 7.

[42] L.G.A. 1894 s. 7(8).
[45] L.G.A. 1933 s. 193(3).
[47] L.G.A. 1933 s. 193(4).
[49] L.G.A. 1933 s. 170.

policies in the parish of any other local authority, public body, government department or public service.

Expenses

Where there is a parish council the expenses of parish meetings and of polls consequent upon them are met by it.[51]

I. PARISH MEETINGS WHERE THERE IS NO SEPARATE PARISH COUNCIL

A parish meeting is not a corporation and is therefore unable to own property or to sue or be sued.[52] Generally speaking it is not a local authority[53] though for certain limited purposes it may be regarded as one.[54]

Its alleged lack of legal personality has not prevented Parliament from enabling it to exercise functions. It may adopt the Adoptive Acts;[55] it may administer allotments; any function of a parish council may be conferred upon it by an order of the county council;[56] it has inherited certain miscellaneous functions from the vestry[57] and has certain powers of appointment, representation and complaint;[57] finally it may appoint committees to administer any of its functions provided that all the acts of such a committee are submitted to it for approval.[58]

J. THE REPRESENTATIVE BODY

The representative body is a puppet corporation which in law exists (subject to the express terms of any grouping order) in every parish with no separate parish council and nowhere else.[59] It consists of the chairman of the parish meeting and the representative of the parish on the rural district council, but if these two offices happen to be combined in the same person, the rural district council must appoint an elector for the parish to act as the second member. This elector, unless he resigns or ceases to be qualified or becomes disqualified, holds office for four years or until the chairman and the member of the rural district council cease to be the same person whichever first occurs.[59]

---

[51] L.G.A. 1933 s. 193(2).
[52] See also L.G.A. 1933 s. 276.   [53] See also L.G.A. 1933 s. 305.
[54] See page 252 (Allotments), page 84 (Superannuation).
[55] L.G.A. 1894 s. 7(1).   [56] L.G.A. 1933 s. 273.   [57] L.G.A. 1894 s. 19.
[58] L.G.A. 1933 s. 90.   [59] L.G.A. 1933 s. 47(3).

The representative body is a corporation with perpetual succession and a name and it may hold land.[60] It signifies its acts under the hands or hands and seals of its members.[61, 62]

Its function is simply to be the depository of the title to parish property; it is really the parish trustee and apart from a power to convene a parish meeting to consider arrangements for providing information relating to the footpaths survey[63] it has no discretion of its own at all but is required in all respects to act in manner directed by the parish meeting.[64]

K. MINUTES

The rules on the signature and admissibility of the minutes of a parish meeting and its committees are in effect the same as those in force for a parish council.[65] A representative body has no minutes.

L. ADMISSION OF THE PUBLIC

The press and public have the same rights of admission to a parish meeting as they have to a meeting of a parish council.[66] It is therefore advisable to set aside a clearly marked place for strangers to avoid confusion when a vote is taken.

[60] L.G.A. 1933 s. 47(3).   [61] L.G.A. 1933 s. 47(4).
[62] For its predecessors in title see page 106.
[63] National Parks Act, 1949 s. 28(3).
[64] L.G.A. 1933 s. 47(4) and P.C.A. 1957 s. 3(s)(b).
[65] See page 61.
[66] Public Bodies (Admission to Meetings) Act, 1960. See page 49.

Records, Books, Documents and Returns

A. CUSTODY AND CUSTODIANS' MUTUAL RIGHTS OF INSPECTION

Before 1894 the public books, writings and papers of the parish and *the three registers* (of baptism, marriage and burial) were in the custody of the incumbent and churchwardens. These documents have since been divided into two groups: on the one hand there are the three registers together with documents containing entries wholly or partly relating to the affairs of the church other than documents specifically directed by law to be kept with the public books, and on the other there are all the other public books and the documents directed to be kept with them.[1] The former group is now in the custody of the incumbent and Parochial Church Council[2] whilst the latter remains in its existing custody as at the 17th November, 1933, until the parish council (or where there is no parish council the parish meeting) otherwise directs.[1] Each side is entitled to have reasonable access to documents in the possession of the other and disputes on custody and access are to be settled by the County Council.[3]

It has been suggested that the parish and parochial church councils might advantageously inspect each other's documents annually and that in the parishes which hold a civic Sunday, such inspection might form part of the ceremonies.

[1] L.G.A. 1933 s. 281.
[2] Parochial Church Councils (Powers) Measure, 1921 s. 4.
[3] L.G.A. 1933 s. 281 (3).

B. DEPOSIT AND SUPERVISION

The manner in which documents are kept and preserved is controlled by four different types of authority, some of whom may make conflicting orders.

Manorial Documents

Manorial documents are subject to a certain control exercised by the Master of the Rolls[4] who may make enquiries regarding their proper preservation and may direct the transfer of documents which are not being properly preserved to museums or other institutions for proper preservation. Such an order does not affect rights of inspection.[5]

Tithes

Documents relating to tithes may be placed in such custody as may be ordered by Quarter Sessions[6] but the county council is equally entitled to make orders for their custody.[7] Until an order is made one copy of the confirmed instrument of apportionment or agreement should be kept by the parish council.[8] Sealed copies (as opposed to originals) of instruments of apportionment are under the jurisdiction of the Master of the Rolls who may determine their places of deposit.[9]

Of the remaining documents those in the hands of the ecclesiastical and of the lay body are supervised respectively by the Bishop[10] and the county council.[11] These supervisory powers are in practice only spasmodically effective.

The county council must periodically inquire how the lay parish records are being preserved and must make preservation orders as it thinks fit; these orders must be obeyed by the parish council (or parish meeting as the case may be).[11] All County councils maintain county record offices and are willing to preserve and maintain any parochial records entrusted to them. Deposit at such record offices makes no difference to ownership or rights of inspection and an undertaking to return at seven days' notice is usually given.

[4] Law of Property Amendment Act, 1924 Second Schedule.
[5] Law of Property Act, 1922 s. 144A(5).   [6] Tithe Act, 1846 s. 17.
[7] See page 100 and Fox v. Pitt 1918 2 K.B. 196..
[8] Tithe Act, 1836, s. 64.   [9] Tithe Act, 1936, s. 36.
[10] Parochial Registers and Records Measure, 1929.
[11] L.G.A. 1933 s. 281(4).

In relation to the three registers[12] the Bishop has powers of inquiry and control over his parochial organisations which are very similar to those possessed by a county council over a parish council,[13] and where a diocesan record office has been established an incumbent may, with the consent of the Bishop and the Parochial Church Council, deposit in it any such register which is not in actual use, and certain other documents; these are deeds and documents of value as historical records or as evidence of legal rights, but do not include registrars' duplicate copies of marriage registers nor the documents deposited in the parish under the Tithe Acts, 1836–1925, or under local or personal tithe acts, nor do they include manorial documents.[14] Where documents which may be voluntarily deposited are exposed to danger of loss or damage the Bishop may order their deposit at the Diocesan Office.[15]

C. PROMOTION OF USE

A parish council may do anything necessary or expedient to enable adequate use to be made of records under its control and in particular it can permit persons with or without charge to inspect and copy them; it can have them indexed and calendared and can publish such indices and calendars and it can hold exhibitions or entrusts its records to others for exhibition.[16]

A parish council may also bear the expense incurred by anyone else in doing to its records what it may do itself or in doing to records of local interest not under its control what it could do if they were.[17] In effect this means that if any records of parish interest are deposited in a museum or with a county archivist, the parish council can pay to have them restored, indexed, calendared or otherwise made useful.

D. SAFES AND REPOSITORIES

Where there is a separate parish council it must either provide proper 'repositories' for its records or request the

[12] See page 95.
[13] Parochial Registers and Records Measure, 1929. s. 1.
[14] Parochial Registers and Records Measure, ss. 3 and 5. See Law of Property Amendment Act, 1924 Second Schedule.
[15] Parochial Registers and Records Measure, 1929 s. 4.
[16] L.G. (Records) Act, 1962 s. 1. [17] ibid. s. 4.

rural district council to do so, in which case the rural district council must comply with the request.[18] Where there is no parish council the rural district council must provide the repositories with the consent of the parish meeting.[19]

The three registers must, subject to any directions given by the Bishop, be kept in an iron chest in the church or at the residence of the incumbent if he lives in the parish.[20]

E. PUBLIC RIGHTS OF INSPECTION

The minutes of a local authority (including a parish meeting [21]) may be inspected by any elector for the area of the authority upon payment of a fee not exceeding 1*s*. 0*d*. and he may copy or make extracts from them.[22] This rule applies also to committee minutes which have been laid before the council for approval.[23] Such electors may also free of charge[24] inspect and copy orders for payment[25] and the financial statement or abstract of accounts of the authority and its treasurer with any auditors' report upon them, and copies must be delivered to such electors upon payment of a reasonable sum.[26] The accounts themselves may be inspected and copied by any member of the council.[27]

Documents which are legally open to inspection must be open at reasonable hours[28] and any person having custody of them who obstructs lawful inspection or copying or who refuses to give copies or extracts to persons entitled to them is liable to a fine of £5.[29]

F. RETURNS

General Information

Parish councils, joint committees and joint boards must make to the Home Secretary or the Minister such reports and returns and give such information on their functions as he

---

[18] L.G.A. 1933 s. 282(1).   [19] L.G.A. 1933 s. 282(2).
[20] Parochial Registers Act, 1812 s. 5, amended by Parochial Registers and Records Measure, 1929 s. 1.
[21] L.G.A. 1933 s. 283(8).   [22] L.G.A. 1933 s. 283(1).
[23] Williams v. Manchester Corporation (1897) 45 W.R. 412.
[24] L.G.A. 1933 s. 283(6).   [25] L.G.A. 1933 s. 283(2).
[26] L.G.A. 1933 s. 283(4).   [27] ibid. s. 283(3).
[28] ibid. s. 283(6).   [29] ibid. s. 283(7).

may require or as may be required by either House of Parliament.[30] Parish meetings are not obliged to comply with these requirements.

Financial Returns

Parish councils and parish meetings are required annually to make a financial return to the Minister showing their income and expenditure[31] and this obligation is enforceable by *mandamus* and by a fine of £20 on the responsible person who fails to make the return.[32] Parish councils must also at request and under similar sanctions make a return within one month showing what provision has been made for loan repayments.[33]

Responsible Persons

Returns required from a parish council must be made by the clerk[34] and financial returns must be certified by the treasurer.[31] Those required from a parish meeting must be made by the chairman.[31]

Financial returns need not be made if a copy of the annual financial statement prepared for purposes of the annual audit[35] has been forwarded to the Minister, unless he otherwise directs.[31]

G. MISCELLANEOUS NOTES ON PARTICULAR DOCUMENTS

The following is a list of some of the more important documents together with suggestions for finding some of them.

Inclosure Awards. If no copy is in the possession of the parish council, inquiry should be made to the Parochial Church Council and incumbent and failing them to the county council and Clerk of the Peace. If this fails to bring a copy to light, the Public Record Office in London should be consulted and in the case of a Yorkshire parish, the deeds registries at Beverley, Northallerton or Wakefield. If the award was made under a private act, application to inspect the act itself may be made to the House of Lords. Some awards are also in the possession of the Land Registry in London.

[30] ibid. s. 284.
[31] ibid. s. 244.
[32] ibid. s. 246.
[33] ibid. s. 199.
[34] ibid. s. 199(1) and s. 244(3)(c)(i).
[35] ibid. s. 222.

Tithe apportionments, parochial agreements, etc. (sometimes loosely called tithe awards). If no copies are in the possession of the parish council, inquiry should be made to the parochial church council and the Diocesan Registry. Some of the original documents are in the possession of the Ministry of Agriculture. If an order of the county council or of the justices has been made, inquiries should be addressed to the person named in the order or his successors in title or their respective solicitors.

Manor rolls, terriers and court rolls. These should be in the hands of the Lord of the Manor. More commonly they will be found in the possession of his solicitor as, or in succession to, the steward of the manor. Sometimes they will have been deposited with a museum, library, record office or learned body, either voluntarily or as a result of an order made by the Master of the Rolls. In such cases the Lord or his solicitor should know where they are. Occasionally, however, they will be found among papers formerly in the possession of the vestry with the result that they may have descended to the parish council and the county council on the one hand or to the parochial church council and (notwithstanding the law) to the Diocesan Registry.

Private Acts of Parliament. Private acts which authorise the compulsory acquisition of land for a railway, canal or similar undertaking, should be in the hands of the clerk of the county council or clerk of the peace of each county in which such land is situated.[36]

Plans and Sections of alterations from the original plan and section approved by Parliament for a railway must be deposited with the Clerks of the Peace and of the relevant parish councils.[37] Such plans should be in the custody of the parish council but the older ones may be in the possession of the parochial church council or even of the Diocesan Registry. Both Houses of Parliament require the local deposit of plans in connection with certain private bills to authorise the construction of certain types of public works.[38]

Local Acts conferring special powers upon a parish council or its predecessors. The county council will have copies.

Statutory Instruments relating to the parish and its boundaries.

---

[36] Lands Clauses Consolidation Act, 1845 ss. 150 and 151.
[37] Railway Clauses Consolidation Act, 1845 ss. 8 to 10.
[38] L.G.A. 1933 s. 280 and House of Commons S.O. (Private Business) 27 and 36 and H.L. S.O. 27 and 36.

Agreements and Arbitration Awards arising out of boundary alterations.

Orders of the County Council on the constitution and functions of the parish council.

Orders and Schemes made by the Charity Commissioners or the Ministry of Education in relation to parochial charities.

Trust Instruments.

Deeds, Leases and Conveyances.

Mortgages and the Mortgage Register.

Written Contracts.

Registers of Baptism, Marriage and Burial.

Copies of Statutory Reports and Returns.

Minutes. Vestry minutes may be found with the parochial church council or in the Diocesan Registry.

H. COMMONS AND GREENS

Where difficulty is experienced in tracing documents required for the registration of a common or village green a parish council can apply for help through the documentary research service of the Commons, Open Spaces and Footpaths Society.

12

Property

A. GENERAL

'Parish property' is a class of property whose rents and profits are applicable (or would be applicable if let) to the *general* benefit of one or more parishes or of their ratepayers, parishioners or inhabitants, and also certain exhausted quarries, but it does not include charitable property not so applicable nor property acquired before 1st April, 1930, by a board of guardians for the relief of the poor.[1]

Corporate land is land belonging to or held in trust for a borough otherwise than for an express statutory purpose.[2]

Not all parish property is necessarily owned by the parish council, and conversely not all property owned by a parish council is necessarily parish property; parish property owned by a parish council may be 'inherited', 'transferred' or 'acquired'; acquired property may either come to the parish council by gift or may have been acquired actively for the purpose of the parish council's functions; actively acquired property may be obtained compulsorily or by agreement and property acquired by agreement may be obtainable by purchase, lease or exchange.

In addition in most parishes there are lands not vested in a public authority where the inhabitants have certain rights and over which the parish council has or may have powers of repair, maintenance, control or contribution.

These and allied classifications are illustrated by the diagram on the next page.

---

[1] See L.G.A. 1933 s. 178 and the definition in s. 305 which codifies the definition in L.G.A. 1929 s. 115(6) and the effect of Corporation of London v. L.C.C. (1931) 1 K.B. 25.
[2] L.G.A. 1933 s. 305.

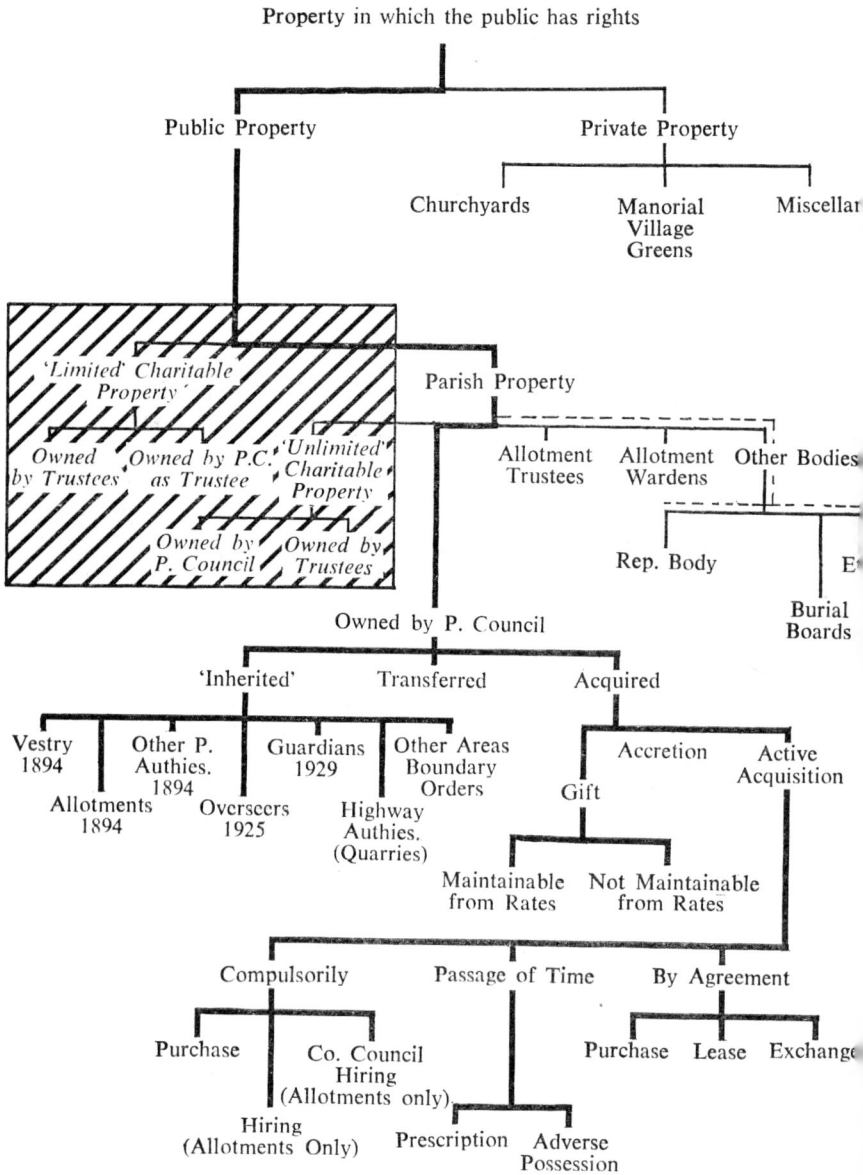

Property in which the public has rights

Public Property

Private Property

Churchyards   Manorial   Miscellar
                     Village
                     Greens

'Limited' Charitable
Property

Owned   Owned by P.C.   'Unlimited'
by Trustees as Trustee   Charitable
                             Property

            Owned by   Owned by
            P. Council   Trustees

Parish Property

Allotment   Allotment   Other Bodies
Trustees   Wardens

                            Rep. Body   E

                            Burial
                            Boards

Owned by P. Council

'Inherited'   Transferred   Acquired

Vestry   Other P.   Guardians   Other Areas   Accretion   Active
1894   Authies.   1929   Boundary   Acquisition
             1894   Orders
    Allotments   Overseers   Highway   Gift
    1894   1925   Authies.
                                  (Quarries)
                                              Maintainable   Not Maintainable
                                              from Rates   from Rates

Compulsorily   Passage of Time   By Agreement

Purchase   Purchase   Lease   Exchange
            Co. Council
            Hiring
       (Allotments only)
    Hiring
(Allotments Only)   Prescription   Adverse
                                        Possession

B. TYPES OF PROPERTY

The following is a list of the main kinds of property owned by a parish council or representative body or in which they or the inhabitants have or may have rights or interests.

Allotment Gardens, Pasture, Grazing Rights and Stints

'Bus and Public Shelters

Chattels including Safes, Chests, Furniture, Typewriters and Books

Churchyards and Burial Grounds

The Church and Vestry

Public Clocks

Cycle Parks and Racks

Fuel Allotments

Investments

Lighting Equipment

Mortuaries and Hearses

Museums

Parish and Village Halls

Parochial Offices provided under the Parochial Offices Act, 1861

Parks, Recreation Grounds, Playing Fields and Children's Playgrounds

Pounds, Pumps, Wells, Hearse houses, etc., of ancient origin

Quarries

Rights of Way (local only)

Schools

Seats

Small Local Undertakings such as Water and Harbour Boards

Undenominational Chapels

Vestry Rooms provided under the Vestries Act, 1850

Village Greens, Commons and Allotments for exercise and recreation

Workhouses, Cottages and other property which were before 14th August, 1834, vested in trustees or the Churchwardens and Overseers for the relief of the poor

War Memorials

C. THEORETICAL EXPOSITION

Like parish meetings the vestries were not generally[3] corporations and had no legal personality. 'Their' property had therefore to be held on their behalf by other persons and so, immediately before the Local Government Act, 1894, was passed, such property was vested in bodies of trustees of varying kinds and composition[4] who had as a rule to obey the directions of the vestry, though sometimes the property was subject to special trusts or to statutory appropriation for a particular purpose. The most important of these trustees were the churchwardens, the overseers and the guardians acting alone or in various combinations, but there also existed, and sometimes still exist, more specialised bodies of which the commonest were burial boards, inspectors of lighting, wardens, trustees, committees or managers of allotments, and commissioners for public baths.

The Act of 1894 secularised the civil administration of all parishes and it therefore became necessary to transfer property held for non-ecclesiastical purposes away from such church officials as held it to the new secular institutions. The authors of the original bill in 1893 had intended that there should be a parish council in every parish to which both property and authority would be transferred but their political opponents forced them to abandon this arrangement in relation to small parishes, and it therefore became necessary to preserve alongside the new parish councils a slightly modernised version of the older system for use in the parishes without separate parish councils. In relation to these numerous parishes the Act therefore did little to reduce the confusion which it had been intended to remedy, more particularly as it became necessary to preserve some of the specialised parish authorities.

D. PROPERTY 'INHERITED' BY
REPRESENTATIVE BODY

In parishes without a separate parish council the Act of 1894 created a corporation consisting of the chairman of a parish meeting and overseers[5] and transferred to it the legal interest in

---

[3] Some select vestries were corporations.
[4] No doubt these persons were in fact trustees but the word is not used here in a technical sense.   [5] L.G.A. 1894 s. 19(6).

all property which would have been transferred to the parish council had one existed.[6] On 1st April, 1927, overseers were abolished and their functions and interests transferred to other bodies;[7] the corporation was accordingly reconstituted in its present form, renamed the 'representative body'[8] and the property was transferred to it; this arrangement was re-enacted in statutory form in 1933.[9]

Deeds, leases, conveyances and other instruments made between 1894 and 1st April, 1927, in connection with property in these small parishes, were accordingly made in the name of the chairman and overseers acting as a corporate body and not as individuals and they will bind the representative body as successor in title.

On 17th July 1957 Inspectors of Lighting were abolished and their property transferred to the representative body.[10]

E. PROPERTY 'INHERITED' BY PARISH COUNCIL

Where the area for which a burial authority administered its acts does not coincide with the area administered by the parish council, the authority remains separately in existence[5] and is the owner of the property which it has acquired for the purposes of its functions. If a parish council is set up whose area coincides with the area of the authority, the latter ceases to exist and its property passes automatically to the parish council.[11]

Vestries and Adoptive Act Authorities, 1894

Most parish councils will have inherited vestry property by the statutory transfer in 1894 of the parish property vested in the overseers or churchwardens and overseers; this included the village greens, and garden, recreational and all other types of allotments,[12] and the property of those adoptive act authorities whose area coincided with the area of the parish council.[13]

---

[5] L.G.A. 1894 s. 19(6).   [6] L.G.A. 1894 s. 19(7).
[7] The Overseers Order 1927 (No. 55) made under authority of R.V.A. 1925 s. 62.
[8] Overseers Order 1927 Art. 7.   [9] L.G.A. 1933 s. 47.
[10] P.C.A. 1957 s. 3(2)(b)   [11] L.G.A. 1894 s. 7(5).
[12] L.G.A. 1894 s. 6(1) and also s. 6(4) which was substantially re-enacted in S.H. and A.A. 1908 s. 33(3).   [13] L.G.A. 1894 s. 7(5).

Overseers, 1927

Where no burial board had been appointed and a parish mortuary existed and had not been acquired by the parish council, the mortuary was transferred to the parish council on 1st April, 1927.[14]

Guardians, 1930

Parish property which was vested in a board of guardians on the 1st April, 1930, including the proceeds of the sale of such property and any securities in which the proceeds had been invested were transferred to the parish council on that day. If the property was held on behalf of two or more parishes, it vested in the appropriate parish councils or representative bodies jointly and where the parishes concerned were grouped, the property was vested in the common parish council unless the county council otherwise provided in the grouping order.[15]

Quarries and Gravel Pits, 1930

It was the normal practice under Inclosure Acts for land to be allotted to provide materials for road making. Such quarries and gravel pits were sometimes allotted for the use of the inhabitants and vested in the Lord of the Manor as trustee, but more often they were vested in the surveyor of highways or other trustees. The surveyor was authorised with the consent of the vestry to sell them (giving the adjoining landowner first refusal) if they became exhausted and with the like consent to purchase others.[16] In due course the parish council succeeded to the functions of the vestry[17] and the surveyor's functions descended to the rural district council as highway authority. On the 1st April, 1930, the functions of the highway authority were transferred to the county council[18] which was obliged, if required by the rural district council, to purchase the quarries or materials belonging to it as highway authority.

The effect of this legislation was only to deal with the materials but not with the land itself which was and remains parish property;[19] of the numerous exhausted quarries, therefore, those which were exhausted before 1894, are usually vested

[14] R.V.A. 1925 and Overseers Order 1927 Arts. 5, 6 and Schedule.
[15] L.G.A. 1929 s. 115.   [16] Highway Act, 1835 s. 48.
[17] L.G.A. 1894 s. 6(a).   [18] L.G.A. 1929 s. 30.
[19] See L.G.A. 1933 s. 305 which is not affected by H.A. 1959.

in the parish council or representative body whilst of the remainder some are vested in rural district councils and others in county councils. None of them, however, can be sold without the consent of the parish council (or parish meeting) and the income, if any, from such properties must be paid into the parochial account. The proceeds of sale must be held in trust for the parish.[20]

Creation of New Parish Councils

If a parish council is created for a single pre-existing parish, the property of the representative body passes to it automatically when the parish council comes into office,[21] but this is not necessarily the case where the new parish council comes into existence as a result of a grouping order for then the parishes in the group retain their representative bodies[22] unless the county council decides to adapt the Local Government Act, 1933, so as to abolish them in the particular instance.[23]

Unclaimed Village Greens and Commons

Where land has been registered as a village green but the owner is unknown the title will be investigated by a Commons Commissioner and if no owner can be identified by him the green will eventually vest in the parish council. If the land is common and subject to a management scheme under the Commons Act, 1899, it will vest in the rural district council unless the management has been delegated to the parish council under the scheme. Where there is no parish council the land will vest in the rural district council.[24]

F. ACQUISITION BY AGREEMENT

A parish council may for the purposes of its functions by agreement acquire by way of purchase, lease or exchange any land in or outside the parish. Land includes any interest or easement or right in, to or over land.[25] As an exchange involves a disposal of parish property certain consents are needed.[26]

---

[20] This appears also to be the law in the Isle of Wight.
[21] L.G.A. 1894 s. 7(6).   [22] L.G.A. 1933 s. 47(3).
[23] L.G.A. 1933 s. 45(2)(d); see also L.G.A. 1929 s. 115(5) and page 19.
[24] Commons Registration Act, 1965 s. 8.
[25] L.G.A. 1933 ss. 167 and 305.   [26] See page 114.

A rural borough may acquire land in exchange for or with capital arising out of its corporate land; such an acquisition need not be made for a statutory purpose.[27]

Where boundary alterations occur, the authorities affected may adjust their property rights and liabilities by agreement or by arbitration in default of agreement. In such cases the right or duty to transfer or receive property will depend upon the terms of the agreement or award, and the title to the property itself will depend upon the deeds executed in pursuance of them.

Transferred Property

Trustees who hold property for the purposes of a public recreation ground or of allotments for the benefit of the inhabitants or any of them or for other charitable purposes other than an ecclesiastical charity may, with the consent of the Charity Commissioners (or in the case of an educational charity of the Minister of Education), transfer the property to the parish council or its appointees upon the same trusts.[28]

Gifts

A parish council may, for any local public purpose, or for the benefit of the inhabitants of the parish or part of it, accept, hold and administer any gift of property so long as the gift is not to be held in trust for an ecclesiastical or eleemosynary charity.[29, 30]

G. ACCRETION

The imperceptible natural increase of land belonging to the parish council and situated on the seashore or beside running water will belong to the council even though the increase is artificially caused by it provided that the act is lawful,[31] but this rule of accretion does not apply where the land is situated beside a lake, canal or pond,[32] nor will it entitle a parish council to claim land artificially reclaimed by someone else.[33]

[27] L.G.A. 1958 Seventh Schedule para. 13(2).
[28] C.A. 1960 s. 37.
[29] L.G.A. 1933 s. 268 and see pages 119 and 122.
[30] For maintenance and improvement of such gifts see page 117.
[31] A.G. v. Chambers (1859) 4 de G. & J. 55 and Mayor of Bradford v. Pickles 1895 A.C. 587.
[32] Trafford v. Thrower (1929) 45 T.L.R. 502.
[33] A.G. of Southern Nigeria v. John Holt and Co. 1915 A.C. 599.

H. COMPULSORY ACQUISITION

Purchase

Unless in any particular case a parish council's power to acquire land is specifically limited to acquisition by agreement,[34] a parish council may make use of a special procedure for compulsory purchase where it is unable to purchase land by agreement and on reasonable terms.[35] Compulsory purchase cannot be used to acquire for allotments land which is part of a park, garden, pleasure ground or home farm or which is needed for the amenity or convenience of a dwelling, or which is woodland unless wholly surrounded by or adjacent to land already acquired by the parish council for the purposes of the Allotments Acts, 1908–1950,[36] and the consent of the Minister of Agriculture must, in the latter case, be obtained.[37]

Where it is proposed compulsorily to acquire land owned inalienably by the National Trust, or by a statutory undertaker such as the Transport Commission, or by a local authority as defined in the Local Loans Act, 1875 (which includes a parish council and a parish meeting), or by any drainage board or joint board whose members are appointed by local authorities, the compulsory purchase order is subject to special parliamentary procedure.[38]

Procedure

The parish council represents the case to the county council and the latter, if satisfied that the representation is true and that it is reasonable to proceed, must hold a local inquiry in the parish.[39] Reasonable public notice must be given[40] in a prescribed form[41] and in the usual manner[42] by the county council which must also serve notice on the owners, tenants and occupiers (other than tenants for a month or less) of the land to be taken. The county council may appoint one or more of its

---

[34] L.G.A. 1933 s. 179(b).   [35] L.G.A. 1933 s. 168(1).
[36] S.H. & A.A. 1908 s. 41(1).
[37] S.H. & A.A. 1908 s. 39(1) amended by Compulsory Acquisition (Authorisation Procedure) Act, 1946, s. 1.
[38] Acquisition of Land (Authorisation Procedure) Act, 1946 s. 8 and see page 202.   [39] L.G.A. 1933 s. 168(1).
[40] The length of notice is not enacted.
[41] L.G.A. 1933 s. 168(2). The form is prescribed in S.R. & O. 1934 No. 363 Form 5.   [42] L.G.A. 1933 s. 287.

members or one of its officers to hold the inquiry[43] and the person so appointed has the same powers as a person who holds an inquiry on behalf of the Minister.[44]

Appeal

After the inquiry is completed and all objections considered, the county council may make a compulsory purchase order which cannot become effective until confirmed by the Minister. A copy of the order and a map must be deposited in the parish and before the order is submitted for confirmation, notice in a prescribed form must be given by the county council[45] to the same individuals as are entitled to notice of the inquiry and in addition it must be advertised in two successive weeks in the local press. The notice must state where the copy of the order and map may be found, the way in which objections may be made and the time limit for objections. After objections have been heard, the Minister may confirm the order with or without modifications.[46]

If the county council refuses to hold an inquiry the parish council may petition the Minister who may hold the inquiry and 'step into the shoes' of the county council for the purpose of making the order.[47]

The confirmed order is carried out by the county council but the land when acquired is conveyed to the parish council[48] which ultimately becomes liable to the vendor for the amount of the compensation[49] and the cost of the conveyance.

Hiring for Allotments

A county council may acquire land compulsorily for the purpose of letting it to a parish council for allotments.[50]

---

[43] L.G.A. 1933 s. 168(1).   [44] L.G.A. 1933 s. 168(6).

[45] This form is prescribed in S.I. 1949 No. 507 Form 4.

[46] The above is merely a summary of a procedure in which the parish council takes very little active part.

[47] L.G.A. 1933 s. 168(7).   [48] L.G.A. 1933 s. 168(3)(b).

[49] For grants payable to parish councils in certain cases see page 138.

[50] Land Settlement (Facilities) Act, 1919 s. 17.

I. OPERATION OF TIME

Prescription and Presumption of Legality

Title to land may be acquired by prescription,[52] and where rights of ownership have been publicly exercised over a long period without challenge the court will presume a lawful origin for the parish council's rights.[53]

Limitation

The time within which an action for the recovery of land may be brought is limited to a fixed period from the time when the right of action accrued. Where the Crown wishes to recover foreshore, the period is 60 years, and in the case of other lands where the Crown or a spiritual or eleemosynary corporation sole intends to bring the action the period is 30 years. In all other cases such actions must be brought within twelve years.[54]

There are rules for ensuring that the rights of action of persons with future interests are preserved until their interests fall into possession and for dealing with cases of concealed fraud.[55]

Now the rules on limitation are purely negative. They merely extinguish at the end of a fixed period[56] the title of people who neglect to defend their property when they were able to do so. The rules do not create a new title in favour of the person in possession and against whom an action should have been brought. Thus it is not sufficient for the latter to show that he was in possession for the appropriate period of time: he must, in order to establish a complete title to the land, be able to prove what persons would be entitled but for limitation and then that all such persons have been barred.

J. PRIVATE PROPERTY SUBJECT TO PUBLIC RIGHTS[57]

In most parishes there are private lands over which the inhabitants have rights of a more or less far-reaching nature. Such rights originate sometimes in custom and sometimes in

---

[52] Blackstone v. Martin (1625) Latch 112 footnote.
[53] Haigh v. West (1893) 2 Q.B. 19. This was a vestry case.
[54] Limitation Act, 1939 s. 4.   [55] ibid. ss. 6, 7, 8, 9 and 11.
[56] ibid. s. 17.   [57] See also Chapter 4.

E

statute—more especially in inclosure acts and the awards made under them.

The most usual lands in which such rights exist are village greens and churchyards, both of which may be controlled and to some extent maintained and managed by the parish council even though they remain in private ownership. The most usual public rights are rights of exercise and recreation, and rights of way.

Village greens must now be registered.

K. SALE AND EXCHANGE OF LAND

With appropriate consents a parish council or representative body may sell any land which is not needed for the purpose for which it was acquired or for which it is being used or may exchange it for other land with or without giving or receiving money for equality of exchange.[58] Such a power cannot, of course, be exercised in breach of any binding trust, covenant or agreement.[59]

Necessary Consents

In all such cases the consent of the parish meeting must be obtained, and in addition the consent in the case of charitable property of the Charity Commissioners or of the Secretary of State for Education and Science (as the case may require)[60] and in other cases of the Minister.[61]

National Trust

A parish council may, with all proper consents, sell any of its property which the National Trust is entitled to hold to the National Trust whether the land is 'needed' or not.[62]

With certain exceptions a rural borough may dispose of land without the consent of a Minister. The exceptions are land held under a local Act and which is either common or under a restriction on sale, open spaces, and land acquired by compulsory purchase.[63]

[58] L.G.A. 1933 s. 170(1).
[59] L.G.A. 1933 s. 179(d).
[60] See pages 127–8.
[61] L.G.A. 1933 s. 170(1) proviso.
[62] National Trust Act, 1937 s. 7(1).
[63] L.G.A. 1933 s. 172 and T. & C.P.A. 1959 s. 26.

L. LETTING OF LAND

A parish council may let its land but some lettings require the consent of other bodies. For this purpose a representative body with the consent of the parish meeting is in the position of a parish council.

Without Consent

A parish council may let its cycle parks for seven days and its other land for a period not exceeding one year without obtaining the consent of anybody.[64]

A parish council may let its charitable lands for allotments under the Allotments Acts, 1908–1950,[64] without the consent of anybody. Such lettings may be required to be subject to special provisions relating to rent and notice but there is no limitation on the length of the lease.

Where land has been acquired by a parish council for the purposes of the Physical Training and Recreation Act, 1937, it may let the land for any period without consent.[65]

Consent Required

A lease of charitable lands exceeding one year and for purposes other than allotments requires the consent of the Charity Commission or of the Secretary of State for Education as the case may be.[66]

A lease of other lands exceeding one year and for purposes other than those of the Physical Training and Recreation Act, 1937, requires the consent of the Minister.[66]

Cycle parks (other than those in a road) may be let for not longer than seven days for each letting but this limitation does not prejudice the right of the parish council to let the land of which the park is a part for a longer period.[67]

Apart from charitable lands there now seems to be no limit on the period for which a rural borough may grant a lease.[63]

M. INVESTMENTS AND PROCEEDS OF SALE

Where parish property has been sold the resulting proceeds and investments or other property into which they had been

---

[63] L.G.A. 1933 s. 172 and T. & C.P.A. 1959 s. 26.
[64] L.G.A. 1933 s. 169 proviso.   [65] P.T. & R.A. 1937 s. 4(1).
[66] L.G.A. 1933 s. 169.   [67] P.C.A. 1957 s. 4(8).

converted before the 17th November, 1933, remain vested and continue to be applied as they were on that date until the Minister otherwise directs.[68] After that date capital received for the disposal of charitable land must be applied in accordance with the directions of the Secretary of State for Education or the Charity Commissioners (as the case may be)[69] and capital received for other land must be applied in such manner as the Minister may approve towards the reduction of debt or otherwise for any purpose for which capital may be applied.[70]

N. *L.A.M.I.T.* AND *C.I.T.*

Funds invested to bring income can now be placed with the Local Authorities Mutual Investment Trust (L.A.M.I.T.) or if charitable with the Charities Investment Trust (C.I.T.); these are approved methods of investment;[71] they are under the same management and have the same address.

O. APPROPRIATION

Land acquired for a purpose is said to be "appropriated" to that purpose and can be used for no other, save as the law permits.

With the consent of the Minister and the Minister of Agriculture, a parish council may appropriate any of its land for allotments or may appropriate its allotment land for any other purpose,[72] but the Ministers may impose conditions as to the repayment of loans and otherwise. A rural borough requires only the consent of the Minister of Agriculture.[73]

A parish council may also appropriate land for an open space[74] and with the Minister's consent small plots of certain lands for cycle parks.

Burial authorities also have special powers of appropriation.[75]

In all other cases a parish council must obtain the consent of the parish meeting and of the Minister and a parish meeting must obtain the consent of the Minister.[76] In these residual

---

[68] L.G.A. 1933 s. 178.   [69] L.G.A. 1933 s. 170(2)(i).
[70] L.G.A. 1933 s. 170(2)(ii).
[71] See Trustee Investments Act, 1961 especially s. 10.
[72] Land Settlement (Facilities) Act, 1919 s. 22.
[73] T. & C.P.A. 1959 s. 23.   [74] Open Spaces Act, 1906 s. 7.
[75] See page 285.   [76] T. & C.P.A. 1959 s. 28.

cases the accounts may have to be adjusted[77] and if the appropriation involves property used or to be used for a function which is grant-aided by a government department, such adjustment must be made as the Minister directs.[78]

P. MAINTENANCE AND IMPROVEMENT

A parish council[79] and a parish meeting[80] have power to execute any works including works of maintenance or improvement in relation to any parish property.[81] So far as gifts for non-statutory purposes are concerned this rule apparently applies only to those which were accepted before the Local Government Act, 1933, came into force,[82] but in the case of gifts accepted after that date the parish council can use its 'free fifth'.

Q. LAND REGISTRATION

Any parish council which owns land can register its title in the Land Registry if it is in one of the compulsory registration areas. This has advantages inasmuch as dealings in the land are simplified and there is thenceforth no doubt of the parish council's title even if the documents are subsequently lost or mislaid.[83]

In addition in these areas registration is compulsory within two months of the happening of certain events. These events are the conveyance on sale of the fee simple (that is full ownership) of the land, the making of a lease for forty years or more, and the assignment on sale of a lease which has forty or more years to run.[84] Where a parish council acquires the land there will generally be little difficulty save that it may be asked to pay part or the whole of the expense of registration, but where the parish council is disposing of it, it will be responsible for seeing that the registration is effected. Failure to register in time results in the grant becoming void unless an extension of time is secured.[85]

---

[77] ibid. s. 24(1).
[78] ibid. s. 24(2) and s. 57.
[79] L.G.A. 1894 s. 8(1)(i).
[80] L.G.A. 1929 s. 115(3).
[81] See page 103.
[82] See page 107.
[83] Land Registration Act, 1925, s. 4 as amended by Land Registration Act, 1966 s. 1.
[84] Land Registration Act, 1925 s. 123.
[85] ibid. s. 123.

The areas of compulsory registration are being steadily extended by Order in Council. At the time of going to press they comprised Kent, Berkshire, Surrey and a number of boroughs and urban areas.

13

Charities and Public Gifts

I t has been necessary to make provision in the law of charities and public gifts for several special principles.

Firstly, it has been necessary to preserve the barrier between the secular and the ecclesiastical and to continue the century-old policy of relieving the parish of direct responsibility for the poor.[1]

Secondly, provision has been made for the fact that many charities have in the past and will in the future benefit more than one parish.

Thirdly, for reasons of convenience there is provision for the continuance in office or the future creation of independent bodies of trustees.

Fourthly, whilst all charities are public not all public gifts are charitable; under the general law only charities are perpetual, and the law has had, without making inroads upon the law of charity, to find a way of preserving non-charitable gifts from destruction under the rule against perpetuities.

Fifthly, it has been the object of Parliament to give to the parish or its elected representatives as much control over a public gift or charity affecting it as may reasonably be expected.

A. THE NATURE OF LEGAL CHARITY

The law of legal charity comprises some of the most abstruse problems of English jurisprudence: it is essentially a matter for experts and in practical questions of difficulty it will always be better to seek advice rather than to rely upon such general statements of principle as are contained in this work.

[1] See L.G.A. 1933 s. 268.

119

Common Characteristics

Valid gifts of property for charitable purposes must be couched in imperative language, the charitable intention of the donor must be beyond question and the property comprised in the gift must be certain.

The question whether a trust is charitable or not depends upon its objects and not upon the character of the trustees, though that character may, of course, be evidence of the nature of the objects.

The objects must be public: that is to say 'a purpose must in order to be charitable be directed to the benefit of the community or a section of the community'.[2] Thus an intention to benefit an individual or particular individuals (even though by so doing poverty will be relieved or education or religion furthered) will not be charitable, but an intention to further a charitable object in the abstract without giving any individual person an enforceable claim on the funds will be charitable.

The purposes of the trust must not be contrary to the policy of the law. Infringements of this rule are now uncommon.

If the objects of a trust fall under one head or classification of charity, they will be valid even if they contravene another.[3, 4]

To escape certain fiscal burdens the trust must be charitable and nothing else[5] but this rigorous rule does not apply in cases of exemption from rating.[6]

Charitable trusts are perpetual and therefore if their objects become obsolete the Crown or its other representatives will intervene as guardians of the public to ensure that the charitable intentions of the donor do not fail and that the funds are re-directed for the public good.[7]

B. CHARITABLE PURPOSES CLASSIFIED

Pemsel's Case

Legal charity is mainly defined by reference to the preamble to the statute 43 Eliz. I cap. 4 which did not so much define charity as give examples of it.[8] The courts have always interpreted the spirit rather than the letter of the statute and in

---

[2] See *Tudor on Charities*, Fifth Ed., pages 11 and 12.
[3] See A.G. v. Lonsdale (1827) 1 Sim. 105 (Education of Sons of Gentlemen).   [4] See below.
[5] See page 128.   [6] See R. & V.A. 1961 s. 11.
[7] See page 127.   [8] Morice v. Bishop of Durham (1804) 9 Ves. 405.

recent times many attempts to classify the extensive case law have been made. The most notable, and potentially misleading, of these attempts was made in 1893[9] in the following manner:— (1) relief of poverty; (2) education; (3) advancement of religion; (4) other purposes beneficial to the community not falling under any of the preceding three heads. A fifth class—recreation —was recognised by statute in 1958.

Relief of Poverty

Gifts for the benefit of the poor either generally or of a particular parish,[10] or for a particular class of poor persons or for institutions benefiting the poor are charitable, and a gift for the poor is none the less charitable because it happens incidentally to benefit the rich, but a trust benefiting the rich exclusively and without any other charitable object cannot be charitable.

Education

Gifts for the advancement of education generally, or for the education of particular classes of persons, are charitable and the advancement of education has been held to include education in particular branches of study,[11] the equipment of a school with a facility for playing a game,[12] or with a sanatorium,[13] the provision of a school treat,[14] the endowment of scholarships[15] and prizes.[13, 16]

On the other hand a gift for the promotion of a scientific or artistic pursuit is not charitable unless it promotes education.[17]

Advancement of Religion

Most, but not quite all, gifts which are technically for the advancement of religion are ecclesiastical charities (with which parish councils are not concerned) but it is customary to include in this class gifts for the maintenance of a churchyard[18] or burial

[9] I.R.C. v. Pemsel (1891) A.C. 583.
[10] Whicker v. Hume (1858) 7 H.L.C. 124.
[11] Re Allsop (1884) I Th. R. 4.
[12] Re Mariette (1915) 2 Ch. 284.
[13] Re Harrow School (1927) 1 Ch. 556.
[14] Re Mellody (1918) 1 Ch. 228.
[15] R. v. Newman (1667) 1 Lev. 284.
[16] Thompson v. Thompson (1844) 1 Coll. 398.
[17] Re Ogden (1909) 25 T.L.R. 382.
[18] Re Vaughan (1886) 33 Ch. D. 187. Re Pardoe (1906) 2 Ch. 184.

F*

ground, even though restricted to members of one sect,[19] gifts for the maintenance of a church[20] and for the provision of a church clock.[21] A gift for the maintenance of a particular tomb is not charitable[22] unless it is in a church.

It is charitable to provide or help to provide facilities for recreation or other leisure time occupation if (but only if) this is done to improve the condition of life of the intended beneficiaries and *either* they need them because of age, youth, infirmity, poverty or social or economic circumstances *or* the facilities are to be open to members or female members of the public.[23] The Recreational Charities Act, 1958, further declares that trusts for these purposes always have been charitable, but as doubt had been shed on this proposition by a High Court decision before the passing of the Act there is provision for saving any proper transactions entered into before 17th December, 1957, in the belief that the law was otherwise than as declared in the Act.[24]

All these rules apply especially to village halls, women's institutes and recreation grounds.

Miscellaneous

Not all trusts which benefit the community are legally charitable and the fourth or residual class of charities is incapable of orderly analysis. In parish administration, however, the following types of trusts which have been held to be charitable, are the most important: gifts for the relief of the rates,[25] or to the parish council in furtherance of its statutory duties;[26] for a burial ground;[27] for supplying public water;[28] for repairing public highways and bridges.[29]

C. NON-CHARITABLE PUBLIC GIFTS

A local authority (including a parish council) may for any local public purpose or for the benefit of the inhabitants of its

[19] Re Manser (1905) 1 Ch. 68.
[20] A.G. v. Ruper (1722) 2 P.Wms. 125.
[21] Re Church Estates Charity Wandsworth (1871) 6 Ch. App. 296.
[22] Masters v. Masters (1718) 1 P.Wms. 422.
[23] Recreational Charities Act, 1958 s. 1.
[24] ibid. s. 3.   [25] Doe d. Preece v. Howells (1831) 2 B. & Ad. 744.
[26] Luckcraft v. Pridham (1877) 6 Ch. D. 205.
[27] Re St Pancras Burial Ground 3 Eq. 175.
[28] Jones v. Williams (1767) Amb. 651.
[29] A.G. v. Corporation of Limerick (1816) Beat. 563.

area or part of it accept, hold and administer any non-charitable gift of property whether real or personal.[30] It may execute any works including works of maintenance and improvement incidental or consequential on the acceptance, ownership and administration of the gift, and if the purpose of the gift is a purpose upon which it has power to spend public money it may defray the cost from the rates.[31] The real effect of this is negative: it means that unless the gift is for a purpose upon which the authority may spend rate funds, it may not defray these expenses from the rate fund, and local authorities are often advised (even by the most reputable authorities[32]) not to accept such gifts without an endowment fund for their maintenance. In parishes such defeatism is seldom if ever justified for, apart from the possibility of using the 'free fifth'[33] or of obtaining ministerial sanction for the necessary expenditure,[34] it is often possible to obtain the necessary funds locally by public subscription or lottery.

D. REGISTRATION AND INDEXES

Public registers of charities are maintained by the Department of Education and Science for 'educational' charities and by the Charity Commission for all the other charities. Oddly enough 'educational' charities include village halls, recreational allotments and playing fields.

County councils keep indexes of local charities which are in fact copies of their local portions of the main register.

It is the duty of charity trustees to register their charity unless it is exempted under the Act of 1960 or excepted by regulations or has no permanent endowment nor any income from property exceeding £15 a year nor the use and occupation of land.[35]

A trust when registered is conclusively presumed for all purposes to be a charity;[36] this is a great practical advantage when recovering tax or negotiating rate settlements.

---

[30] L.G.A. 1933 s. 268(1).   [31] L.G.A. 1933 s. 268(2).
[32] See for instance *Encyclopedia of Local Government Law and Administration.*
[33] See L.G. (Fin. Prov.) Act, 1963 s. 6.
[34] Under the proviso to L.G.A. 1933 s. 228(1).
[35] Charities Act, 1960 s. 4.   [36] ibid. s. 5.

E. REVIEW AND CO-ORDINATION OF CHARITIES

With the consent of the charities concerned a county council may review the working of charities in the county[37] and all councils may make arrangements with a charity for co-ordinating its activities with those of the council concerned.[38]

F. PAROCHIAL CHARITIES

Definition

'Parochial Charity' is a technical term meaning in relation to a parish a charity the benefits of which are confined either to the inhabitants of the parish, or of a single ancient ecclesiastical parish which included that parish or part of it or of an area consisting of that parish and not more than four neighbouring parishes.[39] A reorganisation of parish boundaries sometimes results in a parochial charity ceasing to be technically parochial with the result that the parish councils and parish meetings formerly concerned in its management lose most of their rights.

G. CHARITIES OUTSIDE PARISH ADMINISTRATION

Ecclesiastical and eleemosynary charities cannot be administered by a parish council.

Ecclesiastical

An ecclesiastical charity includes a charity for any spiritual purpose which is lawful or for the benefit of any spiritual person or ecclesiastical officer as such, or (if a building) for a church, chapel, mission room or Sunday school or otherwise for any denomination, or for maintenance of Divine Service in such building, or otherwise for the benefit of any particular church or denomination or of any members thereof as such; and in addition it includes any building which between the 5th March, 1854, and the 5th March, 1894, was provided mainly at the expense of the members of any particular denomination.[40]

---

[37] ibid. s. 11.   [38] ibid. s. 12.
[39] C.A. 1960 s. 45.   [40] L.G.A. 1894 s. 75 and C.A. 1960 s. 45.

A partly ecclesiastical endowment other than a building is regarded as an ecclesiastical charity but must be apportioned by the Charity Commissioners or the Department of Education on application, and provision must be made for the management of the non-ecclesiastical part.[40]

Eleemosynary

An eleemosynary charity is one which exists to distribute its founder's bounty or alms and is said to mean 'an almshouse or charity the trusts of which require or involve a distribution of money or other benefits among individual poor persons'.[41]

H. CHARITIES BEING PARISH PROPERTY

Charities whose proceeds are applicable for the general benefit of one or more parishes are parish property[42] and may, in certain circumstances, be vested in several parish councils or representative bodies jointly.[43]

I. ADMINISTRATION OF CHARITABLE TRUSTS AND APPOINTMENT OF TRUSTEES

Acceptance

A parish council may accept, hold and administer a charitable trust for the general benefit of the parish so long as it is not of an ecclesiastical or eleemosynary character[44] and it may also accept trusteeship of village greens, and recreational, agricultural and other allotments.[45]

Transfer

The trustees of such trusts and trustees who hold property for public purposes may, with the consent of the Charity Commissioners, or the Department of Education, transfer their property to the parish council or its nominees upon the same trusts.[46] The trustees are not bound to transfer, nor the council to accept the property.

[40] L.G.A.1894 s. 75 and C.A. 1960 s. 45.
[41] *L.G. Law and Administration* (1935), Vol. 3, p. 102.
[42] L.G.A. 1933 s. 305.   [43] See page 103.
[44] L.G.A. 1933 s. 268.
[45] Poor Relief Act (1819) s. 17 and L.G.A. 1894 s. 6(c).
[46] C.A. 1960 s. 37(1).

Parochial Charities

Where, however, there exists or it is intended to create a parochial charity not falling within the definition of parish property, the charity is subject to special rules and the parish council has certain rights of appointment of trustees but may not accept the trusteeship itself.

Many parish councils are entitled to appoint trustees under the terms of a trust deed. Apart from rights of this kind they also have powers of appointment accorded them by statute.

Formerly Overseers and Churchwardens

The parish council is entitled to appoint one trustee of every parochial charity in the place of each overseer (if any) who was formerly entitled to be a trustee,[47] and one trustee in place of each churchwarden who was formerly entitled to be a trustee of a non-ecclesiastical charity.[47] Where there is no separate parish council these rights of appointment belong to the parish meeting.[47]

No Popular Element

Where the body of trustees of a non-ecclesiastical parochial charity includes no representative appointed by the council, the parish meeting, or by ratepayers, electors or inhabitants, the council may appoint additional trustees not exceeding the number permitted by the Charity Commissioners, and where the charity is managed by a single person, the trustees may be increased to three, one of whom may be appointed by the parish council.[47]

Vestry

Any power to appoint trustees or beneficiaries of a non-ecclesiastical charity formerly exercisable by the vestry was transferred to the parish council.[47]

Forty-year Moratorium

Save in the case of appointments in lieu of overseers none of the powers of appointment may be exercised within forty years of the foundation of the charity without the consent of the founder or surviving founders.[47]

[47] ibid. s. 37.

Term of Office

Trustees appointed by a parish council hold office for four years but half (as nearly as may be) of those first appointed hold office for only two years.[48]

Audit

The accounts of a parochial charity administered by a parish council form part of its ordinary accounts and are subject to district audit,[49] but where a charity is administered by trustees its accounts do not form part of the parish council's accounts and it is therefore not subject to district audit even though all the trustees are appointed by the parish council.

The audited accounts of all parochial charities other than ecclesiastical charities must be transmitted annually to the parish council or the chairman of the parish meeting if there is no parish council of any parish affected thereby. The parish council or chairman (as the case may be) must lay these accounts before the next parish meeting in whose minute book they must be inserted.[50]

J. CY PRÉS AND SCHEMES

Summary

Obsolete charitable funds are applied 'cy prés' that is to say 'as nearly as possible to that which has failed';[51] it would be unpractical to allow trustees to judge when the original trusts had failed or what objects can be regarded as cy prés the original trusts, and it would equally be impossible for an independent body to do so unless it were armed with extensive powers of inquiry and control. Jurisdiction over charities is vested in the Crown acting through the attorney-general or the Lord Chancellor (depending on the nature of the case), in a visitor, in the High or a County Court, or finally in the Charity Commission or Department of Education and Science. From the point of view of the parish council, the most important of these are the Charity Commission and the Department which in their appropriate spheres exercise the Crown's inherent

[48] C.A. 1960 s. 37 (6).
[49] S.R. & O. Rev. 1904 I.X. Parish Council E, page 155 of 20 April 1900 preserved by L.G.A. 1933 s. 307.   [50] C.A. 1960 s. 32(3).
[51] Ironmongers Company v. A.G. 10 Cl. & F. at page 922.

power of reorganisation by means of so-called schemes for the future management of a given trust.

The draft of any scheme relating to a parochial charity (other than an ecclesiastical charity) must be communicated on or before the publication of the draft order making the scheme to the parish council or chairman of the parish meeting (as the case may be)[52] and a parish council, with the consent of the parish meeting, may appeal within three months to the High Court against the order creating the scheme. A certificate that the matter is a proper one for appeal must be obtained from the Commissioners or the Department of Education, or the leave of a High Court Judge.[53] A parish meeting has no such right.

Where the charity property includes land other than buildings, the scheme must contain a clause permitting the trustees to let the land for allotments.[54] The Charity Commissioners have jurisdiction over allotments for fuel and cultivation, and the Department of Education over allotments for recreation.

K. RELIEF FROM FISCAL BURDENS

Where a trust is established for charitable purposes *only*[55] the trustees may claim exemption from income tax, corporation tax and both capital gains taxes upon most of their investments and in certain circumstances also upon trading profits. The Inland Revenue cannot dispute the charitable status of a trust registered in the Register of Charities.

A gift for charitable *or public* purposes attracts estate duty only if made within a year of the donor's death.

An instrument relating to a poor child apprenticed at the sole charge of a public charity is not liable to stamp duty.

If written notice is given to the rating authority that a property is occupied by a charity or trustees for a charity and wholly or mainly used for charitable purposes and that s. 40(1) of the General Rate Act, 1967, applies to it, then the amount of rates to be collected in respect of it may not exceed one half. The rating authority may also remit the rest; it has in addition power to give remissions to non-profit-making bodies

[52] ibid. s. 21(1).   [53] ibid. s. 18(12).
[54] Allotments Extension Act, 1882 s. 14.
[55] Income Tax Act, 1952 s. 448(3) and Finance Act, 1965 s. 35.

whose *main* objects are charitable, philanthropic or religious or concerned with education, social welfare, science, literature or the fine arts and to similar organisations occupying property mainly for recreation.[56]

L. INVESTMENT

Any charity can place its funds with the Charities Investment Trust which has been approved by the Charity Commissioners. Apart from this charitable trustees have all the powers of investment possessed by local authorities and in addition may invest in company debentures, and, provided that they have divided the fund formally into two equal parts they may invest one part in wider range investments after taking proper advice in writing.[57]

M. DECLARATION OF CHARITABLE TRUSTS

With three (unreal) exceptions a parish council has no power to declare trusts of its property because insofar as the trusts agree with the purposes for which the property was acquired the declaration is unnecessary, and insofar as they are inconsistent with those purposes, they would be unlawful.

There are, however, three cases where trusts can be declared though none of them are true exceptions to the general rule.

Firstly a donor may give property to a parish council upon charitable trusts which the latter is to declare. Here the property is already subject to charitable trusts when accepted by the council which is merely entitled to say what those trusts shall be.

Secondly a parish council may declare charitable trusts of property in a conveyance upon sale for full and valuable consideration. This power arises from the fact that the trusts will only come into operation at the moment when the property ceases to belong to the council. The trusts cannot govern the money or other consideration received for the property sold.

Thirdly a parish council may let its land to 'clubs, societies or organisations having athletic, social or educational objects'.[58] Evidently some of the organisations falling within this class may

[56] General Rate Act 1967 s. 40.
[57] Trustee Investments Act, 1961 see especially s. 2.
[58] P.T. & R.A. 1937 s. 4(1).

be charitable but from the point of view of the parish council they are no different from other tenants. It is, however, sometimes financially advantageous, especially in connection with rating, to make a lease to a charitable organisation.[59]

[59] See above.

14

Finance—Assets

A parish council obtains 'the money which it can call its own' from seven main types of sources; these are public funds, special trusts, rents and payment for services, subscriptions, grants, sales and capital gifts. Of these the first three are always income and the last is capital whilst the remainder may fall under one or other heading according to circumstances.

A rural borough may, in addition, have corporate land.

A. PUBLIC FUNDS AND PAROCHIAL ACCOUNTS

A parochial account is kept by the rating authority (the rural district council) for each parish and into this account is paid the proceeds of any trusts in aid of the parish rates, any contributions made by the Crown in lieu of rates, and such sums as are raised by way of rates for the purposes of parish administration together with any surplus rents from allotments, cycle parking fees and rents and surplus bathing receipts.

The sums required to meet the expenses of a parish council, a parish meeting (including a poll consequent on a parish meeting) and of burial boards are chargeable separately on the parish[1] or area of the board and so is the cost of a parish council election.[2] Where there is a parish council the expenses of the parish meeting (including such a poll) are payable by the parish council[3] but the expenses of a parish council election are payable by the rural district council.[2] All these amounts are paid out of the parochial account.

[1] L.G.A. 1933 s. 193(1).   [2] L.G. Elections Act, 1956 s. 4(2).
[3] L.G.A. 1933 s. 193(2).

Precepts

It is the duty of the rating authority to make and levy the rates and to pay the required sums to the parish council, parish meeting or burial board (as the case may be) in accordance with orders, known as precepts directed to it.[4]

A precept is a peremptory order to the rating authority to pay a named sum by a certain date to the precepting body.[5] A parish council precept is still normally signed by the presiding chairman and two members and countersigned by the clerk. A precept from a parish meeting is signed by the chairman. It need not be a printed document but usually is. Its function is similar to that of a cheque on a bank and so long as it is regular upon its face the rating authority can be compelled to honour it.

A precept may be enforced against the rating authority in two ways. Firstly a parish council may give 21 days' notice that it intends to apply to the Minister for a certificate that the rating authority has refused or through wilful neglect or default failed to raise the necessary rate, or to pay the amount due under the precept; at the expiry of the twenty-one days the application may be made: if the Minister gives the certificate, the parish council becomes entitled to apply to the County Court for a receiver as if it were a secured creditor for the amount due together with 6 per cent. interest per annum thereon, and the receiver may, subject to the direction of the Court, raise the money by or out of the rates or other property of the rating authority together with his own expenses and remuneration.[6] Secondly if (but only if) this remedy is inadequate or inconvenient, application may be made to the High Court for an order of *mandamus*[7] which can ultimately be enforced by imprisonment for contempt of court.[8]

---

[4] General Rate Act 1967 s 2.

[5] The forms of parish precepts were prescribed by S.R. & O. 1895 No. 448 (Parish Council) and No. 449 (Parish Meeting) for the purposes of L.G.A. 1894, s. 11 (Repealed). These forms with appropriate modifications are still in use.

[6] L.G.A. 1933 s. 193(7) applying R.V.A. 1925 s. 13 which amends for this purpose the Local Loans Act, 1875 s. 12 and applies it as amended.

[7] R. v. Poplar Borough Council (No. 1) 1922 1 K.B. 72.

[8] R. v. Poplar Borough Council (No. 2) 1922 1 K.B. 95.

B. LIMITATIONS ON EXPENDITURE

The rules which govern the amount which a parish council may spend are now confused beyond hope of logical exposition and the Redcliffe Maud Commission has proposed that they be abolished. The principal land-marks are the 4d. and 8d. (1·7p and 3·3p) 'rate limits'[9] which fix the size of the rate fund from which general expenditure may be financed. Within these limits, however, expenditure on certain matters (such as the 'free fifth' (·1p) or war memorials)[10] is specially limited, whilst on the other hand funds for expenditure on certain other services are not derived from the limited fund at all but are either limited by the provisions of the particular acts[11] governing those services or are not limited by them. Some, but not all of these statutes, are called 'adoptive acts' because the powers under them could not originally be used until a special procedure for adopting them had been carried out;[12] the necessity for such an adoption was, however, in two cases[13] abolished, though the powers continued to be known as adoptive powers, whilst certain other powers were conferred[14] which could be exercised as if they were adoptive though no formalities of adoption were ever required.

The Rate Limits

A parish council may, on its own responsibility, in any financial year[15] raise a sum equal to the product of a 4d. (1·7p) rate to meet the expense of exercising its 'general' powers and may, with the consent of the parish meeting, raise up to the product of an 8d. (3·3p) rate.[16]

If the consent of the parish meeting is refused or if the parish council wishes to raise more than the product of an 8d. (3·3p) rate, it may apply to the Minister for an order permitting it to raise additional sums.[16] Orders of this kind are made as a rule so as to apply to a single financial year but may be made for longer; this happens most commonly where there are loans to be repaid over a period of years.

---

[9] See below.   [10] See pages 213-7.
[11] See for instance the peculiar provisions of the Allotments Acts.
[12] This procedure differed in each case.
[13] Baths and Wash-houses, Recreation Grounds and Public Walks.
[14] e.g. boating pools.   [15] i.e. any year ending on 31st March.
[16] L.G.A. 1933 s. 193(3).

Calculation

With one exception the amount of the penny rate for the purposes of these rules is calculated on the total rateable value of the parish for the year without any deductions[17] (for instance for the cost of collection) and therefore if, for instance, it costs the product of $\frac{1}{2}d$. or ·3p rate to levy a 4d. or 1·7p rate, the parish council may lawfully require the levy of $4\frac{1}{2}d$. or 2p rate without seeking the consent of the parish meeting. The exception is the limit on expenditure for the benefit of the parish or its inhabitants under s. 6 of the Local Government (Financial Provisions) Act, 1963. In this case the amount is calculated with the same deductions as are made by the rating authority in calculating its penny rate product.[18]

Charities in Aid of the Rates

The income from charities in aid of the rates is paid to the rating authority for the account of the parish; the amount of any precept is charged against this income first, and only when it is exhausted is any call made on the ratepayers, but one effect of the existence of this additional source of income is that more money is available for spending before the rate limit is reached.

Accumulations

Save to maintain a sinking fund in connection with a loan[19] a parish council is not allowed to accumulate funds by precepting for more than its needs in the period covered by the precept plus debts incurred in the previous six months but not yet paid. It is, however, required to take contingencies into account[20] and a surplus will therefore not infrequently but lawfully result. A surplus from this source at the end of one year must therefore be spent before further calls can be made on the rates.

The better opinion is that there is no way of accumulating the 'free fifth' even by making payments from it to a parish accumulations or loans trust, but a similar practical effect of a very

---

[17] L.G.A. 1933 s. 193(3).
[19] See page 152.

[18] L.G.(F.P.)A. 1963 s. 6(6).
[20] R.V.A. 1925 s. 12.

limited kind can sometimes be usefully produced by spacing payments over more than one year.

Where there is an income from sources other than the rates and the parish council's expenses are less than that income, the balance not only can but must be accumulated for the benefit of the parish, and there appears to be no reason why such a surplus should not be invested.

C. SPECIAL TRUSTS

Apart from charities[22] a parish council may have trust funds for special objects. Such funds are commonly given as an endowment for the maintenance of gifts of a type which cannot be maintained from public funds[23] or they may exist to further a particular statutory function such as the provision of a playing field. The corporate lands of a rural borough are often of this character.

Where there is an endowment trust for a non-statutory purpose and the income is not sufficient for maintenance, it is a breach of trust to use the capital for maintenance unless the trust instrument specifically permits such use. It will accordingly be necessary to resort to public subscription[24] or to use the 'free fifth' or to ask the Minister to sanction expenditure from public funds.[25]

Where there is a trust for a statutory function the recurrent (as opposed to capital) costs of that function must be charged against the income of that fund unless the trust instrument otherwise provides.

In general the application of funds of this sort is governed by the terms of the trust deed rather than by the law applicable to public funds.

D. PAYMENTS AND RENTS

Parish councils may receive rents from tenants of their property or for herbage on their land and charges and fees for the use of common pasture, for burials, for admission to playing fields and recreation grounds (but only on days when they may lawfully be closed), for admission to swimming pools, baths,

[22] See chapter 13.   [23] See page 117.
[24] See pages 136 & 140-1.   [25] Under L.G.A. 1933 s. 228(1) proviso.

wash-houses and boating pools and also for the use of the parish hall and other offices.

It is normal for the income from these services to be applied towards the cost of maintaining them and to apply any surpluses in aid of the general rate, but there are a number of exceptional cases connected with the management of allotments[25] and recreation grounds[26] where such surpluses must be 'ploughed back' and not used for any other purpose without special leave.

E. FEES

In certain circumstances fees are payable to a parish council as follows:

1. For each *inspection* of the minutes by an elector . . . . . Not more than 1s. 0d.[27] (5p)
2. For each *copy* of the confirmed byelaws . . . . Not more than 1s. 0d.[27] (5p)
3. For each copy made by the clerk of the Financial Statement or Auditor's Report and given to an elector . . . . . . A reasonable sum[27]
4. For each such copy of the draft byelaws — Not more than 6d. (3p) per 100 words[28]
5. For each ordinary entry of the transfer of a mortgage . . . Not more than 5s. 0d.[29] (25p)
6. For each compensation fund entry of the transfer of a mortgage. — In addition to No. 5 above not more than 1s. 0d. (5p) for every £100 transferred with a minimum equal to the charge for £25[30]

F. SUBSCRIPTIONS

Parish councils commonly[31] and lawfully[32] raise funds by public subscription for their statutory purposes or in order to maintain property which they have no specific power to maintain from public funds and for whose maintenance they have been unable to secure ministerial sanction.[33] In the larger

---

[25] See page 25.   [26] See page 25.
[27] L.G.A. 1933 s. 283 and s. 250.   [28] L.G.A. 1933 s. 283 and s. 250.
[29] L.G.A. 1933 s. 207.   [30] The Forged Transfers Acts, 1891 and 1892.
[31] But the Public Improvements Act, 1860 has been repealed.
[32] L.G.A. 1933 s. 268.   [33] Under L.G.A. 1933 s. 228(1) proviso.

parishes this practice, once common, may be expected to decline as a result of the enactment of the 'free fifth'[34] but in the many smaller parishes where one fifth of a penny rate still produces a very small sum funds are still often raised in this fashion.

Trusts

Money raised by subscription is impressed with a trust. The first object of such a trust is naturally the purpose for which the fund was raised, but if the purpose fails or if, after it has been achieved, there remains a surplus, then, if there is a general charitable intention, the ordinary law of charity applies, but if there was no such intention the money must be returned *pro rata* to those who gave it. To avoid these difficulties, it is desirable to frame the objects of the appeal carefully and to insert a clause stating that if the objects fail or if there is a surplus the fund will be applied in accordance with the directions of the parish meeting.

Street Collections

Regulations with respect to the places where and the conditions under which persons may be permitted in public places to collect money or sell articles for the benefit of charitable or other purposes may be made by any police authority for its own area[35] or by any authority to which a combined police authority has delegated the power of making such regulations.[36] Disobedience may lead to a fine. The regulations usually provide for the production of accounts.

House-to-House Collections

If a house-to-house collection is to be undertaken the promoter (for instance the parish council) must obtain a licence from the police authority or in most cases the chief constable.[37] It is an offence to promote such a collection without a licence or to collect if no licence is in force.

A licence may be refused or if granted may be revoked upon any of six specific grounds which between them are designed to

---

[34] see pages 213-7.
[35] Police, Factories etc. (Miscellaneous Provisions) Act, 1916 s. 5.
[36] Police Act, 1946 s. 3(2)(g).
[37] House to House Collections Act, 1939 s. 1.

prevent such collections degenerating into begging or becoming an encouragement to vagrancy.[38]

The promoter must be prepared to furnish accounts.[39]

G. GRANTS

Parish councils receive relatively much less in grants than any other type of authority, the total for all parish councils amounting to only a few thousand pounds in any year.

Basic Services in Development Areas

A Minister may with Treasury consent make grants to a parish council in a development district to improve an inadequate basic service for which he is responsible.[40] A development district is a locality where a high rate of unemployment exists or is to be expected.[41]

A basic service means the provision of facilities for transport, or of power, lighting or heating, housing, health and other services on which the development of the area or of industry therein depends.[41] Presumably the extension of burial grounds falls within this definition and also the improvement of public lighting and recreational facilities.

Allotments—Water and Unemployment

The Ministry of Agriculture makes grants towards the provision of *water* for allotments under a scheme operated by the National Association of Parish Councils for the Ministry. The most important conditions for the making of a grant are that the land must exceed two acres and that the parish council must own it or have in hand a long unexpired portion of a lease.

If the letting of allotments to the wholly or partially *unemployed* will entail a loss, the parish council may submit proposals to the Minister of Agriculture together with estimates of probable cost, and the Minister may undertake to defray in any year the loss on such estimates as he has approved. If the proposals are subsequently varied without his consent he may

---

[38] ibid. s. 2.
[39] House to House Collections Regulations 1947 S.R. & O. No. 2662.
[40] Local Employment Act, 1960 s. 7.   [41] ibid. s. 1(2).

make such consequential variations in his undertaking as he thinks fit.[42] The parish council must keep separate accounts.

In the rare cases where a parish council has let its land as an agricultural holding for a horticultural production business there seems to be no reason why it should not receive grants under the Horticulture Act, 1960.[43]

Halls

The Department of Education operates a system of grants towards the building and equipment of village halls by voluntary bodies, and there is also a scheme for providing advantageous loans which is administered by the Village Halls Loans Fund of the National Council of Social Service.

Open Spaces

Government grants are available to acquire land (a) to replace an open space where an area is being developed or redeveloped as a whole; or (b) simply for an open space; or (c) to reclaim it from dereliction. In cases (b) and (c) the grant cannot exceed 50%. [43A]

A county council may make grants towards the cost of providing land for use as a public open space.[44] Expenditure ranking for grant may include not only the cost of acquisition but the cost of such clearing and preliminary development as is approved by the council, and the cost of any payment in connection with the imposition of planning restrictions.

Any local authority may make grants towards expenditure for the provision of facilities, including parish halls, swimming pools, and playing fields, under the Physical Training and Recreation Act, 1937.

A county council may support or contribute to the support of public walks or pleasure grounds provided by anyone.[45]

The National Playing Fields Association is prepared to consider applications for grants, usually where they are not available from other sources. Its policy varies from time to time but parish councils wishing to provide or improve

[42] Agricultural Land (Utilisation) Act, 1931 s. 14.
[43] Horticulture Act, 1960 s. 1(1).   [43A] LGA 1966 ss. 7-9.
[44] L.G.A. 1958 s. 56(2).
[45] Open Spaces Act, 1906 s. 14.

playing fields or to provide new types of equipment should always ask the Association for information before proceeding.

Miscellaneous

A highway authority may make grants to a parish council towards the maintenance of a footpath or bridleway.[46]

A county council may contribute to a parish council's expenses in providing litter bins or disposing of the contents.[47]

The Forestry Commission with Treasury consent may make grants or loans for afforestation or replanting.[47A]

H. SALES

Land

Capital received for the disposal of charitable land must be applied in accordance with the directions of the Department of Education or the Charity Commissioners (as the case may be) and capital received for other land must be applied as the Minister may approve towards reducing debt or for any lawful capital purpose.[48]

Chattels

There are no statutory rules governing the sale of other kinds of property such as furniture, but the ordinary rules of good business management do not necessarily require that an article shall be worn out (and unsaleable) before it is replaced.

Difficulties may arise where a service is being discontinued. Cases of this kind have to be decided on individual merits especially where equipment was acquired through the medium of grants) but where there is a substantial unappropriated surplus it should be invested and the income paid in aid of the rates, or used to reduce the parish council's debt whilst a small surplus can be paid in aid of the rates in the current year.

I. CAPITAL GIFTS OF MONEY

It is impossible for a parish council to receive a capital gift of money with no restrictions whatever on its use, for in the absence of special directions of an explicit kind it will be presumed that the gift is for local public purposes or for the benefit

---

[46] Highways (M.P.) Act, 1961 s. 4.   [47] P.H.A. 1961 s. 51(6).
[47A] Forestry Act, 1967 s. 4   [48] L.G.A. 1933 s. 170.

of the inhabitants of the area or of part of it[49], and a parish council has no power to accept a gift for private purposes.

Such gifts should be invested.

J. FUND-RAISING EVENTS

Small Lotteries

A parish council cannot promote a small lottery because it is not a 'society',[50] but a parish loans trust or society for reducing parish rates can do so for the purpose of financing the activities of the parish council. Any organisation in a rural parish which wishes to promote a small lottery must register with the rural district council and must comply with somewhat stringent statutory conditions and other rules.[51]

Whist Drives

On the other hand a parish council is not forbidden to promote a small gaming party to raise money for its purposes provided that five conditions are fulfilled: firstly not more than one payment not exceeding 5s. 0d. must be made by each player in respect of all games played at the entertainment; secondly the amount of the expenses must not exceed the reasonable cost of providing the facilities; thirdly the whole of the proceeds less prizes and expenses must be applied to purposes other than private gain; fourthly there may be only one distribution of prizes and fifthly the total of the prizes must not exceed £20 in value in the case of a single day entertainment or £100 where the entertainment consists of a series on successive days and entry on a later day is conditional upon the entrant having taken part in an earlier day.[52] If two parties are held by the parish council on the same day in the same premises they are treated as a single party.[52] There is no provision for registration of such parties.

The principal effect of the legislation on small gaming parties is to legalise whist drives.

---

[49] See L.G.A. 1933 s. 268.
[50] See the definition in Betting, Gaming and Lotteries Act, 1963 s. 45(1).
[51] See ibid. s. 45 generally.
[52] Gaming Act, 1968 s. 41.

5

Borrowing

A. WHAT IS BORROWING?

With minor exceptions certain consents are needed before a parish council may commit itself to a loan, and though in all ordinary cases it is obvious enough whether the contemplated transaction is a loan or not (and whether therefore the consents are needed) there are a number of borderline cases.

Loans Defined and Distinguished from Bailments

In a contract of loan the lender agrees to appropriate a fixed sum of money to the borrower's order[1] and this may be done either by paying the money to the borrower or to some third party at the borrower's direction or by using the appropriated fund to pay off a debt already owed by the borrower to the lender or by any combination of these methods. In return for this the borrower agrees to appropriate similarly the equivalent or a larger sum at an agreed time and upon agreed conditions (which usually include an obligation to pay interest) to the lender's order. The only subject of a contract of loan is money.

Borrowing by parish councils is governed by a scheme of enactments[2] which is concerned solely with loans of money: a parish council in the course of its work is perfectly entitled to 'borrow' goods or chattels since the temporary custody and use of such things is in law not a loan (since other things than money are involved) but a bailment, and there are no special enactments governing parish councils' bailments.

---

[1] Lyle (B.S.) Ltd v. Chappell (1932) 1 K.B. 691.
[2] L.G.A. 1933 s. 193(4) and Part IX.

Forbearance

A contract to purchase property or goods or to employ services may lawfully include a clause relieving the parish council from the normal obligation to pay the whole of the consideration money at one time, for in such a case the other party is not appropriating money but transferring property or giving services whilst exercising forbearance in requiring full payment. Such contracts are merely varieties of ordinary contracts of sale or service and the forbearance is not an appropriation of money, for no money would be due at all if (for instance) the goods were not delivered. Moreover the fact that forbearance increases the total price does not necessarily introduce a lending element into the contract: a parish council is entitled to pay a reasonable amount for a forbearance of this kind and may indeed be saving the ratepayers by so doing, if it can thus avoid raising a loan.

Hire Purchase

But a provision for deferred payments may at any time be converted into (or rather replaced by) a contract of loan and the question whether this has occurred is one of fact which must be discovered from the intentions of the parties as expressed in the contract, for the same document may contain both an agreement for sale and an agreement for a loan. An agreement providing for the payment of many instalments over a long period or for the payment of interest or both, would raise a presumption of a loan which would be difficult to rebut; it would, however, be rebutted if each instalment of money was payable in return for an instalment of goods or services.

B. PRELIMINARY CONSENTS

Usual Procedure

It is commonly believed that the consent of the parish meeting is always required before a parish council may raise a loan. This, however, is not the case. The normal procedure is divided into two parts, for the parish council is required to obtain the consent of the parish meeting before it incurs 'any expense or liability which will involve a loan'[3] and it is then required to obtain the consent of the Minister to the loan itself.[4]

[3] L.G.A. 1933 s. 193(4) amended by P.C.A. 1957 s. 8.
[4] L.G.A. 1933 s. 195 amended by P.C.A. 1957 s. 8.

Exceptional Cases

There are, however, five cases where this procedure is not followed. No consents are needed where *firstly* the parish council wishes to borrow by way of temporary overdraft or loan pending the receipt of revenue or loan capital or where *secondly* it proposes to reborrow.[5] *Thirdly* if a liability is thrust upon a parish council against its will, only the consent of the Minister to the loan is required; this unusual case can probably only arise where damages have been awarded against a parish council in legal proceedings and it is necessary to raise money quickly to satisfy the judgment. *Fourthly* where it is proposed to borrow to make payments in connection with financial adjustments arising out of boundary alterations, the Minister's consent to the loan is not required but his approval of the loan period is.

Fifthly the Minister has given a general consent to borrowings by parish councils of amounts not exceeding £500 at any one time nor exceeding £500 in any one year, provided that the usual repayment period appropriate to the purpose of the loan is observed.[5A] Therefore in these cases the consent only of the parish meeting is required.

C. PERMITTED USES OF BORROWED MONEY

A parish council may borrow to acquire land or erect buildings and for any purpose for which it is authorised to borrow under any enactment or statutory order, and in addition it may borrow for the execution of any permanent work, the provision of any plant or the doing of *anything* which the parish council has power to execute, provide or do if in the opinion of the Minister the cost should be spread over a term of years.[6]

Unexpended Balances

The balance of borrowed money not required for the purpose for which it was borrowed may be applied with the consent of the Minister and subject to such conditions as he may impose to any purpose for which capital may be applied, but where the

[5] L.G.A. 1933 s. 215.   [5A]Ministry Circular 32/69 and see p 150.
[6] L.G.A. 1933 s. 195 amended by P.C.A. 1957. For borrowing in connection with compensation for loss of employment and with boundary adjustments see Chapter 3.

F

money was borrowed from the Public Works Loan Board, the consent of the Board is also required.[7]

The balance of borrowed money not needed for the purpose for which it was borrowed may be applied at the discretion of the parish council towards the repayment of a different outstanding loan or for a purpose for which loan consent has been obtained or both, or in addition with the Minister's consent to any purpose to which capital may be applied.[8] If, however, the balance is an old one controlled by the rules which existed before 1st August, 1963, and if in addition the Minister's consent (and that of the Public Works Loans Board) to its application was obtained before that date, then the money must continue to be applied in accordance with that consent and the conditions attached to it.[9]

D. MODE OF BORROWING

Except in the case of temporary loans a parish council may only borrow by way of mortgage[10] or by way of automatic charge (equivalent to but simpler than a mortgage) under an agreement with the Public Works Loans Board.[11]

A parish council loan is a narrow range trustee security requiring advice.[12]

A Burial Board may borrow by way of terminable annuity not exceeding thirty years.[13]

E. SECURITY FOR LOANS

All money borrowed by a parish council must be charged indifferently on all the revenues of the council.[14]

It is doubtful whether the parish council's property can be charged as well, but since in case of default such a charge might lead to the alienation of the property, the specific consent of the parish meeting and of the Minister should be sought before a charge on the property is given. It is, in any case, most undesirable that the property should be mortgaged

[7] L.G.A. 1933 s. 202.   [8] L.G. (F.P.) Act, 1963 s. 10.
[9] L.G. (F.P.) Act, 1963 s. 10 and L.G.A. 1933 s. 202.
[10] L.G.A. 1933 s. 196.   [11] Public Works Loans Act, 1965 s. 2.
[12] Trustee Investments Act, 1961, s. 1 & Schedule I Part II.
[13] Burial Act, 1857 s. 21.   [14] L.G.A. 1933 s. 197.

because some bodies which give advantageous loans will only do so for the development of property which is free of debt.

F. PRIORITY OF LOANS

Mortgages and automatic charges created on or after 1st June, 1934, rank equally without any priority; priorities or rights to priority existing by virtue of mortgages made before that date are not affected by this rule which also has no application in the case of temporary unsecured loans.[15]

G. SOURCES OF LOAN CAPITAL

The Public Works Loans Board has power to lend to parish councils for any purpose for which they may borrow money.[16]

The willingness of the Board to lend and the conditions upon which its loans are made depend upon the financial policy of the government and therefore no account of these topics can safely be given here. Borrowing from private sources, though more complicated, is often cheaper in the long run.

A county council may borrow for the purpose of lending to a parish council[17] and the Minister may by order impose conditions either generally or in a particular case.[18] So far as parish councils are concerned the most important general condition relates to the method of repayment.[19]

The Village Halls Loan Fund of the National Council of Social Service will lend money for the building or improvement of a village hall upon the security of the land and buildings and of personal guarantors provided that there is no other charge on the property and that no work has been undertaken before the application has been approved.

In considering the provision or improvement of any open-air recreational facility, a parish council would be well advised to make inquiries with the National Playing Fields Association before deciding to borrow elsewhere.

[15] L.G.A. 1933 s. 197 and P.W.L.A. 1965 Schedule para. 9.
[16] Local Authorities Loans Act, 1945 s. 2.
[17] L.G.A. 1933 s. 195.   [18] L.G.A. 1933 s. 200.
[19] See page 151.

Subject to the vagaries of government policy there is no reason why parish councils should not, like other authorities, borrow from private individuals.[20]

It is sometimes possible to finance both statutory and voluntary activities in a parish by means of a parish loans trust. As it is inconvenient for borrowers to execute a large number of small mortgages, a trust can be created as a collecting agency for the purpose of lending money in lump sums to the parish council or charitable and quasi-public bodies such as a village hall committee. The trustees raise funds by receiving gifts or loans in large or small sums or by any other lawful means and lend the aggregates to the bodies needing the money. In this way the inhabitants (even children) can invest quite small sums in a local project which interests them despite the rule that a parish council can only borrow by mortgage.

H. FORM OF MORTGAGE, MORTGAGE TRANSFER AND CHARGE

Mortgage and mortgage transfers for loans other than loans from the Public Works Loans Board[21] are made by a deed in a form prescribed by the Minister.[22, 23]

Mortgages with the Board must be in a form prescribed by it but the fact that a mortgage is executed by the Secretary to the Board is conclusive evidence that it is in the prescribed form.[25]

Agreements with the Board providing for an automatic charge are made in a form settled by the Board. None of these documents need now be stamped.

I. LOANS REGISTER

The clerk must keep a register of mortgages and automatic charges and must enter within fourteen days of their creation

---

[20] In the spring of 1956 the London County Council borrowed ten million pounds from a single private lender.
[21] See page 146.   [22] L.G.A. 1933 ss. 205 and 206.
[23] L.G. (Forms of Mortgages and Transfers) Regulations, 1934 S.R. & O. No. 620.
[24] P.W.L.A. 1875 s. 32.   [25] For stamp duties see page 163.

the number and date, the names and descriptions of the parties to it and the amount borrowed, *as stated in the deed.*

Where there is a change of person entitled to a mortgage the deed must be produced to the clerk, and in addition: where the change is caused by transfer the duly executed transfer must be produced; where the change is caused by death, the probate of the will or letters of administration of the estate of the deceased must be produced; in other cases of transmission (such as bankruptcy or company liquidation) satisfactory evidence of transmission must be produced. Thereupon the date of transfer or transmission and the particulars of the new owner may be entered by the clerk upon payment of a fee (fixed by the parish council) not exceeding 5*s.* (25*p*). The fact that the entry has been made should then be endorsed on the deed (not the transfer) and signed by the clerk before return.

Owners of mortgages are responsible for notifying changes of name and address and the clerk must on being satisfied thereof enter such changes on the register.

The register must be open at all reasonable times to public inspection without charge and any custodian of it who obstructs inspection is liable to a fine of £5.

A clerk who refuses or wilfully neglects to make an entry required by law is liable to a fine of £20.[27]

Notices of trusts cannot lawfully be entered on the register.[28]

The parish council is entitled to treat the last person appearing in the register as exclusively entitled to the mortgage to which the entry relates. Where without sufficient cause an entry is wrong or unnecessary delay arises in making it, a court may order the register to be rectified. If the amount involved does not exceed £500 the county court may make the order. In other cases the order is made by the High Court.

In proceedings for rectification the Court may decide any question which it may be necessary or expedient to decide including any questions of title.[29]

J. RECEIPTS IN SPECIAL CASES

Where persons are jointly entitled under a mortgage any one of them can give an effectual receipt for the interest thereon

[27] L.G.A. 1933 s. 207.   [28] L.G.A. 1933 s. 209.
[29] L.G.A. 1933 s. 208.

unless the parish co ncil is notified to the contrary; but the receipt of the guardian of an infant (that is a 'minor') is a sufficient discharge for any money payable to the infant in respect of the mortgage.[30]

K. COMPENSATION FOR FORGED TRANSFERS

A parish council may make compensation for loss arising from a transfer of a mortgage by means of a forgery, and may impose reasonable restrictions on transfers and powers of attorney to guard against such loss.

It may provide a compensation fund by accumulating income or transfer fees (which for this purpose may amount to not more than 1s. (5p) for every £100 transferred with a minimum of 3d (1p)) or by insurance or in any other way it thinks fit; alternatively it may borrow in order to make compensation in a particular case but the loan period must not exceed five years; transfer fees may be applied towards the service of such a loan.

Subrogation

Where the parish council has made compensation it has, without prejudice to its other rights, all the rights against the person responsible for the loss as the person compensated would have had.[31]

L. PERIOD OF LOAN

A parish council must repay a loan within the period which it, with the consent of the Minister, determines, but the period must not exceed 80 years where the loan was raised to acquire allotments, 5 years where the loan is raised for compensation for a forged transfer, or 60 years in any other case.[32]

The considerations influencing the Minister in determining the period include the durability of the works, the overall saving when loan periods are reduced, the desirability of each generation paying for its own works, the possibility of obsolescence in design and the possibility that changes in population may make the works unnecessary.

[30] L.G.A. 1933 s. 210.　　[31] The Forged Transfers Acts, 1891 and 1892.
[32] L.G.A. 1933 s. 198.

These principles work out in the following practical fashion:—

Purchase of land for allotments (including cost of fencing if fencing is required as part of the terms of purchase) } 80 years

Purchase of other land
Housing
Compensation under Town and Country Planning Acts } 60 years

New buildings and structures other than houses } 40 years

Furniture, Machinery
Works of Repair and renewal } 20 years

Professional fees not associated with works
Office Machinery
Other } 10 years

If leasehold land is purchased the maximum period is the duration of the lease if the unexpired part of it is less than 80 or 60 years as the case may be. If existing buildings are purchased the maximum period will not exceed the district valuers estimate of their useful life unless there is to be a government grant based on some other period, or the land is to be redeveloped.[32A]

M. METHOD OF REPAYMENT

Money borrowed from a county council must be repaid by equal yearly or half yearly instalments of principal or of principal and interest combined.[33] Loans from other sources may be repaid by these methods or by means of a sinking fund or partly by one and partly by another or other of these methods.[34]

With two exceptions the first instalment must be paid within a year or in the case of half yearly repayments within six months of the date of borrowing.[35]

The exceptions are as follows:—

Firstly in the case of loans from the Public Works Loans Board repayment may commence at any date within five years of borrowing allowed by the Board[36] and the Treasury may on

[32A] Min. of H. & L.G. Circular 32/69.
[33] County Councils (Loans for Advances to Parish Councils) Order 1934 S.R.O. 621 Art. 2(2).   [34] L.G.A. 1933 s. 212.
[35] For 'date of borrowing' where a temporary loan is raised see page 154.
[36] Public Works Loans Act, 1875 s. 11 and Local Authorities Loans Act, 1945 s. 4.

the recommendation of the Board suspend repayment of the Board's loans for a period not exceeding five years.[37]

Secondly there are permissive rules on the suspension of annual provision for the repayment of loans which differ according to whether the money was borrowed before or after 31st July, 1963. Where the money was borrowed *before* that date for the construction alteration or extension of revenue-producing works, the annual provision for repayment may be suspended for such a limited period and subject to such conditions as the Minister may determine. The period is limited to five years or the time during which the expenditure remains unremunerative, whichever is the shorter. Where the money was borrowed *after* that date for similar purposes or for the acquisition of land in connection with them or where land was appropriated or operations completed after that date, the annual provision for repayment may be suspended for not more than five years commencing at any time before five years from the end of the loan period, or the parish council may for the same period borrow money to pay the interest, or it may do both.[38]

Separate Accounts

Where (as in the case of allotments) separate accounts have to be kept, the service of the loan to meet expenditure under that account must be charged to it.

N. OPERATION OF SINKING FUNDS

Instead of repaying a loan by instalments a parish council will find it wise to consider and may decide to establish a sinking fund which may be 'accumulating' or 'non-accumulating'.

The advantage is that the fund is invested and parish councils do not pay income or capital gains or corporation taxes.

A non-accumulating sinking fund is built up by equal annual contributions of such an amount that the fund will equal the total debt at or before the end of the loan period.

An accumulating fund is built up from rather smaller equal annual contributions of capital together with contributions of compound interest on the amount in the fund each year.

[37] Public Works Loans Act, 1875 s. 37 and Local Authorities Loans Act, 1945 s. 4.
[38] L.G.A. 1933 s. 198(2).

The rate of compound interest is prescribed by the Minister by order.[39]

Obligation to Invest

Except where the sinking fund is about to be used for the repayment of the debt all money paid to a sinking fund must immediately be invested in permissible 'trustee investments'. The parish council has power to vary or transpose these investments as it considers prudent.[39]

The range of permissible trustee investments is considerable. It is divided into two classes, namely narrower range investments not requiring advice[40] and narrower range investments requiring advice.[41] In the case of the latter the parish council must obtain advice in writing[42] from a person whom it reasonably considers qualified by his ability in and practical experience of financial matters. In addition there is power to invest in L.A.M.I.T.

Anticipation

A parish council may at any time apply the whole or any part of the sinking fund towards the discharge of the loan for which it was formed, but if it was an accumulating fund the council must continue to contribute the sums which would have accumulated had the money not been paid out.[43]

Adjustments

If at any time it appears that the sinking fund is not building up quickly enough the parish council may—and if required by the Minister must—increase the contributions either temporarily or permanently,[44] and similarly it may increase its contributions in order to accelerate repayment of the debt.[44]

If in the Minister's opinion the sinking fund is building up too quickly or is enough to enable the debt to be repaid within the loan period he may (as the case may be) permit the parish council to reduce or suspend its contributions to the fund.[44]

---

[39] L.G.A. 1933 s. 213.
[40] See Trustee Investment Act, 1961 First Schedule Part I.
[41] ibid. Part II.　　　　　　　　[42] ibid. s. 6 (4) & (5).
[43] L.G.A. 1933 s. 213.　　　　　　[44] L.G.A. 1933 s. 214.

F*

If after the whole of the debt has been repaid there remains a surplus in the sinking fund the money may with the Minister's consent be applied to other capital purposes.[45]

Destination of Investment Income

The income from sinking fund investments is always paid to the parochial account and not retained in the sinking fund itself. Where, however, the fund is cumulative the contributions from the account to the sinking fund are increased at the compound interest rate approved by the Minister.[46]

O. BORROWING WITHOUT CONSENT

There are three kinds of loans which a parish council may raise without obtaining the consent of anyone.

Loans Pending Revenue

A parish council may borrow by way of temporary overdraft or loan (whether from the bank or otherwise) pending the receipt of revenue from any source, for the purpose of defraying expenses chargeable in the current year *and taken into account in the estimates* for that year.[47] In borrowing under this head a parish council should take care that sufficient precepts for the period have been issued because interest paid on an overdraft caused by insufficient precepts is surchargeable.[48]

Temporary Loans on Capital Account

A parish council may similarly borrow pending the receipt of money for a loan already sanctioned. For purposes of the rules on repayment the principal loan if actually raised is deemed to have been raised at the date of the temporary loan.[49]

Reborrowing

A parish council may reborrow to pay off a loan forthwith or to replace other money used temporarily during the preceding

---

[45] L.G.A. 1933 s. 213. Compare the rule on unexpended balances of loans, see page 145.   [46] L.G.A. 1933 s. 213.
[47] L.G.A. 1933 s. 215 (1) (a).   [48] See page 184.
[49] L.G.A. 1933 s. 215 (1) (b) and (2).

twelve months to repay a loan when it was always intended to replace that other money by borrowed money.

Reborrowing is not permissible to make any payment to a sinking fund or to replace money previously borrowed which has been paid off by other means such as instalments, sinking fund, sale of land or capital applicable to repayment other than money borrowed for the purpose.

Reborrowed capital is for purposes of repayment regarded as part of the original loan; the Minister may extend the time for repayment but not beyond the maximum period allowable for the original loan.[50]

P. RETURNS AND DEFAULT ORDERS

Within one month of being so requested the clerk must make a return to the Minister showing how the parish council has provided for the repayment of its loans. It must contain the particulars required by the Minister and must be certified by the treasurer or other person responsible for keeping the accounts and (if required) verified by a statutory declaration made by the latter. A person who fails to make the return may be fined £20, and the making of the return is enforceable by *mandamus* whether the guilty person has been fined or not.[51]

Default Orders

If it appears that the parish council has failed to pay or appropriate any sum which it should have done or to set apart any sum required for a sinking fund or has applied any part of a sinking fund to an unauthorised purpose the Minister may direct the parish council to set aside or apply a sum (not exceeding the amount in default) by a certain date, and the parish council must notify the Minister when such order has been complied with. The order is enforceable by *mandamus*.[52]

Q. PARISH MEETINGS

A parish meeting has no power to borrow save for the purposes of a joint burial committee.[53, 54]

[50] L.G.A. 1933 s. 216.　　　[51] L.G.A. 1933 s. 199.
[52] L.G.A. 1933 s. 199.　　　[53] See page 283.
[54] Local Government (Joint Committees) Act, 1897 s. 1(3).

R. REDUCING THE DEBT BURDEN

The table at the end of this Chapter shows for various interest rates and repayment periods the half yearly annuity payments which have to be made to a lender from whom a parish council has borrowed £100. The total cost of the operation can be calculated by multiplying the amount of each payment by the number of payments. In practice at any given moment the rate of interest for long periods will be slightly higher (say $\frac{1}{2}$ per cent.) than the rate for short ones.

If a parish council wishes to provide its people with the best possible services it will in most cases be forced to create debt. Provided that proper prudence is used there is no reason to be alarmed at this for the people will by this means enjoy advantages earlier than otherwise. Moreover, the parish council acquires a solid asset such as a hall or a playing field in return for its outlay.

There are several legitimate ways, frequently neglected by parish councils, in which the debt burden created by these operations can be kept down or its cost reduced.

Instalment Payments

For comparatively small operations it will sometimes be possible to avoid borrowing at all by inducing the contractor to accept payment in instalments spread over more than one financial year.[55] If this will result in his receiving some of his money sooner than he would otherwise expect, he will have no reason to charge interest on later payments. In this way some of the advantages of debt creation are obtained without cost to the ratepayers and without any need for loan consents.

Short Periods

Interest rates for short periods are, as already noticed, usually slightly lower than those obtainable for long ones at any given moment, and in any event the shorter a loan period the less will be paid in the total of interest payments. There are therefore advantages in preferring short loan periods to long ones. These advantages may, however, be offset by inflation (reflected over a long period by rising rateable values) and by the state of the market in gilt edged securities.[56]

[55] See page 144.　　　　[56] See page 157.

Reborrowing

The rate of interest at which money can be borrowed fluctuates under the influence of factors related to the general prosperity of the country. If a parish council has had to borrow at a high rate of interest it is entitled when market rates fall to borrow at the new lower rates and use the money to pay off the original loan. In this way the capital debt will remain the same in amount but the interest payable will be less. Reborrowing of this kind can be repeated whenever interest rates fall sufficiently to make it worth while.

It should, however, be observed that a lender will sometimes be in a position to require an increased rate of interest when interest rates rise.

Sinking Fund Management

Since parish councils, in common with other local authorities, have ceased to pay income tax on their investments and are liable neither for corporation tax nor for the capital gains taxes, the establishment of a sinking fund to amortize debt has become more attractive and important, particularly when interest rates are high, for it is then that the numerous low interest trustee 'dated' stocks can be purchased at less than the full amount at which they will eventually be repaid. For example on 15th July, 1964, long-term loans could be obtained in the market only at $6\frac{1}{2}$ per cent. or more; if then a parish council borrowed £7,500 at $6\frac{1}{2}$ per cent. until 1979 (fifteen years) the first annual instalment due to the non-accumulating sinking fund on 15th July, 1965, was £500. On that day £100 worth of $3\frac{1}{2}$ per cent. Electricity Stock 1976–1979 could be bought in the market for about £70 and therefore (allowing for commissions and expenses) the £500 could be used to buy about £710 worth of this stock. Since the full amount (£710) is repayable in 1979 to the parish council, the latter, at a cost of £500 to the ratepayers has really set aside £710 towards the repayment of its own debt.

Moreover, the interest (in this example) received on the stock would amount to a yield of just over 4·9 per cent. on the £500 invested, thus reducing the future cost to the ratepayers of £500 of the debt covered by the investment to just over $1\frac{1}{2}$ per cent. per annum.

Conclusion

By purchasing dated stocks below par when interest rates are high and by reborrowing when they fall, a vigilant parish council can do a great deal to lighten the burden on its ratepayers. Sound advice is obviously desirable and so when borrowing any substantial sum a parish council ought to consult a stockbroker or accountant on the establishment of a sinking fund, and on investments.

Annual rate of interest	Number of years in which the loan is to be repaid 5	10	15	20	25	30	40	60	80*
	£ s. d.	£ s. d.	£ s. d.	£ s. d.	£ s. d.	£ s. d.	£ s. d.	£ s. d.	£ s. d.
2½	10 14 0	5 13 7¾	4 0 4¼	3 3 10	2 14 0½	2 7 7	1 19 8¼	1 12 3¼	1 8 11¾
3	10 16 10½	5 16 6	4 3 3¼	3 6 10¼	2 17 1¾	2 10 9½	2 3 1¼	1 16 0½	1 13 0¾
3½	10 19 9	5 19 4½	4 6 3	3 9 11¼	3 0 4¼	2 14 1¼	2 6 7¾	1 19 11¾	1 17 4
4	11 2 7¾	6 2 3¾	4 9 3½	3 13 1¼	3 3 7¾	2 17 6½	2 10 3¾	2 4 1¼	2 1 9
4½	11 5 7	6 5 3½	4 12 4¾	3 16 4¼	3 7 0½	3 1 0¾	2 14 1½	2 8 4¼	2 6 3¾
5	11 8 6¼	6 8 3½	4 15 6¾	3 19 8	3 10 6¼	3 4 8½	2 18 0¾	2 12 8¾	2 10 11¾
5½	11 11 5¾	6 11 4	4 18 9¼	4 3 0¾	3 14 1	3 8 5¼	3 2 1	2 17 2½	2 15 8¾
6	11 14 5½	6 14 5¼	5 2 0½	4 6 6¼	3 17 8¾	3 12 3¼	3 6 2¾	3 1 9¼	3 0 6½
6½	11 17 5½	6 17 6¾	5 5 4¼	4 10 0¾	4 1 5½	3 16 2¼	3 10 5½	3 6 5¼	3 5 4¾
7	12 0 5¾	7 0 8¾	5 8 9	4 13 7¾	4 5 3¼	4 0 2¼	3 14 9¼	3 11 1¾	3 10 3½
7½	12 3 6¼	7 3 11	5 12 2	4 17 3¾	4 9 1¾	4 4 3	3 19 2	3 15 11	3 15 2½
8	12 6 7	7 7 2	5 15 8	5 1 0½	4 13 1	4 8 5	4 3 7½	4 0 8½	4 0 2
8½	12 9 8	7 10 5	5 19 2½	5 4 10	4 17 1½	4 12 8	4 8 2		
9	12 12 9	7 13 9	6 2 9½	5 8 8½	5 1 3	4 16 11	4 12 9		
9½	12 15 3	7 17 1	6 6 5	5 12 7	5 5 4	5 0 0½	4 17 4		
10	12 19 0½	8 0 5½	6 10 1	5 16 6½	5 9 6½	5 5 7½	5 2 0½		

* Allotments only.

EXAMPLE. If it is desired to borrow £5,000 for 20 years at 6 per cent., follow the 6% line as far as the 20 year column where the figure £4 6*s*. 6¼*d*. appears. As this is the periodical payment appropriate to £100 it will be necessary to multiply it by 50 giving a periodical payment of £215 1*s*. 0½*d*. The total cost of the loan will be this figure multiplied by the number of payments (i.e. 40) = £8,602 1*s*. 8*d*.

Miscellaneous Liabilities

A. ESTATE DUTY

If a gift is made to a parish council for a charitable or public purpose and the donor dies within *one* year the parish council may be liable to repay the amount of any estate duty leviable on that part of the donor's estate represented by the gift.[1] A gift made more than a year before death escapes the duty and the phrase 'charitable or public purposes' covers any gift which a parish council may lawfully accept.[2]

B. INCOME, CORPORATION, AND CAPITAL GAINS TAXES AND BETTERMENT LEVY
P.A.Y.E.

If a parish council has employees who are paid a regular wage or salary it will be required to make the appropriate tax-deductions from the amount payable to the employee and account for them to the Inland Revenue.

Parish councils, burial boards, joint committees and joint boards consisting wholly of members appointed by local authorities are exempt from income tax on their income and from corporation tax and both capital gains taxes. The same exemptions apply to parish councils' associations.[3]

Local authorities are not liable to betterment levy.[3A]

---

[1] See Customs & I.R. Act, 1881 s. 38(2), Finance Act, 1894 s. 2(1)(c) and Finance (1909–10) Act, 1910 s. 59(1).

[2] See Blair v. Duncan (1902) A.C. 37 where it was asserted that a gift to a regimental fund or even to a political party would be within the meaning of the word 'public'.

[3] Finance (No. 2) Act, 1965 s. 66.   [3A] Land Commission Act, 1967 s. 56

C. LICENCES

Parish halls are often used for entertainments; parish councils have very little power to provide entertainments, but their property is often let to organisations and individuals which can and do provide them.

This is not the place for an explanation of the law of licensing which is enormous, complicated and obscure.[4] As, however, the failure to obtain the necessary piece of paper may have unfortunate consequences even for the most innocent, anyone who wishes to organise public dances, theatrical and cinematographic performances or billiards, or who wishes to have alcoholic refreshments provided on such occasions is advised to make sure that he has complied with the law.

D. STAMP DUTIES

Audit

The most important stamp duty with which a parish council is concerned is the audit stamp duty[5] which is leviable upon a figure calculated in the following manner:—the income and expenditure during the year are added together and from the total is deducted receipts from loans, loans repaid from money borrowed or to be borrowed and grants from government departments; the final figure thus obtained is the amount upon which the duty is payable as follows:—

Where the amount on which Stamp Duty is payable does not exceed		the sum shall be
	£25	5s. 0d. (25p.)
Exceeds £25 but does not exceed £50		10s. 0d. (50p.)
£50	£100	£1
£100	£250	£2
£250	£500	£3
£500	£1,000	£5
£1,000	£2,500	£8
£2,500	£5,000	£12
£5,000	£10,000	£20
£10,000	£25,000	£35

[4] The 73rd (1965) Edition of *Paterson's Licensing Acts* runs to 1,613 pages of text, 244 pages of index and 158 pages of forms, making a total of 2,015 pages. This is not the fault of the successive editors of this admirable work to which on all occasions the reader is referred.

[5] L.G.A. 1933 s. 221 and Audit Stamp Duty Order, 1938, S.R. & O. No. 793.

Mortgages and Automatic Charges

No stamp duty has been payable upon loans raised since 31st July, 1967.[6]

Conveyances and Transfers on Sale

Transfers of British government or parliamentary stocks are not liable to stamp duty, and for stock substituted for Bank of England stock and those Dominion and Colonial stocks which are trustee stocks the duty is reduced.

Where a transfer or conveyance of land contains a statement certifying that the transaction thereby effected does not form part of a larger transaction or of a series of transactions in respect of which the amount or value or aggregate amount or value of the consideration exceeds £5,500, no stamp duty is payable and where the value of the transaction exceeds that sum but is less than £7,000 the effective rate of duty is halved.[9]

Subject to the above exceptions stamp duty on conveyances of property or transfers of shares amounts to *about* 2 per cent. of the capital value of the transaction.[7]

National Trust etc.

A voluntary conveyance to a non-profit-making body incorporated by a special act (such as the National Trust) for the purposes of an open space or for its preservation for the nation is free of stamp duty.[10]

Contracts before Decimalization

An agreement for a matter not worth £5 or for an allotment lease at an annual rent of 10s. 0d. without premium, or for the hire of a labourer or menial servant need not be stamped,[11] but other agreements should until 15th February 1971 be signed over a 6d. stamp by the first person to execute it.[12] The 6d. stamp duty is abolished as from that day.

---

[6] Finance Act, 1967 s. 29. [7] Stamp Act, 1891 and Finance Act, 1947 s. 52.
[9] Finance Act, 1963 s. 55 as ammended by Finance Act, 1967 s. 27.
[10] Finance (1909–10) Act, 1910 s. 74.   [11] Stamp Act, 1891 s. 21.
[12] ibid. s. 22.

Receipts before Decimalization

Receipts for £2 or upwards must be stamped with a 2*d.* stamp except receipts for money paid as a tax or for the purchase of government or Bank of England stock or for dividends thereon, or for money deposited in a bank for the parish council's account; receipts contained in some other instrument already liable to be stamped do not require a stamp.

Anyone who gives an unstamped receipt for £2 or more or who refuses to stamp such a receipt, or who splits receipts to avoid stamp duty, or who gives a receipt for less than £2 for a payment of £2 or more, may be fined £10.[13]

As paid cheques are now evidence of receipt[14] these rules are obsolete in many cases, and in any case the 2*d.* stamp duty is abolished as from 15th February 1971.

E. LIABILITY TO RATES

With a modern exception in favour of poorer ratepayers and another to the disadvantage of the owners of unoccupied premises, rates are basically a personal charge levied upon a subject in respect of the occupation of property; and though Crown land occupied by a subject is rateable they are strictly speaking not payable by the Crown itself. In practice the Crown makes voluntary contributions in lieu of rates and these are assessed and paid on the same basis as if the Crown were rateable. Disputes about exceptional cases—particularly in connection with lighting—do however arise occasionally.

With a few exceptions local authorities including parish councils are subject to the same rules of liability to rates as everyone else. The purpose of the following paragraphs is to indicate the occasions when the rules enure to the advantage of a parish council or parochial charity.

Property of Public Resort

Recreation grounds, parks, village greens, 'bus shelters and other property owned and maintained upon statutory trusts by the parish council for the use of the public and to which the

---

[13] ibid. s. 103.   [14] Cheques Act, 1957 s. 3.

public resort by right, are occupied by the public at large which is not a rateable occupier. Accordingly rates are not payable in respect of these properties any more than a private person is rateable for a public right of way across his property.[15]

Parks, recreation and pleasure grounds, public walks, open spaces and playing fields if provided or managed by a parish council are treated for rating purposes as if dedicated to perpetual public use so long as they are available for the time being for the free and unrestricted use of the public.[16]

Allotments

Allotments, as agricultural land, are not rateable.[17]

Local Acts, Orders, and Highway Act 1865

Within limits rating privileges conferred by local acts and orders (often of ancient date) are preserved[18] and property exempted from statute duty or highway rate before 1835 remains exempt from that part of the rate attributable to the repair of the highways.[19] If created before 22 December 1925 these local privileges subsist only if continued by a scheme in force in 1967 or if enjoyed in practice then.

Not Charitable

A parish council cannot as such claim the rating privileges accorded to charitable and similar organisations[20] and will therefore be liable to pay rates on the parish hall unless it is let to such an organisation.[21]

Appeals

Appeals against assessment and other methods of resisting liability or payment of rates are discussed in Chapter 20.

[15] See the 'Brockwell Park Case' (Lambeth Overseers v. L.C.C. 1897 A.C. 625), the 'Putney Bridge Case' (Hare v. Overseers of Putney 1881 7 Q.B.D. 223), and Trustees of Mitcham Golf Course v. Ereaut 1937 3 All. E. 450.
[16] General Rate Act, 1967 s. 44.
[17] s. 26.
[18] s. 117.See also Wilts. Valuation Committee v. Boyce and The Same v. Ramsbury Rating Authority and Orchard (1948) 2 K.B. 125.
[19] s. 117
[20] R. & V. (Misc. Prov.) Act, 1955 s. 8(1) proviso.   [21] See page 128.

F. DRAINAGE CHARGES

Agricultural land and buildings not within an internal drainage district excluding rough grazing and woodlands may be assessed to the *general* drainage charge payable to a River Board which may in addition levy a *special* drainage charge for carrying out works in the interests of agriculture. The special charge can only be levied under authority of a scheme approved by the Minister of Agriculture. These charges will sometimes be leviable on allotments.[22]

G. TITHE REDEMPTION ANNUITIES

Many properties, some of which are owned by parish councils, are charged with Tithe Redemption Annuity.[23]

Unless redeemed the annuity is charged upon all lands which were subject to tithe rent charge on 2nd October, 1936[24] and is payable yearly on 1st October[25] until and including 1st October, 1996.

The land to be charged and the amount payable may be shown in an Annuities Register which when sealed is conclusive.

Redemption and Reduction

A parish council may at any time free such of its land as is chargeable by paying to the Inland Revenue a lump sum calculated in accordance with the Tithe Act, 1936, and with rules made by the Treasury. The Board is bound on application to inform the parish council of the sum required.[26] In 1965 the remaining 31 years of annuity could be redeemed for slightly less than 15 years' purchase.

A parish council may also pay capital sums of not less than £25 to the Board and this has the effect of reducing, upon similar principles, the amount of the annuity.

An annuity is redeemable compulsorily whenever land still charged with it is now sold[27], or where it amounts to £3

[22] Land Drainage Act, 1961 ss. 1–3 and Agriculture (Misc. Prov.) Act, 1968 Part II.

[23] For a complete and very learned statement of the history and law of this tangled subject see *Millard's Tithes*, Third Edition (1938).

[24] Tithe Act, 1936 s. 13(1).   [25] ibid. s. 47.(1)

[26] ibid. s. 15.   [27] Finance Act, 1962 s. 32.

or less, or where it is charged upon land divided or about to be divided into numerous plots for building or other purposes,[28] but the Board may remit very small annuities if the cost of collection does not warrant their continuance.[29]

H. CORN RENTS

Corn rents are payments charged on land in lieu of tithes when the old tithe system in a parish had become unworkable as a result of a private inclosure act. They are redeemable.[30]

I. SUBSCRIPTIONS

A parish council may pay reasonable subscriptions annually or otherwise to any association of local authorities formed to consult upon matters of common interest and for the discussion of matters relating to local government, or to such associations of officers and of members of local authorities as may be approved by the Minister.[31]

J. INSURANCE

Like other authorities a parish council may insure its members against accident when on duty.[32]

A parish council may, moreover, insure its property against loss or destruction because it is bound to preserve the property held by it as a trustee for the public and to conduct its affairs in a prudent and businesslike fashion: the right to effect such insurance is inherent in the duties of preservation and maintenance laid upon parish councils by law.

Similarly where a risk exists a parish council may (and ought to) protect the ratepayers against claims and litigation costs arising out of injury and damage to members of the public.

[28] ibid. s. 11. amended by Finance Act, 1958 s. 38(3).
[29] ibid. s. 10.　　　　　　[30] See Corn Rents Act, 1963.
[31] L.G.A. 1948 s. 129. Amended by L.G.(F.P.)A. 1963 s. 3.
[32] L.G.A. 1948 ss. 130 and P.C.A. 1957 s. 9.

Neglect of this precaution may lead to a heavy imposition on the rates.[33]

While it is obviously unnecessary to insure against every remote risk a parish council would be wise to review its work at intervals and consider whether it is adequately insured or whether there are new risks against which insurance is advisable. The following are the main types of policy in which a parish council may be interested:—

1. *Public Liability* to protect the ratepayers against claims for accidents caused to members of the public as a result of the parish council's activities.

2. *Loss of Property* by fire, burglary and the like. There is a type of comprehensive policy in this class known as an 'All Risks' policy. Such a policy should be carefully studied because most of them are so riddled with exceptions and exclusions that the name is misleading.

3. *Fidelity* to protect the council against the loss of cash in the hands of its employees.

4. *Members' Accidents* to cover members on duty. Such a policy is generally necessary only where meetings are numerous and distances long.

K. ALLOWANCES TO MEMBERS

Mayor's Allowance

A rural borough council may pay to the mayor a reasonable allowance to meet the expenses of his office.[34]

Other Allowances

Since 1948 a parish council has been able to pay four types of allowances to its members, namely for travel, subsistence, financial loss and conferences. Payments for such allowances are not subject to the rate limits[35] but are subject to conditions and limitations prescribed by the Minister.[36]

---

[33] An accident which occurred in 1947 led in 1951 to an action against the Stone Parish Council. In 1954 judgment was given against the Council for £17,500 which was reduced to £9,000 in the Court of Appeal. These sums take no account of the high legal costs which may be expected in such a protracted case.

[34] L.G.A. 1958 7th Sched. par. 5.   [35] L.G.A. 1948 s. 114(5).

[36] L.G.A. 1948 s. 117.

General Conditions and Limitations

A claimant for financial loss, travelling and subsistence allowance must claim in a prescribed form or on a form to a like effect.[37] If possible the parish council must give tickets or warrants instead of cash[38]; and it must keep detailed records of payments and the persons to whom they are made and these must be open to public inspection.[39] Where a claimant is travelling for more than one body, arrangements are made to reduce the amount payable by each.[40]

Travel

Travel allowance must not exceed the amount of the ordinary or any available cheap fare: and the fare allowed is the first-class fare by steamer and the second-class rail fare unless the parish council determines upon first-class rail fares either generally or specially. The amount may be increased for Pullman or similar supplements, reservation of seats, deposit and porterage of luggage. If a sleeping car is used the overnight subsistence allowance is reduced by one-third. For taxi fares the amount allowable is normally the equivalent only of the fare by public transport, but in an urgent case the full taxi fare may be allowed.

Amounts at rates which vary for the type of vehicle may be paid where a member uses his own vehicle, if such use would be in the public interest or would involve a substantial saving. The rate for a hired car must not exceed the amount which would have been payable had the car belonged to the member.

The rate for travel by air must not exceed the cost of travelling by the equivalent ground service plus the consequent saving (if any) of financial loss and subsistence allowance, but a parish council may resolve that the saving in time is so substantial as to justify the payment of air fares and thereupon the ordinary or available cheap fare may be paid or the actual fare if neither of these is available.

Subsistence

Subsistence allowances may be paid for periods of absence exceeding 4 hours (not involving an overnight stay) from home:

---

[37] S.I. 1948 No. 1784 as amended by S.I. 1949 No. 457 and 1952 No. 535 Art. 4.   [38] ibid. Art. 5.   [39] ibid. Art. 6.   [40] ibid. Art. 7.

the amounts vary for periods of 4 to 8 hours, 8 to 12 hours and over 12 hours. Special rates are allowed for overnight absences in respect of each complete period of 24 hours absent and there may be supplements for a stay in London or for an annual conference approved by the Minister.[41]

Financial Loss

Financial loss allowance may be paid for loss of earnings or additional expense suffered or incurred to enable a member to perform an approved duty outside the parish.[42] It is limited to an amount fixed from time to time by the Minister.[43]

Conferences (Expiring Rules)

A parish council may in certain cases pay the reasonable expenses of individual attendances by members at conferences and meetings. The number of attendances per annum is *unlimited* in the case of meetings organised by a local authority or government department to consider boundary changes, or meetings organised to instruct parish councillors as such in their work. In addition a limited number of attendances per annum is permitted for other meetings and conferences, for instance, of parish councils' associations: this number depends upon the population of the parish as follows:—

10,000 and over	9 attendances per year
5,000 to 10,000	7 attendances per year
Under 5,000	5 attendances per year

Over and above these, conference allowance is payable for the triennial national conference of the National Association of Parish Councils.[44] New regulations abolishing all numerical restrictions are expected in the course of 1970. The power to pay conference allowances includes power to purchase reports of them.

[41] S.I. 1948 No. 1784 as amended by S.I. 1949 No. 457 and 1952 No. 535 Art. 4.
[42] L.G.A. 1948 s. 112.
[43] L.G.(M.P.)A. 1953, s. 16 and S.I. 1954 No. 398.
[44] L.G.A. 1933 s. 267 as amended by L.G.A. 1948 s. 113(3). See also S.I. 1965 No. 1666.

L. ALLOWANCES TO OFFICERS

Expenses properly incurred by an officer as such may[45] and indeed must be defrayed by the parish council because they have been incurred on the council's behalf.

M. NATIONAL INSURANCE

A parish council will be liable for national insurance contributions payable for a *full time employee* and may recover such an employee's contribution from him; but most employees will be on a part time or casual basis only and sometimes an employment is disregarded in considering whether there is a liability. The main relevant *disregarded employments* are:—

1. Casual employments.
2. Employment for less than 8 hours a week where weekly earnings are normally less than £2.
3. Part time clerical work after 6 p.m. or outside normal working hours.
4. Unpaid or part time caretaking.
5. Reliefs for gymnasium, lavatory or park attendance if earning less than £2 a week.
6. Lamplighters and lampcleaners.
7. Part time youth leaders.
8. Part time caretakers and record keepers at burial grounds if earning less than £2 a week[46]

In the common case of a person with more than one employer the liability for contributions rests, in general, upon the person who first employs him or who first pays him in any given employment week.[47]

N. INDUSTRIAL INJURIES INSURANCE

Whether or not national insurance contributions are payable a parish council will be liable for industrial injuries insurance unless it can show either that the employment is casual, or that

---

[45] L.G.A. (F.P.) Act, 1963 s. 5.   [46] S.I. 1957 No. 2175.
[47] S.I. 1948 No. 1274 Art. 8.

the work is part time and that the employee is not employed as an 'officer or servant' and that there is no contract of service; for this purpose a contract of service need not be in writing.[48]

O. REDUNDANCY PAYMENTS

It appears that a parish council may be liable for redundancy payments[49] where an employee is not otherwise entitled to compensation for loss of office. The circumstances in which this might happen are not likely to be very common.

P. SELECTIVE EMPLOYMENT TAX AND PAYMENTS

Since 5th September, 1966, Local Authorities including Parish Councils have been liable to pay if necessary selective employment *tax* in respect of any employee in any week where they are liable to pay an employer's national insurance contribution for that employee.[50] The Minister and the Secretary of State for Wales (whichever is appropriate) are empowered to make *payments* for the benefit of Local Authorities including Parish Councils. The amount of these is related to the amount of selective employment tax paid.

The amount of the tax is laid down by statute but the amount of the payment, on the contrary, is not but is fixed by the appropriate minister with the consent of the Treasury. It follows that the payment can be as much as, or more, or less than the tax; indeed it need not be paid at all, and the rates of payment can differ as between England and Wales.

The sums are actually received by the Rural District Council and credited by it to the parochial account of the parish concerned[51] so that the ratepayers do not eventually suffer. As the rural district council has to claim the amount from the appropriate minister, it is essential that a parish council which is paying the tax should inform the rural district council of the fact so that its payments can be included in the claim.

---

[48] S.I. 1948 No. 1456.   [49] Redundancy Payments Act. 1965.
[50] Finance Act, 1966 s. 44.
[51] Selective Employment Payments Act. 1966 s. 4.

17

Accounts and Financial Administration

L ike every other local authority a parish council may buy, own or sell property and goods, employ servants and contractors, and give or receive services. These transactions are connected with each other, with the parish council and with the ratepayers by the passing of money. An effective accounting system provides an accurate record of the origin, quantity, whereabouts and disposal of the council's property and money in a form which will make mistakes obvious.

A. INSPECTION

Large authorities can adopt accounting systems which are so detailed and dovetailed that administrative irregularities will come to light automatically; but few parish councils have funds or dealings which would justify elaborate systems because the expense and trouble of maintaining them would exceed the possible losses caused by not doing so. It is sometimes, therefore, desirable for parish council accounts to be supplemented by systematic or regular (but not necessarily frequent) inspections by the council or members specially deputed. This is important in connection with property which is not in the custody of the council itself such as certain parish documents[1] and individual allotments, and with equipment which is liable to deteriorate such as rollers and tennis nets.

If such inspection is instituted an up-to-date inspection book in the form of a summarised inventory with columns for each

[1] See Chapter 11.

inspection should be provided. Some parish councils make such
inspections the duty of the vice-chairman.[2]

B. RECEIVING SMALL SUMS (TICKETS AND TURNSTILES)

Parish councils often derive substantial income from the
receipt of large numbers of small sums such as *admission charges*
to tennis courts, bowling greens, bathing pools, recreation and
camping grounds, or as *use charges* for towels or boats. The
giving of hand-written receipts in these circumstances is
wasteful of resources and an intolerable nuisance to the public

The simplest way both to give a receipt and keep a primary
record is to use roll tickets which must be machine numbered
consecutively. To reduce the possibility of confusion, the ticket
should be of different colours for different amounts or uses.

In conjunction with the tickets a ticket register should be
kept showing progressively the rolls in use (identified by
number, colour and letter); at the beginning of each day the
first unused number should be entered: this number should be
the same as the number entered at the end of the previous day
At the end of the day the number of the first unused ticket
should be entered. The difference between the number
multiplied by the amount of each ticket should equal the
money collected. The book should also show how much was
banked, the amounts brought in and carried down and the
totals of each day. A register of this kind ruled in columns is not
difficult to enter up and is a considerable safeguard against
irregularity.

Where a turnstile is in use instead of tickets, it should be self
recording and a turnstile register should be kept in the same
way as a ticket register.

C. RECEIVING LARGER SUMS (RECEIPT BOOKS)

For larger sums (such as rent) it is desirable though not
essential to use official receipt forms printed with the council's
name. The manifold carbon receipt book is better than the

[2] See page 79.

counterfoil type because it has to be written only once and exactly reproduces the original. The receipts should be machine numbered in duplicate, the original being torn out and the copy remaining in the book.

A register of receipt books should be kept showing the date when each was acquired and the dates when it was begun and finished. If a receipt book is issued out permanently the person to whom it is issued should be required to sign for it and the person issuing it should also sign at the same time.

D. PAYMENTS TO THE BANK
(PAYING-IN BOOKS)

Money ought to be paid into the bank at the earliest possible opportunity.[3] The parish council is required to provide a paying-in book with counterfoils or duplicates for the use of anyone who pays money into its account or the account of its treasurer.[4] The person paying in must enter on a slip and its counterfoil particulars of the payments into the bank and in the case of cheques, the amount of each cheque and some reference, such as the number of the receipt given or the name of the debtor, which will connect the cheque with the debt. In addition if a cheque was not received in discharge of a debt that fact must be noted.

The paying-in book must be produced on demand to the parish council or district auditor.[4]

E. MATERIALS

Orders

Orders for goods should always be in writing. Machine numbered carbon duplicate books are normally the most satisfactory.

Orders, unless very small, should have the *previous* approval of the council but in an emergency it may be necessary to order without specific authority; nevertheless all orders must ultimately be submitted for approval.

[3] See above, page 168.
[4] Accounts (Payment into Bank) Order, 1922 S.R. & O. No. 1404.

Records

Stock books should be kept showing particulars of each item, when and where purchased and showing also the date of issue and the date and place of use. Records of this kind are particularly desirable where the council owns numbers of small objects such as tennis balls or perishable equipment such as cricket nets.

It is also desirable to keep a register of plant and equipment such as old iron chests, mowers, rollers, tennis court markers or pleasure boats. This sort of equipment, especially if it is of an old-fashioned pattern, is easily forgotten and notwithstanding size and weight quite capable of being lost.[5]

Lighting

A parish council which maintains public lighting[6] should have a large-scale map upon which each light is marked and numbered. Where a parish council maintains its lights itself labour and materials can be booked to each light by number; in this way the cost of each light can be quickly calculated and the parish council will be put on inquiry if one regularly costs more than the others.

F. ACCOUNT BOOKS AND FINANCIAL STATEMENTS

Forms are not prescribed generally for the accounts of parish authorities but a form of *annual financial statement* is.[7] This provides a clear guide to the type of accounts which should be kept; and as it must be completed in duplicate for the annual audit the council should keep its books in such a way that they correspond as nearly as possible with the form itself.

The parish council and the chairman of a parish meeting is required to keep accounts of actual receipts and payments[8] and

[5] It is said that the government of Ireland once lost a battery of heavy guns; the author has experience of a parish council which mislaid a half-ton roller.

[6] See Chapter 25.

[7] For Parish Councils and parish meetings S.I. 1961 No. 251; for Joint Committees other than under the Burial Acts S.R. & O. 1900 No. 300; for Joint Committees under the Burial Acts S.R. & O. 1902 No. 361. The two last were amended by the Financial Statements (District Audit) Regs. 1938 S.R. & O. No. 794 and by S.I. 1951 No. 922.

[8] L.G.A. 1933 s 193(9).

the financial statement is designed to enable these to be summarised; a *Receipts and Payments Book* should therefore be kept in which sums actually paid out and received are recorded in order of date. Small parish councils may find it unnecessary to keep any other account book, but larger ones, perhaps administering several adoptive acts and charities, may find it convenient to keep a separate receipts and payments book for each service.

Separate Accounts

Separate accounts *must* be kept for allotments[9] and apparently also for a forged transfer compensation fund.[10]

The treasurer (if any) should keep a *Treasurer's Receipts and Payments Book* and if, as is usual, someone has authority to make small disbursements in cash he should keep a *Petty Cash Book* in the form of a receipts and payments book.

G. BILLS

Apart from disbursements of sums under £1 (petty cash) bills should be numbered consecutively and when they are submitted to the council for approval they should be initialled by the chairman. When they have been paid they should with the receipt (or paid cheque) attached, be carefully filed in order of number in files (such as box or clutch files) from which they cannot be unintentionally detached.

Bills should be itemised and the council should refuse to consider a bill which does not set out with reasonable clarity the goods or services for which payment is demanded.

H. TIME SHEETS AND WAGES BOOKS

Where a parish council employs labour on a time basis the time sheet is really the bill for work done. Like any other bill it should be specific, setting out the nature of each job and the time taken to do it. If the council employs a foreman he should certify the time sheets.

[9] A.A. 1908 s. 54(1).
[10] This seems to follow from the terms of the Forged Transfer Acts, 1891 and 1892.

G

The wages book (or sheet) is compiled primarily from the time sheets. It shows the employee's name, the rates of pay, the hours worked, the total gross wages earned and the deductions for taxation, superannuation, and so forth together with the employer's contributions, and finally the net amounts payable by the parish council to the employee, the Inland Revenue and the Ministry of National Insurance.

I. PAYMENT OF BILLS

By Cheque

When the payment of a bill has been authorised and the amount exceeds £1, a cheque should be made out and signed by two members of the council[11] who should also initial the counterfoil. It is desirable (but not legally essential) that cheques should be signed at council meetings.

It was a common practice to have a form of receipt stamped or printed on the back of each cheque but this is no longer desirable because since 17th October, 1957, any cheque which appears to have been paid by the banker upon whom it is drawn is evidence that the person to whom the cheque is made out (the creditor) has received the sum payable by the cheque. It is not, however, by itself evidence that any particular debt owed to the creditor has been paid and therefore a covering letter should be sent stating that the cheque is sent in payment of a particular debt, or better still the cheque can be marked in such a way that there is a cross reference to the bill on it; it is undesirable to insist upon a separate receipt, for the multiplication of the formalities of receipt was the very thing which the Cheques Act was intended to abolish. If a cheque is crossed 'Account payee only' the banker becomes liable if the money finds its way into the hands of any other person.

It is desirable to write on each cheque the number of the bill to which it relates.[12]

In Cash

Payments of sums under £1 are commonly made from a *Petty Cash Imprest* of a few, say, five, pounds in the hands of the clerk or treasurer. When small bills are paid the transaction is

---

[11] L.G.A. 1933 s. 193(8). [12] Especially in view of the Chues Act, 1957.

entered in the petty cash book and a receipt or signature obtained. At each meeting the book should be presented and initialled in the same way as a bill, and a cheque should be issued to bring the imprest up to the original amount.

J. FINANCIAL YEAR

The Financial Year begins on 1st April and ends on 31st March.[13]

K. STANDING ORDERS ON CONTRACTS

Contracts made by a parish council or committee of a parish council must be made in accordance with standing orders.[14]

The purpose of such orders is to ensure that all tenders for the work receive the same treatment and to regulate the procedure followed by the clerk in dealing with them. It is sometimes desirable to relate them to an approved list of contractors kept by the rural district council.

[13] L.G.A. 1933 s. 223.   [14] See page 190.

18

Audit

A. WHAT ACCOUNTS ARE AUDITED?

The accounts of every parish council, parish meeting or committee of either, of any joint committee of which a parish council is a constituent authority[1] and of any officer who handles money or property for which he should account to the council[2] are liable to district audit. Charities administered by a parish council are audited as part of the council's accounts but not charities to which the parish council merely appoints trustees even if it appoints all the trustees.

If a parish council or parish meeting has no financial transactions in a given year and the clerk or chairman so certifies no audit will be held.

B. TIME FOR AUDIT

The audit takes place annually as soon as may be after the close of the financial year on 31st March.[3] An extraordinary audit may take place at any time.[4]

C. EXTRAORDINARY AUDIT

The Minister may at any time direct an extraordinary audit and it may be held after three days' notice in writing to the authority or persons whose accounts are to be audited.

All the statutory rules relating to ordinary audits apply to extraordinary audits except those relating to the preparation of

[1] L.G.A. 1933 s. 219.   [2] L.G.A. 1933 s. 241.
[3] L.G.A. 1933 s. 223.   [4] L.G.A. 1933 s. 236.

the financial statement, the deposit of the accounts and supporting documents for public inspection and the giving of public
notice thereof.[5]

D. PROCEDURE BEFORE ORDINARY AUDIT
Notice

The accounts must be made up to 31st March[6] and balanced[7]
and then the financial statement[8] in the prescribed form must
be prepared.[9] Meanwhile the clerk (or chairman of the parish
meeting) asks the auditor for an appointment which must be
fixed for such a day that at least fourteen (that is sixteen[10]) days'
public notice of the audit can be given. Having secured his
appointment the clerk gives the necessary sixteen days' public
notice of the audit and of the deposit of the accounts for public
inspection; notice is given in the usual manner[11] and when it has
been given the clerk must immediately send to the auditor a
certificate that he has given it.[12]

Deposit of Accounts

Seven clear days before the audit a copy of every account
duly made up and balanced and all account books, deeds, contracts, accounts, vouchers and receipts relating to the accounts
must be deposited at the 'appropriate office' of the parish
council and must be open to inspection at all reasonable hours
by all interested persons, who may make copies or extracts
without payment.[13] An interested person includes his agent.[14]

In most cases the 'appropriate office' is the place where the
clerk transacts his business as clerk and is nearly always in his
home. It is desirable that the accounts should be deposited in the
parish but if the office is outside the parish their deposit there is
not illegal if it is in the neighbourhood.

Anyone who fails to make up the accounts or who alters them
after making up without obtaining the consent or directions of

---

[5] L.G.A. 1933 s. 236.   [6] L.G.A. 1933 s. 223.
[7] L.G.A. 1933 s. 224(1).   [8] See page 184.
[9] L.G.A. 1933 s. 222(1).
[10] R. v. Salop Justices (1838) 8 Ad. & El. 173.
[11] L.G.A. 1933 s. 224(3).   [12] S.R. & O. 1934 No. 1188.
[13] L.G.A. 1933 s. 224(1).
[14] R. v. Bedwellty U.D.C. ex p. Price (1934) 1 K.B. 333.

the auditor, or who obstructs lawful inspection, may be fined up to £5.[15]

E. PROCEEDINGS AT AUDIT

Evidence

The auditor may in writing under his hand require the production of any document which he thinks necessary for the audit and may require anyone holding or accountable for such a document to appear before him at the audit and may require him to make and sign a declaration as to the correctness of the document. Anyone who fails to comply with the auditor's requirements may be fined up to £2 and anyone who knowingly makes or signs a false declaration may on conviction be imprisoned for a maximum of two years or fined or both.[16]

Electors' Rights

Any elector for the area to which the accounts relate may be present or represented and may object to the accounts.[17]

Duties of Auditor

The auditor must *disallow* every item which is contrary to law; he must *surcharge* upon the person or persons responsible any disallowed expenditure, any sum which should have been brought into account but which was not so brought, and the amount of any loss or deficiency caused by negligence or misconduct; and he must *certify* the amount due from any person surcharged.[18]

In addition he must on application by any person aggrieved by his decision on any matter to which that person has objected or by anyone aggrieved by a disallowance or surcharge state in writing the reason for his decision.[19]

'The effect of a *disallowance* is that the item (or the part thereof which is disallowed) is expunged from the accounts.'[20] The auditor cannot disallow any item of expenditure which has been sanctioned by the Minister.[21] He is entitled to disallow not

---

[15] L.G.A. 1933 s. 224(2).
[16] L.G.A. 1933 s. 225 and Perjury Act, 1911 s. 5.
[17] L.G.A. 1933 s. 226(1).   [18] L.G.A. 1933 s. 228.
[19] L.G.A. 1933 s. 226(2).
[20] Hurle-Hobbs, *Law Relating to District Audit.*
[21] L.G.A. 1933 s. 228(1) proviso.

only unlawful expenditure, but where expenditure upon a lawful object has (objectively speaking) been excessive or unreasonable or improper, he may disallow the amount by which the expenditure exceeds the reasonable figure.[22]

The effect of a *surcharge* is to impose a personal liability upon a person surcharged for the amount of a loss caused by his act or omission. Only a member, officer or servant of the council may be surcharged;[23] a mere contractor or other stranger cannot be treated in this way.

A surchargeable loss includes interest or loss of interest arising from failure to issue a sufficient precept or to collect other revenues,[24] and misconduct which leads to a surcharge includes the passing of a resolution after its illegality has been brought to the notice of the council.[25]

Conclusion

At the end of the proceedings the auditor must certify on each copy of the financial statement, in the prescribed form, the amount of expenditure audited and allowed subject to disallowances and surcharges (if any), the fact that the regulations relating to the statement have been obeyed and that he has ascertained by audit the correctness of the statement.[26]

One copy of the statement must then be stamped for the appropriate amount,[27] the auditor must then cancel the stamp and forward the stamped copy to the Minister.[28]

F. PROCEEDING AFTERS AUDIT

The unstamped copy of the financial statement is retained by the parish authority which must within seven days of the end of the audit give public notice that it is available for public inspection at all reasonable hours by any elector for the area of the authority.[29]

Within fourteen days of the completion of the audit the auditor must send a report of the audit to the Minister.[30]

[22] Roberts v. Hopwood 1925 A.C. 578.
[23] Re Dickson (1948) 2 K.B. 95.   [24] L.G.A. 1933 s. 228(2).
[25] Davies v. Cowperthwaite (1938) 2 All. E. 685.
[26] L.G.A. 1933 s. 228.   [27] See page 162.
[28] L.G.A. 1933 s. 222.
[29] Audit Regulations 1934 S.R. & O. No. 1188 Art. 7.
[30] L.G.A. 1933 s. 227 proviso.

Surcharge Certificates

The auditors' surcharge certificates must state the amount of the surcharge, and the name of the person from whom the money is due and must be signed and dated.[31] Sums due under a certificate must be paid to the treasurer within fourteen days of the date of the certificate or within fourteen days of the adverse conclusion or abandonment of any appeal or application for relief in respect of the certificate.[32]

A sum which has become payable under a certificate is recoverable summarily or otherwise as a civil debt on complaint or action taken by or under the direction of the auditor at the expense of the parish council.[33] Proceedings in a court of summary jurisdiction may be taken at any time within nine months of the debt becoming due.[34]

G. APPEALS AND APPLICATIONS FOR RELIEF

Within six weeks of the conclusion of the audit an 'aggrieved objector' or a person aggrieved by a disallowance may give notice of *appeal* against the auditor's decision and a person aggrieved by a surcharge may give notice of appeal or lodge an *application for relief* or both.

An appeal involves the contention that the auditor's decision is wrong and ought to be quashed or reduced; an application is based on the contention that whether the auditor's decision is right or wrong the applicant acted reasonably or in the belief that his action was lawful.

Appeal Tribunal

If the amount involved exceeds £500 the appeal is made to the High Court; in other cases it may be made to the High Court or to the Minister.[35] If an application for relief is made at the same time as an appeal it must be made to the same tribunal as the appeal; if there is no appeal, the application may be made to whichever tribunal an appeal might have been made.[36]

---

[31] Audit Regulations 1934 S.R. & O. No. 1188 Art. 9.
[32] L.G.A. 1933 s. 232.   [33] L.G.A. 1933 s. 234.
[34] L.G.A. 1933 s. 233.   [35] L.G.A. 1933 s. 229.
[36] L.G.A. 1933 s. 230.

Procedure

Appeals and applications to the High Court are made by originating notice of motion in the Queen's Bench Division.[37]

Where an appeal or application is to be made to the Minister a personal hearing by a person appointed by the Minister may be demanded, and a member of the Council on Tribunals may attend any such hearing.[36A]

The auditor should be asked to enter the reasons for his decision in the account book in which the certificate is entered and the book should be presented to him for that purpose. An exact copy of these reasons and a copy of the certificate including the signature and date should be forwarded to the Ministry together with the appeal or application which should be made by letter on foolscap paper and signed by the appellant or applicant in his own hand. The letter should contain a very full statement of the grounds upon which the appeal is made and of the facts which it is desired to lay before the Minister, and any relevant documents and copies of council resolutions should be enclosed with it. It is usually desirable to take advice before writing such a letter.

Effect of Appeals and Applications

On appeal the tribunal may confirm, vary or quash the decision and may remit the case to the auditor with such directions as it thinks fit for giving effect to its decision.[38]

On an application for relief the tribunal may relieve the applicant wholly or partly from personal liability,[39] and its decision is final.[40]

The tribunal's decision may also affect the qualifications of the person concerned for office.[41]

Appeal from the Minister

The Minister may at any stage (and must if required by the court) state a case for the opinion of the High Court on an appeal, but otherwise his decision is final.[42] Appeals from the Minister, therefore, arise only on points of law.

[36A] L.G.A. 1933 s. 231 (2) and Tribunals and Inquiries Act 1966 s. 4.
[37] See R.S.C. Order 55B rr 59–70.   [38] L.G.A. 1933 s. 229.
[39] L.G.A. 1933 s. 230.   [40] L.G.A. 1933 s. 230.
[41] See page 33.   [42] L.G.A. 1933 s. 229.

Costs

The auditor's costs in defending an allowance, disallowance or surcharge are paid by the parish authority unless the tribunal otherwise orders.[43]

[43] L.G.A. 1933 s. 234.

19

Miscellaneous Administrative Matters

A. PUBLIC NOTICES

Save as otherwise expressly provided by a particular enactment any public notice required to be given by a parish council, chairman of a parish meeting or joint committee of parish councils must be given by affixing the notice on or near the principal door of each Anglican[1] church or chapel in the parish and by posting it in some conspicuous place or places in the parish and in addition in such other manner as appears to be desirable for giving publicity to the notice,[2] such as by proclamation or advertisement in the press, or the employment of a town crier. Expenditure upon such publicity must be reasonable in all the circumstances.

A notice of any meeting open to the public by statute must in addition be posted at the parish council's offices (if any) and if none then in a central and conspicuous place.[3]

Proclamation in church or at the church door during or after divine service is prohibited.[4]

Penalties

Anyone who destroys, tampers with, pulls down, injures or defaces any board on which a byelaw, notice or other matter is put by authority of the Minister or the parish council or any advertisement, placard, bill or notice put up by a parish council is liable to a fine not exceeding £20.[5]

[1] Caiger v. St Mary's Vestry (1881), 50 L.J.M.C. 59.
[2] L.G.A. 1933 s. 287.
[3] Public Bodies (Admission to Meetings) Act, 1960 s. 1(4).
[4] Parish Notices Act, 1837 s. 1.
[5] L.G.A. 1933 s. 289 as amended by Criminal Justice Act 1967 Schedule 3

Fixtures, Bulletins

In an increasing number of parishes a monthly bulletin of future events and fixtures is published, usually by voluntary effort. A parish council can assist this enterprise from the 'free fifth', but apart from this it can pay to ensure that its own official notices are inserted.

B. SERVICE OF DOCUMENTS

Notices, orders and documents required to be sent, delivered or served upon a parish council, its clerk or chairman must be left at or sent by post to the office of the parish council. Similar communications for a parish meeting go to the chairman.[6]

A document contained in a letter which is properly addressed stamped and posted is deemed, unless the contrary is proved, to have been served when the letter would have been delivered in the ordinary course of post,[7] but this rule applies only to documents to be served under acts passed since 1st January, 1890.

Documents required by law to be sent by registered post may be sent by recorded delivery.[8]

C. CONTRACTS

A parish council may make all contracts necessary for the discharge of its functions.[9] Accordingly a contract made in pursuance of action which is *ultra vires* is itself *ultra vires*.

Form and Standing Orders

With the exception of contracts for the sale of land and contracts of guarantee, a contract is no longer required by the general law to be in writing,[10] but on the other hand all contracts made by a parish council or committee thereof must be made in accordance with standing orders made by the parish council. These standing orders must, in the case of contracts for the supply of goods or materials or for the execution of works, require that, except as otherwise provided in the standing orders, notice of intention to contract shall be published and tenders invited, and must regulate the manner of publication

---

[6] L.G.A. 1933 s. 286.   [7] Interpretation Act, 1889.
[8] Recorded Delivery Service Act, 1962 s. 1.   [9] L.G.A. 1933 s. 266.
[10] Law Reform (Enforcement of Contracts) Act, 1954.

and invitation. Persons contracting with a parish council are not bound to inquire whether the standing orders have been complied with.[11]

Contracts need not be sealed if they are for work done or goods supplied in the ordinary course of business with the approval of the council or its authorised agent, but as a general rule all contracts of a substantial nature should be signed by two members of the council under authority of a resolution.

If an order is given for the supply of goods or the giving of services and no price is named, the parish council will be liable for the true value of the goods or services (*quantum meruit*) if they are actually supplied or given.

D. BYELAWS GENERALLY

Byelaws must be made under the hands and seals of two members and have no effect until confirmed.[12] In most cases the confirming authority is the Home Secretary.[13] Model byelaws have been issued by the Home Office on public bathing (VIII), baths and washhouses (IX), pleasure grounds (X), pleasure boats (XII), cemeteries (XIV) and mortuaries (XV). Where it is desired to pass a byelaw which departs from a standard model it is wise to consult the Home Office beforehand.

Procedure

At least one month before application for confirmation is made, notice of intention to apply must be advertised in a local newspaper and a copy of the proposed byelaws must be available for inspection at all reasonable hours at the parish council's offices. A copy, at a price not exceeding 6*d*. (3*p*) per 100 words, must be furnished to every person applying for it.[14]

The confirming authority may confirm or refuse to confirm and may fix the date when the byelaws are to come into operation, but if no date is so fixed they come into operation one month after confirmation;[15] they must be printed or reproduced by some mechanical process such as rotaprinting, and open to free inspection at all reasonable times and copies must be furnished to any applicant at a price not exceeding 1*s*. 0*d*.[16] (5*p*)

[11] L.G.A. 1933 s. 266. [12] L.G.A. 1933 s. 250(2).
[13] S.R. & O. 1946 No. 1757.
[14] L.G.A. 1933 s. 250 sub-sections (3) to (5).
[15] L.G.A. 1933 s. 250 (6). [16] L.G.A. 1933 s. 250(7).

Penalties

Byelaws may fix reasonable fines recoverable on summary conviction not exceeding the amount fixed by the enabling act or if no amount is fixed not exceeding £20, and in the case of a continuing offence £2 for each day during which the offence continues after conviction.[17] If a byelaw was made before 1st January, 1968 and in it the maximum penalty specified for an offence was £5, then the maximum penalty was automatically raised to £20 on that day.[17A]

Proof

The manner in which byelaws are proved in legal proceedings is described in Chapter 20.

E. SAFEGUARDS FOR OTHER INTERESTS

There are some functions which parish councils cannot exercise or cannot exercise in particular ways without observing procedures which are intended to safeguard the interests of private individuals and other public authorities. The safeguards which are peculiar to the provision of 'bus shelters[18] are explained elsewhere, but there are also safeguards connected with the provision of cycle parks and the placing upon land or premises of seats, shelters other than 'bus shelters, public clocks, and lighting equipment.

Where it is proposed to erect any of these installations it may be necessary to obtain certain consents even (in some rare cases) if they are to be placed upon the parish council's own property.

The person from whom such consents must be obtained are the owner and occupier in the case of private property (including public paths across it and places obstructing access to it),[19] and certain public authorities in the case of highways (other than public paths) and land abutting onto them.[20] The private owners and occupiers have an absolute right to withhold their consent; the public authorities, however, must not do so unreasonably but may impose reasonable conditions including a condition requiring removal in due course.[21]

[17] L.G.A. 1933 s. 251 as amended by Criminal Justice Act 1967 Schedule 3.
[17A] ibid. s. 92 (3).
[18] See page 276.　　　　　　[19] P.C.A. 1957 s. 5(1)(a) and (b).
[20] For details see the table in P.C.A. 1957 s. 5(1)(c).
[21] P.C.A. 1957 s. 5(2).

Disputes on reasonableness are to be settled by an arbitrator who is appointed in default of agreement by the Minister of Transport and Civil Aviation unless the Minister is himself a party to the dispute when the arbitrator is appointed by the President of the Institution of Civil Engineers.[22]

F. RACIAL DISCRIMINATION

It is illegal for any local or other public authority[23] to refuse or neglect to afford access to any person to any place of public resort on grounds of colour, race, or ethnic or national origin.[24] A place of public resort is any place whether a building or not to which the public is invited or entitled to come[25] and the offence consists in failing or refusing to give access to all comers upon the same terms.

G. NOTE ON DEFINITIONS

Interpretation Act

All the Local Government Acts must be construed in the light of the definitions contained in the Interpretation Act, 1889, unless the contrary appears. Amongst these the following are the commonest:—

Month means calendar month.

Person includes any body of persons corporate or unincorporate.

Writing includes any mode of representing or reproducing words in a visible form.[26]

In addition, unless the context otherwise requires, the words other than 'parish' defined in section 100 of the Local Government Act, 1888, are used in the same sense in the Act of 1894[27] which contains further definitions;[28] the 'vocabulary' thus created is used but not used consistently in the acts of 1929, 1933 and 1948: the Act of 1933 in particular contains a very large number of definitions[29] for its own peculiar purposes.

---

[22] P.C.A. 1957 s. 5(3).   [23] Race Relations Act, 1965 s. 1(2)(d).
[24] ibid. s. 1(1) and 1(3).   [25] Glynn v. Symmonds 1952 2 All. E.R. 47.
[26] Interpretation Act, 1889.   [27] L.G.A. 1894 s. 75(2).
[28] L.G.A. 1894 s. 75(2).   [29] L.G.A. 1933 s. 305.

Sundays and Holidays

Where the day or last day required or permitted for doing anything under the Local Government Act, 1933, falls on a Sunday, Christmas Day, Good Friday, Bank Holiday, or day of public mourning or thanksgiving, the day concerned is deemed to be the first day after, which is not one of those days.[30]

References to Population

The population of a parish is deemed to be the population according to the last published official census save where otherwise expressly provided,[31] but in the Local Government Act, 1933, and later acts, the census population of a local government area is that found in the Registrar General's Report, provided that it is not a provisional report.[32]

H. PLANNING PERMISSION

Generally speaking planning permission is needed for 'development', that is to say building, engineering and similar operations, material changes in the use of land or buildings and the display of advertisements; alterations not affecting the appearance of a building, and the use of land or buildings for agriculture or forestry are not 'development' and in addition some kinds of 'development' may be undertaken without planning permission:[33] These include the erection and maintenance of gates, fences and other means of enclosure not exceeding 4 feet in height beside a road or 7 feet elsewhere,[34] small ancillary buildings and equipment on land owned or maintained for the purposes of the parish council's functions, lampposts, shelters and seats, drinking fountains, refuse bins and baskets, and 'bus queue barriers.[35]

I. THE TIME ELEMENT

Waiting periods or periods of notice play an important part in all official procedures. The following is a list of most of those affecting parish councils.

[30] L.G.A. 1933 s. 295. [31] L.G.A. 1933 s. 296(1).
[32] L.G.A. 1933 s. 296(2). [33] S.I. 1950/728. [34] Ibid. Class II.
[35] Ibid. Class XIII

Subject	Period or dates	Notice given by and to
Audit		
Extraordinary	3 days	Minister to Parish Council
Ordinary	14 clear days	Parish Council to Public
Deposit of Accounts	7 ,, ,,	,, ,, ,, ,,
Completion of Audit	Within 7 days after audit	,, ,, ,, ,,
Payment against consequence of surcharge	14 days	—
Appeal against disallowance	6 weeks	—
Boundaries		
Public Inquiry	10 days	County Councils to Public
Proposal in Order not considered at Public Inquiry	21 days	,, ,, ,, ,,
Appeal to Minister against Order	6 weeks	—
Byelaws		
Application to Secretary of State	1 month	Parish Council to Public
Churchyards		
Closure Order	1 month 10 days	Minister to Public Minister to the Parochial Church Council
Removal of Tombstones	3 months	Parish Council to Public
Application for faculty to remove monuments	1 month	—
Commons		
Registration	1st Jan. 1967 to 31st Dec. 1969	—-

Subject	Period or dates	Notice is given by and to
Elections		
Timetable	21 weekdays	Returning Officer to Public
Claims for expenses	14 days from election day	—
Payment of expenses	Within 21 days from election day	—
Licensing		
Applications for new licences, removals and transfers	21 days	Applicant to Parish Council
Manoeuvres		
Application for Order	2 months	Minister for the Army to Parish Council
Loans		
Return of Provision for Repayment	1 month	Minister to Parish Council
Meetings		
Parish Council	3 clear days	Clerk or Convener to Public
Agenda	,, ,, ,,	Clerk or Conveners to members of Parish Council
Parish Meeting— Ordinary	7 days	Conveners to Public
Resolutions to establish, dissolve Parish Council to group and adopt adoptive power	14 days	,, ,, ,,
Statutory Resolution	28 days	Conveners to Public
Persistent Absence from Meetings	6 months	

Subject	*Period or Dates*	*Notice given by and to*
Term of Office		
Chairman and Vice-Chairman	One Annual Meeting to the next	—
Parish Councillors	The period of office of the R.D. Councillor (usually three years)	--

J. NEW TOWNS

The site of a new town is designated by the Minister[36] who makes an order after consulting any local authorities including parish councils[37] who appear to him to be concerned. Notice of intention to make the order must be published in local newspapers and served on county and district councils involved, and may be served on the parish councils. A public inquiry must be held into objections validly made within the time limit specified in the order, and when the order has eventually been made, notice must again be given to those bodies who received the original notice and to the objectors to give them an opportunity to challenge the legality (as opposed to the expediency) of the order in the courts. This challenge must be made within six weeks of the second notice.

Where land or rights over land are needed for the purposes of the new town and new town corporation, the highway authority and the Minister of Transport respectively can acquire them compulsorily, subject, however, to special parliamentary procedure if owned by a parish council, or voluntarily. Once acquired in this way the purposes for which the land was previously used can be overridden: public[38] and private[39] rights of way can be extinguished; subject to planning permission being obtained, burial grounds can be cleared and used for other purposes,[40] and commons, open spaces and fuel and field garden allotments can be put to other uses.[41]

As the boundaries of a designated area are usually settled without regard to the boundaries of the local parishes some

---

[36] New Towns Act, 1965, s. 1(1). [37] ibid. s. 54.
[38] ibid. s. 23. [39] ibid. s. 19. [40] ibid. s. 20. [41] ibid. s. 21.

adaptation of the parish organisation becomes desirable very early in the development. At Harlow and Bracknell joint committees of the parish councils were set up for the area; these committees wielded most of the effective power of their constituent parish councils and a growing number of the rural district councils' powers was delegated to them as time went on. This made the transition to urban status an easy process.

20

Legal and Similar Business and Inquiries

A. GENERAL CONSIDERATIONS

Insurance

Litigation is expensive and the potential cost to the rate-payers has been increased by the introduction of the Legal Aid Scheme; for in cases where a parish council is forced into contested proceedings by a legally-aided opponent it will generally be compelled to bear its own costs even if it succeeds. For this reason all parish councils which own any substantial property or which operate extensive services should insure and be certain that their insurance policy will cover them against the cost of any legal proceedings which may arise from the risks insured.

Preparing Cases

The importance of making an early start with the preparation of a case and the collection of evidence cannot be overstressed. This is equally essential in legal proceedings and in administrative inquiries. Witnesses' memories grow dim over long periods, and a good case hurriedly prepared may be lost because those who have to conduct it have not had time in which either to collect sufficient evidence or to reflect upon it; and where professional assistance is not or cannot be procured such reflection is doubly necessary.

B. LEGAL PROCEEDINGS

General Rules

If a parish council thinks that it is expedient for the promotion or protection of the interests of the inhabitants it may

199

prosecute or defend legal proceedings.[1, 2, 3] There is also a special right to take proceedings to protect an ownerless common.[3] In addition and independently of these statutory rights, it may as a local authority and trustee for the ratepayers have recourse to the ordinary rights which trustees have to defend their own position as such and the rights of the beneficiaries, and this enables it to take or defend proceedings with the object of defending its constitution, property, or rights.[4]

Representation

A parish council may, by resolution, authorise any member or officer (but no one else[5]) to conduct proceedings on its behalf in a *Court of Summary Jurisdiction* or to appear in such proceedings even though he is not a solicitor.[6] The authority must be given before proceedings are commenced.[7] A *County Court* has power to allow a corporation to appear before it otherwise than by solicitor or by solicitor and counsel.[8] Otherwise the rule that a corporation must appear by counsel in legal proceedings applies to parish councils.

Briefs and Retainers

If a solicitor is retained for legal proceedings the retainer should be under seal.[9]

A barrister may accept a brief from a clerk of a local authority who is not a solicitor.[10]

A parish council may in all proper cases take and pay for professional legal advice. This right is a necessary incident to its functions as a public authority, as well as a logical consequence of its power to take legal proceedings.

---

[1] L.G.A. 1933 s. 276.

[2] For a special limitation in the case of allotments see A.A. 1922 s. 16 and page 196.

[3] Commons Registration Act, 1965 s. 9 and see page 226.

[4] Per Jessel M.R. in A.G. v. Mayor of Brecon (1878) 10 Ch.D. 204 at pages 214–219.

[5] Kyle v. Barbor (1888) 58 L.T. 229.   [6] L.G.A. 1933 s. 277.

[7] Bowyer Philpott and Payne Ltd v. Mather (1919) 1 K.B. 419.

[8] Kinnell & Co. v. Harding Wace & Co. (1918) 1 K.B. 405.

[9] Arnold v. Poole Corporation (1842) 2 Dowl. (NS) 574.

[10] Annual Statement of the General Council of the Bar, 1927, page 8

Evidence of Constitution

It is not necessary to prove the name, area and constitution of a parish council in legal proceedings, but this rule does not deprive a party in the proceedings of any right of objection which he would have had if it did not exist.[11]

Evidence of Byelaws

Byelaws are proved by the production of a printed copy endorsed with a certificate signed by the clerk that the parish council made the byelaws, that the copy is a true copy, that it was confirmed on a specified date and that it came into operation on a specified date.[12]

Welsh

Any person so desiring may speak Welsh in legal proceedings in Wales or Monmouthshire, but in courts other than magistrates courts it may be necessary to give prior notice.[12A]

C. PROCEEDINGS IN PARLIAMENT

Private Bills

A parish council cannot promote a private bill in Parliament[13] but may, like other local authorities, oppose any private bill which threatens its existence as a corporation or would prejudicially affect its rights, powers, privileges or property[14] or the interests of the ratepayers.[15] No local authority may promote a bill to alter an area of local government before 22nd July, 1973.[16]

Opposition in committee to private bills is normally conducted through parliamentary agents and is a somewhat expensive procedure.[17] A parish council will seldom wish to conduct such opposition alone, but may nevertheless assist other or wealthier authorities by offering a member of the parish council to be called as a local witness on behalf of that other authority. Nevertheless parish councils may sometimes wish to

[11] L.G.A. 1933 s. 278.　　　　　　　[12] L.G.A. 1933 s. 252.
[12A] Welsh Language Act, 1967.　　　[13] L.G.A. 1933 s. 253.
[14] L.G.A. 1933 s. 258 and R. v. Mayor of Brecon (1878) L.R. 10 Ch. D. 153.
[15] R. v. White (1884) 16 Q.B.D. 358.　　[16] L.G.A. 1958 s. 35.
[17] In 1960 the House of Lords, despite opposition from the promoters, heard a petition by the Brookthorpe-with-Waddon parish council against a British Transport Commission Bill under which it was proposed to take land in the parish not the property of the council. The council's case was conducted by its clerk.

petition against bills, in which case it is important to have regard to the time-table which is normally followed:—

Time-table

A petition for a bill with a copy of the bill annexed is deposited by the promoters at the House of Commons or the House of Lords on or before 27th November in each year and advertised, and copies of the bill become available for sale, both in London and in the district to which it relates, on 4th December. A petition against a bill must be made to the House of Commons on or before 30th January and to the House of Lords on or before 6th February. If the bill passes its first House a petition may be made to the second House.

Procedure

Petitions on private bills are heard by a committee of each House and the proceedings resemble those of a court.

Where a parish council cannot afford the expense of a petition it should request a Member of Parliament or a Peer to oppose the bill on second reading or at the report or third reading stage. The second reading takes place before the committee stage, the report and third reading afterwards.

Special Parliamentary Procedure

Certain orders, especially orders for the compulsory purchase of land belonging to local authorities (including parish councils) are required to be laid before Parliament and to undergo special parliamentary procedure. As in private bill procedure the time-table is very important. The following is a summary

The body promoting the order must first of all comply with all the requirements of the enabling Act concerning the publication and service of notices, the consideration of objections and the holding of inquiries. If that act contains no such requirements, the rules in the First Schedule of the Statutory Order (Special Procedure) Act, 1945, must be followed. The responsible Minister (that is the Minister who would be able to confirm the order if it were not subject to special parliamentary procedure) then gives at least three days' notice in the *London Gazette* of his intention to lay the order before Parliament and thereafter lays it before both Houses with a certificate setting out the requirements and that they have been complied with Without this certificate the order cannot be confirmed.

An objector then has twenty-one days within which to petition Parliament against the order. There are two sorts of petitions: a *petition for amendment* which must specify the amendments desired, and a *petition of general objection* which prays for the rejection of the whole order. These two types of petitions must be submitted in different documents. At the expiry of this first period of twenty-one days, the order and any petitions against it are considered by the chairman who must report on them to the Houses and especially whether the petitions disclose substantial grounds of objection and are fit to be received. There follows a second period of 21 days called the resolution period; if during this period a house resolves to annul the order, it becomes void—but can be resubmitted. If no such resolution is passed then petitions against it may be referred to a Joint Committee of the two Houses. Petitions of general objection must be specifically referred; petitions for amendment certified by the chairmen are referred automatically. If no petitions are referred the order comes into force at the end of the resolution period or any later date mentioned in it.

After a third period of three weeks for counter petitions against any petitions for amendment, the Joint Committee holds a hearing similar to the proceedings on a private bill.[18]

Parliamentary Commissioner (Ombudsman)

Complaints to the Ombudsman against maladministration must be made by an individual through a member of the House of Commons. They cannot be made by local authorities.

D. PROCEEDINGS RELATING TO RATES

A parish council which is a ratepayer has the same rights as any other ratepayer to resist the payment of or dispute the extent of its liability to rates. There are four different types of proceedings in which different issues may be raised.

Firstly a *proposal* in writing may be made to the valuation officer to alter the assessment of a property or to delete it from the valuation list, and if after negotiation it is rejected or objected to, an appeal may be made to the Local Valuation Court and from there to the Lands Tribunal. Alternatively the dispute may be referred to arbitration under the Arbitration Act, or the Lands Tribunal may be appointed arbitrator;

[18] See generally Statutory Orders (Special Procedure Acts) 1945 and 1965.

reference to arbitration must be in writing. Secondly an *appeal* may be made against a *rate* to the next practicable Quarter Sessions. Thirdly *a distress warrant may be resisted* before the Court of Summary Jurisdiction. Lastly a person aggrieved by a distress (as opposed to a warrant) may *appeal* to Quarter Sessions against the *distress*.

General Rule

Nothing may be raised in an appeal to Quarter Sessions against a rate which might have been raised in a proposal, but an objection which can be used in an appeal against a rate can be urged on an appeal against a distress.

Until a proposal is decided the amount payable cannot exceed the amount paid in the previous rating period. The grounds of such an appeal are therefore restricted to such matters as the purpose or legality of the rate and the area in which it is to be levied.

Notice

A parish council or chairman of a parish meeting is entitled to fourteen clear days' notice from any appellant to Quarter Sessions against a rate.

E. PUBLIC LOCAL INQUIRIES

A local inquiry may be held on behalf of any government 'department' (including any Board or Commissioners) authorised 'to determine any difference, to make or confirm any order, to frame any scheme or to give any consent, confirmation, sanction or approval to any matter or otherwise to act' under the Local Government Act, 1933, or where the Secretary of State or the Minister is authorised to hold an inquiry under any enactment relating to the functions of a local authority.[19]

Such inquiries are usually held by an inspector appointed by the department concerned. He may administer oaths, and may summon in writing any witness to attend and bring relevant documents, but if a witness must travel more than ten miles from his home, his travelling expenses must be paid or tendered. Documents of title cannot be required unless they relate to the title of a local authority.

[19] L.G.A. 1933 s. 290.

Costs

The department may order any local authority or party to pay the department's costs (including five guineas a day for the inspector) and these costs when certified are recoverable as a debt to the Crown or summarily as a civil debt. It may also make orders as to the costs of the parties and any party can make such an order a rule of court.[19]

These procedural provisions have been applied in whole or in part in a very large number of cases where local authorities and ministries have powers of inquiry under other legislation. Amongst the most important of these are Town and Country Planning, Coast Protection and Trunk Roads. A parish council may appear and be represented at such an inquiry and may pay the expenses (including the expense of witnesses) of such representation; if the inquiry concerns the parish council as an authority or as an owner of property it may pay the expenses from its ordinary funds; where it appears solely to represent the views of the inhabitants it seems that the costs would have to be paid from the free fifth.

Where a county council holds an inquiry under the Local Government Act, 1933, on application from the council of a county district or parish or from such electors of a district or parish as are entitled to make the application, the expenses incurred by the county council are paid by the district or parish council or parish meeting concerned, unless the county council otherwise determines. Where the inquiry is held otherwise than on such application the county council pays.[20]

F. SUMMARY JURISDICTION

Compensation for Damage ('Damages')

Damages up to £20 may be recovered summarily in a magistrates' court for damage caused by negligence to any lamp, lamppost, notice board, fence, rail, post, shelter or other equipment provided by a parish council in a street or public place.[21] Where property is damaged maliciously the magistrates have a similar power to award compensation up to £100 upon conviction.[22]

[20] L.G.A. 1933 s. 291.   [21] P.H.A. 1961 s. 81.
[22] Criminal Justice Administration Act, 1914 s. 14.

Where damages or compensation required exceed these amounts these convenient remedies are not available, and the parish council must proceed in the County or High Court.

Limitation of Time

Except as otherwise provided by a particular act a Court of Summary Jurisdiction cannot deal with a criminal or civil case unless the information or complaint has been laid or made within six months of the date of the offence or matter of complaint.[23] Unless the right to prosecute is limited by statute[24] any person may lay an information where the offence is not a matter merely of private grievance.[25]

Costs—Criminal

On the summary trial of an information the accused may, on conviction, be ordered to pay a part or the whole of the prosecutor's costs, but if he is under seventeen the costs payable by him must not exceed the amount of the fine imposed, and in any case if the fine is under 5s. 0d. (25p) costs are only to be awarded in special circumstances. If the information is dismissed the prosecutor may be ordered to pay the costs of the accused.[26]

Costs—Civil

Subject to the provisions of any particular act enabling a magistrate's court to order a successful party to pay the other party's costs, a magistrate's court has on the hearing of a complaint a discretion to order the unsuccessful party to pay some or all of the successful party's costs.[27] The amount may include witness expenses as well as solicitor's fees.

Both in civil and in criminal cases the amount of the costs is incorporated in the order of the court; a party who wishes his costs to be paid by the other side, should ask the court to incorporate the necessary clause in the order.

[23] Magistrates Courts Act, 1952 s. 104.   [24] e.g. P.H.A. 1936 s. 298.
[25] R. v. Hicks (1855) 19 J.P. 515.
[26] See Costs in Criminal Cases Act, 1952 s. 6.
[27] Magistrates Courts Act, 1952 s. 55.

21

Parish Councils and Village Life

T he usefulness of a parish council may be considered in terms of voluntary activities and legal powers. The voluntary activities arise from the versatility of village life. The membership of the parish and parochial church councils is sometimes interchangeable, and the members of the parish council may unite in their persons the majority of the leading positions in all the parish clubs and societies. A parish council so constituted is locally influential even if it seldom exercises its legal powers, and it is in a position to focus the effort and opinion of those by whom it is elected. At times of celebration, agitation or crisis a strong and representative parish council can be a powerful factor in the stability of the community of neighbours.

A. SPECIFIC POWERS CLASSIFIED

The powers of a parish council can be classified in a number of ways, none of which are wholly satisfactory, but such classifications have their value as an aid to an understanding of the system, and the following is a brief account of them.

Origin

The legal powers of parish councils and other parish authorities are commonly classified according to their origin into powers inherited from the vestry,[1] powers inherited from the churchwardens,[2] from the churchwardens and overseers, or overseers alone,[3] 'additional' powers conferred in 1894,[4] and miscellaneous powers conferred in and since 1894.

---

[1] L.G.A. 1894 s. 6(1)(a).   [2] L.G.A. 1894 s. 6(1)(b).
[3] L.G.A. 1894 s. 6(1)(c).   [4] L.G.A. 1894 s. 8(1).

Juridical Nature

From many points of view a classification by juridical nature is sometimes more convenient, namely into powers of provision and service, powers of supervision, consultation and complaint, powers of appointment and powers of bye-legislation.

Financial Order

Thirdly the legal powers may be considered from the point of view of the financial resources behind them and the limitations placed by law upon those resources. There are general powers whose expense is governed by the rate limits; adoptive powers which can only be exercised after a special procedure of adoption has been carried out but whose expense is not governed by the rate limits; wider powers restrained neither by the rate limits nor by adoptive procedure; delegated powers whose expense is borne wholly or partly by another authority; powers whose expense is borne by some fund other than the rates; and powers involving no expenditure.

Degree of Independence

Fourthly powers may be considered from the standpoint of the formalities which are needed before they can be exercised. Some can be exercised without any,[5] others require the previous intervention of one,[6] two[7] and sometimes even three other bodies.

Ancillary Powers

In addition to the functions which may be conferred expressly by statute, local authorities have supplementary or so called ancillary powers which are necessary for the exercise of the principal functions or which may logically be deduced from them; for instance, power to maintain a building is inherent in power to provide it and includes authority to insure it against destruction; the obligation to keep proper records, minutes and accounts and to issue notices implies power to make adequate office arrangements, and to purchase stationery; the conduct of public affairs involves an obligation to be businesslike and therefore to obtain proper advice when necessary, to employ fir

---

[5] e.g. the purchase of land.
[6] e.g. to go beyond the 4*d.* rate limit (parish meeting).
[7] e.g. to sell land (the parish meeting and the Minister).

persons and to give employees reasonable means of ascertaining the nature of their functions and of improving their skill.

Common Law Powers

Parish councils are in the peculiar position of having had some common law powers conferred upon them by statute. Cases of the kind are probably not very important but insofar as they occur, they occur because the powers, duties and liabilities of the vestry (including the inhabitants whether assembled in vestry or not and any select vestry by statute or common law[8]) were conferred upon parish councils in 1894[9] except insofar as they relate to the affairs of the church or to ecclesiastical charities or have been transferred from the vestry to some other authority. Where, therefore, it can be shown that a vestry exercised a power by a custom enforceable at common law, that power will have descended in the absence of legislative interference to the parish council, and it is, for instance, by virtue of common law that some parish councils are entitled to meet in the vestry or even in the church; and there are probably a number of parish councils which have exceptional powers by local custom.

Local Acts

Parish councils sometimes exercise functions which have been conferred upon them by local acts.[10] Parish councils should make inquiries with county councils concerning such local acts which nowadays are mostly promoted in Parliament by the latter. Counties where local acts confer special powers on parish councils or parish meetings include Berkshire, Cheshire, Cumberland, Derbyshire, Devon, Durham, Glamorgan, Essex, Gloucester, Hertford, Kent, Lancashire, Monmouth, Nottingham, Somerset, Surrey and the West Riding of Yorkshire.

B. *ULTRA VIRES*

Parish councils are statutory corporations and 'have therefore only such powers as are conferred upon them by statute and will be restrained by the courts if they act *ultra vires*';[11] after due

---

[8] L.G.A. 1894 s. 75(2).   [9] L.G.A. 1894 s. 6.
[10] L.G.A. 1894 s. 52(5).
[11] Halsbury's *Laws of England* 3rd (Simonds) Edition Vol. 24 p. 602. Article by C. E. Scholefield on Local Government (1958).

H

allowance is made for ancillary powers[12] this means in theory that a parish council (or any other local authority) can do nothing whatever without express statutory permission. The inconveniences, not to say absurdities, inherent in this rule if pushed to its logical conclusion have led to a number of limitations in its application, and to some exceptions now recognised by statute.

Expenditure

The commonest method by which the rule is enforced is through the medium of district audit; for where a local authority acts *ultra vires* (beyond its powers) any resulting expenditure must be disallowed by the auditor and surcharged upon those responsible.[13] This deals with most of the cases which matter because illegal expenditure is the main subject in which ratepayers are likely to be interested.

There are, however, three important enactments which prevent excessive rigour in applying the auditor's powers. First the parish council may spend up to one-fifth of a penny rate in any one year, (the 'Free Fifth') for the benefit of the inhabitants or the parish.[14]

Secondly it is possible to apply to the Minister for a special sanction for extra-statutory expenditure;[15] the effect of such a sanction is that the auditor has no power to disallow the expenditure. The need for such sanctions has considerably decreased since the enactment of the 'Free Fifth' in 1963, but where applications still have to be made they should, and in practice will, be refused if the effect of the sanction requested is to enable a local authority to make recurrent payments, for to give a sanction of this kind would amount indirectly to conferring a new power not contemplated by Parliament.

Thirdly where expenditure has been disallowed those concerned may apply to be exonerated from the resulting surcharge.[16]

Misuse of Property

It will be observed that the foregoing exceptions o the rule of *ultra vires* relate only to unauthorised expenditure and

---

[12] See page 208.
[13] See page 183.
[14] For details see below, pages 213–217.
[15] LGA 1933 s 228 (1) proviso
[16] See page 185.

cannot legalise something which would be illegal on other grounds. Expenditure which led to the commission of a crime or (more probably) a trespass or a breach of trust might still lead to proceedings in the courts based upon the nature of the acts complained of.

In practice the general public has an interest in public property being used for the purposes for which it was acquired and therefore proceedings are sometimes taken in the courts to restrain local authorities from putting property acquired for one purpose to a different use.[17] These vexations can now be avoided in most instances by reappropriation.[18]

Total Absence of Powers

Action can be taken to restrain a local authority by injunction from doing something for which it has no statutory authority even though it involves or has so far involved no expenditure. In practice such actions are very rare and brought only by plaintiffs whose property or commercial interests are seriously and adversely affected. It would be unusual for a parish council to put itself into such a position.

Contracts

An important effect of the rule of *ultra vires* is that a contract made by a local authority for a purpose not authorised by statute is void and consequently the parish council cannot be sued upon it;[19] it also seems that the parish council cannot attempt to enforce such a contract.[20]

C. CONTROLS IN GENERAL

As if the doctrine of *ultra vires* were not enough, English local government is riddled with controls. Many of these (such as the need to obtain agreement for a loan, a sale of land, the creation of a museum, the imposition of a byelaw or the formulation of a table of burial fees) are exercised by a department of the central government. Others (of which planning is the most important) are administered by other local authorities. The

[17] See A.G. v. Westminster City Council (1924) 2 Ch. 416 C.A.
[18] See pages 116–117.
[19] See Ashbury Railway Carriage Co. v. Riche (1875) L.R. 71 HL 653.
[20] See the opinion of Cheshire & Fifoot in *Law of Contract* 6th Ed. page 366 with which the author respectfully agrees.

details appear elsewhere: here it may be worth noticing certain general characteristics which they exhibit as a class.

For practical reasons, the more distant the controlling authority the more it has to depend upon local secondary sources for information. An application to the Ministry of Transport for a speed limit will invariably result in the Ministry consulting the Chief Constable; an application to sell land brings in the district valuer and possibly the land commissioner as well; negotiations for a loan may involve specialist bodies such as the Regional Council for Sport, depending on the purpose of the loan. Even where planning powers are not delegated, a planning application may lead to inquiries through the district council. It follows that a friendly acquaintanceship with the other authorities and the local representatives of central departments is a part of sound administration; as government becomes more centralised its importance is increasing.

Controls are not necessarily negative: in addition to the fairly numerous cases where something cannot legally be done without somebody else's consent there are the more subtle forms of control exercised through the manipulation of funds: it may, for instance, sometimes be difficult without great determination to carry out some operation (such as laying out a playing field) with local resources alone. A grant from another body may be a great relief to the ratepayers: the body that offers grants may impose conditions which if habitually enforced may amount to a policy. If the proportion of the grant to proposed expenditure is high the conditions may not seem very onerous in comparison with the advantages achieved, and so the money is difficult to refuse. Thus grant administering bodies (not all of which are statutory) can and do exercise a strong influence in parish administration; in theory their ideas can be rejected: in fact acceptance of them can be a good deal less than voluntary. The control, theoretically partial, is effective. Again the funds are administered by central and by local bodies: amongst them are the Department of Education, the Village Halls Loan Fund of the National Council of Social Service and the Carnegie Trust, and these have to rely for guidance upon local organisations whom they trust. As a result, Rural Community Councils and Councils of Social Service usually act as a channel for negotiations with the appropriate central body.

One of the ways in which the exercise of these various forms of control can be rationalised is through the proper use of Parish Councils' Associations, whose local function (amongst others) is to obtain general principles to guide their administration. It is consequently no accident that parish councils' organisations are often closely associated with rural community councils and in some cases have played a leading part in forming them.

D. THE FREE FIFTH

Subject to certain formalities a parish council may spend up to one-fifth ($\cdot 1p$) of a penny rate for any purpose which in the parish council's opinion is in the interests of the area or its inhabitants.

Parish meetings do not have this power.

Practical Effects

In terms of money the enactment has the following effects: (Column A is the annual amount which may be spent. Column B the number of parish councils which may spend it). The figures relate to 6,976 parish councils in 1964.

A Amount £	B Number of Councils	A Amount £	B Number of Councils
2–10	3,025	60–80	256
10–20	1,547	80–100	168
20–30	660	100–120	102
30–40	417	120–140	69
40–50	337	140–200	102
50–60	185	Over 200	130

In the 'over £200 class' there were some very high figures.

The effects on existing law must be considered in the light of these financial facts. Some things have now become lawful but are still not always possible to some parish councils.

Accounts and Resolutions

A separate account of expenditure must be kept and be open to public inspection and (which is a corollary) expenditure under the section must be *specifically authorised by resolution*. It is not enough to plead at audit that if an item is unauthorised by a statute the section will cover it. The following form of resolution may be regarded as suitable:

'*Resolved that the Council in accordance with its powers under section* 6 *of the Local Government (Financial Provisions) Act,* 1963, *should incur the following expenditure which, in the opinion of the Council is in the interests of the area or its inhabitants:*

(here set it out)

Calculation of Amount

The fifth of a penny rate is calculated not in the manner used for calculating the 4*d*. (1·7*p*) and 8*d*. (3·3*p*) rate limits but in that used by the rural district council for raising its own rate. This produces a slightly smaller sum. The rural district council should be asked to supply the correct figure.

Nature of the Power

The parish council, not the auditor, is the judge of what is or is not in the interests of the parish or inhabitants provided that there is some ground (however slight) on which such a judgment can be properly based. Extravagance apart, the expenditure could only be challenged if there were no ground at all. Difficult borderline cases will doubtless occur but mostly this distinction will be obvious enough.

Though the section may not be used if there is already a power conferred upon the parish council by some other enactment, it should be observed that this does not prevent it being used to effect something which another type of authority has power to do. A parish council can spend its free fifth on a public lavatory though the rural district council is the public health authority.

Moreover, the powers of an existing statute must be used if there are any. The principle of this is simple enough, but the exact application may sometimes be complicated by the last words of sub-section (1) of the section.

There is a prohibition against 'Expenditure for a purpose for which they are either unconditionally or subject to a *limitation* or to the *satisfaction of any condition* authorised or required by or by virtue of any enactment other than this section to make any payment.'

A limitation appears to mean a statutory clog on the exercise of a power within a place where it can otherwise be exercised without the limitation. The most obvious examples are the limit of one and one-third (·6*p*) of a penny rate on expenditure on war memorials and the limit of a 2*d*. (1*p*) rate on the deficit on the Allotments Account. It does not seem to refer to a geographical limitation: thus a parish council can under the War Memorials Acts only maintain, repair and protect a war memorial in the parish; therefore it can spend money under the section for a memorial outside; nor does it seem to apply to the definition of a power itself; a parish council could use the section to pay for doing something to a war memorial which was not maintenance, repair or protection, e.g. it could resite it. An omission is not a limitation.

The satisfaction of any condition refers to something which is required to be done by a parish council before it can exercise a power which it already has. For example, under Section 5 of the Parish Councils Act, 1957, it is required to obtain certain consents before exercising its powers to place seats and shelters in particular positions. The section cannot be used to evade such conditions but, on the other hand, it could be used to pay for seats, or shelters in situations (such as private property) which were not authorised by the Act of 1957 at all.

Actual Uses

The following are examples of actual uses to which the power is known to have been put by parish councils:

Class 1. *Small Public Properties*

Seat outside the parish
Car park
Film projector
Kerbing, resurfacing road
    or market
Public telephone
Culvert
Public lavatory
Village surgery

Memorial plaques
Repair of a Bier-house
Set of parish china
Invalid wheel chair
Mobile W.C. for Harvest
    Festival
Doctor's car radio
Bus turning bay
Duckhouse for village pond

Class 2. *Preservation or Restoration of Old Objects or Buildings*

Churches and chapels
Windmill
Market and village cross
Pounds
Jubilee Arch

Stocks, firehooks, pinfolds
Biers
Contribution to Local
    Preservation Society

Class 3.   *Improvement of Appearance of Villages*

Civic Trust type 'face lift' scheme
Planning competition
Garden competition prizes
Best-kept village competition
Village sweeper
Junk disposal
Tidying land of unknown ownership
Removal of slaughter house
Landscaping
Local garden centre
Litter competitions
Enterprise 'Neptune'
Beach cleansing
Clearance of commons
Planting trees, shrubs and flowers

Class 4.   *Influence*

Public inquiries
Propaganda for Civic Centre project
Support of organisations such as River Thames
Society, Railway Protection Association
Contribution to Anti-Third London Airport Campaign

Class 5.   *Ceremonial and Entertainment*

Christmas trees
Sports prizes
Civic entertainments and services
Flags
Chains or badges of office
Beating bounds
Chairman's allowance
Flower shows, festivals, and fairs
Exhibitions
Local Eisteddfods, concerts, dances and Gymkhanas
Fireworks Displays

Class 6.   *Safety*

Fencing dangerous places
Road warden
Old People's Distress Cards and Lights
Lectures on artificial respiration
Ambulance competition entries
Life-belts and lifeguards
First-aid post
Inshore rescue service
Safety competitions
Road markings
Safety posts and bollards
Accident committees
Flood prevention

Class 7.   *Public Information*

Signs (bus stop, footpath, or village)
Public maps
Parish handbooks, guides and histories
Hotel list
Chairman's annual report
Tourist leaflets
Letters of welcome to newcomers

Parish fixture lists and bulletins

Information bureau
Local Publicity Association

Class 8. *Contributions to Voluntary Bodies without Premises*

Play groups and youth clubs

Theatre and music groups, bands

Class 9. *Social Welfare*

Flood relief
New ambulance
Citizens' Advice Bureau
Meals on wheels
Marriage guidance and family planning
Village librarian
Day nursery
Mobile Physiotherapy unit

Assistance for schemes or organisations concerned with the handicapped
Welfare organisations
Sickness fund
Contribution to Almshouses
Collection of medicines from distant dispensaries
Samaritans and 'Task Force'

Class 10. *Recognition of Public Service*

Testimonials on retirement

Gratuity to youths making historical discoveries

Class 11. *Miscellaneous*

Essay competitions
Co-operative Christmas crib
Flower and vegetable show
Purchase of South-East Study

Restocking of river with trout
Repair of sheepwash
Repair of slipway
Village handyman

Class 12. *Communications*

Local bus
Repair of ford
'No parking' signs

Temporary roads, private streets
Traffic survey

Class 13. *Educational*

History and Local Government Lectures
Compilation of village history

Further Education Grant
Duke of Edinburgh's scheme

E. VOLUNTARY ACTIVITIES

In most parishes (leaving aside the very large and the very small) there is a meeting point between the statutory or

H*

official organisation of the state and the voluntary bodies. With increasing frequency this meeting point is the parish council itself for, as already observed, its membership often includes the most influential personalities in those voluntary bodies. The most effective parish administration is one in which there is a marriage of minds between the statutory and the voluntary sides of rural organisation. The older settled form of village life is giving way to something more mobile and already those who live in the parish of their birth are in a minority. A village has to maintain its social life by a more self-conscious effort than was formerly needed, and this has led (since World War II) to the widespread rise of village societies of all kinds and often to the creation of national organisations of such societies and of parish councils.

The table at the end of this chapter represents a conspectus of the kind of activity which nowadays leads to the formation of a voluntary organisation and will indicate the ways in which help from the official or statutory side may be needed: broadly these consist in preliminary encouragement, trusteeship or the provision of premises (especially for meetings) or land, or a judicious combination of all these.

Most of the activities in the table will breed separate committees which need to meet somewhere in addition to the gatherings which the activities themselves involve.

Weaknesses of Voluntary Bodies

In any fair-sized village it will be found that a high proportion of the activities mentioned are either in progress or desired; some of them must in their nature be confined to daylight hours and are therefore restricted to the young, the unemployed or to week-ends; others in practice have to be restricted to evenings. Tastes vary: it is not possible to be in more than one place at once or to have two functions in the same place at the same time; in younger families someone has to stay at home to mind the baby, and there is always the pub. Bringing all these factors into account and making allowances for cross-membership most voluntary organisations will obviously be small and poor. If a village has 1,000 inhabitants and its people indulge in only half the activities in the table, the average attendance per activity is unlikely to exceed 30, and the composition of each 30 will be changing continually.

The main weaknesses of such bodies are that they are hard to launch, liable to disintegrate, and mostly unable to provide their own premises or land. Parish councils are equipped by law to provide most of the remedies for these defects.

Encouragement at the Start

A parish council can legitimately[21] spend from the free fifth to encourage the formation or development of some potentially valuable parish organisation. Apart from this, however, parish councils can help a new body by lending equipment or premises and by helping them to publicise their objects and meetings on parish notice boards and in parish bulletins.[22] A parish council should ensure that its willingness to do these things is known.

Permanence

Most voluntary societies have funds and small bank accounts. If a society disintegrates and those entitled to operate the accounts die or leave the district or become otherwise disengaged, these balances may be wasted. This happens all too often.

A parish council, being a corporation, never dies and this fact can be used to provide the required stiffening in two ways. Where funds or other property are provided with charitable or public objects it can itself act as trustee for the benefit of the organisations interested; this often happens in the case of village halls. Its advantage is that no further appointment is necessary; the disadvantage that the funds have to be brought into account for the purposes of audit stamp duty. Alternatively the parish council can be given power to nominate the trustees instead of acting as a trustee itself; this can be done whether or not the objects of the fund are charitable or public, and no question of district audit or audit stamp duty arises.

Lands and Buildings

The legal powers of parish councils to provide or help to provide lands and buildings for voluntary activities are very comprehensive.[23] The practical problem is to provide an adequate and also economical substructure for a vigorous social life. Some villages have no meeting place: others have too many all in poor condition; lands have often been acquired

---

[21] See page 213 onward.   [22] See page 190.

[23] See Chapters 22 and 23.

haphazardly and without relation to each other or so that they are no longer adequate for their purpose, or simple or cheap to maintain; and bad siting and over-specialisation of types and poor insulation and heating leads to underuse.

The ideal is a recreational and community centre[24] comprising all the necessary lands and buildings (with a caretaker's residence) the whole being situated so that it is not difficult for anyone in the village to walk to it. Such an ideal is worth stating even if it is rarely attainable.

A glance at the table[24] will show that if the design is well thought out many different activities can be accommodated in one building, namely the village or parish hall[25] with which a pavilion can sometimes be combined. A stage or platform is equally desirable for a play, a parish meeting, a dance band, or a lecture. Changing rooms can serve both actors and cricketers. The eventual (if not immediate) ownership and use of a projector should be foreseen. There should be a separate place for smaller meetings, a kitchen and lavatories. Some halls have a room with a separate door for occasional use as a village surgery; others have an outside booth with a coin box telephone. There must be a reasonable degree of bodily comfort; audiences become restive on ill-designed chairs and soon disperse in the cold. Insulation, double windows, and storage or infra-red heating are good investments. The capital cost may at first seem high but the important factor in the long run is the cost (both on maintenance and on capital account) *per hour of actual use*. A village cannot afford a building which is not used.

Similar principles apply in satisfying other demands. Playing fields should be laid out so that they are capable of use both in winter and in summer and if land of the right sort is scarce or prohibitively expensive, facilities for games playing in enclosures (such as tennis or bowls) or in small buildings (such as fives) should be considered.

---

[24] p. 221.

[25] By a convention 'village hall' means a hall managed under a charitable trust deed usually modelled on that provided by the National Council of Social Service; 'parish hall' means a hall provided and managed by a Parish Council under its statutory powers. 'Community centre' means much the same but is in a town. It is not here used in this restricted sense.

	Sports and Games				Cultural	Welfare	Social and Official
	Vigorous		Non-vigorous				
	I(L)	II(S)	I(L)	II(S)			
In the Open Air	Football Cricket Archery	Netball Tennis	Camping	Bowls			Fêtes
In Buildings	Gymnastics Dancing	Squash Fives Rackets	Billiards Bingo	Chess, etc. Cards* Darts	Debating Societies Literary* Dramatic Musical Local History* Archaeological* Civic Societies Horticultural Exhibitions Best-kept Village	Old People Play-groups Nursery Schools Youth Clubs Welfare Cars Meals on Wheels	Church Functions Dances Occasional Celebrations Parish Council Parochial Church Council British Legion
Water	Swimming Boating Sailing			Fishing			

I(L) = Large resources needed II(S) = Smaller resources needed * = Often occur in private houses

22

Open Air and Exercise

Parish councils have substantial and variegated powers relating to open-air and other recreational facilities; they are derived from a series of general enactments passed in the course of more than a century and may also be derived from local (especially inclosure) acts. It is difficult to reconcile all these powers.

A. VILLAGE GREENS AND RECREATIONAL ALLOTMENTS

A village green is strictly speaking a piece of land (usually but not necessarily common or waste of the manor) where the inhabitants have by enforceable custom a right to indulge in lawful sports and pastimes.[1] The term is, however, often used to include a recreational allotment, which is a piece of land set aside under an Inclosure Award for the recreation of the inhabitants. Such allotments were sometimes made in substitution for old village greens and sometimes the village green was converted into a recreational allotment, whilst sometimes the old village green kept some of its older characteristics and acquired some new ones as well. From 1845 onwards recreation allotments were (save in exceptional cases) required to be made as a condition of inclosure,[2] and were awarded under general

---

[1] Fitch v. Rawling (1795) 2 Hy. Bl. 393 (games, sports and pastimes in a particular close). Hall v. Nottingham (1875) 1 Ex. D. 1 (maypole in old glebe). Warwick v. Queen's College, Oxford (1870) L.R. 10 Eq. 105 (sports on a common and unfenced green). See also the definition in Commons Registration Act, 1965, s. 22.

[2] Inclosure Act, 1845 s. 30.

legislation;[3] most of them ultimately came to be controlled or owned by the parish council or parish meeting.[4]

On such allotments the parish authority may let the herbage and must apply the rents towards maintenance and the payment of taxes, rates and tithe redemption charges. Surplus rents may be used to acquire new recreational allotments or to improve or acquire field gardens and for no other purpose;[5] it follows that where there is no lawful opportunity for expenditure the income must be accumulated.[6]

The Charity Commissioners may modify the provisions in an inclosure act which relate to recreational and other allotments on application from any parish council or parish meeting interested[7] except in Epping Forest, the New Forest and the Forest of Dean.

Registration

A parish council should register all land believed to be a village green with the county council whether it owns it or not and if it owns it or claims ownership that should be registered as well. Where there is no parish council the chairman of the parish meeting should do this, and register ownership or claims in the name of the representative body.

Where the ownership of a green is unclaimed and an investigation by a Commons Commissioner fails to reveal an owner the green will eventually vest in the parish council if there is one and in the rural district council if there is no parish council.

Some lands habitually used as village greens may turn out to be roadside wastes.[8]

B. REGULATION SCHEMES FOR COMMONS[9]

A rural district council (after three months' notice by advertisement[10]) may make a scheme for the management of

---

[3] Inclosure Act, 1845 s. 75. Commons Act, 1876 s. 27. Commons Act, 1879 s. 2. Commons Act, 1899 s. 16.

[4] For the descent of these allotments to the parish council see pages 106–8.

[5] ibid. s. 75. Commons Act, 1876 s. 27. Commons Act, 1879 s. 2. Commons Act, 1899 s. 16.

[6] See page 257.   [7] Commons Act, 1899 s. 18.

[8] See page 270.

[9] For the special situation which can arise in a New Town see page 198.

[10] Commons Act, 1899 s. 2.

any common in the district with a view to the expenditure of money on drainage, levelling, improvement and the making of byelaws,[11] and may delegate any power of management under the scheme to a parish council,[12] which may contribute to the expense of preparing and executing the scheme (including any compensation to be paid).[13]

Schemes of this sort are only intended to simplify the bringing into use of commons for purposes of recreation, and as they may interfere with the agricultural uses they require the approval of the Minister of Agriculture, and may be vetoed by either the Lord of the Manor or one-third (by value) of the commoners. The Minister of Agriculture may hold a local inquiry before approving a scheme.[14]

Byelaws made under a regulation scheme require the confirmation of the Home Secretary.[15]

Regulation schemes cannot be made for a metropolitan common, or for one which is regulated by a provisional order made under the Inclosure Acts, 1845–1882, or which is subject to byelaws made by a parish council under Section 8 of the Local Government Act, 1894.[16, 17]

Metropolitan Commons

A common any part of which is in the Metropolitan Police District as defined in 1866 is a metropolitan common;[18] it may not be inclosed[19] and, subject to the making of any schemes, the public is entitled to rights of access for air and exercise over it unless the county council resolves that the public be excluded, and the resolution is approved by the Minister of Agriculture.[20]

C. PUBLIC ACCESS TO RURAL COMMONS

The Lord of a Manor or other person such as a parish council entitled to the soil may by deed revocable or irrevocable give the public a right of access to a rural common, and this right

[11] ibid s. 1.   [12] ibid. s. 4.   [13] ibid. s. 5.   [14] ibid. s. 2.
[15] S.R. & O. 1946 No. 1757 Art. 3(1) and Schedule.
[16] Commons Act, 1899 s. 14.   [17] See page 231.
[18] Metrop. Commons Act, 1866 s. 4.   [19] ibid. s. 5.
[20] The Law of Property Act, 1925 s. 193(1).

begins when the deed is deposited with the Minister of Agriculture[21] who may by scheme made on application by the Lord impose limitations or conditions upon such right;[22] these must be published.[23]

Any person who brings a vehicle on to such a common without lawful authority or who camps or lights fires or fails to observe any of the limitations or conditions commits an offence for which he may be fined a sum not exceeding £2.[24]

D. PROTECTION OF OWNERLESS COMMONS

If land is registered as a common but no one is registered as the owner, a parish council or any other local authority in whose area it lies may take such steps to protect it against illegal interference as would be open to an owner in possession, and may also launch criminal proceedings for any offence committed in respect of the land.[25] Primarily these powers enable the parish council to warn off trespassers, prevent encroachments and institute proceedings whether criminal or civil as may be appropriate to the situation, but it also enables the council sometimes to execute works.

These powers will last only so long as Parliament has not decided on the future of these ownerless commons; no such decision is probable before 1972.

E. OPEN SPACES ACT POWERS

General Power

A[26] parish council may (with the appropriate consents) convey, with or without conditions, land to a local authority for any or no consideration, for the purpose of its being preserved as an open space, for the enjoyment of the public, and may similarly accept[27] or appropriate land for that purpose.[28]

The remaining provisions of the Open Spaces Act, 1906, fall into two classes and certain safeguards.

---

[21] Law of Property Act, 1925 s. 193(2)
[22] ibid. s. 193(1)b().
[23] ibid. s. 193(3).
[24] ibid. s. 193(4).
[25] Commons Registration Act, 1965 s. 9.
[26] O.S.A. 1906 s. 7.
[27] ibid. s. 7(1).
[28] ibid. s. 7(2).

Freeedom to Transfer

The first class makes possible the transfer to parish councils (amongst others) of certain kinds of lands which are open spaces in fact but to whose transfer legal obstacles would otherwise exist. Accordingly trustees of open spaces under local and private acts,[29] trustees of open spaces held otherwise than under such acts,[30] charitable trustees of open spaces,[31] owners of land subject to rights of exercise and recreation vested in neighbouring owners or occupiers,[32] and owners of disused burial grounds[33] may after obtaining the consents proper to each case[34] convey or let the land or transfer its management or entire or partial control to the parish council. Usually but not invariably the land must be held upon the same trusts as bound the previous owner and in each class of case the type of agreement is defined in the act.[34]

Acquisition

The second class confers upon a parish council numerous powers of acquisition and administration. It may acquire by agreement and for any valuable, nominal or no consideration the freehold or lease of or any limited interest in or any right or easement in on or over any open space[35] or burial ground[35] in the parish or outside; and it may undertake the entire or partial care, management or control whether any interest in the soil is transferred to it or not; and for these purposes it may make any agreement with any person authorised to convey or agree with reference to such land or with any person interested therein.[36]

Trusts

Subject to any conditions under which the estate, interest or control was acquired, the parish council is bound to hold the land in trust to allow and with a view to the enjoyment thereof by the public as an open space and under proper control and regulation, and for no other purpose, and must maintain it in a good and decent state.[37, 38]

---

[29] ibid s. 2. [30] ibid. s. 3. [31] ibid. s. 4 [32] ibid. s. 5.
[33] ibid. s. 6 disused burial ground is defined in s. 20.
[34] The details will be found in O.S.A. 1906 ss. 2–6 and 8.
[35] These are specially defined in O.S.A. 1906 s. 20.
[36] O.S.A. 1906 s. 9. [37] O.S.A. 1906 s. 11(1).
[38] For the special circumstances which can arise in a New Town see page 197.

Administrative Powers

For the purpose of carrying out the trusts a parish council may
enclose the land with proper railings and gates and may drain
level, lay out, turf, plant, ornament, light, provide with seats and
otherwise improve it, and do all such works and employ such
officers and servants as may be requisite.[37]

Consecrated Land

In the case of consecrated land the powers of management
may not be exercised until a faculty or licence has been obtained
from the Bishop.[39]

Games

Games may not be played in a burial ground without the
consent, in the case of consecrated land, of the Bishop (given by
licence or faculty), and in the case of other land of the person
from whom the estate, interest or control was obtained. Such
consent may be given subject to conditions.[40]

Tombstones

A parish council may move or remove headstones, tombstones
or monuments in a disused burial ground but if it wishes to do
so, it must at least three months beforehand, prepare a statement
sufficiently describing by name, date and other necessary particulars the tombstones and monuments in the ground, and this
statement must be deposited with the clerk and must be open to
public inspection; it must then on three occasions advertise in a
newspaper circulating in the area its intention, the existence and
place of deposit of the statement and the hours when it is open
to inspection, and in addition it must place a copy of the
advertisement on the door of the church (if any) and send a copy
by post to any known near relatives.[41] Further, if the ground is
consecrated the parish council must wait for at least one month
after the appearance of the last of the advertisements and must
then apply for a faculty or licence to the Bishop. No monuments
or tombstones in consecrated ground may be moved until such
licence or faculty has been obtained.[41]

---

[37] O.S.A. 1906 s. 10.   [39] O.S.A. 1906 s. 11 (1)
[40] O.S.A. 1906 s. 11(2).   [41] O.S.A. 1906 s. 11(3) and (4).

No building other than a church or chapel may be erected on a disused burial ground.[42]

Byelaws

For open spaces managed under the act a parish council may, with the approval of the Home Secretary, make byelaws to regulate their use (for instance for games), preserve order, prevent nuisances and for the removal of persons infringing the byelaws. Penalties may be imposed and are recoverable summarily.[43]

Extension to Other Property

A parish council is entitled to exercise the powers of the act respecting open spaces and burial grounds transferred to it under the act in relation to open spaces and burial grounds of a similar nature which may be vested in it by any other title.[44]

Co-operation

In carrying out the act a parish council may act jointly with any other parish council or local authority, and there is a right of mutual contribution.[45]

Exceptions

The Open Spaces Act, 1906, cannot apply to Royal Parks, land vested in the Crown or the Duchy of Lancaster, land belonging to the Honourable Societies of the Inner and Middle Temples, or any metropolitan common.

F. CONTRIBUTIONS TO THE NATIONAL TRUST

With the Minister's consent the parish council (like other local authorities) may contribute to the expenses of the National Trust in acquiring, maintaining or preserving any land (or building) in or in the neighbourhood of the parish.[46]

[42] Disused Burial Grounds Act, 1884, amended by O.S.A. 1887 s. 4.
[43] O.S.A. 1906 s. 15 and S.R. & O. 1947 No. 1757.
[44] O.S.A. 1906 s. 12.   [45] ibid. s. 16.
[46] National Trust Act, 1937 s. 7(2).

G. RECREATION GROUNDS AND PUBLIC WALKS

A parish council alone or jointly with any other parish council may acquire land for a recreation ground and for public walks and may execute any necessary works for those purposes.[47] This power is not subject to the rate limits.[48]

H. PLAYING FIELDS, GYMNASIA AND CAMPING

A parish council or other local authority may acquire, lay out, provide with suitable buildings and otherwise equip and maintain lands in or outside the parish for gymnasia, playing fields, holiday camps or camping sites.[49] They may contribute to expenses of any other parish council or local authority in so doing and in addition they make contributions[50] or loans[51] (upon any terms they think fit) to any non-profit-making voluntary organisation providing these facilities.[52] They may also manage the lands themselves with or without charge for use or admission or may let them at a nominal or other rent to such a voluntary organisation.[49] There is no limit on the length of the lease which may be granted, and the Minister's consent to a lease for more than one year is not required.

Many parish councils provide playing fields under these powers or encourage them to be provided, The rapid growth of public interest in camping may eventually lead to the use of the other powers.

There are important financial consequences arising from the wording of the legislation. It is, legally speaking, possible to precept for funds which are then lent or granted outright to a voluntary organisation, or money can (with the appropriate consents) be borrowed by the parish council and granted or lent upon similar or different terms to the voluntary body. All these combinations appear in practice, though direct management is the normal mode.

---

[47] L.G.A. 1894 s. 8(1) sub-sections (b) (i) and (k).
[48] P.C.A. 1957 s. 1(3).   [49] P.T. & R.A. 1937 s. 4(1).
[50] ibid. ss. 4(5).   [51] P.T. & R.A. 1958.
[52] P.T. & R.A. 1937 s. 4(4) and 9.

There is power to acquire land compulsorily for these purposes, but no grants can be made to a voluntary body without premises except from the free fifth.

I. GENERAL POWERS

In relation to any recreation ground, village green, open space, or public walk which is for the time being under its control or to the expense of which it has contributed,[53] a parish council has certain important powers of management, improvement, provision of pleasure boats, and bye-legislation. The parish council's right to exercise these powers does not depend upon its having any legal interest in the land, but, on the other hand, it is limited by special provision in the various acts under which the lands may have been acquired, and must not be exercised in a manner which is inconsistent with those acts.

Improvement and Use

Accordingly a parish council may lay out, plant, improve and maintain the land[54] and may support or contribute to the support or purchase of public walks or pleasure grounds provided by any person and whether they are in the parish or not so long as they are situated conveniently for the inhabitants;[54] it may provide and let or licence someone to provide and let pleasure boats together with the necessary buildings and equipment;[55, 56] it may close the land for not more than twelve days in the year and grant its use (free or for payment) to any public charity or institution or for any agricultural, horticultural or other show or for any other public purpose, or may use it for any such show or purpose itself, and on 'closed' days admission to the land may be free or for such payment as is directed by the parish council; this power of closure, however, may not be exercised so as to close the land on a Sunday nor for more than six days consecutively nor so as to close more than a quarter of the total 'recreational land' available on a Bank Holiday or at Christmas, Good Friday, or a day of public mourning or thanksgiving.[57, 58]

[53] L.G.A. 1894 s. 8(1)(d).
[54] P.H.A. 1875 s. 164 first sentence as amended by P.H.A. (Amendment) Act, 1890 s. 45.
[55] P.H.A. (Amendment) Act, 1890 s. 44(2).   [56] P.H.A. 1961 s. 54.
[57] P.H.A. (Amendment) Act, 1890 s. 44(1).   [58] P.H.A. 1936 s. 53.

Byelaws for Land and Boating

Moreover a parish council may make byelaws for the regulation of the land and for the removal of any person infringing the byelaws;[59] and may also make byelaws on the naming and numbering of boats, the numbers of persons to be carried in them, boathouses and mooring places, rates of hire, qualifications of boatmen and for securing their good and orderly conduct while in charge of a boat.[60]

The parish council may also execute any works incidental to or consequential on the exercise of any of these powers.[61]

The powers connected with boating are not subject to the rate limits.[62]

J. 'ACCESS LAND'

Where land is subject to an access agreeement [63]between a local planning authority and a landowner, or to an access order,[64] a person who enters such land for open-air recreation cannot be treated as a trespasser unless he does damage or goes upon 'excepted land' such as agricultural land other than rough grazing, nature reserves, the curtilage of a house, private parks, gardens and pleasure grounds so used at the date of the agreement or order, surface workings for minerals and quarries, land used for a rail- or tramway, golf course, racecourse or aerodrome or for a statutory undertaking, and land upon which certain works are in course of erection.[65] An access agreement or order cannot confer these rights in respect of rural commons upon which there is a public right of access conferred by deed deposited with the Minister of Agriculture.[66]

K. SWIMMING POOLS AND BATHING PLACES

Management

A parish council or other local authority may provide open or covered public swimming baths and bathing places and may

---

[59] P.H.A. 1875 s. 164 second sentence.
[60] P.H.A. (Amendment) Act, 1890 s. 44(2).
[61] L.G.A. 1894 s. 8(1)(i).   [62] P.H.A. 1961 s. 54.
[63] Under N. Parks Act, 1949 s. 64.   [64] ibid. s. 65.
[65] ibid. s.60.   [66] ibid. s. 60(5)(h) and see page 225.

lay the necessary pipes to them.[67] Subject to one month's public notice they may fix charges for admission and use.[67] They may also close them temporarily so as to grant their exclusive use (either free or for payment) to a school or club or to persons organising swimming practices or contests, aquatic sports or other entertainments or may organise such events themselves[68] and between 1st October and the 30th April they may close the pool and use or allow it to be used or let it for such purpose and subject to such conditions as they think fit.[69]

Expenditure

Expenditure on the provision of these swimming facilities is not subject to the rate limits.[70]

Plastic Pools and Solar Heating

Formerly very expensive, the capital cost of pools has been revolutionised in the less pretentious cases by the introduction of plastic pools laid on sand. These are safe, durable and cheap. Running expenses can also be reduced and the useful annual season considerably extended by the use of a simple solar heat exchanger.[71]

Byelaws

A parish council may make byelaws for the regulation of its swimming places and of any person resorting thereto and for excluding undesirable persons. The byelaws may provide for penalties and for the removal of persons infringing them. A printed copy or abstract must be exhibited at the bathing place.[72]

L. GRANTS

Grants available at the time of going to press are discussed in Chapter 14.

---

[67] P.H.A. 1936 ss. 221(b), 222, 227, 230 and P.T. & R.A. 1937 s. 4(3).
[68] P.H.A. 1936 s. 225.   [69] ibid. s. 226.
[70] L.G.A. 1933 s. 193(3) and P.C.A. 1957 1st Schedule.
[71] A covered pool at Charbury belonging to Admiral the Hon. Sir R. Plunkett-Ernle-Erle-Drax maintains a temperature exceeding 65° regularly from mid-March to November.
[72] P.H.A. 1936 s. 223.

M. FACILITIES FOR COUNTRYSIDE VISITORS

The Countryside Commission may prepare schemes for experimental projects for facilitating the enjoyment of the countryside. It must consult such bodies (including parish councils) as appear to it to have an interest, and the schemes must be confirmed by the Minister.[73]

Country parks, with or without facilities for sailing, boating, bathing and fishing may be provided by the councils of counties, boroughs, districts and Greater London and by the Common Council of the City of London. They can also provide camping and picnic sites with the necessary road access, car parks and conveniences, and in the case of commons in which a public right of access exists they can provide on or near them means for facilitating their enjoyment by persons going there for open air recreation. In all these cases, however, the providing authority must first obtain the consent of the county council, consult the rural district council and inform the parish council or chairman of the parish meeting.[74]

[73] Countryside Act, 1968 s. 4.　　　[74] ibid. ss. 6–10.

23

Social and Educational Projects

A. HALLS AND CENTRES

All the powers possessed by local authorities including parish councils for providing or encouraging the provision of playing fields, gymnasia and camping or holiday sites[1] are equally available for providing or encouraging halls and (so called) community centres for the use of clubs, societies or organisations with athletic, social or educational objects. It is difficult to imagine an organisation (other than a criminal conspiracy) which is not covered by this power.

Whereas direct management of facilities for exercise is the normal (but not invariable) method, in the case of halls and centres the converse is the case, and experience has shown that it is usually (but not always) better for halls and centres to be let to voluntary management committees constituted under a model trust deed drawn up by the National Council of Social Service, and consisting of representatives from the voluntary bodies in the parish together with nominees appointed by the parish council and parish meeting.

One reason for the relative success of village halls managed in this way is that government funds have since 1947 been readily available through the Department of Education for them; another that they are not subject to certain restrictions in entertainments.

Wardens and Leaders

Parish councils may also provide and where necessary arrange training for wardens, teachers and leaders so that effective use can be made of the facilities provided.[2] This has been found to be an effective way of combating vandalism.

---

[1] See page 230. [2] P.T. & R.A. 1937 s. 4(1).

Entertainments

Halls and other premises provided under the Physical Training and Recreation Act, 1937, may be used for the provision by the parish council or any other person of entertainments or for meetings, but an entertainment provided by a parish council must not consist of a stage play, variety show or film (other than a film illustrating questions relating to health or disease), nor must theatrical costumes or scenic or theatrical accessories be used.[3] This practically confines these entertainments to music, but it should be noted that the power to permit entertainments is much wider if the main use of a building (or part of it) is as a museum.[4]

Grants

The Department of Education has power to make grants to voluntary organisations for the purposes of the Act.[5]

In practice such grants are made only to an organisation constituted under an approved trust deed in such a way that the organisation is a charity and so subject to the department's charitable jurisdiction.

Parish Hall and Offices

A parish council may by itself or in combination with any other parish council acquire or provide and furnish buildings in which to transact the business of the parish council or of the parish meeting or any other parish business and for public meetings and assemblies, or may contribute towards the expense incurred by any other parish council or person in doing so.[6]

The Offices, Shops and Railway Premises Act, 1963, does not apply where the clerk does his work at home[7] nor where the time worked in the office does not exceed 21 hours a week.[8]

B. LANDS FOR LITERARY AND SCIENTIFIC INSTITUTES AND SCHOOLS

A parish council or parish meeting may, with the consent of the Minister[9] (or in the case of charity lands of the Charity

---

[3] P.T. & R.A. 1937 incorporating and amending P.H.A. 1925 s. 70.
[4] See page 237.   [5] P.T. & R.A. 1937 s. 3 but see page 139.
[6] L.G.A. 1933 s. 127. For the rght to use other meeting places see pages 47-8.   [7] s. 2.   [8] . 3.
[9] Literary and Scientific Institutions Act, 1854 s. 6 and 8.

Commissioners) convey land not exceeding one acre for each
institute to a literary or scientific institute[10] but it reverts if it
ceases to be used for the purposes of the institute.[11] Grants may
be made to any number of institutes.[12]

Similarly, land to the same quantity may be conveyed for a
school, schoolmaster's residence or otherwise for the education
of the poor,[13] but there is no provision for reverter and there
may not be more than one such site in the same *ecclesiastical*[14]
parish.[15]

C. MUSEUMS

A parish council may apply to the Secretary of State for
Education for consent to provide a museum and he may give
such consent subject to conditions which he may vary or revoke.[16]
A parish council thus empowered may with his consent transfer
its museum or collections to another authority.[17]

Once empowered to provide a museum the parish council
may make admission charges (but must have regard to local
education needs and the interests of children and students[18])
and it may contribute to the expenses of museums elsewhere.[19]
It may also make byelaws imposing fines or permitting offenders
to be excluded or removed.[20]

Museum premises so provided may be used for other purposes
(whether for payment or free) such as meetings, exhibitions,
films, musical performances and other events of an educational
or cultural nature.[21]

A county council which maintains a museum cannot charge
the expense upon a parish whose council maintains one without
the consent of the latter[22] but the Secretary of State may make it
a condition of his consent that such consent shall be given.

Expenditure is not subject to the rate limits.[23]

There is no power of compulsory purchase.

---

[10] ibid. s. 1.   [11] ibid. s. 4.   [12] ibid. s. 10.
[13] School Sites Act, 1841 ss. 2 and 6.   [14] School Sites Act, 1851.
[15] School Sites Act, 1841 s. 9.
[16] Public Libraries and Museums Act, 1964 s. 12(1).
[17] ibid. s. 12(2).   [18] ibid. s. 13.   [19] ibid. s. 14.   [20] ibid. s. 19.
[21] ibid. s. 20. Contrast the restrictions on entertainments in village halls
(see page 236).
[22] ibid. s. 21(1) and (2).   [23] P.C.A. 1957 1st Schedule.

24

Appearance of Villages

Parish councils can statutorily take a certain part in maintaining or improving the general appearance of villages, and they and the parish meeting can also exert a persuasive influence to the same effect on other authorities, intending developers and residents. The sum total of these powers is greater than is sometimes supposed.

A. KEY BUILDINGS AND SITES

Many villages have a visual focus of which the church and its churchyard is usually the most conspicuous; other striking features may include village greens, memorials or market crosses, tithe barns, avenues or clumps of trees, ponds, and verges. These things individually or in combination set the character of the village: they may be good or bad, well designed or ugly, well or badly sited. Under modern conditions it will be rare for a parish council to be wholly powerless in dealing with them, for where a specific power is lacking the 'free fifth'[1] is generally available even if it is not always adequate. The following paragraphs are examples of the uses to which specific powers have been put.

Where a churchyard is open a parish council may contribute to its maintenance.[2] This can be used, in the case of an impecunious Parochial Church Council either to improve the appearance of an unkept churchyard or, by taking the financial burden of churchyard maintenance off the Parochial Church Council to help that body to improve the appearance of the church.

---

[1] L.G.(F.P.) Act, 1963 s. 6.   [2] P.C.A. 1957 s. 10.

In some places the degradation of village greens by parking and litter is becoming a serious problem; and some seem to be disappearing through encroachment, erosion and clutter. This process can be reversed by a judicious combination of measures; prosecutions for litter can be launched,[3] and publicised, and litter baskets can be provided.[6] Large stones or posts and chains can be placed to hinder vehicles,[4] and drivers can be prosecuted for damaging the surface.[5] If the green is big enough local clubs can be encouraged to play games on it and take an interest in it,[4] and sometimes trees or shrubs can be planted.

Often a village can be improved by tree planting or tree preservation. There is power to plant verges with the consent of the Highway Authority when they form part of the highway,[7] and in other cases the power to provide public walks can be invoked. Where trees are privately owned the County Council can be asked to make a preservation order or in an appropriate case an open space agreement can be negotiated.[8]

There are instances where neglected village ponds have been rescued and made agreeable to the eye, and subsequently stocked with goldfish to keep down the mosquitoes.

B. VILLAGE OR CIVIC SOCIETIES

No village will ever look better than its people want. If a parish council can set in motion the process of village improvement by paying attention to the key sites, the general level can often be maintained by voluntary action through a village civic society organised with the help of the Civic Trust. The formation of such a society can by itself be a valuable service to a village, and a parish council can encourage or even initiate the process by providing a meeting place, offering help with publicity and subscribing to its funds.[9] The Society can embark on undertakings of wide scope once its membership is reasonably large. It can organise street and house improvement schemes similar to the Magdalen Street Scheme in Norwich; it can act as the organising body in Best-kept Village Competitions and in garden and window box competitions—for which the parish

[3] Litter Act, 1958 s. 1(2).   [4] L.G.A. 1894 s. 8.
[5] Inclosure Act, 1857 s. 12.   [6] Public Health Act, 1961 s. 51.
[7] Health Act, 1959 s. 82.   [8] O.P.A. 1906 s. 10.
[9] From the free fifth.

council can provide prizes[10] and it can by persuasion or pressure help to eliminate eyesores and derelict buildings.

C. GOOD DESIGN

Apart from buildings parish councils provide a surprisingly large amount of street furniture such as lamp-posts, bus shelters, litterbins, public seats and notice boards. These are not always as apt for their purpose or as durable or as suitable for their surroundings as they might be because the existence of better designs is not invariably known. Well-designed articles of the kind used by parish councils are usually worth their higher price because they look better and last better and because they attract vandalism less. Moreover the habitual planting of cheap or ill-designed objects in public places diminishes the moral authority of a parish council interested in the amenity of the village. A parish council which intends to provide street furniture can usually obtain independent information on designs through its Association or the Civic Trust and should invariably do so before placing large contracts.[11]

D. PLANNING

It is common sense to give parish councils an opportunity to express their opinion on proposals affecting the appearance of the village or the environment of its people, especially as reorganisation enlarges the area of the planning authorities and of the district councils to whom they delegate their functions. Recognition of this is becoming increasingly widespread and unofficial arrangements of varying effectiveness have been made in many areas accordingly.[12]

The essential is that a parish council should be able to give to the planning authority sensible advice without delay. For this it needs a reasoned idea of the future of the village and an expeditious procedure. The reasoned idea implies some sort of

[10] See page 216.
[11] At the time of writing (1965) there has for several years past been an exhibition of street furniture beside County Hall in London.
[12] A bill to place these arrangements on a statutory basis was introduced in the Commons in 1964, but failed to secure a debate because another bill was filibustered: M.P.s received over 3000 letters in support, not only from parish councils.

I

plan even if it is only a very rough one: this can be, and sometimes is, drawn up by parish councillors relying on their detailed knowledge of the parish. In practice some professional help may be necessary but can be kept within very narrow limits; elaborate documents similar to those produced in county planning offices are unnecessary for this purpose. The required expeditious procedure can take several forms which all have two features in common: the planning authority having only a statutory two months[13] within which to decide a planning application, the parish council needs to be notified of the application *at the beginning of the two months*, and it should be given only a short period (say two or three weeks) within which to make its comments. Such a procedure if vigorously applied need cause no delay whatever.[14]

E. ROADSIDE VERGES

With the consent of the Highway Authority a parish council may, in any publicly repairable highway, plant trees and shrubs and plants and lay out grass verges; it may fence or otherwise protect them or similar plantings effected by private persons. These powers must not be exercised so as to obstruct public rights of passage or so as to be a nuisance to a frontager. Expenditure is subject to the rate limits.[15]

F. MANOEUVRES

Manoeuvres can only be held under authority of a manoeuvres order which defines the area in which they may be held. At least two months before the order is to be made, a draft of it must be sent to every parish council in the area. Manoeuvres under an order may not last more than three months and no further order for the same area may be made within five years without the consent of the county council and (in the case of the New Forest) of the Verderers.[16]

During the currency of the order a manoeuvres commission has power to pay compensation for damage and to impose

---

[13] In real life they often take longer.
[14] For Public Inquiries see page 204.
[15] H.A. 1959 s. 82 and Highways (Misc. Provisions) Act, 1961 s. 5.
[16] Manoeuvres Act, 1959 s. 1.

requirements on owners of property; disregard of such requirements destroys the right to compensation.[17] Petty Sessions also
have power on application from the military authorities and
after seven days' notice, to close highways and footpaths during
certain hours of the day.[18]

[17] ibid. ss. 5–7.   [18] ibid. s. 3.

25

Public Lighting

A. SUMMARY

L ighting is of three major kinds, namely open space lighting, road lighting and footway lighting.

Open Space Lighting

Any parish council may light an open space acquired or controlled under the Open Spaces Act, 1906, without any need for adoption formalities,[1] but the expense of so doing falls within the rate limits.

Road Lighting

A highway authority may provide *road lighting* in any highway for which it is responsible[2]. Road lighting is any such lighting other than footway lighting.[3] On 1st April, 1967, all road lighting (including lamps, apparatus and property) was transferred from the lighting authority to the highway authority, and agreements can be made respecting the transfer, and defining the property and rights to be transferred.[4] In default of agreement disputes are settled by the Minister of Transport unless he is a party to the dispute in which case the matter is settled by arbitration.

Where the Highway Authority is the Minister no liability for outstanding loans or loan charges can be transferred to him,[5]

---

[1] P.C.A. 1957, s. 8(1) and O.S.A. 1906, s. 10.
[2] L.G.A. 1966 s. 28.   [3] ibid. s. 31.
[4] ibid. s. 31 and see below.   [5] ibid. s. 31 (2).

but where it is a county council, the agreement may deal with the transfer of such liabilities.

A highway authority can delegate its road lighting powers to a lighting authority which exercises them as agent. Works and expenditure must be approved by the highway authority; the lighting authority must comply with any requirements on the manner in which works are to be carried out, and with any directions about the terms of agreements made with contractors, and works must be carried out to the satisfaction of the highway authority.[6]

If a road lighting system provided under a delegation agreement is not in proper repair or condition the highway authority can by notice require it to be put in order, and if the notice is not complied with the highway authority may do the work itself.[7]

Delegation agreements may be terminated by notice. Such a notice must not be given in the last three months of a calendar year and must not take effect until 1st April in the year after which it is given.[8]

Footway Lighting

Footway lighting is lighting where either no lamp is more than 13 feet above the ground, or no lamp is more than 20 feet above ground and there is in addition at least one interval exceeding 50 yards between adjacent lamps in the system,[9] but the Minister may by order vary these definitions.

Lighting authorities may provide or, as the case may be, continue to provide footway lighting, but even these systems are liable to transfer to the highway authority in any one of three contingencies. The first is where the lighting authority itself alters the system so that it ceases to comply with the definition of footway lighting; the second is where the Minister alters the definition and the system does not comply with the new definition; the third is where the highway authority proposes to provide road lighting along the same road and gives notice to that effect to the lighting authority.[10] In each of these cases the method of transfer is the same as if it had happened on 1st April, 1967.

[6] ibid. s. 30 (1) (2)   [7] ibid. s. 30 (3)   [8] ibid. s. 30 (5)   [9] ibid. s. 32 (1)
[10] ibid. s. 32 (2) (3)

B. CREATION AND CESSATION OF POWERS

Rural District Council

A rural district council may light streets (up to footway standard) markets and public buildings[11] in any parish in respect of which it has been invested with urban powers by an order of the Minister of Housing and Local Government;[12] on such an order being made the parish council's adoptive lighting powers, if any, come to an end[13] and if none they cannot be adopted while the order is in force. It may, however, delegate these powers to a parish council.

Parish Council and Parish Meeting

A parish council (or parish meeting where no parish council exists) may provide footway lighting under the Lighting Section (Section 3) of the Parish Councils Act, 1957.

The Lighting Section is in force in every place where on the 17th July, 1957, the Lighting and Watching Act, 1833, was in force[6] and in addition it may be adopted elsewhere for the whole of a parish or for any part of a parish in which a parish meeting is authorised or required to be held by an enactment other than the lighting section[7] by a simple majority at a parish meeting held upon 14 days' notice[8] for the area for which it is to be adopted. If it is already in force in part of a parish it may sometimes[14] be adopted for another area by a meeting for that other area[15] and as a result there will be two separate lighting systems with separate accounts and differential rates. In the alternative it may be adopted for the whole of the parish or sometimes[14] for an area exceeding the old area in size by a meeting held for the whole parish or the enlarged area; in this case the former lighting area will be merged in the larger unit.[15]

If the parish is not lit by the rural district council no further formalities are necessary, but if it is, the resolution of adoption is not effective until the Minister has given his consent;[16] he may only give such consent after consultation with the rural district

---

[11] P.H.A. 1875 s. 161.   [12] ibid. s. 163.
[13] P.C.A. 1957 s. 3(4).
[14] See the wording of P.C.A. 1957 s. 3(3) which has caused great difficulties. There cannot be many cases where the powers can now be adopted for part of a parish.
[15] P.C.A. 1957 s. 3(3).   [16] P.C.A. 1957 s. 3(3) proviso.

council and if he is satisfied that the parish is not in fact being adequately lit by the latter.[16]

The section once adopted cannot be abandoned, but it ceases to have effect if the Minister confers lighting powers upon the rural district council.[17]

Where a road hitherto lit by a parish council or parish meeting becomes a special road[18] an order may authorise or even require the special road authority to light the road concurrently with or to the exclusion of the parish authority.[19] The Minister of Transport makes the order if he is providing the special road, otherwise the Highway Authority makes it and he confirms it.[20]

C. ADMINISTRATIVE AUTHORITIES

Wherever a parish is represented upon a parish council the latter (either alone or in combination with other parish lighting authorities)[21] is the administering authority under the section and where there is no parish council the section is administered by the parish meeting which may, but is not bound to, appoint a committee for the purpose. Where parishes provided lighting in concert before 1894, the relevant parish councils, parish meetings or urban districts appointed a joint committee[22] and, whilst this procedure is still available now, where the lighting authorities concerned do not include an urban district it will be more convenient to use the power of combination under the Parish Councils Act, 1957.[23]

In cases where the Lighting Section ceases to be effective because lighting powers have been conferred upon the rural district council, the parish council's lighting property is dealt with as if the Minister's order were an order making an alteration of authorities.[24] There is no express provision for the opposite case but no doubt a similar procedure would be followed.

[16] 16 P.C.A. 1957 s. 3(3) proviso.　　[17] P.C.A. 1957 s. 3(4).
[18] H.A. 1959 s. 11.　　[19] ibid. s. 13(1)(e).
[20] ibid. s. 13(2).
[21] P.C.A. 1957 s. 6.
[22] L.G.A. 1894 s. 53(2).　　[23] See page 72.
[24] P.C.A. 1957 s. 3(4) and L.G.A. 1933 ss. 148(1), 150 and 151.

D. POWERS

The powers of the section may be used to light any highway except a 'special road'[25] but including any footpath or bridleway and any other road, lane, footway, square, court, alley or passage whether a thoroughfare or not and also any other place to which the public has access.[26] It is not necessary that the lighting equipment shall be actually situated in those places so long as they are designed to light them, for the parish lighting authority is expressly empowered (subject, however, to important safeguards[27]) to cause the apparatus to be installed on or against any premises or in such other places as may be convenient.[28]

Parish lighting authorities may provide and maintain such lamps, lamp-posts and other materials and apparatus as they think fit, contract for the supply of gas, electricity or other means of lighting and employ with or without remuneration the necessary maintenance and superintendent staff.[29] They also have a power of contribution towards the expense incurred by any other parish council or person in the provision of lighting,[30] and there is also power to combine.[30]

E. FINANCE

The expenses of lighting under the Open Spaces Act, 1906, are subject to the rate limits and are chargeable upon the whole parish in the ordinary way.

The expenses of lighting under the Lighting Section are not subject to the rate limits[31] and are chargeable only upon the area where the section is in force.

F. FRONTAGERS' LIABILITY IN PRIVATE STREETS

In ordinary cases the expense of lighting installations must be defrayed by the lighting authority, but in private streets it is

[25] See page 248. [26] P.C.A. 1957 s. 3(1) and s. 7.
[27] See page 192. [28] P.C.A. 1957 s. 3(1)(b).
[29] P.C.A. 1957 s. 3(1)(a), (c) and (d).
[30] P.C.A. 1957 s. 6 and see page 72.
[31] P.C.A. 1957 s. 3(8) and L.G.A. 1933 s. 193(3) as amended by P.C.A. 1957 s. 15 and First Schedule.
I*

occasionally possible to impose the cost on private person:
with the result that the frontager will pay in the end. This car
be important in the case of new housing estates whether built by
a local authority or by a private developer, but the occasions for
taking advantage of the law are fugitive, and vigilance is necessary to ensure that the opportunity does not slip away.

The Two Codes

The Code of 1892 is in force in all rural districts. The Advance
Payments Code only in certain rural districts to which the
Minister may add.[32]

Of these two codes the Code of 1892[33] empowers a county
council to resolve to execute certain works (including lighting
in a private street and the cost of this operation is eventually
apportioned between the frontagers. There is provision for
publishing specifications, hearing objections to them by the
magistrates, apportioning the cost and hearing appeals to the
magistrates against the apportionments, and finally for recover
ing the sums due. There is also an independent right of appea
in some cases to the Minister. Once the procedure has been
completed the street becomes a highway maintainable at the
public expense and nothing more can be done. It follows that
when a housing estate is being built, efforts should be made to
ensure that the county council includes lighting to the satisfact
ion of the parish council in the specification.

The Advance Payments Code[34] (where in force) lays down
that anyone who erects a building on a road may be required to
deposit or secure a sum which will suffice to pay for the cost of
such works (including lighting) as may have to be carried out
in future under the Code of 1892. The deposit exonerates the
frontager from future liability and efforts should therefore be
made to ensure that the cost of lighting is included in the
estimate.

[32] In 1965 the advance payments code was in force in the whole of
part of 13 counties
[33] H.A. 1959 ss. 174–188.   [34] H.A. 1959 ss. 192–199.

26

Common Pasture
and Allotments for Cultivation

Strictly speaking an allotment is a piece of land *allotted* to a person or for a particular purpose under an Inclosure Award, but the word soon came to mean land allotted for a public purpose, such as recreation or poor relief,[1] and finally land which is let essentially in small plots for cultivation. These, however, are lay, not legal usages, and though definitions exist for the purposes of particular acts there is no general technical definition.

A. DEFINITIONS AND DISTINCTIONS

Poor allotments were cultivation allotments provided as part of the general poor law.[2]

Fuel allotments were provided under Inclosure Acts and Awards as compensation for turbary, estovers and other fuel rights. They may be let for cultivation only if not needed for the provision of fuel.[3]

Field gardens are cultivation allotments provided under the general Inclosure Acts from 1845 onwards.[4]

Parochial charity allotments are allotments carved out of lands held for the purposes of parochial charities.[5]

An *allotment garden* is a plot not exceeding forty poles which is wholly or mainly cultivated by the occupier to produce

---

[1] It is often used in this sense in statutes.
[2] See Poor Relief Act, 1819 and 1831; Crown Lands Allotments Act, 1831. All the relevant provisions of these acts have now been repealed.
[3] A.A. 1832 ss. 1 and 2.
[4] Inclosure Act, 1845 s. 31. See also ss. 34, 73 and 87.
[5] Allotments Extension Act, 1882, now repealed except for s. 6

vegetables or fruit for consumption by himself and his family.[6] It cannot be *agricultural land* for the purposes of the Agriculture Act, 1947,[7] nor is it an *agricultural holding* within the Agricultural Holdings Act, 1948,[8] because an agricultural holding is the aggregate of agricultural land comprised in a contract of tenancy (other than 'tied land') and which is used for a trade or business, or land which is designated as agricultural land by the Ministry of Agriculture.

B. OWNERSHIP AND TRUSTS OF ALLOTMENTS

Usually allotments (whatever their origin) will nowadays be vested in the parish council or representative body[9] but exceptional cases still occur where they have not been transferred. The commonest exceptions are charitable trustees who may but are not bound to transfer,[10] but it seems that fuel and other such allotments[11] should have been surrendered to the parish councils and parish meetings long ago.[12]

Whatever their origin allotments are managed as one unit; the great majority are provided under the Allotments Acts, 1908–1950, but these acts apply whether the allotments are provided under them or not;[12] nevertheless the trusts upon which a given allotment was originally held will remain in force.

C. OBLIGATION TO PROVIDE ALLOTMENT GARDENS

A parish council must formally consider any written request by six or more electors to operate the Allotments Acts[13] and in addition if it is of the opinion that there is a demand it is bound to provide allotments[14] but the duty is restricted to the provision of allotment gardens.[15] It would be difficult for a parish council to be of any other opinion in the face of a resolution from a well-attended parish meeting.

---

[6] A.A. 1922 s. 22(1).   [7] Agriculture Act, 1947 s. 109(1).
[8] Agricultural Holding Act, 1948 s. 1.
[9] L.G.A. 1894 s. 6(1)(c) and s. 19 and Overseers Order, 1927 Arts. 4(2) and 7, and S.H. & A.A. 1908 ss. 33 and 61.
[10] S.H. & A.A. 1908 s. 33(2) and L.G.A. 1894 s. 14.
[11] See A.A. 1832 ss. 1 and 3 and Allotments Management Act, 1873 s. 1.
[12] S.H. & A.A. 1908 s. 33.   [13] S.H. & A.A. s. 23(2).
[14] S.H. & A.A. s. 23(1).   [15] A.A. 1950 s. 9.

Default

Where a parish council or parish meeting fails in its duty to provide any or enough allotments the county council must provide them; any financial surplus on the county council's allotments must be paid in aid of the parish rate and the county council may delegate the management, or on request transfer the allotments to the parish council or parish meeting.[16]

If the county council similarly makes default the Minister of Agriculture may, after holding a local inquiry, transfer the county council's power of providing allotments to officials nominated by himself.[17]

D. BUILDINGS AND ADAPTATION OF LAND

The allotments authority may improve and adapt land for letting for allotments by draining, fencing, dividing, acquiring approaches, making roads and otherwise as the authority thinks fit and this power of adaptation includes power to erect buildings and adapt existing buildings, but so that no more than one house is erected for occupation with any one allotment nor with an allotment of less than one acre.[18]

On the other hand in the case of poor and fuel allotments,[19] buildings are prohibited and in the case of field gardens[20] they are not only prohibited but the parish council or trustees must pull them down if put up.

E. LETTING, SUB-LETTING AND RENT[21]

Poor and Fuel Allotments

In the case of poor and fuel allotments, the parish council or parish meeting must meet annually in the first week of September to receive applications from industrious cottagers of good character for allotments which must be let in amounts not exceeding one acre for each person for a yearly tenancy beginning with Michaelmas.[22] The rent must be that which is normally obtainable for land of the same quality in the parish[23] and is

[16] S.H. & A.A. 1908 s. 24.
[17] S.H. & A.A. 1908 s. 24(4) and A.A. 1926 s. 22(2).
[18] S.H. & A.A. 1908 s. 26.   [19] A.A. 1832 s. 10.
[20] Inclosure Act, 1845 s. 109.   [21] For Stamp Duty see page 164.
[22] A.A. 1832 s. 3.   [23] A.A. 1832 s. 1.

payable in a single sum at the end of the year,[24] and the land must be properly cultivated so as to maintain its fertility.[25]

If the rent is four weeks in arrear, or if at the end of the year the parish council or parish meeting is of the opinion that the land has not been properly cultivated, a week's notice to quit may be served. Arrears of rent and the land itself may be recovered by proceedings in a Court of Summary Jurisdiction.[26]

Field Gardens

Field gardens must be offered to the poor of the parish in plots not exceeding a quarter of an acre on tenancies for a year or from year to year upon such terms as the parish council or parish meeting thinks fit, but free of all rates and taxes[27] and at a fair agricultural rent if sufficient to cover the rates, taxes and tithe rent charges.[28] If they cannot be let in these amounts and at these rents, they may be let in plots not exceeding one acre at the best annual rent (without premium or fine) and on such terms that they may be resumed at twelve months' notice.[28]

If the rent is forty days in arrear or if at any time after the third month of the tenancy the tenant is not carrying out the terms of the tenancy or has gone to live more than a mile from the parish, a month's notice to quit must be given. If he lives in the parish this must be served on him: if he lives outside, it must be affixed to the church door.[29]

Arrears of rent are recoverable by distress or other ordinary means,[30] but possession may be recovered by application to a County Court.[31] [32] The Small Tenements Recovery Act, 1838, will shortly cease to have effect.

Large Modern Allotments

'Modern' allotments under the Allotments Acts, 1908–1950, must not exceed five acres per person without the consent of the county council,[33] and may not without the consent of the parish council or parish meeting be sub-let.[33] There is no limit on the permissible duration of the lease;[34] the rent must be such as a

---

[24] A.A. 1832 s. 4.
[25] A.A. 1832 s. 2.
[26] A.A. 1832 ss. 5, 6 and 7.
[27] Inclosure Act, 1845 s. 109.
[28] Commons Act, 1876 s. 26.
[29] Inclosure Act, 1845 s. 110.
[30] ibid. s. 112.
[31] ibid. s. 111.
[32] Small Tenements Recovery Act; Rent Act 1965
[33] S.H. & A.A. 1908 s. 27.
[34] L.G.A. 1933 s. 169 proviso.

tenant can reasonably be expected to pay for the land on the terms on which it is in fact let to him but may be less if there exist special circumstances affecting him personally which render it proper to reduce it.[35] It is, therefore, possible within limits[36] to help old age pensioners and the unemployed through these allotments. If the rent is 25s. 0d. (125p) a year or less the whole of it may be demanded in advance; in other cases not more than one quarter's rent may be required in advance.[37]

In relation to modern allotments which are not allotment gardens[38] the rules on arrears, breaches of covenant, departure from the parish and (with one exception) the consequent notice to quit together with their relevant legal remedies are the same as the rules relating to field gardens. The exception is that if a tenant no longer resides in the parish, notice to quit may be exhibited at the allotment instead of at the church door.[39]

Holders of modern allotments may have certain compensation rights and accordingly the court may stay delivery of possession until any compensation due has been made or secured.[40]

Allotment Gardens

The rules on the letting and rent of allotment gardens are the same as those for other modern allotments, but the rules on determination of tenancies are far more rigid. Such a tenancy may (notwithstanding any agreement to the contrary) only be ended in six ways:

Notice to Quit

Firstly notice to quit must be of at least one year's duration expiring on or after 29th September or on or before 6th April in any year.[41]

Re-entry for breach

Secondly there is a right of re-entry if the tenant fails to pay the rent or breaks any term or condition of the tenancy or becomes bankrupt or compounds with his creditors, or where the tenant is an association if it goes into liquidation.

[35] A.A. 1950 s. 10(1).
[36] See page 258.
[37] A.A. 1950 s. 10(2).
[38] A.A. 1922 s. 1.
[39] S.H. & A.A. 1908 s. 30.
[40] S.H. & A.A. 1908 s. 30 and see pages 258–260.
[41] A.A. 1922 s. 1(a) amended by A.A. 1950 s. 1.

Re-entry in the Contract

In the remaining four cases the right of re-entry can only be exercised if it is contained in or affects the contract of tenancy; they are (thirdly) re-entry of land let by a corporation and needed for a railway, dock, canal water or other public undertaking (other than agricultural land); in this case three months' written notice is required save in an emergency; (fourthly) re-entry upon land acquired for housing under the Housing Acts and now required by a local authority for housing; (fifthly) re-entry upon land acquired by a local authority for one of its statutory purposes and now required for that purpose; (sixthly) re-entry after three months' written notice upon land required for building, mining or other industrial purposes or for roads or sewers connected therewith.[42]

Most of these cases will only affect the parish council's or parish meeting's relationship with its tenants where the land has been taken on lease and sub-let, but care must be taken in allotments agreements to make provision for them, and it is generally simplest to word such agreements so that the parish council's rights of entry on allotment gardens shall be similar to those provided by law for field gardens.[43]

Agricultural Holdings

If an allotment exceeds forty poles and is let for commercial cultivation because nobody can be found to cultivate it for personal consumption, it may become an agricultural holding and the special rules on notice to quit agricultural holdings will apply. Broadly speaking such notices are *invalid* if they purport to terminate a tenancy before the end of twelve months from the end of the current year of the tenancy[44] and in addition a valid notice to quit cannot operate if the tenant has within one month of service served a counter notice and if after such counter notice the Minister of Agriculture does not consent to the notice to quit.[45]

Covenant Against Commercial Use

It is, therefore, desirable that where allotment land is to be let in plots exceeding forty poles the tenant should be required

---

[42] A.A. 1922 s. 1(b) to (e).

[43] See page 254.

[44] Agricultural Holdings Act, 1948 s. 23.

[45] ibid. s. 24.

to covenant that the land is to be cultivated exclusively for his own consumption.

F. RULES

Modern Allotments

A parish council or parish meeting may make allotments rules and submit them to the Minister of Agriculture for confirmation. The confirmed rules are binding upon all persons.[46] The rules may contain provisions to prevent undue preferences, to define the qualifications of tenants, the length of notice to quit and the conditions of cultivation and rent. They may be published as the authority thinks fit and free copies must be given on demand.

G. SURPLUS RENTS

'Surplus rents' are the sums remaining after payment of all rates, taxes, and administration expenses.

Surplus rents of *fuel allotments*[47] must be applied in the purchase of fuel for distribution in winter to the poor settled in or near the parish,[48] but and therefore it will be possible to apply the income to some other purpose by obtaining a scheme from the Charity Commissioners. Whether it is desirable to do so will depend largely upon the price of coal.

Surplus rents of *poor allotments* are applied in aid of the parish rate.[49]

Surplus rents of *parochial charity allotments* are applied for the purposes of the charity.

Surplus rents of *field gardens* must be applied to improving, or hiring or purchasing additional land for field gardens,[50] or recreation grounds.[51] The money may not be used for any other purposes and must, therefore, be accumulated if no opportunity for lawful expenditure occurs.

Surplus rents of *ordinary allotments* cannot be applied for any purpose except allotments without the consent of the Minister.[52]

[46] S.H. & A.A. 1908 s. 28.
[47] Poor Allotments Management Act, 1873 s. 13.   [48] A.A. 1832 s. 8.
[49] Poor Allotments Management Act, 1873 s. 14.
[50] Commons Act, 1876 s. 27.   [51] Commons Act, 1899 s. 16(1).
[52] S.H. & A.A. 1908 s. 54.

H. PERMITTED DEFICIT AND THE RATE LIMITS

Except in the case of approved schemes for the unemployed (where there is no limit)[53] a parish authority must so manage its ordinary allotments that its deficit thereon in any year does not exceed the product of a 2d. ($\cdot 8p$) rate[54] but for this calculation it is not necessary to include expenses of land acquisition other than purchase price, rent or compensation, nor expenses of road making nor sinking fund charges for loans raised in connection with the purchase of the land.

Expenditure under the Allotment Acts, 1908–1950, is not subject to the rate limits.[55]

I. ALLOTMENT MANAGERS

Allotment managers may be appointed; they may consist partly of members of the parish council and partly of locally resident ratepayers or wholly of ratepayers. They may do anything in relation to the management of allotments which the council could do and may incur expenses up to a limit authorised by the council, and any such expenses are deemed to be expenses of the parish council.[56]

J. COMPENSATION AT THE END OF TENANCIES (OTHER THAN ALLOTMENT GARDENS)

Parties cannot contract out of their rights to and liabilities for compensation but may by agreement increase the rights of the tenant.

Prohibited Improvements

A parish council may in writing prohibit improvements and if a tenant is aggrieved by such prohibition he may appeal to the Minister of Agriculture who may confirm, vary or annul the prohibition. His decision is final.[57] A tenant is not entitled to

[53] Agricultural Land (Utilization) Act, 1931 s. 14(9).
[54] A.A. 1922 s. 16 amended by A.A. 1950 s. 11.
[55] L.G.A. 1933 s. 193(3) and P.C.A. 1957 First Schedule.
[56] S.H. & A.A. 1908 s. 29.   [57] S.H. & A.A. 1908 s. 47.

compensation for an improvement which has been effectively prohibited.[58]

Compensation Crops

A tenant (provided that he has carried out the improvement himself[59]) may claim compensation for the 'compensation crops' which include permanent fruit trees and bushes, strawberry plants, asparagus, rhubarb and other vegetable crops likely to be productive for two or more years.[60]

Removables

The tenant may before, but not after, the expiration of the tenancy remove any trees, bushes, toolhouse, shed, greenhouse, fowl-house or pigsty for which he has no claim to compensation.[61] In the alternative he may, even though the allotment exceeds two acres,[61] claim compensation for crops (including fruit), for labour expended and manure applied, for fruit trees and bushes planted with the previous written consent of the authority and for drains, outbuildings, pigstys, fowl-houses and other structural improvements made at the tenant's expense and with such consent. From the amount of such claim is deducted amounts due for rent, breach of contract, and wilful or negligent damage.[62] In case of dispute the amount is settled by a valuer appointed by the local County Court Judge upon written application by either party, and is recoverable if not paid within 14 days as a debt within the ordinary jurisdiction of the County Court.[63]

Compensation of Parish Council or Meeting by Landlord

Subject to any provisions to the contrary in the tenancy agreement the parish council or meeting is entitled on quitting land which it has hired for allotments to compensation for the 'compensation crops' and in addition (if such improvement was necessary to adapt the land for allotments) for the erection, alteration or enlargement of buildings, formation of silos, laying down of permanent pasture, making and planting osier beds, making of water meadows, irrigation works, gardens, roads,

---

[58] Agriculture Act, 1947 s. 22.
[59] S.H. & A.A. 1908 2nd Schedule Part I.
[60] S.H. & A.A. 1908 s. 47(4).
[61] S.H. & A.A. 1908 s. 47(3) and A.A. 1922 s. 3(5).
[62] A.A. 1922 s. 3(2) and (3).   [63] A.A. 1922 s. 3(4) and 6(1).

bridges, water courses, ponds, wells, reservoirs or works for agricultural water supply and fences; for planting hops, orchards or fruit bushes; for protecting young trees; for reclaiming waste; for warping and weiring; for embankments and sluices against floods; for wire work in hop gardens; for drainage; for removal of bracken, gorse tree roots, boulders and other obstructions and for permanent sheep dips.[64]

Moreover in the case of land let to it since 4th August, 1922,[65] where the tenancy is determined by notice to quit or re-entry for industrial, housing, or statutory purposes or for purposes of a public undertaking,[66] the parish council or meeting may claim compensation for growing crops and manure,[67] and also for disturbance up to the amount of one year's rent.[68]

K. COMPENSATION AT THE END OF ALLOTMENT GARDENS TENANCY

A tenant of an allotment garden has the same rights of compensation for growing crops, manure and disturbance against the parish council as the parish council has against a superior landlord and may exercise them in like circumstances and in cases where the parish authority's tenancy has come to an end.[69, 70]

He may also, before but not after the end of the tenancy, remove fruit trees and bushes and any erection, fencing or other improvement provided by him, making good any damage done in the process.[71]

Compensation may also be recovered from a foreclosing mortgagee as if he were the landlord[71] and a tenant who compensates an outgoing tenant is entitled to claim for improvements as if he had made them himself.[72]

L. ARBITRATION AND VALUATION

Act of 1908

Compensation disputes under the Act of 1908 are settled by an *arbitrator* appointed by the parties or in default of agreement

---

[64] S.H. & A.A. 1908 2nd Schedule Part II.
[65] A.A. 1922 s. 2(6).   [66] See page 256.   [67] A.A. 1922 s. 2
[68] A.A. 1950 s. 3.   [69] A.A. 1922 s. 2.   [70] A.A. 1950 s. 3.
[71] A.A. 1922 s. 4.   [72] A.A. 1922 s. 5.

by the Minister of Agriculture and the arbitration is held under the Agricultural Holdings Act, 1923, and not under the Arbitration Act, 1950. The arbitrator may state a case for the opinion of the County Court whence an appeal may be made to the Court of Appeal.

Act of 1922

Compensation disputes under the Act of 1922 are settled by a valuer.

The essential difference between the two procedures is that an arbitrator decides upon evidence placed before him by the parties whereas a valuer uses his own knowledge and skill.

M. SALES AND EXCHANGES OF ALLOTMENT LAND

Poor and recreational allotments may be exchanged for better land under orders made on application by the parish council or trustees by the Ministry of Agriculture.[73]

Field gardens may be sold with the approval of the Ministry of Agriculture for the purchase within a reasonable time of other land to be held upon the same trusts.[74]

Modern allotments must not be sold without the consent of the Minister and the Minister of Agriculture.[75]

Fuel and Field Garden Allotments can be acquired compulsorily for the purposes of a New Town and the land used for other purposes.[76]

N. ASSOCIATIONS

A parish council or parish meeting may let allotments to persons working on a co-operative system provided that the system is approved by the Minister of Agricultur.[77]

Lettings to allotments associations are now made under the parish councils or meetings ordinary letting powers.

[73] See Inclosure Acts, 1845 s. 149, 1852 s. 21. For appropriations see page 107.   [74] Commons Act, 1876 s. 27.
[75] A.A. 1925 s. 8 amended by Agricultural Land (Utilisation) Act, 1931 Schedule 2.   [76] See page 197.
[77] S.H. & A.A. 1908 ss. 27(6) and 61(4) and Agriculture Act 1947 s. 52(4)

O. COMMON PASTURE

A parish authority may acquire land, stints and other alienable common rights and let them to tenants of allotments.[78] If it wishes to provide common pasture for other people it must apply to the county council for a scheme.[79]

Common lands and rights of common such as pasture must be registered with the county council.[80]

P. REPORTS AND FINANCIAL STATEMENT

Where land is purchased or leased under the Allotments Acts 1908–1950, the parish authority must record the purchase price or rent and must include it in the annual report which it is required to make to the Minister of Agriculture.[81]

A financial statement relating to allotments must be prepared annually and must within one month of the end of every financial year be available for public inspection without fee.[82]

---

[78] ibid. s. 42.   [79] ibid. s. 34.
[80] Commons Registration Act, 1965.
[81] S.H. & A.A. 1908 s. 59 and A.A. 1925 s. 13.
[82] S.H. & A.A. 1908 s. 54.

27

Health, Housing, Inns and Clocks

A. WASHHOUSES, LAUNDERETTES AND BATHS

A parish council may provide open or covered public baths and washhouses, with or without drying grounds and may lay the necessary pipes and make charges and byelaws of a nature similar to those which apply to swimming facilities.[1] Washing machines and the rising age of the population may make these powers increasingly useful.[2]

The expenses are not subject to the rate limits.[3]

B. WATER

A parish council may utilise any well, spring or stream in the parish and provide facilities for obtaining water therefrom and may execute the necessary consequential works, but not so as to interfere with any private right or the powers of any other authority. It may also contribute to the expenses of any other parish council or person in doing these things.[4]

In 1936 public works for the gratuitous supply of water were vested in the rural district council which may close them or restrict their use if it considers that they are no longer needed or are irremediably polluted.[5]

---

[1] P.H.A. 1936 ss. 221(a), 222, 223 and 227. See page 232.
[2] See P.H.A. 1936 s. 271. There is at least one parish council launderette.
[3] L.G.A. 1933 s. 193(3) and P.C.A. 1957.   [4] P.H.A. 1936 s. 125.
[5] P.H.A. 1936 s. 124 converted the parish pump into the rural district pump.

C. DRAINAGE

A parish council may drain, clean or cover or otherwise deal with any pond, pool, ditch, gutter or place containing or used for the collection of any drainage, filth, stagnant water or matter likely to be prejudicial to health, but not so as to interfere with any private right or any public drainage, sewerage or sewage disposal works, and may carry out any incidental or consequential works or contribute to the expense incurred by any other person in so doing.[6]

D. NOTICE OF SEWERAGE WORKS

A rural authority which proposes to carry out any sewerage works must notify the parish council (or parish meeting if there is no parish council) of any parish where the works are to be carried out *before it adopts the plans.*[7]

E. LITTER

Bins

A parish council may provide, cleanse and empty litter bins in public places and erect anti-litter notices. Such bins and notices cannot be placed in open spaces without the consent of the controlling authority nor on land not forming part of a street without the consent of the owner and occupier. In addition certain other consents may be needed.[8] Refuse and litter collected may be sold.

The county council may contribute to the expenses of the parish council in providing litter bins.[9]

Prosecutions

A parish council has power to prosecute offences against the Litter Act, 1958.[10] These offences relate to certain kinds of anti-social behaviour in places in the open air (including shelters) where the public is entitled or permitted to be without payment. A person in such a place is forbidden to throw down, drop or deposit *in, into or from* that place anything whatsoever in

---

[6] P.H.A. 1936 s. 260(1).   [7] P.H.A. 1936 s. 15(4).
[8] These are much the same as for a 'bus shelter, see page 276.
[9] P.H.A. 1961 s. 51.   [10] s.1(2).

such circumstances as to cause, contribute to, or tend to lead to the defacement by litter of any place in the open air. It is a defence to a charge to show that the act was permitted by law or by the person or authority controlling the place where the thing was deposited. An offender may be fined up to £10.[11]

F. NOISE

A parish council has power to prosecute persons who unlawfully operate loudspeakers in a street.[12]

G. APPLICATIONS FOR URBAN HEALTH POWERS

A parish council or 100 or one-third of the electors (whichever is the less) may apply to the Minister for an order conferring, with respect to the parish, upon the rural district council certain urban public health powers.[13] These powers relate to the repair of drains,[14] the provision of W.C.s in industrial premises,[15] the removal of manure from stables,[16] the regulation of certain trades[17] and the making and cleaning of culverts.[18]

H. HOUSING COMPLAINTS

Parish councils, parish meetings, any justice of the peace or any four local government electors may complain to the county council that the rural district council has failed to exercise its powers under the Housing Act, 1957, and the Housing (Financial Provisions) Act, 1958.[19] If the county council is of the opinion that the complaint should be investigated it may hold a public inquiry, and if satisfied that the complaint is true, it may transfer the power in question to itself by order.[19]

If, on a representation made to the Minister by a justice of the peace, four electors or otherwise, it appears to him that a county council has failed or refused to make an order which should have been made or has made a defective order he may make the

---

[11] s. 1(1).
[13] P.H.A. 1936, s. 13(2).
[15] P.H.A. 1936 s. 46.
[17] P.H.A. 1936 ss. 107 and 108.
[19] Housing Act, 1957 s. 171(1).

[12] Noise Abatement Act, 1960.
[14] P.H.A. 1936 s. 41.
[16] P.H.A. 1936 s. 80.
[18] P.H.A. 1936 ss. 263 and 264.

order himself or remedy the defect.[20] Upon a similar representation that the county council has failed to exercise its transferred powers he may hold a public inquiry and either direct the county council to exercise the powers or transfer them to himself.[21]

Slum Houses

If a parish council, justice of the peace, or four electors complain to the Medical Officer of Health in writing that a house is unfit for human habitation or that any area ought to be treated as a clearance area, the Medical Officer of Health is placed under a duty forthwith to make an inspection and to report in writing to the Housing Authority stating the facts and whether in his opinion the house is unfit or the area should be so treated.[22] This report (which is called a 'representation') must be considered by the Housing Authority as soon as may be.[23]

I. INNKEEPERS' LICENCES

In four cases concerned with licensing an applicant must give twenty-one days notice to the parish council or (if none) to the Chairman of the parish meeting together with his name and address, the situation of the premises to be licensed and (with one exception) certain other particulars. The cases and other particulars are:

New Justices Licence: the applicant's trade or calling during the six months preceding the application and the kind of licence for which application is to be made.

Renewal of Justices Licence

Ordinary and Special Removal of Licence: the premises from which and to which removal is sought.

Order to extend drinking hours in restaurant where dancing or other entertainment is permitted: the applicant's trade or calling during the six months preceding the application.[24]

The annual licensing meeting of the justices takes place in the first fourteen days of February.[25]

J. LAVATORY TURNSTILES

If a parish council provides a public lavatory access to it may not be impeded by turnstiles.

---

[20] Housing Act, 1957 ss. 171(5).   [21] ibid. s. 172
[22] ibid. s. 157 (1).   [23] ibid. s. 157(2).
[24] Licensing Act 1964 ss. 3 and 71 and Schedule 2.
[25] ibid. Schedule I Part II.

K. PUBLIC CLOCKS

A parish council may provide and light public clocks in the parish, and, subject to safeguards,[26] it may install them on or against any premises or in any convenient situation. It may, moreover, maintain any public clock whether provided by it or some other person.[27] For these purposes it may combine with any other parish council or parish meeting with like powers or may contribute to their expenses or to those of any other person in providing lighting or maintaining a public clock; it is therefore possible, for instance, for a parish council to maintain or help to maintain a church clock.[28]

[26] See page 192.   [27] P.C.A. 1957 s. 2.
[28] P.C.A. 1957 ss. 2 and 6.

28

Powers relating to Communications

A. CREATION AND ACQUISITION OF RIGHTS OF WAY

Rights Held in Trust

A parish council may by agreement acquire *any right of way* in or in an adjoining parish the acquisition of which is beneficial to the inhabitants of the parish or part of it, and may execute any necessary works (including maintenance and improvement) or may contribute to the expense of, or combine with any other parish council in so doing.[1] This power is not limited to footpaths but may include bridle, drift and carriageways and the effect of using it is to create a private right of way held in trust for the inhabitants. The main value of this power is to create approaches to playing fields and other public properties.[2]

The acquisition of a right of way does not necessarily involve ownership of the strip of soil along which it passes but in an appropriate case this soil could be acquired if it were needed.

Dedication Agreements

In addition a parish council may make an agreement with a landowner for the dedication of a highway in the parish or an adjoining parish and has in relation to such a highway the same powers as if it had acquired it.[3]

---

[1] L.G.A. 1894 s. 8(1), ss. (g) (i) and (k).
[2] For the making of roads and approaches in connection with allotments see page 253.   [3] H.A. 1959 s. 33.

B. PROTECTION OF RIGHTS OF WAY AND ROADSIDE WASTES

If a highway in the rural district or in an adjoining rural district in the county is unlawfully obstructed or if a roadside waste in the district is unlawfully encroached upon, the parish council may impose upon the rural district council a duty to take proper proceedings to remove the obstruction or encroachment, by making an official representation which the rural district council must obey unless satisfied that it is incorrect; if it fails or refuses to take action the parish council may petition the county council and if the latter so resolves, the power of the rural district council to take the proceedings will be transferred to the county council.[4]

The power of representation does not derogate from the general right of a parish council to take legal proceedings for the promotion or protection of its inhabitants[5] (as, for instance, where the guilty party is the rural district council itself) but enables it in most such cases to impose the cost of litigation on some other authority.

It is an offence to drive a motor vehicle on a footpath or bridleway except a vehicle for cleaning or repairing it, but a bicycle may now legally be ridden on a bridleway.[6]

Misleading Notices

It is an offence to exhibit a false or misleading notice likely to deter the public from using a public path shown on the definitive or revised footpath survey map. The offender is liable, upon the prosecution of the highway authority only, to a fine not exceeding £5, to be ordered to remove the notice within a period of not less than four days, and to be fined a further £2 for every day on which he fails to comply with the order.[7]

C. DIVERSIONS AND CLOSURES

Public and private rights of way can be extinguished over land acquired compulsorily for the purposes of a New Town.[8]

Public rights of way can be suspended for short daily periods during military manoeuvres.[9]

[4] H.A. 1959 s. 116(3) to (7) but see sub.-s. (10) for the Isle of Wight.
[5] L.G.A. 1933 s. 276.
[6] R.T.A. 1960 s. 18 and P.H.A. 1961 s. 49, and Countryside Act, 1968 s. 30.
[7] N. Parks Act, 1949 s. 57.   [8] See page 198.
                                        [9] See page 243.

Stopping up and Diverting Roads etc.

In the case of a highway other than a trunk or special road a highway authority may apply to the magistrates' court for authority to stop it up or divert it on the ground that it is unnecessary or that a diversion will be more commodious to the public. If the highway is a classified road the parish council or, if none, the chairman of the parish meeting must, amongst others, be given at least 28 days' notice and is entitled to appear before the magistrates' court and be heard.[10] Any other person likely to be aggrieved may also be heard and this presumably includes a parish council of a neighbouring parish.

If, however, the highway is an unclassified road the highway authority must give notice that it proposes to make the application to both the rural district council and the parish council or chairman of the parish meeting, and if within two months any of these give notice to the highway authority that they have refused their consent, the highway authority may not make the application at all.[11]

Any two magistrates of the court may view the highway in question; the court cannot authorise a diversion without the written consent of the planning authority and of all those with legal interests in the land over which the diversion is to be made,[12] and an order can reserve a footway or bridleway.[13]

Public Path Extinguishment

Whilst the magistrates' court procedure is only available to highway authorities and applies, apart from trunk and special roads to all highways including footpaths and bridleways, rural district councils have a special procedure available to them alone for extinguishing by order a public right of way over any footpath or bridleway in their district. The rural district council can only make such an order (called a public path extinguishment order) on the ground that the path or way is not needed for public use.[14] If the order is opposed it must be confirmed by the Minister and before it is submitted to him for confirmation the rural district council must give at least 28 days' notice in the *London Gazette*, a local newspaper and to the parish council or parish meeting, and must post a notice near the land concerned.

[10] H.A. 1959 s. 108(5), (6) and 12th Schedule.
[11] H.A. 1959 s. 108(2).   [12] H.A. 1959 s. 108(7).
[13] H.A. 1959 s. 108(3).   [14] H.A. 1959 s. 110(1).

The Minister may hold a public inquiry and is bound to do so if the objector is a local authority including a parish council, or parish meeting where there is no parish council. If the order is not opposed the rural district council may confirm the order itself.[15]

A similar procedure exists for the diversion of public footpaths and bridleways but the order cannot be made unless the new line is substantially as convenient to the public as the old. Where the order is to be made upon the representation of a landowner the latter may be required as a condition of the making of the order, to contribute to the expenses or compensation resulting from the diversion.[16]

Ploughing Up

A farmer may plough up a public path across a field but must give seven days' notice to the highway authority before he does so (under pain of a fine not exceeding £2)[17] and he must make the surface good within six weeks of giving the notice or, if none is given within three weeks after ploughing under pain of a fine not exceeding £10 and £1 for every day after conviction on which the failure continues.[18] The county council may extend the time or divert the footpath for a period not exceeding three months.

The rule on making good is almost unworkable unless the county council notifies the parish council, and the latter is prepared to see that the work is done and report failure.

D. RALLIES

It is an offence to organise a motor vehicle trial on a footpath or bridleway without the county council's authorisation which must not be given unless the owner and occupier of the land have given their consent in writing.[19]

E. FOOTPATHS SURVEY

A county council is bound to consult the parish council or parish meeting (where there is no parish council) in the preparation of the footpaths survey and the parish council or representative body must convene a parish meeting to consider the

[15] H.A. 1959 s. 110(4) and Countryside Act, 1968 s. 31.
[16] H.A. 1959 s. 111.   [17] H.A. 1959 s. 119.
[18] H.A. 1959 s. 119 and Countryside Act, 1968 s. 29.
[19] R.T.A. 1960 s. 17.

nformation to be provided for the survey.[20] A similar procedure must be followed if on the five-yearly review of the particulars n the definitive maps and statements[21] it becomes necessary to evise them.[22]

F. WORKS ON FOOT- AND BRIDLEPATHS

Repair and Maintenance

A parish council may repair and maintain any public foot-path in a parish other than those beside a public road, and any ridleway but this does not relieve any other authority or erson whose duty it may be to repair them.[23] Unless there is n agreement or condition to the contrary the landowner is ound to keep gates and stiles safe and to the standard of epair necessary to prevent unreasonable interference with sers, but may claim a quarter of his expenses from the highway uthority. If he fails in his duty, the latter may do the work t his expense after 14 days' notice.[24]

mprovement

Except where rights of way have been acquired on trust or reated under a dedication agreement[25] a power to repair and naintain does not include a power to improve, but reasonable xpenditure designed to reduce maintenance costs in the future s not improvement, nor is expenditure upon an improvement f the public right would become inoperative without it.

ignposting

A highway authority may in consultation with a landowner ignpost a footpath or bridleway along its length; it *must* do o at every point where they leave a metalled road unless the arish council or chairman of the parish meeting agrees that t is unnecessary. In addition any other person, including a arish council may provide signposts along a footpath or ridleway with the consent of the highway authority.[25A]

G. LIABILITY FOR THE STATE OF HIGHWAYS

A parish council has a power but no duty to repair public ot- and bridlepaths and cannot therefore be made liable for heir condition if they fall into disrepair. It is only if someone is njured by a positive act of the parish council (for instance,

---

[20] ibid., s. 28.   [21] ibid. s. 33.   [22] ibid. s. 34
[23] H.A. 1959 s. 46   [24] Countryside Act, 1968 s. 28.
[25] See page 269.   [25A] Countryside Act, 1968 s. 27.

K

by leaving an unlit obstruction at night) that the parish counci
may be liable in damages to that person.

Highway Authority

The duty of a highway authority to maintain publicly
repairable highways in a proper state of repair is more positive
and can be enforced by court proceedings. The complainant
begins by serving a notice requiring the highway authority (or
other person who may be liable) to state whether it admits that
the way is a highway and that it is liable to maintain it. If the
necessary notice of admission is not forthcoming within a
month, Quarter Sessions may order it to put the highway in
proper repair within a reasonable time specified in the order
If the notice of admission is given the complainant can within
six months obtain a similar order from the local magistrates
court. If the time allowed by the order expires without the
work having been done the complainant may apply to the
magistrates who may authorise him to do it himself and recover
the cost.[26]

Standards for New Footpaths and Bridlepaths

Where a new footpath or bridleway has been created by
agreement with a local authority other than a parish council o
by order the highway authority certifies what work needs to be
done; the Minister may quash or vary such a certificate on
appeal by the local authority and where this has happened the
liability to repair is limited to the standard which obtained
before the certificate was quashed or as established by the
variation.[27]

H. CYCLE PARKS AND RACKS

Purchase and Appropriation

A parish council may by purchase, order, or appropriation
provide and maintain within the parish structures or places
suitable for the parking of bicycles or motorcycles. So far as the
purchase of land for the purpose is concerned the ordinary rules
on compulsory purchase and purchase by agreement apply; the
parish council may also with the consent of the Minister appro
priate part of any recreation ground or playing field provided
or maintained by it or part of any open space controlled or
maintained by it; but appropriation of this sort cannot extend

[26] H.A. 1959 ss. 59–60.   [27] See H.A. 1959 s. 30.

to an area exceeding 800 square feet or one-eighth of the land concerned nor to land held for purposes other than those of section 8 of the Local Government Act, 1894, the Open Spaces Act, 1906, and the Physical Training and Recreation Act, 1937.

Order

Alternatively the Parish Council may, subject to the safe-guards,[28] adapt and by order authorise the use of any part of a 'road', that is to say any of the places where a parish lighting authority may put lamps. Such an order cannot authorise the creation of a cycle park so as to be a nuisance or so as unreason-ably to prevent access to adjoining premises or the use of the 'road' by anyone entitled to use it.

Attendants and Byelaws

A parish council which has provided a parking place may employ parking attendants with or without remuneration, and may make byelaws (subject to the confirmation of the Home Secretary) as to their use, the conditions upon which they may be used and the parking charges. Where a parking place is in a 'road' however, the byelaws cannot provide for charges. Copies of byelaws must be posted at every place to which they relate.

Liability for Losses

In the case of a cycle park in a 'road' a parish council cannot be made liable for loss of or damage to any vehicle parked there or its fittings or contents.

Letting

A parish council may let its parking places other than those in a 'road' but no single letting must exceed seven days; this restriction is not, however, to prejudice the right under other enactments of the parish council to let the land of which the park forms a part.[29]

I. 'BUS SHELTERS AND SEATS AT 'BUS STOPS

A parish council (or other local authority) may provide and maintain 'bus shelters 'or other accommodation' at 'bus stops

[28] See page 192.   R.T. Regulation Act, 1967 ss. 46–50.

or land abutting a 'bus route for the use of intending passengers and may make agreements with the 'bus operators or any other local authority for such provision and maintenance including agreements on the manner in which the cost is to be defrayed.[30]

Consultation and Consents

The Commissioner of the Metropolitan Police must be consulted on the position if it is to be erected in the Metropolitan Police District,[31] and the power may not be exercised in certain other cases without obtaining the consent of certain persons or bodies, viz. :—

In or on land abutting any highway for which there is a highway authority other than the local authority, the highway authority's consent must be obtained.

The consent of the undertakers must be obtained if the shelter is to be placed in any highway belonging to or repairable by any railway, dock, harbour, canal, inland navigation or passenger road transport undertakers and forming the approach to any station, dock, wharf, or depot belonging to them.

In the case of a bridge or approaches to a bridge the consent of the person in whom the bridge is vested must be obtained, and where the bridge carries a highway over a railway canal or inland navigation or where a bridge carries a railway canal or inland navigation over a highway, the consent of the relevant undertakers must also be obtained.

If the shelter is to be placed in a position obstructing or interfering with any existing access to any land or premises abutting on a highway, the consent of the owner must be obtained.[32]

Disputes

Consent must not be unreasonably withheld but may be given subject to reasonable conditions including a condition that it shall be removed after a period if reasonably required by the person giving the consent. Disputes on reasonableness with the Minister of Transport are to be settled by an arbitrator to be appointed in default of agreement by the President of the Institute of Civil Engineers, and disputes with other persons are to be settled by the Ministry of Transport.[33]

[30] L.G.(M.P.) Act, 1953 s. 4.   [31] L.G.(M.P.) Act, 1953 s. 4(3).
[32] L.G.(M.P.) Act, 1953 s. 5. The owner is defined in P.H.A. 1936 s. 343
[33] L.G.(M.P.) Act, 1953 s. 5.

If the shelter or accommodation obstructs access to tele-graphic lines the parish council must at request either remove it or pay to the Postmaster General the additional cost of gaining access.[34] Similar provisions apply to sewers, pipe subways or wires belonging to or maintained by a local authority or any gas, electricity, water, hydraulic power, tramcar or trolley under-takers. Disputes on the amount payable are settled by arbitra-tion or (if the amount does not exceed £50 and either party so requests) by a Court of Summary Jurisdiction.[35]

A parish council may maintain 'bus shelters and other accommodation and queue-barriers erected without statutory authority before 14th July, 1953.[36]

J. OTHER SHELTERS AND SEATS

Subject to safeguards[37] a parish council may provide and maintain seats and shelters in, or on, any land abutting on any road' within the parish; for this purpose a 'road' excludes a special road'[38] but includes any highway, road, lane, footway, square, court, alley or passage to which the public has access.[39]

K. POSTAL FACILITIES

If a parish council or parish meeting (where there is no parish council) considers that it would benefit the parish that a post office, telegraphic office or other facility should be provided in or outside the parish for the inhabitants it may guarantee any expected loss which the Postmaster General may sustain.[40]

A rural district council may exercise similar powers but the consent of the parish council or parish meeting is required if the facilities to be provided for a parish are to be situated outside its boundaries.[41]

It takes two to make such an agreement and post office reluctance has recently made such agreements very rare. In practice the need arises most often in connexion with public

---

[34] L.G.(M.P.) Act, 1953 s. 6(1).
[35] L.G.(M.P.) Act, 1953 s. 6 and P.H.A. 1936 s. 278.
[36] L.G.(M.P.) Act, 1953 s. 7.   [37] See page 192.
[38] See page 248.   [39] P.C.A. 1957 ss. 1(1) and 7.
[40] Post Office Act, 1953 s. 51.   [41] Post Office Act, 1953 s. 51.

telephones and it is usually simpler and more effective to pro-vide coin box telephones as part of the equipment of a hall but in a position where it is accessible when the hall is closed.

29

Powers Relating to the Dead

A. WAR MEMORIALS

A parish council or parish meeting may maintain, repair and protect any war memorial whether vested in it or not, and may adapt it so as to serve as a memorial for any war subsequent to that for which it was erected.[1] Expenditure must not exceed the equivalent of one and one-third of a 1d. (·6p) rate.[2]

B. MORTUARIES

Provision

A parish council may, and if required by the Minister must, provide a mortuary or post-mortem room, and may make bye-laws with respect to its management and the charges for its use.[3]

A burial authority under the burial acts other than a parish council, may, with the consent of the parish meeting, provide a mortuary.[4]

Disposal of Bodies

A parish council which has provided a mortuary may provide for the burial of the bodies received into it[5] but the burial expenses are chargeable to the deceased's estate.[6]

Where there is no ascertainable person responsible for the burial of the deceased, it is the duty of the rural district council to provide for the burial of the body,[7] but the parish council may do so if it wishes.

[1] W.M.A. 1923 ss. 1 and 3 amended by L.G.A. 1948 s. 133.
[2] W.M.A. 1923 s. 2(a) amended by L.G.A. 1929 s. 75(1) and P.C.A. 1957 s. 8(2).   [3] P.H.A. 1936 s. 198.
[4] B.A. 1852 s. 42, B.A. 1853 s. 7 and L.G.A. 1894 s. 7(3).
[5] P.H.A. 1936 s. 198.   [6] Rees v. Hughes (1948) K.B. 517.
[7] National Assistance Act, 1948 s. 50.

C. HEARSES

Where the burial acts have been adopted a parish council or burial board may make such arrangements as it thinks fit for facilitating the conveyance of bodies from the parish or place of death to any place of burial;[8] this includes the purchase, housing and maintenance of a hearse or bier.

D. POWER OF CONTRIBUTION

A parish council may contribute towards the expenses incurred by any other person in maintaining any place where the remains of the inhabitants are or may be buried.[9]

The uses of this sweepingly defined power are not confined to publicly-owned burial places nor to those vested in ecclesiastical authorities nor even to places situated in the parish. It extends to places of all denominations and even to those in private lands. Expenditure is subject to the rate limits.

E. CLOSED AND DISUSED CHURCHYARDS

Order in Council

Parishioners have a right of burial in their churchyard even when it is full. It is, therefore, necessary on sanitary grounds that there should be a regular procedure for extinguishing this right when the churchyard ceases to be usable. This is done by an Order in Council made on the representation of the Minister.[10] At least one month's public notice must be given and also at least ten days' notice to the parochial church council.[11] Such an order cannot apply to Jewish or Quaker or private non-parochial burial grounds unless it specifically mentions them,[12] and its operation may be postponed or varied by a later order.[11] Its effect is merely to make further burials unlawful; it does not alter the legal responsibility for maintenance.

Certificate

A closed churchyard accordingly is maintainable by the parochial church council and in a parish where there is no other

---

[8] B.A. 1852 s. 41. See also *Brooke Little on Burials*, Third Ed., page 168.
[9] P.C.A. 1957 s. 10.
[10] For special circumstances which can arise in a New Town see page 197.
[11] B.A. 1853 s. 1.   [12] B.A. 1855 s. 2.

burial authority, the parochial church council may recover the cost of repair from the rating authority by means of a certificate which is in effect a precept. Where, however, the parish is represented on a parish council the position is entirely different; so long as the parochial church council maintains the closed churchyard at its own expense, it retains control of it, but if once it issues a certificate to recover the cost from the rating authority, its functions and liabilities with respect to the maintenance and repair of the churchyard pass automatically to the parish council whether it wants them or not.[13] A certificate issued in these circumstances is sometimes called a final certificate.

Effect of Final Certificate

A final certificate can only be issued for expenses already incurred, and the amount for which it is issued must be paid by the rating authority to the parochial church council and charged upon the parish, but the amount is not charged against the parish council and is not, therefore, taken into account in computing the parish council's expenditure for the purposes of the rate limits. A final certificate may be issued for any amount.

No final certificate can be issued until after an Order in Council has been made and therefore a parish council cannot be required to maintain a churchyard which is disused but not closed.

A final certificate does not transfer to the parish council the ownership or any other legal interest in the churchyard. As a result, for instance, the fruit of any trees would continue to belong to the person entitled to it before the certificate was given.

Standard of Maintenance

The body responsible for a closed churchyard is bound to maintain it in decent order and also do the necessary repair to the walls and other fences.[14] This probably means that the churchyard must be maintained in such a state that it would not offend the susceptibilities of a reasonable Christian, and that the maintaining body must do such repairs to the walls and fences as are necessary to this end. There is accordingly a legal obligation to bring an 'indecent' closed churchyard up to a

[13] B.A. 1855 s. 18 and L.G.A. 1933 s. 169(2).
[14] B.A. 1855 s. 18.
K*

standard of decency (even at great expense) but the Burial Acts do not permit a higher standard than this.

Open Spaces Act

If the parish council wishes to effect improvements beyond the standard of decency, it may, however, use its powers under the Open Spaces Act, 1906.[15]

The expense of maintaining a closed churchyard or burial ground is charged on the parish *in which it is situated*.[16]

F. BURIAL GROUNDS AND CEMETERIES

A *burial ground* is a place for the interment of the dead which has been provided under the Burial Acts, 1852–1906. In rural districts the only authorities for administering burial grounds are parish councils, burial boards and joint burial committees.

A *cemetery* is a similar place provided under the Public Health (Interments) Act, 1879. None of the burial authorities may provide a cemetery.

There is no difference to the naked eye.

G. ADOPTION OF BURIAL POWERS

Where the Burial Acts have not been adopted a parish meeting may at any time be convened for the whole or part of a parish[17] to consider whether a burial ground shall be provided, and it must be convened if the Minister gives notice that he intends to make representations to the Queen in Council that the parish churchyard or burial ground be closed.[18]

Fourteen days' notice is required.[18]

A resolution that a burial ground be provided is deemed to be an adoption of the burial acts;[19] a copy of the resolution of adoption signed by the chairman must be forwarded to the Minister,[20] together with a certified copy of the notice convening the meeting, a statement of the votes cast and, if a poll was held, a statement by the returning officer of the result.

---

[15] See page 226.
[16] R. v. The Burial Board of Bishop Wearmouth (1879) 5 Q.B.D. 67.
[17] B.A. 1852 s. 10, 1855 s. 12 and 1857 s. 5.   [18] B.A. 1855 s. 3.
[19] L.G.A. 1894 s. 7(8).   [20] B.A. 1852 s. 10.

H. ADMINISTRATIVE AUTHORITIES

Where there is a parish council it becomes the burial authority,[21] otherwise it becomes necessary to appoint a burial board. A burial board may be appointed for the whole or for a part of a parish whether the relevant area has previously had a separate burial ground[22] or not,[23] but if it is desired to provide a burial ground for more than one parish[24] or within a parish for more than one area any one of which already has a burial ground, a joint board may be appointed provided that the previous sanction of the Minister is obtained.[25] A joint board consists of the boards of the respective areas acting as one,[26] and it may be dissolved at any time before it has provided a burial ground.[27] This type of arrangement is unlikely to be made nowadays because parish meetings may concur in providing a joint burial ground and may agree on the apportionment of the expenses;[28] and it will then be comparatively simple to appoint a joint committee even though it will be necessary for a parish meeting (where there is no separate parish council) to obtain an order from the county council empowering it to appoint members to such a committee.[29]

In a few cases where burial boards existed before 1894 for areas comprised in more than one parish, the authorities concerned were required to appoint a joint committee.[30] A few of these old committees still exist.

A burial board is elected by the parish meeting or by poll in the usual manner.[31] The cost of a poll is borne as part of the expenses of administering the act.[32]

Meetings of all burial authorities must be open to the public.[33]

I. CONSTITUTION OF A BURIAL BOARD

A burial board, whether singular or joint, is a corporation with perpetual succession, a common seal and power to hold land.[34]

[21] L.G.A. 1894 s. 7(7).   [22] B.A. 1855 s. 12.
[23] B.A. 1857 s. 5.   [24] B.A. 1857 s. 10 R. & V.A. 1925 s. 68(4).
[25] B.A. 1860 s. 4.   [26] B.A. 1852 s. 23.   [27] B.A. 1857 s. 1.
[28] B.A. 1852 s. 23.   [29] Under L.G.A. 1933 s. 273.
[30] L.G.A. 1894 s. 53.   [31] B.A. 1852 s. 11.
[32] Burial Boards (Contested Elections) Act, 1885.
[33] Public Bodies (Admission to Meetings) Act, 1960 Schedule.
[34] B.A. 1852 s. 24.

Singular Board

A burial board for a single area consists of not less than three nor more than nine members who must be ratepayers, but the incumbent is qualified whether he is a ratepayer or not.[35] Members retire annually by thirds but remain eligible and they may resign in writing addressed to the chairman of the parish meeting.[35] The parish meeting may fill a casual vacancy within one month of its arising but if it fails to do so the vacancy may be filled by co-option.[36]

Joint Board

A joint board may consist of any number not being less than three times nor more than nine times the number of areas for which it acts, and the number of members appointed by each area is settled by agreement.[37]

Quorum

The quorum of a burial board is three,[38] and any two members may by written summons at forty-eight hours' notice convene a meeting, which must also be publicly notified.[39]

J. SPECIAL RULES ON FINANCES OF BURIAL BOARDS

A burial board may borrow with the consent of the parish meeting and of the Minister for providing a burial ground and chapels.[40] It may reborrow.[41] The Public Works Loan Board has power to lend to a burial board.[42]

A burial board may borrow by mortgage or automatic charge[43] or (unlike a parish council) by terminable annuity for a life or lives or for years not exceeding thirty.[44]

The accounts are audited annually in March by two persons (not being members) appointed annually by the parish meeting.[45]

---

[35] B.A. 1852 s. 11.
[37] B.A. 1852 s. 23.
[39] B.A. 1852 s. 13.
[41] B.A. 1854 s. 9.
[43] P.W.L.A. 1965.
[45] B.A. 1852 s. 18.

[36] B.A. 1855 s. 4.
[38] B.A. 1852 s. 14.
[40] B.A. 1852 s. 20
[42] B.A. 1852 s. 21.
[44] B.A. 1857 s. 21.

K. PROVISION OF BURIAL GROUNDS

Land or Other Facilities

The burial authority must provide burial facilities with all convenient speed.[46] This may be done by purchasing a cemetery or contracting for a right of burial in a cemetery, but the normal and convenient practice is to provide a ground in the parish though it may be outside it if necessary.[47] If more than one burial ground is to be provided the Home Secretary's approval must be obtained.[48] Parish or charity land may be appropriated with the consent of the parish meeting and the Minister, but charity land must only be taken subject to conditions laid down by the Chancery Division of the High Court.[49]

100 *Yard Rule*

Land must not be used for burials within a hundred yards of a dwelling house (measured from its walls in a straight line to the grave[50]) without the written consent of the owner, lessee and occupier of any pre-existing house.[51] Breach of this rule makes the offender liable to a fine not exceeding £10.[52]

Procedure

The land chosen should preferably have a medium soil; it should not be on a slope but should be well drained, and the site should be such that there will be no risk of contaminating water supplies. At two burials per grave, one acre may be expected to last seventy years for each 2,000 inhabitants; the amount of land to be bought should suffice to provide graves for at least the duration of the loan period.

Having chosen the proposed site, outline planning permission should be obtained; trial boreholes should then be sunk and the Medical Officer of Health should be asked to certify the suitability of the soil. If the owner will not permit entry, the parish council should serve a notice of entry for between three and fourteen days under the Lands Clauses etc. Act, Section 84, and then enter the land. It remains liable for any damage and for fencing the holes.

[46] B.A. 1852 s. 25. [47] B.A. 1852 s. 26.
[48] B.A. 1857 s. 3 and B.A. 1900 1st Schedule. [49] B.A. 1852 s. 29.
[50] Wrights Case (1887) 18 Q.B.D. 783 Monflet v. Cole (1872) **L.R.** 8 Exch. 32.
[51] B.A. 1855 s. 9 and B.A. 1906 s. 1. [52] B.A. 1855 s. 8.

Next the District Valuer should be asked to negotiate a price and at the same time the Minister's approval for the site should be requested. When this has been received, but not before, the parish council should start proceedings for raising a loan and (if the owner is unwilling to sell) for compulsory purchase[53] and should apply for planning approval for the actual layout of the site. The land should then actually be purchased, conveyed to the parish council and laid out in accordance with the terms of planning approval, and having regard to the 100 yard rule.

A burial ground provided under the burial acts is to be the burial ground of the parish,[54] and it may be laid out and embellished as may be fitting and proper.[55]

Consecration

Application may be made to the Bishop for the consecration of such part of a burial ground as is approved by the Home Secretary; if no such application is made within a reasonable time after a request has been made on that behalf, the Home Secretary, on being satisfied of public demand and that the fees have been paid or secured, may make the application himself and thereupon the burial authority must make the necessary arrangements for the consecration.[56] The consecrated portions must be permanently marked off from the unconsecrated but no wall is necessary.[57]

The Home Secretary's approval is also required if land is to be specially allotted for the use of any other denomination.

A burial authority has a general power of management regulation and control[58] and can therefore determine such matters as layout, design and treatment of monuments and whether or not kerbs should be used or mounds levelled. These powers cannot be used capriciously so as, for instance, to infringe rights acquired by someone else under a contract.[59]

L. MANAGEMENT

Fees for Plots, etc.

A burial authority may sell the exclusive right of burial in a plot either in perpetuity or for a limited period, the right to

[53] See page 111.
[54] B.A. 1852 s. 32.
[55] B.A. 1852 s. 30.
[56] B.A. 1900 s. 1.
[57] B.A. 1857 s. 11.
[58] B.A. 1852 s. 38.
[59] For removal of monuments in disused burial grounds see page 228.

construct a vault and to erect monuments and inscriptions,[60] but disputes as to the fitness of an inscription in the consecrated portion of a burial ground must be determined by the Bishop.[61] The fees and charges are fixed by the burial authority and may be altered with the consent of the parish meeting[62] and the approval of the Minister.[63] They must be printed and exhibited in a conspicuous place in the burial ground.[64]

Minister's and Sexton's Fees

A burial authority must fix a table of fees for actual services rendered by any minister of religion and the sexton. The table must be submitted to the Home Secretary who may approve it with or without modifications. The fees must be the same in respect of burials in consecrated and in unconsecrated ground. If the authority fails to make a table, the Home Secretary may make it himself.[65]

The fees are collected by the burial authority and paid over to the person concerned by agreement or in default of agreement as directed by the Home Secretary.[65]

Regulations and Inspection

The Minister may make regulations for the protection of public health and the maintenance of public decency in burial grounds and places for the reception of bodies before burial[66] and may cause them to be inspected whether such regulations have been made or not.[67]

Regulations have in fact been made. Grave spaces must measure at least $9' \times 4'$ for adults and either $6' \times 3'$ or $4\frac{1}{2}' \times 4'$ for children under twelve; only one body may be buried at one time in a common earthen grave except in the case of members of the same family; no unwalled grave may be opened, in the case of adults for at least 14 years after burial and in the case of a child for at least eight save to bury another member of the same family; at least one foot of earth must always be left undisturbed above a coffin, and coffins in vaults or walled graves must be bricked in so as to be air-tight and the bricks never disturbed.

[60] B.A. 1852 s. 33.   [61] B.A. 1852 s. 38.
[62] B.A. 1852 s. 34.   [63] B.A. 1855 s. 7.
[64] B.A. 1852 s. 34.   [65] B.A. 1900 s. 3.
[66] B.A. 1852 s. 44. The regulations are not printed in the series of Statutory Rules and Orders.   [67] B.A. 1855 s. 8.

Offences

It is an offence for anyone having the care of a burial ground to obstruct inspection or to violate, neglect or fail to comply with the regulations. The maximum fine is £10.[68]

It is an offence wilfully to destroy or injure any building, wall or fence belonging to a burial ground or to destroy or injure any tree or plant therein or to daub or disfigure any wall thereof or put up any bill therein or on any wall or wilfully to destroy, injure or deface any monument, tablet or inscription or to do any wilful damage in the burial ground, or to play any game, or discharge firearms (save at a military funeral) or unlawfully to disturb a funeral. Offenders are liable to forfeit a sum not exceeding £5 to the burial authority for each offence.[69]

Troops on manoeuvres are not allowed to enter a burial ground.[70]

M. PROVISION OF CHAPELS

A burial authority at its own cost may provide a chapel but neither it nor the land upon which it is built must be consecrated or appropriated for the special use of a particular denomination.[71]

On the other hand it may at the request and expense of residents erect a denominational chapel upon land appropriated to the use of such denomination. Where such a request is made and the necessary funds are tendered or secured the Home Secretary may order the burial authority to erect the chapel if it neglects or refuses to comply with the request, and such an order may be enforced by *mandamus*.[71]

N. WALES AND MONMOUTH

On 31st March, 1920,[72] churchyards and burial grounds belonging to the Welsh church were vested in the Welsh Church Commissioners;[73] those given as private benefactions since 24th March, 1662/3[74] were soon transferred to the

[68] B.A. 1855 s. 8.
[69] B.A. 1852 s. 40 and Cemeteries Clauses Act, 1847 ss. 58 and 59.
[70] Manoeuvres Act, 1958 s. 2(2)(b).   [71] B.A. 1900 s. 2.
[72] Welsh Church (Temporalities) Act, 1919 s. 2.
[73] Welsh Church Act, 1914 s. 4.
[74] ibid. s. 7 and Calendar (New Style) Act, 1750 s. 1.

Representative Body of the Church in Wales;[75] the majority of the remainder (comprising, amongst others, most of the old churchyards) were vested in the Welsh Representative Body in 1st December, 1946.[76]

Transferred Churchyards

In a certain number of cases (the so-called 'transferred' churchyards) the churchyard or burial ground was transferred to the existing incumbent and at the termination of the incumbency to the burial authority, if any, and if none to the parish council or the representative body *of the Parish*.[77] If the burial ground adjoins a church vested in the Welsh Representative Body it is held subject to a right of way for clergy and worshippers; funerals are forbidden during hours of Divine Service; the authority must maintain any road or path through the burial ground and where any land is needed for enlargement of the church it may be so used.[78] Subject to these 'four rules' the churchyard is to be held at the death of the incumbent as if it were a burial ground under the Burial Acts and as if the Burial Acts were in force in the parish, and accordingly if there was no parish council a burial board has to be constituted.[79] The burial authority or parish council may agree with the Welsh Representative Body for the transfer of the churchyard to the latter and thereupon the 'four rules' and the burial acts cease to apply to it in the manner set out in the Welsh Church Act, 1914.[80]

Duties of Welsh Representative Body

The Welsh Representative Body must maintain its burial grounds in decent order[81] and on a burial ground vesting in the Body any liability under any other enactment or at common law or by custom ceases.[82] Accordingly a parish council is not bound to maintain a closed churchyard in respect of which a certificate has been given once it is vested in the Welsh Representative Body.

[75] Welsh Church Act, 1914 s. 8(a).
[76] Welsh Church (Burial Grounds) Act, 1945 s. 1 and S.R. & O. 1946 No. 1538.
[77] Welsh Church Act, 1914 s. 8(b).   [78] ibid. s. 24(3).   [79] ibid. s. 24(4).
[80] Welsh Church (Burial Grounds) Act, 1945 s. 2.
[81] ibid. s. 3(1).   [82] ibid. s. 3(2).

O. CREMATION

Any burial authority (including a parish council and a burial board) may provide a crematorium.[83]

Such a crematorium must not without the written consent of the owner, lessee and occupier be within two hundred yards of a house, nor must it be within fifty yards of a highway nor in the consecrated part of a burial ground[84] and burnings may not take place unless the site and plans have been approved by the Minister nor until the burial authority has certified to the Home Secretary that it is complete in accordance with the plans and properly equipped.[85]

The maintenance and inspection of crematoria and the circumstances in which cremations may take place are regulated by order of the Home Secretary[86] and breach of the regulations is subject to heavy penalties.[87] He also has power to fix fees for burial services[88] and medical certificates.[89] Fees for burnings are fixed by the Minister.[90]

An incumbent may but is not bound to officiate at a cremation service but if he refuses, any other priest of the Established Church may do so with the permission of the Bishop and at the request of the executor or of the burial authority.[91]

Whilst it is true that only larger parish councils can afford to provide crematoria, there is no reason why a number of them should not provide one jointly.

---

[83] Cremation Act, 1902 ss. 2 and 4.   [84] ibid. s. 5.
[85] Cremation Act, 1952 s. 1.
[86] Cremation Act, 1902 s. 7 amended by Cremation Act, 1952 s. 2.
[87] Cremation Act, 1902 s. 8.   [88] ibid. s. 12.
[89] Cremation Act, 1952 s. 3.   [90] Cremation Act, 1902 s. 9.
[91] ibid. s. 11.

APPENDIX

Note

Parliament has dealt somewhat hardly with parish law and many enactments have been amended, partially repealed, extended, restricted or reinterpreted.

In the text which follows, irrelevant and repealed legislation has so far as possible been omitted together with sections and schedules effecting the relevant repeals. Where later acts have altered the meaning of previous legislation the dangerous words in the previous act are printed in *italics*. The amendments made by the Decimal Currency Act, 1969 have been included at the appropriate points but the act itself is not printed.

Enactments whose effect is restricted to parish authorities other than parish councils are printed between square brackets.

As few people, even the present author, ever seem to need to wade through the legislative jungle of the Burial and Cremation Acts, these have been omitted from this edition.

It should be assumed, unless the contrary is evident, that legislation dealing with parish councils applies equally to rural boroughs.

Extracts from Legislation

Inclosure Act, 1845

15. And be it enacted, That no Town Green or Village Green shall be subject to be inclosed under this Act; provided that in every Case in which an Inclosure of Lands in the Parish in which such Town Green or Village Green may be situate shall be made under the Authority of this Act it shall be lawful for the *Commissioners*, if they shall think fit, to direct that such Town Green or Village Green, provided such Green be of equal or greater Extent, be allotted to the Churchwardens and Overseers of the Poor of such Parish, in trust to allow the same to be used for the Purposes of Exercise and Recreation, and the same shall be allotted and awarded accordingly, in like Manner, and with the like Provisions for making or maintaining the Fences thereof, and preserving the Surface thereof, and draining and levelling the same where Occasion shall require, as herein-after directed concerning the Allotments to be made for the Purposes of Exercise and Recreation; and such Green may be so allotted in addition to other Land which may be allotted for the Purposes of Exercise and Recreation, or, if the *Commissioners* shall think it sufficient, may be allotted in substitution for other Land which might have been required to be allotted for such Purpose; and in every Case in which such Town Green or Village Green shall adjoin Land subject to be inclosed under this Act, and shall not be separated from such Land by Fences or known Bounds, the *Commissioners* shall, in the Provisional Order concerning such Inclosure, set out a Boundary Line between such Green and the adjoining Land, and shall in their annual General Report mention and describe such Boundary.

30. And be it enacted, That in the Provisional Order of the *Commissioners* concerning the Inclosure under the Provisions of this Act of any Waste Land of any Manor on which the Tenants of such Manor have Rights of Common, or of any other Land subject to Rights of Common which may be exercised at all Times of the Year for Cattle *levant and couchant* or to any Rights of Common which may be exercised at all Times of the Year, and which shall *not be limited by Number or Stints*, it shall be lawful for the *Commissioners* to require, and in their Provisional Order to specify, as One of the Terms and Conditions of such Inclosure, the Appropriation of an Allotment for the Purposes of Exercise and Recreation for the Inhabitants of the Neighbourhood, ... and if in the provisional order for such inclosure the *Commissioners* shall not have required the appropriation of an allotment for the purposes of exercise and recreation, the *Commissioners* shall in their annual general report state the grounds on which they shall have abstained from requiring such appropriation.

31. And be it enacted, That in the provisional order of the *Commissioners* concerning the inclosure under the provisions of this Act of any waste land of any manor on which the tenants of such manor have rights of common, or of any land whatsoever subject to rights of common which may be exercised at all times of the year for cattle *levant and couchant as aforesaid*, or to any rights of common which may be exercised at all times of the year, and which shall *not be limited by number or stints*, it shall be lawful for the *Commissioners* to require and specify as one of the terms and conditions of such inclosure the appropriation of such an allotment for the labouring poor as the *Commissioners* shall think necessary, with reference to the circumstances of each particular case, and if in the provisional order for such inclosure the *Commissioners* shall not have required the appropriation of an allotment for the labouring poor the *Commissioners* shall in their annual general report state the grounds on which they shall have abstained from requiring such appropriation.

72. And be it enacted, That the valuer acting in the matter of any inclosure shall allot to the *Surveyor of the Highways* for the time being of the parish in which the land proposed to be inclosed, or any part thereof, shall be situate, and to his successors for ever, such part of the land proposed to be inclosed as by the instructions given to such valuer shall have been directed to be appropriated for supplying stone, gravel, or other materials for the repairs of roads and ways, as aforesaid, or in case no such instructions shall have been given in this behalf, and the valuer shall think an allotment necessary for the purposes aforesaid, such part as the valuer shall think fit; and such allotments shall be inclosed and fenced as the valuer shall direct, and shall from the confirmation of the award be vested in *the surveyor of the highways* within the said parish for the time being, in trust for the purposes aforesaidt and the grass and herbage of such allotments shall belong to such persons as by the valuer shall be directed, and if he shall make no such direction then such *surveyor* shall from time to time let any such allotment, reserving the right to get and take away such stone, gravel, and other materials when and as he shall think fit, for the most money that can be obtained for the same.

73. And be it enacted, That the valuer acting in the matter of any inclosure shall and may, in pursuance of the directions of or in any manner not inconsistent with the directions of the provisional order of the *Commissioners*, or any Act hereafter to be passed, or the instructions given to such valuer as aforesaid, set out and allot such part of the lands to be inclosed as by such provisional order or Act or instructions respectively shall have been directed to be appropriated as a place of exercise and recreation for the inhabitants of the said parish and neighbourhood; and such allotment shall,

be made and awarded to the *church-wardens and overseers* for the time being of the parish in which the same shall be situated, and shall be held by the *churchwardens and overseers* for the time being of the said parish for the purposes aforesaid, and shall be in the first instance fenced, and, where occasion shall require, drained and levelled by the valuer, the expense in such case to be considered part of the expenses of the inclosure, or shall be fenced by any person to whom adjoining land shall be allotted, as the valuer may direct; and the fences of such allotment shall for ever afterwards be repaired and maintained, and the surface thereof kept drained and level, by such *churchwardens and overseers*, or by the *churchwardens and overseers* of the several parishes interested therein, in such proportions and manner as shall be directed by the valuer, out of the rents to be received for the herbage of the said allotment, or out of the *poor rate* of the said parish or respective parishes, or otherwise; and the grass and herbage growing upon such allotment may be from time to time let by the *churchwardens and overseers* in whom the same shall be vested, and the rents which shall be received by them for the same shall be by them from time to time applied, in the first place, in maintaining and repairing the fences of the said allotment, and keeping the surface thereof drained and level, as aforesaid, and the valuer shall in like manner set out and allot such part of the land to be inclosed as by such provisional order or act or instructions as aforesaid shall have been directed to be appropriated as an allotment for the labouring poor unto the *churchwardens and overseers of the poor* of the parish in which such allotment shall be situate, and the said valuer shall in like manner, in pursuance of the directions of or in any manner not inconsistent with the directions of such provisional order or act or instructions as aforesaid, set out and allot, for the other public purposes mentioned in such provisional order or act or instructions as aforesaid, such parts of the land to be inclosed as shall have been thereby respectively directed to be set apart for such purposes, and such allotments shall be made to such persons respectively, with such regulations and provisions as to the fencing, maintenance, use, and enjoyment thereof respectively, as the valuer, with the approbation of the *Commissioners*, shall direct; and in every case in which the valuer with such approbation of the *Commissioners*, shall not think it necessary or proper to direct the same to be otherwise made, such allotments shall be made to the *churchwardens and overseers of the poor* for the time being of the parish in which such allotments shall be situate; and all allotments which shall be made to the *churchwardens and overseers* under this act shall be held by the *churchwardens and overseers of the poor* for the time being in the same manner and with the same legal powers and incidents as if the same allotments were lands belonging to the parish, but in trust nevertheless for the purposes for which the same shall be allotted, and subject, as to the said allotment for the labouring poor, to the provisions in relation thereto herein-after contained, and as to all other such allotments, subject to such directions for the maintenance, fencing, management, and use thereof as the valuer, with the approbation of the *Commissioners*, may think fit.

74. *Words repealed empowering the Commissioners to allot land for exercise and recreation to persons entitled to an allotment* the person to whom the land so to be appropriated shall be allotted, and all future owners thereof, shall, unless it shall be otherwise directed by the award, be subject to the obligation of maintaining the fences of such land, and of preserving the surface thereof in good condition, and of permitting such land to be at all times used for exercise and recreation by the inhabitants of the parish and neighbourhood, and, subject to such obligations, the herbage of such land shall belong to the person to whom such land shall be so allotted.

87. And be it enacted, That where the freemen or burgesses of any city or borough, or the householders or inhabitant householders of any town or place, or any class or description of such freemen, burgesses, householders or inhabitant householders, or any other persons as a class, shall be entitled to rights of common or other rights over the lands to be inclosed, it shall be lawful for the valuer to award in respect of such rights one or more allotment or allotments, for the benefit of the class so entitled, to any two or more trustees, who shall be nominated by the majority at such meeting as herein-after mentioned, or in case two or more trustees shall not be nominated at such meeting, then to such trustees as the *Commissioners* shall approve, with provisions for the appointment of new trustees from time to time, or to the *churchwardens and overseers of the poor* of the parish in which each allotment shall be situate, in trust for the parties entitled to the right in respect of which the allotment shall be made; and it shall be also lawful for the valuer, having regard to such instructions, if any, as may have been resolved on at such meeting as hereafter mentioned, or to such instructions as shall be given by the *Commissioners* in this behalf, to direct in what manner and under what regulations such allotment shall be occupied or enjoyed by the persons from time to time entitled to the benefit thereof, and (in case the valuer, having regard to such instructions, shall think fit,) to give directions and powers for the letting of such allotment from year to year, or for any term of years, subject to such provisions and restrictions as the said valuer, with the approbation of the *Commissioners*, shall think fit, and for the receipt of the money to arise from such letting, and for the application of such money for the benefit of the persons entitled to the benefit of the allotment, and to give all such directions and provisions for the fencing, draining, and management of such allotment, as the valuer may think expedient.

88. Provided also, and be it enacted, That it shall be lawful for the valuer, with the approbation of the *Commissioners* and of such meeting as herein-

after mentioned, to sell and dispose of the whole or any part of any allotment to which any such class of persons as aforesaid shall be entitled under this Act; and the allotment or any part thereof so sold shall be conveyed by the *Commissioners* as the purchaser shall direct, and the *Commissioners* shall sign a receipt for the purchase money, which shall be a sufficient discharge for the same; and the purchase money arising from the sale, or the surplus thereof after payment thereout of any expenses to which the same shall be liable, shall, with the approbation of the *Commissioners*, be paid to any trustee or trustees, upon trust for the investment thereof, with provisions for the appointment of new trustees from time to time, and for the application of the interest and annual produce of such investment to such purposes, for the benefit of the persons who would have been entitled to such allotment, or the part thereof so sold, in case the same had not been sold, as the *Commissioners* shall approve, and by the final award in the matter of such inclosure direct.

108. The allotment which upon any inclosure under this Act shall be made to the labouring poor, shall be under the management *of the incumbent of the parish or ecclesiastical district in which such allotment shall be situate* (*or the officiating minister for the time being nominated by the incumbent for that purpose*), *the churchwarden, if there be but one, or* (*if there be more than one*) *one of the churchwardens for the time being of such parish, and two other persons who shall be rated to the relief of the poor in such parish* and such *churchwarden* where there is more than one *churchwarden* shall be yearly named, and such two other persons shall be yearly chosen and appointed, at the same time, and by the same persons, and in the same manner, as the *overseers of the poor* for such parish shall be chosen and appointed, and shall continue in office in like manner until the next appointment of *overseers*, or until others are named and chosen and appointed in their stead; and such *incumbent* (*or officiating minister*), *churchwarden* and two other persons for the

time being shall be styled 'the allotment wardens' of the parish, and shall manage and let the said allotment as thereinafter provided, and all things by this act authorised to be done by such allotment wardens may be done by any two of them, and in the event of the death or retirement from office of any one or more of the said allotment wardens the surviving or continuing wardens may act as if no such vacancy had happened.

109. The *allotment wardens* shall from time to time let the allotment under their management in gardens not exceeding a quarter of an acre each to such poor inhabitants of the parish for one year, or from year to year, at such rents, payable at such times, on such terms and conditions, not inconsistent with the provisions of this act, as they shall think fit: provided always, that the *Commissioners* may frame such regulations, not inconsistent with the provisions of the act, for the letting of such allotments as aforesaid, as they may think advisable, and such regulations shall be obligatory on the *allotment wardens* during five years from the date thereof or during such shorter period as the *Commissioners* shall direct; provided also, that the gardens so to be let shall be let free of all tithe or tithe rent-charge (if any), rates, taxes, and assessments whatsoever, and shall before the first letting thereof, and once at least in every ten years after such first letting, be valued by a competent person to be appointed by the *allotment wardens* for that purpose, who shall estimate the full rent which the same would be worth to be let by the year for farming purposes, all tithe or tithe rent-charge, rates, taxes, and assessments, being borne by the landlord, and shall verify such valuation by solemn declaration under the statute; . . . and the *allotment wardens* shall, for the purposes of all rates and taxes, be deemed the occupiers of such allotment and shall pay all rates and taxes, tithes and tithe rent-charge (if any), in respect thereof: provided always, that no building whatsoever shall, under any such letting as aforesaid or otherwise, on any pretence, be erected for or used as a dwelling on any such garden or on any part of any such allotment; and in case any such building shall be erected or used as aforesaid contrary to this provision, the *allotment wardens* shall forthwith pull down the same, and sell and dispose of the materials thereof, and the produce of such sale shall be applicable in like manner as the rents of such gardens.

110. If the rent reserved upon the letting of any garden by the *allotment wardens* shall at any time be in arrear for 40 days, or if at any time during the tenancy, being not less than three calendar months after the commencement thereof, it shall appear to the *allotment wardens* that the occupier of such garden shall not have duly observed the terms and conditions of his tenancy, or shall have gone to reside more than one mile out of the parish, then and in every such case the *allotment wardens* shall serve a notice upon such occupier, or in case he shall have gone to reside out of the parish, shall affix the same to the door of the church of the parish, determining the tenancy at the expiration of one month after such notice shall have been so served or affixed, and thereupon such tenancy shall be determined accordingly: . . .

111. In case upon the determination of any such tenancy as aforesaid the occupier of any such garden shall refuse to quit and deliver up possession thereof, or if any other person shall unlawfully enter upon, take, or hold possession of any such garden, or of any part of such allotment, the *allotment wardens* may recover possession by proceedings in the County Court.

112. All rents payable in respect of the allotment under the management of the *allotment wardens* shall be payable to *such wardens*, who shall have the same remedies for recovery thereof by distress and otherwise as if the legal estate of and in such allotment were vested in them under this Act; and such rents shall be applicable, in the first place, to the payment of all rates, taxes, tithes tithe rent-charge, and of the rent-charge charged on such allotment under the provisions of this act, and of all expenses incurred by the *allotment wardens* in the execution of their trusts and powers under this act; . . .

Cemeteries Clauses Act, 1847

58. **Penalty for damaging the Cemetery.**—Every person who shall wilfully destroy or injure any building, wall or fence belonging to the cemetery, or destroy or injure any tree or plant therein, or who shall daub or disfigure any wall thereof, or put up any bill therein or on any wall thereof, or wilfully destroy, injure, or deface any monument, tablet, inscription, or gravestone within the cemetery, or do any wilful damage therein, shall forfeit for every such offence a sum not exceeding £20.

59. **Disturbances and Nuisances in Cemetery.**—Every person who shall play at any game or sport, or discharge firearms, save at a military funeral, in the cemetery, or who shall wilfully and unlawfully disturb any persons assembled in the cemetery for the purpose of burying any body therein, or who shall commit any nuisance within the cemetery, shall forfeit for every such offence a sum not exceeding £10.

Inclosure Act, 1852

14. Notwithstanding the provisions in the Inclosure Act, 1845 with reference to the fencing of allotments for exercise and recreation, and of town greens and village greens allotted for such purposes, it shall be lawful for the *Commissioners*, by an order under their seal, in such cases as they shall see fit, to direct that such allotments, town greens, and village greens respectively shall be distinguished by metes and bounds, but not fenced.

Inclosure Act, 1857

12. Protecting from Nuisances town and village greens and allotments for exercise and recreation And whereas it is expedient to provide summary means of preventing nuisances in town greens and village greens, and on land allotted and awarded upon any inclosure under the said acts as a place for exercise and recreation: if any person wilfully cause any injury or damage to any fence of any such town or village green or land, or wilfully and without lawful authority lead or drive any cattle or animal thereon, or wilfully lay any manure, soil, ashes, or rubbish, or other matter or thing thereon, or do any other act whatsoever to the injury of such town or village green, or land, or to the interruption of the use or enjoyment thereof as a place for exercise and recreation, such person shall for every such offence, upon a summary conviction thereof before two justices, upon the information of any *churchwarden or overseer* of the parish in which such town or village green or land is situate, or of the person in whom the soil of such town or village green or land may be vested, forfeit and pay, in any of the cases aforesaid, and for each and every such offence, over and above the damages occasioned thereby, any sum not exceeding £20; and it shall be lawful for any such *churchwarden or overseer* or other person as aforesaid to sell and dispose of any such manure, soil, ashes, and rubbish, or other matter or thing as aforesaid; and the proceeds arising from the sale thereof, and every such penalty as aforesaid, shall, as regards any such town or village green not awarded under the said acts or any of them to be used as a place for exercise and recreation, be applied *in aid of the rates for the repair of the public highways in the parish*, and shall, as regards the land so awarded, be applied by the person or persons in whom the soil thereof may be vested in the due maintenance of such land as a place for exercise and recreation; and if any manure, soil, ashes, or rubbish be not of sufficient value to defray the expense of removing the same, the person who laid or deposited such manure, soil, ashes, or rubbish shall repay to such *churchwarden or overseer* or other person as aforesaid the money necessarily expended in the removal thereof; and every such penalty as aforesaid shall be recovered in manner provided by the Summary Jurisdiction Act, 1848, and the amount of damage occasioned by any such offence as aforesaid shall, in case of dispute be determined by the justices by whom the offender is convicted; and the payment of the amount of such damage, and the repayments of the money necessarily expended in the removal of any manure, soil, ashes, or rubbish, shall be enforced in like manner as any such penalty.

Public Health Act, 1875

Section 164. Any urban authority may purchase or take on lease, lay out, plant, improve and maintain lands for the purpose of being used as public walks or pleasure grounds, and may support or contribute to the support of public walks or pleasure grounds provided by any person whomsoever.

Any urban authority may make byelaws for the regulation of any such public walk or pleasure ground, and may by such byelaws provide for the removal from such public walk or pleasure ground of any person infringing any such byelaws by any officer of the urban authority or constable.

Local Loans Act, 1875

34. 'For the purposes of this Act . . . "Local Authority" means . . . any authority whatsoever having power to levy a rate, as in this Act defined, also any prescribed authority.' . . . A 'rate' means a rate the proceeds of which are applicable to public local purposes and leviable on the basis of an assessment in respect of property and includes any sum which, though obtained in the first instance by a precept certificate or other document requiring payment from some authority or officer, is or can be ultimately raised out of a rate; and the levy of a rate includes the issue and enforcement of any such precept certifi- cate or document as aforesaid; and expressions relating to the levy and the assessment and making of a rate shall be construed accordingly: 'Local rate' means any rate as before defined which a local authority have power to levy or charge by way of mortgage or other- wise.

Commons Act, 1876

7. In any provisional order in relation to a common, the *inclosure commissioners* shall, in considering the expediency of the application, take into consideration the question whether such application will be for the benefit of the neighbour- hood, and shall, with a view to such benefit, insert in any such order such of the following terms and conditions (in this act referred to as statutory provi- sions for the benefit of the neighbour- hood) as are applicable to the case; that is to say,

(1) that free access is to be secured to any particular point of view; and
(2) that particular trees or objects of historical interest are to be pre- served; and
(3) that there is to be reserved, where a recreation ground is not set out, a privilege of playing games or of enjoying other species of recrea- tion at such times and in such manner and on such parts of the common as may be thought suit- able, care being taken to cause the least possible injury to the persons interested in the common; and
(4) that carriage roads, bridle paths, and footpaths over such common are to be set out in such direc- tions as may appear most com- modious; and
(5) that any other specified thing is to be done which may be thought equitable and expedient, regard being had to the benefit of the neighbourhood.

19. Whereas by several awards made under the authority of inclosure acts prior to the year 1845, fuel allotments for the poor have been set out and awarded, and vested in divers persons and bodies of persons as trustees of such allotments: and whereas under the provisions of the Inclosure Acts, 1845– 1868, and the several acts of Parliament and awards made thereunder, allot- ments for recreation grounds and field gardens have been set out and awarded to the *churchwardens and overseers* of parishes and other persons: and where- as power exists or is claimed under divers acts of parliament, to divert such allotments from the uses declared by parliament respecting the same: be it enacted, that . . . notwithstanding any- thing in any other act contained, it shall not be lawful (save as hereinafter mentioned) to authorise the use of or to use any such allotment, or any part thereof, for any other purpose than those declared concerning the same by the act of parliament and award, or either of them, under which the same has been set out: . . .

26. . . . *Allotment wardens,* if they are unable to let the allotments under their management, or any portion thereof, to the poor inhabitants of the parish in gardens not exceeding a quarter of an acre, may let the same or any unlet portion thereof, in gardens not exceed- ing an acre each to such inhabitants as aforesaid: further, it shall be the duty of *allotment wardens* to offer the gardens under their management to the poor inhabitants of the parish at a fair agricultural rent, if from time to time sufficient to satisfy all rates, taxes, tithes, tithe rent-charge, and the rent charge charged on the said allotments under the provisions of 'the General Inclosure Act, 1845' but not otherwise, instead of at such rent as is required by the said act. Moreover, if in any parish the *allotment wardens* are unable to let the allotments under their management, or any portion thereof, to the poor inhabitants of the parish in such quantities and at such rents as aforesaid, they may let the same, or such portion as may be unlet to any person whatever at the best annual rent which can be obtained for the same, without any premium or fine, and on such terms as may enable the *allotment wardens* to resume possession thereof within a period not exceeding twelve months, if it should at any time be required for such poor inhabitants as aforesaid.

This section shall apply to all land allotted to the poor for the purpose of cultivation under any inclosure act whatever, whether public or private, whether under the management of *allotment wardens*, *feoffees*, trustees, rector, or vicar and churchwardens, *overseers*, managers, or any other person or persons whatever, and whether at present cultivated or uncultivated, so that all such persons as aforesaid shall have like powers and duties as are hereinbefore given to and imposed upon *allotment wardens*.

27. The surplus rents arising from recreation grounds shall . . . be applied to all or any of the following purposes, and to no other purpose; that is to say, in improving the recreation grounds or any of them in the same parish or neighbourhood, or maintaining the drainage and fencing thereof, or in hiring or purchasing additional land for recreation grounds in the same parish or neighbourhood; and the surplus rents arising from field gardens shall, be applied to all or any of the following purposes and to no other purpose; that is to say, in improving the field gardens or any of them in the same parish or neighbourhood, or maintaining the drainage and fencing thereof, or in hiring or purchasing additional land for field gardens in the same parish or neighbourhood.

The trustees of any recreation ground and the *allotment wardens* of any field gardens may, with the approval of the *inclosure commissioners*, sell all or any part of the allotment vested in them, and out

of the proceeds of such sale purchase any fit and suitable land in the same parish or neighbourhood: provided, that the land so purchased shall be held in trust for the purposes for which the allotment so sold as aforesaid was allotted, and for no others; and provided, that the *inclosure commissioners* shall not sanction any such sale as aforesaid unless and until it shall be proved to their satisfaction that land more suitable for the purposes for which the allotment proposed to be sold was allotted may and will be forthwith purchased; and the proceeds of any such sale shall be paid to the *inclosure commissioners*, and shall remain in their hands until such purchase of other land as aforesaid.

28. The trustees of recreation grounds, where such trustees are the *overseers or churchwardens* of a parish, and the *allotment wardens* of field gardens, shall, from time to time, and at such intervals of not less than three years nor more than five years, as the *inclosure commissioners* direct, make such reports to the said *commissioners* in respect of the recreation grounds and field gardens under their management, with such particulars of the rents received by them, as the *commissioners* may require.

29. An encroachment on or inclosure of a town or village green, also any erection thereon or disturbance or interference with or occupation of the soil thereof which is made otherwise than with a view to the better enjoyment of such town or village green or recreation ground, shall be deemed to be a public nuisance, and if any person does any act in respect of which he is liable to pay damages or a penalty under section 12 of the said Inclosure Act, 1857, he may be summarily convicted thereof upon the information of any inhabitant of the parish in which such town or village green or recreation ground is situate, as well as upon the information of such persons as in the said section mentioned.

This section shall apply only in cases where a town or village green or recreation ground has a known and defined boundary.

Commons (Expenses) Act, 1878

4. The *Commissioners* may, if they think fit, specify in any provisional order for the regulation of a common, as one of the terms and conditions of the regulation, the appropriation of an allotment for the labouring poor, and the provisions of the Inclosure Acts 1845 to 1876, with respect to such allotments made upon the inclosure of a common shall apply to any such allotment made on the regulation of a common.

Commons Act, 1879

2. The improving the field gardens, or any of them, to which the 27th section of the Commons Act, 1876, applies, in the same parish or neighbourhood, or maintaining the drainage and fencing thereof, shall be one of the purposes to which the surplus rents arising from recreation grounds shall be applied.

Commonable Rights Compensation Act, 1882

3. Any moneys heretofore paid or hereafter to be paid by any railway or other public company or body corporate or otherwise under the provisions of the Lands Clauses Act, 1845, and any act incorporated therewith, or of any other act of parliament, to any local authority as specified in the schedule to this act, or to the *churchwardens and* *overseers* of a parish, in respect of any recreation ground or allotment for field gardens taken under the powers of any such act or acts of parliament shall be applied in manner provided by the Inclosure Acts 1845 to 1878, as amended by the Commons Act, 1879, with respect to the surplus rents arising from recreation grounds and field gardens respectively.

SCHEDULE

Situation of Land	Local Authority
... Elsewhere than within the metropolis or the district of an urban sanitary authority ...	... The *churchwardens and overseers* of the parish.

Disused Burial Grounds Act, 1884

2. Interpretation *See now Open Spaces Act, 1906, s. 20 for definition of the expressions 'burial ground',*[1] *'disused burial ground'*[1] *and 'building'.*[1]

3. No buildings to be erected upon disused burial grounds except for enlargement, etc. It shall not be lawful to erect any buildings upon any disused burial ground, except for the purpose of enlarging a church, chapel, meeting house, or other places of worship.

4. Saving for buildings already sanctioned Nothing in this Act shall prevent the erection of any building on a disused burial ground for which a faculty has been obtained before the passing of this Act.

5. Saving of burial grounds sold by Act of Parliament Nothing in this Act contained shall apply to any burial ground which has been sold or disposed of under the authority of any Act of Parliament.

[1] Strictly speaking these definitions are inserted in this act by the Open Spaces Act, 1887, s. 4.

Local Government Act, 1888

100. The expression 'urban authority' means, until the establishment of district councils as aforesaid, an urban sanitary authority; and after their establishment, the district council of an urban county district:

The expression 'person' includes any body of persons, whether corporate or unincorporate:

... where an area is authorised or directed by this Act to be assessed to any contributions or rates, the same shall unless otherwise provided by law, be assessed according to the standard or basis for the county rate:

The expression 'property' includes all property, real and personal, and all estates interests, easements, and rights, whether equitable or legal, in, to, and out of property real and personal, including things in action, and registers, books, and documents; and when used in relation to any quarter sessions, clerk of the peace, justices, board, sanitary authority, or other authority, includes any property which on the appointed day belongs to, or is vested in, or held in trust for, or would but for this Act have, on or after that day, belonged to, or been vested in, or held in trust for, such quarter sessions, clerk of the peace, justices, board, sanitary authority, or other authority:

The expression 'powers' includes rights, jurisdiction, capacities, privileges, and immunities:

The expression 'duties' includes responsibilities and obligations:

The expression 'liabilities' includes liability to any proceeding for enforcing any duty or for punishing the breach of any duty, and includes all debts and liabilities to which any authority are or would but for this Act be liable or subject to, whether accrued due at the date of the transfer or subsequently accruing, and includes any obligation to carry or apply any money to any sinking fund or to any particular purpose:

The expression 'powers, duties, and liabilities,' includes all powers, duties, and liabilities conferred or imposed by or arising under any local and personal Act:

The expression 'expenses' includes costs and charges:

The expression 'costs' includes charges and expenses:

Interpretation Act, 1889

Section 19. Meaning of 'person' in future Acts.—In this Act and in every Act passed after the commencement of this Act the expression 'person' shall, unless the contrary intention appears, include any body of persons corporate or unincorporate.

Section 20. Meaning of 'writing' in past and future Acts.—In this Act and in every other Act whether passed before or after the commencement of this Act expressions referring to writing shall, unless the contrary intention appears, be construed as including references to printing, lithography, photography, and other modes of representing or reproducing words in a visible form.

Section 32(2). Where an Act passed after the commencement of this Act confers a power to make any rules, regulations or byelaws, the power shall, unless the contrary intention appears, be construed as including a power, exercisable in the like manner and subject to the like consent and conditions, if any, to rescind, revoke, amend, or vary the rules, regulations or byelaws.

Public Health Acts Amendment Act, 1890

44. '(1) An urban authority may on such days as they think fit (not exceeding 12 days in any one year, nor 6 consecutive days excluding Sundays on any one occasion) close to the public any park or pleasure ground provided by them or any part thereof, and may grant the use of the same, either gratuitously or for payment, to any public charity or institution, or for any agricultural, horticultural, or other show, or any other public purpose, or may use the same for any such show or purpose; and the admission to the said park or pleasure ground, or such part thereof, on the days when the same shall be so closed to the public may be either with or without payment, as directed by the urban authority, or, with the consent of the urban authority, by the society or persons to whom the use of the park or pleasure ground, or such part thereof, may be granted: Provided that no such park or pleasure ground shall be closed on any Sunday but on any bank holiday or on Christmas Day or Good Friday or on a day appointed for public thanksgiving or mourning a local authority shall not have power . . . to close any park or pleasure ground or part thereof if the area so closed together with any other area so closed exceeds one quarter of the total area of all the parks or pleasure grounds provided by the local authority.

(2) An urban authority may either themselves provide and let for hire, or may licence any person to let for hire, any pleasure boats on any lake or piece of water in any such park or pleasure ground, and may make byelaws for regulating the numbering and naming of such boats, the number of persons to be carried therein, the boathouses and mooring places for the same, and for fixing rates of hire and the qualifications of boatmen, and for securing their good and orderly conduct while in charge of any boat.'

Local Government Act, 1894

[5 March 1894]

Powers and Duties of Parish Councils and Parish Meetings

5. (2) As from the appointed day—
(*b*) references in any Act to the churchwardens and overseers shall, as respects any rural parish, except so far as those references relate to the affairs of the church, be construed as references to the *overseers* . . .

6. Transfer of certain powers of vestry and other authorities to parish council (1) Upon the parish council of a rural parish coming into office, there shall be transferred to that council:—

(*a*) The powers, duties, and liabilities of the vestry of the parish except—
   (i.) so far as relates to the affairs of the church or to ecclesiastical charities; and

   (ii.) any power, duty, or liability transferred by this Act from the vestry to any other authority:

(*b*) The powers, duties, and liabilities of the churchwardens of the parish, except so far as they relate to the affairs of the church or to charities, or are powers and duties of *overseers* . . .

(*c*) The powers, duties, and liabilities of the overseers or of the churchwardens and overseers of the parish with respect to—
   (ii.) the provision of parish Books or matters relating thereto, and
   (iii.) the holding or management of parish property, not being property relating to affairs of the church or held for an ecclesiastical charity, and the holding or management of village

greens, or of allotments, whether for recreation grounds or for gardens or otherwise for the benefit of the inhabitants or any of them.

7. (1) As from the appointed day, in every rural parish the parish meeting shall, exclusively, have the power of adopting any of the following Acts, inclusive of any Acts amending the same (all which Acts are in this Act referred to as 'the adoptive Acts'); namely:—

(a) . . . .

(b) . . . .

(c) The Burial Acts, 1852 *to 1885*;

(3) Where under any of the said Acts the consent or approval of, or other act on the part of, the vestry of a rural parish is required in relation to any expense or rate, the parish meeting shall be substituted for the vestry, and for this purpose the expression 'vestry' shall include any meeting of ratepayers or voters.

(4) Where there is power to adopt any of the adoptive Acts for a part only of a rural parish, the Act may be adopted by a parish meeting held for that part.

(5) Where the area under any existing authority acting within a rural parish in the execution of any of the adoptive Acts is co-extensive with the parish, all powers, duties, and liabilities of that authority shall, on the parish council coming into office, be transferred to that council.

(6) This Act shall not alter the incidence of charge of any rate levied to defray expenses incurred under any of the adoptive Acts, and any such rate shall be made and charged as heretofore, and any property applicable to the payment of such expenses shall continue to be so applicable.

(7) When any of the adoptive Acts is adopted for the whole or part of a rural parish and the parish has a parish council, the parish council shall be the authority for the execution of the Act.

(8) For the purposes of this Act the passing of a resolution to provide a burial ground under the Burial Acts, 1852 *to 1885*, shall be deemed an adoption of *those* Acts.

8. Additional powers of parish council (1) A parish council shall have the following additional powers, namely, power—

(*b*) To provide or acquire land for a recreation ground and for public walks; and

(*c*) to apply to the *Board of* Agriculture under section 9 of the Commons Act, 1876; and

(*d*) to exercise with respect to any recreation ground, village green, open space, or public walk, which is for the time being under their control, or to the expense of which they have contributed, such powers as may be exercised by an urban authority under section 164 of the Public Health Act, 1875, or section 44 of the *Public Health Acts Amendment Act, 1890,* in relation to recreation grounds or public walks, and sections 183 to 186 of the Public Health Act, 1875, shall apply accordingly as if the parish council were a local authority within the meaning of those sections; and

(*g*) *to acquire by agreement any right of way, whether within their parish or an adjoining parish, the acquisition of which is beneficial to the inhabitants of the parish or any part thereof;* and

(*i*) to execute any works (including works of maintenance or improvement) incidental to or consequential on the exercise of any of the foregoing powers, or *in relation to any parish property*, not being property relating to affairs of the church or held for an ecclesiastical charity; and

(*k*) to contribute towards the expense of doing any of the things above mentioned, or to agree or combine with any other parish council to do or contribute towards the expenses of doing any of the things above mentioned.

(4) Notice of any application to the *Board of Agriculture* in relation to a common shall be served upon the council of every parish in which any part of the common to which the application relates is situate.

19. Provisions as to small parishes

In a rural parish not having a separate parish council, the following provisions shall, as from the appointed day, but subject to provisions made by a grouping order, if the parish is grouped with some other parish or parishes, have effect:—

(4) All powers, duties, and liabilities of the vestry shall, except so far as they relate to the affairs of the Church or to ecclesiastical charities, or are transferred by this Act to any other authority, be transferred to the parish meeting;

(8) The provisions of this Act with respect to a complaint to a county council of a default by a district council, shall apply with the substitution of the parish meeting for the parish council;

26. Duties and powers of district council as to . . . rights of common . . .

(2) A district council may with the consent of the county council for the county within which any common land is situate aid persons in maintaining rights of common where, in the opinion of the council, the extinction of such rights would be prejudicial to the inhabitants of the district; and may with the like consent exercise in relation to any common within their district all such powers as may, under section 8 of the Commons Act, 1876, be exercised by an urban sanitary authority in relation to any common referred to in that section; and notice of any application to the *Board of Agriculture* in relation to any common within their district shall be served upon the district council.

(3) A district council may, for the purpose of carrying into effect this section, institute or defend any legal proceedings, and generally take such steps as they deem expedient.

52. (5) All enactments in any Act, whether general or local and personal,

relating to any powers, duties, or liabilities transferred by this Act to a parish council or parish meeting from justices or the vestry or overseers or churchwardens and overseers shall, subject to the provisions of this Act and so far as circumstances admit, be construed as if any reference therein to justices or to the vestry, or to the overseers, or to the churchwardens and overseers, referred to the parish council or parish meeting as the case requires, and the said enactments shall be construed with such modifications as may be necessary for carrying this Act into effect.

53. Supplemental provisions as to adoptive Acts (1) Where on the appointed day any of the adoptive Acts is in force in a part only of a rural parish, the existing authority under the Act, or the parish meeting for that part, may transfer the powers, duties, and liabilities of the authority to the parish council, subject to any conditions with respect to the execution thereof by means of a committee as to the authority or parish meeting may seem fit, and any such conditions may be altered by any such parish meeting.

(2) If the area on the appointed day under any authority under any of the adoptive Acts will not after that day be comprised within one rural parish, the powers and duties of the authority shall be transferred to the parish councils of the rural parishes wholly or partly comprised in that area, or, if the area is partly comprised in an urban district, to those parish councils and the district council of the urban district, and shall, until other provision is made in pursuance of this Act, be exercised by a joint committee appointed by those councils. Where any such rural parish has not a parish council the parish meeting shall, for the purposes of this provision, be substituted for the parish council.

(3) The property, debts, and liabilities of any authority under any of the adoptive Acts whose powers are transferred in pursuance of this Act shall continue to be the property, debts, and liabilities of the area of that authority, and the proceeds of the property shall be credited, and the debts and liabilities

and the expenses incurred in respect of the said powers, duties, and liabilities, shall be charged to the account of the rates or contributions levied in that area, and where that area is situate in more than one parish the sums credited to and paid by each parish shall be apportioned in such manner as to give effect to this enactment.

(4) The county council on the application of a parish council may, by order, alter the boundaries of any such area if they consider that the alteration can properly be made without any undue alteration of the incidence of liability to rates and contributions or of the right to property belonging to the area, regard being had to any corresponding advantage to persons subject to the liability or entitled to the right.

66. Nothing in this Act shall affect the trusteeship, management, or control of any elementary school.

67. Transfer of property and debts and liabilities Where any powers and duties are transferred by this Act from one authority to another authority—

(1) All property held by the first authority for the purpose or by virtue of such powers and duties shall pass to and vest in the other authority, subject to all debts and liabilities affecting the same; and

(2) The latter authority shall hold the same for the estate, interest, and purposes, and subject to the covenants, conditions, and restrictions for and subject to which the property would have been held if this Act had not passed, so far as the same are not modified by or in pursuance of this Act; and

(3) All debts and liabilities of the first authority incurred by virtue of such powers and duties shall become debts and liabilities of the latter authority, and be defrayed out of the like property and funds out of which they would have been defrayed if this Act had not passed.

75. Construction of Act (1) The definition of 'parish' in section 100 of the Local Government Act, 1888, shall not apply to this Act, but, save as afore-said, expressions used in this Act shall, unless the context otherwise requires, have the same meaning as in the said Act.

(2) In this Act, unless the context otherwise requires—

The expression 'trustees' includes persons administering or managing any charity or recreation ground, or other property or thing in relation to which the word is used.

The expression 'ecclesiastical charity' includes a charity, the endowment whereof is held for some one or more of the following purposes:—

(a) for any spiritual purpose which is a legal purpose; or

(b) for the benefit of any spiritual person or ecclesiastical officer as such; or

(c) for use, if a building, as a church, chapel, mission room, or Sunday school, or otherwise by any particular church or denomination; or

(d) for the maintenance, repair, or improvement of any such building as aforesaid, or for the maintenance of divine service therein; or

(e) otherwise for the benefit of any particular church or denomination, or of any members thereof as such.

Provided that where any endowment of a charity, other than a building held for any of the purposes aforesaid, is held in part only for some of the purposes aforesaid, the charity, so far as that endowment is concerned, shall be an ecclesiastical charity within the meaning of this Act; and the *Charity Commissioners* shall, on application by any person interested, make such provision for the apportionment and management of that endowment as seems to them necessary or expedient for giving effect to this Act.

The expression shall also include any building which in the opinion of the *Charity Commissioners* has been erected or provided within forty years before the passing of this Act mainly by or at the cost of members of any particular church or denomination.

The expression 'affairs of the church' shall include the distribution of offertories or other collections made in any church.

The expression 'vestry' in relation to a parish means the inhabitants of the parish whether in vestry assembled or not, and includes any select vestry either by statute or at common law.

The expression 'elementary school' means an elementary school within the meaning of the Elementary Education Act, 1870.

The expression 'local and personal Act' includes a Provisional Order confirmed by an Act and the Act confirming the Order.

The expression 'prescribed' means prescribed by order of the *Local Government Board*.

Commons Act, 1899

[9th August 1899]

PART I.

REGULATION OF COMMONS.

1. Power for district council to make scheme for regulation of common (1) The council of an urban or rural district may make a scheme for the regulation and management of any common within their district with a view to the expenditure of money on the drainage, levelling, and improvement of the common, and to the making of byelaws and regulations for the prevention of nuisances and the preservation of order on the common.

(2) The scheme may contain any of the statutory provisions for the benefit of the neighbourhood mentioned in section 7 of the Commons Act, 1876.

(3) The scheme shall be in the prescribed form, and shall identify by reference to a plan the common to be thereby regulated, and for this purpose an ordnance survey map shall, if possible, be used.

2. Procedure for making scheme (1) Not less than three months before the making of a scheme under this Part of this Act the council shall give the prescribed notice of their intention to make it, and shall state thereby where copies of the draft of the scheme may be obtained, and where the plan therein referred to may be inspected. They shall also send to the *Board* of Agriculture as soon as possible a copy of the draft and plan.

(2) During the three months afore-said any person may obtain copies of the draft on payment of a sum not exceeding sixpence per copy, and may inspect the plan at the prescribed place, and may make in writing to the *Board* of Agriculture any objection or suggestion with respect to the scheme or plan.

(3) After the expiration of the said three months the *Board* of Agriculture shall take into consideration any objections or suggestions so made, and for that purpose may, if they think fit, direct that an inquiry be held by an officer of the *Board*.

(4) The *Board* of Agriculture may by order approve of the scheme, subject to such modifications, if any, as they may think desirable, and thereupon the scheme shall have full effect.

Provided that if, at any time before the Board have approved of the scheme, they receive a written notice of dissent either—

(a) from the person entitled as lord of the manor or otherwise to the soil of the common; or

(b) from persons representing at least one-third in value of such interests in the common as are affected by the scheme,

and such notice is not subsequently withdrawn, the Board shall not proceed further in the matter.

3. Management of regulated common The management of any common regulated by a scheme made by a district council under this Part of this Act shall be vested in the district council.

4. Provision for delegation of powers of district council to parish

council A rural district council may delegate to a parish council any powers of management conferred by this Part of this Act on the district council in relation to any commons within the parish, and thereupon the *Public Health Acts* shall apply as if the parish council were a parochial committee.

5. Power for parish council to contribute to expenses A parish council may agree to contribute the whole or any portion of the expenses of and incidental to the preparation and execution of a scheme for the regulation and management of any common within their parish (including any compensation paid under this Act) . . .

6. Provision for compensation No estate, interest, or right of a profitable or beneficial nature in, over, or affecting any common shall, except with the consent of the person entitled thereto, be taken away or injuriously affected by any scheme under this Part of this Act without compensation being made or provided for the same by the council making the scheme, and such compensation shall, in case of difference, be ascertained and provided in the same manner as if it were for the compulsory purchase and taking, or the injurious affecting, of lands under the Lands Clauses Acts.

7. Power for district council to acquire property in regulated common A district council may acquire the fee simple or any estate in or any rights in or over any common regulated by a scheme under this Part of this Act by gift or by purchase by agreement, and hold the same for the purposes of the scheme . . .

8. Digging of gravel Section 20 of the Commons Act, 1876 (which relates to the digging of gravel), shall apply to any common regulated by a scheme under this Part of this Act.

9. Power to amend scheme The power to make a scheme under this Part of this Act shall include power to amend or supplement any such scheme.

10. Provisions as to byelaws The provisions with respect to byelaws contained in sections 182 *to* 186 both inclusive, of the *Public Health Act*, 1875,

and any enactment amending or extending those sections, shall apply to all byelaws made in pursuance of a scheme under this Part of this Act, and any fine imposed by any such byelaw shall be recoverable summarily and be payable to the council in whom the management of the common is vested.

11. Expenses (1) All expenses incurred by the *Board* of Agriculture in relation to a scheme under this Part of this Act, and all expenses of and incidental to the preparation and execution of the scheme (including any compensation paid under this Act) shall be paid by the district council.

(3) A district council may for the purposes of this Act borrow money . . .

12. Power for urban district council to contribute towards expenses The council of any urban district may, with a view to the benefit of the inhabitants of their district, and subject to the approval of the *Local Government Board*, enter into an undertaking with any other council making or having made a scheme under this Part of this Act to contribute any portion of the expenses incurred by that council in executing the scheme.

14. Saving for commons regulated under other Acts A scheme under this Part of this Act shall not apply to any common which is or might be the subject of a scheme made under the Metropolitan Commons Acts, 1866 to 1878, or is regulated by a Provisional Order under the Inclosure Acts, 1845 to 1882, or has been acquired, or managed as an open space, under the powers of the Corporation of London (Open Spaces) Act, 1878, or any Act therein referred to, or is the subject of any private or local and personal Act of Parliament having for its object the preservation of the common as an open space, or is subject to byelaws made by a parish council under section 8 of the Local Government Act, 1894.

15. Definitions In this Part of this Act, unless the context otherwise requires—

The expression 'common' shall include any land subject to be inclosed under the Inclosure Acts, 1845 to 1882, and any town or village green;

The expression 'prescribed' shall mean prescribed by regulations made by the Board of Agriculture.

PART II.

MISCELLANEOUS.

16. Surplus rents from field gardens and recreation grounds (1) Surplus rents arising from field gardens may, in addition to the purposes for which they are now applicable, be applied for any of the purposes for which surplus rents arising from recreation grounds may be applied.

(2) Surplus rents arising from any field garden, or recreation ground may be applied towards the redemption of any . . . tithe rentcharge, or other charge on the garden or ground.

18. Power to modify provisions as to recreation grounds, &c. Any provisions with respect to allotments for recreation grounds, field gardens or other public or parochial purposes contained in any Act relating to inclosure or in any award or order made in pursuance thereof, and any provisions with respect to the management of any such allotments contained in any such Act, order, or award, may, on the application of any district or parish council interested in any such allotment, be dealt with by a scheme of the *Charity Commissioners* in the exercise of their ordinary jurisdiction, as if those provisions had been established by the founder in the case of a charity having a founder.

21. Annual report to Parliament . . . the *Board* of Agriculture shall include in an annual report to Parliament a statement of their proceedings under Part I of this Act and under the Metropolitan Commons Acts, 1866 to 1878, during the year ending the 31st day of December then last past, with such particulars as to their proceedings under the last-mentioned Acts as are required by section 21 of the Metropolitan Commons Act, 1866.

22. Restrictions on inclosures under scheduled Acts (1) A grant or inclosure of common purporting to be made under the general authority of any of the Acts mentioned in the First Schedule hereto or any Act incorporating the same, or any provisions thereof shall not be valid unless it is either—

(a) specially authorised by Act of Parliament; or

(b) made to or by any Government Department; or

(c) made with the consent of the *Board* of Agriculture.

(2) The *Board* of Agriculture, in giving or withholding their consent under this section, shall have regard to the same considerations, and shall, if necessary, hold the same inquiries as are directed by the Commons Act, 1876, to be taken into consideration and held by the *Board* before forming an opinion whether an application under the Inclosure Acts shall be acceded to or not.

23. . . . This repeal shall not affect the construction or effect of any local and personal Act of Parliament passed before the commencement of this Act, whereby any provisions of the said enactments are intended to be incorporated.

24. Short title This Act . . . shall read with the Inclosure Acts, 1845 to 1882.

SCHEDULES.

FIRST SCHEDULE.

ENACTMENTS relating to INCLOSURES subject to restriction under the Act.

Session and Chapter.	Title or Short Title.
43 Eliz. c. 2. - -	The Poor Relief Act, 1601.
17 Geo. 3. c. 53. - -	The Clergy Residences Repair Act, 1776.
51 Geo. 3. c. 115. - -	The Gifts for Churches Act, 1811.
58 Geo. 3. c. 45. - -	The Church Building Act, 1818.
1 & 2 Will. 4. c. 42.	The Poor Relief Act, 1831.
1 & 2 Will. 4. c. 59.	The Crown Lands Allotments Act, 1831.
5 & 6 Will. 4. c. 69. -	The Union and Parish Property Act, 1835.
4 & 5 Vict. c. 38. - -	The Schools Sites Act, 1841.
8 & 9 Vict. c. 18. - -	The Lands Clauses Consolidation Act, 1845.
17 & 18 Vict. c. 112. -	The Literary and Scientific Institutions Act, 1854.

Open Spaces Act, 1906

[4th August 1906]

LOCAL AUTHORITIES.

1. Each of the following bodies shall be a local authority for the purposes of this Act, namely—

The council of any county, of any municipal borough, or of any district:

The common council of the city of London:

Any parish council.

POWER TO TRANSFER OPEN SPACES AND BURIAL GROUNDS TO LOCAL AUTHORITIES.

2. Power of trustees under local Act to transfer open space to local authority or admit other persons to enjoyment thereof (1) Where an open space is, in pursuance of a local or private Act of Parliament, placed under the care and management of trustees or other persons (in this section referred to as trustees), with a view to the preservation and regulation thereof as a garden or open space, the trustees may, in pursuance of a special resolution, and with the consent, signified by a special resolution, of the owners and occupiers of any houses which front upon the open space, or of which the owners and occupiers are liable to be specially rated for the maintenance of the open space,—

(*a*) convey, for or without any consideration, to any local authority, their estate or interest in the open space or, if they have no such estate or interest, transfer to any local authority the entire care and management of the open space, to the end that the space may be preserved for the enjoyment of the public; or

(*b*) grant, for or without any consideration, to any local authority any term of years or other limited interest in or any right or easement over the open space; or

(*c*) make any agreement with any local authority for the opening to the public of the open space and the care and management thereof by the local authority, either at all times or at any specified time or times; or

(*d*) notwithstanding anything in the

Act or any instrument under which the trustees are constituted or act, admit persons not owning, occupying, or residing in any house fronting on the open space to the enjoyment of the open space, either at all times or at any specified time or times and regulate the admission of such persons thereto on such terms and conditions as the trustees think proper.

(2) Where the freehold of the open space and the freehold of all or the greater part of the houses round the open space are vested in the same person the powers conferred by this section shall not be exercised without the consent of that person.

(3) Any such conveyance, transfer, grant, or agreement shall be made, if the trustees are a corporation, by an instrument under the common seal of the trustees, and if the trustees are not a corporation, by an instrument under the hands and seals of any five of the trustees or of all the trustees if for the time being they are less than five in number.

(4) Any conveyance, transfer, grant, or agreement under this section shall be deemed a good execution of the trusts, powers, and duties imposed or conferred upon the trustees by the Act or instrument under which they are constituted or act, and where the trustees convey their entire interest in, or transfer the entire care and management of, the open space they shall, on the execution of the conveyance or transfer, be relieved and discharged from all trusts, powers, and duties under the Act or instrument or otherwise with reference to the open space.

(5) The trustees shall hold any purchase money or rent paid for or in respect of the open space in trust for the benefit of the persons or class of persons for whose benefit the open space was previously preserved and managed by the trustees, or, as the case may be, for the benefit of the objects to which any rates previously imposed in respect of the open space had been applied, and

such persons or class of persons shall be discharged either absolutely, or, if the grant was for a term of years or other limited interest, during the continuance of that interest, from any special rate or other obligation previously imposed on them in respect of the open space.

3. Transfer to local authority of spaces held by trustees for purposes of public recreation (1) Where any land is held by trustees (not being trustees elected or appointed under any local or private Act of Parliament) upon trust for the purposes of public recreation, the trustees may, in pursuance of a special resolution, transfer the land to any local authority by a free gift absolutely or for a limited term, and, if the local authority accept the gift, they shall hold the land on the trusts and subject to the conditions on and subject to which the trustees held the same, or on such other trusts and subject to such other conditions (so that the land be appropriated to the purposes of public recreation) as may be agreed on between the trustees and the local authority with the approval of the *Charity Commissioners*.

(2) Subject to the obligation of the land so transferred being used for the purposes of public recreation, the local authority may hold the land as and for the purposes of an open space under this Act.

4. Transfer by charity trustees of open space to local authority (1) When an open space is vested in trustees, other than such as are mentioned in the foregoing provisions of this Act, for any charitable purpose and as part of their trust estate, and it appears to the majority of the trustees that the open space is no longer required for the purposes of their trust, or may with advantage to the trust be dealt with under this section, the trustees may, in pursuance of a special resolution, and with the sanction of an order of the *Charity Commissioners* or with that of an order of the Court to be obtained as hereinafter provided, convey or demise the open space to any local authority on such terms as they may agree, and the local authority shall thenceforth be

L*

entitled to hold the same as an open space on the terms and under the conditions specified in the conveyance or demise, or on such terms or under such conditions as may be so authorised or approved, or as the court may from time to time order, as the case may be.

(2) The court for the purposes of this section shall be either the High Court or the county court of the district in which the whole or any part of the open space is situate.

(3) An order of the court for the purposes of this section may be made upon application by the trustees, in manner directed by rules of court, and the court, before making any order, may direct such inquiries to be made, such consents to be obtained, and notice to be given to such persons, as to the court seem expedient, and may make such order thereon as in the discretion of the court appears proper.

5. Transfer to local authority by owners of open spaces subject to rights of user (1) Where any open space is subject to rights of user for exercise and recreation in the owners or occupiers, or both, of any houses round or near the same, whether the rights are secured by covenant or not, the owner of the open space may, with the consent, signified by a special resolution, of such owners or occupiers, or both, as the case may require,—

(*a*) convey to any local authority his estate or interest in the open space in trust for the enjoyment of the public; or

(*b*) grant to any local authority in trust as aforesaid any term of years or other limited interest in or any right or easement over the open space; or

(*c*) make an agreement with any local authority for the opening to the public of the open space and the care and management thereof by the local authority either at all times or at any specified times:

and thereupon the owner shall be discharged from any liability to any person entitled to any right of user in respect of any act done in accordance with the consent so given.

(2) Where any person has any term of years or other limited interest in any such open space this section shall apply to him with reference to that interest in like manner as it applies to the owner of the open space.

(3) Where any open space is used as a place of exercise and recreation for the inhabitants of certain houses, and the property and right of user is vested in one or more persons as owners or occupiers of the houses, those owners and occupiers (if any) may convey to a local authority in trust for the public a right to enter upon, use, and enjoy the open space subject to such terms and conditions as may be agreed upon.

6. Transfer of disused burial grounds to local authority The owner of any disused burial ground may convey the burial ground to, or grant any term of years or other limited interest therein to, or make any agreement with, any local authority for the purpose of giving the public access to the burial ground, and preserving the same as an open space accessible to the public and under the control of the local authority, and for the purpose of improving and laying out the same.

7. Power of corporation, &c. to convey land for open space (1) Any corporation (other than a municipal corporation) or persons having power, either with or without the consent of any other corporation or persons, to sell any land may, but with the like consent (if any), convey, for or without any consideration, to any local authority that land, or any part thereof, for the purpose of the same being preserved as an open space for the enjoyment of the public under this Act, and may so convey the same with or without conditions, and the local authority may accept the land for that purpose, and, if conditions are imposed, subject to such conditions.

(2) Where a corporation having power under this section to convey land are themselves a local authority, this section shall enable the authority to appropriate their land as an open space

for the enjoyment of the public, and shall, with the necessary modifications, apply to the appropriation in like manner as it applies to the conveyance.

8. Special resolutions and consents (1) A resolution shall for the purposes of this Act be a special resolution when it has been—

(*a*) passed by a majority of at least two-thirds of the persons present at a meeting summoned as hereinafter provided; and

(*b*) confirmed by another resolution passed by a majority of at least two-thirds of the persons present at a meeting summoned as hereinafter provided and held after an interval of not less than one month from the first meeting.

A meeting of trustees for the purposes of this Act shall be summoned by a notice stating generally the object of the meeting, which notice shall be left at, or sent by post, at least one month before the date of the meeting, to the last known or usual place of abode of each trustee.

(3) A meeting of owners and occupiers of houses under this Act shall be summoned by a notice stating generally the object of the meeting, which notice shall be left at, or sent through the post to, each of such houses, at least one month before the date of the meeting, and shall be inserted as an advertisement at least three times in any two or more papers circulating in the neighbourhood.

(4) If at any meeting of trustees or of owners and occupiers under this Act a resolution with respect to an open space is rejected, no meeting of the trustees, or, as the case may be, the owners or occupiers, shall be called or held with the same object and with respect to the same open space until the expiration of three years from the date of the rejection.

(5) A meeting of owners or occupiers of houses for the purposes of this Act shall not be held between the first day of August in one year and the thirty-first day of January in the following year.

9. Power of local authority to acquire open space or burial ground A local authority may, subject to the provisions of this Act,—

(*a*) acquire by agreement and for valuable or nominal consideration by way of payment in gross, or of rent, or otherwise, or without any consideration, the freehold of, or any term of years or other limited estate or interest in, or any right or easement in or over, any open space or burial ground, whether situate within the district of the local authority or not; and

(*b*) undertake the entire or partial care, management, and control of any such open space or burial ground, whether any interest in the soil is transferred to the local authority or not; and

(*c*) for the purposes aforesaid make any agreement with any person authorised by this Act or otherwise to convey or to agree with reference to any open space or burial ground, or with any other persons interested therein.

10. Maintenance of open space and burial grounds by local authority A local authority who have acquired any estate or interest in or control over any open space or burial ground under this Act shall, subject to any conditions under which the estate, interest, or control was so acquired—

(*a*) hold and administer the open space or burial ground in trust to allow, and with a view to, the enjoyment thereof by the public as an open space within the meaning of this Act and under proper control and regulation and for no other purpose; and

(*b*) maintain and keep the open space or burial ground in a good and decent state,

and may inclose it or keep it inclosed with proper railings and gates, and may

drain, level, lay out, turf, plant, ornament, light, provide with seats and
otherwise improve it, and do all such
work and things and employ such
officers and servants as may be requisite
for the purposes aforesaid or any of
them.

**11. Special provisions as to
management of burial grounds and
removal of tombstones** (1) A local
authority shall not exercise any of the
powers of management under this Act
with reference to any consecrated
burial ground unless and until they are
authorised so to do by the licence or
faculty of the bishop.

(2) The playing of any games or
sports shall not be allowed in any burial
ground in or over which a local authority have acquired any estate, interest,
or control under this Act, except that—

(a) in the case of a consecrated burial
ground, the bishop by licence or
faculty; and

(b) in the case of any burial ground
which is not consecrated, the
persons from whom the local
authority have acquired the
estate, interest, or control in or
over the same

may expressly sanction any such use of
the burial ground, and may specify any
conditions as to the extent or nature of
such use.

(3) In the case of any disused burial
ground, at least three months before
removing or changing the position of
any tombstone or monument, a local
authority shall—

(a) prepare a statement sufficiently
describing by the name and date
appearing thereon the tombstones
and monuments standing or
being in the ground, and such
other particulars as may be necessary, and shall cause this statement to be deposited with the
clerk of the local authority, and
to be open to inspection by all
persons; and

(b) insert an advertisement of the
intention to remove or change the

position of such tombstones and
monuments three times at least in
some newspaper circulating in
the neighbourhood, and by that
advertisement give notice of the
deposit of the statement hereinbefore described, and of the place
at which and the hours within
which the same may be inspected;
and

(c) place a notice in terms similar to
the advertisement on the door of
the church (if any) to which the
burial ground is attached, and
deliver or send by post a notice to
any person known or believed by
the local authority to be a near
relative of any person whose
death is recorded on any such
tombstone or monument.

(4) In the case of a consecrated
ground, no tombstone or monument
shall be removed or its position changed
without a licence or faculty from the
bishop, and no application for such
licence or faculty shall be made until
the expiration of one month at least
after the appearance of the last of such
advertisements as aforesaid:

Provided that on an application for a
licence or faculty nothing shall prevent
the bishop from directing or sanctioning
the removal or change of position of any
tombstone or monument, if he is of
opinion that reasonable steps have been
taken to bring the intention to effect
such removal or change of position to
the notice of some person having a
family interest in the tombstone or
monument.

(5) A licence or faculty for the purposes of this section may be granted by
the bishop of the diocese within which
the consecrated burial ground is situate
on the application of the local authority
who have acquired any estate, interest,
or control in or over the burial ground,
and may be granted subject to such
conditions and restrictions as to the
bishop may seem fit.

**12. Powers over open spaces and
burial grounds already vested in
local authority** A local authority may
exercise all the powers given to them

by this Act respecting open spaces and burial grounds transferred to them in pursuance of this Act in respect of any open spaces and burial grounds of a similar nature which may be vested in them in pursuance of any other statute, or of which they are otherwise the owners.

13. Provision for compensation No estate, interest, or right of a profitable or beneficial nature in, over, or affecting an open space or burial ground shall, except with the consent of the person entitled thereto, be taken away or injuriously affected by anything done under this Act without compensation being made for the same; and such compensation shall be paid by the local authority by whom the estate, interest, or right is taken away or injuriously affected, and shall, in case of difference, be ascertained and provided in the same manner as if the same were compensation for lands purchased and taken otherwise than by agreement or injuriously affected under the Lands Clauses Acts.

14. Power of county councils as to public walks or pleasure grounds A county council may ... support or contribute to the support of public walks or pleasure grounds provided by any person whomsoever.

15. Byelaws (1) A local authority may, with reference to any open space or burial ground in or over which they have acquired any estate, interest, or control under this Act, make byelaws for the regulation thereof, and of the days and times of admission thereto, and for the preservation of order and prevention of nuisances therein, and may by such byelaws impose penalties recoverable summarily for the infringement thereof, and provide for the removal of any person infringing any byelaw by any officer of the local authority or police constable.

(2) All byelaws made under this Act by any local authority shall be made—

(e) in the case of a municipal borough or district or parish council, subject and according to the provisions with respect to

byelaws contained in sections *182 to 186 of the Public Health Act* 1875, and those sections shall apply to a parish council in like manner as if they were a local authority within the meaning of that Act, except that byelaws made by a parish council need not be under common seal.

(3) The trustees or other persons having the care and management of any open space, who in pursuance of this Act admit to the enjoyment of the open space any persons not owning, occupying, or residing in any house fronting thereon, shall have the same powers of making byelaws as are conferred on a committee of the inhabitants of a square by section 4 of the Town Gardens Protection Act, 1863, and that section shall apply accordingly.

16. Power of local authorities to act jointly Any two or more local authorities may jointly carry out the provisions of this Act and may make any agreement on such terms as may be arranged between them for so doing and for defraying the expenses of the execution of this Act, and any local authority may defray the whole or any part of the expenses incurred by any other local authority in the execution of this Act.

18. Borrowing A local authority may borrow for the purposes of this Act. . . .

SUPPLEMENTAL.

19. Savings This Act shall not apply to—

(a) the royal parks nor
(b) any land belonging to His Majesty in right of His Crown or of His Duchy of Lancaster; nor
(d) any metropolitan common within the meaning of the Metropolitan Commons Acts, 1866 to 1898; nor
(e) any land belonging to either of the honourable Societies of the Inner Temple and Middle Temple.

20. Definitions In this Act, unless the context otherwise requires,—

The expression 'open space' means any land, whether inclosed or not, on which there are no buildings or of which not more than one-twentieth part is covered with buildings, and the whole or the remainder of which is laid out as a garden or is used for purposes of recreation, or lies waste and unoccupied:

The expression 'owner'—

(a) used in relation to an open space (not being a burial ground), means any person in whom the open space is vested for an estate in possession during his life or for any larger estate;

(b) used in relation to a house, includes any person entitled to any term of years in the house;

(c) used in relation to a burial ground, means the person in whom the freehold of the burial ground is vested whether as appurtenant or incident to any benefice or cure of souls or otherwise:

The expression 'occupier' used in relation to a house, means the person rated to the relief of the poor in respect of the house:

The expression 'burial ground' includes any churchyard, cemetery, or other ground, whether consecrated or not, which has been at any time set apart for the purpose of interment:

The expression 'disused burial ground' means any burial ground which is no longer used for interments, whether or not the ground has been partially or wholly closed for burials under the provisions of a statute or Order in Council:

The expression 'building' includes any temporary or movable building.

23. Repeal

(a) Nothing in this repeal shall affect the validity or operation of any byelaw made under any enactment so repealed, but all such byelaws shall continue in force as if made under that Act, and may be revoked and altered accordingly; and

(b) Nothing in this repeal shall affect any order of a county council under any enactment repealed investing a parish council with the powers of the Open Spaces Acts, 1877 to 1890, and every parish council in respect of which such an order has before the commencement of this Act been made, shall be deemed to be a parish council invested with the powers of this Act by an order of the council of the county within wh:ch the parish is situate.

24. Commencement of Act This Act shall come into operation on the 1st day of January 1907.

Small Holdings and Allotments Act, 1908

[1st August 1908]

PART II.

ALLOTMENTS.

Provision of Allotments

23. Duty of certain councils to provide allotments (7) If the council of any borough, urban district, or parish are of opinion that there is a demand for allotments . . . in the borough, urban district, or parish, . . . the council shall provide a sufficient number of allotments, and shall let such allotments to persons . . . resident in the borough, district, or parish, and desiring to take the same.

(2) On a representation in writing to the council of any . . . parish, by any six registered parliamentary electors or ratepayers resident in the . . . parish, that the circumstances of . . . parish are such that it is the duty of the council

to take proceedings under this Part of this Act therein, the council shall take such representation into consideration.

24. Duty of county councils to act in default of district and parish councils (1) It shall be the duty of a county council to ascertain the extent to which there is a demand for allotments by any person or by an association to which allotments may be let under this act in the several urban districts . . . and rural parishes in the county, or would be a demand if suitable land were available, and the extent to which it is reasonably practicable, having regard to the provisions of this Act, to satisfy any such demand, and for that purpose to co-operate with such authorities, associations, and persons as they think best qualified to assist them, and take such other steps as they think necessary.

(2) The county council, if satisfied that the circumstances are such that land for allotments should be acquired by them under this section, shall pass a resolution to that effect, and thereupon the powers and duties of the . . . parish council under the provisions of this Act relating to allotments shall be transferred from that council to the county council, and the county council, in substitution for that council, shall proceed to acquire land in accordance with this Act, and otherwise execute this Act in the district or parish.

Provided that this section shall not affect the property in, or any powers or duties of the . . . parish council in relation to, any land which, before the passing of the resolution, was acquired by the . . . parish council under this Act, or any enactment repealed by this Act.

(3) Where the powers of the . . . parish council are, by virtue of this section, transferred to the county council, the following provisions shall have effect:—

(a) The provisions of this Act relating to allotments shall apply with the modifications necessary for giving effect to this section;

(b) The county council may borrow for the purposes of those provisions subject to the conditions, in the manner, and on the security of the rate, subject to, in, and on the security of which the . . . parish council might have borrowed under those provisions. The council shall have power to charge the said rate with the repayment of the principal and interest of the loan, and the loan with the interest thereon shall be repaid by . . . or parish council in like manner, and the charge shall have the like effect, as if the loan were lawfully raised and charged on that rate by the district or parish council;

(c) The county council shall keep separate accounts of all receipts and expenditure under this section;

(d) All sums received by the county council in respect of any land acquired under this section or the corresponding provision of any enactment repealed by this Act, otherwise than from any sale or exchange, in so far as they are not required for the payment of expenses incurred by them in respect of such land, shall be paid to the . . . parish council;

(e) The county council may delegate to the . . . parish council any powers under this Act relating to the management of the allotments, and the letting and use thereof, and the recovery of the rent and of possession thereof; and, subject to the terms of the delegation, all expenses and receipts arising in the exercise of the powers so delegated shall be paid and dealt with as expenses and receipts of the . . . parish council under this Act;

(f) The county council, on the request of the . . . parish council, may, by order under their seal, transfer to that council all or any of the powers, duties, property, and liabilities vested in and imposed on the council by virtue of this section or the corresponding provision of any enactment repealed by this Act, as regards the district or parish, and the property so transferred shall be deemed to have been acquired by that council under this Act, and that council shall act accordingly.

(4) If the *Board* are, in relation to any ... rural parish, satisfied, after holding a local inquiry at which the county council and the council of the ... parish, and such other persons as the person holding the inquiry may in his discretion think fit to allow, shall be permitted to appear and be heard, that the county council have failed to fulfil their obligations under this section, the Board may by order transfer to the *Commissioners* all or any of the powers of the county council under this section in relation to the ... parish, and this section shall apply as if references to the *Commissioners* were substituted for references to the county council and with such other adaptations as may be made by the order.

Powers of Councils in relation to the provision of Allotments

25. Acquisition of land for purpose of Act (1) The council of a ... parish may, for the purpose of providing allotments, by agreement purchase or take on lease land, whether situate within or without their ... parish or may purchase such land compulsorily in accordance with the provisions of this Act and of the Acquisition of Land (Authorisation Procedure) Act 1946, in that behalf.

26. Improvement and adaptation of land for allotments (1) The Council of a parish may improve any land acquired by them for allotments and adapt the same for letting in allotments, by draining, fencing, and dividing the same, acquiring approaches, making roads and otherwise, as they think fit, and may from time to time do such things as may be necessary for maintaining such drains, fences, approaches, and roads, or otherwise for maintaining the allotments in a proper condition.

(2) The council may also adapt the land for allotments by erecting buildings and making adaptations of existing buildings, but so that not more than one dwelling-house shall be erected for occupation with any one allotment; and no dwelling-house shall be erected for occupation with any allotment of less than one acre.

27. Provisions as to letting (3) One person shall not hold any allotment or allotments acquired under this Part of this Act, or any enactment hereby repealed, exceeding five acres:

Provided that any part of the land acquired by a council for the purposes of allotments which exceeds five acres may be adapted for letting and let as an allotment, if the county council are satisfied by the council that it is convenient and desirable that it should be so let and consent to such letting accordingly.

(4) An allotment shall not be sublet.

(5) If at any time an allotment cannot be let in accordance with the provisions of this Act and the rules made thereunder, the same may be let to any person whatever at the best annual rent which can be obtained for the same, without any premium or fine, and on such terms as may enable possession thereof to be resumed within a period not exceeding twelve months if it should at any time be required to be let under the provisions aforesaid.

(6) A council shall have the same power of letting one or more allotments to persons working on a co-operative system or to an association formed for the purposes of creating or promoting the creation of allotments *as may be exercised as respects small holdings by a county council.*

28. Rules as to letting allotments (1) Subject to the provisions of this Act, a ... parish council may make such rules as appear to be necessary or proper for regulating the letting of allotments under this Act, and for preventing any undue preference in the letting thereof, and generally for carrying the provisions of this Part of this Act into effect.

(2) Rules under this section may define the persons eligible to be tenants of allotments, the notices to be given for the letting thereof, the size of the allotments, the conditions under which they are to be cultivated, and the rent to be paid for them.

(3) *All such rules shall make provision for reasonable notice to be given to a tenant of any allotment of the determination of his tenancy.*

Rules under this section shall not be of any force unless and until they have been confirmed by the *Board* in like manner and subject to the like provisions as in the case of byelaws required to be confirmed by the *Local Government Board* under the Public Health Acts.

(4) Rules for the time being in force under this section shall be binding on all persons whatsoever; and the council shall cause them to be from time to time made known, in such manner as the council think fit, to all persons interested, and shall cause a copy thereof to be given gratis to any inhabitant of the district or parish demanding the same.

29. Management of allotments (1) The council of a . . . parish may from time to time appoint, and, when appointed, remove allotment managers of land acquired by the council for allotments, and the allotment managers shall consist either partly of members of the council and partly of other persons, or wholly of other persons, so that in either case such other persons be persons residing in the locality and contributing to the rate out of which the expenses of the council under this Act are paid.

(2) The proceedings and powers of allotment managers shall be such as, subject to the provisions of this Act, may be directed by the council; the allotment managers may be empowered by the council to do anything in relation to the management of the allotments which the council are authorised to do and to incur expenses to such amount as the council authorise, and any expenses properly so incurred shall be deemed to be expenses of the council under this Act.

30. Recovery of rent and posses-sion of allotments (1) The rent for an allotment let by a council in pursuance of this Act, and the possession of such an allotment in the case of any notice to quit, or failure to deliver up possession thereof as required by law, may be recovered by the council as landlords, in the like manner as in any other case of landlord and tenant.

(2) If the rent for any allotment is in arrear for not less than forty days, or if it appears to the council that the tenant of an allotment not less than three months after the commencement of the tenancy thereof has not duly observed the rules affecting the allotment made by or in pursuance of this Act, or is resident more than one mile out of the . . . parish for which the allotments are provided, the council may serve upon the tenant, or, if he is residing out of the borough, . . . or parish, leave at his last known place of abode in the borough, . . . or parish, or fix in some conspicuous manner on the allotment, a written notice determining the tenancy at the expiration of one month after the notice has been so served or affixed, and thereupon the tenancy shall be determined accordingly:

(3) Upon the recovery of an allotment from any tenant, the court directing the recovery may stay delivery of possession until payment of the compensation (if any) due to the outgoing tenant has been made or secured to the satisfaction of the court.

32. Sale of superfluous or unsuit-able land (1) Where the council of any . . . parish are of opinion that any land acquired by them for allotments or any part thereof is not needed for the purpose of allotments, or that some more suitable land is available, they may, with the sanction of the county council, sell or let such land otherwise than under the provisions of this Act, or exchange the land for other land more suitable for allotments, and may pay or receive money for equality of exchange.

(2) The proceeds of a sale under this Act of land acquired for allotments, and any money received by the council on any such exchange as aforesaid by way

of equality of exchange, shall be applied in discharging, either by way of a sinking fund or otherwise, the debts and liabilities of the council in respect of the land acquired by the council for allotments, or in acquiring, adapting, and improving other land for allotments, and any surplus remaining may be applied for any purpose for which capital money may be applied, and which is approved by the *Local Government Board*; and the interest thereon (if any) and any money received from the letting of the land may be applied in acquiring other land for allotments, or shall be applied in like manner as receipts from allotments under this Act are applicable.

33. Transfer of allotments to borough, district, and parish councils (1) The allotment wardens under the Inclosure Acts, 1845 to 1882, having the management of any land appropriated under those Acts either before or after the passing of this Act for allotments or field gardens for the labouring poor of any place, may, by agreement with the council of the . . . parish, within whose . . . parish that place is wholly or partly situate, transfer the management of that land to the council, upon such terms and conditions as may be agreed upon with the sanction, as regards the allotment wardens, of the Board, and thereupon the land shall vest in the council.

(3) Where, as respects any rural parish, any Act constitutes any persons wardens of allotments, or authorises or requires the appointment or election of any wardens, committee, or managers for the purpose of allotments, the powers and duties of the wardens, committee, or managers shall, subject to the provisions of this Act, be exercised and performed by the parish council, or, in the case of a parish not having a parish council, by persons appointed by the parish meeting, and it shall not be necessary to make the said appointment or to hold the said election.

(4) The provisions of this Act relating to allotments shall apply to land vested in, or the management whereof has been transferred to a council under this section or the corresponding provision of any enactment repealed by this Act in like manner as if the land had been acquired by the council under the general powers of this Part of this Act.

Supplemental

34. Power to make scheme for provision of common pasture (1) Where it appears to the council of any . . . parish that, as regards their . . . parish, land can be acquired for affording common pasture at such price or rent that all expenses incurred by the council in acquiring the land and otherwise in relation to the land when acquired may reasonably be expected to be recouped out of the charges paid in respect thereof, and that the acquisition of such land is desirable in view of the wants and circumstances of the labouring population, the council may submit to the council of the county in which the . . . parish is wholly or partly situate a scheme for providing such common pasture.

(2) The county council, if satisfied of the expediency of such scheme, may by order authorise the council which submitted it to carry it into effect, and, upon such an order being made, the provisions of this Act relating to allotments shall, with the necessary modifications, apply in like manner as if 'allotments' in those provisions included common pasture, and 'rent' included a charge for turning out an animal:

Provided that the rules made under those provisions may extend to regulating the turning out of animals on the common pasture, to defining the persons entitled to turn them out, the number to be turned out, and the conditions under which animals may be turned out, and fixing the charges to be made for each animal, and otherwise to regulating the common pasture.

PART III.

GENERAL.

Acquisition of Land

38. Purchase of land by agreement For the purpose of the purchase of land by agreement under this Act by a council, the provisions of Part I of the Compulsory Purchase Acts 1965 (so far as applicable) other than sections 4 to 8, section 10, subsections (1) to (5) of section 23 and section 31 shall apply and section 178 of the Public Health Act, 1875, shall apply as if the council were referred to therein.

39. Procedure for compulsory acquisition of land (1) Where a council propose to purchase land compulsorily under this Act, the council may be authorised so to do by the Minister of Agriculture and Fisheries.

(2) *Where a council propose to hire land compulsorily, the council may submit to the Board an order for the compulsory hiring of the land specified in the order for a period not less than fourteen nor more than thirty-five years, and the provisions of Part I of the First Schedule to this Act shall apply to the order in like manner as it applies to an order for compulsory purchase, with the substitution of 'hiring' for 'purchase', and with the modifications set out in Part II of that Schedule.*

(3) An order under the last foregoing sub-section shall be of no force unless and until it is confirmed by the *Board*, and the *Board* may subject to the provisions of the First Schedule to this Act confirm the order either without modification or subject to such modifications as they think fit, and an order when so confirmed shall become final and have effect as if enacted in this Act; and the confirmation by the *Board* shall be conclusive evidence that the requirements of this Act have been complied with, and that the order has been duly made and is within the powers of this Act.

(4) An order for the compulsory purchase *or hiring* of land under this Act may provide for the continuance of any existing easement or the creation of any new easement over the land authorised to be acquired, and every such order shall, if so required by the owner of the land to be acquired, provide for the creation of such new easements as are reasonably necessary to secure the continued use and enjoyment by such owner and his tenants of all means of access, drainage, water supply, and

other similar conveniences, theretofore used or enjoyed by them over the land to be acquired: *Provided that, notwithstanding anything contained in this sub-section, no new easement created by or in pursuance of the order over land hired by a council shall continue beyond the determination of such hiring.*

(5) In determining the amount of any disputed compensation under any such order, no additional allowance shall be made on account of the purchase *or hiring* being compulsory.

(6) *Where land authorised to be compulsorily hired by an order under this section is subject to a mortgage, any lease made in pursuance of the order by the mortgagor or mortgagee in possession shall have the like effect as if it were a lease authorised by section 18 of the Conveyancing and Law of Property Act, 1881.*

(7) Where the council proposing to acquire land compulsorily is a parish council, the council shall, instead of themselves making and submitting to the Board the order, represent the case to the county council, and thereupon the county council may, on behalf of the parish council, exercise the powers in relation to compulsory purchase *or hiring* conferred on councils by this Act, and the order shall be carried into effect by the county council, but the land shall be assured or demised to the parish council, and all expenses incurred by the county council shall be paid by the parish council:

Provided that, if the parish council are aggrieved by the refusal of the county council to proceed under this section, the parish council may petition the *Board*, and thereupon the *Board*, after such inquiry as they think fit, may make such an order as the county council might have made, and this sub-section shall apply as if the order had been made by the county council.

(8) If, after the determination of the amount of the compensation (*including in the case of land hired compulsorily the rent*) to be paid to any person in respect of his interest in the land proposed to be compulsorily acquired, it appears to the council that the land cannot be let for small holdings or

allotments, as the case may be, at such a rent as will secure the council from loss, the council may at any time within six weeks after the determination of the amount by notice in writing withdraw any notice to treat served on that person or on any other person interested in the land, and in such case any person on whom such a notice of withdrawal has been served shall be entitled to obtain from the council compensation for any loss or expenses which he may have sustained or incurred by reason or in consequence of the notice to treat and of the notice of withdrawal, and the amount of such compensation shall, in default of agreement, be determined by arbitration . . .

40. Powers of certain limited owners to sell and lease land for small holdings or allotments (1) Any person having power to lease land for agricultural purposes for a limited term, whether subject to any consent or conditions or not, may, subject to the like consent and conditions (if any), lease land to a council for the purposes of small holdings or allotments for a term not exceeding thirty-five years, either with or without such right of renewal as is conferred by this Act in the case of land hired compulsorily for those purposes.

(2) The like powers of leasing may be exercised, in the case of land forming part of the possessions of the Duchy of Lancaster, by the Chancellor and Council of the Duchy of Lancaster by deed under the seal of the Duchy in the name of His Majesty His heirs and successors, and, in the case of land forming part of the possessions of the Duchy of Cornwall, by the Duke of Cornwall or other the persons for the time being having power to dispose of land belonging to that Duchy.

(3) The like powers of leasing may be exercised in the case of glebe land or other land belonging to an ecclesiastical benefice by the incumbent thereof with the consent of the *Ecclesiastical* Commissioners alone upon such terms and conditions and in such manner as the *Ecclesiastical* Commissioners may approve.

41. Restrictions on the acquisition of land (1) No land shall be authorised by an order under this Act to be acquired compulsorily which at the date of the order forms part of any park garden, or pleasure ground, or form part of the home farm attached to and usually occupied with a mansion house or is otherwise required for the amenity or convenience of any dwelling-house, or which is woodland not wholly surrounded by or adjacent to land acquired by a council under this Act . . .

(2) A council in making, and the *Board* in confirming, an order for the compulsory acquisition of land shall have regard to the extent of land held or occupied in the locality by any owner or tenant and to the convenience of other property belonging to or occupied by the same owner or tenant, and shall, so far as practicable, avoid taking an undue or inconvenient quantity of land from any one owner or tenant, and for that purpose, where part only of a holding is taken, shall take into consideration the size and character of the existing agricultural buildings not proposed to be taken which were used in connection with the holding, and the quantity and nature of the land available for occupation therewith, and shall also, so far as practicable, avoid displacing any considerable number of agricultural labourers or others employed on or about the land.

42. Grazing rights, &c., to be attached to small holdings or allotments (1) The powers of a council to acquire land for small holdings or allotments shall, subject to the restrictions by this Act imposed, include power to acquire land for the purpose of letting to tenants of small holdings and allotments rights of grazing and other similar rights over the land so acquired, and to acquire for that purpose stints and other alienable common rights of grazing.

(2) Any rights created or acquired by

he council under this section shall be
et to tenants of small holdings or allotments in such manner and subject to
uch regulations as the council think
expedient.

Provisions affecting Land acquired

**44. Power of council to renew
tenancy of land compulsorily hired**
(1) Where a council has hired land
compulsorily for small holdings or
allotments, the council may, by giving
to the landlord not more than two years
nor less than one year before the expiration of the tenancy notice in writing,
renew the tenancy for such term, not
being less than fourteen nor more than
thirty-five years, as may be specified in
the notice, and at such rent as, in
default of agreement, may be determined by valuation by a valuer appointed by the Board, but otherwise on
the same terms and conditions as the
original lease, and so from time to
time:

Provided that, if on any such notice
being given, the landlord proves to the
satisfaction of the *Board* that any land
included in the tenancy is required for
the amenity or convenience of any
dwelling-house, then such land shall be
excluded from the renewed tenancy.

(2) In assessing the rent to be paid
under this section the valuer shall not
take into account any increase in the
value of the holding—

(a) due to improvements in respect
of which the council would have
been entitled to compensation, if
instead of renewing the tenancy
the council had quitted the land
on the determination of the tenancy; or

(b) due to any use to which the land
might otherwise be put during
the renewed term, being a use in
respect of which the landlord is
entitled to resume possession of
the land under this Act; or

(c) due to the establishment by the
council of other small holdings or
allotments in the neighbourhood;

or any depreciation in the value of the
land in respect of which the landlord
would have been entitled to compensation if the council had so quitted the
land as aforesaid.

**45. Interchange of land for small
holdings and allotments** A county
council may sell or let to a . . . parish
council for the purpose of allotments
any land acquired by them for small
holdings, and a . . . parish council may
sell or let to the county council for the
purpose of small holdings any land
acquired by them for allotments . . .

**46. Power to resume possession
of land hired compulsorily** (1)
Where land has been hired by a council
compulsorily for small holdings or
allotments, and the land or any part
thereof at any time during the tenancy
thereof by the council is shown to the
satisfaction of the *Board* to be required
by the landlord to be used for building,
mining, or other industrial purposes, or
for roads necessary therefor, it shall be
lawful for the landlord to resume possession of the land or part thereof upon
giving to the council twelve months'
previous notice in writing of his intention so to do or such shorter notice as
may be required by the order for the
compulsory hiring of the land; and, if a
part only of the land is resumed, the
rent payable by the council shall as
from the date of resumption be reduced
by such sum as in default of agreement
may be determined by valuation by a
valuer appointed by the Board.

**47. Compensation for improve-
ments** (1) Where a council has let a
small holding or allotment to any tenant, the tenant shall as against the
council have the same rights with
respect to compensation for the improvements mentioned in Part I of the
Second Schedule to this Act as he
would have had if the holding had been
a holding to which section 42 of the
Agricultural Holdings Act, 1908, applied:

Provided that the tenant shall not be
entitled to compensation in respect of
any such improvement if executed contrary to an express prohibition in
writing by the council affecting either
the whole or any part of the holding or

allotment; but, if the tenant feels aggrieved by any such prohibition, he may appeal to the *Board*, who may confirm, vary, or annul the prohibition, and the decision of the *Board* shall be final.

(2) Where land has been hired by a council for small holdings or allotments, the council shall (subject to any provision to the contrary in the agreement or order for hiring) be entitled at the determination of the tenancy on quitting the land to compensation under the Agricultural Holdings Act, 1908, for any improvement mentioned in Part I of the Second Schedule to this Act, and for any improvement mentioned in Part II of that Schedule which was necessary or proper to adapt the land for small holdings or allotments, as if the land were a holding to which section 42 of the Agricultural Holdings Act, 1908, applied, and the improvements mentioned in Part II of the said Schedule were improvements mentioned in Part III of the First Schedule to the Agricultural Holdings Act, 1908:

Provided that, in the case of land hired compulsorily, the amount of the compensation payable to the council for those improvements shall be such sum as fairly represents the increase (if any) in the value to the landlord and his successors in title of the holding due to those improvements.

(3) The tenant of an allotment to which Part II of this Act applies may, if he so elects, claim compensation for improvements under the Allotments and Cottage Gardens Compensation for Crops Act, 1887, instead of under the Agricultural Holdings Act, 1908, as amended by this section, notwithstanding that the allotment exceeds two acres in extent.

(4) A tenant of any small holding or allotment may, before the expiration of his tenancy, remove any fruit and other trees and bushes planted or acquired by him for which he has no claim for compensation, and may remove any to l-house, shed, greenhouse, fowl-house, or pigsty built or acquired by him for which he has no claim for compensation. (Note. See also Opencast Coal

Act, 1958 s. 41 and Schedule 8

48. Provisions as to glebe land In the case of glebe land or other lan belonging to an ecclesiastical benefic hired by a council for the purposes o small holdings or allotments—

(1) The provisions of the Ecclesias tical Dilapidations Act, 1871, shall no during the continuance of the tenanc be applicable to the buildings upon th land.

(2) *relates to disposal of buildings o determination of a tenancy of ecclesiastic property.*

52. Borrowing powers (2) Th Public Works Loans Commissioner may, in manner provided by the Publi Works Loans Act, 1875, lend an money which may be borrowed by county council for such purposes a aforesaid:

Provided that—. . .

(*b*) if the *Local Government Board* mak a recommendation to that effect the period for which the loan i made by the Public Works Loan Commissioners may exceed th period allowed under the Publi Works Loans Act, 1875, and th Acts amending that Act, but th period shall not exceed the perio recommended by the *Local Gov ernment Board*, nor, where th purpose of the loan is the pur chase of land, eighty years, or i any other case fifty years; and

53. (2) All expenses incurred by th county council in executing the saic provisions in any . . . parish on defaul of a . . . parish council, or incurred b the county council in or incidentally to a local inquiry under those provisions shall be paid in the first instance out o the county fund as expenses for genera county purposes, and, unless defrayec out of moneys received by the council ir respect of any land acquired under those provisions otherwise than by sale o exchange, or out of money borrowed a before in this Act mentioned, shall, when the powers and duties of the . . . parish council under those provisions are transferred to the county council in pursuance of this Act, be repaid to the county council as a debt by the . . . parish council.

(4) The council of a . . . parish may borrow for the purposes of acquiring, improving and adapting land for allotments—

(5) Sections 242 and 243 of the Public Health Act, 1875, relating to loans by the Public Works Loan Commissioners to a local authority, shall apply . . . with the necessary adaptations, to a loan to a parish council under the *Local Government Act*, 1894, or to a county council lending money to a parish council under that Act, where the purpose for which the loan is required by the parish council is the acquisition, improvement, or adaptation of land under Part II of this Act, in like manner as if those sections were herein re-enacted and in terms made applicable thereto.

54. Separate accounts of receipts and expenditure (1) Separate accounts shall be kept of the receipts and expenditure of a council under this Act with respect to small holdings or allotments, and any such receipts shall, subject to the provisions of this Act, be applicable to the purposes of small holdings or allotments, but not for any other purpose except with the consent of the *Local Government Board*; and, for the purpose of the provisions relating to the audit of accounts, any persons appointed under this Act by a council to exercise and perform powers and duties as to the management of allotments shall be deemed to be officers of the council.

(2) The council of a parish shall within one month after the end of every financial year of the council cause an annual statement, showing their receipts and expenditure with respect to allotments for that year and their liabilities outstanding at the end of that year, to be deposited at some convenient place in the parish, and any ratepayer may without fee inspect and take copies of the statement.

57. Local inquiries (1) The Board . . . and . . . officers of the Board shall have for the purpose of an inquiry in pursuance of this Act the same powers as the *Local Government Board* and

their inspectors respectively have for the purpose of an inquiry under the Public Health Acts.

(2) Notices of the inquiries shall be given and published in accordance with such general or special directions as the Board may give.

(3) A local inquiry by a county council for the purposes of the provisions of this Act relating to allotments shall be held by such one or more members of the small holdings and allotments committee of the council or by such officer of the council or other person as that committee may appoint to hold the inquiry.

58. Arbitrations and valuations (1) All questions which under this Act are referred to arbitration shall, unless otherwise expressly provided by this Act, be determined by a single arbitrator in accordance with the Agricultural Holdings Act, 1908.

(3) The remuneration of an arbitrator or valuer appointed under this Act shall be fixed by the Board.

59. Annual report to Parliament The *Board* shall make an annual report to Parliament of their proceedings, under this Act, and also of the proceedings of the several county, borough, district, and parish councils under this Act, and for that purpose every such council shall, before such date in every year as the Board may fix, send to the Board a report of their proceedings under this Act during the preceding year.

60. Saving for existing tenancies Nothing in this Act shall affect the rights and obligations under any tenancy created under any enactment repealed by this Act.

61. (1) For the purposes of this Act:—
The expression 'allotment' includes a field garden:

The expressions 'agriculture' and 'cultivation' shall include horticulture and the use of land for any purpose of husbandry, inclusive of the keeping or breeding of live stock, poultry, or bees, and the growth of fruit, vegetables, and the like:

The expression 'prescribed' means prescribed by regulations made by the *Board*:

The expression 'landlord', in relation to any land compulsorily hired by a council, means the person for the time being entitled to receive the rent of the land from the council.

(2) In this Act and in the enactments incorporated with this Act the expression 'land' shall include any right or easement in or over land.

(3) For the purposes of this Act, any expenses incurred by a council . . . in the purchase or redemption of any quit rent, chief rent, tithe, or other rentcharge, or other perpetual annual sum issuing out of land . . . shall be deemed to have been incurred in the purchase of the land.

(4) In this Act references to a parish council shall, in the case of a rural parish not having a parish council, include references to the parish meeting.

(5) Any notice required by this Act to be served or given may be sent by *registered* post.

FIRST SCHEDULE.

Part I.

Provisions as to the Compulsory Acquisition of Land by a Council.[1]

(1) The order shall be in the prescribed form, and shall contain such provisions as the *Board* may prescribe for the purpose of carrying the order into effect, and of protecting the council and the persons interested in the land, and shall incorporate, subject to the necessary adaptations, the Lands Clauses Acts and sections 77 to 85 of the Railways Clauses Consolidation Act, 1845, but subject to this modification, that any question of disputed compen-

[1] This schedule no longer applies in the case of Compulsory Acquisition but still relates to compulsory hiring. See s. 39(2).

sation shall be determined by a single arbitrator appointed by the *Board*, who shall be deemed to be an arbitrator within the meaning of the Lands Clauses Acts, and the provisions of those Acts with respect to arbitration shall, subject to the provisions of this schedule, apply accordingly.

(2) The order shall be published by the council in the prescribed manner, and such notice shall be given both in the locality in which the land is proposed to be acquired and to the owners, lessees, and occupiers of that land, as may be prescribed.

(3) If within the prescribed period no objection to the order has been presented to the *Board* by a person interested in the land, or if every such objection has been withdrawn, the *Board* shall, without further inquiry, confirm the order, but, if such an objection has been presented and has not been withdrawn, the *Board* shall forthwith cause a public inquiry to be held in the locality in which the land is proposed to be acquired, and the council and all persons interested in the land and such other persons as the person holding the inquiry in his discretion thinks fit to allow shall be permitted to appear and be heard at the inquiry.

(4) Before confirming the order the *Board* shall consider the report of the person who held the inquiry, and all objections made thereat.

(5) The arbitrator shall, so far as practicable, in assessing compensation act on his own knowledge and experience, but, subject as aforesaid, at any inquiry or arbitration held under this schedule the person holding the inquiry or arbitration shall hear, by themselves or their agents, any authorities or parties authorised by or under this Act to appear, and shall hear witnesses, but shall not, except in such cases as the *Board* otherwise direct, hear *counsel or expert witnesses*.

(7) In construing, for the purposes of this schedule or any order made thereunder, any enactment incorporated with the order, this Act together with the order shall be deemed to be the special Act and the council shall be

eemed to be the promoters of the
undertaking . . .

(8) *relates to disposal of purchase money
and compensation for ecclesiastical property.*

PART II.

PROVISIONS AS TO THE
COMPULSORY HIRING OF
LAND BY A COUNCIL.

(1) The *Board* shall make regulations
for the purpose of carrying the order
into effect and of protecting the
council and the persons interested in the
land, and the order shall incorporate
such regulations, together with such
provisions of the Lands Clauses Acts
and of sections 77 to 85 of the Railways
Clauses Consolidation Act, 1845, as
may, subject to the prescribed adaptations, appear to the Board necessary or
expedient for that purpose.

(2) The order authorising the land
to be hired compulsorily shall determine the terms and conditions of the
hiring other than the rent, and in
particular—

(a) shall provide for the insertion in
the lease of covenants by the
council to cultivate the land in a
proper manner and to pay to the
landlord at the determination of
the tenancy on the council
quitting the land compensation
for any depreciation of the land
by reason of any failure by the
council, or any person deriving
title under them, to observe such
covenants, or by reason of any
user of the land by the council or
such person as aforesaid, and
(unless otherwise agreed) to keep
the buildings and premises demised in repair; and

(b) shall not authorise the breaking
up of pasture unless the *Board* are
satisfied that it can be so broken
up without depreciating the value
of the land, or that the circumstances are such that small holdings or allotments as the case may

be cannot otherwise be success-
fully cultivated; and

(c) shall not, except with the consent
of the landlord, confer on the
council any right to fell or cut
timber or trees or any right to
take, sell, or carry away any
minerals, gravel, sand, or clay,
except so far as may be necessary
or convenient for the purpose of
erecting buildings on the land or
otherwise adapting the land for
small holdings or allotments, and
except upon payment of compensation for minerals, gravel, sand,
or clay so used.

(3) The determination of—

(a) The amount of the rent to be paid
by the council for the land compulsorily hired;
(b) The amount of any other compensation to be paid by the
council to any person entitled
thereto in respect of the land
or any interest therein, or in
respect of improvements executed on the land or otherwise;
and
(c) Where part only of a holding held
for an unexpired term is hired,
the rent to be paid for the residue
of the holding during the remainder of that term;

shall in default of agreement be by
valuation by a single valuer appointed
by the *Board*: Provided that, if the land
hired is in the occupation of a tenant,
he may, by notice in writing served on
the council before the determination of
his tenancy, require that any claim by
him against the council which, under
the Agricultural Holdings Act, 1908,
might be referred to arbitration under
that Act, shall be so referred, and in
such case those claims shall be determined by arbitration under that Act
and not by valuation under this Act.

(4) The valuer, in fixing the rent to
be paid for the land compulsorily hired,
shall take into consideration the rent
(if any) at which the land has been let
and the annual value at which the land

is assessed for purposes of income tax or rating, the loss (if any) caused to the owner by severance, the terms and conditions of the hiring (including any reservation of sporting or fishing rights), and all the other circumstances connected with the land, but shall not make any allowance in respect of any use to which the land compulsorily hired might otherwise be put by the owner during the term of hiring, being a use in respect of which the owner is entitled to resume possession of the land under this Act.

(5) Any compensation awarded to a tenant in respect of any depreciation of the value to him of the residue of his holding caused by the withdrawal from the holding of the land compulsorily hired shall, as far as possible, be provided for by taking such compensation into account in fixing the rent to be paid for the residue of the holding during the remainder of the term for which it is held by the tenant.

(6) Any person interested in any valuation shall give the valuer all such assistance, information, and explanations as he may require and shall produce to the valuer, or give him access to, all such books, accounts, vouchers, and other documents relating to the land to be compulsorily hired as he may reasonably require for the purposes of valuation, and such expenses as the council shall consider or as the valuer certifies to have been properly incurred by any person in furnishing such assistance, information, and explanations or otherwise, in relation to the valuation, shall be paid by the council.

(7) On the determination of any tenancy created by compulsory hiring any questions as to the amount due by the council for depreciation shall in default of agreement be determined by arbitration.

SECOND SCHEDULE.

Improvements referred to in Section Forty-seven.

Part I.

(1) Planting of standard or other fruit trees permanently set out;

(2) Planting of fruit bushes permanently set out;

(3) Planting of strawberry plants;

(4) Planting of asparagus, rhubarb, and other vegetable crops which continue productive for two or more years.

Part II.

(1) Erection, alteration, or enlargement of buildings;

(2) Formation of silos;

(3) Laying down of permanent pasture;

(4) Making and planting of osier beds;

(5) Making of water meadows or works of irrigation;

(6) Making of gardens;

(7) Making or improving of roads or bridges;

(8) Making or improving of watercourses, ponds, wells, or reservoirs, or of works for the application of water power or for supply of water for agricultural or domestic purposes;

(9) Making or removal of permanent fences;

(10) Planting of hops;

(11) Planting of orchards or fruit bushes;

(12) Protecting young fruit trees;

(13) Reclaiming of waste land;

(14) Warping or weiring of land;

(15) Embankments and sluices against floods;

(16) The erection of wirework in hop gardens;

(17) Drainage.

(18) Provision of permanent sheep-dipping accommodation;

(19) in the case of arable land, the removal of bracken, gorse, tree roots, boulders, and other like obstructions to cultivation.

Land Settlement (Facilities) Act, 1919

[19 August 1919]

2. Power of entry on land (1) *Where an order for the compulsory purchase of land has been made, and where necessary confirmed, under the principal Act, whether such order was made before or after the passing of this Act, the council entitled to purchase the land under the order may, at any time after a notice to treat has been served, and on giving not less than fourteen days' notice to each owner, lessee and occupier of the land, enter on and take possession of the land or such part thereof as is specified in the notice without previous consent or compliance with sections 84 to 90 of the Lands Clauses (Consolidation) Act, 1845, but subject to the payment of the like compensation for the land of which possession is taken and interest thereon as would have been payable if the provisions of those sections had been complied with:*

Provided that, where a council have so entered on land, the council shall not be entitled to exercise the powers conferred by subsection (8) of section 39 of the principal Act.[1]

[NOTE. The above wording of this subsection applies only to compulsory hiring.]

(1) *Where the council authorised to purchase any land compulsorily under the principal Act have, by virtue of paragraph (3) of the Second Schedule to the Acquisition of Land (Authorisation Procedure) Act, 1946, entered on the land, the council shall not be entitled to exercise the powers conferred by subsection (8) of section 39 of the principal Act.*

[1]In its relation to compulsory hiring this subsection reads as printed above. In relation to compulsory acquisition it now reads as follows:—

(1) Where the council authorised to purchase any land compulsorily under the principal Act have, by virtue of paragraph (3) of the Second Schedule to the Acquisition of Land (Authorisation Procedure) Act, 1946, entered on the land the council shall not be entitled to exercise the powers conferred by subsection (8) of section 39 of the principal Act.

[NOTE. This wording applies to compulsory purchase.]

(2) Where a council have agreed for the purposes of the principal Act, to purchase land subject to the interest of the person in possession thereof, and that interest is not greater than that of a tenant for a year, or from year to year, then at any time after such agreement has been made the council may, after giving not less than fourteen days' notice to the person so in possession, enter on and take possession of the land or of such part thereof as is specified in the notice without previous consent, but subject to the payment to the person so in possession of the like compensation for the land of which possession is taken, with such interest thereon as aforesaid, as if the council had been authorised to purchase the land compulsorily and such person had, in pursuance of such power, been required to quit possession before the expiration of his term or interest in the land, but without the necessity of compliance with sections 84 to 90 of the Lands Clauses (Consolidation) Act, 1845.

(3) Where a notice of entry under this section relates to land on which there is a dwelling-house and the length of notice is less than three calendar months, the occupier of the dwelling-house may, by notice served on the council within ten days after the service on him of the notice of entry, appeal against such notice, and in any such case the appeal shall be determined by an arbitrator under and in accordance with the provisions of the Second Schedule of the Agricultural Holdings Act, 1908 (except that the arbitrator shall, in default of agreement, be appointed by the President of the Surveyors' Institution), and the council shall not be entitled to enter on the land under this section except on such date and on such conditions as the arbitrator may award.

(4) This section shall with such necessary adaptations as may be prescribed apply in the case of an order

authorising the compulsory hiring of land, or of an agreement to hire land.

8. Sales of glebe For the purpose of a sale of land under the Ecclesiastical Leasing Acts to a council or to the *Board* of Agriculture and Fisheries for the purposes of the principal Act or the Small Holding Colonies Acts, 1916 and 1918, the consent of the patron to the sale shall not be necessary.

16. Amendment of section 41 of principal Act (1) An order under the principal Act may, notwithstanding anything in section 41 thereof, author-ise the compulsory acquisition—

(a) of any land which at the date of the order forms part of any park or of any home farm attached to and usually occupied with a mansion house, if the land is not required for the amenity or con-venience of the mansion house; or

(b) of a holding of fifty acres or less in extent or any part of such a holding.

(2) Where it is proposed to acquire any land forming part of a park or any such home farm, or, except where re-quired for purposes of allotments, a holding of fifty acres or less in extent or of an annual value not exceeding one hundred pounds for the purposes of income tax, or any part of such a hold-ing, the order authorising the acquisi-tion of the land shall not be valid unless confirmed or made by the *Board* of Agriculture and Fisheries.

(3) A holding to which the preceding subsection applies shall not in whole or in part be compulsorily acquired under the principal Act by . . . a council where it is shown to the satisfaction of . . . the council that the holding is the principal means of livelihood of the occupier thereof, except where the occuper is a tenant and consents to the acquisition.

17. Power of county council to acquire land for letting to parish council for allotments A county council may acquire land for the pur-pose of leasing it to the council of a parish within the county for the pro-vision of allotments, and the provisions

of the principal Act relating to the acquisition, and to proceedings in relation to the acquisition, of land fo the purpose of providing small holding shall apply to such acquisition as if the land were to be acquired for the pro vision of small holdings.

19. Power of entry to inspect land A council, with a view to ascertaining whether any land is suitable for any purpose for which the council has powe: to acquire land under the principa Act, may by writing in that behal authorise any person (upon production if so required, of his authority), to ente and inspect the land specified in the authority, and anyone who obstructs o impedes any person acting under and ir accordance with any such authority shall be liable on summary convictior to a fine not exceeding twenty pounds

21. Provisions as to allotments (1) The council of any . . . parish may purchase any fruit trees, seeds, plants fertilizers or implements required for the purposes of allotments cultivated as gardens, whether provided by the council or otherwise, and sell any article so purchased to the cultivators, or, in the case of implements, allow their use, at a price or charge sufficient to cover the cost of purchase.

(2) The powers conferred by the pre-ceding subsection shall be exercisable by a council only where in the opinion of the council the facilities for the pur-chase or hire of the articles therein referred to from a society on a co-operative basis are inadequate.

(3) Rules made by a council under section 28 of the principal Act, shall, unless otherwise expressly provided, apply to an allotment, though held under a tenancy made before the rules come into operation.

(5) Stamp duty shall not be payable on any lease or agreement for the letting of any allotment or garden, whether provided under the principal Act or otherwise, or on any duplicate or counterpart of any such lease or agree-ment where the rent does not exceed ten shillings per annum and no premium is paid.

22. Power of appropriation of

and (1) A council of a . . . parish may, in a case where no power of appropriation is otherwise provided, with the consent of the *Board* of Agriculture and *Fisheries* and the *Local Government Board*, and subject to such conditions as to the repayment of any loan obtained for the purpose of the acquisition of land or otherwise as the last-mentioned *Board* may impose,—

(*a*) appropriate for the purpose of allotments *any land held by the council for other purposes* of the council; or

(*b*) appropriate for other purposes of the council land acquired by the council for allotments.

23. Agreements as to compensation where land is let for provision of allotments Where land is let for the provision of allotments either to a council under the principal Act or to an association formed for the purpose of creating or promoting the creation of allotments, the right of the council or association to claim compensation from the landlord on the determination of the tenancy shall be subject to the terms of the contract of tenancy, notwithstanding the provision of any Act to the contrary:

Provided that this section shall not prejudice or affect any right on the part of a person holding under a tenancy granted by the council or association to claim compensation from the council or association on the determination of his tenancy.

Part IV.

General.

28. Provisions as to commons and open spaces (1) Any land which is, or forms part of, a metropolitan common within the meaning of the Metropolitan Commons Act, 1866, or which is subject to regulation under an order or scheme made in pursuance of the Inclosure Acts, 1845 to 1899, or under any local Act or otherwise, or which is or forms part of any town or village green, or of any area dedicated or appropriated as a public park, garden, or pleasure ground, or for use for the purposes of public recreation, shall not be appropriated under this Act by a council for small holdings or allotments, and shall not be acquired by a council or by the *Board* of Agriculture and Fisheries under the principal Act except under the authority of an order for compulsory purchase made under the principal Act, which so far as it relates to such land shall be provisional only, and shall not have effect unless it is confirmed by Parliament.

(2) The *Board* of Agriculture and Fisheries, in giving or withholding their consent under this Act to the appropriation and in confirming an order for compulsory acquisition by a council for the purpose of small holdings or allotments of any land which forms part of any common, and in the exercise by the *Board* of their powers of acquiring land under this Act, shall have regard to the same considerations and shall hold the same inquiries as are directed by the Commons Act, 1876, to be taken into consideration and held by the *Board* before forming an opinion whether an application under the Inclosure Acts shall be acceded to or not. Any consent by the *Board* of Agriculture and Fisheries for the appropriation of land forming part of any common for the purpose of small holdings or allotments shall be laid before Parliament while Parliament is sitting, and, if within twenty-one days in either House of Parliament a motion is carried dissenting from such appropriation the order of the Board shall be cancelled.

(3) Where an order for compulsory purchase to which this section applies or a consent by the *Board* to the appropriation of land provides for giving other land in exchange for the common or open space to be purchased or appropriated, the order for compulsory purchase or an order made by the *Board* in relation to the consent for appropriation may vest the land given in exchange in the persons in whom the

common or open space purchased or appropriated was vested subject to the same rights, trusts, and incidents as attached to the common or open space and discharges the land purchased or appropriated from all rights, trusts, and incidents to which it was previously subject.

(4) Nothing in the principal Act shall be deemed to authorise the acquisition of any land which forms part of the trust property to which the National Trust Act, 1907, applies.

32. Construction (1) This Act, so far as it amends the principal Act, shall be construed as one with that Act, and references in this Act to the principal Act, or to any provision of the principal Act, shall, where the context permits be construed as references to the principal Act, or the provisions of the principal Act as amended by this Act.

34. Short title This Act may be cited as the Land Settlement (Facilities) Act, 1919, and the Small Holdings and Allotments Acts, 1908 and 1910, and so much of this Act as amends those Act may be cited together as the Small Holdings and Allotments Acts, 1908 to 1919.

Allotments Act, 1922

1. Determination of tenancies of allotment gardens (1) Where land is let on a tenancy for use by the tenant as an allotment garden or is let to any local authority or association for the purpose of being sub-let for such use the tenancy of the land or any part shall not (except as hereinafter provided) be terminable by the landlord by notice to quit or re-entry, notwithstanding any agreement to the contrary, except by—

(a) [1]a twelve months' or longer notice to quit expiring on or before the 6th day of April or on or after the 29th day of September in any year; or

(b) re-entry, after three months' previous notice in writing to the tenant, under a power of re-entry contained in or affecting the contract of tenancy on account of the land being required for building, mining, or any other industrial purpose or for roads or sewers necessary in connection with any of those purposes; or

(c) re-entry under a power in that behalf contained in or affecting the contract of tenancy in the case of land let by a corporation or company being the owners or lessees of a railway, dock, canal, water, or other public undertak-

[1]As amended by Allotments Act, 1950.

ing on account of the land being required by the corporation, or company, for any purpose (not being the use of the land for agriculture) for which it was acquired or held by the corporation, or company, or has been appropriated under any statutory provision, but so that, except in a case of emergency, three months notice in writing of the intended re-entry shall be given to the tenant; or

(d) re-entry under a power in that behalf contained in or affecting the contract of tenancy, in the case of land let by a local authority (being land which was acquired by the local authority before the passing of this Act under the Housing Acts, 1890 to 1921) on account of the land being required by the local authority for the purposes of those Acts, and, in the case of other land let by a local authority, after three months' previous notice in writing to the tenant on account of the land being required by the local authority for a purpose (not being the use of land for agriculture) for which it was acquired by the local authority, or has been appropriated under any statutory provision; or

(e) re-entry for non-payment of rent or breach of any term or condition of the tenancy or on account of the tenant becoming bankrupt or compounding with his creditors, or where the tenant is an association, on account of its liquidation.

(2) This section shall apply to a tenancy current at the date of the passing of this Act, but not so as to affect the operation of any notice to quit given, or proceedings for recovery of possession commenced, before that date.

(3) Where under any contract of tenancy to which this section applies, made before the passing of this Act, the tenancy is either by express provision or by implication made terminable by the landlord by notice to quit expiring on a date between the 6th day of April and the 29th day of September, the tenancy shall be terminable by him on the 29th day of September, and any such notice to quit given in accordance with the contract shall have the effect of a notice to quit on that day.

(4) [1]This section shall not apply to land held by or on behalf of the Admiralty, War Department, Air Council, or *Minister of Supply*, and so let as aforesaid when possession of the land is required for naval, military, or air force purposes or for purposes of the *Ministry of Supply*, as the case may be.

2. Compensation on quitting allotment gardens (1) Where under any contract of tenancy land is, before or after the passing of this Act, let for use by the tenant as an allotment garden, the tenant shall, subject to the provisions of this section and notwithstanding any agreement to the contrary, be entitled at the termination of the tenancy, on quitting the land, to obtain from the landlord compensation as provided by this section.

(2) [1]Subject to the provisions of this section, compensation shall be recoverable under this section only if the tenancy is terminated by the landlord by notice to quit or by re-entry, under

paragraph (b), (c) or (d) of subsection (1) of the last preceding section.

(3) The compensation recoverable from the landlord under this section shall be for crops growing upon the land in the ordinary course of the cultivation of the land as an allotment garden or allotment gardens, and for manure applied to the land.

(4) A tenant whose tenancy is terminated by the termination of the tenancy of his landlord shall be entitled to recover from his landlord such compensation (if any) as would have been recoverable if his tenancy had been terminated by notice to quit given by his landlord.

(6) This section shall also apply to any contract of tenancy made after the passing of this Act by which land is let to any local authority or association for the purpose of being sublet for use by the tenants as allotment gardens and, notwithstanding that the crops have been grown and the manure applied by the tenants of the local authority or association. Section 23 of the Land Settlement (Facilities) Act, 1919, shall not apply to land let after the passing of this Act to any local authority or association for the purpose of being sub-let for use by the tenants as allotment gardens.

(7) This section shall apply to the termination of the tenancy of the whole or any part of the land the subject of a contract of tenancy.

(8) Except as provided by this section or by the contract of tenancy, the tenant of land under a contract of tenancy to which this section applies shall not be entitled to recover compensation from the landlord at the termination of the tenancy.

(9) If the tenancy of the tenant is terminated on the 29th day of September or the 11th day of October, or at any date between those days, either by notice to quit given by the landlord or by the termination of the tenancy of the landlord, the tenant whose tenancy is so terminated shall be entitled at any time within twenty-one days after the termination of the tenancy to remove any crops growing on the land.

[1] As amended by Allotments Act, 1950.

(10) This section shall not apply to any tenancy which is terminated by the effluxion of time before the date of the passing of this Act, or, where a notice to quit has been given, re-entry has been made or proceedings for recovery of possession have been commenced before that date.

3. Provision as to cottage holdings and certain allotments (1) The foregoing provisions of this Act as to determination of tenancies of allotment gardens and compensation to a tenant on quitting the same shall not apply to any parcel of land attached to a cottage.

(2) In the case of any allotment within the meaning of this section (not being an allotment garden), the tenant shall, on the termination of his tenancy by effluxion of time, or from any other cause, be entitled, notwithstanding any agreement to the contrary, to obtain from the landlord compensation for the following matters:—

(a) For crops, including fruit, growing upon the land in the ordinary course of cultivation and for labour expended upon and manure applied to the land; and

(b) For fruit trees or bushes provided and planted by the tenant with the previous consent in writing of the landlord, and for drains, outbuildings, pigsties, fowlhouses, or other structural improvements made or erected by and at the expense of the tenant on the land with such consent.

(3) Any sum due to the landlord from the tenant in respect of rent or of any breach of the contract of tenancy under which the land is held, or wilful or negligent damage committed or permitted by the tenant, shall be taken into account in reduction of the compensation.

(4) The amount of the compensation shall, in default of agreement, be determined and recovered in the same manner as compensation is, under this Act, to be determined and recovered in the case of an allotment garden.

(5) *The Agricultural Holdings Acts,* 1908

to 1921, shall, in the case of an allotment within the meaning of this section to which those Acts apply, have effect as if the provisions of this section as to the determination and recovery of compensation were substituted for the provisions of those Acts as to the determination and recovery of compensation, and a claim for compensation for any matter or thing for which a claim for compensation can be made under this section, may be made either under those Acts or under this section, but not under both.

(6) The compensation in respect of an improvement made or begun on an allotment (not being an allotment garden) before the passing of this Act shall be such (if any) as could have been claimed if this Act had not been passed.

(7) In this section the expression 'allotment' means any parcel of land, whether attached to a cottage or not, of not more than two acres in extent, held by a tenant under a landlord and cultivated as a farm or a garden, or partly as a garden and partly as a farm.

4. Further provision as to allotment gardens and allotments (1) A tenant of land held under a contract of tenancy to which any of the foregoing provisions of this Act apply may, before the termination of the tenancy, remove any fruit trees or bushes provided and planted by the tenant and any erection, fencing or other improvement erected or made by and at the expense of the tenant, making good any injury caused by such removal.

(2) A tenant of land held under a contract of tenancy to which any of the foregoing provisions of this Act apply and which is made with a mortgagor but is not binding on the mortgagee, shall, on being deprived of possession by the mortgagee, be entitled to recover compensation from him as if he were the landlord and had then terminated the tenancy, but subject to the deduction from such compensation of any rent or other sum due from the tenant in respect of the land.

5. Rights of tenant who has paid

compensation to outgoing tenant
Where a tenant of an allotment has paid compensation to an outgoing tenant for any fruit trees or bushes or other improvement, he shall have the same rights as to compensation or removal as he would have had under this Act if the fruit trees or bushes had been provided and planted or the improvement had been made by him and at his expense.

6. Assessment and recovery of compensation (1) The compensation under the foregoing provisions of this Act, and such further compensation (if any) as is recoverable under the contract of tenancy shall, in default of agreement, be determined by a valuation made by a person appointed in default of agreement by the judge of the county court having jurisdiction in the place where the land is situated, on an application in writing being made for the purpose by the landlord or tenant, and, if not paid within fourteen days after the amount is agreed or determined, shall be recoverable upon order made by the county court as money ordered to be paid by a county court under its ordinary jurisdiction, is recoverable.

(2) The proper charges of the value or the valuation shall be borne by the landlord and tenant in such proportion as the valuer shall direct, but be recoverable by the valuer from either of the parties and any amount paid by either of the parties in excess of the amount (if any) directed by the valuer to be borne by him shall be recoverable from the other party and may be deducted from any compensation payable to such party.

7. Application to Crown lands The foregoing provisions of this Act shall not apply to any land of which possession was taken by or on behalf of any Government department under the enactments relating to the Defence of the Realm or the regulations made thereunder and possession of which has been continued by virtue of any enactment, or to any land forming part of a royal park; but, save as aforesaid, the foregoing provisions of this Act shall apply to land vested in His Majesty in right of the Crown or the Duchy of Lancaster, and to land forming part of the possessions of the Duchy of Cornwall, and, except as otherwise hereinbefore expressly provided, to land vested in any Government department for public purposes.

8. (3) Notwithstanding anything contained in any other enactment, counsel shall not be heard in any arbitration under this Act or as to compensation payable for land acquired for allotments under the Allotments Acts unless the Minister otherwise directs.

(4) No land shall be authorised by an order under the Allotments Acts to be hired compulsorily for the purposes of allotments which at the date of the order is pasture land if it is proved to the satisfaction of the Minister that arable land which is equally suitable for the purpose of allotments to the pasture land proposed to be compulsorily hired is reasonably available for hiring by the council.

(5) Paragraph 2 (*b*) of Part II of Schedule I to the Small Holdings and Allotments Act, 1908 (which restricts the breaking up of pasture compulsorily hired) shall not apply to land compulsorily hired for the provision of allotment gardens.

11. Determination of questions arising on resumption of land (1) Where land has been let to a local authority or to an association for the purpose of being sub-let for use as allotment gardens, or is occupied by a council under the powers of entry conferred by this Act, and the landlord, or the person who but for such occupation would be entitled to the possession of the land, proposes to resume possession of the land in accordance with the provisions of this Act for any particular purpose, notice in writing of the purpose for which resumption is required shall be given to the local authority or association.

(2) The local authority or association may, by a counter notice served within twenty-one days after receipt of such notice on the person requiring possession, demand that the question as to

M

whether resumption of possession is required in good faith for the purpose specified in the notice shall be determined by arbitration under and in accordance with the provisions of the Second Schedule to the Agricultural Holdings Act, 1908.

(3) Possession of the land shall not be resumed until after the expiration of the said period of twenty-one days or the determination of such question as aforesaid where such determination is demanded under this section.

(4) This section shall not apply to any case where resumption of possession is required by a corporation or company being the owners or lessees of a railway, dock, canal, water, or other public undertaking.

12. Time limit for serving notice to treat for compulsory acquisition of land (1) Where an order has been made for the compulsory acquisition of any land and notice to treat thereunder is not served by the acquiring authority within three calendar months after the date of the said order, or where confirmation of the said order is necessary, then after the date of the confirmation thereof the order so far as it relates to land in respect of which notice to treat has not been so served shall become null and void.

(2) Where an order has so become null and void as respects any land, no order authorising the compulsory acquisition of that land or any part of such land shall, if made within three years after the expiration of the said three calendar months, be valid, unless confirmed by the Minister, or be so confirmed, unless it is proved to the satisfaction of the Minister that there are special reasons justifying the failure to exercise the powers under the original order and the making of the order submitted for confirmation.

16. Limitation on expenditure on allotments and rents to be charged (1) [1]A council *shall not* take any proceedings under the provisions of the Allotments Acts relating to allotments, unless in the opinion of the council the

[1] As amended by Allotments Act, 1950.

expenses of the council incurred under those provisions (other than such expenses as are hereinafter specified) may reasonably be expected, after the proceedings are taken to exceed the receipts of the council under those provisions by no greater amount than would be produced by a rate of *twopence* ($\cdot$8p) in the pound.

(2) For the purposes of this section, expenses and receipts shall be calculated in such manner as the Minister of Housing and Local Government may direct, and shall include expenses and receipts in respect of land acquired whether before or after the passing of this Act:

Provided that such expenses shall not include—

(a) expenses in relation to the acquisition of land other than the purchase price or rent, or other compensation payable in respect of the land;
(b) expenses incurred in making roads to be used by the public;
(c) sinking fund charges in respect of loans raised in connection with the purchase of land.

18. Financial provisions (1) ... the provisions of subsection (2) of section 52 of the Small Holdings and Allotments Act, 1908, relating to loans by the Public Works Loan Commissioners for small holdings shall extend to money borrowed by any such council for the purpose of providing allotments.

19. Penalty for damage to an allotment garden (1) Any person who by any act done without lawful authority or by negligence causes damage to any allotment garden or any crops or fences or buildings thereon shall be liable on summary conviction to a penalty not exceeding £20, but this provision shall not apply unless notice of this provision is conspicuously displayed on or near the allotment garden.

21. Provision as to parts of New Forest now used for allotment gardens (1) Notwithstanding anything in any other Act, the *Commissioners of Woods* may let for any term to a local authority under the Allotments Acts, and the local authority may take for the purpose of providing allotment gardens any land in the Forest (as defined in the New Forest Act, 1877) which is vested in His Majesty and was on the 5th day of April, 1922, being used for the provision of allotment gardens, and, with the consent of the Minister, such further land in the forest not exceeding sixty acres, as may be agreed between the *Commissioners of Woods* and the Verderers of the Forest:

Provided that, if at any time any land so let is used for any purpose other than the provision of allotment gardens, the lease shall become void and the land shall revert to His Majesty and be held in the same manner as it was held before its use for the provision of allotment gardens and subject to the same rights and liabilities so far as practicable.

(2) While a lease under this section has effect any land let thereunder shall be free from all rights of common and all other similar rights and privileges except the right of the public to use any highway on the land.

(3) *relates to division of rent between the Commissioners and the Verderers.*

22. Interpretation (1) For the purposes of this Act, where the context permits—

The expression 'allotment garden' means an allotment not exceeding forty poles in extent which is wholly or mainly cultivated by the occupier for the production of vegetable or fruit crops for consumption by himself or his family;
The expression 'landlord' means in relation to any land the person for the time being entitled to receive the rents and profits of the land:
The designations of landlord and

tenant shall continue to apply to the parties until the conclusion of any proceedings taken under this Act in respect of compensation and shall include the legal personal representative of either party;
The expression 'council' shall, in the case of a rural parish not having a parish council, mean the parish meeting;
The expression 'industrial purpose' shall not include use for agriculture or sport, and the expression 'agriculture' includes forestry, horticulture, or the keeping and breeding of livestock;
The expression 'the Allotments Acts' means the provisions of the Small Holdings and Allotments Acts, 1908 to 1919, which relate to allotments and this Act;
The expression 'Minister' means the Minister of *Agriculture and Fisheries*;
The expression 'sinking fund charges' includes any charges for the repayment of loans whether by means of a sinking fund or otherwise.

(3) Compensation recoverable by a tenant under this Act for crops or other things shall be based on the value thereof to an incoming tenant.

(4) Where land is used by the tenant thereof as an allotment garden, then, for the purposes of this Act, unless the contrary is proved—

(a) the land shall be deemed to have been let to him to be used by him as an allotment garden; and
(b) where the land has been sublet to him by a local authority or association which holds the land under a contract of tenancy, the land shall be deemed to have been let to that authority or association for the purpose of being sub-let for such use as aforesaid.

War Memorials
(*Local Authorities' Powers*) *Act, 1923*

1. Expenditure in maintenance, &c., of war memorials A local

authority may incur reasonable expenditure in the maintenance, repair and protection of any war memorial within their district whether vested in them or not.[1]

2. Any expenditure to be incurred under this Act by a local authority shall—

(a) in the case of a parish council or parish meeting, be limited to an amount which will not involve a rate exceeding a *penny* (·**6p**) in the pound for any financial year.

3. Application The provisions of this Act shall not apply to a war memorial provided or maintained by a local authority in the exercise of any other statutory power.

4. Definition In this Act the expression 'local authority' means the council of a . . . parish, and the parish meeting of a rural parish with no parish council.

Allotments Act, 1925

1. Interpretation In this Act, unless the context otherwise requires—

'Allotment' means an allotment garden as defined by the Allotments Act, 1922, or any parcel of land not more than five acres in extent cultivated or intended to be cultivated as a garden or farm, or partly as a garden and partly as a farm;

'Commissioners' means the Public Works Loans Commissioners;

'The Act of 1922' means the Allotments Act, 1922.

8. Sale, &c., of land used as allotments Where a local authority has purchased or appropriated land for use as allotments the local authority shall not sell, appropriate, use, or dispose of the land for any purpose other than use for allotments without the consent of the Minister of *Agriculture and Fisheries* after consultation with the *Minister of Health*, and such consent may be given unconditionally or subject to such conditions as the Minister thinks fit, but shall not be given unless the Minister is satisfied that adequate pro-

vision will be made for allotment holders displaced by the action of the local authority or that such provision is unnecessary or not reasonably practicable, and where such consent is obtained the sanction of the county council under section 32 of the Small Holdings and Allotments Act, 1908, shall not be required.

13. Records of purchase price, rent, and rateable value of land acquired Where land is purchased or leased by a local authority under the Allotments Acts, 1908 to 1922, or this Act, the local authority shall record the purchase price or rent agreed to be paid for the land, and the gross value or gross estimated rental at which the land is assessed for rating purposes at the date of its acquisition, where it is separately so assessed, or the apportioned part thereof as estimated by the local authority, where it is not so separately so assessed, and the particulars so recorded shall be included by each local authority in their annual report to the *Minister of Agriculture and Fisheries* under section 59 of the Small Holdings and Allotments Act, 1908.

[1] As amended by L.G.A. 1948

Small Holdings and Allotment Acts, 1926

17. Amendment of law as to the acquisition of land . . .[1]

(3) For removing doubts as to the effect of the Acquisition of Land (Assessment of Compensation) Act, 1919, it is hereby declared:—

(*a*) that the said Act does not apply to the determination of a dispute as to the amount of compensation payable on the withdrawal of a notice to treat under subsection (8) of section 39 of the principal Act;

(*b*) that the said Act has not affected the power of the Minister under paragraphs (5) and (6) of Part I of the First Schedule to the principal Act to give directions with respect to the hearing of . . . expert witnesses . . . and that any directions so given . . . apply to arbitrations before an official arbitrator both when assessing the compensation in the case of the compulsory purchase of land and when assessing the rent or other compensation to be paid in the case of the compulsory hiring of land.

18. Provisions as to land compulsorily hired (1) Where a council in pursuance of the powers conferred by section 44 of the principal Act have given notice to the landlord of land compulsorily hired by them to renew the tenancy, it shall be lawful for the council to withdraw the notice at any time not less than three months before

[1] As amended by LGA 1958 and 1966.

the expiration of the tenancy if it appears to the council that the rent assessed in pursuance of the said section is such as will involve loss to the council, but in any such case the landlord shall be entitled to obtain from the council compensation for any loss or expenses which he may have sustained or incurred by reason or in consequence of the notice to renew and of the notice to withdraw, such compensation to be determined in like manner as the compensation for withdrawal of notice to treat under subsection (8) of section 39 of the principal Act.

(2) A notice to resume possession of the whole or part of land hired by a council compulsorily for small holdings or allotments given under section 46 of the principal Act shall not be valid if given before it has been shown to the satisfaction of the Minister that the land, possession of which is proposed to be resumed, is required for such a purpose as is mentioned in that section, and where an applicant has failed to satisfy the Minister that any land is required for such a purpose, any further application to the Minister with a view to the resumption of possession of the same land or any part of it for the same purpose shall not be entertained if made within two years after the previous application.

22. (2) Any references in any other Act to the Small Holdings Commissioners shall be construed as references to such officers of the Ministry of Agriculture and Fisheries as the Minister may appoint for the purpose.

Overseers Order, 1927

(S.R. & O. 1927 No. 55)

At the Court at Buckingham Palace the 7th day of February, 1927.

PRESENT,

The King's Most Excellent Majesty in Council.

. . . His Majesty, by and with the advice of His Privy Council, is pleased to order, and is hereby ordered, as follows:—

Preliminary

1. (1) This Order . . . save as otherwise expressly provided shall come into operation on the 1st day of April, 1927.

2. (1) The Interpretation Act, 1889, applies to the interpretation of this Order as it applies to the interpretation of an Act of Parliament.

(2) In this Order, unless the context otherwise requires—

'Parish' has the same meaning as in subsection (4) of Section 68 of the Rating and Valuation Act, 1925;

'Property' includes all property, real and personal, and all estates, interests, easements, and rights, whether equitable or legal, in, to, and out of property real and personal, including things in action, and registers, books, and documents;

'Rating Authority' means the council of any county borough, urban district or rural district;

'Rural parish' means a parish in a rural district;

'The Act of 1925' means the Rating and Valuation Act, 1925;

'The appointed day' means the 1st day of April, 1927;

'The Minister' means the *Minister of Health*.

(3) Where rural parishes are grouped under a common parish council, any reference in this Order to the parish council shall include a reference to the grouped parish council, but where the powers or duties in connection with which the expression is used are excluded by the grouping order from the powers or duties exercisable by the parish council, any reference in this Order to the parish council shall be read as a reference to the parish meeting of each of the grouped parishes.

Holding or Management of Parish Property, Village Greens and Allotments

4. (1) The powers and duties of the overseers, or of the churchwardens and overseers, of any urban parish with respect to the holding or management of parish property (not being property relating to affairs of the church or held for an ecclesiastical charity within the meaning of the Local Government Act, 1894), and the holding or management of village greens, or of allotments, whether for recreation grounds or for gardens or otherwise for the benefit of the inhabitants or any of them, and whether of that parish or of that parish conjointly with other parishes, are hereby transferred to the rating authority.

(2) The powers and duties of overseers, or of the churchwardens and overseers, mentioned in paragraph (1) of this article, as respects any rural parish not having a separate parish council and to which sub-section (6) of Section 19 of the Local Government Act, 1894, applies, are hereby transferred to the parish meeting.

(3) Where immediately before the appointed day the overseers, or the

churchwardens and overseers, of any urban parish are associated with any other persons in the holding or management of parish property, village greens or allotments to which this article applies, the powers and duties of the overseers, or of the churchwardens and overseers, in relation to such holding or management, are hereby transferred to such number of persons, not exceeding the number of overseers, or of churchwardens and overseers (as the case may be) as may be appointed by the rating authority, and shall be exercised and performed by the persons so appointed jointly with the persons associated with them.

(4) Paragraph (3) of this article shall extend to any rural parish, and if the parish has a parish council with the substitution for the rating authority of the parish council, and if the parish has not a parish council with the substitution for the rating authority of the parish meeting.

Other Powers and Duties of Overseers

5. (1) The powers and duties of overseers, or of the churchwardens and overseers, under the enactments mentioned in the schedule to this Order are hereby transferred to the local authorities or persons mentioned in the third, fourth and fifth columns of that schedule, and those enactments shall have effect accordingly.

Transfer of Property

6. (1) All property held by overseers, or by the churchwardens and overseers, for the purposes or in the exercise or performance of any powers or duties transferred by the foregoing provisions of this Order shall by virtue of this Order pass to and vest in the authority to whom the powers and duties are transferred, subject to all debts and liabilities affecting the same.

7. (2) On the appointed day, or if the first appointment under the proviso to paragraph (1) of this article is made after the appointed day by the rural district council, on the day on which the appointment is made by them, the legal

interest in all property vested in the body corporate consisting of the chairman of the parish meeting and overseers shall, by virtue of this Order, be transferred to and vest in the representative body of the parish.

(3) If on the appointed day the representative body constituted by this article is not complete, the persons who immediately before that day constitute the body corporate consisting of the chairman of the parish meeting and overseers shall continue to constitute that body corporate until the representative body is complete.

(4) Any reference in any Act or document to the corporate body consisting of the chairman of the parish meeting and overseers of a parish shall be read as a reference to the corporate body constituted by this article.

Trustees under Local Acts

8. Where immediately before the appointed day the overseers of any parish are members *ex officio* of a body of trustees incorporated by a local Act, and property the income whereof is applicable in aid of the poor rate or otherwise for the general benefit of the ratepayers, parishioners or inhabitants of a parish is vested in those trustees, such number of persons, not exceeding the number of the overseer trustees, as the rating authority shall appoint, shall be trustees in place of the overseers.

Term of Office of Trustees, &c. Vacancies

12. (1) The term of office of a trustee or member of a corporate body appointed under a power conferred by this Order shall, subject to the provisions of this Order, be four years.

(2) Any trustee appointed under a power conferred by this Order may, by a notice signed by him and delivered to the appointing authority, resign his office as trustee, and a copy of the notice shall forthwith be sent by him to the clerk or chairman of the trustees.

(3) Any member of a corporate body appointed by a rural district council under a power conferred by this Order

may, by a notice signed by him and delivered to the clerk of that council, resign his office as member.

(4) The body in whom by this Order is vested the power of appointing trustees or members of a corporate body shall fill, as soon as practicable, any vacancy in the office.

(5) Nothing in this article shall affect the power of the Minister, to prescribe the term of office of a trustee or other person in any order made under a power conferred by this Order.

Enactments as to expenditure and receipts of Overseers

13. (1) Save as otherwise provided in this Order—

(a) Any enactment authorising expenses to be defrayed by overseers and either expressly providing or conveying by implication that the expenses shall be defrayed from the poor rate of a parish; and

(b) any enactment authorising fines, fees, allowances, income from an endowment, or other receipts to be applied in aid of the poor rate of a parish, and either expressly providing or conveying by implication that the receipts are to be so applied by overseers; and

(c) any order or direction given under any enactment referred to in this article;

shall have effect with the substitution for the overseers of the rating authority, and for the poor rate of the general rate or the poor rate, or, where the area for which the rate is made comprises more than one parish, of that portion of the general rate or poor rate which is levied on the parish.

(2) Where under sub-section (3) of Section 41 of the Education Act, 1921, as amended by this article, a county council direct money arising from an endowment to be paid to the rating authority, they shall specify the parish or parishes for whose benefit the money is by the rating authority to be applied and the proportions in which the money is so to be applied.

Service and Signature of Documents

14. Save as otherwise provided by this Order, where any enactment or order provides for the service upon or transmission to the overseers, or the churchwardens and overseers, of a parish of any document, the enactment or order shall have effect in its application to—

(2) a rural parish under a parish council, as if it provided for the service of the document on or its transmission to the *chairman* of the parish council; or

(3) a rural parish not under a parish council as if it provided for the service of the document on or its transmission to the chairman of the parish meeting.

15. (1) Any document required to be signed by the overseers, or by the churchwardens and overseers, of a parish and relating to powers or duties transferred by this Order to a local authority may, save as otherwise in this Order provided, be signed by the clerk to the local authority.

(2) Any document required to be signed by the overseers, or by the churchwardens and overseers, of a parish and relating to powers or duties transferred by this Order to a chairman, officer or other person, may be signed by that person.

Expenses of Execution of Transferred Powers, &c.

16. (1) Any expenses incurred in the exercise or performance of those powers and duties of overseers which by this Order are transferred to—

(a) the parish council or chairman of the parish council, or to the parish meeting or chairman of the parish meeting, shall be defrayed as part of the general expenses of the parish council or parish meeting as the case may require;

(2) Subject to the provisions of this Order, any expenses incurred in the exercise or performance of those powers and duties which by this Order are transferred to the rating authority, or to the clerk to the rating authority, shall be defrayed by the rating authority, and shall be chargeable by them to the account of the parish in respect of which the expenses were incurred.

Supplemental Provision as to Property Transferred

17. Where by or in pursuance of this Order property is transferred from overseers to another authority—

(1) The authority to whom the property is transferred shall hold the property for the estate, interest and purposes, and subject to the covenants, conditions, and restrictions for and subject to which the property would have been held if this Order had not been made, so far as the same are not modified by or in pursuance of the Act of 1925; and

(2) All debts and liabilities incurred by overseers in respect of or otherwise affecting the property shall become debts and liabilities of the authority to whom the property is transferred and shall, subject to the provisions of the Act of 1925, be defrayed from the like property and funds from which they would have been defrayed if this Order had not been made.

Exceptional Areas

18. (2) If any difficulty arises in connection with the application of this Order to any exceptional area, as defined in Section 67 of the Act of 1925, or otherwise in bringing into operation in an exceptional area any of the provisions of this Order, the *Minister* may, by order, remove the difficulty or do anything which appears to him necessary or expedient for bringing the said provisions into operation.

(3) An order of the Minister under this article may modify the provisions of this Order in so far as may appear to the *Minister* necessary or expedient for carrying his order into effect, and may provide for any necessary adjustment of property and liabilities.

Savings

19. This Order shall have effect subject to the provisions of the Act of 1925.

20. The abolition of the office of overseer shall not, nor shall anything contained in this Order,—

(2) affect the transfer by the Local Government Act, 1894, to parish councils of any powers, duties and liabilities of overseers, or affect any powers as to charities conferred on parish councils by that Act.

21. Nothing in this Order shall prejudice or affect any right or interest in any charitable endowment, or the jurisdiction of the Charity Commissioners or the *Board of Education* over any charitable endowment.

22. This Order shall have effect subject to the provisions of any future Order made under Section 62 of the Act of 1925.

M. P. A. Hankey.

M*

The Schedule

ENACTMENTS CONFERRING POWERS OR IMPOSING DUTIES ON OVERSEERS
AND DESTINATION OF POWERS AND DUTIES.

Enactment. (1)	Subject-matter. (2)	Destination in rural parishes—	
		under a parish council. (4)	not under a parish council. (5)
The Burial Act, 1852 (15 & 16 Vict. c. 85) s. 42, as extended by the Burial Act, 1853 (16 & 17 Vict. c. 134) s. 7.	Provision of mortuary where no burial board appointed.	The parish council. The parish	— —
The Reserve Forces Act, 1882 (45 & 46 Vict. c. 48) s. 24 and as applied by any other enactment or by Order in Council.	Publication and service of notices by overseers.	The chairman of the parish council.	The chairman of the parish meeting.

Local Government Act, 1929

75. Adaptation of enactments imposing limits on expenditure of local authorities (1) Subject as hereinafter provided, any provision of *any enactment*[1] imposing a limit upon the expenditure of a local authority for any purpose in any year by reference to any specified rate poundage shall, have effect as if for the limit thereby imposed there were substituted such a limit as would be imposed if the specified rate poundage were increased by $33\frac{1}{3}\%$, or such higher percentage as the Minister may by order in any special case allow.

(2) An order under this section shall be laid before Parliament as soon as may be after it is made.

(3) For the purposes of this section—

(*a*) a provision shall be deemed to

impose a limit upon the expenditure of a local authority by reference to a specified rate poundage, if the effect of the provision is that the expenditure is—

(i) not to involve a rate of not exceeding a specified sum in the pound; or

(ii) not to exceed the amount which would be produced by a rate of a specified sum in the pound, whether or not the expenditure is to be defrayed or the amount raised out of rates;

and any sum so specified as aforesaid is in this section referred to as a 'specified rate poundage':

(*b*) a provision that if the expenditure of a local authority exceeds in any

[1] Not now including the Allotments Act.

year any specified rate poundage any functions of the authority are to cease or be suspended, shall be deemed to impose a limit upon the expenditure of the authority.

115. Parish property

(3) The council of any county borough or urban district and the parish meeting of any rural parish not having a parish council may exercise the powers of executing works in relation to parish property which are by paragraph (*i*) of subsection (1) of section 8 of the Local Government Act, 1894, conferred on parish councils.

(6) For the purposes of this Section ... 'parish property' means any property the rents and profits of which are applicable or, if the property were let, would be applicable to the general benefit of one or more parishes, or the ratepayers, parishioners or inhabitants thereof, but does not include—

(*a*) property given or bequeathed by way of charitable donation or allotted in right of some charitable donation or otherwise for the poor persons of any parish or parishes if the income of the property is not applicable to the general benefit of the ratepayers or other persons as aforesaid;

(*b*) property acquired by a board of guardians for the purposes of their functions in the relief of the poor.

Agricultural Land (Utilisation) Act, 1931

11. Power to arrange for management by local authorities of small holdings and allotments provided by Minister or for the transfer thereof to such authorities (1) Any small holdings or allotments provided by the Minister and any land acquired by him for the purposes of small holdings or allotments in exercise of the powers conferred on him by this Part of this Act may, by arrangement between him and the local authority, be either—

(*a*) controlled and managed by the authority as agents for the Minister; or

(*b*) transferred to the authority on such terms as may be agreed between the Minister and the authority and approved by the Treasury.

(2) Any small holdings, allotments, or land transferred to a local authority under this section shall be deemed to have been acquired by the authority under the Small Holdings and Allotments Acts.

(3) In this section the expression 'local authority' means ... in relation to any allotment or to land acquired for allotments, the council of the ... parish or any county council acting in default of such a council as aforesaid.

13. (3) Where the Minister determines to exercise in any ... parish the powers conferred by this section, he shall give notice of his determination to the council thereof.

(4) Every such council as aforesaid shall furnish to the Minister such information as he may require for the purposes of this section.

(5) Any of the powers and duties conferred on the Minister by this section, except the power of acquiring land or of disposing of it otherwise than for use as allotments, may, by arrangement between him and the council of any county, or ... parish, or with any society having as its object or one of its objects the provision or the profitable working of allotments, be exercised and performed by the council or society as agents for the Minister.

14. Power of Minister to defray losses incurred by local authorities in providing allotment gardens for unemployed persons (1) Where it appears to the council of any ... parish, or to any county council acting in default of such a council as aforesaid, that the provision of any allotment gardens required for the purpose of their being let to unemployed persons, or persons who are not in full-time employment, resident in the . . . parish, who desire to take them will entail a loss, the council may submit their proposals to the Minister together with estimates in the prescribed form of the expenses (whether on capital or income account) in relation thereto likely to be incurred by the council and of the sums likely to be received by the council by way of rent or otherwise.

(2) If the Minister approves the proposals and estimates of the council, either without modifications or with such modifications as he may require, the Minister may, subject to such conditions as to records, certificates, audit or otherwise, as with the approval of the Treasury he may determine, undertake to defray in any year the loss shown in the approved estimates as likely to be incurred in that year by the council in providing allotment gardens for such persons as aforesaid in accordance with the proposals.

(3) Neither subsections (1) and (2) of section 16 of the Allotments Act, 1922, nor section 4 of the Allotments Act, 1925 (which impose limits on the expenditure of councils on the provision of allotments) shall apply to any expenses incurred in accordance with proposals and estimates approved by the Minister under this section.

(4) If proposals after having been approved by the Minister under this section are subsequently varied without his consent, the Minister shall defray only such part as he thinks fit of the annual loss aforesaid and of any additional loss attributable to the variation.

(5) The Minister may, after the date of the commencement of this Act, approve proposals and estimates submitted to him for the purposes of this section before that date, but where the land to which any proposals relate has been acquired before the 1st day of January, 1931, or is after the commencement of this Act acquired without the consent of the Minister, this section shall apply with respect to such ex-

penses only as are incurred in equipping the land and adapting it for allotment gardens for letting to unemployed persons or persons who are not in full-time employment.

(6) A council shall keep separate accounts with respect to all their transactions under this section and shall furnish to the Minister such information as he may require as to such transactions.

(7) The Minister shall with the concurrence of the Treasury make regulations for carrying this section into effect.

15. Unemployed persons not to vacate allotments on obtaining employment Where an allotment has been let to an unemployed person or to a person not in full-time employment in accordance with the provisions of either of the last two foregoing sections, his tenancy of the allotment shall not be terminated without his consent on the ground only that he has ceased to be an employed person or a person not in full-time employment.

16. Power of Minister to make grants for assisting in the provision of seeds, fertilisers and equipment for unemployed persons (1) The Minister may, in accordance with regulations made by him with the approval of the Treasury, make grants or advances to any county council or to the council of any borough, urban district or parish, or to any society having as its object or one of its objects the profitable working of allotments, for the purpose of assisting the council or society in the provision of seeds, fertilisers and equipment for unemployed persons or persons who are not in full-time employment for whom allotments are provided; and the regulations made under this section may, notwithstanding anything in section 21 of the Land Settlement (Facilities) Act, 1919, provide for empowering any such council, where necessary, to sell seeds, fertilisers or equipment purchased with such assistance as aforesaid and to allow the use of such equipment, at a price or charge less than that sufficient to cover the cost of purchase.

20. Interpretation and construction (1) In this Part of this Act, unless the context otherwise requires—

'Small Holdings and Allotments Acts' means the Small Holdings and Allotments Acts, 1908 to 1926, the Allotments Acts, 1908 to 1925, and this Act;

(2) Except where the context otherwise requires, references in this Part of this Act to any enactment or to any provision of any enactment shall be construed as references to that enactment or provision as amended by any subsequent enactment, including this Part of this Act, and this Part of this Act shall, except so far as it applies to Scotland, be construed as one with the Small Holdings and Allotments Acts, 1908 to 1926, and the Allotments Acts, 1908 to 1925.

25. (1) . . . Part II of this Act and the Small Holdings and Allotments Acts, 1908 to 1926, may be cited as the Small Holdings and Allotments Acts, 1908 to 1931, and so much of the said Part II as relates to allotments and the Allotments Acts, 1908 to 1925, may be cited as the Allotments Acts, 1908 to 1931.

Local Government Act, 1933

PART I.

35A.[1] (1) The councillors of a rural district shall be called 'rural district councillors'.

(2) The councillors for each rural district shall be elected by the local government electors for the district in manner provided by this Act and Part I of the Representation of the People Act, 1949.

(3) The term of office of rural district councillors shall be three years, and the following provisions shall have effect with respect to their retirement, that is to say:—

(a) in the case of a rural district other than one falling within paragraph (b) or (c) of this subsection, one-third, as near as may be having regard to the provisions of section one of the Local Government Elections Act, 1956, of the whole number of councillors for the district shall retire in every year on the twentieth day of May;

(b) in the case of a rural district comprising only two rural parishes which are not grouped together under a common parish council but either or both of which has a separate parish council or is

grouped under a common parish council with a neighbouring parish or parishes in another rural district, the district councillors representing one of the parishes shall retire together in one year of each triennial period on the twentieth day of May and those representing the other parish shall retire together in another year of that period on the twentieth day of May;

(c) in the case of a rural district co-extensive with a rural parish which has a separate parish council or is grouped under a common parish council with a neighbouring parish or parishes in another rural district, or of a rural district comprising only two rural parishes grouped together under a common parish council (whether or not they are so grouped with a neighbouring parish or parishes in another rural district), the district councillors representing that parish or, as the case may be, those parishes shall retire together in every third year on the twentieth day of May:

Provided that, in the case of a rural district the councillors whereof do not regularly retire simultaneously, the county council, if they consider, on request made by a resolution of the rural

---

[1] This section was inserted by Local Government Elections Act, 1956.

district council passed by not less than two-thirds of the members voting on the resolution, that it would be expedient to provide for the simultaneous retirement of all the councillors for the district, may by order give directions to that effect, and where an order giving such directions as aforesaid has been made (whether before or after the commencement of this Act), the councillors for that district shall retire together in every third year on the twentieth day of May.

(4) Where any such order has been made with respect to the simultaneous retirement of rural district councillors, the county council may, on the like request, by order rescind the first-mentioned order, and the rescinding order shall provide for all matters necessary or proper for giving effect thereto.

(5) The places of rural district councillors who are required by or by virtue of this section to retire on the twentieth day of May in any year shall be filled by the newly elected councillors who shall come into office on that day.

(6) A county council may, for the purpose of regulating the retirement of rural district councillors in cases where they do not regularly retire simultaneously, direct in which year or years of each triennial period the councillors for each electoral area in the district shall retire:

Provided that—

(a) no direction shall be given under this subsection which has the effect of specifying different years of retirement for councillors who are required by section one of the Local Government Elections Act, 1956, to retire simultaneously; and

(b) in exercising their powers under this subsection, the county council shall so far as practicable secure that the councillors who have been district councillors for the longest time without re-election shall retire before the other councillors for the district.

43. Parish meetings and councils

(1) For every rural parish there shall be a parish meeting, and subject to the provisions of this Act, for every rural parish or group of parishes having a parish council immediately before the commencement of this Act there shall continue to be a parish council.

(2) If a rural parish has not a separate parish council, the county council shall by order establish a parish council for that parish—

(a) if the population of the parish is three hundred or upwards; or

(b) if, in the case of a parish having a population of two hundred or upwards but under three hundred, the parish meeting of the parish so resolve,

and the county council may, in the case of a parish having a population of less than two hundred, by order establish a parish council for that parish if the parish meeting so resolve.

(3) Where a rural parish is co-extensive with a rural district, then, unless the county council otherwise direct, a parish council shall not be elected for that parish, and the rural district council shall, in addition to their own functions, have the functions of, and be deemed to be, the parish council.

(4) An order establishing a parish council for a rural parish shall make such provision as appears to the county council to be necessary for the election of a parish council in manner provided by this Part of this Act.

(5) An order establishing a parish council for a parish included in a grouping order, as hereinafter defined, or in a like order made, whether before or after the commencement of this Act, under any other Act, shall make such provision as appears to the county council to be necessary for separating the parish from the group, and for the alteration or dissolution of the parish council of the group.

44. Power to dissolve parish councils in small parishes (1) Where the population of a rural parish having a separate parish council is less than two hundred, the parish meeting may petition the county council for the dissolution of the parish council, and thereupon the county council may by order dissolve the parish council, and from such date as may be specified in the order this Act shall apply to that parish as to a parish not having a separate parish council.

(2) Where a petition for an order under this section is rejected, another petition for the same purpose may not be presented within two years from the presentation of the previous petition.

45. Orders for grouping parishes, dissolving groups, and separating a parish from a group (1) The parish meeting of a rural parish may apply to the county council for an order grouping the parish with some neighbouring parish or parishes in the same county under a common parish council, and the county council may thereupon make an order (in this Act referred to as 'a grouping order') accordingly:

Provided that—

(*a*) no parish shall be so grouped *without the consent of the parish meeting of that parish*; and

(*b*) unless the county council for special reasons otherwise direct, the grouped parishes shall be within the same rural district.

(2) A grouping order or the like order under Part II of the Local Government Act, 1958, shall make the necessary provisions—

(*a*) for the name of the group;

(*b*) for there being a parish meeting for each of the parishes included in the group;

(*c*) for the election, in manner provided by this Part of this Act and any rules made thereunder, of separate representatives on the parish council for each parish;

(*d*) for the application to the parishes included in the group of any provisions of the Local Government Act, 1894, with respect to the appointment of trustees and to beneficiaries of a parochial char-

ity, and of any provisions of this Act with respect to the custody of parish documents, so as to preserve the separate rights of each parish.

and the order may provide for the consent of the parish meeting of a parish being required to any particular act of the parish council, and for any other necessary adaptations of this Act to the group of parishes, or to the parish meetings of the parishes in the group.

(3) The county council may, on the application of the council of a group of parishes or of the parish meeting of any parish included in a group of parishes, make an order dissolving the group, and an order so made shall make such provision as appears to the county council to be necessary for the election of a parish council or councils for any parish or parishes in the group.

In this subsection a reference to a group of parishes includes a reference to a group of parishes formed by an order made before the commencement of this Act or formed by an order under Part II of the Local Government Act, 1958.

46. Provisions as to orders An order made by a county council under any of the last three preceding sections may contain such incidental, consequential and supplemental provisions as appear to the county council to be necessary or proper for bringing the order into operation and giving full effect thereto, including provisions for the transfer of officers and for the adjustment of property, rights, and liabilities as between parishes and groups of parishes, and upon such order being made the provisions of Part VI of this Act with respect to the transfer of officers and with respect to financial adjustments between public bodies affected by an order shall apply as if the order was an order made under the Part of this Act.

47. Constitution and powers of parish meetings, &c. (1) The parish meeting of a rural parish shall consist of the local government electors for the parish.

(2) Any act of a parish meeting may be signified by an instrument under the hands, or, if an instrument under seal is required, under the hands and seals, of the person presiding at the meeting and two other local government electors present thereat, and any instrument purporting to have been so executed shall, until the contrary is proved, be deemed to have been so executed.

(3) In a rural parish not having a separate parish council the chairman of the parish meeting and the councillor or councillors for the time being representing the parish on the rural district council shall be a body corporate by the name of 'the representative body' with the addition of the name of the parish, or, if there is any doubt as to the latter name, of such name as the county council after consultation with the parish meeting of the parish direct, and shall have perpetual succession:—

Provided that, if the parish is represented on the rural district council by one councillor only, and that councillor is also the chairman of the parish meeting, the rural district council shall appoint a local government elector for the parish to be a member of the representative body of the parish, and the person so appointed shall, unless he resigns or ceases to be qualified or becomes disqualified, hold office as such member until the expiration of a term of four years, or until the offices of rural district councillor representing the parish and chairman of the parish meeting cease to be held by the same person, whichever first occurs.

(4) The representative body of a rural parish shall in all respects act in manner directed by the parish meeting, and any act of that body may be signified by an instrument under the hands, or, if an instrument under seal is required, under the hands and seals, of the members thereof, and any instrument purporting to have been so executed shall, until the contrary is proved, be deemed to have been so executed.

48. Constitution and powers of parish council (1) A parish council shall consist of the chairman and parish councillors, and shall have all such functions as are vested in the council by this Act or otherwise.

(2) The parish council shall be a body corporate by the name of the parish council with the addition of the name of the parish or, if there is any doubt as to the latter name, of such name as the county council after consultation with the parish meeting of the parish direct, and shall have perpetual succession.

(3) Any act of a parish council may be signified by an instrument under the hands, or, if an instrument under seal is required, under the hands and seals, of two members of the council, and any instrument purporting to have been so executed shall, until the contrary is proved, be deemed to have been so executed.

49. Chairman and vice-chairman of parish council or meeting (1) The chairman of a parish council shall be elected annually by the council from among the councillors or persons qualified to be councillors of the parish.

(2) The election of the chairman shall be the first business transacted at the annual meeting of the council.

(3) The chairman shall, unless he resigns or ceases to be qualified or becomes disqualified, continue in office until his successor is elected.

(4) During his term of office the chairman shall continue to be a member of the council, notwithstanding the provisions of this Act relating to the retirement of parish councillors at the end of three years.

(5) The parish council may appoint a member of the council to be vice-chairman of the council.

(6) The vice-chairman shall, unless he resigns or ceases to be qualified or becomes disqualified, hold office until immediately after the election of a chairman at the next annual meeting of the council and during that time shall continue to be a member of the council, notwithstanding the provisions of this Act relating to the retirement of parish councillors at the end of three years.

(7) Subject to any standing orders made by the parish council, anything authorised or required to be done by, to

or before the chairman may be done by, to or before the vice-chairman.

(8) In a rural parish not having a separate parish council, the parish meeting shall, subject to any provisions of a grouping order, at their annual assembly choose a chairman for the year who shall continue in office until his successor is elected.

50. Number and term of office of parish councillors (1) The number of parish councillors for each parish or group of parishes, shall be such number, not being less than five nor more than twenty-one, as may be fixed from time to time by the county council.

(2) The term of office of parish councillors shall be three years, and they shall retire together on the 20th day of May in every third year, and their places shall be filled by the newly elected councillors who shall come into office on that day.

52. Wards for election of parish councillors[1] (1) If a county council, on receipt of proposals made by the parish council of, or by not less than one-tenth of the local government electors for, a parish, are satisfied—

(a) that the area or population of the parish is so large, or different parts of the population are so situate, as to make a single election of parish councillors impracticable or inconvenient; or

(b) that it is desirable for any reason that certain parts of the parish should be separately represented on the parish council,

the county council may by order divide the parish for the purpose of the election of parish councillors into wards, to be called parish wards, and fix the boundaries of, and the number of parish councillors to be elected for, each parish ward.

(2) In the division of a parish into parish wards regard shall be had to—

(a) the population of the parish according to the last published census for the time being;

[1] See L.G.E A. 1956 s. 3.

(b) the evidence of any considerable change of population since that census;

(c) the area of the parish;

(d) the distribution and pursuits of the population; and

(e) all the other circumstances of the case.

(3) An order made under this section may be revoked or varied by the county council on application made by the parish council of, or by not less than one-tenth of the local government electors for, the parish.

(4) Where a parish is not divided into parish wards, there shall be one election of parish councillors for the whole parish.

(5) Where a parish is divided into parish wards, there shall be a separate election of parish councillors for each ward.

55. Omission to hold election, &c. (1) If any difficulty arises with respect to an election of parish councillors or of an individual parish councillor, or to the first meeting of a parish council after an ordinary election of such councillors, or if, from an election not being held, or being defective, or otherwise, a parish council have not been properly constituted, the county council may by order make any appointment or do anything which appears to them necessary or expedient for the proper holding of such election or meeting, and properly constituting the council, and may, if it appears to them necessary, direct the holding of an election or meeting, and fix the dates for any such election or meeting.

(2) If a parish council become unable to act, whether from failure to elect or otherwise, the county council may order a new election to be held, and may by order make such provision as seems expedient for authorising any person to act temporarily in the place of the parish council and of the chairman thereof.

(3) An order made under this section may modify the provisions of this Act . . . so far as may appear to the county

council necessary or expedient for carrying the order into effect.

PART II.

57. Qualifications for election and holding office as member of local authority A person shall, unless disqualified by virtue of this Act or any other enactment, be qualified to be elected and to be a member of a local authority if he is of full age and a British subject, and—

(a) he is a local government elector for the area of the local authority; or

(c) he has during the whole of the twelve months preceding the day on which he is nominated as a candidate resided in the area of the local authority; or,

(d) in the case of a member of a parish council, he has either during the whole of the twelve months preceding the day on which he is nominated as a candidate or since the 25th day of March in the year preceding the year of election resided either in the parish or within three miles thereof.

58. Re-election A person ceasing to hold any office to which he is elected under this Act, shall, unless he is not qualified or is disqualified, be eligible for re-election.

59. Disqualifications for office as member of local authority (1) Subject to the provisions of this section, a person shall be disqualified for being elected or being a member of a local authority if he—

(a) holds any paid office or other place of profit (other than that of mayor, chairman or sheriff) in the gift or disposal of the local authority or of any committee thereof; or

(b) is a person who has been adjudged bankrupt, or made a composition or arrangement with his creditors; or

(d) has within five years before the day of election or since his election been surcharged to an amount exceeding £500 by a district auditor; or

(e) has within five years before the day of election or since his election been convicted in the United Kingdom, the Channel Islands or the Isle of Man of any offence and ordered to be imprisoned for a period of not less than three months without the option of a fine; or

(f) is disqualified for being elected or for being a member of that authority under any enactment relating to corrupt or illegal practices; or

(g) in the case of the council of a borough, is an elective auditor of the borough;

Provided that . . .

(ii) the disqualification attaching to a person by reason of his having been adjudged bankrupt shall cease,—

(a) if the bankruptcy is annulled either on the ground that he ought not to have been adjudged bankrupt, or that his debts have been paid in full, on the date of the annulment; or

(b) if he is discharged with a certificate that the bankruptcy was caused by misfortune without any misconduct on his part, on the date of his discharge; or

(c) in any other case, on the expiration of five years from the date of his discharge;

(iii) the disqualification attaching to a person by reason of his having made a composition or arrangement with his creditors shall cease,—

(a) if he pays his debts in full, on the date on which the payment is completed; or

(b) in any other case, on the expiration of five years from the date on which the terms of the deed of composition or arrangement are fulfilled;

(v) for the purposes of paragraphs (*d*) and (*e*) of this subsection, the ordinary date on which the period allowed for making an appeal or application with respect to the surcharge or conviction expires or, if such an appeal or application is made, the date on which the appeal or application is finally disposed of or abandoned or fails by reason of the non-prosecution thereof, shall be deemed to be the date of the surcharge or conviction, as the case may be.

(2) A paid officer of a local authority who is employed under the direction of a committee or sub-committee of the authority, any member of which is appointed on the nomination of some other local authority, shall be disqualified for being elected or being a member of that other local authority.

60. Validity of acts done by unqualified person The acts and proceedings of any person elected to an office under this Act and acting in that office, shall, notwithstanding his disqualification or want of qualification, be as valid and effectual as if he had been qualified.

61. (4) A person elected to the office of chairman of a parish council or parish councillor shall, in the case of the chairman, at the meeting at which he is elected and, in the case of a councillor, at the first meeting of the parish council after his election, or in either case if the council at that meeting so permit at a later meeting fixed by the council, make in the presence of a member of the council and deliver to the council a declaration of acceptance of office in a form prescribed by the Secretary of State, and if he fails so to do his office shall thereupon become vacant.

(5) Any person before whom a declaration is authorised to be made under this section may take the declaration.

62. Resignation A person elected to any office under this Act may at any time resign his office by writing signed by him (in this Act referred to as the 'notice of resignation') and delivered—

(*d*) in the case of a parish councillor, to the chairman of the parish council; and

(*e*) in the case of a chairman of a parish council or of a parish meeting, to the parish council or parish meeting, as the case may be,

and his resignation shall take effect upon the receipt of the notice of resignation by the person or body to whom it is required to be delivered.

63. Vacation of office by failure to attend meetings, &c. (1) If a member of a local authority fails throughout a period of six consecutive months to attend any meeting of the local authority, he shall, unless the failure was due to some reason approved by the local authority, cease to be a member of the authority:

Provided that—

(*a*) attendance as a member at a meeting of any committee or sub-committee of the local authority, or at a meeting of any joint committee, joint board or other body to which any of the functions of the local authority have been delegated or transferred, shall be deemed for the purposes of this subsection to be attendance at a meeting of the local authority;

(*b*) a member of any branch of His Majesty's naval, military or air forces when employed during war or any emergency on any naval, military or air force service, and a person whose employment in the service of His Majesty in connection with war or any emergency is such as, in the opinion of the Minister, to entitle him to relief from disqualification on account of absence, shall not cease to be a member of a local authority by reason only of failure to attend meetings of the local authority if the failure is due to that employment;

64. Declaration by local authority of vacancy in office in certain cases

Where a member of a local authority—

(a) ceases to be qualified to be a member of the authority; or

(b) becomes disqualified for being a member of the authority for any reason other than by reason of a surcharge, or of a conviction, or of a breach of any enactment relating to corrupt or illegal practices; or

(c) ceases to be a member of the authority or to hold the office of mayor of a borough by reason of failure to attend meetings of the local authority or by reason of absence from the borough, as the case may be,

the local authority shall, except in any case in which a declaration has been made by the High Court under this Part of this Act, forthwith declare his office to be vacant and signify the vacancy by notice signed by the clerk of the authority and affixed to the offices of the authority.

Casual Vacancies

65. Date of casual vacancies

For the purpose of filling a casual vacancy in any office for which an election is held under this Act, the date on which the vacancy shall be deemed to have occurred shall be—

(a) in the case of non-acceptance of office by any person who is required to make and deliver a declaration of acceptance of office, upon the expiration of the period appointed under this Part of this Act for the delivery of the declaration;

(b) in the case of resignation, upon the receipt of the notice of resignation by the person or body to whom the notice is required to be delivered;

(c) in the case of death, upon the date of death;

(d) in the case of a disqualification by reason of a surcharge or conviction, upon the expiration of the ordinary period allowed for making an appeal or application with respect to the surcharge or conviction or, if an appeal or application is made, upon the date on which that appeal or application is finally disposed of or abandoned or fails by reason of non-prosecution thereof;

(e) in the case of an election being declared void on an election petition, upon the date of the report or certificate of the election court;

(f) in the case of a person ceasing to be qualified to be a member of a local authority, or becoming disqualified for any reason other than those mentioned in the foregoing paragraphs of this section, or ceasing to be a member of a local authority by reason of failure to attend meetings, . . . upon the date on which his office is declared to have been vacated either by the High Court or by the council, as the case may be; . . .

66. Filling of casual vacancy in case of chairman, mayor or alderman

(1) On a casual vacancy occurring in the office of chairman of a . . . parish council, an election to fill the vacancy shall be held not later than the next ordinary meeting of the council held after the date on which the vacancy occurs, or if that meeting is held within fourteen days after that date, then not later than the next following ordinary meeting of the council, and shall be conducted in the same manner as an ordinary election.

(2) Where the office vacant is that of chairman of a . . . parish council, a meeting of the council for the election may be convened by the clerk of the authority.

(3) In a rural parish not having a separate parish council, a casual

vacancy in the office of chairman of the parish meeting shall be filled by the parish meeting, and a parish meeting shall forthwith be convened for the purpose of filling the vacancy.

67. Filling of casual vacancies (6) A casual vacancy among parish councillors shall be filled by the parish council, and the council shall forthwith be convened for the purpose of filling the vacancy.

74. Provisions as to ballot boxes, &c. (1) Any ballot boxes, fittings and compartments provided for parliamentary elections out of moneys provided by Parliament may, on request, be lent to the returning officer . . . at a poll consequent on a parish meeting upon such terms and conditions as the Treasury may determine.

(2) Any ballot boxes, fittings and compartments provided by or belonging to a local authority shall, on request, and if not required for immediate use by that authority, be lent to the returning officer . . . at a poll consequent on a parish meeting upon such terms and conditions as may be agreed.

Meetings and Proceedings

75. Meetings and proceedings of local authorities The provisions of Parts I to V of the Third Schedule to this Act shall have effect as respects the meetings and proceedings of local authorities and of committees thereof:

76. Disability of members of authorities for voting on account of interest in contracts, &c. (1) If a member of a local authority has *any pecuniary interest*, direct or indirect, in any contract or proposed contract or other matter, and is present at a meeting of the local authority at which the contract or other matter is the subject of consideration, he shall at the meeting, as soon as practicable after the commencement thereof, disclose the fact, and shall not take part in the consideration or discussion of, or vote on any question with respect to, the contract or other matter:

Provided that this section shall not apply to an interest in a contract or other matter which a member may have as a ratepayer or inhabitant of the area, or as an ordinary consumer of gas, electricity or water, or to an interest in any matter relating to the terms on which the right to participate in any service, including the supply of goods, is offered to the public.

(2) For the purposes of this section a person shall (subject as hereafter in this subsection provided) be treated as having indirectly a pecuniary interest in a contract or other matter, if—

(a) he or any nominee of his is a member of a company or other body with which the contract is made or is proposed to be made or which has a direct pecuniary interest in the other matter under consideration; or

(b) he is a partner, or is in the employment, of a person with whom the contract is made or is proposed to be made or who has a direct pecuniary interest in the other matter under consideration:

Provided that—
(i) this subsection shall not apply to membership of, or employment under, any *public body*;
(ii) a member of a company or other body shall not, by reason only of his membership, be treated as being so interested if he has no beneficial interest in any shares . . . of that company or other body.

'(2A)[1] Where a member of a local authority has indirectly a pecuniary interest in a contract or other matter and would not fall to be treated as having such an interest but for the fact that he has a beneficial interest in shares of a company or other body, then, if the total nominal value of those shares does not exceed £500 or one hundredth of the total nominal value of the issued share capital of the company

[1] This subsection was inserted by L.G.A. 1948 and amended by L.G.(M.P.)A. 1953.

or body, whichever is the less, so much of subsection (1) of this section as prohibits him from taking part in the consideration or discussion of, and from voting on any question with respect to, the contract or other matter shall not apply to him, without prejudice, however, to the duty of disclosure imposed by the said subsection (1):

Provided that where the share capital of the company or other body is of more than one class, this subsection shall not apply if the total nominal value of all the shares of any one class in which he has a beneficial interest exceeds one hundredth part of the total issued share capital of that class of the company or other body'.

(3) In the case of married persons living together the interest of one spouse shall, if known to the other, be deemed for the purposes of this section to be also an interest of that other spouse.

(4) A general notice given in writing to the clerk of the authority by a member thereof to the effect that he or his spouse is a member or in the employment of a specified company or other body, or that he or his spouse is a partner or in the employment of a specified person, or that he or his spouse is the tenant of any premises owned by the authority, shall, unless and until the notice is withdrawn, be deemed to be a sufficient disclosure of his interest in any contract, proposed contract or other matter relating to that company or other body or to that person or to those premises which may be the subject of consideration after the date of the notice.

(5) The clerk of the authority shall record in a book to be kept for the purpose particulars of any disclosure made under subsection (1) of this section, and of any notice given under sub-section (4) thereof, and the book shall be open at all reasonable hours to the inspection of any member of the local authority.

(6) If any person fails to comply with the provisions of sub-section (1) of this section, he shall for each offence be liable on summary conviction to a fine

not exceeding £200, unless he proves that he did not know that a contract, proposed contract, or other matter in which he had a pecuniary interest was the subject of consideration at the meeting.

(7) A prosecution for an offence under this section shall not be instituted except by or on behalf of the Director of Public Prosecutions.

(8) The county council, as respects a member of a parish council may, subject to such conditions as the county council or the Minister, as the case may be, may think fit to impose, remove any disability imposed by this section in any case in which the number of members of the local authority so disabled at any one time would be so great a proportion of the whole as to impede the transaction of business, or in any other case in which it appears to the county council or the Minister, as the case may be, that it is in the interests of the inhabitants of the area that the disability should be removed.

(9) A local authority may by standing orders provide for the exclusion of a member of the authority from a meeting of the authority whilst any contract, proposed contract or other matter in which he has such an interest as aforesaid is under consideration.

(10) In this section, the expression 'shares' includes stock and the expression 'share capital' shall be construed accordingly.

77. Parish meetings (1) Parish meetings shall be held, and the proceedings thereat shall be conducted, in accordance with the provisions of Part VI of the Third Schedule to this Act.

(2) The chairman of a parish council shall be entitled to attend a parish meeting for the parish whether he is or is not a local government elector for the parish, but, if not such an elector, he shall not be entitled to give any vote at the meeting except a casting vote.

78. Parish meeting for parish wards, &c. Where a parish meeting is required or authorised to be held for a parish ward or other part of a parish, then—

(*a*) the persons entitled to attend and vote at the meeting, or to vote at any poll consequent thereon, shall be the local government electors registered in respect of qualifications in that parish ward or part of the parish; and

(*b*) the provisions of this Act with respect to parish meetings for the whole of a parish, including the provisions with respect to the convening of a parish meeting by local government electors, shall apply as if the parish ward or part of the parish were the whole parish.

Part III.

85. Appointment of committees

(1) A local authority may appoint a committee for any such general or special purpose as in the opinion of the local authority would be better regulated and managed by means of a committee, and may delegate to a committee so appointed, with or without restrictions or conditions, as they think fit, any functions exercisable by the local authority either with respect to the whole or a part of the area of the local authority, except the power of levying, or issuing a precept for, a rate, or of borrowing money.

(2) The number of members of a committee appointed under this section, their term of office, and the area, if any, within which the committee is to exercise its authority, shall be fixed by the local authority.

(3) A committee appointed under this section (other than a committee for regulating and controlling the finance of the local authority or of their area may include persons who are not members of the local authority:

Provided that at least two-thirds of the members of every committee shall be members of the local authority.

(4) Every member of a committee appointed under this section who at the time of his appointment was a member of the local authority by whom he was appointed shall, upon ceasing to be a member of the authority, also cease to be a member of the committee:

Provided that for the purposes of this section a member of a local authority shall not be deemed to have ceased by reason of retirement to be a member of the authority, if he has been re-elected a member thereof not later than the day of his retirement.

(5) Nothing in this section shall authorise the appointment of a committee for any purpose for which the local authority are authorised or required to appoint a committee by any other enactment (including any enactment in this Act) for the time being in force.

87. Parochial committees

(1) A rural district council may, at a meeting specially convened for the purpose, appoint for any one or more contributory places within their district a parochial committee consisting either wholly of members of the district council or partly of such members and partly of local government electors for such contributory place or places, as the council may determine:

Provided that, where a parochial committee is appointed consisting partly of members of the district council and partly of other persons, those other persons shall, as respects any contributory place which consists of a parish having a separate Parish Council, be, or be selected from, the members of the parish council.

(2) A rural district council may delegate to a parochial committee, with or without restrictions or conditions, as they think fit, any functions exercisable by them within the contributory place or places for which the committee is formed, except the power of levying a rate or borrowing money.

(3) If a rural district council refuse to appoint a parochial committee for a contributory place after receiving a request to that effect from the parish council or parish meeting of a parish which is wholly or in part comprised in the contributory place, the parish council or parish meeting may petition the Minister and the Minister may by

order direct the rural district council to appoint a parochial committee for that contributory place.

88. Delegation of powers to parish council (1) A rural district council may delegate to a parish council any functions which, under the preceding section, may be delegated to a parochial committee, and thereupon that section shall apply as if the parish council were a parochial committee.

(2) Where functions are delegated to a parish council under this section, the parish council, in the discharge of those functions, shall act as agents for the rural district council.

89. Committees for parts of rural parishes Where a parish council have any functions which are to be discharged in a part only of the parish, or in relation to a recreation ground, building or property held for the benefit of a part only of the parish, and that part of the parish has a defined boundary, the council shall, if required by a parish meeting held for that part of the parish, appoint annually a committee, consisting partly of members of the council and partly of other persons representing the said part of the parish to discharge such functions.

90. Committees of parish meetings (1) In a rural parish not having a separate parish council the parish meeting may, subject to any provisions made by a grouping order, appoint a committee from amongst the local government electors for the parish for any purpose which, in the opinion of the parish meeting, would be better regulated and managed by means of such a committee.

(2) All acts of a committee appointed under this section shall be submitted to the parish meeting for approval.

91. Appointment of joint committees (1) A *local authority* may concur with any one or more *other local authorities* in appointing from amongst their respective members a joint committee of those authorities for any purpose in which they are jointly interested, and may delegate to the committee, with or without restrictions or conditions, as they think fit, any

functions of the local authority relating to the purpose for which the joint committee is formed, except the power of levying, or issuing a precept for, a rate, or of borrowing money:—

Provided that, where a local authority concur in appointing a joint committee for the discharge of any functions which under any enactment the authority are authorised or required to discharge through a committee appointed under that enactment, and that enactment contains any special provisions with respect to the constitution and functions of that committee (including any provisions with respect to the appointment of persons who are not members of the local authority), those provisions shall apply to the constitution and functions of the joint committee with such modifications, if any, as the case may require.

(2) Subject to the provisions of this section, the number of members of a joint committee appointed under this section, the term of office of the members thereof, and the area, if any, within which the joint committee is to exercise its authority, shall be fixed by the appointing authorities.

(3) Every member of a joint committee appointed under this section who at the time of his appointment was a member of the local authority by whom he was appointed, shall, upon ceasing to be a member of that authority, also cease to be a member of the joint committee:—

Provided that for the purposes of this subsection a member of a local authority shall not be deemed to have ceased by reason of retirement to be a member of the authority, if he has been re-elected a member thereof not later than the day of his retirement.

(4) Nothing in this section shall authorise the appointment of a joint committee for any purpose for which the appointing local authorities are authorised or required to appoint a joint committee by any other enactment for the time being in force.

92. Joint committees for parts of parishes Where a parish council can be required under this Part of this Act to appoint a committee consisting partly of members of the council and partly of other persons, that requirement may also be made in the case of a joint committee, and shall be duly complied with by the parish councils concerned at the time of the appointment of such committee.

93. Expenses and accounts of joint committees (1) The expenses incurred by a joint committee appointed under this Part of this Act shall be defrayed by the local authorities by whom the committee is appointed in such proportions as they may agree upon, or in case of disagreement as may be determined—

(a) in any case in which a county council, the Greater London Council, the Council of a London borough or the council of a county borough are an appointing authority, and in any case in which the appointing authorities include the councils of county districts situate in different counties, by the Minister; and

(b) in any other case, by the county council.

(2) The accounts of a joint committee appointed under this Part of this Act shall be made up yearly to the 31st day of March, and where the appointing authorities consist only of the councils of boroughs, and the accounts of the joint committee are not subject to audit by a district auditor under the provisions of Part X of this Act, they shall be audited by the auditor or auditors of the accounts of such one of the appointing authorities as may be agreed upon.

94. Disqualification for membership of committees and joint committees A person who is disqualified under Part II of this Act for being elected or being a member of a local authority shall be disqualified for being a member of a committee or sub-committee of that authority, or for being a representative of that authority on a joint committee appointed by agreement between the authority and

other local authorities, whether the committee, sub-committee or joint committee are appointed under this Part of this Act or under any other enactment, . . .

Provided that a person shall not by reason of his being a Teacher in, or being otherwise employed in, any school, college or other educational institution maintained or assisted by a local education authority, be disqualified for being a member of any committee or sub-committee of any local authority—

(c) appointed under this Act for purposes connected with the execution of the Public Libraries and Museums Act, 1964;

or for being a representative of a Local Authority on a joint committee appointed by agreement between the authority and other local authorities for any such purpose aforesaid.

95. Disability for voting on account of interest in contracts, &c. Section 76 of this Act shall apply in respect of members of a committee or sub-committee of a local authority or of any joint committee appointed by agreement between local authorities, whether the committee, sub-committee or joint committee are appointed under this Part of this Act or under any other enactment, as that section applies in respect of members of local authorities, subject to the following modifications:—

(a) as respects members of a committee or sub-committee, references to meetings of the committee or sub-committee shall be substituted for references to meetings of the local authority, and the right of persons who are members of the committee or sub-committee but not members of the local authority to inspect the book to be kept under sub-section (5) of the said section shall be limited to an inspection of the entries in the book relating to members of the committee or sub-committee; and (*b*) as respects members of any such joint committee as aforesaid, references to meetings of the joint committee shall be substituted for references to meetings of the local authority, and references to the clerk to the joint committee for references to the clerk of the authority.

96. Standing orders, &c. (1) A local authority appointing a committee, and local authorities who concur in appointing a joint committee, either under this Part of this Act or under any other enactment, may make, vary and revoke standing orders respecting the quorum, proceedings and place of meeting of the committee or joint committee, but subject to any such standing orders the quorum, proceedings and place of meeting shall be such as the committee or joint committee may determine.

(2) The person presiding at a meeting of a committee or joint committee appointed either under this Part of this Act or under any other enactment shall have a second or a casting vote.

Part IV.

114. Clerk and treasurer of parish council (1) A parish council may appoint one of their number to be clerk of the council without remuneration.

(2) If no member of the council is so appointed, the council may appoint some other fit person to be their clerk with such reasonable remuneration as they may determine.

(3) Where a parish council act as a parochial committee by delegation from the rural district council, they shall be entitled whilst so acting to the services of the clerk of the rural district council, unless the district council otherwise direct.

(4) A parish council may appoint one of their own number or some other fit person to be treasurer, without remuneration.

General

115. Appointment of standing deputies. (1) A local authority who under this Part of this Act appoint a clerk, treasurer . . . shall have power to appoint a deputy of that officer for the purpose of acting in the place of the officer whenever the office is vacant or the holder thereof is for any reason unable to act, and any person appointed as a deputy under this section shall, when acting as such and subject to the terms of his appointment, have all the functions of the holder of the office . . .

(2) A local authority may pay to a person appointed as a deputy under this section, other than a deputy clerk of a parish council who is a member of the council, or a deputy treasurer of a parish council, such reasonable remuneration as they may determine.

(3) A person appointed as a deputy under this section shall hold office during the pleasure of the local authority.

116. Appointment of temporary deputies (1) If the office of clerk of the authority, or treasurer . . . is vacant, or the holder of the office is for any reason unable to act, and no deputy has been appointed under the provisions of the last preceding section, or the deputy so appointed is unable to act, the local authority may appoint a person to act temporarily in that office, and any person so appointed shall, subject to the terms of his appointment, have all the functions of the holder of the office:

(2) The local authority may pay to a person appointed under this section, other than a member of a parish council who is appointed to act for the clerk of the council or a person appointed to act for the treasurer of a parish council, such reasonable remuneration as they may determine.

119. Security to be given by Officers (3) In the case of the treasurer of a parish council, the parish council shall either require the officer to give, or may themselves take, such security for the faithful execution of his office as may be directed by the county council.

(4) A local authority shall, in the case of persons not employed by them, and

may in any other case, defray the cost of any security given or taken under this section, and every such security shall be produced to the auditor or auditors at the audit of the accounts of the local authority.

120. Accountability of officers (1) Every officer employed by a local authority, whether under this Act or any other enactment, shall at such times during the continuance of his office, or within three months after his ceasing to hold it, and in such manner, as the local authority direct, make out and deliver to the authority, or as they direct, a true account in writing of all money and property committed to his charge, and of his receipts and payments, with vouchers and other documents and records supporting the entries therein, and a list of persons from whom or to whom money is due in connection with his office, showing the amount due from or to each.

(2) Every such officer shall pay all money due from him to the treasurer of the . . . parish, or otherwise as the local authority may direct.

(3) If any such officer—

(a) refuses or wilfully neglects to make any payment which he is required by this section to make; or

(b) after three days' notice in writing, signed by the clerk of the authority or by three members thereof, and given or left at his usual or last known place of residence refuses or wilfully neglects to make out or deliver to the authority, or as they direct, any account or list which he is required by this section to make out and deliver, or any voucher or other document or record relating thereto, or to give satisfaction respecting it to the authority or as they direct;

a court of summary jurisdiction having jurisdiction where the officer is or resides may, on complaint, by order require him to make such payment or delivery or to give such satisfaction.

(4) Nothing in this section shall affect any remedy by action against any such officer or his surety, except that the officer shall not be both sued by action and proceeded against summarily for the same cause.

121. Notice of termination of and retirement from appointments held during pleasure (1) Notwithstanding any provision in this Act or any other enactment that a person holding any office shall hold the office during the pleasure of a local authority, there may be included in the terms on which he holds the office a provision that the appointment shall not be terminated by either party without giving to the other party such reasonable notice as may be agreed, and where, at the commencement of this Act, an officer of a local authority holds office upon terms which purport to include such a provision, that provision shall, as from the commencement of this Act, be deemed to be valid.

(2) A provision in this Act or any other enactment that a person holding any office shall hold the office during the pleasure of a local authority shall not affect any right or obligation of the officer to retire on attaining any specified age or on the happening of any specified event in pursuance of any enactment or scheme relating to superannuation allowances which is applicable to the officer.

122, Members of local authorities not to be appointed as officers A person shall, so long as he is, and for twelve months after he ceases to be, a member of a local authority, be disqualified for being appointed by that authority to any paid office, other than to the office of chairman, mayor or sheriff.

123. Disclosure by officers of interest in contracts (1) If it comes to the knowledge of an officer employed, whether under this Act or any other enactment, by a local authority, that a contract in which he has any *pecuniary interest*, whether direct or indirect (not being a contract to which he is himself a party), has been, or is proposed to be, entered into by the authority or any committee thereof, he shall, as soon as practicable, give notice in writing to the authority of the fact that he is interested therein.

For the purposes of this section an officer shall be treated as having indirectly a pecuniary interest in a contract or proposed contract if he would have been so treated by virtue of *sub-section (2) or sub-section (3) of section 76 of this Act* had he been a member of the authority.

(2) An officer of a local authority shall not, under cover of his office or employment, exact or accept any fee or reward whatsoever other than his proper remuneration.

(3) If any person fails to comply with the provisions of sub-section (1) or contravenes any of the provisions of sub-section (2) of this section, he shall for each offence be liable on summary conviction to a fine not exceeding £200.

(4) References in this section to a local authority shall include a reference to a joint committee appointed under Part III of this Act.

PART V.

127. Provision of offices, &c. by parish council A parish council may—

(a) acquire or provide and furnish buildings to be used for the purpose of transacting the business of the parish council or of the parish meeting or any other parish business, and for public meetings and assemblies; or

(b) combine with any other parish council for the purpose of acquiring or providing and furnishing any such buildings; or

(c) contribute towards the expense incurred by any other parish council or by any other person in acquiring or providing and furnishing a building suitable for use for any of the aforesaid purposes.

128. Use of schoolroom, &c. in rural parish (1) If in a rural parish

there is no suitable public room vested in the parish council or in the representative body of the parish, as the case may be, which can be used free of charge, a suitable room in the school-house of a public *elementary* school, or a suitable room the expense of maintaining which is payable out of any rate, may be used, free of charge, at all reasonable times and after reasonable notice, for any of the following purposes, that is to say, for the purpose of—

(a) the parish meeting or any meetings of the parish council; or

(b) an inquiry held in pursuance of a direction given by the *Minister* or by any other Government department or by a local authority; or

(c) meetings convened by the chairman of the parish meeting or by the parish council; or

(d) the administration of public funds within or for the purposes of the parish where such funds are administered by any committee or officer appointed either by the parish meeting or parish council or by a county or district council:

Provided that nothing in this sub-section shall—

(i) authorise the use of a room used as part of a private dwelling-house; or

(ii) authorise any interference with the hours during which a room in a school-house is used for educational purposes; or

(iii) authorise any interference with the hours during which a room used for the purposes of the administration of justice or for the purposes of the police, is used for those purposes.

(2) If, by reason of the use of a room for any of the purposes mentioned in the last foregoing subsection, any expense is incurred by the persons having control over the room, or any damage is done to the room or to the building of which the room is part or to its appurtenances,

or to the furniture of the room or the apparatus for instruction, the expense or the cost of making good the damage shall be defrayed, in the case of an inquiry as part of the expenses of the inquiry, and in any other case as expenses of the parish meeting or parish council.

(3) If any question arises under this section as to what is reasonable or suitable, it may be determined—

(a) in the case of a room in a schoolhouse, by the *Minister* of Education;

(b) in the case of a room used for the purposes of the administration of justice or for the purposes of the police, by the Secretary of State;

(c) in any other case, by the Minister.

140. Alterations of boundaries of counties, boroughs, &c. (1) Whenever proposals are made to the Minister by a county council for the purpose of effecting any of the following changes, namely—

(a) the alteration or definition of the boundaries of the county;

(b) the union of the county with any other county or with any county borough; or

(c) the division of the county; . . .

or whenever proposals are made to the Minister by the council of a county borough for the purpose of effecting any of the following changes, namely—

(i) the alteration of the boundaries of the borough; or

(ii) the union of the borough with any other borough, or the inclusion in the borough of an urban or rural district; or

(iii) the union of the borough with a county,

the Minister shall, unless for special reasons he thinks that the proposals ought not to be entertained, cause a local inquiry to be held, and may make an order for giving effect to the proposals or for such other alteration as he may deem expedient, or may refuse to make the order:

Provided that, an order under this section shall not have effect until approved by a resolution of each House of Parliament.

[NOTE: See L.G.A. 1958 8th Schedule paragraph 7(2)]

Part VI.

141. Alteration of urban or rural districts and parishes, &c. (1) Where a county council consider, either on the receipt of proposals from a local authority or otherwise, that a prima facie case exists for any of the following changes, namely—

(a) *an alteration or definition of the boundaries of an urban or rural district or of a parish; or*

(b) *the division of an urban or rural district or of a parish; or*

(c) *the transfer of any part of an urban or rural district to another such district, whether urban or rural, or the transfer of any part of a parish to another parish; or*

(d) *the union of an urban or rural district with any other such district, whether urban or rural, or the union of a parish with another parish; or*

(e) *the conversion of a rural district or any part of a rural district into an urban district, or of an urban district or any part of an urban district into a rural district; or*

(f) *the formation of a new urban or rural district or parish;*

the county council shall cause a local inquiry to be held.

(2) The county council shall cause such notice as may be prescribed of the local inquiry and of the matters to be considered thereat to be given both in the locality and to the local authorities appearing to the county council to be concerned, and to the Minister and to such other Government departments as may be prescribed, and any local authority or person appearing to the

county council to be concerned shall be entitled to appear at the local inquiry.

(3) If the county council are satisfied, after holding the local inquiry, that any such change as aforesaid is desirable, they may make an order giving effect to the change and shall submit the order to the Minister for confirmation:

Provided that, before making an order giving effect to a change not considered at the local inquiry, the county council shall cause such notice as may be prescribed of the proposed change to be given both in the locality and to all local authorities appearing to the county council to be concerned, and those authorities shall be given an opportunity of making representations thereon.

(4) The county council shall send copies of the order to the Minister and to any other Government department to which notice of the local inquiry was required to be sent, and shall publish in one or more local newspapers circulating in the locality affected a notice stating that the order has been made, that a copy thereof is open to inspection at a specified place in the locality, and that petitions with respect thereto may be made to the Minister within six weeks after the publication of the notice.

(5) If within six weeks after publication of the notice referred to in the last preceding subsection any local authority, or any number of local government electors for a county district or for any ward of a county district or for any parish affected by the order, not being less than one hundred or one-third of the total number of those electors, whichever is the less, petition the Minister to disallow or modify the order, and the petition is not withdrawn, or if either the county council or any local authority by whom the proposals were originally made, on being informed by the Minister that he intends to refuse to confirm the order, request him to hold a local inquiry, the Minister shall, before taking further action, cause a local inquiry to be held.

(6) If proposals under subsection (1) of this section have been made by a

local authority, and the county council refuses or neglects to hold a local inquiry or to make an order under this section the authority who made the proposals may apply to the Minister, and the Minister may, after giving the county council and all local authorities and persons appearing to him to be concerned an opportunity of making representations, make any such order as the county council might have made.

(9) In this section the expression 'local authority' includes the parish meeting of a rural parish not having a separate parish council.

142. Confirmation of order by Minister (1) Subject as aforesaid, the Minister may confirm an order made under the last preceding section with or without modifications, or may refuse to confirm the order, whether or not a petition against it has been presented to him, but before making any modification in an order the Minister shall give notice of the proposed modification to all local authorities concerned, and those authorities shall be given an opportunity of making representations thereon, and if in any case in which the Minister has not already caused a local inquiry to be held the county council or any local authority by whom the proposals were originally made request the Minister to hold a local inquiry, the Minister shall cause a local inquiry to be held.

(2) In this section the expression 'local authority' includes the parish meeting of a rural parish not having a separate parish council.

143. Adjustment of boundaries of counties and county boroughs (2) The Minister may, on a joint representation being made by a county council and the council of a county borough, after holding a local inquiry, except in cases where he is satisfied that an inquiry is unnecessary, by order, alter the boundary between the county and the county borough.

144. Accretions from the sea, &c. Every accretion from the sea, whether natural or artificial, and any part of the sea-shore to the low-water mark, which does not at the commencement of this

Act form part of a parish, shall for all purposes of local government be annexed to, and incorporated with, the parish or parishes which such accretion or part of the sea-shore adjoins, in proportion to the extent of the common boundary, and every such accretion or part of the sea-shore annexed to and incorporated with a parish under this section shall be annexed to and incorporated with the county district and county, or the county borough, as the case may be, in which that parish is situate.

145. Alteration of local boundaries consequent on alteration of watercourse (1) Where, in the exercise of any powers conferred by the Land Drainage Act, 1930, a watercourse forming a boundary line between two or more areas of local government is straightened, widened or otherwise altered so as to affect its character as a boundary line, the drainage board or other persons under whose authority the alteration is made shall forthwith send notice of the alteration to the Minister, and the Minister, if satisfied that a new boundary line may conveniently be adopted, shall, by order of which notice shall be published in such manner as he thinks fit, declare that such line as may be specified in the order (whether or not consisting wholly or in part of the line of the watercourse as altered) shall be substituted as the boundary line for the former line of the watercourse, and thereupon the limits of the areas of which the watercourse, when unaltered, was the boundary shall be deemed to be varied accordingly.

(3) Where the Minister incurs any expenses in or in connection with the exercise of the powers conferred on him by this section, he may make such orders as he thinks fit with respect to the parties by whom or the funds or rates out of which those expenses or any part thereof are to be borne, and any sum payable to the Minister by virtue of any such order may be recovered as a debt due to the Crown.

147. Power to change name of district or parish (2) The council of . . . a borough to which the 7th Schedule of the Local Government Act, 1958 applies may change the name of any urban parish situate in the borough.

(4) In the case of a rural parish, the county council may, at the request of the parish council or of the parish meeting of the parish, change the name of that parish.

(5) Every change of name made in pursuance of this section shall be published in such manner as the council of the county may direct, and shall be notified to the Secretary of State, the Minister, and to the *Minister of Agriculture and Fisheries*.

(6) A change of name made under this section shall not affect any rights or obligations of any parish, district, council, authority, or person, or render defective any legal proceedings, and any legal proceedings may be commenced or continued as if there had been no change of name.

148. Supplemental provisions as to alterations of areas (1) A scheme or order made under this Part of this Act may contain such incidental, consequential, transitional or supplemental provisions with respect to administrative and judicial arrangements as may appear to be necessary or proper for the purposes or in consequence of the scheme or order and for giving full effect thereto (including provisions applying, amending or repealing any Act) and without prejudice to the generality of the foregoing provision may provide for all or any of the following matters, that is to say, the scheme or order—

(a) may provide for the abolition or establishment, or the restriction or extension of the jurisdiction, of any public body in or over any part of the area affected by the scheme or order;

(b) may provide for the name of any altered area;

(c) may provide for the adjustment or alteration of the boundaries of any area affected by the scheme or order, or of any parishes or districts wholly or in part situate within any such area, or for the union of any such parishes or parts thereof, and for the constitution and election of the public bodies in any such area;

(d) may deal with the functions or area of jurisdiction of any public body, court of quarter sessions, justices of the peace, stipendiary magistrate, coroner, sheriff, lieutenant, custos rotulorum, clerk of the peace, and other officers (including police officers) within the area affected by the scheme or order, and with the costs and expenses of any such public bodies, sessions, persons, or officers as aforesaid;

(e) may determine the status of any area affected by the scheme or order as a component part of any larger area, and may extend to any altered area the provisions of any local Act or statutory order which were previously in force in a portion of the area, or exclude from the application of any local Act or statutory order any part of the altered area to which it previously applied, so, however, that such extension or exclusion shall not, without their consent, affect the powers or duties of any statutory undertakers;

(f) may make temporary provision for meeting the debts and liabilities of the various public bodies affected by the scheme or order, for the management of their property, and for regulating the duties, position, and remuneration of officers affected by the scheme or order;

(g) may provide for the transfer of any writs, process, records, and documents relating to or to be executed in any part of the area affected by the scheme or order, and for determining questions arising from such transfer;

(h) may provide for the adjustment of any property, debts, and liabilities affected by the scheme or order and for the continuance in office of any public body for the purposes of such adjustment:

Provided that a scheme or order which provides for the extension of any provision relating to a gas or electricity undertaking and contained in a local Act or statutory order, or for the exclusion of any part of an area from the application of any such provision, shall not be made or confirmed by the Committee of Council or the Minister except with the consent of the Board of Trade or the Minister of Transport, as the case may require.

(2) An order made under this Part of this Act may, as respects any area affected by the order, contain such incidental, consequential, or supplemental provisions as may be necessary for—

(a) the division or redivision of the area into electoral divisions or wards, the constitution of new electoral divisions or wards, and the alteration of the boundaries of electoral divisions or wards; and

(b) the total number of councillors and aldermen (if any), the apportionment of councillors amongst electoral divisions or wards or parishes, the assignment of existing councillors to altered electoral divisions or wards or parishes, and the first election of councillors for any new or altered area, electoral division, ward or parish and for the first election of aldermen (if any).

149. Miscellaneous provisions relating to orders (1) An order may be made for amending any order previously made in pursuance of this Part of this Act, or of any corresponding enactment repealed by this Act, and may be made by the same authority and after the same procedure and subject to compliance with the like conditions as the original order.

(2) An order made under this Part of this Act may amend any local Act or statutory order.

Provided that an order which provides for the amendment of any provisions relating to a gas or electricity undertaking and contained in a local Act or statutory order shall not be made or confirmed by the Minister except with the consent of the Board of Trade or the Minister of Transport, as the case may require.

150. Transfer and compensation of officers (1) *A scheme or order made under this Part of this Act may contain provisions as to the transfer of existing officers affected by the scheme or order, and shall contain provisions for—*

   (a) *the protection of the interests of any such existing officers; and*
   (b) *the payment, by such local authority as may be determined by or under the scheme or order, of compensation to any existing officer who by virtue of the scheme or order, or of anything done in pursuance of or in consequence of its provisions, suffers any direct pecuniary loss by reason of the determination of his appointment or the diminution of his emoluments, and for whose compensation for that loss no other provision is made by any enactment or statutory order for the time being in force.*

(2) *An existing officer who, at any time within five years after the date on which the scheme or order comes into operation, relinquishes office by reason of his having been required to perform duties which are not analogous to, or which are an unreasonable addition to, those which he was required to perform immediately before that date shall be deemed for the purposes of the scheme or order to have had his office determined in consequence of the scheme or order, and, unless the contrary is shown, to have suffered direct pecuniary loss in consequence of the scheme or order by reason of such determination.*

(3) *An existing officer whose appointment is determined or whose emoluments are reduced within five years after the date on which the scheme or order comes into operation, because his services are not required or his duties are diminished (no misconduct being established), shall be deemed, unless the contrary is shown, to have suffered direct pecuniary loss in consequence of the scheme or order.*

(4) *A scheme or order made under this Part of this Act and providing for the payment of compensation to existing officers shall incorporate the provisions set out in the Fourth Schedule to this Act.*

(5) *For the purposes of this section—*
   (a) *the expression 'office' means any place, situation or employment . . . and the expression 'officer' has a corresponding meaning; and*
   (b) *the expression 'existing officer' means an officer who holds office on the date on which the scheme or order is made, or on such other date or dates as may be specified in the scheme or order.*

(6) *The payment of a lump sum by a local authority by way of compensation to an existing officer under a scheme or order made under this Part of this Act shall be a purpose for which the local authority may borrow.*

[NOTE: See L.G.A. 1958 s. 60(2).]

151. Financial adjustments (1) Any public bodies affected by any alteration of areas or authorities made by an order under this Part of this Act may from time to time make agreements for the purpose of adjusting any property, income, debts, liabilities and expenses (so far as affected by the alteration) of, and any financial relations between, the parties to the agreement.

(2) The agreement may provide for the transfer or retention of any property, debts, and liabilities, with or without any conditions, and for the joint use of any property, and for the transfer of any functions, and for payment by either party to the agreement in respect of property, debts, functions, and liabilities so transferred or retained, or of such joint user, and in respect of the remuneration or compensation payable to any officer or person, and that either by way of capital sum or of a terminable annuity for a period not exceeding that allowed by the Minister.

(3) In default of an agreement as to any matter requiring adjustment, such adjustment shall be referred to the arbitration of a single arbitrator agreed upon by the parties, or in default of agreement appointed by the Minister, and the award of the arbitrator may provide for any matter for which an agreement might have provided.

(4) Any sum required to be paid by a public body for the purpose of an adjustment under this section, may be

N

paid out of such fund or rate as may be specified in the agreement or award, or if no fund or rate is so specified, either out of the fund or rate from which the general expenses of the public body are defrayed, or out of such other fund or rate as the public body, with the approval of the *Minister*, may direct.

(5) For the purpose of paying any capital sum required to be paid by a public body for the purposes of an adjustment under this section—

(a) a local authority may borrow without the consent of any sanctioning authority, but so that the sum borrowed shall be repaid within such period as the authority, with the consent of the Minister, may determine;

(b) any other public body having power under any enactment or statutory order to borrow may borrow under that enactment; and

(c) a public body having no power under any enactment or statutory order to borrow may be empowered by the order to borrow in such manner and in accordance with such conditions as may be therein provided and may borrow accordingly.

(6) . . . capital money received by [a] public body in respect of an adjustment under this section shall be applied in such manner as the *Minister* may approve towards the discharge of any debt of the body or otherwise for a purpose for which capital money may be applied.

Part VII.

167. Power of parish council to acquire land A parish council may, for the purpose of any of their functions under this or any other public general Act, by agreement acquire, whether by way of purchase, lease, or exchange, any land whether situate within or without the parish.

168. Compulsory purchase of land on behalf of parish council (1) If a parish council are unable to purchase by agreement and on reasonable terms suitable land for any purpose for which they are authorised to acquire land, they may represent the case to the council of the county in which the parish is situate, and if on any such representation the county council are satisfied that suitable land for the said purpose cannot be purchased on reasonable terms by agreement and that the circumstances are such as to justify the county council in proceeding under this section, the county council shall cause a local inquiry to be held in the parish by such one or more members, or such officer, of the council as the council may appoint for the purpose.

(2) The county council shall publish in the parish in the prescribed manner a notice of the proposed inquiry, and shall serve on the owners, lessees, and occupiers (except tenants for a month or any period less than a month), of the land proposed to be taken notice thereof in the prescribed form.

(3) After the inquiry has been completed, and all objections made by persons interested have been considered, the county council may make and submit to the Minister an order for the compulsory purchase of the land, or any part thereof, and the provisions of this Part of this Act relating to compulsory purchase orders shall apply to an order made under this section, subject to the following modifications:—

(a) if no objection is duly made by any of the persons upon whom notices are required to be served, or if all objections so made are withdrawn, it shall be obligatory on the Minister, if he is satisfied that the proper notices have been published and served, to confirm the order with or without modification;

(b) the order shall be carried into effect by the county council, but the land, when acquired, shall be conveyed to the parish council, and accordingly in construing for the purposes of this section and of the order any enactment incorporated in the order the parish council in whom the land is to be vested and the county council by whom the land is to be acquired shall, as the case may require, be deemed to be the promoters of the undertaking or the company;

(c) it shall not be necessary for the county council to publish any notice stating that the order has been made and the purpose for which the land is required.

(4) The county council in making and the Minister in confirming an order under this section shall have regard to the extent of land held in the neighbourhood by any owner, and to the convenience of other property belonging to the same owner, and shall, so far as is practicable, avoid taking an undue or inconvenient quantity of land from any one owner.

(6) The person holding an inquiry under this section on behalf of a county council shall have the same powers as a person appointed by the Minister under this Act to hold an inquiry.

(7) If a county council refuse to make an order under this section, the parish council may petition the Minister, and the Minister, after holding a local inquiry, may, if he thinks proper, make the order, and this section shall apply as if the order had been made by the county council and confirmed by the Minister.

169. Power of parish council to let land A parish council, or in the case of a rural parish not having a separate parish council the representative body of the parish with the consent of the parish meeting, may let any land vested in them which is held for charitable purposes with the sanction of an order of the *Charity Commissioners*, and may let any other land vested in them with the consent of the Minister:

Provided that no order or consent shall be required where the term for which the land is let does not exceed one year, and in the case of land held

for charitable purposes, no order shall be required if the letting is for the purpose of allotments under the Allotments Acts, 1908 to 1950.

170. Power of parish council to sell or exchange land (1) A parish council, or in the case of a rural parish not having a separate parish council the representative body of the parish may, with the consent of the parish meeting—

(a) sell any land which they may possess and which is not required for the purposes for which it was acquired or is being used; or

(b) exchange any land which they may possess for other land, either with or without paying or receiving any money for equality of exchange:

Provided that no land held for charitable purposes shall be sold or exchanged without the sanction of an order of the *Charity Commissioners* and no other land shall be sold or exchanged without the consent of the Minister.

(2) Capital money received in respect of a transaction under this section shall be applied—

(i) in the case of a sale or exchange of land held for charitable purposes, in accordance with any directions given under the Charities Act, 1960; and

(ii) in any other case, in such manner as the Minister may approve towards the discharge of any debt of the parish council or parish meeting, or otherwise for any purpose for which capital money may be applied.

173. Lands belonging to Duchy of Lancaster The Chancellor and Council of the Duchy of Lancaster may sell to a local authority any land belonging to His Majesty in right of the said duchy which the local authority think fit to purchase, and the land may be assured to the local authority . . .

176. Application of Lands Clauses Acts to purchases by agreement Where under this Part of this Act a local authority are authorised to acquire land by agreement, the provisions of Part 1 of the Compulsory Purchase Act 1965 (so far as applicable) other than sections 4 to 8, section 10 and section 31 shall apply and in the said Part I as so applied the word 'land' shall have the meaning assigned to it in this Act.

177. Payment of purchase or compensation money by one local authority to another (1) Any purchase money or compensation payable in pursuance of this Part of this Act by a local authority in respect of any land acquired from another local authority which would, but for this section, be required to be paid into court in manner provided by the Lands Clauses Acts may, if the Minister consents, instead of being paid into court, be paid and applied as the Minister may determine.

(2) A decision of the Minister under this section shall be final.

178. Application of proceeds of sale of parish property Where property representing the proceeds of sale of parish property is held at the commencement of this Act for the benefit of a parish, the property and the income thereof shall continue to be applied to the purposes to which they were applied immediately before the commencement of this Act, until the *Minister* otherwise directs.

179. Savings Nothing in this Part of this Act shall—

(d) authorise the disposal of land by a local authority, whether by sale, lease, or exchange, in breach of any trust, covenant or agreement binding upon the authority; or

(e) effect any power to sell, mortgage, alienate or lease corporate land in pursuance of an agreement made on or before the 5th day of June 1835, or of a resolution entered in the books of a body corporate on or before that date; or

(f) where under any enactment or statutory order conferring on a local authority a power to acquire land the power is expressly limited to acquisition by agreement, confer on the local authority power to acquire land compulsorily for the purposes of that enactment or statutory order.

Part VIII.

190. General and special expenses of rural authority (1) The expenses incurred by a rural district council in the discharge of their functions shall be divided into general expenses and special expenses.

(2) All expenses incurred by a rural district council not declared by or under this Act or any other enactment or statutory order to be special expenses shall be general expenses.

(3) The Minister may, by order, on the application of a rural district council, declare any expenses incurred by that council to be special expenses separately chargeable on such contributory place or places in the district as may be specified in the order, and, if the said expenses are declared to be chargeable on more than one contributory place, the order may apportion the expenses amongst the contributory places: . . .

(4) Where any expenses of a rural district council are payable as special expenses, the council may determine to contribute as part of their general expenses such sums as appear to them to be reasonable in or towards defraying such expenses, and to treat the remainder, if any, as special expenses.

(5) Where any special expenses have been incurred for the common benefit of any two or more contributory places, the rural district council may, subject to the apportionment, if any, contained in an order made under subsection (3) of this section, apportion the expenses in such proportions as they think just between those contributory places, and any expenses so apportioned to any contributory place shall be a separate charge on that contributory place.

192. Power of rural district council to levy rates

(2) Amounts leviable by a rural district council by means of a rate shall be chargeable—

(a) in the case of amounts leviable to meet liabilities in respect of general expenses, on the whole of the district; and

(b) in the case of amounts leviable to meet liabilities in respect of special expenses, on the part of the district chargeable separately therewith.

193. Expenses of parish councils, &c.[1] (1) The sums required to be raised to meet the expenses of a parish council or of a parish meeting (including the expenses of a poll consequent on a parish meeting) shall be chargeable separately on the parish.

(2) In a parish having a separate parish council the expenses of the parish meeting (including the expenses of any poll consequent on a parish meeting) shall be paid by the parish council.

(3) The sums required to be raised in any financial year to meet the expenses *of a parish council* (other than expenses mentioned in the First Schedule to the Parish Councils Act, 1957) shall not, *without the consent of the parish meeting*, exceed an amount equal to a rate of *fourpence* (**1·7p**) in the pound, calculated on the total rateable value as set out in the valuation list in force at the commencement of the financial year, or such higher rate as the Minister may by order as respects any particular parish allow, and shall *in no case* exceed an amount equal to a rate of *eightpence* (**3·3p**) in the pound, calculated as aforesaid, or such higher rate as the Minister may by order as respects any particular parish allow.

(4) A parish council shall not, without the consent of the parish meeting, incur any expense or liability which will involve a loan.

Amended by P.C.A. 1957 s. 15.

(5) In a parish not having a parish council, the sums required to be raised in any financial year to meet the expenses of the parish meeting (other than expenses under the Allotments Acts, 1908 to 1950) when added to the expenses of any authority under any of the adoptive Acts or the Public Libraries and Museums Act, 1964, shall not exceed an amount equal to a rate of *eightpence* (**3·3p**) in the pound, calculated as aforesaid, or such higher rate as the Minister may by order as respects any particular parish allow.

(6) For the purpose of obtaining sums necessary to meet the expenses of a parish councillor or of a parish meeting, the parish council, or the chairman of the parish meeting of a parish not having a separate parish council, shall issue precepts to the council of the rural district in which the parish is situate.

(8) Every cheque or other order for the payment of money by a parish council shall be signed by two members of the council.

(9) Every parish council and the chairman of the parish meeting for a rural parish not having a separate parish council shall keep such accounts as may be prescribed of the receipts and payments of the council or parish meeting, as the case may be.

(10) An order made by the Minister under this section may be altered or revoked by an order made in like manner as the original order.

(11) Nothing in this section shall alter the incidence of charge of any rate levied to defray expenses incurred under any of the adoptive Acts.

194. Savings for revenues from undertakings, &c. Nothing in this Part of this Act shall—

(a) be deemed to require or authorise a local authority to apply or dispose of the surplus revenue arising from any undertaking carried on by them otherwise than in accordance with the provisions of any enactment or statutory order relating to the undertaking.

PART IX.

195. Purposes for which money may be borrowed A local authority may, with the consent of the sanctioning authority, or in the case of a parish council with the consent of the Minister, borrow such sums as may be required for any of the following purposes, that is to say:—

(*a*) for acquiring any land which the local authority have power to acquire:

(*b*) for erecting any building which the local authority have power to erect:

(*c*) for the execution of any permanent work, the provision of any plant, or the doing of any other thing which the local authority have power to execute, provide, or do, if, in the opinion of the sanctioning authority or, in the case of a parish council, in the opinion of the Minister, the cost of carrying out that purpose ought to be spread over a term of years:

(*d*) in the case of a local authority being a county council, for the purpose of lending to a parish council any money which the parish council are authorised to borrow:

(*e*) for any other purpose for which the local authority are authorised under any enactment, including any enactment in this Act, or under any statutory order, to borrow:

Provided that the consent of the sanctioning authority shall not be required to a borrowing by a county council for the purposes of paragraph (*d*) of this section.

196. Modes of borrowing (1) Where a local authority are authorised to borrow money, they may, subject to

the provisions of this Part of this Act, raise the money . . .

Provided that a parish council shall not borrow *otherwise than by way of mortgage*.

[NOTE: See P.W.L.A. 1965.]

197. Security for borrowing and priority of securities (1) All moneys borrowed by a local authority, whether before or after the commencement of this Act, shall be charged indifferently on all the revenues of the authority.

(2) Subject to the provisions of this section, *all securities* created by a local authority, whether under this Act or under any other enactment or statutory order, shall rank equally without any priority.

(3) Nothing in this section shall—

(*a*) apply to any money borrowed by way of temporary loan or overdraft without security; or

(*b*) affect any priority existing at, or any right to priority conferred by a security created before, the commencement of this Act.

198. Period for repayment of moneys borrowed (1) Every sum borrowed under this Part of this Act shall be repaid within such period as the local authority, with the consent of the sanctioning authority, may determine:

Provided that the period for the repayment of a sum so borrowed shall not exceed [80 years] in the case of a sum borrowed [for the acquisition of land for use as allotments] or, in any other case, the period of sixty years. [Note: The words in brackets are in the Eighth Schedule].

(2) *Where any sum is borrowed by a local authority for the purpose of meeting expenditure on the construction of new, or the extension or alterations of existing, works forming or to form part of an undertaking of a revenue-producing character, it shall be lawful for any annual provision required to be made by the local authority for the repayment of the sum so borrowed to be suspended for such period (not being a period longer than the period during which the expenditure remains unremunerative, or the period of five years*

from the commencement of the financial year next after that in which the expenditure commences to be incurred, whichever is the shorter) and subject to such conditions as the sanctioning authority may determine.

[NOTE: See L.G.(F.P.)A. 1963 s. 8(1) and (9)]

199. Return to Minister (1) The clerk of a local authority shall, within one month after being requested so to do by the Minister, transmit to the Minister a return showing the provision made by the local authority for the repayment of moneys borrowed by the authority.

(2) The return shall show such particulars, shall be made up to such date and shall be in such form, as the Minister may require, shall be certified by the treasurer or other person whose duty it is to keep the accounts of the authority, and shall, if so required by the Minister, be verified by a statutory declaration made by that person.

(3) If it appears to the Minister from any return made under this section or otherwise that a local authority—

(a) have failed to pay any instalment or annual payment required to be paid: or

(b) have failed to appropriate to the discharge of any loan any sum required to be so appropriated:

(c) have failed to set apart any sum required for a sinking fund: or

(d) have applied any portion of a sinking fund to a purpose other than those authorised;

the Minister may by order direct that such sum as is specified in the order, not exceeding the amount in respect of which default has been made, shall be paid or applied in the manner and by the date set out in the order, and the authority shall notify the Minister as soon as the order has been complied with.

(4) An order made under the last preceding sub-section may be enforced, at the instance of the Minister, by mandamus.

(5) If a return required to be made

under this section is not made, the person in default shall be liable, on summary conviction, to a fine not exceeding £20, and notwithstanding the recovery of any such fine the making of the return may be enforced, at the instance of the Minister, by mandamus.

(6) The provisions of this section shall be in substitution for, and not in addition to, any requirement under any other enactment or statutory order to make a return as to the provision made by a local authority for the repayment of borrowed moneys.

200. Charge of service of loan to particular account Where a loan is raised to meet any expenditure of a local authority which is chargeable to a particular account, there shall be debited to that account all sums required for repayment of the principal of the loan, or for payment of interest thereon, or for making payments to any sinking fund established for the purposes thereof.

201. Conditions of borrowing by county council for loan to parish council (1) In relation to borrowing by a county council for the purpose of lending to a parish council, the *Minister* may by order impose conditions to be observed either generally or in any particular case in addition to the conditions to be observed in relation to borrowing for other purposes.

(2) An order made under this section may be altered or revoked by an order made in like manner as the original order.

202. Balance of unexpended moneys *The balance of any money borrowed by a local authority and not required for the purposes for which the money was borrowed may, with the consent of the Minister, and subject to any conditions which he may impose, be applied to any other purpose for which capital money may be applied:*

Provided that nothing in this section shall dispense with the necessity of the consent of the Public Works Loan Commissioners in any case in which such consent is required under section 9 of the Public Works Loans Act, 1881.

[NOTE: See L.G.(F.P.)A. 1963 s. 10.]

203. Lenders relieved from certain inquiries A person lending money to a local authority shall not be bound to inquire whether the borrowing of the money is or was legal or regular or whether the money raised was properly applied, and shall not be prejudiced by any illegality or irregularity in the matters aforesaid or by the misapplication or non-application of any such money.

205. Form of mortgage A mortgage created under this Part of this Act shall be by deed made in the prescribed form or in a form to the like effect:

Provided that in the case of a loan made by the Public Works Loan Commissioners the mortgage shall be in such form as may be prescribed under the Public Works Loans Acts, 1875 to 1882.

206. Transfer of *mortgage* The person entitled to a *mortgage* created by a local authority, may transfer it by deed made in the prescribed form or in a form to the like effect.

207. Register of mortgages (1) The clerk of a local authority shall keep at the office of the authority a register of *mortgages* created by the authority under this Part of this Act (in this Part of this Act referred to as 'the register').

(2) Within 14 days after the date of a *mortgage* the clerk of the authority shall cause an entry to be made in the register of the number and date thereof, of the names and descriptions of the parties thereto, and of the amount borrowed, as stated in the *deed.*

(3) On production to the clerk of the authority of the *deed of mortgage*, and—

(a) in the case of a transfer of a *mortgage*, of a duly executed deed of transfer:

(b) in the case of a transmission of a *mortgage* by the death of a person solely entitled thereto or of the survivor of persons jointly entitled thereto, of probate of the will or letters of administration of the estate of the deceased:

(c) in the case of a transmission of *mortgage* otherwise than as aforesaid, of satisfactory evidence of the transmission,

and on payment of such sum, if any, not exceeding five shillings, as the authority may determine the clerk of the authority shall cause an entry to be made in the register of the date of the transfer or transmission, and of the name and description of the person becoming entitled thereunder to the *mortgage.*

(4) Any change of name or address on the part of a person entitled to a *mortgage* shall forthwith be notified to the clerk of the authority, who, on being satisfied thereof, shall alter the register accordingly.

(6) The register shall be open at all reasonable hours to public inspection without payment.

(7) If any person,—

(a) having the custody of the register, refuses inspection of the register to any person; or

(b) being required under this section to make an entry in the register, refuses or wilfully neglects so to do,

he shall be liable, on summary conviction, to a fine not exceeding, in the case of an offence under paragraph (a) of this subsection, £5, or, in the case of an offence under paragraph (b) of this subsection, £20.

208. Title to mortgage and rectification of register (1) A local authority shall be entitled to treat as exclusively entitled to a *mortgage*, in relation to which entries have been duly made in the register, the person appearing by the latest of those entries to be entitled thereto.

(2) If the name of any person is, without sufficient cause, entered in or omitted from the register, or default is made or unnecessary delay takes place in making any entry required to be made in the register, the High Court or, where the sum involved does not exceed £500, the county court may, on application by the person aggrieved or by the local authority, make an order for the rectification of the register.

(3) On any proceedings under this section the court may decide any

question relating to the title of any party thereto to have his name entered in or omitted from the register and generally any question which it may be necessary or expedient to decide for the purpose of the rectification of the register.

209. Notice of trusts No notice of any trust, expressed, implied or constructive, affecting a mortgage created by a local authority shall be entered in the register or be receivable by the authority or by any officer of the authority.

210. Receipts on behalf of joint holders and infants (1) Where two or more persons are jointly entitled to a mortgage created by a local authority any one of those persons may give an effectual receipt for any interest thereon, unless notice in writing to the contrary has been given to the local authority by any other of those persons.

(2) The receipt of the guardian of an infant shall be a sufficient discharge to a local authority for any money payable to the infant in respect of a mortgage created by the local authority.

211. Appointment of receiver (1) If at any time any principal money or interest due under a mortgage created by a local authority remains unpaid for a period of two months after demand in writing, the person entitled thereto may, without prejudice to any other remedy, apply to the High Court for the appointment of a receiver, and the Court may, if they think fit, appoint a receiver on such terms and with such powers as the Court think fit:

Provided that no such application shall be entertained unless the sums due to the applicant, or in the case of a joint application by two or more persons the aggregate sums due to them, amount to not less than £500.

(2) The Court may confer upon the receiver any such powers of collecting, receiving and recovering the revenues of the local authority, and of making, collecting and recovering rates, and of issuing and enforcing precepts, as are possessed by the local authority or their officers.

212. Repayment of moneys borrowed on mortgage (1) Every sum borrowed by a local authority by way of *mortgage* shall be paid off either by equal yearly, half-yearly or quarterly instalments of principal, or of principal and interest combined, or by means of a sinking fund, or partly by one of those methods and partly by another or others of them.

(2) Subject to the provisions of *subsection (2) of section 198 of this Act*, the payment of the first instalment or the first payment to the sinking fund shall be made within twelve months or, where the moneys are repayable by half-yearly instalments, within six months or, where the moneys are repayable by quarterly instalments, within three months from the date of borrowing.

[NOTE: See L.G.(F.P.)A. 1963 s. 8(6)].

213. Sinking fund (1) If a local authority determine to repay by means of a sinking fund any sums borrowed under this Part of this Act by way of *mortgage*, the sinking fund shall be formed and maintained either—

(a) by payment to the fund throughout the fixed period of such equal annual sums as will be sufficient to pay off within that period the moneys for the repayment of which the sinking fund is formed; or

(b) by payment to the fund throughout the fixed period of such equal annual sums as, with accumulations at a rate not exceeding the prescribed rate, or such other rate as the Minister may in any particular case approve, will be sufficient to pay off within that period the moneys for the repayment of which the sinking fund is formed.

In this Part of this Act a sinking fund formed under paragraph (a) of this subsection is referred to as 'a non-accumulating sinking fund,' and a sinking fund formed under paragraph (b) thereof as 'an accumulating sinking fund.'

(2) Every sum paid to a sinking fund shall, unless applied in repayment of the moneys for the repayment of which the

sinking fund is formed, or in such other manner as may be authorised by an enactment, be immediately invested in statutory securities (other than securities created by the local authority), and the local authority may from time to time vary and transpose the investments.

(3) In the case of an accumulating sinking fund, the interest received in any year from the investment of the sums set apart for the purposes of the sinking fund shall form part of the revenue for that year of the county fund or general rate fund, as the case may be, but the contribution to be made to the sinking fund out of the county fund or general rate fund, as the case may be, shall in that year be increased by a sum equal to the interest that would have accrued to the sinking fund during that year if interest had been accumulated therein at the rate per cent. per annum on which the annual payments to the sinking fund are based.

(4) A local authority may at any time apply the whole or any part of a sinking fund in or towards the discharge of the moneys for the repayment of which the sinking fund was formed:

Provided that, in the case of an accumulating sinking fund, the local authority shall pay into the fund each year and accumulate during the residue of the fixed period a sum equal to the interest which would have been produced by such sinking fund or part thereof so applied if invested at the rate per cent. per annum on which the annual payments to the sinking fund are based.

(5) Any surplus of a sinking fund remaining after the discharge of the whole of the moneys for the repayment of which it was formed shall be applied to such capital purpose as the local authority, with the consent of the Minister, may determine.

(6) Subsection (2) of this section shall apply to a sinking fund established by a local authority under any enactment for the repayment of moneys borrowed by way of mortgage, and subsections (3), (4) and (5) of this section shall apply to an accumulating sinking fund so established, in like manner as they respectively apply to a sinking fund or an accumulating sinking fund established under this Part of this Act.

(7) In the application of this section to a sinking fund formed by a parish council, references to the county fund or general rate fund shall be read as references to the fund out of which the expenses of the council are defrayed.

214. Adjustments of sinking fund (1) If at any time it appears to the local authority that the amount in a sinking fund, together with the sums which will be payable thereto in accordance with the provisions of this Part of this Act, and, in the case of an accumulating sinking fund, with the accumulations thereon, will not be sufficient to repay within the fixed period the moneys for the repayment of which the sinking fund is formed, the local authority shall, either temporarily or permanently, make such increased payments to the sinking fund as will cause the sinking fund to be sufficient for that purpose, and if it appears to the Minister that any such increase is necessary, the local authority shall increase the payments to such extent as the Minister may direct.

(2) If the local authority desire to accelerate the repayment of any moneys borrowed by way of mortgage, they may increase the amounts payable to the sinking fund.

(3) If the amount in a sinking fund, together with the sums which will be payable thereto in accordance with the provisions of this Part of this Act, and also, in the case of an accumulating sinking fund, together with the accumulations thereon, will in the opinion of the Minister be more than sufficient to repay within the fixed period the moneys for the repayment of which the sinking fund is formed, the local authority may reduce the payments to the sinking fund either temporarily or permanently to such amounts as will in the opinion of the Minister be sufficient to repay within the fixed period the moneys for the repayment of which the sinking fund is formed.

(4) If at any time the amount in a sinking fund, together with the accumulations thereon in the case of an accumulating sinking fund, will in the opinion of the Minister be sufficient to repay the moneys for the repayment of which the sinking fund is formed within the fixed period, the Minister may authorise the local authority to suspend the annual payments to the sinking fund until the Minister otherwise directs.

(5) This section shall apply to a sinking fund established by a local authority under any other enactment for the repayment of moneys borrowed by way of mortgage in like manner as it applies to a sinking fund established under this Part of this Act.

215. Temporary loans, &c. (1) A local authority may, without the consent of any sanctioning authority, borrow by way of temporary loan or overdraft from a bank or otherwise, any sums which they may temporarily require—

(a) for the purpose of defraying expenses (including the payment of sums due by them to meet the expenses of other authorities) pending the receipt of revenues receivable by them in respect of the period of account in which those expenses are chargeable and taken into account in the estimates made by the local authority for that period;

(b) for the purpose of defraying, pending the raising of a loan which the authority have been authorised to raise, expenses intended to be defrayed by means of the loan.

(2) Where money is borrowed in pursuance of paragraph (b) of the preceding subsection and subsequently such a loan as is mentioned in that paragraph is raised, then for the purposes of the provisions of this Part of this Act regulating the repayment of that loan, the loan shall, to the extent of the sum borrowed under the said paragraph, be deemed to have been raised at the time when the borrowing under the said paragraph took place.

216. Power to re-borrow (1) A local authority may, without the consent of any sanctioning authority, borrow for the purpose of—

(a) paying off any moneys previously borrowed by the local authority which are intended to be repaid forthwith; or

(b) replacing moneys which, during the preceding twelve months, have been temporarily applied from other moneys of the local authority in repaying moneys previously borrowed, and which at the time of such repayment it was intended to replace by borrowed moneys:

Provided that a local authority shall not have power to borrow under this section—

(a) for the purpose of making any payment to a sinking fund or of paying any instalment or making any annual payment which has or may become due in respect of borrowed moneys; or

(b) for the purpose of replacing any moneys previously borrowed which have been repaid

    (i) by instalments or annual payments; or

    (ii) by means of a sinking fund; or

    (iii) out of moneys derived from the sale of land; or

    (iv) out of any capital moneys properly applicable to the purpose of the repayment, other than moneys borrowed for that purpose.

Note: See P.W.L.A. 1964 s. 6.

(2) Any moneys borrowed under this section shall, for the purposes of repayment, be deemed to form part of the original loan, and shall be repaid within that portion of the fixed period which remains unexpired, and the provisions which are for the time being applicable to the original loan shall apply to the moneys borrowed under this section:

Provided that the authority who sanctioned the original loan may, upon application made to them for that purpose, extend the period for repayment of the moneys borrowed under this section so as to expire on such date as they think fit, not being later than the expiration of the maximum period which might have been permitted for the repayment of the original loan.

218. Definitions In this Part of this Act, unless the context otherwise requires, the following expressions have the meanings hereby assigned to them—

'fixed period' means the period originally fixed as the period within which the moneys borrowed are to be repaid;

'revenues' in relation to a local authority includes the county fund or general rate fund, as the case may be, and all rates, Exchequer contributions and other revenues, whether arising from land or undertakings or from any other source, receivable by the local authority;

'sanctioning authority' means—

(c) . . . the Minister;

'statutory securities' means any security in which trustees are for the time being authorised by law to invest trust moneys, and any mortgage, bond, debenture, debenture stock, stock or other security created by a local authority, other than annuities, rentcharges, or securities, transferable by delivery.

PART X.

219. Authorities and officers whose accounts are subject to district audit The following accounts shall be subject to audit by a district auditor under this Part of this Act, that is to say,—

(a) the accounts of every . . . parish council, and of every parish

meeting for a rural parish not having a parish council;

(b) the accounts of any committee appointed by any such council or parish meeting;

(c) the accounts of any joint committee constituted under Part III of this Act or under any enactment repealed by this Act, of which one or more of the constituent authorities are a . . . parish council . . .

(d) any other accounts which are made subject to audit by a district auditor by virtue of any enactments or statutory order . . .

Provided that in relation to any audit of accounts under paragraph (d) of this section this Part of this Act shall have effect subject to the provisions of the relevant enactment or statutory order.

222. Financial statement and certificate of expenditure (1) Where any accounts of an authority are audited by a district auditor, the authority shall prepare and submit to the district auditor at every audit a financial statement of those accounts, in duplicate, in the prescribed form and containing the prescribed particulars.

(2) The district auditor, at the conclusion of the audit, shall certify on each copy of the financial statement, in the prescribed form, the amount of the expenditure so audited and allowed, and further, that the regulations with respect to the statement have been duly complied with, and that he has ascertained by the audit the correctness of the statement.

(3) One copy of the financial statement shall have the stamp charged under this Part of this Act affixed thereon, and at the conclusion of the audit the district auditor shall cancel the stamp.

(4) The district auditor shall, immediately after the conclusion of the audit, send the stamped copy of the financial statement to the Minister.

(5) If an authority fail to comply with the provisions of this section with respect to a financial statement, the authority,

and, if a clerk of the authority is appointed, the clerk, or if no clerk is appointed but there is a treasurer or other officer whose duty it is to keep the accounts which ought to be comprised in the financial statement, the treasurer or other officer, shall be liable, on summary conviction, to a fine not exceeding twenty pounds and notwithstanding the recovery of any such fine, compliance with the provisions of this section may be enforced, at the instance of the Minister, by mandamus.

223. Accounts to be made up and audited yearly All accounts which are subject to audit by a district auditor shall be made up yearly to the 31st day of March, or to such other date as the Minister may either generally or in any special case direct, and shall be audited as soon as may be thereafter.

224. Deposit of accounts (1) A copy of every account which is subject to audit by a district auditor, duly made up and balanced, and all rate books, account books, deeds, contracts, accounts, vouchers and receipts relating to the accounts, shall be deposited in the appropriate office of the authority, and shall for seven clear days before the audit be open at all reasonable hours to the inspection of all persons interested, and any such person shall be at liberty to make copies of or extracts from the deposited documents, without payment.

(2) If any officer of the authority duly appointed in that behalf neglects to make up the aforesaid accounts and books, or, except with the consent of, or in accordance with directions given by, the district auditor, alters, or allows to be altered, the aforesaid accounts and books when so made up and deposited, or having the custody of such accounts and books refuses to allow inspection thereof, he shall be liable on summary conviction to a fine not exceeding £5.

(3) Before each audit the authority, on receiving from the auditor the requisite appointment, shall, by advertisement in one or more local newspapers circulating in the district, give at least fourteen days' notice of the deposit of accounts required by this section, and the production of the newspaper containing such notice shall be sufficient proof of such notice in any legal proceeding:

Provided that in the case of the audit of the accounts of a parish council or of a parish meeting or of a joint committee of parish councils, the authority shall, in lieu of giving notice by advertisement, give at least fourteen days' public notice of the deposit of the accounts.

225. Production of and declarations as to documents (1) A district auditor may by writing under his hand require the production before him of all books, deeds, contracts, accounts, vouchers, receipts and other documents which he may deem necessary for the purpose of the audit, and may require any person holding or accountable for any such document to appear before him at the audit or any adjournment thereof, and may require any such person to make and sign a declaration as to the correctness of the document.

(2) If any person neglects or refuses to comply with any such requirement, he shall be liable on summary conviction to a fine not exceeding forty shillings, and if any person knowingly and wilfully makes or signs any such declaration which is untrue in any material particular, he shall be deemed to be guilty of an offence under section 5 of the Perjury Act, 1911.

226. Right of objection (1) A local government elector for the area to the accounts of which the audit relates may be present or may be represented at the audit and may make any objection to the accounts before the auditor.

(2) The district auditor shall, on the application of any person who is aggrieved by his decision on any matter with respect to which that person has made an objection, or of any person aggrieved by a disallowance or surcharge made by the auditor, state in writing the reasons for his decision.

227. Report to local authority Within fourteen days after the completion of the audit of the accounts of an authority the auditor shall report on the accounts audited and examined, and shall send the report to the authority, and the authority shall take the report into consideration at their next ordinary meeting or as soon as practicable thereafter:

Provided that in the case of a parish council or parish meeting or of any joint committee appointed by parish councils or parish meetings the report shall, in lieu of being sent to the authority, be sent to the Minister.

228. Power and duties of the auditor (1) It shall be the duty of the district auditor at every audit held by him—

(a) to disallow every item of account which is contrary to law;

(b) to surcharge the amount of any expenditure disallowed upon the person responsible for incurring or authorising the expenditure;

(c) to surcharge any sum which has not been duly brought into account upon the person by whom that sum ought to have been brought into account;

(d) to surcharge the amount of any loss or deficiency upon any person by whose negligence or misconduct the loss or deficiency has been incurred;

(e) to certify the amount due from any person upon whom he has made a surcharge;

(f) to certify at the conclusion of the audit his allowance of the accounts, subject to any disallowances or surcharges which he may have made:

Provided that no expenses paid by an authority shall be disallowed by the auditor, if they have been sanctioned by the Minister.

(2) Any loss represented by a charge for interest or any loss of interest shall be deemed to be a loss within the meaning of this section, if it arises from failure through wilful neglect or wilful default to make or collect such rates or to issue such precepts as are necessary to cover the expenditure of the authority for any financial year (including any expenditure incurred in any previous year and not covered by rates previously levied or precepts previously issued), or to collect other revenues.

229. Appeals against decisions of auditors (1) Any person who is aggrieved by a decision of a district auditor on any matter with respect to which he made an objection at the audit, and any person aggrieved by a disallowance or surcharge made by a district auditor may, where the disallowance or surcharge or other decision relates to an amount exceeding £500, appeal to the High Court, and may in any other case appeal either to the High Court or to the Minister.

(2) The Court or Minister on such an appeal shall have power to confirm, vary or quash the decision of the auditor, and to remit the case to the auditor with such directions as the Court or Minister thinks fit for giving effect to the decision on appeal, and if the decision of the auditor is quashed, or is varied so as to reduce the amount of the surcharge to £500 or less, the appellant shall not be subject to the disqualification by reason of the surcharge imposed by Part II of this Act.

(3) Where an appeal is made to the Minister under this section, he may at any stage of the proceedings, and shall, if so directed by the High Court, state in the form of a special case for the opinion of the Court any question of law arising in the course of the appeal, but save as aforesaid the decision of the Minister shall be final.

230. Applications for relief (1) In the case of a surcharge, the person surcharged may, whether or not he appeals under the preceding section, apply to the tribunal (whether the High Court or the Minister) to whom he appeals or, if he does not appeal, to the tribunal (whether the High Court or the Minister) to whom he might have appealed, for a declaration that in relation to the subject matter of the surcharge he acted reasonably or in the belief that his action was authorised by law, and the Court or Minister, if satisfied that there is proper ground for doing so, may make a declaration to that effect.

(2) Where such a declaration is made the person surcharged, if by reason of

the surcharge he is subject to the disqualification imposed by Part II of this Act, shall not be subject to that disqualification, and the Court or Minister may, if satisfied that the person surcharged ought fairly to be excused, relieve him either wholly or in part from personal liability in respect of the surcharge, and the decision of the Court or Minister under this section shall be final.

231. Supplemental provisions as to appeals and applications (1) Provision shall be made by rules of court for limiting the time within which appeals and applications may be made to the High Court under this Part of this Act, and for securing that where an application is made public notice of the hearing shall be given, and for enabling any local government elector for the area of the authority whose accounts were subject to the audit to appear at the hearing and object.

(2) Where under this Part of this Act an appeal or application is made to the Minister, the appellant or applicant shall be entitled, if he so desires, to a personal hearing by a person appointed for the purpose by the Minister.

232. Payment of sums certified to be due. Every sum certified by a district auditor to be due from any person shall be paid by that person to the treasurer of the authority within fourteen days after it has been so certified, or, if an appeal or application with respect to that sum has been made, within fourteen days after the appeal or application is finally disposed of or abandoned or fails by reason of the non-prosecution thereof.

233. Recovery of sums certified to be due (1) Any sum which is certified by a district auditor to be due and has become payable shall, on complaint made or action taken by or under the direction of the district auditor, be recoverable either summarily or otherwise as a civil debt.

(2) In any proceedings for the recovery of such a sum, a certified signed by a district auditor shall be conclusive evidence of the facts certified, and a certificate signed by the treasurer

of the authority concerned or other officer whose duty it is to keep the accounts that the sum certified to be due has not been paid to him shall be conclusive evidence of non-payment, unless it is proved that the sum certified to be due has been paid since the date of the certificate.

Unless the contrary is proved, a certificate purporting to be signed by a district auditor, or by the treasurer of the authority or other officer whose duty it is to keep the accounts, shall be deemed to have been signed by such auditor, treasurer or other officer, as the case may be.

(3) Notwithstanding anything in the Summary Jurisdiction Acts, proceedings before a court of summary jurisdiction to recover sums certified by a district auditor to be due may be commenced at any time before the expiration of nine months from the date of the disallowance or surcharge, or, in the event of an appeal or application being made to the High Court or to the Minister, before the expiration of nine months from the date on which the appeal or application is finally disposed of or abandoned or fails by reason of non-prosecution thereof.

235. Power to regulate audit (1) The Minister may make regulations generally with respect to the preparation and audit of accounts which are subject to audit by a district auditor, including—

(a) the financial transactions which are to be recorded in the accounts;

(b) the mode of keeping the accounts of the authority and their officers, and the form of those accounts;

(c) the mode in which, if it is so prescribed, the accounts are to be certified by the authority or any officer of the authority;

(d) the publication of the time and place of holding the audit;

(e) the persons by whom the accounts are to be produced for audit;

(f) the mode of conducting the audit;

(g) the form of certificates to be given by district auditors;

(h) the deposit and inspection of the accounts as audited, and the publication of information with respect thereto;

(i) the making of an abstract of the accounts as audited.

(2) If any person wilfully neglects or disobeys any regulation made under this section, he shall be liable, on summary conviction, for a first offence to a fine not exceeding £5, and for a second or subsequent offence to a fine not exceeding £20.

(3) Regulations made under this section shall be laid before each House of Parliament as soon as may be after they are made.

236. Extraordinary audits (1) The Minister may at any time direct a district auditor to hold an extraordinary audit of any accounts which are subject to audit by a district auditor.

(2) An extraordinary audit held under this section shall be deemed to be an audit for the purposes of this Part of this Act, and the provisions of this Part of this Act, other than those requiring the authority to prepare and submit a financial statement of the accounts, to deposit copies of the accounts and documents relating thereto for public inspection and to give notice thereof by advertisement, shall apply accordingly.

(3) An extraordinary audit may be held after three days' notice in writing given to the authority or persons whose accounts are to be audited.

241. Audit of accounts of officers Where an officer of an authority receives any money or property on behalf of the authority, or receives any money or property for which he ought to account to the authority, the accounts of the officer shall be audited by the auditor of the accounts of the authority, with the same powers, incidents and consequences as in the case of those accounts.

Part XI.

244. Returns of local finance to be made to Minister (1) Subject to the provisions of this section, a return shall be made to the Minister for each year ending on the 31st day of March, or on such other day as may be prescribed, of the income and expenditure of every local authority, and of the parish meeting for every rural parish not having a separate parish council.

(2) Subject to the provisions of this section, a return shall be made to the Minister for each year ending on the 31st day of March, or on such other day as may be prescribed, of all sums levied or received in respect of the general rate . . . or of any of the following rates, taxes, tolls or dues, and of the expenditure of any such sums, that is to say—

(a) any church rate, whether leviable under the common law or the Church Building Acts, 1881 to 1884, or any other enactment;

(b) any drainage rate or other rate, scot or tax in connection with land drainage, whether leviable under the Land Drainage Act, 1930, or any other enactment or statutory order, or by charter, usage or custom;

(d) any tolls or dues leviable under any enactment relating to markets, bridges or harbours;

(e) any other compulsory rates, taxes, tolls or dues:

Provided that nothing in this subsection shall extend to—

(i) rates, taxes, tolls or dues levied for the public revenue of the United Kingdom; or

(ii) tolls or dues taken by any statutory undertakers carrying on business for profit, or by any company within the meaning of the Companies Act, 1929, as revenues of their undertaking; or

(iii) tolls or dues taken by prescription or otherwise as private property.

(3) The returns required to be made under this section shall—

(a) be in such form, and contain such particulars, as the Minister may direct;

(b) be sent to the Minister—

(i) within one month after the completion of the audit of the accounts of the local authority, parish meeting, or other authority or person, as the case may be, for the year in respect of which the return is required to be made; or

(ii) if the audit of those accounts is not completed within six months after the end of the said year, at the expiration of those six months; or

(iii) if the accounts are not required to be audited, within six months after the end of the said year;

(c) be made—

(i) in the case of a return relating to the income and expenditure of a local authority, by the clerk of the authority;

(ii) in the case of a return relating to the income and expenditure of a parish meeting, by the chairman of the parish meeting;

(iii) in the case of a return under subsection (2) of this section, where the power to levy, or to precept for the levying of, the rate, tax, toll, or due, is vested in a corporate body, by their clerk, or if there is no clerk by the treasurer or other person whose duty it is to keep the accounts of that body, and in any other case by the person or body of persons in whom that power is vested.

(4) Where under the preceding subsection a return is required to be made by the clerk of an authority or by the clerk to a corporate body, the return shall be certified by the treasurer or other person whose duty it is to keep the accounts of the authority or corporate body.

(5) Where any accounts are subject to audit by a district auditor and a copy of the financial statement relating to those accounts is sent to the Minister under Part X of this Act, a return of the income and expenditure comprised in such statement need not, unless the Minister so requires, be sent to the Minister under this Part of this Act, and the copy shall, for the purposes of this Part of this Act, be deemed to be a return made under this Part of this Act.

246. Penalties (7) If any person fails to make a return which he is required to make under this Part of this Act, he shall be liable, on summary conviction, to a fine not exceeding £20, and notwithstanding the recovery of any such fine the making of the return may be enforced, at the instance of the Minister, by mandamus.

(2) Where a return is required to be made under this Part of this Act by a body of person unincorporate, they shall severally be liable in respect of any failure to make such return.

247. Returns required to be made under other enactments Where under any enactment, whether passed before or after the commencement of this Act, any return relative to any rate, tax, toll or due (other than such as are levied for the public revenue of the United Kingdom) is required to be sent to a Secretary of State or to any other Government department, a duplicate thereof shall in like manner be sent to the Minister, and any person failing to send such duplicate shall be subject to the like penalties as a person failing to make a return under this Part of this Act.

PART XII.

250. Procedure, Etc. for making byelaws (1) The following provisions of this section shall apply to byelaws to be made by a local authority by virtue of—

(a) this Act; or

(b) the Public Health Acts, 1875 to 1932 (not being byelaws made under section thirteen of the Public Health Acts Amendment Act, 1890); or

(c) any enactment in force at the date of the commencement of this Act and incorporating or applying sections 182 to 186 of the Public Health Act, 1875, or any of those sections . . .; or

(d) any local Act passed before the eleventh day of August, 1875, being byelaws made for any purpose similar to which, bye-laws may be made under the Public Health Acts, 1875 to 1932; or

(e) any enactment passed after the commencement of this Act and conferring on any local authority a power to make byelaws.

(2) The byelaws shall be made . . . in the case of byelaws made by a parish council, under the hands and seals of two members of the council, and shall not have effect until they are confirmed by the confirming authority.

(3) At least one month before application for confirmation of the byelaws is made, notice of the intention to apply for confirmation shall be given in one or more local newspapers circulating in the area to which the byelaws apply.

(4) For at least one month before application for confirmation is made, a copy of the byelaws shall be deposited at the offices of the authority by whom the byelaws are made, and shall at all reasonable hours be open to public inspection without payment.

(5) The authority by whom the bye-laws are made shall, on application, furnish to any person a copy of the byelaws, or of any part thereof, on payment of such sum, not exceeding sixpence for every hundred words contained in the copy, as the authority may determine.

(6) The confirming authority may confirm, or refuse to confirm, any byelaw submitted under this section for confirmation, and may fix the date on which the byelaw is to come into operation, and if no date is so fixed the byelaw shall come into operation at the expiration of one month from the date of its confirmation.

(7) A copy of the byelaws, when confirmed, shall be printed and deposited at the offices of the authority by whom the byelaws are made, and shall at all reasonable hours be open to public inspection without payment, and a copy thereof shall, on application, be furnished to any person on payment of such sum, not exceeding one shilling for every copy, as the authority may determine.

(8) The clerk of a rural district council shall send a copy of every byelaw made by the council, and confirmed, to the clerk of the parish council of every parish to which they apply, or in the case of a parish not having a separate parish council to the chairman of the parish meeting of the parish, and the clerk of the parish council or chairman of the parish meeting, as the case may be, shall cause the copy to be deposited with the public documents of the parish.

The copy so deposited shall at all reasonable hours be open to public inspection without payment.

(9) . . .

(10) In this section the expression 'the confirming authority' means the authority or person, if any specified in the enactment (including any enactment in this Act) under which the bye-laws are made, or in any enactment incorporated therein or applied thereby, as the authority or person by whom the byelaws are to be confirmed, and in the case of byelaws made under any enactment incorporating or applying section 23 of the Municipal Corporations Act, 1882, or section 16 of the Local Government Act, 1882, means the Secretary of State or, if the subject-matter of the byelaws is such that the Minister would have been the confirming authority had they been made

under the last preceding section, the Minister:

Provided that, where under or by virtue of any enactment the power of an authority or person specified as aforesaid to confirm byelaws has been transferred, the authority or person to whom that power has been transferred shall be deemed to be the authority or person specified as aforesaid.

251. Fines for offences against byelaws

Byelaws to which the last preceding section applies may contain provisions for imposing on persons offending against the byelaws reasonable fines, recoverable on summary conviction, not exceeding such sum as may be fixed by the enactment conferring the power to make the byelaws, or, if no sum is so fixed, the sum of £20, and in the case of a continuing offence a further fine not exceeding such sum as may be fixed as aforesaid, or, if no sum is so fixed, the sum of 40 shillings for each day during which the offence continues after conviction therefor.

252. Evidence of byelaws

The production of a printed copy of a byelaw purporting to be made by a local authority, upon which is endorsed a certificate purporting to be signed by the clerk of the authority stating—

- (a) that the byelaw was made by the authority;
- (b) that the copy is a true copy of the byelaw;
- (c) that on a specified date the byelaw was confirmed by the authority named in the certificate or, as the case may require, was sent to the Secretary of State and has not been disallowed;
- (d) the date, if any, fixed by the confirming authority for the coming into operation of the byelaw;

shall be prima facie evidence of the facts stated in the certificate, and without proof of the handwriting or official position of any person purporting to sign a certificate in pursuance of this section.

Part XIII

266. Contracts of local authorities

(1) A local authority may enter into contracts necessary for the discharge of any of their functions.

(2) All contracts made by a local authority or by a committee thereof shall be made in accordance with the standing orders of the local authority, and in the case of contracts for the supply of goods or materials or for the execution of works, the standing orders shall—

- (a) require that, except as otherwise provided by or under the standing orders, notice of the intention of the authority or committee, as the case may be, to enter into the contract shall be published and tenders invited; and
- (b) regulate the manner in which such notice shall be published and tenders invited:

Provided that a person entering into a contract with a local authority shall not be bound to inquire whether the standing orders of the authority which apply to the contract have been complied with, and all contracts entered into by a local authority, if otherwise valid, shall have full force and effect notwithstanding that the standing orders applicable thereto have not been complied with.

267. Conferences of local authorities

A local authority . . . may, in such cases and subject to such conditions as may be prescribed, pay any reasonable expenses incurred by members . . . of the authority or of any committee thereof, in attending a conference or meeting convened by one or more local authorities, or by any association of local authorities, for the purpose of discussing any matter connected with the discharge of the functions of the authority, and any reasonable expenses incurred in purchasing reports of the proceedings of any such conference or meeting:

Provided that nothing in this section shall affect the provisions of any other enactment for the time being in force authorising the payment of expenses incurred by members of a local authority in attending any conference or meeting, or authorise a local authority to defray any expenses to which such enactment applies except in accordance with the provisions of that enactment.

[NOTE: See L.G.(F.P.)A. 1963 ss. 1 and 5.]

Acceptance of Gifts

268. Acceptance of gifts of property (1) Subject to the provisions of this section a local authority may accept, hold and administer any gift of property, whether real or personal, for any local public purpose, or for the benefit of the inhabitants of the area or of some part thereof, and may execute any works (including works of maintenance or improvement) incidental to or consequential on the exercise of the powers conferred by this section.

(2) Where the purposes of the gift are purposes for which the local authority are empowered to expend money raised from a rate, they may, subject to any condition or restriction attaching to the exercise of that power, defray expenditure incurred in the exercise of the powers conferred by the last preceding subsection out of money so raised.

(3) This section shall not authorise the acceptance by a local authority of property which, when accepted, would be held in trust for an ecclesiastical charity or for an eleemosynary charity.

(4) Nothing in this section shall affect any powers exercisable by a local authority under or by virtue of the Education Acts, 1921 to 1933.

269. Transfer of powers, &c. (2) Where after the commencement of this Act a certificate is given under the provisions of the Burial Act, 1855 . . . in a rural parish having a parish council, in order to obtain repayment from the general rate fund of the expenses of maintaining or repairing a closed churchyard, the functions and liabilities of the parochial church council of the parish with respect to the maintenance and repair of the churchyard shall, by virtue of this Act, be transferred . . . to the parish council . . .

272. Power to confer functions of urban district councils on rural district councils (1) The Minister may by order confer on rural district councils the functions of urban district councils under any public general Act, and apply to rural districts the provisions of any such Act relating to urban districts.

(2) The powers conferred on the Minister by this section shall be in addition to, and not in substitution for, the powers conferred on him by section 276 of the Public Health Act, 1875, or by any enactment applying that section.

273. Power to confer functions of parish council on parish meeting (1) On the application of the parish meeting of a rural parish not having a separate parish council the county council may, subject to the provisions of the grouping order if the parish is grouped with any other parish, by order confer on the parish meeting any functions of a parish council.

(2) A copy of every order made under this section shall be sent by the county council to the Minister.

276. Power of local authorities to prosecute or defend legal proceedings Where a local authority deem it expedient for the promotion or protection of the interests of the inhabitants of their area, they may prosecute or defend any legal proceedings.

277. Appearance of local authorities in legal proceedings A local authority may by resolution authorise any member or officer of the authority, either generally or in respect of any particular matter, to institute or defend on their behalf proceedings before any court of summary jurisdiction or to appear on their behalf before a court of summary jurisdiction in any proceedings instituted by them or on their behalf or against them, and any member or officer so authorised shall be entitled to institute or defend any such proceedings and, notwithstanding anything contained in the Solicitors Act, 1932, to conduct any such proceedings although he is not a certificated solicitor.

278. Name of local authority need

not be proved In any proceedings instituted by or against a local authority it shall not be necessary to prove the corporate name of the local authority or the constitution or limits of their area:

Provided that nothing in this section shall prejudice the right of a defendant to take or avail himself of any objection which he might have taken or availed himself of if this Act had not been passed.

280. Deposit of plans, &c. with clerk of authority, &c. (1) In any case in which a map, plan or other document of any description is deposited with the clerk of a local authority, or with the chairman of a parish council or parish meeting, pursuant to the standing orders of either House of Parliament or to any enactment (including any enactment in this Act) or statutory order, the clerk or chairman, as the case may be, shall receive and retain the document in the manner and for the purposes directed by the standing orders or enactment or statutory order, and shall make such memorials and endorsements on, and give such acknowledgments and receipts in respect of the document, as may be so directed.

(2) Subject to any provisions to the contrary in any other enactment or statutory order, a person interested in any such map, plan or other document deposited as aforesaid may, at all reasonable hours, inspect and make copies thereof or extracts therefrom on payment to the person having custody thereof of the sum of one shilling for every such inspection, and of the further sum of one shilling for every hour during which such inspection continues after the first hour.

(3) If a person having the custody of any map, plan or other document as aforesaid obstructs any person in inspecting the document or making a copy thereof or extract therefrom, he shall be liable, on summary conviction, to a fine not exceeding £5.

(4) All documents required by any enactment or statutory order to be deposited with the parish clerk of a rural parish shall, in the case of a parish having a separate parish council be deposited with the clerk or, if there is no clerk, with the chairman of the council, and in the case of a parish not having a separate parish council, be deposited with the chairman of the parish meeting.

281. Custody of parochial documents (1) The custody of registers of baptisms, marriages and burials, and of all other books and documents containing entries wholly or in part relating to the affairs of the church or to ecclesiastical charities, except documents directed by law to be kept with the public books, writings, and papers of a parish, shall remain as provided by the existing law unaffected by this Act.

(2) All other public books, writings, and papers of a parish, and all documents directed by law to be kept therewith, shall either remain in their existing custody or be deposited in such custody as may be directed—

(*b*) in the case of a rural parish having a separate parish council by the parish council;

(*c*) in the case of a rural parish not having a separate parish council, by the parish meeting.

(3) The incumbent and churchwardens on the one part, and the council or parish meeting referred to in the preceding subsection on the other, shall have reasonable access to all such books, documents, writings, and papers as are referred to in this section, and any difference as to such custody or access shall be determined in the case of a parish in a county borough, by the Minister, and in any other case, by the county council.

(4) Every county council shall from time to time inquire into the manner in which the public books, writings, papers, and documents under the control of a parish council or parish meeting are kept with a view to the proper preservation thereof, and shall make such orders as they think necessary for such preservation, and those orders shall be complied with by the parish council or parish meeting.

282. Provision of depository for parochial documents (1) . . . in the case of a rural parish having a separate parish council the parish council or, if the parish council so request, the council of the rural district in which the parish is situate, shall provide proper depositories for all the public books, writings, papers and documents belonging to the parish for which no provision is otherwise made.

(2) In the case of a rural parish not having a separate parish council, the council of the rural district in which the parish is situate, shall, with the consent of the parish meeting of the parish, provide proper depositories for all the public books, writings, papers and documents under the control of the parish meeting.

283. Inspection of documents (1) The minutes of proceedings of a local authority shall be open to the inspection of any local government elector for the area of the authority, on payment of a fee not exceeding one shilling, and any such local government elector may make a copy thereof or an extract therefrom.

(2) A local government elector for the area of a local authority may inspect and make a copy of or extract from an order for the payment of money made by the local authority.

(3) The accounts of a local authority and of the treasurer of a local authority shall be open to the inspection of any member of the authority, and any such member may make a copy thereof or an extract therefrom.

(4) The *abstract of the accounts* of a local authority and of the treasurer of a local authority, and any report made by an auditor on those accounts, shall be open to the inspection of any local government elector for the area of the authority, and any such local government elector may make a copy thereof or an extract therefrom, and copies thereof shall be delivered to any such local government elector on payment of a reasonable sum for each copy.

(6) A *document* directed by this section to be open to inspection shall be so open at all reasonable hours, and, except

where otherwise expressly provided, without payment.

(7) If a person having the custody of any *document* in this section mentioned:—

(*a*) obstructs any person entitled to inspect the document or to make a copy thereof or extract therefrom in inspecting the document or making a copy or extract; or

(*b*) refuses to give copies or extracts to any person entitled to obtain copies or extracts,

he shall be liable, on summary conviction, to a fine not exceeding £5.

(8) This section shall apply to the minutes of proceedings and to the accounts of a parish meeting as if that meeting were a local authority within the meaning of this Act.

[NOTE: See L.G.(F.P.)A. 1963 s. 6.]

284. Reports and returns Every local authority and every joint committee or joint board appointed jointly by two or more local authorities shall make to the Secretary of State or to the *Minister* such reports and returns, and give him such information with respect to their functions, as he may require, or as may be required by either House of Parliament.

286. Service of notices on local authorities, &c. (1) Any notice, order or other document required or authorised by this Act, or by any other enactment or statutory order, to be sent, delivered or served to or upon a local authority or to or upon the clerk or chairman of a local authority, shall be addressed to the local authority or to the clerk or chairman, as the case may be, and left at, or sent by post in a prepaid letter to, the offices of the local authority.

(2) In the case of documents required or authorised to be sent or delivered to, or served upon, a parish meeting, the document shall be left with, or sent by post in a prepaid letter to, the chairman of the parish meeting.

287. Public notices (1) Save as otherwise expressly provided, a public notice required to be given by a local authority, shall be given—

(a) by affixing the notice to the offices of the local authority or, in the case of a parish council, on or near the principal door of each church or chapel in the parish; and

(b) by posting the notice in some conspicuous place or places within the area of the local authority; and

(c) in such other manner, if any, as appears to the local authority to be desirable for giving publicity to the notice.

(2) This section shall apply to a public notice required to be given by the chairman of a parish meeting or by a joint committee of parish councils as it applies to public notices required to be given by a parish council.

287A. Service of notices by local authority (1) Any document to which this section applies, being a document required or authorised to be served on any person, shall be deemed to be duly served—

(a) where the person to be served is a company, if the document is addressed to the secretary of the company at its registered office or at its principal office or place of business, and is either—
　(i) sent by post, or
　(ii) delivered at the registered office, or at the principal office or place of business of the company;

(b) where the person to be served is a partnership, if the document is addressed to the partnership at its principal place of business, identifying it by the name or style under which its business is carried on, and is either—
　(i) sent by post, or
　(ii) delivered at the said place of business;

(c) where the person to be served is a public body, or a corporation, society or other body, if the document is addressed to the clerk, secretary, treasurer or other head officer of that body, corporation or society at its principal office, and is either—
　(i) sent by post, or
　(ii) delivered at that office;

(d) in any other case, if the document is addressed to the person to be served, and is either sent to him by post or delivered at his residence or place of business.

(2) Any document to which this section applies, being a document required or authorised to be served on the owner or occupier of any premises may be addressed 'the owner' or 'the occupier,' as the case may be, of those premises (naming them) without further name or description, and shall be deemed to be duly served—

(a) if the document so addressed is sent or delivered in accordance with paragraph (d) of the foregoing subsection; or

(b) if the document so addressed, or a copy thereof so addressed, is delivered to some person on the premises or, where there is no person on the premises to whom it can be delivered, is affixed to some conspicuous part of the premises.

(3) Where a document to which this section applies is served on a partnership in accordance with this section, the document shall be deemed to be served on each partner.

(4) For the purpose of enabling any document to be served on the owner of any premises, the local authority may by notice in writing require the occupier of the premises to state the name and address of the owner thereof, and if the occupier refuses or wilfully neglects to do so, or wilfully misstates the name and address of the owner, he shall, unless in the case of a refusal he shows cause to the satisfaction of the court for his refusal, be liable on summary conviction in respect of

each offence to a fine not exceeding five pounds.

(5) This section applies to any notice, order or other document which is required or authorised by any enactment or any instrument made under an enactment to be served by or on behalf of a local authority, or by an officer of a local authority, not being a document to the service of which the provisions of some enactment other than this section or some instrument made under an enactment are applicable.

(6) For the purposes of this section, a notice, order or other document shall be deemed to be a notice, order or other document which is required or authorised to be served on a person if it is required or authorised to be notified, given or transmitted, or (in the case of a demand) if it is required or authorised to be made, to that person, and in this section the expressions 'served' and 'service' shall be construed accordingly.

287B. Authentication of documents
(1) Any notice, order or other document which a local authority are authorised or required by or under any enactment (including any enactment in this Act) to give, make or issue may be signed on behalf of the authority by the clerk of the authority or by any other officer of the authority authorised by the authority in writing to sign documents of the particular kind or the particular document, as the case may be.

(2) Any document purporting to bear the signature of the clerk of the authority or of any officer stated therein to be duly authorised by the authority to sign such a document or the particular document, as the case may be, shall be deemed, until the contrary is proved, to have been duly given, made or issued by the authority of the local authority.

In this subsection the word 'signature' includes a facsimile of a signature by whatever process reproduced.

(3) Where any enactment or instrument made under an enactment makes, in relation to any document or class of documents, provision with

respect to the matters dealt with by one of the two foregoing subsections, that subsection shall not apply in relation to that document or class of documents.

289. Penalty for destroying notices, &c. Any person who destroys, tampers with, pulls down, injures, or defaces—

(a) any board on or to which any byelaw, notice or other matter put up by the authority of the Minister or of a local authority is inscribed or affixed; or

(b) any advertisement, placard, bill or notice put up by or under the direction of a local authority,

shall in respect of each offence be liable, on summary conviction, to a fine not exceeding £20.

290. Power of government departments to direct inquiries (1) Where any department are authorised by this Act to determine any difference, to make or confirm any order, to frame any scheme, or to give any consent, confirmation, sanction or approval to any matter, or otherwise to act under this Act, and where the Secretary of State or the Minister is authorised to hold an inquiry, either under this Act or under any other enactment relating to the functions of a local authority, they or he may cause a local inquiry to be held.

(2) For the purpose of any such inquiry, the person appointed to hold the inquiry may by summons require any person to attend, at such time and place as is set forth in the summons, to give evidence or to produce any documents in his custody or under his control which relate to any matter in question at the inquiry, and may take evidence on oath, and for that purpose administer oaths, or may, instead of administering an oath, require the person examined to make and subscribe a declaration of the truth of the matter respecting which he is examined:

Provided that—

(a) no person shall be required, in

obedience to such a summons, to go more than ten miles from his place of residence, unless the necessary expenses of his attendance are paid or tendered to him; and

(*b*) nothing in this section shall empower the person holding the inquiry to require the production of the title, or of any instrument relating to the title, of any land not being the property of a local authority.

(3) Every person who refuses or wilfully neglects to attend in obedience to a summons issued under this section, or to give evidence, or who wilfully alters, suppresses, conceals, destroys, or refuses to produce any book or other document which he may be required to produce for the purposes of this section, shall, in respect of each offence, be liable on summary conviction, to a fine not exceeding £50 or to imprisonment for a term not exceeding six months, or to both such fine and imprisonment.

(4) Where a department cause any such inquiry to be held, the costs incurred by them in relation to that inquiry (including such reasonable sum *not exceeding five guineas a day* as they may determine for the services of any officer engaged in the inquiry) shall be paid by such local authority or party to the inquiry as the department may direct, and the department may certify the amount of the costs so incurred, and any amount so certified and directed by the department to be paid by any authority or person shall be recoverable from that authority or person either as a debt to the Crown or by the department summarily as a civil debt.

(5) The department may make orders as to the costs of the parties at any such inquiry and as to the parties by whom such costs shall be paid, and every such order may be made a rule of the High Court on the application of any party named in the order.

(7) This section shall extend to local inquiries held by the Minister of Transport under the provisions of the Local Government Act, 1929, or the Ferries (Acquisition by Local Authorities) Act, 1919.

(8) In this section the expression 'department' includes the Secretary of State, the Minister, the Minister of Transport, and any Board or Commissioners, and the expression 'enactment' includes an enactment in an order brought into operation in accordance with the provisions of the Statutory Orders (Special Procedure) Act, 1945.

291. Inquiries by county councils
(1) Where a county council hold a local inquiry under this Act on the application of the council of a county district or parish, or of any local government electors for a county district or parish authorised to make such application, the expenses incurred by the county council in relation to the inquiry (including the expenses of any committee or person authorised by the county council to hold the inquiry) shall, unless the county council otherwise determine, be paid by the council of that county district or parish, or in the case of a parish not having a separate council, by the parish meeting of the parish.

(2) Subject as aforesaid, the expenses incurred by a county council in connection with inquiries, held by them under this Act shall be paid by the county council.

295. Provisions as to Sundays, &c. (1) Where the day or the last day on which any thing is required or permitted by or in pursuance of *this Act* to be done is a Sunday, Christmas Day, Good Friday, bank holiday or a day appointed for public thanksgiving or mourning, the requirement or permission shall be deemed to relate to the first day thereafter which is not one of the days before mentioned.

(2) Where under the foregoing provisions of this section an election is postponed, the day on which the election is held shall be treated as the day of election for all purposes of *this Act* relating to that election:

Provided that, where a day is declared to be a bank holiday, or day of public thanksgiving or mourning.

nothing in this subsection shall affect the validity of any act done in relation to an election before or on the date of the declaration.

296. References to population (2) For the purposes of this Act and of any enactment passed after the commencement of this Act relating to local government, references to the last published census shall, as regards any local government area, be construed as references to the last census in respect of which the Registrar-General has, in pursuance of the Act under which the census was taken, published a report giving the population of that area, not being a report which is, or purports to be, of a provisional nature.

305. Definitions In this Act, unless the context otherwise requires, the following expressions have the meanings hereby assigned to them—

'Affairs of the church' has the same meaning as in the Local Government Act, 1894;

'Contributory place' means—
(a) a rural parish no part of which is included in a *special drainage district* formed under the Public Health Act, 1875;
(b) a special drainage district formed under that Act; and
(c) in the case of a rural parish part of which forms, or is included in, a *special drainage district* formed as aforesaid, such part of the parish as is not comprised within that drainage district;

'County' means administrative county;

'County district' means a non-county borough, urban district or rural district;

'District council' means an urban district council or a rural district council;

'District councillor' means an urban district councillor or a rural district councillor;

'Ecclesiastical charity' has the same meaning as in the Local Government Act, 1894;

'Emoluments' includes all salary, wages, fees, poundage and other payments paid or made to an officer as such for his own use, including the money value of any apartments, rations or other allowances in kind appertaining to his office, but does not include payments for overtime or any sum paid to him to cover travelling expenses, cost of office accommodation, assistance of deputies, or clerical, or other assistance;

'Enactment' includes any enactment in a provisional order confirmed by Parliament;

'Financial year' means the period of twelve months ending on the 31st day of March;

'Land' includes any interest in land and any easement or right in, to or over land;

'Local authority' means the council of a county, county borough, county district or *rural parish. . .* ;

'Local government elector' or 'elector' means a person registered as a local government elector in the register of electors in accordance with the provisions of the Representation of the People Acts;

'Officer' includes a servant;

'Parish property' means—

(a) property, the rents and profits of which are applicable or, if the property were let, would be applicable to the general benefit of one or more parishes, or the ratepayers, parishioners or inhabitants thereof, but does not include—
(i) property given or bequeathed by way of charitable donation or allotted in right of some charitable donation or otherwise for the poor persons of any parish or parishes, if the income of the property is not applicable to the general benefit of the ratepayers or other persons as aforesaid;
(ii) property acquired by a board of guardians before

the first day of April, 1930, for the purposes of their functions in the relief of the poor; and

(b) land allotted to, or otherwise acquired by, a parish, whether in the name of the surveyor of highways or other trustees, or generally, for the purpose of the supply of materials for the repair of the public roads and highways in the parish and also for the repair of private roads therein, or for some other purpose, public or private, where the materials in the land are exhausted or are not suitable or required, and the land is not available for that other purpose, if any;

'Prescribed' means prescribed by regulations and, except where some other prescribing authority is specified, prescribed by regulations made by the Minister;

'Property' includes all property, real and personal, and all estates, interests, easements and rights whether equitable or legal, in, to, and out of property, real and personal;

'Public body' includes a local authority and any trustees, commissioners or other persons who, as a public body and not for their own profit, act under any enactment or statutory order for the improvement of any place or for the supply to any place of water, gas or electricity, or for providing or maintaining a cemetery or market in any place, and any other authority having powers of levying, or issuing a precept for, any rate for public purposes, and, for the purposes of Part VI of this Act, includes a body which is a compensation authority for the purposes of the Licensing (Consolidation) Act, 1910, and an insurance committee constituted under the National Health Insurance Act, 1924, and the expression 'district' means, in relation to a public body other

than a local authority, the area for which the public body acts;

'Sale' includes a sale in consideration of a chief rent, rent charge or other similar periodical payment, and the expressions 'sell' and 'purchase' have corresponding meanings;

'Statutory order' means any order, rule or regulation made under any enactment;

'Statutory undertakers' means any persons authorised by an enactment or statutory order to construct, work or carry on any railway, canal, inland navigation, dock, harbour, tramway, gas, electricity, water, or other public undertaking;

'The Adoptive Acts' means—

(c) The Burial Acts, 1852 to 1906;

'Undertaking' means, in relation to a local authority, the provision of water, gas, electricity, transport or any other public service which the local authority are authorised to undertake.

307. Repeals (1) . . .

Provided that—

(i) nothing in this repeal shall affect any byelaw in force at the commencement of this Act, and any byelaw for good rule and government and for prevention and suppression of nuisances in force at the commencement of this Act shall have effect as if made under this Act and may be amended or revoked and enforced accordingly;

(v) nothing in this section shall affect any appointment, agreement or resolution made, direction or notice given, proceedings taken or other thing done under any enactment repealed by this Act, and every such appointment, agreement, resolution, direction, notice, proceedings or other thing shall, so far as it could have been made, given, taken or done under this Act, have effect as if it had been made, given, taken or done under the corresponding provision of this Act:

(2) Any document referring to any Act or enactment repealed by this Act shall be construed as referring to this Act or to the corresponding enactment, if any, in this Act.

(3) The mention of particular matters in this section shall not be held to prejudice or affect the general application of section 38 of the Interpretation Act, 1889, with regard to the effect of repeals.

THIRD SCHEDULE

PART IV.

PARISH COUNCILS.

1. Days of meetings (1) A parish council shall in every year hold an annual meeting and at least three other meetings.

(2) The annual meeting of a parish council shall be held on or within fourteen days after the 20th day of May in every year.

(3) The first meeting of a parish council constituted after the commencement of this Act shall be convened by the chairman of the parish meeting at which the first parish councillors are nominated.

(5) A meeting of a parish council shall not be held in premises licensed for the sale of intoxicating liquor, except in cases where no other suitable room is available for such meeting, either free of charge or at a reasonable cost.

2. Convening meetings (1) The chairman of a parish council may call a meeting of the council at any time.

(2) If the chairman refuses to call a meeting of the council after a requisition for that purpose, signed by two members of the council, has been presented to him, or if, without so refusing, the chairman does not call a meeting within seven days after such requisition has been presented to him, any two members of the council, on that refusal or on the expiration of those

seven days, as the case may be, may forthwith convene a meeting of the council.

(3) Three clear days at least before a meeting of a parish council—

(a) notice of the time and place of the intended meeting shall be affixed in some conspicuous place in the parish, and where the meeting is called by members of the council the notice shall be signed by those members and shall specify the business proposed to be transacted thereat;

(b) a summons to attend the meeting specifying the business proposed to be transacted thereat and signed by the clerk of the council shall be left at or sent by post to the usual place of residence of every member of the council:—

Provided that want of service of the summons on any member of the council shall not affect the validity of a meeting.

3. Chairman of meeting (1) At a meeting of a parish council the chairman of the council, if present, shall preside.

(2) If the chairman of the council is absent from a meeting of the council, the vice-chairman of the council, if present, shall preside.

(3) If both the chairman and vice-chairman of the council are absent from a meeting of the council, such councillor as the members of the council present shall choose shall preside.

4. Quorum Subject to the provisions of Part V of this Schedule, no business shall be transacted at a meeting of a parish council unless at least one-third of the whole number of members of the council are present thereat:—

Provided that in no case shall the quorum be less than three members.

5. Mode of voting The mode of voting at meetings of a parish council shall be by show of hands, and on the requisition of any member of the council the voting on any question shall be recorded so as to show whether each member present and voting gave his vote for or against that question.

PART V.

PROVISIONS RELATING TO LOCAL AUTHORITIES GENERALLY.

1. Decision of questions (1) Subject to the provisions of any enactment (including any enactment in this Act) all acts of a local authority and all questions coming or arising before a local authority shall be done and decided by a majority of the members of the local authority present and voting thereon at a meeting of the local authority.

(2) In the case of an equality of votes the person presiding at the meeting shall have a second or a casting vote.

2. Names . . . to be recorded The names of the members present at a meeting of a local authority shall be recorded.

3. Minutes (1) Minutes of the proceedings of a meeting of a local authority, or of a committee thereof, shall be drawn up and entered in a book kept for that purpose, and shall be signed at the same or next ensuing meeting of the local authority or, as the case may be, at the same or any subsequent meeting of the committee by the person presiding thereat, and any minute purporting to be so signed shall be received in evidence without further proof.

(2) Until the contrary is proved, a meeting of a local authority or of a committee thereof in respect of the proceedings whereof a minute has been so made and signed shall be deemed to have been duly convened and held, and all the members present at the meeting shall be deemed to have been duly qualified, and where the proceedings are proceedings of a committee, the committee shall be deemed to have been duly constituted and to have had power to deal with the matters referred to in the minutes.

4. Standing orders Subject to the provisions of this Act, a local authority may make standing orders for the regulation of their proceedings and business and may vary or revoke any such orders.

5. Vacancies . . . not to invalidate meetings The proceedings of a local authority or of a committee thereof shall not be invalidated by any vacancy among their number, or by any defect in the election or qualification of any member thereof.

6. Quorum in cases of disqualification Where more than one-third of the members of a local authority become disqualified at the same time, then, until the number of members in office is increased to not less than two-thirds of the whole number of members of the local authority, the quorum of the local authority shall be determined by reference to the number of members of the local authority remaining qualified instead of by reference to the whole number of members of the local authority.

PART VI.

PARISH MEETINGS.

1. Days and hours of meetings (1) The parish meeting of a rural parish shall assemble annually on some day between 1st March and 1st April, both inclusive, in every year.

(2) Subject as aforesaid, parish meetings shall be held on such days and at such times and places as may be fixed by the Parish Council, or, if there is no Parish Council, by the chairman of the parish meeting;

Provided that in a rural parish not having a separate parish council the parish meeting shall, subject to any provisions made by a grouping order, assemble at least twice in every year.

(3) The proceedings at a parish meeting shall not commence earlier than six o'clock in the evening.

(4) A parish meeting shall not be held in premises licensed for the sale of intoxicating liquor, except in cases where no other suitable room is available for such meeting either free of charge or at a reasonable cost.

2. Convening meetings (1) A parish meeting may be convened by—

(a) the chairman of the parish council; or

(b) any two parish councillors; or

(c) in the case of a parish not having a parish council, the chairman of the parish meeting, or any person representing the parish on the rural district council; or

(d) any six local government electors for the parish.

(2) Not less than seven clear days before a parish meeting, public notice thereof shall be given specifying the time and place of the intended meeting and the business to be transacted thereat, and signed by the convener or conveners of the meeting:

Provided that if any business proposed to be transacted at a parish meeting relates to the establishment or dissolution of a parish council or to the grouping of the parish with another parish, or to the adoption of any of the *adoptive Acts*, not less than fourteen days' notice of the meeting shall be given.

(3) A public notice of a parish meeting shall be given—

(a) by affixing the same to or near the principal door of each church or chapel in the parish; and

(b) by posting the same in some conspicuous place or places in the parish; and

(c) in such other manner, if any, as appears to the persons convening the meeting to be desirable for giving publicity to the notice.

3. Chairman of meeting (1) If the chairman of a parish council is present at a parish meeting for the parish . . . he shall preside at the meeting.

(2) In a rural parish not having a separate parish council the chairman of the parish meeting shall preside over all assemblies of the parish meeting at which he is present.

(3) If the chairman of the parish council or the chairman of the parish meeting, as the case may be, is absent from . . . an assembly of the parish meeting, the parish meeting may appoint a person to take the chair, and that person shall have, for the purpose

of that meeting, the powers and authority of the chairman.

4. Business A parish meeting may discuss parish affairs and pass resolutions thereon.

5. Determination of questions (1) Subject to the provisions of this Act, each local government elector may, at a parish meeting or at a poll consequent thereon, give one vote and no more on any question.

(2) A question to be decided by a parish meeting shall, in the first instance, be decided by the majority of those present at the meeting and voting thereon, and the decision of the person presiding at the meeting as to the result of the voting shall be final unless a poll is demanded thereon.

(3) In the case of an equality of votes the person presiding at the meeting shall have a second or a casting vote.

(4) A poll may be demanded, before the conclusion of a parish meeting, on any question arising thereat:

Provided that a poll shall not be taken unless either the person presiding at the meeting consents, or the poll is demanded by not less than five, or one-third, of the local government electors present at the meeting, whichever is the less.

(5) A poll consequent on a parish meeting shall be a poll of those entitled to attend the meeting as local government electors and shall be taken by ballot in accordance with rules made by the Secretary of State, . . . and the provisions of the local elections rules in the *second Schedule of the Representation of the People Act, 1949, and of the enactments mentioned in subsection (1) of section 165 of that Act shall, subject to any adaptations, alterations or exceptions made by the first-mentioned rules*, apply in the case of a poll so taken as if it were a poll for the election of parish councillors.

Rules made under this subparagraph shall be laid before each House of Parliament as soon as may be after they are made.

6. Minutes (1) Minutes of the proceedings of a parish meeting, or of a committee thereof shall be drawn up and entered in a book provided for that purpose, and shall be signed at the same or the next ensuing assembly of the parish meeting, or meeting of the committee, as the case may be, by the person presiding thereat, and any minute purporting to be so signed shall be received in evidence without further proof.

(2) Until the contrary is proved, a parish meeting, or meeting of a committee thereof, in respect of the proceedings whereof a minute has been so made and signed shall be deemed to have been duly convened and held, and all the persons present at the meeting shall be deemed to have been duly qualified, and where the proceedings are proceedings of a committee, the committee shall be deemed to have been duly constituted and to have had power to deal with the matters referred to in the minutes.

7. Standing orders (1) Subject to the provisions of this Act, a parish council may make, vary, and revoke standing orders for the regulation of the proceedings and business at parish meetings for the parish.

(2) In a rural parish not having a separate parish council the parish meeting may subject to the provisions of this Act, regulate their own proceedings and business.

FOURTH SCHEDULE.

Provisions as to the Determination and Payment of Compensation to Officers.

1. Procedure . . . (1) For the purpose of enabling a claim for compensation to be assessed the claimant shall deliver to the local authority with the claim a statement containing such particulars as may be prescribed.

(2) The said statement shall be accompanied by a statutory declaration that it is a true statement to the best of the knowledge, information and belief of the claimant.

(3) The authority shall forthwith take the claim into consideration and assess the just amount of compensation, if any, and shall forthwith inform the claimant of their decision.

(4) If a local authority fail to inform any claimant of their decision on his claim within six months after it has been delivered to them, the Minister may, on application made to him by the claimant, direct the authority to do so within such time, not being less than one month, as may be specified in the direction.

(5) A claimant, if so required by any member of the local authority by notice sent through the clerk of the authority, shall attend at a meeting of the authority, or of any committee appointed by the authority for the purpose and answer on oath, which any justice of the peace present may administer, all questions asked by any member of the authority or committee touching the matters set forth in his claim and in the said statement, and shall further produce all books, papers and documents in his possession or under his control relating to the claim.

2. General considerations to be applied For the purpose of determining whether compensation is payable to an officer and, if so, the amount of such compensation, regard shall be had to—

(a) The conditions upon which his appointment was made;
(b) The nature of his office;
(c) All the other circumstances of the case;

3. . . . Lump sums . . . Compensation may be awarded either by way of an annual sum or by way of a lump sum representing the capital value of an annual sum.

4. Assessment of compensation for determination of whole-time office (1) The annual sum payable as compensation in respect of the determination of a whole-time office shall not exceed the aggregate of the following sums—

(i) for every year of the officer's

service one-sixtieth of an amount equal to the annual pecuniary loss which he has sustained by reason of the determination of the office;

(ii) in the case of service for twenty years or upwards, a sum equal to ten-sixtieths of the said amount; in the case of service for fifteen years and less than twenty years, a sum equal to seven-sixtieths of the said amount; in the case of service for ten years and less than fifteen years, a sum equal to five-sixtieths of the said amount; in the case of service for five years and less than ten years, a sum equal to three-sixtieths of the said amount; in the case of service for less than five years, a sum equal to one-sixtieth of the said amount; and

(iii) in the case of an officer who was appointed as a specially qualified person or who before his appointment had been employed (otherwise than in an office within the meaning of this Schedule) as a deputy, assistant or clerk by a permanent officer for the purpose of the discharge of the latter's official duties, such additional sum, if any, not exceeding ten-sixtieths of the said amount, as the local authority in their discretion and in consideration of his special qualifications or of his previous employment, as the case may be, may think fit to award:

Provided that the compensation shall not in any event exceed two-thirds of the said amount.

(2) In assessing the amount of any pecuniary loss sustained by an officer by reason of the determination of his office regard shall be had as respects any emoluments either—

(a) to the amount of those emoluments received by him in respect of that office immediately before the material date; or

(b) to the average amount of those emoluments received by him in respect of that office during the period of five years next before the material date or such shorter period as may be reasonable in the circumstances.

(3) In assessing the amount of any pecuniary loss sustained by an officer by reason of the determination of his office regard shall also be had to—

(a) any increase of the emoluments enjoyed by the officer at the material date which he has obtained by virtue of the scheme or order or of anything done in pursuance of or in consequence of the scheme or order; and

(b) the emoluments of any office or other public appointment which he would have obtained on or after the material date if he had accepted an offer made to him.

(4) For the purpose of assessing any compensation payable in respect of the loss of a whole-time office or of any two or more offices which in the aggregate involve the whole-time service of the officer, any previous period of part-time service shall be treated as though it were whole-time service for a proportionately reduced period.

(5) Where the material date has occurred at any time other than at the expiration of a complete year of the officer's service, the portion then expired of that year shall, for the purpose of calculating any period of service under this paragraph, be treated as a complete year if it exceeds six months, and if it does not shall be ignored.

5. Assessment of compensation for determination of part-time appointment In the case of a claim for compensation in respect of the determination of a part-time office, the compensation, if any, which would have been payable if the office had been a whole-time office may be reduced by one quarter or by such other amount, if any, as may in the circumstances be reasonable:

Provided that no reduction shall be

made in the case of an officer who immediately before the material date held two or more offices and who devoted the whole of his time to the duties of such offices.

6. Assessment of compensation for diminution of emoluments In the case of an officer who suffers any diminution of the emoluments of an office, the compensation shall not exceed a sum bearing the same proportion to the amount of compensation which could have been awarded if his office had been determined, as the amount by which the emoluments of the office are diminished bears to the amount of those emoluments before diminution.

7. War service to be reckoned in determining compensation If an officer was temporarily absent from his office during the late war whilst serving in His Majesty's forces, or the forces of the Allied or Associated Powers, either compulsorily or with the sanction or permission of the authority in whose employment he was immediately before such temporary absence, such period of temporary absence shall be reckoned as service under that authority:

Provided that in the case of an officer who, after the 11th November, 1918, voluntarily extended his term of service in the forces, no period of absence during any such extension shall be reckoned.

8. Right of appeal If the claimant is aggrieved by the failure of the local authority to inform him of their decision upon his claim within the time required by any direction of the Minister, or by the refusal of the authority to grant any compensation, or by the amount of compensation assessed, the claimant may, within three months after the failure, or after the date on which he receives notice of the decision of the authority, as the case may be, appeal to the Minister, and the Minister shall consider the case and determine whether any compensation, and if so what amount, ought to be granted to the claimant, and his determination shall be final.

9. Date on which compensation commences The sum payable as com-

pensation shall be or commence to be payable at the date fixed by the local authority on granting the compensation, or, in case of appeal, by the Minister, and shall be recoverable as a debt due from the authority.

10. Suspension of compensation (1) If a person receiving compensation under the scheme or order—

(*a*) obtains any office or other public appointment; or

(*b*) receives, by virtue of the scheme or order, or of anything done in pursuance of or in consequence of the scheme or order, any increase of the emoluments which were enjoyed by him at the date as at which the compensation was assessed,

he shall not, so long as he holds that office or other public appointment or receives those increased emoluments, be entitled to receive any greater sum by way of compensation in respect of the office for which compensation is awarded than would make up the amount, if any, by which the emoluments which he is receiving falls short of the emoluments of the office in respect of which compensation was awarded:

Provided that where a person held two or more offices at the date as at which the compensation was assessed or has been awarded compensation in respect of two or more offices, the Ministry may, on the application of that person or of any authority by whom the compensation is payable, modify the operation of the foregoing sub-paragraph in relation to that person so far a is, in the opinion of the Minister, necessary in order equitably to meet the circumstances of the case.

(2) Where an officer to whom compensation has been awarded under any scheme or order subsequently becomes entitled to a superannuation allowance in respect of any office or other public appointment which he has accepted after the material date, and in calculating the amount of such allowance account is taken of any period of service

o

in respect of which compensation is payable, then, if the compensation does not exceed such part of the super-annuation allowance as is attributable solely to that service, the compensation shall cease to be payable, and if it exceeds such part of the superannuation allowance as aforesaid, it shall be reduced by an amount equal to that part of the allowance.

11. Forms The Minister may prescribe the form of any notice, statement, award or other document to be used in connection with a claim for compensation, and the forms so prescribed or forms as near thereto as circumstances admit, shall be used in all cases to which the forms are applicable.

12. Interpretation For the purposes of this Schedule—

'Office' means any place, situation or employment, and includes the office of superintendent registrar, registrar of births and deaths, registrar of marriages, and the office of teacher in a public elementary school maintained but not provided by a local education authority, and 'officer' has a corresponding meaning;

'Public appointment' means any employment the emoluments of which are payable out of public funds;

'Scheme or order' means a scheme or order made under Part VI of this Act and incorporating this Schedule;

'Service' means whole-time or part-time service in any office after the officer has attained the age of eighteen years;

'Material date' means the date on which the determination of office or diminution of emoluments, as the case may be, takes effect.

Public Health Act, 1936

1. (2) In this Act the following expressions have the meanings hereby assigned to them:—

'local authority' means the council of a borough, urban district or rural district;

'rural authority' means the council of a rural district;

'parish,' in relation to a common parish council acting for two or more grouped parishes, means those parishes:

12. Constitution and dissolution of special purpose areas in rural districts (1) A rural authority may, with the approval of the Minister, constitute any part of their district a special purpose area for the purpose of charging thereon exclusively the expenses ... of any ... works the expenses of which are declared by or under any enactment (including any enactment in this Act) to be special expenses.

(2) Special drainage districts constituted under section 277 of the Public Health Act, 1875, or under the corresponding provisions of any earlier Act, shall be known as and styled special purpose areas, and references in any Act or other document to special drainage districts shall be construed accordingly.

13. Power of Minister to invest particular rural authority with urban powers (1) The Minister, on an application made to him in accordance with the provisions of this section, may by order—

(a) declare any provisions of this Act which are in force in boroughs and urban districts to be in force in any particular rural district, or in any particular contributory place in a rural district; and

(b) invest the council of the rural district, as respects the district or, as the case may be, as respects that particular contributory place, with all or any of the functions of an urban authority under this Act, either unconditionally or subject to such conditions as may be specified in the order as to the time, area or manner during, at or in which those functions are to be discharged.

(2) An application for the purposes of this section may be made by—

(a) the council of the rural district;
(b) the council of the county in which the district is situate;
(c) the parish council of any parish situate in the district; or
(d) any number of local government electors for the district or for any contributory place therein, not being less than 100 or one-third of the total number of those electors, whichever is the less:

Provided that, where the application is made by the council of a parish or by local government electors for a contributory place, the order of the Minister shall not confer upon the rural district council any new power, except in relation to, or to a part of, that parish or, as the case may be, that contributory place.

Sewerage and sewage disposal

14. It shall be the duty of every local authority to provide such public sewers as may be necessary for effectually draining their district for the purposes of this Act, and to make such provision, by means of sewage disposal works or otherwise, as may be necessary for effectually dealing with the contents of their sewers.

15. Provision of public sewers (4) Where a rural authority propose to carry out works for the sewerage of any part of their district, they shall, before adopting plans for the works, give notice of their proposals to the parish council of each parish to be served by the works, or, in the case of a parish not under a parish council, to the parish meeting.

23. General duty of local authority to maintain public sewers It shall be the duty of every local authority to maintain, cleanse and empty all public sewers vested in them, subject, however, to their right under the next succeeding section to recover in certain cases the expenses, or a part of the expenses, incurred by them in maintaining a length of a public sewer.

30. Sewage, &c. to be purified before discharge into streams, canals, &c. Nothing in this Part of this Act shall authorise a local authority to construct or use any public or other sewer, or any drain or outfall, for the purpose of conveying foul water into any natural or artificial stream, watercourse, canal, pond or lake, until the water has been so treated as not to affect prejudicially the purity and quality of the water in the stream, watercourse, canal, pond or lake.

31. Local authority not to create any nuisance A local authority shall so discharge their functions under the foregoing provisions of this Part of this Act as not to create a nuisance.

WATER SUPPLY.

General duties and powers of local authority

111. Duty of local authority with respect to water supplies within their district It shall be the duty of every local authority—

(i) to take from time to time such steps as may be necessary for ascertaining the sufficiency and wholesomeness of the water supplies within their district; and
(ii) for the purpose of securing, so far as is reasonably practicable, that every house and school has available within a reasonable distance a sufficient supply of wholesome water for domestic purposes—
(a) to provide a supply of water to every part of their district in which danger to health arises from the insufficiency or unwholesomeness of the existing supply, and a general scheme of supply is required and can be carried

out at a reasonable cost; and

(*b*) without prejudice to their obligations under the preceding subparagraph, to exercise their powers under this Part of this Act of requiring owners of houses to provide a supply of water thereto.

115. Purity of water . . . A local authority who supply water under this Act shall secure that the water in any waterworks belonging to them from which water is supplied for domestic purposes is wholesome.

Public wells, pumps, &c.

124. Certain public pumps, wells and cisterns &c. vested in local authority (1) All public pumps, wells, cisterns, reservoirs, conduits, and other works used for the gratuitous supply of water to the inhabitants of any part of the district of a local authority shall vest in and be under the control of the authority, and the authority may cause the works to be maintained and supplied with wholesome water, or may substitute, maintain and supply with wholesome water other such works equally convenient.

(2) If the local authority are satisfied that any such works are no longer required, or that the water obtained from any such works is polluted and that it is not reasonably practicable to remedy the cause of the pollution, they may close those works or restrict the use of the water obtained therefrom.

(3) Subject to the provisions of this Act, a local authority may construct any works for supplying water for the gratuitous use of any inhabitants who desire to take it not for sale but for domestic purposes.

125. Power of parish council to utilise wells, springs or streams for obtaining water (1) A parish council may utilise any well, spring or stream within their parish and provide facilities for obtaining water therefrom, and may execute any works, including works of maintenance or improvement, incidental to, or consequential on, any exercise of that power:

Provided that nothing in this subsection shall be construed as authorising them to interfere with the rights of any person, or as restricting, in the case of a public well or other works, any powers of the local authority under the last preceding section.

(2) A parish council may contribute towards the expenses incurred by any other parish council, or by any other person, in doing anything authorised by the preceding subsection.

(3) Nothing in this section shall derogate from any obligation of a district council with respect to the supply of water.

198. Provision of mortuaries and post-mortem rooms (1) A local authority or a parish council may, and if required by the Minister shall, provide—

(*a*) a mortuary for the reception of dead bodies before interment;
(*b*) a post-mortem room for the reception of dead bodies during the time required to conduct any post-mortem examination ordered by a coroner or other duly authorised authority;

and may make byelaws with respect to the management, and charges for the use, of any such place provided by them.

(2) A local authority or parish council may provide for the interment of any dead body which may be received into their mortuary.

Part VIII.

Baths, Washhouses, Bathing Places, &c.

Provision of baths, &c.

221. Power of local authority to provide baths, bathing places and washhouses A local authority may provide—

(a) public baths and washhouses, either open or covered, and with or without drying grounds;

(b) public swimming baths and bathing places, either open or covered,

or any of those conveniences.

222. Charges for use of baths, &c. (1) Subject to the provisions of this section, a local authority may make such charges for the use of, or for admission to, any baths, washhouse, swimming bath or bathing place under their management as they think fit.

(2) One month at least before fixing any charges to be made under this section, the local authority shall publish by advertisement in a local newspaper circulating in their district a notice stating their intention to consider a proposed table of charges and naming a place where a copy of the proposed table may be inspected at all reasonable hours by any person free of charge.

223. Byelaws for regulation of baths, &c. (1) A local authority may make byelaws for the regulation of any baths, washhouses, swimming baths and bathing places under their management, and for the regulation of persons resorting thereto, including the exclusion therefrom of undesirable persons.

Any such byelaws may, in addition to providing for the imposition of penalties, empower any officer of the local authority to exclude or remove from any baths, washhouse, swimming bath or bathing place under the management of the authority any person contravening any of the byelaws applicable to the premises in question.

(2) A printed copy, or abstract, of the byelaws relating to any baths, washhouse, swimming bath or bathing place shall be exhibited in a conspicuous place therein.

224. Baths, &c., to be public places for certain purposes Any baths, washhouse, swimming bath or bathing place under the management of a local authority shall be deemed to be a public and open place for the pur-

poses of any enactment relating to offences against decency.

225. Use of baths and bathing places for swimming contests, &c., or by schools or clubs (1) A local authority may close temporarily to the public any swimming bath or bathing place under their management and may—

(a) grant, either gratuitously or for payment, the exclusive use thereof to a school or club, or to persons organising swimming practices or contests, aquatic sports or similar entertainments; or,

(b) themselves use it for such practices, contests, sports or entertainments.

(2) The authority may make, or authorise the making of, charges for admission to, or for the use of, any swimming bath or bathing place while it is closed to the public under this section.

226. Closing of baths and bathing places during winter months, and use for other purposes (1) A local authority may, during any period between the first day of October and the last day of the following April, close any swimming bath or bathing place under their management, and may, at any time when it is closed, use it, or allow it to be used, or let it, for such purposes, and upon such conditions, as they think fit, and may adapt it for the purpose of being so used or let:

(2) The power of the local authority to make byelaws under the foregoing provisions of this Part of this Act shall extend to the making of byelaws with respect to a swimming bath or bathing place when used for any purpose authorised by this section.

(3) Nothing in this section shall authorise the use of a swimming bath or bathing place for the public performance of stage plays, for public music, public music and dancing, or other public entertainment of the like kind, or for cinematograph exhibitions, unless such licence as may be required for the

use of a place for the purpose in question has been obtained, or such notices as may be required by subsection (2) of section 7 of the Cinematograph Act, 1909, have been duly given, and any terms, conditions or restrictions attached to the grant of such licence, or any regulations or conditions made or imposed under the said subsection (2), shall apply, notwithstanding anything in any byelaw made by virtue of this section.

(4) The local authority shall be responsible for any breach of any such conditions as aforesaid which may occur during any entertainment given on the premises by their permission.

227. Power of local authority to lay pipes for purposes connected with baths, &c. Subject to the provisions of Part XII of this Act with respect to the breaking open of streets, a local authority may provide, lay down and maintain such pipes and apparatus as may be necessary for conducting water to or from any baths, washhouse, swimming bath or bathing place which is under their management, or which they propose to provide.

228. Power of trustees to sell existing baths, &c., to local authority The trustees of any public baths, washhouse, swimming bath or bathing place may, with the consent of the committee of management, if any, sell or lease the baths, washhouse, swimming bath or bathing place to a local authority.

229. Power of statutory undertakers to supply water, gas or electricity to baths, &c., on favourable terms Any statutory undertakers supplying water, gas or electricity may supply water, gas or electricity to any public baths, washhouse, swimming bath or bathing place, either without charge or on such other favourable terms as they think fit.

230. Power of parish council to provide baths, bathing places and washhouses (1) A parish council may provide baths, washhouses, swimming baths and bathing places, or any of them, either within or without their parish, and, for that purpose shall have

the like powers as the local authority of the district have under the foregoing provisions of this Part of this Act, and accordingly in those provisions any reference to a local authority or their district shall be construed as including a reference to a parish council or their parish.

Watercourses, ditches, ponds, &c.

259. Nuisances in connection with watercourses, ditches, ponds, &c. (1) The following matters shall be statutory nuisances for the purposes of Part II of this Act, that is to say—

(a) any pond, pool, ditch, gutter or watercourse which is so foul or in such a state as to be prejudicial to health or a nuisance;

(b) any part of a watercourse, not being a part ordinarily navigated by vessels employed in the carriage of goods by water, which is so choked or silted up as to obstruct or impede the proper flow of water and thereby to cause a nuisance, or give rise to conditions prejudicial to health:

Provided that in the case of an alleged nuisance under paragraph (b) nothing in this subsection shall be deemed to impose any liability on any person other than the person by whose act or default the nuisance arises or continues.

260. Power of parish council, or local authority, to deal with ponds, ditches, &c. (1) A parish council may—

(a) deal with any pond, pool, ditch, gutter or place containing, or used for the collection of, any drainage, filth, stagnant water, or matter likely to be prejudicial to health, by draining, cleansing or covering it, or otherwise preventing it from being prejudicial to health, but so as not to interfere with any private right, or with any public drainage, sewerage or sewage disposal works;

(b) execute any works, including works of maintenance or improvement, incidental to or consequential on any exercise of the foregoing power;

(c) contribute towards the expenses incurred by any other person in doing anything mentioned in this subsection.

(2) Without prejudice to their right to take action in respect of any statutory nuisance, a local authority may exercise any powers which a parish council may exercise under this section.

266. Savings (1) The powers conferred by the foregoing provisions of this Part of this Act shall not be exercised—

(i) with respect to any stream, watercourse, ditch or culvert within the jurisdiction of a land drainage authority, except after consultation with that authority;

Provided that nothing in this subsection shall apply in relation to the taking of proceedings in respect of a statutory nuisance.

(2) Nothing in the foregoing provisions of this Part of this Act shall prejudice or affect the powers of any railway company or dock undertakers to culvert or cover in any stream or watercourse, or without the consent of the railway company or dock undertakers concerned, extend to any culvert or covering of a stream or watercourse constructed by a railway company and used by them for the purposes of their railway, or constructed by dock undertakers and used by them for the purposes of their undertaking.

Supplemental as to powers of councils

271. Interpretation of 'provide' (1) Any power of a council under this Act to provide buildings or other premises for any purpose includes power to equip them with such furniture, apparatus and instruments as may be reasonably necessary to enable them to be used for that purpose.

(2) Any power of a council under this Act to provide buildings or other premises, accommodation, equipment, or vehicles for any purpose includes power to enter into agreements with any other council or any person for the use, upon such terms as may be agreed, of any suitable buildings, premises, accommodation, equipment or vehicles provided by, or under the control of, that other council or that person, and, if it appears convenient, for the services of any staff employed in connection therewith.

(3) A council who provide buildings or other premises, accommodation, equipment or vehicles for any of the purposes of this Act may, on such terms (including terms with respect to the services of any staff employed by them) as may be agreed, permit the use thereof by any other council authorised by or under this, or any other Act, to make such provision.

Powers of the Minister

312. Confirmation of byelaws The Minister shall be the confirming authority as respects byelaws made under this Act.

321. Complaint by county council to Minister of default of council of county district If it appears to a county council that the council of any county district within their county have made default in discharging any of their functions under this Act, the county council may complain to the Minister, and thereupon the Minister shall cause a local inquiry to be held into the matter.

322. Power of Minister to enforce exercise of powers by local authorities, &c., in default (1) If—

(i) a complaint is made to the Minister that any council, port health authority or joint board have failed to discharge their functions under this Act in any case where they ought to have done so; or

(ii) the Minister is of opinion that an

investigation should be made as to whether any council, port health authority or joint board have failed as aforesaid, the Minister may cause a local inquiry to be held into the matter.

324. Provisions as to exercise by Minister of functions of body in default (1) Where under the last but one preceding section the Minister has by order transferred to himself any functions of a council, port health authority or joint board, any expenses incurred by him in discharging the said functions shall be paid in the first instance out of moneys provided by Parliament, but the amount of those expenses as certified by the Minister shall on demand be paid to him by the body in default, and shall be recoverable by him from them as a debt due to the Crown, and that body shall have the like power of raising the money required as they have of raising money for defraying expenses incurred directly by them.

(2) The payment of any such expenses as aforesaid shall, to such extent as may be sanctioned by the Minister, be a purpose for which a local authority, port health authority or joint board may borrow money in accordance with the statutory provisions relating to borrowing by such an authority or board.

325. In any case where under this Part of this Act an order has been made by the Minister transferring to a county council or to himself any functions of a council, port health authority or joint board, the Minister may at any time by a subsequent order vary or revoke that order, but without prejudice to the validity of anything previously done thereunder; and when any order is so revoked the Minister may, either by revoking order or by a subsequent order, make such provision as appears to him to be desirable with respect to the transfer, vesting and discharge of any property or liabilities acquired or incurred by the county council or by him in discharging any of the functions to which the order so revoked related.

Savings

328. Powers of Act to be cumulative All powers and duties conferred or imposed by this Act shal[1] be deemed to be in addition to, and not in derogation of, any other powers and duties conferred or imposed by Act of Parliament, law or custom, and, subject to any repeal effected by, or other express provision of, this Act, all such other powers and duties may be exercised and shall be performed in the same manner as if this Act had not been passed.

343. Interpretation 'Owner' means the person for the time being receiving the rackrent of the premises in connection with which the word is used, whether on his own account or as agent or trustee for any other person, or who would so receive the same if those premises were let at a rackrent.

Physical Training and Recreation Act, 1937

4. Extension of powers of local authorities (1) A local authority may acquire, lay out, provide with suitable buildings and otherwise equip, and maintain lands, whether situate within or without their area, for the purpose of gymnasiums, playing fields, holiday camps or camping sites, or for the purpose of centres for the use of clubs, societies or organisations having athletic, social or educational objects, and may manage those lands and buildings themselves, either with or without a charge for the use thereof or admission thereto, or may let them, or any portion thereof, at a nominal or other rent to any person, club, society or organisation for use for any of the purposes aforesaid.

The authority may also provide and, where necessary, arrange for the training of, such wardens, teachers and leaders as they may deem requisite for securing that effective use is made of the facilities for exercise, recreation and social activities so provided.

(2) Section seventy of the Public Health Act, 1925 (which relates to the use of public offices for entertainments and the like), shall apply in relation to any premises provided by a local authority under the preceding subsection as if those premises were offices for the transaction of business, and as if any local authority as defined by this Act were a local authority for the purposes of the said section seventy.

(3) A county council . . . may provide public swimming baths and bathing places under Part VIII of the Public Health Act, 1936, and, accordingly, in sections 221 to 229 of that Act any reference to a local authority or their district shall, in relation to public swimming baths and bathing places, be construed as including a reference to a county council or their county . . .

(4) A local authority may contribute towards expenses incurred by another local authority, whether under this or any other Act, or by a voluntary organisation, in providing or maintaining within the area of the contributing authority, or on a site where it will benefit any of the inhabitants of that area, anything mentioned in subsection (1) of this section, or a swimming bath or bathing place.

(5) Section 69 of the Public Health Act, 1925, and so much of the Museums and Gymnasiums Act, 1891, as relates to gymnasiums, shall cease to have effect and any property held by a local authority for the purposes of the enactments thus repealed shall, without any necessity for formal appropriation, be held by them for the purposes of this section.

9. Interpretation In this Act, unless the context otherwise requires—

'local authority' means the council of a county, county borough, metropolitan borough, county district or parish . . .

'voluntary organisation' means any person or body of persons, whether corporate or unincorporate, carrying on, or proposing to carry on, an undertaking otherwise than for profit.

Education Act, 1944

Management of Primary Schools and Government of Secondary Schools

17. Constitution of managers and governors (1) For every county school and for every voluntary school there shall be an instrument providing for the constitution of the body of managers or governors of the school in accordance with the provisions of this Act, and the instrument providing for the constitution of the body of managers of a primary school is in this Act referred to as an instrument of management, and the instrument providing for the constitution of the body of governors of a secondary school is in this Act referred to as an instrument of government.

(2) The instrument of management or the instrument of government, as the case may be, shall be made in the case of a county school by an order of the local education authority and in the case of a voluntary school by an order of the Minister.

(3) Subject to the provisions of this Act and of any trust deed relating to the school:—

(*a*) every county primary school and every voluntary primary school shall be conducted in accordance with rules of management made by an order of the local education authority; and

(*b*) every county secondary school and every voluntary secondary school shall be conducted in accordance with articles of government made in the case of a county school by an order of the local education authority and approved by the Minister, and in the case of a voluntary school by an order of the Minister; and such articles shall in particular determine the functions to be exercised in relation to the school by the local education authority, the body of governors, and the head teacher respectively.

(4) Where it appears to the Minister that any provision included or proposed to be included in the instrument of management, rules of management, instrument of government, or articles of government, for a county school or a voluntary school is in any respect inconsistent with the provisions of any trust deed relating to the school, and that it is expedient in the interests of the school that the provisions of the trust deed should be modified for the purpose of removing the inconsistency, he may by order make such modifications in the provisions of the trust deed as appear to him to be just and expedient for that purpose.

(5) Before making any order under this section in respect of any school, the Minister shall afford to the local education authority and to any other persons appearing to him to be concerned with the management or government of the school an opportunity of making representations to him with respect thereto, and in making any such order the Minister shall have regard to all the circumstances of the school, and in particular to the question whether the school is, or is to be, a primary or secondary school, and, in the case of an existing school, shall have regard to the manner in which the school has been conducted theretofore.

18. Managers of primary schools (1) The instrument of management for every county primary school serving an area in which there is a minor authority shall provide for the constitution of a body of managers consisting of such number of persons, not being less than six, as the local education authority may determine:—

Provided that two-thirds of the managers shall be appointed by the local education authority and one-third

shall be appointed by the minor authority.

(2) The instrument of management for every county primary school serving an area in which there is no minor authority shall provide for the constitution of a body of managers constituted in such manner as the local education authority may determine.

(3) The instrument of management for every voluntary primary school shall provide for the constitution of a body of managers consisting of such number of persons not being less than six as the Minister may, after consultation with the local education authority, determine:—

Provided that—

(a) if the school is an aided school or a special agreement school, two-thirds of the managers shall be foundation managers; and, if the school is a controlled school, one-third of the managers shall be foundation managers;

(b) where the school serves an area in which there is a minor authority, then of the managers who are not foundation managers not less than one-third nor more than one-half shall be appointed by the minor authority and the remainder shall be appointed by the local education authority; and

(c) where the school serves an area in which there is no minor authority, all the managers who are not foundation managers shall be appointed by the local education authority.

19. Governors of secondary schools (1) The instrument of government for every county secondary school shall provide for the constitution of a body of governors consisting of such number of persons appointed in such manner as the local education authority may determine.

(2) The instrument of government for every voluntary secondary school shall provide for the constitution of a body of governors of the school consisting of such number of persons as the Minister

may after consultation with the local education authority determine:
Provided that—

(a) where the school is a controlled school, one-third of the governors shall be foundation governors and two-thirds of the governors shall be appointed by the local education authority;

(b) where the school is an aided school or a special agreement school, two-thirds of the governors shall be foundation governors and one-third of the governors shall be appointed by the local education authority.

20. Grouping of schools under one management (1) A local education authority may make an arrangement for the constitution of a single governing body for any two or more county schools or voluntary schools maintained by them, and any such arrangement may relate exclusively to primary schools, or exclusively to secondary schools or partly to primary schools and partly to secondary schools:

Provided that an authority shall not make any such arrangement with respect to a voluntary school except with the consent of the managers or governors thereof.

(2) The governing body constituted in pursuance of any such arrangement as aforesaid shall, if all the schools to which the arrangement relates are county schools, consist of such number of persons appointed in such manner as the local education authority may determine.

(3) Where all or any of the schools to which any such arrangement relates are voluntary schools, the governing body constituted in pursuance of the arrangement shall consist of such number of persons appointed in such manner as may be determined by agreement between the local education authority and the managers or governors of those schools, or, in default of such agreement, by the Minister.

(4) The local education authority, in making any such arrangement as aforesaid which relates to a primary school serving an area in which there is a minor authority, shall make provision for securing that the minor authority is adequately represented upon the governing body constituted in pursuance of the arrangement.

(5) Every arrangement made under this section may, if it does not relate to any voluntary school, be terminated at any time by the local education authority by which it was made, and any such arrangement which relates to such a school may be terminated by agreement between the local education authority and the governing body constituted in pursuance of the arrangement, or, in default of such agreement, by one year's notice served by the local education authority on the said governing body or by one year's notice served by the said governing body on the local education authority.

(6) While an arrangement under this section is in force with respect to any schools, the provisions of the last three foregoing sections as to the constitution of the body of managers or governors shall not apply to the schools, and for the purposes of any enactment the governing body constituted in accordance with the arrangement shall be deemed to be the body of managers or governors of each of those schools, and references to a manager or governor in any enactment shall, in relation to every such school, be construed accordingly.

21. Proceedings of managers and governors (1) Any manager or governor of a county school or of a voluntary school may resign his office, and any such manager or governor appointed by a local education authority or by a minor authority shall be removable by the authority by whom he was appointed.

(2) The provisions of the Fourth Schedule to this Act shall have effect with respect to the meetings and proceedings of the managers or governors of any county school or voluntary school.

(3) The minutes of the proceedings of the managers or governors of any county school or voluntary school shall be open to inspection by the local education authority.

114. . . .

'Minor authority' means, in relation to any school maintained by the local education authority for a county, the council of any borough (other than county borough) or urban district or rural parish which appears to the local education authority to be the area served by the school, so, however, that where it appears to the local education authority that the area served by the school is a rural parish which has no parish council, the parish meeting of that parish shall be the minor authority, and where it appears to the local education authority that a school serves the area of two or more minor authorities, that expression shall be construed as referring to all those minor authorities acting jointly;

FOURTH SCHEDULE.

MEETINGS AND PROCEEDINGS OF MANAGERS AND GOVERNORS.

1. The quorum of the managers or governors shall not be less than three, or one-third of the whole number of managers or governors, whichever is the greater.

2. The proceedings of the managers or governors shall not be invalidated by any vacancy in their number or by any defect in the election, appointment or qualification of any manager or governor.

3. Every question to be determined at a meeting of the managers or governors shall be determined by a majority of the votes of the managers or governors present and voting on the question, and where there is an equal division of votes the chairman of the meeting shall have a second or casting vote.

4.[1] The managers or governors shall hold a meeting at least once in every school term.

5. A meeting of the managers or governors may be convened by any two of their number.

6. The minutes of the proceedings of the managers or governors shall be kept in a book provided for the purpose.

[1] As amended by Education Act, 1948

Town and Country Planning Act, 1947

49. (8) Section 3 of the Acquisition of Land (Authorisation Procedure) Act, 1946 (which enables the Minister of Town and Country Planning to extinguish certain public rights of way over land acquired under that Act) shall apply in relation to land acquired before the commencement of that Act by a local authority, being—

(a) land acquired compulsorily under any such enactment as is specified in paragraph (a) of subsection (1) of section one of that Act; or
(b) land acquired by agreement for a purpose such that the land could have been so acquired compulsorily.

Local Government Act, 1948

PART VI.

111. Bodies to which Part VI applies and members thereof (1) This Part of this Act shall apply to the following bodies, that is to say,—

(a) the councils of . . . rural parishes;
(g) any joint committee, joint board, joint authority or other combined body all the members of which

are representatives of local authorities.

(2) For the purposes of this Part of this Act, a member of a committee or sub-committee of a body to which this Part of this Act applies shall be deemed to be a member of that body.

112. Financial loss allowance (1) A member of a body to which this Part of this Act applies shall be entitled to receive a payment by way of financial loss allowance *not exceeding such amount as may be prescribed* where—

(a) loss of earnings which he would otherwise have made; or
(b) additional expense (other than expense on account of travelling or subsistence) to which he would not otherwise have been subject,

is necessarily suffered or incurred by him for the purpose of enabling him to perform any approved duty as a member of that body:

(2) A member of a parish council shall not be entitled to any payment under this section in respect of any approved duty as a member of that council performed within the area of the parish.

113. Travelling allowance and subsistence allowance (1) A member of a body to which this Part of this Act applies shall be entitled to receive payments, at rates which shall be determined by the body but which shall not exceed those prescribed, by way of travelling allowance or subsistence allowance where expenditure on travelling or, as the case may be, on subsistence is necessarily incurred by him for the purpose of enabling him to perform any approved duty as a member of that body:

Provided that—

(a) a member of the council of a . . . rural parish shall not be entitled to any payments under this section in respect of the performance of any approved duty within the area of that council;
(c) without prejudice to paragraph

(a) of this proviso a member of a body shall not be entitled to a payment under this section by way of subsistence allowance in respect of the performance of an approved duty except in respect of a duty performed at a distance of more than three miles from his usual place of residence.

114. Bodies by whom payments by way of allowances are to be made (1) Any amounts by way of allowances payable under this Part of this Act—

(c) . . . shall be payable by the body as a member of which the person claiming payment performed the approved duty in respect of which the right to payment under this Part of this Act arises.

(3) Where a body to which this Part of this Act applies has power, otherwise than under this Part of this Act, to defray expenses incurred by any person in respect of which that person is entitled to a payment by way of allowance under this Part of this Act, that power shall not be so exercised as to defray those expenses otherwise than in accordance with the provisions of this Part of this Act, but subject as aforesaid nothing in this Part of this Act shall affect any other power of the body to defray expenses.

115. Meaning of 'approved duty' In this Part of this Act, the expression 'approved duty', in relation to a member of a body, means any of the following duties, that is to say,—

(a) attendance at a meeting of the body, or of any committee or sub-committee thereof;
(b) the doing of any other thing approved by the body for the purpose of, or in connection with, the discharge of the functions of the body, or of any committee or sub-committee thereof;
(c) *attendance as a representative of the body at a conference or meeting convened by one or more bodies to which*

this Part of this Act applies or by any association of such bodies, where the body has power, under any statutory provision other than this Act, to defray the expenses incurred in such attendance; or

(*d*) where, in pursuance of a duty imposed on or a power granted to the body by any statutory provision or Royal Charter, he has been appointed by or on the nomination of the body to be a member of any such other body as may be prescribed, not being a body to which this Part of this Act applies, the doing of anything as a member of that other body for the purpose of the discharge of the functions of that other body:

117. Regulations for the purposes of Part VI (1) The Minister may make regulations as to the manner in which the provisions of this Part of this Act are to be administered, and in particular, and without prejudice to the generality of the preceding provision, may make regulations—

(*a*) providing for the avoidance of duplication in payments under this Part of this Act, or between payments under this Part of this Act and under any other Act, where, in any one period of twenty-four hours, a person performs approved duties as a member of more than one body to which this Part of this Act applies, or, as the case may be, becomes entitled to payments both under this Part of this Act and under any other Act, and for the determination of the body or bodies by whom any payments to which that person is entitled are to be made, and, where such payments are to be made by more than one body, for the apportionment between those bodies of the sums payable;

(*b*) prescribing anything which under this Part of this Act is to be prescribed;

(*c*) specifying the forms to be used

and the particulars to be provided for the purpose of claiming payments under this Part of this Act;

(*d*) providing for the publication by a body to which this Part of this Act applies, in the minutes of that body or otherwise, of details of payments made under this Part of this Act.

(2) The power to make regulations conferred by this section shall be exercisable by statutory instrument, and any statutory instrument under this section shall be laid before Parliament after it is made.

PART VII.

129. Subscriptions to local government associations The council of a . . . rural parish may pay reasonable subscriptions, whether annually or otherwise, to the funds—

(*a*) of any association of local authorities formed for the purpose of consultation as to the common interests of those authorities and the discussion of matters relating to local government, or

(*b*) of such associations of officers or members of local authorities, being associations formed for the purposes aforesaid, as may be approved by the Minister.

130. Insurance . . . against accidents to members (1) A local authority may enter into a contract with any person whereby, in consideration of payments by the authority by way of premium or otherwise, that person undertakes to pay to the authority such sums as may be provided in the contract in the event of any member of the authority meeting with a personal accident, whether fatal or not, while he is engaged on the business of the authority.

(2) Any sum received by the authority under any such contract shall, after deduction of any expenses incurred in

the recovery thereof, be paid by them to, or to the personal representatives of, the member of the authority in respect of an accident to whom that sum is received.

(3) The provisions of the Life Assurance Act, 1774, shall not apply to any such contract, but any such contract shall be deemed for the purposes of the Assurance Companies Acts, 1909 to 1946, to be a policy of insurance upon the happening of personal accidents.

131. Disability of members of local authorities for voting on account of interest in contracts, &c. *Subsections* (1), (2) *and* (3) *amend s. 76 of the Local Government Act, 1933.*

(4) In the said section 76 and in section 123 of the said Act of 1933 (which relates to the disclosure by officers of local authorities of interest in contracts), references to a local authority shall be construed as including references to a divisional executive constituted under the Education Acts, 1944 and 1946, or the National Health Service Act, 1946, and, for the purposes of the said section 123, an officer of a local authority who carries out any duties under the control of such an executive shall be deemed, in relation to those duties, to be an officer of that executive.

133. War memorials (1) *Amends section 1 of the War Memorials (Local Authorities' Powers) Act, 1923.*

(2) The matters on which expenditure may be incurred under the said section one shall include the alteration of any memorial to which that section applies so as to make it serve as a memorial in connection with any war subsequent to that in connection with which it was erected and the correction of any error or omission in the inscription on any such memorial.

Part VIII.

141. Payments to councils to be for general expenditure (1) Any sums received under Part I of this Act,—

(*d*) by the council of a rural parish or of a group of rural parishes, or by a parish meeting or the representative body of a parish, shall be receipts in respect of expenses in relation to which a precept is issuable in respect of the whole of the parish or group of parishes.

(2) The reference in subsection (1) of this section to sums received by any council includes a reference to sums the payment whereof is effected by making a deduction from the amount due under a precept.

National Parks and Access to the Countryside Act, 1949

28. Provision of information by other local authorities (1) Before carrying out a survey[1] under the last foregoing section the surveying authority shall consult with the councils of county districts and parishes in the area of the authority as to the arrangements to be made for the provision by such councils of information for the purposes of the survey.

[1] This refers to the footpaths survey. By section 34 this procedure is also applied to the periodical revisions of the maps and statements.

(2) Where the surveying authority and any such council as aforesaid are unable to agree as to the said arrangements, they shall refer the matter to the Minister and he shall determine what arrangements are to be made.

(3) Any arrangements made under this section for the provision of information by a parish council shall require the council to cause a parish meeting to be held for the purpose of considering the information to be provided by the council; and any arrangements so made for the provision of information

by the council of a rural district shall, as respects each parish in the district not having a parish council, require the representative body of the parish or a member of that body to cause a parish meeting to be held for the purpose of considering the information to be provided by the district council in relation to the parish.

(4) **Representations and objections as to draft maps and state-** ments It shall be the duty of any such council as aforesaid to collect and furnish to the surveying authority such information, in such manner and at such time, as may be provided for by arrangements agreed or determined under this section; and the said duty shall be enforceable by mandamus on the application of the surveying authority.

Allotments Act, 1950

[26 October 1950]

Allotments

1. Extension of length of notices to quit allotment gardens (1) *Amends Paragraph* (a) *of subsection* (1) *of section* 1 *of the Allotments Act,* 1922.

(2) This section shall not affect the operation of a notice to quit given before the passing of this Act.

2. Cesser of restrictions on right of tenant of an allotment garden to compensation for crops and manure (1) *Amends subsection* (2) *of section* 2 *of the Allotments Act,*1922.

(2) This section shall not have effect in relation to a tenancy terminated by virtue of a notice to quit given before the passing of this Act.

3. Compensation to tenant of an allotment garden for disturbance (1) Where a tenancy under which land let, whether before or after the passing of this Act, for use by the tenant as an allotment garden or to a local authority or association for the purpose of being sub-let for such use is terminated, as to the whole or any part of the land comprised in the tenancy—

(a) by re-entry under paragraph (b), (c) or (d) of subsection (1) of section 1 of the Allotments Act, 1922; or

(b) where the landlord is himself a tenant, by the termination of his tenancy; or

(c) where the landlord is a local authority who have let the land under section 10 of the Allotments Act, 1922, by the termina-

tion of the right of occupation of the authority;

the tenant shall, notwithstanding any agreement to the contrary, be entitled, on quitting the land or that part thereof, as the case may be, to recover from the landlord compensation for the disturbance of an amount determined in accordance with subsection (2) of this section.

(2) The amount of any compensation recoverable under this section shall be—

(a) where the tenancy terminates as to the whole of the land, an amount equal to one year's rent of the land at the rate at which rent was payable immediately before the termination of the tenancy;

(b) where the tenancy terminates as to part of the land, an amount bearing to the amount mentioned in the foregoing paragraph the same proportion that the area of that part bears to the area of the whole of the land.

(3) Compensation under this section shall be in addition to any compensation to which the tenant may be entitled under the Allotments Act, 1922.

(4) Subsection (2) of section 4 of the Allotments Act, 1922 (which enables the tenant of an allotment garden to recover compensation from a mortgagee who deprives him of possession) shall apply to compensation under this

section as it applies to compensation under that Act.

(5) This section shall not have effect in relation to a tenancy which has terminated before the date of the passing of this Act or terminates after that date in consequence of a notice given or of legal proceedings commenced before that date.

4. Right of landlord of an allotment garden to compensation for deterioration (1) Where the tenant of land let, whether before or after the passing of this Act, on a tenancy for use by the tenant as an allotment garden quits the land on the termination of the tenancy, the landlord shall, notwithstanding any agreement to the contrary, be entitled to recover from the tenant compensation in respect of any deterioration of the land caused by failure of the tenant to maintain it clean and in a good state of cultivation and fertility.

(2) The amount of any compensation recoverable under this section shall be the cost, as at the date of the tenant's quitting the land, of making good the deterioration.

(3) Where the tenant of land let on a tenancy for use by him as an allotment garden has remained therein during two or more tenancies, his landlord shall not be deprived of his right to compensation under this section in respect of deterioration of the land by reason only that the tenancy during which an act or omission occurred which in whole or in part caused the deterioration was a tenancy other than the tenancy at the termination of which the tenant quits the land.

(4) This section shall not have effect in relation to a tenancy which has terminated before the date of the passing of this Act or terminates after that date in consequence of a notice given or of legal proceedings commenced before that date.

5. Set-off of compensation against rent, &c. (1) Out of any money payable to a tenant by way of compensation under section 2 of the Allotments Act, 1922, or section 3 of this Act, the landlord shall be entitled to deduct any

sum due to him from the tenant under or in respect of the tenancy (including any sum due by way of compensation under section 4 of this Act).

(2) Out of any money due to the landlord from the tenant under or in respect of the tenancy (including any money due by way of compensation under section 4 of this Act), the tenant shall be entitled to deduct any sum payable to him by the landlord by way of compensation under section 2 of the Allotments Act, 1922, or section 3 of this Act.

6. Exclusion of cottage holdings, and provisions as to war-time allotments The foregoing provisions of this Act shall not apply to any parcel of land attached to a cottage, *and the said provisions, other than those of section 2, shall not apply to land let by a local authority under Regulation 62A of the Defence (General) Regulations, 1939;* and in any document embodying an arrangement for the cultivation or use of land made in pursuance of the Cultivation of Lands (Allotments) Order, 1939, as originally made, or of that order as amended by the Cultivation of Lands (Allotments) Order, 1941, any reference to compensation to which a person would have been entitled if the arrangement had been a letting under a contract of tenancy of the land for use as an allotment garden or for sub-letting in allotment gardens shall be construed in like manner as if this Act apart from section two thereof had not passed.

[NOTE: See Emergency Laws (M.P.) Act, 1953, s. 5(1). The regulations were revoked in 1952 with a saving for existing allotments.]

7. Application of provisions of the Allotments Act, 1922, for purposes of preceding sections Section 6 of the Allotments Act, 1922 (which relates to the determination and recovery of compensation under the foregoing provisions of that Act) and section 7 of that Act (which provides for the application of those provisions to Crown lands) shall have effect as if the references to those provisions included references to the foregoing provisions of this Act, and subsection (4) of section 22 of that Act (which provides, amongst other things, that, for the purposes of that Act, where land is used by the tenant thereof as an allotment garden, it shall, unless the contrary is proved, be deemed to have been let to him to be used as an allotment garden) shall have effect as if the reference to that Act included a reference to this Act.

8. *Amends Subsection (4) of section 1 of the Allotments Act, 1922.*

9. Restriction of obligations of local authorities to provide allotments The obligation under the Allotments Acts, 1908 to 1931, of the council of a parish and of the parish meeting of a rural parish not having a parish council to provide allotments shall—

(*a*) . . . be limited to the provision of allotment gardens;

10. Rents to be charged for allotments let by local authorities (1) Land let by a council under the Allotments Acts, 1908 to 1931, for use as an allotment shall be let at such rent as a tenant may reasonably be expected to pay for the land if let for such use on the terms (other than terms as to rent) on which it is in fact let:

Provided that land may be let by a council as aforesaid to a person at a less rent if the council are satisfied that there exist special circumstances affecting that person which render it proper for them to let the land to him at a less rent.

(2) Not more than a quarter's rent for land let by a council as mentioned in subsection (1) of this section shall be required to be paid in advance:

Provided that this subsection shall not apply where the yearly rent is twenty-five shillings or less.

(3) In this section the references to a council shall be construed as including references to the parish meeting of a rural parish not having a parish council.

12. Abolition of contractual restrictions on keeping hens and rabbits (1) Notwithstanding any provision to the contrary in any lease or tenancy or in any covenant, contract or undertaking relating to the use to be made of any land, it shall be lawful for the occupier of any land to keep, otherwise than by way of trade or business, hens or rabbits in any place on the land and to erect or place and maintain such buildings or structures on the land as are reasonably necessary for that purpose:

Provided that nothing in this subsection shall authorise any hens or rabbits to be kept in such a place or in such a manner as to be prejudicial to health or a nuisance or affect the operation of any enactment.

Supplementary

13. Expenses and receipts *Parliament to defray Ministers' expenses and Ministers' receipts to be paid to the Exchequer.*

14. Interpretation (1) In this Act the expressions 'allotment garden' and 'landlord' have the same meanings as they have for the purposes of the Allotments Act, 1922, and the provisions of subsection (1) of section 22 of that Act relating to the continued application to parties of the designations of landlord and tenant shall apply for the purposes of this Act as they apply for the purposes of that Act.

(2) References in this Act to any other enactment shall, except so far as the context otherwise requires, be construed as references to that enactment as amended by any subsequent enactment, including this Act.

15. Short title, citation (1) This Act may be cited as the Allotments Act, 1950, and the Allotments Acts, 1908 to 1931, and this Act may be cited together as the Allotments Acts, 1908 to 1950.

Post Office Act, 1953

51. (3) Where the council of any rural district, or the parish council of a parish, or in the case of a parish not having a parish council the parish meeting, consider that it would be for the benefit, in the case of a rural district council, of any contributory place or places within their district or, in the case of a parish council or parish meeting, of their parish, that any post or telegraph office should be established, or any additional postal or other facilities should be provided, by the *Postmaster-General* whether within or without the area to be benefited, that council or meeting may undertake to pay to the *Postmaster-General* any loss he may sustain by reason of the establishment or maintenance of the office or the provision of the facilities; and any expenses incurred by a rural district council in pursuance of such an undertaking may be defrayed as special expenses chargeable on the contributory place or places to be benefited:

Provided that a rural district council shall not exercise their powers under this subsection as respects an office established or facilities provided outside a contributory place proposed to be charged unless the parish council, or if there is no parish council the parish meeting, of any parish wholly or partly situated in the contributory place consent to the exercise of the powers.

Local Government (*Miscellaneous Provisions*) Act, 1953

Powers of local authorities in respect of omnibus shelters, etc.

4. Provision of omnibus shelters, etc. (1) Subject to the following provisions of this Act, a local authority may provide and maintain in any highway within their district which is comprised in the route of public service vehicles, or on any land abutting on such a highway, shelters or other accommodation at stopping places on the route for the use of persons intending to travel on such vehicles.

(2) Any local authority, or any persons authorised to run public service vehicles, may enter into and carry into effect any agreement with a local authority with respect to the provision and maintenance of shelters or other accommodation under this section by the last-mentioned authority; and any such agreement may in particular provide for the payment by the first-mentioned authority or persons of the whole or any part of the cost of the provision and maintenance of the shelter or accommodation.

(3) A local authority shall consult the Commissioner of Police of the Metropolis with regard to the position of any shelter or other accommodation which they propose to provide under this section in a highway in the metropolitan police district.

(4) In this and the next three following sections, 'local authority' includes the council of a rural parish; the references to public service vehicles shall be construed in like manner as if they were contained in the Road Traffic Act, 1960, it being assumed that so much of section 117(1) of that Act as excludes tramcars and trolley vehicles were omitted.

5. Consents to exercise of powers under s. 4 (1) A local authority shall not have power by virtue of the last foregoing section to provide a shelter or other accommodation in any such situation or position as is described in the first column of the following Table, except with the consent of the person described in relation thereto in the second column of that Table:—

TABLE

In any highway for which there is a highway authority other than the local authority, or on land abutting on any such highway.	The highway authority.
In any highway belonging to and repairable by any railway, dock, harbour, canal, inland navigation or passenger road transport undertakers and forming the approach to any station, dock, wharf or depot of those undertakers.	The undertakers.
On any bridge not vested in the local authority or on the approaches to any such bridge.	The authority or other person in whom the bridge is vested.
On any bridge carrying a highway over any railway, canal or inland navigation, or on the approaches to any such bridge, or under any bridge carrying a railway, canal or inland navigation over a highway.	The railway, canal or inland navigation undertakers concerned.
In a position obstructing or interfering with any existing access to any land or premises abutting on a highway.	The owner (as defined by the Public Health Act, 1936) of the land or premises.

(2) Any consent required by this section in respect of a shelter or other accommodation shall not unreasonably be withheld but may be given subject to any reasonable conditions including a condition that the local authority shall remove the shelter or other accommodation either at any time or at or after the expiration of a period if reasonably required so to do by the person giving the consent.

(3) Any dispute between a local authority and a person whose consent is required under this section whether that consent is unreasonably withheld or is given subject to reasonable conditions, or whether the removal of any shelter or other accommodation in accordance with any condition of the consent is reasonably required shall—

(a) in the case of a dispute between the local authority and the Minister of Transport, be referred to and determined by an arbitrator to be appointed in default of agreement by the President of the Institution of Civil Engineers;

(b) in any other case, be referred to and determined by the Minister of Transport.

6. Supplementary provisions as to omnibus shelters, etc. (1) Where a shelter or other accommodation is provided by a local authority under section 4 of this Act in a position obstructing access to any telegraphic line as defined by the Telegraph Act, 1878, and the Postmaster-General notifies the local authority that he requires to obtain access to that line, the authority shall, unless they temporarily *remove*[1] the shelter or accommodation for the purpose of affording such access, or so much thereof as is necessary for that purpose, be liable to repay to the Postmaster-General so much of the expenses reasonably incurred by him in obtaining such access as is attributable to the situation of the shelter or accommodation.

(2) The provisions of the foregoing subsection shall apply in relation to any sewers, pipe-subways, pipes, wires or other apparatus belonging to or maintained by any local authority or any gas, electricity, water, hydraulic power, tramcar or trolley vehicle undertakers, as they apply in relation to any such telegraphic line as is therein mentioned, and as if for any reference therein to the Postmaster-General there were substi-

[1] See P.C.A. 1957 s. 5(5).

tuted a reference to the local authority or the undertakers, as the case may be.

(3) Any dispute as to the amount (if any) payable by a local authority under the foregoing provisions of this section shall be determined in accordance with subsection (2) of section 278 of the Public Health Act, 1936.

7. Maintenance of existing bus shelters and queue barriers (1) *Shelters and queue barriers provided before the Act may continue to be maintained.*

(2) The provisions of sections 5 and 6 of this Act shall apply to the maintenance of any accommodation under this section, and to accommodation maintained thereunder, as they apply to the provision of accommodation under section 4 of this Act and to accommodation provided under that section; but where any consent required under the said section 5 has been given by any authority or person before the com-mencement of this Act in respect of the provision of any accommodation to which this section applies, nothing in this subsection shall be construed as requiring any further consent on the part of that authority or person in respect of the maintenance of that accommodation.

15. *Amends Local Government Act, 1933, Section 76(2A).*

16. Financial loss allowances to members of local authorities, etc. *Amends subsection (1) of section 112 of the Local Government Act, 1948.*

(2) A statutory instrument containing regulations made under section 117 of the said Act, being regulations made for the purposes of section 112 of that Act as amended by this section, shall be subject to annulment in pursuance of a resolution of either House of Parliament.

Auxiliary Forces Act, 1953

41. (1) Notices required in pursuance of this Act or of the orders and regulations in force thereunder to be given to men of the Territorial Army or of the Royal Auxiliary Air Force shall be served or published in such manner as may be prescribed and, if so served or published, shall be deemed to be sufficient notice.

(2) Every constable and other parish officer shall, when so required by or on behalf of the Defence Council, conform with the orders and regulations for the time being in force under this Act with respect to the publication and service of notices, and in default shall be liable on summary conviction to a fine not exceeding twenty pounds.

(3) In the last foregoing subsection the expression 'parish officer' means in an urban parish the clerk to the rating authority, in a rural parish having a parish council the chairman of the parish council, and in any other rural parish the chairman of the parish meeting.

Local Government Elections Act, 1956

1. Synchronisation of rural district and parish elections (1) After the year 1957, in each of the cases mentioned, with respect to rural parishes, in the first column of the First Schedule to this Act, the elections of rural district and parish councillors mentioned, in relation to that case, in the second and third columns of that Schedule, shall be held in the same year and on the same day, and the councillors whose places are filled by the newly elected councillors shall accordingly retire simultaneously.

(2) In each of the said cases, the polls at the elections which, by virtue of the foregoing subsection, are required to be held simultaneously shall be taken together, and paragraph (c) of subsection (1) of section 29 of the Act of

1949 (which requires provision to be made by district and parish election rules for the taking together, so far as practicable, of the polls at certain elections of rural district and parish councillors) shall cease to have effect at the end of the said year.

(3) Nothing in this section shall be construed as affecting, in relation to a group of parishes, the requirement imposed by subsection (2) of section 50 of the Act of 1933 that parish councillors shall retire together.

2. Provisions consequential on section 1 of this Act (1) As from the first day of June, 1957,—

(a) the Act of 1933, the Act of 1948 and the Act of 1949 shall have effect subject to the amendments specified in Part I of the Second Schedule to this Act, being amendments consequential on the foregoing section; and

(b) the provisions of Part II of that Schedule shall have effect for the purpose of, and in connection with, the securing of compliance with the requirements of that section.

(2) Where the regular retirement of all the rural district councillors elected for a parish, for the several wards of a parish or for a combination of parishes would, apart from this Act, take place in the year 1959 or the year 1960, then, unless the term of office of those councillors is varied by an order under Part II of the Second Schedule to this Act, the parish councillors who are required by this Act to retire simultaneously with the first-mentioned councillors shall, instead of retiring in the year 1958, continue in office until the twentieth day of May in the year 1959 or the year 1960, as the case may be, or, if that day is a bank holiday or day appointed for public thanksgiving or mourning, the first day thereafter which is not a Sunday, bank holiday or day so appointed.

3. Wards for rural district elections (1) A rural parish divided into parish wards shall not, for the purpose of the first ordinary election held after the year 1957 of councillors for the rural district within which the parish is situate or any subsequent election of such councillors, be divided into wards any one of which is not co-extensive with a parish ward or a combination of parish wards.

(2) A rural borough divided into . . . wards shall not for the purposes of the election of councillors for the rural district in which the rural borough is situate be divided into wards any one of which is not co-extensive with a rural borough ward or a combination of rural borough wards.

4. Payment of expenses of elections of district and parish councillors

(2) The council of a rural district shall pay—

(a) all expenses properly incurred in relation to the holding of an election of rural district councillors for the district, not exceeding such scale as may be fixed by the county council, so far as the scale is applicable; and

(b) all expenses properly incurred in relation to the holding of—

(i) an election of rural borough councillors for a rural borough within the district, an election of parish councillors for a parish within the district which has a separate parish council; and

(ii) an election, for a parish within the district which is grouped under a common parish council with a neighbouring parish or parishes (whether within or outside the district), of the separate representatives on that council for the first-mentioned parish,

not exceeding in either case such scale as may be fixed by the county council, so far as the scale is applicable;

and all such expenses as are mentioned in paragraph (b) of this subsection shall be defrayed as special expenses separately chargeable on the parish in question.

(3) Where the poll at an election of rural district councillors is taken together with the poll at an election of rural borough councillors or parish councillors, one half of the cost of taking the combined polls shall be treated as attributable to the holding of each election.

(4) The foregoing provisions of this section shall have effect in lieu of subsection (4) of section 29 of the Act of 1949 as respects every election of urban district councillors, rural district councillors or parish councillors, being an election the day of which falls on or after the first day of November, 1956.

5. Polls consequent on parish meetings (1) *Amends sub-paragraph (5) of paragraph 5 of Part VI of the Third Schedule to the Act of 1933.*

7. Savings (1) Any scale of expenses fixed, or having effect as if fixed, under subsection (4) of section 29 of the Act of 1949, being a scale in force immediately before the first day of November, 1956, shall continue in force and have effect as if fixed under section 4 of this Act.

(2) Any rules having effect by virtue of sub-paragraph (5) of paragraph 5 of Part VI of the Third Schedule to the Act of 1933, being rules in force immediately before the passing of this Act, shall continue in force and have

effect as if made under the sub-paragraph substituted for the said sub-paragraph (5) by subsection (1) of section 5 of this Act.

(3) Any order or direction made or given, or having effect as if made or given, under any provision of section 35 of the Act of 1933, being an order or direction in force immediately before the first day of June 1957, shall, so far as it could have been made or given under any provision of the sections substituted for the said section 35 by paragraph 1 of the Second Schedule to this Act, continue in force and have effect as if made or given under that provision.

8. Interpretation and extent (1) ...

(2) In this Act—

(a) the expressions 'the Act of 1933', 'the Act of 1948' and 'the Act of 1949' mean, respectively, the Local Government Act, 1933, the Representation of the People Act, 1948; and the Representation of the People Act, 1949;

(b) references to the Act of 1933 shall be construed as references to that Act as amended by any subsequent enactment (including, except where the context otherwise requires this Act).

(c) *defines a rural borough and its wards*

SCHEDULES
FIRST SCHEDULE
COMBINED ELECTIONS

| Case | Elections to be combined | |
	Rural district elections	Parish elections
1. Where a rural parish having a separate parish council is neither divided into wards for the purpose of the election of rural district councillors nor combined with one or more other parishes for that purpose.	Ordinary elections of rural district councillors for the parish.	If the parish is not divided into parish wards, ordinary elections of parish councillors for the parish. If the parish is divided into parish wards, ordinary elections of parish councillors for all the wards.

Case	Elections to be combined	
	Rural district	Parish elections
2. Where a rural parish having a separate parish council is divided into wards for the purpose of the election of rural district councillors.	Ordinary elections of rural district councillors for all the wards.	If the parish is not divided into parish wards, ordinary elections of parish councillors for the parish. If the parish is divided into parish wards, ordinary elections of parish councillors for all the wards.
3. Where a rural parish having a separate parish council is combined with one or more other parishes for the purpose of the election of rural district councillors.	Ordinary elections of rural district councillors for the combined parishes.	If the parish is not divided into parish wards, ordinary elections of parish councillors for the parish. If the parish is divided into parish wards, ordinary elections of parish councillors for all the wards.
4. Where a rural parish is grouped under a common parish council with a neighbouring parish or parishes (whether the grouped parishes are within the same rural district or not) and is neither divided into wards for the purpose of the election of rural district councillors nor combined with one or more other parishes for that purpose.	Ordinary elections of rural district councillors for the parish.	If the parish is not divided into parish wards, ordinary elections of the separate representatives for the parish on the common parish council. If the parish is divided into parish wards, ordinary elections of such representatives as aforesaid for all the wards.
5. Where a rural parish is both grouped under a common parish council with a neighbouring parish or parishes (whether the grouped parishes are within the same rural district or not) and divided into wards for the purpose of the election of rural district councillors.	Ordinary elections of rural district councillors for all the wards.	If the parish is not divided into parish wards, ordinary elections of the separate representatives for the parish on the common parish council. If the parish is divided into parish wards, ordinary elections of such representatives as aforesaid for all the wards.

Case	Elections to be combined	
	Rural district	Parish elections
6. Where a rural parish is both grouped under a common parish council with a neighbouring parish or parishes (whether the grouped parishes are within the same rural district or not) and combined with one or more other parishes for the purpose of the election of rural district councillors.	Ordinary elections of rural district councillors for the combined parishes.	If the parish is not divided into parish wards, ordinary elections of the separate representatives for the parish on the common parish council. If the parish is divided into parish wards, ordinary elections of such representatives as aforesaid for all the wards.

SECOND SCHEDULE

Consequential Amendments of Enactments and Provisions for securing simultaneous Retirement of Councillors

Part I

Consequential Amendments of Enactments

1. *Substitutes two new sections for section 35 of the Act of* 1933.

2. *Amends subsection* (2) *of section 50 of the Act of* 1933.

4. In accordance with paragraphs 1 and 2 of this Schedule—

(a) in paragraph 3 of the Sixth Schedule to the Act of 1948, the words 'sections thirty-five and fifty of, and' and the words 'the day of retirement of district and parish councillors and'; and

(b) in the Table set out in sub-paragraph (1) of paragraph 5 of the Eighth Schedule to the Act of 1949, the words 'Subsection (2) of section thirty-five';

shall cease to have effect.

Part II

Provisions for securing simultaneous Retirement of Councillors

5. In addition to the powers conferred on them by the Act of 1933, a county council shall, for the purpose of securing compliance, as respects rural districts and rural parishes within the county, with the requirements of section one of this Act and the requirements of the Act of 1933 with respect to the retirement of councillors, have power by order—

(a) to direct that any rural district councillors who would, apart from the direction, regularly retire in a particular year shall retire instead in such earlier or later year as may be specified in the order on the twentieth of May or, if that day is a Sunday, bank holiday or day appointed for public thanksgiving or mourning, the first day thereafter which is none of them; and

(b) to effect any necessary extension or reduction of the term of office of any parish councillors who are required to retire simultaneously with any rural district councillors:

Provided that the power conferred by this paragraph—

(i) shall not be so exercised as to

postpone the ordinary day of retirement of a councillor from the year in which, apart from the direction, he would regularly retire to a year other than the next or the next but one; and

(ii) shall not be so exercised as to effect a reduction in the term of office of a councillor unless the county council are satisfied that it is not reasonably practicable to attain the object of the order by extending his term of office.

6. Where an order under the last foregoing paragraph directs that a rural district councillor shall retire in a year later than that in which, apart from the direction, he would have regularly retired and, on the date of the making of the order, there exists in the office of that councillor a casual vacancy to which subsection (3) of section 67 of the Act of 1933 applies, an election to fill the vacancy shall be held under that section as if the vacancy had occurred on that date; and where an order under that paragraph directs that a rural district councillor shall retire in a year earlier than that in which, apart from the direction, he would have regularly retired and, on the date of the making of the order, there exists in the office of that councillor a casual vacancy to which, by virtue of the order, that subsection becomes applicable, then if, before the date of the making of the order, the day of election to fill that vacancy has been fixed under that section, the election shall be held as if the order had not been made.

8. During his term of office the chairman or vice-chairman of a rural district council or parish council whose retirement as a councillor falls to be determined by virtue of the provisions of this Act or an order thereunder shall, notwithstanding those provisions, continue to be a member of the council.

9. A copy of every order made under this Part of this Schedule shall be sent to the Secretary of State and to the Minister of Housing and Local Government.

Parish Councils Act, 1957

[17 July 1957]

PART I

POWERS TO PROVIDE PUBLIC AMENITIES

1. Power to provide seats and shelters in roads (1) Subject to the provisions of section five of this Act, a parish council may provide and maintain seats and shelters for the use of the public and cause them to be installed or erected in proper and convenient situations, in, or on any land abutting on, any road within the parish.

(2) In parishes in which the Public Improvements Act, 1860 (in this section referred to as 'the Act of 1860') has effect the powers conferred by this section shall be in substitution for any powers under that Act to place seats and shelters.

(3) The Act of 1860 (which, in so far as it relates to the provision of recreation grounds and public walks by parish councils has been superseded by section 8 of the Local Government Act, 1894, and, in so far as it confers powers on other local authorities, has been superseded by other enactments) shall cease to have effect; and accordingly for the purposes of subsection (3) of section 193 of the Local Government Act, 1933 (which limits the sums which may be required to be raised in any financial year to meet the expenses of a parish council, other than expenses under the Act of 1860 and certain other Acts) any expenditure by a parish council in providing or acquiring land for a recreation ground or public walk under subsection (1) of the said section 8, or in exercising any powers under the said subsection (1) in relation to a recreation ground or public walk provided under that subsection or under the Act of 1860, shall be left out of account.

2. Power to provide public clocks

A parish council may provide, maintain and light such public clocks within the parish as they consider necessary, and (subject to the provisions of section 5 of this Act) may cause them to be installed on or against any premises or in any other place the situation of which may be convenient.

3. Power to light roads and public places (1) Where this subsection has effect in any parish or part of a parish, the parish council or, if there is no parish council, the parish meeting, may (subject to the provisions of section 5 of this Act) for the purpose of lighting the *roads* and other public places in the parish, or in that part of the parish, as the case may be,—

(*a*) provide and maintain such lamps, lamp posts and other materials and apparatus as they think necessary;

(*b*) cause such lamps, lamp posts and other materials and apparatus to be erected or installed on or against any premises or in such other places as may be convenient;

(*c*) contract with any person for the supply of gas, electricity or other means of lighting; and

(*d*) employ, with or without remuneration, such persons as may be necessary for the maintenance and superintendence of anything provided under this subsection.

(2) Subject to the provisions of subsection (4) of this section, subsection (1) of this section shall have effect in place of the Lighting and Watching Act, 1833, in every parish or part of a parish in which that Act was in force immediately before the commencement of this Act; and—

(*a*) in a parish having a parish council, all property, debts and liabilities of any inspectors under that Act shall vest in the parish council;

(*b*) in a parish not having a parish council, all such property, debts and liabilities shall vest in the representative body of the parish,

subject to such directions as may be given by the parish meeting under section 47 of the Local Government Act, 1933 (which provides that the representative body shall in all respects act in manner directed by the parish meeting).

(3) Subject to the provisions of subsection (4) of this section, subsection (1) of this section shall also have effect—

(*a*) in every parish for which it is adopted by the parish meeting; and

(*b*) in every part of a parish for which it is adopted by a parish meeting which, apart from this section, is authorised or required to be held for that part;

and the said subsection (1) may be adopted as aforesaid notwithstanding that it already has effect in any area within the parish or part of a parish for which it is so adopted:

Provided that the said subsection (1) shall not be adopted for any parish or part of a parish in respect of which a rural district council has the powers of an urban authority under section 161 of the Public Health Act, 1875 (which confers powers of lighting on urban authorities) except with the consent of the Minister of Housing and Local Government, and the Minister shall not give his consent unless he is satisfied on the application of the parish meeting of the parish or part of a parish for which it is proposed to adopt the said subsection (1), and after consultation with the rural district council, that the rural district council is not exercising the said powers in relation to that parish or part of a parish in such a manner as to provide adequate lighting of the roads and other public places therein.

(4) Where, by an order under section 276 of the said Act of 1875, a rural district council is invested with the powers of an urban authority under the said section 161 in respect of any area in which subsection (1) of this section has effect, the said subsection (1) shall

cease to have effect in that area, and the supplementary provisions set out in subsection (1) of section 148 and in sections 150 and 151 of the Local Government Act, 1933, shall for the purposes of this section apply in relation to the order as if it were an order made under Part VI of that Act making an alteration of authorities.

(5) Not less than fourteen days' notice shall be given of any parish meeting at which it is proposed to adopt subsection (1) of this section, or to transact any business relating to an application to the Minister of Housing and Local Government for his consent to the adoption of that subsection or any other business relating to the adoption of that subsection; and accordingly for the purposes of sub-paragraph (2) of paragraph 2 of Part VI of the Third Schedule to the Local Government Act, 1933 (which provides that fourteen days' notice shall be given of a parish meeting at which any business proposed to be transacted relates to the adoption of any of the adoptive Acts, or certain other matters) the expression 'the adoptive Acts' shall include the said subsection (1).

(6) Where subsection (1) of this section has effect in part only of a parish, any rate levied to defray expenses incurred under this section shall be charged on that part of the parish only.

(8) Any expenditure by a parish council under this section shall be left out of account for the purposes of subsection (3) of section 193 of the Local Government Act, 1933 . . .

(10) In this section 'road' includes a highway comprised in the route of a special road . . . being a highway in relation to which a parish council or parish meeting, as the case may be, are exercising the powers conferred by subsection (1) of this section on the date on which a scheme made under section 11 of the [Highways] Act, 1959, authorising the provision of the special road comes into force.

5. Provisions as to consents and access (1) A parish council or parish meeting shall not have power by virtue of the foregoing provisions of this Part of this Act to provide any seat, shelter, clock, lamp or lamp post, any other material or apparatus—

(a) on any land or premises not forming part of a road, or in a position obstructing or interfering with any existing access to any such land or premises, except with the consent of the owner and the occupier of the land or premises; or

(b) in any road which is not a highway or in any public path, except with the consent of the owner and the occupier of the land over which the road or path runs; or

(c) in any such situation or position as is described in the first column of the following Table, except with the consent of the persons described in relation thereto in the second column of that Table.

TABLE

In any trunk road or any other road maintained by the Minister of Transport and Civil Aviation, or on land abutting on any such road.	The Minister.
In any road which is a highway (other than a trunk road or a road maintained as aforesaid or a public path) or on land abutting on any such road.	The county council.
In any road which is a highway belonging to and repairable by any railway, dock, harbour, canal, inland navigation or passenger road transport undertakers and forming the approach to any station, dock, wharf or depot of those undertakers.	The undertakers concerned.

On any bridge carrying a highway over any railway, dock, harbour, canal or inland navigation, or on the approaches to any such bridge or under any bridge carrying a railway, canal or inland navigation over a highway.

The railway, dock, harbour canal or inland navigation undertakers concerned.

(2) Any consent required by paragraph (c) of subsection (1) of this section shall not unreasonably be withheld, but may be given subject to any reasonable conditions, including a condition that the parish council or parish meeting, as the case may be, shall remove any thing to the provision of which the consent relates either at any time or at or after the expiration of a period if reasonably required so to do by the person giving the consent.

(3) Any dispute between a parish council or parish meeting and a person whose consent is required under paragraph (c) of subsection (1) of this section whether that consent is unreasonably withheld or is given subject to reasonable conditions, or whether the removal of any thing to the provision of which the consent relates in accordance with any condition of the consent is reasonably required, shall—

(a) in the case of a dispute between the parish council or parish meeting and the Minister of Transport and Civil Aviation, be referred to and determined by an arbitrator to be appointed in default of agreement by the President of the Institution of Civil Engineers; and

(b) in any other case be referred to and determined by the Minister of Transport and Civil Aviation, who may cause a local inquiry to be held for the purpose;

and section two hundred and ninety of the Local Government Act, 1933, shall apply in relation to a local inquiry held under this subsection as it applies in relation to such an inquiry held under that Act.

(4) Section six of the Local Government (Miscellaneous Provisions) Act, 1953 (which makes provision as to access to telegraphic lines, sewers, pipe-subways, pipes, wires and other apparatus) shall apply in relation to a thing provided by a parish council or parish meeting under this Part of this Act, and to the council or meeting by which the parking place or other thing is so provided, as it applies in relation to a shelter or other accommodation provided, and to the local authority by which it is provided, under section four of that Act.

6. Supplementary powers (1) A parish council or parish meeting may contribute towards—

(a) the reasonable expenses incurred by any person in doing anything which by virtue of the foregoing provisions of this Act that council or meeting has power to do; and

(b) the expenses incurred by any other parish council or parish meeting in exercising their powers under any such provision as aforesaid.

(2) Where before the commencement of this Act any parish council or parish meeting have provided anything which, after the said commencement, could be provided by them under any of the foregoing provisions of this Act, or where either before or after the said commencement any other person has provided any such thing, the parish council or parish meeting shall have the like power to maintain that thing as if it had been provided by them under those provisions.

(3) Without prejudice to any other power of combination, a parish council or parish meeting having powers under any of the foregoing provisions of this Act may by agreement combine with any other parish council or parish meeting having the same powers for the purpose of exercising those powers.

7. Interpretation of Part I In this Part of this Act except so far as the context otherwise requires—

'in' in a context referring to things in a road includes a reference to things under, over, across, along or upon the road;

'owner' has the meaning assigned to it by section 343 of the Public Health Act, 1936;

'public path' has the meaning assigned to it by section 27 of the National Parks and Access to the Countryside Act, 1949;[1]

'road' means any highway (including a public path) and any other road, lane, footway, square, court, alley or passage (whether a thoroughfare or not) to which the public has access, but does not include a special road (as defined by the Highways Act, 1959).

[1] i.e. 'a highway being either a footpath or a bridleway.'

PART II

EXTENSION AND ADAPTATION OF OTHER POWERS

8. Powers to be exercisable without reference to county council (1) Every parish council shall be a local authority for the purposes of the Open Spaces Act, 1906, whether or not invested with the powers of that Act by the council of the county within which the parish is situate.

(2) *Abolishes the need for the approval or consent of the county council to expenditure on War Memorials and in connection with loans.*

9. Power of parish councils to insure against accidents to members In the application to England and Wales of section 130 of the Local Government Act, 1948 (which empowers certain local authorities to insure against accidents to their members), the expression 'local authority' shall include a parish council.

10. Power to contribute towards expenses of burial grounds A parish council may contribute towards the expenses incurred by any other person in maintaining any place of interment in which the remains of inhabitants of the parish are or may be interred.

PART III

MISCELLANEOUS

12. *Amends Section 50 of the Local Government Act to increase the maximum number of parish councillors to twenty-one.*

14. Interpretation (1) Any reference in this Act to any other enactment shall, except so far as the context otherwise requires, be construed as a reference to that enactment as amended or applied by or under any other enactment, including this Act.

(2) In this Act 'parish', in relation to a common parish council acting for two or more grouped parishes, means those parishes.

FIRST SCHEDULE

EXPENSES TO BE LEFT OUT OF ACCOUNT FOR PURPOSES OF LOCAL GOVERNMENT ACT, 1933, s. 193(3)

1. Any expenditure under the Burial Acts, 1852 to 1906.

2. Any expenditure under the Public Libraries and Museums Act, 1964.

3. Any expenditure incurred in providing or acquiring land for a recreation ground or public walk under subsection (1) of section 8 of the Local Government Act, 1894, or in exercising any powers under the said subsection (1) in relation to a recreation ground or public walk provided under that subsection or under the Public Improvements Act, 1860 or in exercising any powers under section 54 of the Public Health Act, 1961.

4. Any expenditure under the Allotments Acts, 1908 to 1950.

5. Any expenditure under Part VIII of the Public Health Act, 1936.

6. Any expenditure under Part VI of the Local Government Act, 1948.

7. Any expenditure under section 3 of this Act.

Recreational Charities Act, 1958

[13th March, 1958]

1. General provision as to recreational and similar trusts, etc. (1) Subject to the provisions of this Act, it shall be and be deemed always to have been charitable to provide, or assist in the provision of, facilities for recreation or other leisure-time occupation, if the facilities are provided in the interests of social welfare

Provided that nothing in this section shall be taken to derogate from the principle that a trust or institution to be charitable must be for the public benefit.

(2) The requirement of the foregoing subsection that the facilities are provided in the interests of social welfare shall not be treated as satisfied unless—

(a) the facilities are provided with the object of improving the conditions of life for the persons for whom the facilities are primarily intended; and

(b) either—
(i) those persons have need of such facilities as aforesaid by reason of their youth, age, infirmity or disablement, poverty or social and economic circumstances; or
(ii) the facilities are to be available to the members or female members of the public at large.

(3) Subject to the said requirements, subsection (1) of this section applies in particular to the provision of facilities at village halls, community centres and women's institutes, and to the provision and maintenance of grounds and buildings to be used for purposes of recreation or leisure-time occupation, and extends to the provision of facilities for those purposes by the organising of any activity.

3. Savings and other provisions as to past transactions (1) Nothing in this Act shall be taken to restrict the purposes which are to be regarded as charitable independently of this Act.

(2) Nothing in this Act—

(a) shall apply to make charitable any trust, or validate any disposition, of property if before the 17th day of December, 1957, that property or any property representing or forming part of it, or any income arising from any such property, has been paid or conveyed to, or applied for the benefit of, the persons entitled by reason of the invalidity of the trust or disposition; or

(b) shall affect any order or judgment made or given (whether before or after the passing of this Act) in legal proceedings begun before that day; or

(c) shall require anything properly done before that day, or anything done or to be done in pursuance of a contract entered into before that day, to be treated for any purpose as wrongful or ineffectual.

(3) Except as provided by subsections (4) and (5) of this section, nothing in this Act shall require anything to be treated for the purposes of any enactment as having been charitable at a time before the date of the passing of this Act, so as to invalidate anything done or any determination given before that date.

Land Powers (Defence) Act, 1958

Stopping up and diversion of highways

8. Stopping up and diversion of highways (1) The powers conferred on the Minister of Transport and Civil Aviation by section 49 of the Town and Country Planning Act, 1947 (which empowers that Minister to authorise by order the stopping up or diversion of a highway where he is satisfied that it is necessary to do so to enable land to be developed) shall also be exercisable where—

> (a) land is, or is to be, used by a Secretary of State, the Admiralty or the Minister of Supply for the purposes of an installation provided or to be provided for defence purposes, or is used by a manufacturer of aircraft as an airfield wholly or mainly in connection with the manufacture of aircraft for defence purposes; and
>
> (b) the Minister of Transport and Civil Aviation is satisfied that, for the land to be so used efficiently without danger to the public, it is necessary that a highway should be stopped up or diverted.

(2) Where, in the circumstances specified in paragraphs (a) and (b) of the foregoing subsection, it appears to the Minister of Transport and Civil Aviation that it is not necessary that the highway should be stopped up or diverted for more than a limited period, an order under the said section 49, including an order made by virtue of subsection (7) of that section (which authorises the stopping up or diversion of a highway temporarily stopped up or diverted under any other enactment) instead of providing for the permanent stopping up or diversion of the highway may provide for its stopping up or diversion during such period as may be prescribed by or under the order and for its restoration at the expiration of that period:

Provided that, for the purposes of any subsequent order by virtue of the said subsection (7), any order made by virtue of the foregoing provisions of this subsection shall be regarded as having been made otherwise than under the said section 49.

(3) Any order made by virtue of the last foregoing subsection which provides for the provision of another highway in substitution for a highway stopped up by the order may also contain such provisions as appear to the Minister of

Transport and Civil Aviation to be expedient for the stopping up, at the expiration of the period prescribed by or under the order, of that other highway and for the original highway to be reconstructed at the expense of such of the Ministers referred to in paragraph (a) of subsection (1) of this section as may be specified in the order and thereafter maintained by any person who would for the time being have been liable for its maintenance if it had never been stopped up.

(4) For the purposes of the making of any order under the said section 49—

> (a) by virtue of subsection (1) or (2) of this section; or
>
> (b) by virtue of subsection (7) of the said section 49 for the permanent stopping up or diversion of a highway temporarily stopped up or diverted by virtue of the said subsection (2),

the Sixth Schedule to the said Act of 1947 (which relates to the procedure to be followed in connection with the making of orders under that section) shall have effect as if—

> (i) in sub-paragraph (b) of paragraph 1 of that Schedule (which requires a copy of the draft order and of any relevant map or plan to be available for inspection during a period of three months); and
>
> (ii) in paragraph 4 of that Schedule (which relates to procedure where an objection is received before the end of that period),

for the words 'three months' there were substituted the words 'thirty days'.

9. Supplementary provisions with respect to stopping up and diversion of highways (1) The powers to make orders conferred on the *Minister of Transport and Civil Aviation*—

> (a) by section 15 of the Requisitioned Land and War Works Act, 1945, with respect to the permanent stopping up or diversion of a high-

way which has been stopped up or diverted in the exercise of emergency powers or as respects which a Minister has certified as mentioned in subsection (1) of section 3 of the Requisitioned Land and War Works Act, 1948; and

(b) by section 16 of the said Act of 1945 with respect to the use and maintenance until other provision is made by or under any Act of certain works placed along, across, over or under a highway in the exercise of emergency powers or for war purposes.

shall include power to vary or revoke any previous order made under the section in question; and subsection (1) of section 20 of the said Act of 1945

(which restricts the period during which orders may be made under the said section 15 or 16) shall not apply to any order so far as it is made by virtue of this subsection.

(3) Any person authorised in that behalf by the Minister of Transport and Civil Aviation or a local authority may enter on any land for the purpose of surveying it in connection with, or with proposals for, the diversion, provision or improvement of any highway by virtue of an order under the said section 15, and the provisions of the Fourth Schedule to this Act shall have effect in relation to the powers conferred by this subsection.

In this subsection and in the said Fourth Schedule the expression 'local authority' means the council of a county, borough or urban district. . . .

Local Government Act, 1958

PART II

REVIEWS OF LOCAL GOVERNMENT AREAS IN ENGLAND AND WALES

19. Scope of proposals for special review areas In relation to proposals on the review of a special review area, the following paragraphs were added thereto:—

(a) the alteration of the area of a county district;

(b) the constitution of a new non-county borough by the amalgamation of a non-county borough with one or more other county districts;

(c) the constitution of a new urban or rural district by the amalgamation of areas being urban or rural districts or by the aggregation of parts of county districts or the separation of a part of a county district;

(d) the abolition of an urban district or rural district;

(e) the conversion of a rural district into an urban district or of an urban district into a rural district.

(2), (3) and (4) *Provisions on the contents of reports*

23. Power of Minister to give effect to proposals (1) *Proposals of the Commission made on any review held in pursuance of section 17 of this Act may be given effect by order of the Minister. . . .*

24. Power of Minister to initiate changes in default of proposals of Commission

Note. ss. 23 and 24 were repealed by the Local Government (Termination of Reviews) Act, 1967, saving however any report, proposals or notification submitted by the Local Government Commission for England before 10th February, 1966 or for Wales before 1st January, 1963.

P

County Reviews

28. Holding of reviews by county councils (1) *It shall be the duty of each county council in England and Wales to review the circumstances of the county districts within the county and to make such proposals as are hereinafter authorised for effecting changes appearing to the county council desirable in the interests of effective and convenient local government.*

(3) Subject to the provisions of this section, the changes which may be put forward in proposals of a county council are changes to be produced by any of the following means or any combination of those means (including the application of any of the following paragraphs to an area constituted or altered under any of those paragraphs):—

- (*a*) any such means as are specified in paragraphs (*a*) to (*e*) of section 19 of this Act;
- (*b*) the inclusion of a non-county borough in a rural district;
- (*c*) the alteration of the area of a borough so included or of a parish;
- (*d*) the constitution of a new parish by the amalgamation of parishes, by the aggregation of parts of areas within the same rural district, or by the separation of part of an area;
- (*e*) the abolition of a parish;
- (*f*) the grouping of two or more parishes under a common parish council.

(5) The Seventh Schedule to this Act shall apply to boroughs included in rural districts.

29. Procedure on county reviews
(2) *Forthwith after the review is completed, the county council shall submit to the Minister a report on the review together with the proposals as to changes, if any, which they consider desirable, and shall send copies of the report and any proposals to the councils of the county districts in the area to which the review related, and shall publish in one or more local newspapers circulating in those county districts a notice*

that the report has been submitted to the Minister, stating whether any proposals have been made and that copies of the report and any proposals are available for inspection at a specified place within the county, and that representations with respect to any proposals may be made to the Minister within two months of the publication of the notice.

(4) *The Minister shall consider any proposal submitted to him by the county council and any representations with respect thereto which have been made by the council of any borough or urban or rural district or parish council or parish meeting, or by any local government electors, being a council, meeting or electors affected thereby, and may then if he thinks fit make an order giving effect to the proposals or any of them, with or without modifications:*

Provided that if an objection with respect to any proposal is made by any such council or meeting as aforesaid affected thereby, and is not withdrawn, the Minister shall not make an order giving effect to the proposal without first holding a local inquiry into the objection.

(6) *If it appears to the Minister after consultation with such authorities as appear to him to be concerned, that there is a prima facie case for making any change within the powers of a county council on the review, and that the county council have failed to make a proposal for the purpose, the Minister shall publish in one or more local newspapers circulating in the county districts affected a notice stating—*

- (*a*) *that he has it under consideration to make the change;*
- (*b*) *that a copy of his proposals is open to inspection at a specified place within the county; and*
- (*c*) *that representations with respect thereto may be made to him within two months of the publication of the notice;*

and the Minister, after considering any representations duly made, and, if any objections are made by the county council or the council of a borough or urban or rural district or a parish council or parish meeting and are not withdrawn, after holding a local inquiry with respect to the proposals to which the objections relate, may make an order effecting the change or such modified change as appears to him to be expedient.

Provided that where the county council have not submitted proposals they shall not be treated for the purposes of this subsection as having failed to make any particular proposal unless the Minister has fixed a date for the purposes of the foregoing subsection and that date has passed.

Note. Under the Local Government (Termination of Reviews) Act, 1967 the obligation imposed upon county councils by s. 28 ceased on 31st August, 1966 and except for the parts printed in roman type, ss. 28 and 29 were repealed saving any report or proposals made by a county council before or on that day.

The following orders were made:—

Place and Year		S.I. Number
Salop	1966	1966 No. 8
Salop (No. 2)	1966	1966 No. 1529
Herefordshire (Bromyard and Ledbury)	1967	1967 No. 1940
Cornwall (St. Austell with Fowey)	1967	1967 No. 1941
Bedford (Borough of Bedford)	1967	1967 No. 1786
Worcestershire (Droitwich)	1967	1967 No. 1787
Cornwall (Lostwithiel)	1968	1968 No. 5
Cornwall (Padstow)	1968	1968 No. 6

32. County reviews: consequential provisions as to joint boards Where it appears to the appropriate Minister that in consequence of the provisions of any order made or to be made on a review held under section 28, . . . of this Act, being provisions for changing the area or status of any local authority, it is expedient to dissolve, or vary the constitution, functions or area of, a joint board constituted under any enactment other than this Act, the appropriate Minister may by order dissolve the board or, as the case may be, make the variation; and sec-

tion 27 of this Act shall apply in relation to a joint board of which the constitution, functions or area have been varied by an order under this section as it applies in relation to the joint boards mentioned in that section.

General provisions relating to Part II

35. Restriction on promotion of Bills for changes of local government areas or status (1) No local authority shall have power to promote a Bill for forming any new area of local government, or for altering, or altering the status of, any area of local government, before the expiration of fifteen years from the commencement of this Act.

(2) Without prejudice to the foregoing subsection the council of a borough shall not promote a Bill for the purpose of constituting the borough a county borough unless the population of the borough is one hundred thousand or more.

(3) In subsection (1) of this section 'area of local government' means a county, a borough, an urban or rural district, or a parish.

38. Consequential and transitional arrangements relating to Part II (1) An order under this Part of this Act may contain such incidental, consequential, transitional or supplementary provisions as may be necessary or proper for the purposes or in consequence of the order and for giving full effect thereto; and nothing in any other provision of this Act shall be construed as prejudicing the generality of this subsection.

(2) Such provisions as are mentioned in the foregoing subsection may be made with respect to administrative and judicial arrangements and with respect to the transfer and management or custody of property (whether real or personal), may provide for applying, amending or repealing any Act, and may provide for any of the matters specified in paragraphs (*a*) to (*h*) of subsection (1) of section 148 of the Act of 1933; and subsections (2) and (3) of that section . . . shall apply to such

orders as are mentioned in the foregoing subsection.

(3) *An order under this Part of this Act constituting a new borough by the amalgamation of county boroughs, the division of a county borough, or the amalgamation of a non-county borough with other county districts may make provision for the charter of the new borough, by applying thereto, with any necessary exceptions or modifications, the charter of any amalgamated borough, or of the divided borough, as the case may be, or, in the case of an amalgamation including two or more boroughs, by applying as aforesaid to the new borough provisions of charters of two or more amalgamated boroughs or the charter of one and provisions of the charter of one or more of the others.*

(5) *In submitting their proposals under this Part of this Act . . . a county council may include recommendations as to the provision to be made in any order of the Minister in pursuance of subsections (1) to (4) of this section.*

Note. Repealed but for savings see notes to ss. 23 and 24, and 28 and 29.

39. Financial provisions (1) Sections 151 and 152 of the Act of 1933 shall apply to orders under this Part of this Act.

41. Revocation of orders (1) Any order of the Minister made on a review under this Part of this Act may be varied or revoked by order of the Minister made in accordance with the following provisions of this section.

(2) The Minister shall prepare a draft of the varying or revoking order, shall send copies of the draft to such local or public authorities as appear to him to be concerned, and shall give public notice, in such manner as appears to him sufficient for informing persons likely to be concerned, that the draft has been prepared, that a copy thereof is available for inspection at a place specified in the notice and that representations with respect thereto may be made to the Minister within two months of the publication of the notice.

(3) The Minister shall consider any representations duly made with respect to the draft and may then if he thinks fit make an order either in the form of the draft or subject to modifications, so

however that if any objection to the draft is duly made by any authority appearing to the Minister to be affected thereby, and is not withdrawn, the Minister shall not make the order without first holding a local inquiry into the objection.

(4) The foregoing section shall apply to an order under this section as it applies to the order varied or revoked.

43. Boundaries between English and Welsh areas not to be affected *Nothing in this Part of this Act shall be construed as enabling any alteration of areas to be made so as to alter the boundary between an area in England and one in Wales.*

Note. Repealed but for savings see notes to ss. 23-4 and ss. 28-9.

44. Provisions as to Cinque Ports (1) No change of area or status effected *under this Part of this Act* or under section 149 of the Act of 1933 shall affect the continuance of the Confederation of the Cinque Ports.

(2) An order under *this Part of this Act or* the said section 141 affecting any port or ancient town of the Confederation may make provision for securing the continued discharge of functions in relation to the Confederation (including, but without prejudice to the generality of the foregoing, provision for the preservation so far as necessary for the purposes of this section, and with or without modifications, of any existing corporation), for appropriating property or providing funds for the discharge of functions as aforesaid, and otherwise for securing that anything required or authorised to be done by, to, or in relation to the Confederation or any Court thereof may continue to be done.

(3) Subsection (5) of section 38 of this Act shall apply in relation to the foregoing provisions of this section as it applies in relation to subsections (1) to (4) of that section.

45. Saving for Prerogative The enabling provisions of this Part of this Act shall be deemed to be in addition to, and not in derogation of, the powers exercisable by Her Majesty by virtue of Her royal prerogative.

PART IV

GENERAL AND SUPPLEMENTARY

General amendments relating to local government finance

56. Contributions by county councils to expenses ... (2) A county council may make any contribution the council think fit towards expenditure of the council of a borough to which the Seventh Schedule to this Act applies or by a parish council or parish meeting in connection with the exercise of the functions of the council or meeting relating to public open spaces.

Supplementary provisions

59. Change of name of county or borough (1) The council of a . . . borough may with the consent of the Minister change the name of the . . . borough.

(2) Where the name of a borough is changed in pursuance of this section the charter of the borough shall have effect as if the new name were substituted for the old in the name of the borough and its corporation.

(3) Every change of name made in pursuance of this section shall be published in such manner as the Minister may direct.

(4) A change of name made in pursuance of this section shall not affect any rights or obligations of any county, of any borough, or of any council, authority, or person, or render defective any legal proceedings, and any legal proceedings may be commenced or continued as if there had been no change of name.

60. Transfer and compensation of officers (1) Any order under Part II of this Act or scheme under Part III thereof may contain provisions as to the transfer of existing officers affected by the order or scheme and shall contain provisions for the protection of the interests of any such existing officers.

(2) Provision shall be made, by regulations made by such Minister as may be determined by the Treasury to be appropriate in relation to the persons to whom the regulations relate, for the payment by such authority as may be prescribed by or determined under the regulations, but subject to such exceptions or conditions as may be so prescribed, of compensation to or in respect of persons who are, or who but for any national service of theirs would be, the holders of any such place, situation or employment as may be so prescribed and who suffer loss of employment or loss or diminution of emoluments which is attributable to the provisions of any such order or scheme as is mentioned in subsection (1) of this section or of any scheme or order under sections 43 to 45, or Part VI, of the Act of 1933; and so much of section 150 of that Act as provides for compensation shall not apply to any scheme or order under the said Part VI, but without prejudice to any instrument to which it is applied by any other enactment.

(3) Regulations under the foregoing subsection may include provision as to the manner in which and the person to whom any claim for compensation under this section is to be made, and for the determination of all questions arising under the regulations.

(4) In this section—

'existing officer', in relation to an order or scheme, means an officer serving on such date or dates as may be specified in the order or scheme in relation to him;

'national service' means any such service in any of Her Majesty's forces or other employment (whether or not in the service of Her Majesty) as may be prescribed by regulations under this section;

'officer' includes the holder of any place, situation or employment.

(5) Any regulations under this section shall be subject to annulment in pursuance of a resolution of either House of Parliament.

62. Minor and consequential amendments The enactments specified in the Eighth Schedule to this Act shall have effect, as respects England and Wales, subject to the amendments specified in that Schedule, being minor amendments or amendments consequential on the foregoing provisions of this Act.

63. General provisions as to local inquiries (1) Without prejudice to any requirement under the foregoing provisions of this Act, a Minister may cause a local inquiry to be held for the purpose of any of his functions under this Act.

(2) Subsections (2) to (5) of section 290 of the Act of 1933 (which relate to the giving of evidence at inquiries and the payment of costs) shall apply to all inquiries held for the purposes of this Act.

65. Ascertainment of population Save as otherwise expressly provided, for the purposes of Parts II to IV of this Act the population of an area shall be taken to be its population as estimated in the latest estimate published by the Registrar General for England and Wales.

66. Interpretation (1) In this Act, except where the context otherwise requires, the following expressions have the meanings hereby assigned to them respectively, that is to say:—

'Act of 1933' means the Local Government Act, 1933;

'Act of 1948' means the Local Government Act, 1948;

'Act of 1955' means the Rating and Valuation (Miscellaneous Provisions) Act, 1955;

'Area Board' means a Board constituted under the Electricity Act, 1947, 'the Generating Board' means the Central Electricity Generating Board, and 'Electricity Board' means the Generating Board or an Area Board;

'borough' includes any description of borough;

'county functions' and 'district functions' have the meanings assigned by subsection (2) of section 20 of this Act:

'expenditure' includes sums paid by virtue of a precept or other instrument or by way of contribution;

'functions' means powers or duties;

'Gas Board' means an Area Board constituted under the Gas Act, 1948, for an area in England or Wales;

'joint board' includes a combined authority or joint committee;

'Minister' means the Minister of Housing and Local Government;

'appropriate Minister' means, in relation to any matter, the Minister in charge of the Government Department concerned or primarily concerned with that matter;

'parish' means a rural parish;

(2) In Parts II to IV of this Act, except where the context otherwise requires, the expression 'local authority' means the council of a county, county borough or county district and in the said Part II includes the Council of the Isles of Scilly.

(4) References in this Act to any enactment shall be construed as references to that enactment as amended by any subsequent enactment, including this Act.

SEVENTH SCHEDULE

BOROUGHS INCLUDED IN RURAL DISTRICTS

Status of boroughs included in rural districts

1.—(1) On the inclusion of a borough in a rural district—

(a) the Municipal Corporations Act, 1882, and the provisions of the Act of 1933 relating to boroughs shall cease to apply to it;

(b) any other provision made with respect to local authorities, or the areas, functions or officers of local authorities, by any enactment passed or instrument made before the commencement of this Act, except a provision as to any matter as to which provision is made by this Act, shall apply in relation to the borough as it applies in relation to a parish having a separate parish council,

except as otherwise provided in this Schedule.

(2) References in any enactment or instrument (whether passed or made before or after the commencement of

this Act) to a borough shall be construed, except as otherwise provided in this Schedule, as not including a borough which has been included in a rural district, and, in any provision applied by sub-paragraph (1) of this paragraph, references to a parish council and the chairman of such a council shall be construed as including respectively the council and the mayor of such a borough.

(3) On the inclusion of a borough in a rural district any power under its charter to make byelaws shall, except as otherwise provided by the order effecting the inclusion, cease, but without prejudice to any power of the council of the borough under the provisions applied by sub-paragraph (1) of this paragraph.

(4) Notwithstanding the inclusion of a borough in a rural district any parish comprised in the borough shall remain an urban parish.

Power to act by council

2. The corporation of a borough which has been included in a rural district shall be capable of acting by the council of the borough.

Name of corporation

3. On the inclusion of a borough in a rural district the corporate name of its inhabitants shall be changed by the omission of the word 'aldermen'.

Status and composition of council

4.—(1) The council of a borough which has been included in a rural district shall be a local authority within the meaning of the Act of 1933 and shall consist of the mayor and councillors.

(2) There shall be no parish meeting for such a borough, and any power exercisable, under the provisions applied by sub-paragraph (1) of paragraph 1 of this Schedule, by a parish meeting shall in the case of such a borough be exercisable by the council thereof and so much of those provisions as requires the consent of the parish meeting, and section 45 of the Act of 1933 (which enables a county council

on the application of a parish meeting to group parishes under a common parish council) shall not apply to such a borough.

Mayor and deputy mayor

5.—(1) The mayor of a borough which has been included in a rural district shall be elected annually by the council from among the councillors or persons qualified to be councillors of the borough.

(2) The election of the mayor shall be the first business transacted at the annual meeting of the council.

(3) The mayor shall, unless he resigns or ceases to be qualified or becomes disqualified, continue in office until his successor is elected.

(4) During his term of office the mayor shall continue to be a member of the council, notwithstanding the provisions of this Schedule relating to the retirement of councillors.

(5) The council may pay to the mayor for the purpose of enabling him to meet the expenses of his office such allowance as the council may think reasonable.

(6) The mayor shall have precedence in all places in the borough, but this sub-paragraph shall not affect Her Majesty's royal prerogative.

(7) The mayor may appoint a member of the council to be deputy mayor.

(8) The deputy mayor shall, unless he resigns or ceases to be qualified or becomes disqualified, hold office until immediately after the election of a mayor at the next annual meeting of the council and during that time shall continue to be a member of the council, notwithstanding the provisions of this Schedule relating to the retirement of councillors.

(9) Subject to any standing orders made by the council of the borough, anything authorised or required to be done by, to or before the mayor may be done by, to or before the deputy mayor.

Number and election of councillors

6.—(1) The number of councillors of a borough which has been included in a rural district shall be such number, not being less than five nor more than twenty-one, as may be fixed from time to time by the Minister.

(2) The term of office of councillors shall be three years and shall begin and end on the twentieth day of May, except that a person elected to fill a casual vacancy among councillors shall hold office from the date of his election until the date on which the person in whose place he was elected would have been due to retire.

(3) The councillors shall be elected by the local government electors for the borough except that a casual vacancy among councillors shall be filled by the council, which shall be convened forthwith for that purpose.

(4) An order for the inclusion of a borough in a rural district may divide it into wards for the purpose of the election of councillors; and (without prejudice to the generality of paragraph 1 of this Schedule) sections 52 and 55 of the Act of 1933 shall apply in relation to boroughs included in rural districts, and the wards and councillors of such boroughs, as they apply in relation to parishes, parish wards and parish councillors.

Town clerk and other officers

9.—(1) the person appointed under section 114 of the Act of 1933 as applied by paragraph 1 of this Schedule to be clerk of the council of a borough which has been included in a rural district shall be styled town clerk.

(2) The council of a borough which has been included in a rural district shall have power, in addition to that conferred by the said section 114 as so applied, to appoint such officers and servants (who shall hold office or be employed during the pleasure of the council) as the council think necessary for the efficient discharge of the functions of the council, and may pay to any person appointed under this sub-paragraph such reasonable remuneration as they may determine.

Power to take security

10. The council of a borough which has been included in a rural district shall have the same power under section 119 of the Act of 1933 to take security as if the borough had not been so included, and any officer appointed by the council from among their number shall for the purposes of that section be deemed to be an officer employed by them.

Additional expenses of council

11. An order for the inclusion of a borough in a rural district may modify subsection (3) of section 193 of the Act of 1933 in its application to the borough by adding such expenses as may be specified in the order to those which are exempted from the limit imposed by that subsection on the sums that may be raised to meet the expenses of the council.

Saving for boroughs being counties and boroughs having separate commissions of the peace

12.—(1) Paragraph 1 of this Schedule shall not affect the application or construction of any enactment in so far as it refers to a borough as an area being a county of itself or having a sheriff or an area for which justices are appointed or an area having a separate court of quarter sessions, except that section 171 of the Municipal Corporations Act, 1882 (which relates to the appointment of coroners) shall not apply to a borough which has been included in a rural district.

Provisions as to land

13.—(2) Without prejudice to any power to acquire land under the provisions applied by sub-paragraph (1) of paragraph 1 of this Schedule, where a borough has been included in a rural district any power under its charter to acquire land shall cease, but (whether or not its charter confers any such power) the council for the borough shall have power to acquire land in exchange for, or with capital money arising from, corporate land of the borough.

(3) For the purposes of their functions under subsection (1) of section 25 of the Justices of the Peace Act, 1949

EIGHTH SCHEDULE

(which relates to the provision of court houses) the council of a borough which has been included in a rural district shall have the same powers of acquiring or appropriating land as if it had not been so included.

(4) Sections 163 and 172 and paragraph (*a*) of section 217 of the Act of 1933 (which confer powers of appropriation of land and disposal of corporate land and contain savings for mortgages) shall apply in relation to a borough which has been included in a rural district as they apply in relation to a borough not so included.

(5) In this paragraph 'corporate land' has the same meaning as in the Act of 1933.

Application of enactments relating to trusts, freemen, and records and documents

14. The following enactments shall apply in relation to a borough which has been included in a rural district as they apply in relation to a borough not so included, that is to say, sections 134 and 135 of the Municipal Corporations Act, 1882, and Part XIV, subsection (2) of section 279 and subsection (5) of section 283 of the Act of 1933.

Saving for charter

15. The inclusion of a borough in a rural district shall not affect the provisions of its charter except in so far as they are inconsistent with the foregoing provisions of this Schedule or with any provision of the order effecting the inclusion or of any order amending that order.

Surrender of charter

16. Where a borough has been included in a rural district no petition shall be presented for the amendment of its charter or the grant to it of an amending or supplementary charter; but if a petition is presented for the acceptance of a surrender of its charter the Minister may by order provide for the conversion of the borough into a parish, and section 38 of this Act shall apply accordingly.

7.—(2).—. . . the following provisions shall have effect where proposals are made to the Minister as mentioned in the said section 140:—

(*a*) the local authority making the proposals shall deposit in the office of the authority such maps illustrating the proposals as the Minister may require, and the maps so deposited shall be available for inspection, without payment, at all reasonable hours by local or public authorities or other persons concerned;

(*b*) notice of the submission of the proposals and of the deposit of the maps, together with copies of the proposals and such maps as the Minister may require, shall be sent to every county council, borough council, urban or rural district council, parish council and parish meeting appearing to the council submitting the proposals to be concerned, and the notice shall indicate that representations with respect to the proposals may be made to the Minister within six weeks of the giving of the notice;

(*c*) the like notice shall be published in the London Gazette and in one or more newspapers circulating in the locality to which the proposals relate;

(*d*) the requirement of the said subsection (1) that the Minister shall cause a local inquiry to be held before making an order shall not apply if the Minister is satisfied in any particular case that an inquiry is unnecessary.

8.—(1) Section 141 of the Act of 1933 shall have effect as if for the changes specified in subsection (1) thereof there were substituted the changes to be produced by any such means or combination of means as is specified in subsection (3) of section 28 of this Act, excluding the means specified in paragraph (*f*) of that subsection but including the constitution of new urban parishes by the amalgamation of urban parishes; and in subsection (7) of the said section 141 for the words from 'alteration' to 'parts thereof' there shall be substituted the words 'constitution of new urban parishes by the amalgamation of urban parishes'.

(2) The Minister shall not be required to hold a local inquiry before taking further action under subsection (5) of the said section 141 in any case where he is satisfied that the holding of the inquiry is unnecessary.

(3) An order of the Minister confirming an order under the said section 141 constituting a new borough by the amalgamation of a non-county borough with other county districts may make provision for the charter of the new borough, by applying thereto, with any necessary exceptions or modifications, the charter of any amalgamated borough, or, in the case of an amalga-mation including two or more boroughs, by applying as aforesaid to the new borough provisions of charters of two or more amalgamated boroughs or the charter of one and provisions of the charters of one or more of the others.

9. In section 143 of the Act of 1933, subsection (1) shall cease to have effect, and subsection (2) of that section shall be amended as follows:—

(a) the subsection shall apply to a joint representation by two county councils as it applies to a joint representation by a county council and a county borough council;

(b) the reference to altering the boundary shall include a reference to any transference of part of the county or county borough, as the case may be, but not so as to authorise the abolition of any county district.

Litter Act, 1958

[7th July 1958]

1. Penalty for leaving litter (1) If any person throws down, drops or otherwise deposits in, into or from any place in the open air to which the public are entitled or permitted to have access without payment, and leaves, any thing whatsoever in such circumstances as to cause, contribute to, or tend to lead to, the defacement by litter of any place in the open air, then, unless that depositing and leaving was authorised by law or was done with the consent of the owner, occupier or other person or authority having the control of the place in or into which that thing was deposited, he shall be guilty of an offence and be liable on summary conviction to a fine not exceeding ten pounds; and for the purposes of this subsection any covered place open to the air on at least one side and available for public use shall be treated as being a place in the open air.

(2) In England and Wales, without prejudice to the powers of any other person, any of the following bodies shall have power to institute proceedings for an offence under this section committed within their area or on land controlled or managed by them, that is to say, the council of a county, . . . non-county borough, urban district, rural district or rural parish, the Common Council of the City of London, a joint body constituted solely of two or more such councils as aforesaid, and a joint board such as is provided for by section 8 of the National Parks and Access to the Countryside Act, 1949.

Physical Training and Recreation Act, 1958

1. Power to make loans to voluntary organisations (1) The power conferred on local authorities by sub-section (4) of section 4 of the Physical Training and Recreation Act, 1937 (which relates to contributions by local authorities towards expenses of providing and maintaining gymnasiums, playing fields, swimming baths and other facilities) shall include power for a local authority to make a loan to a voluntary organisation for meeting (wholly or in part) any expenses of that organisation, being expenses towards which the local authority could make a contribution under that subsection:

Provided that a loan shall not be made in the exercise of that power for meeting any expenses of maintenance, or for meeting any other expenses which are not of such a description as to be properly chargeable to capital account.

(2) Any loan made by a local authority under the power referred to in the preceding subsection may be made upon such terms as the authority think fit.

3. Interpretation In this Act the expressions 'local authority' and 'voluntary organisation' shall have the same meanings as those assigned to them in the Physical Training and Recreation Act, 1937.

Manoeuvres Act, 1958

[18th December 1958]

1. Power to authorise execution of manœuvres (1) Subject to the provisions of this section, Her Majesty may from time to time by Order in Council authorise the execution of defence manœuvres within such area (in this Act referred to as 'the manœuvres area') and during such period (in this Act referred to as 'the manœuvres period'), being a period not exceeding three months and beginning not less than nine months after the date on which the Order is made, as may be specified in the Order; and any such Order (in this Act referred to as a 'manœuvres Order')—

(a) shall define the manœuvres area both by description and by reference to a map, the latter definition prevailing in the case of any discrepancy; and

(b) without prejudice to the power of Her Majesty to authorise any persons to take part in the manœuvres, shall indicate the description of military, naval or air force formations, and the number of such formations of each description, which, at the time notice of the intention to make the Order was first published in accordance with subsection (3) of this section, were intended so to take part.

(2) No land shall be included in a manœuvres area more than once in any period of five years except—

(a) in the case of land in England or Wales, with the consent of the council of the county or county borough in which the land is situated and, if the land is situated in the New Forest, with the consent of the Verderers of the New Forest;

Provided that for the purposes of this subsection a manœuvres Order under which no manœuvres are executed shall be disregarded.

(3) No recommendation shall be made to Her Majesty in Council to make a manœuvres Order unless—

(a) not less than two months before the date on which the Order is to be made, a draft of the Order has been sent—

(i) to each of the following authorities any part of whose area is included in the manœuvres area, that is to say, any local authority, any river board, the Conservators of the River Thames, the Lee Conservancy Catchment Board, any parish council in England or Wales . . .

(ii) if any part of the New Forest is so included, to the Verderers of the New Forest; and

(iii) except when the whole of the manœuvres area is in Scotland, to the *National Parks Commission*,

and notice of the intention to make the Order has been published in local newspapers which between them circulate in all local authority areas which are wholly or partly so included; and

(*b*) a draft of the Order has been laid before, and approved by a resolution of, each House of Parliament.

2. Powers exercisable for purposes of manœuvres (1) Subject to the provisions of this Act, any persons taking part with the authority of Her Majesty in the manœuvres authorised by a manœuvres Order (in this Act referred to as 'authorised forces') may, under the direction of the *Secretary of State*, within the manœuvres area and during the manœuvres period—

(*a*) pass over, and encamp, construct works not of a permanent character and execute defence manœuvres on, any land; and

(*b*) supply themselves with water from any source of water and, for that purpose, dam up any running water:

Provided that water shall not by virtue of this subsection be dammed up in such manner as to interfere with the carrying on of any trade or industry, or be taken from any source of supply belonging to a private owner or public authority in such quantities as to reduce the water available for use by the persons entitled to use that source of supply below what is shown to be required by those persons.

(2) The foregoing subsection shall not authorise entry on or interference with—

(*b*) any place of worship or ground attached thereto, or any burial ground;

(*c*) any school or ground attached thereto;

Provided that nothing in this subsection shall restrict the use by the authorised forces of any highway or park.

(3) The officer directing the manœuvres shall take care that there is no interference with earthworks, ruins or other remains of antiquarian or historical interest, or with any picturesque or valuable timber or other natural features of exceptional interest or beauty, and shall be empowered to prevent trespass or damage to property by persons not belonging to those forces, and shall as soon and as far as practicable cause all lands used under the powers conferred by this section to be restored to their previous condition.

(4) Subject to section three and to subsection (1) of section 8 of this Act, nothing in this Act shall prejudicially affect any public right or any right of common.

3. Powers to close highways (1) Where, in the case of, or of any part of, any highway which is a trunk road or a special road within the meaning of the *Special Roads Act*, 1949, or which is repairable *by the inhabitants at large*, being a highway or part situated within the manœuvres area, an application for the purpose is made by a person authorised in that behalf by the *Secretary of State*, and not less than seven days' notice of the intention to make the application has been published in one or more newspapers circulating generally in the district in question, two or more justices of the peace sitting in petty session in the petty sessions area within which that highway or part of a highway is situated may, if they think fit, by order—

(*a*) subject to such terms and conditions as may be required by the justices for the protection of individuals or of the public or of public bodies, suspend for any part of the manœuvres period not exceeding twelve hours, or

(*b*) authorise any officer in command of the authorised forces or any part thereof, being a general or field officer or an officer of corresponding naval or air force rank, to make an order suspending for a time not exceeding six hours in any one day of the said period,

any right of way over that highway or that part of a highway.

(2) In the case of any other highway or part of a highway, being a highway or part situated within the manœuvres area, two justices of the peace may, if they think fit, on the application of a person authorised in that behalf by the *Secretary of State*, by order—

(a) suspend for any part of the manœuvres period not exceeding forty-eight hours, or

(b) authorise any such officer as aforesaid to make an order suspending for a time not exceeding six hours in any one day of the said period,

any right of way over that highway or part of a highway, being a highway or part within the jurisdiction of those justices.

(3) The officer directing the manœuvres shall cause such public notice of any order made under paragraph (a) of either of the two foregoing subsections as the justices may require to be given not less than twelve hours before the order comes into force, and provide for the giving of all reasonable facilities for traffic whilst the order is in force; and any officer making an order by virtue of paragraph (b) of either of the two foregoing subsections shall take such steps as in the circumstances he may consider practicable for giving publicity to his intention to make that order and shall give all reasonable facilities for traffic whilst that order is in force.

(4) The justices acting for the purposes of this section shall not be persons belonging to the authorised forces.

4. Manœuvres commissions (1) Whenever a manœuvres Order is made, a commission (in this Act referred to as a 'manœuvres commission') shall be formed . . . [*the rest of the section lays down the membership*].

5. Powers of manœuvres commissions to give directions (1) Subject to section 6 of this Act, a manœuvres commission formed in connection with a manœuvres Order may issue such directions as the commission may consider necessary or expedient for the purpose of avoiding damage or disturbance in consequence of the execution of the manœuvres authorised by the Order beyond what is necessary for the effective carrying out of those manœuvres.

(2) Any such directions shall be so framed as to impose requirements either on the authorised forces or on, or on any class of, occupiers of land, being land comprised within the manœuvres area or land in the vicinity of land so comprised.

(3) Requirements imposed by the directions on the authorised forces may, where the Commission consider it necessary or expedient for avoiding damage or disturbance, include provisions precluding those forces from entering upon land specified in the directions or from using a source of water so specified, or restricting entry upon such land or the use of such land or such a source of water by those forces, notwithstanding that the land or source of water is within the manœuvres area and it shall be the duty of the officer directing the manœuvres to issue such instructions to the authorised forces as, in the opinion of that officer, will secure compliance with any such requirements.

(4) If, where a requirement has been imposed by any such directions on the occupier of any land, that occupier without reasonable cause refuses or fails to comply with that requirement and in consequence thereof any livestock of his is injured, or any other property of his is damaged, he shall not be entitled to compensation in respect of that injury or damage under section 7 of this Act.

(5) Where, by virtue of subsection (3) of section 4 of this Act, two manœuvres commissions have been formed in connection with any manœuvres Order, the power to issue directions conferred

by this section may be exercised by those commissions either separately in relation to their respective parts of the manœuvres area or jointly in relation to the whole of that area.

6. Supplementary provisions as to issue of directions (1) Where a manoeuvres commission formed in connection with a manœuvres Order propose to issue any directions under the last foregoing section, the commission shall consult the *Secretary of State for War* and such other authorities or organisations as they consider appropriate, and shall send to every local authority any part of whose area is comprised within the manœuvres area the following documents, that is to say—

(a) a draft of the directions; and

(b) a copy of the Order,

together with a notice specifying the time (not being less than twenty-one days) within which, and the manner in which, representations may be made to the commission with respect to the draft directions.

(2) A local authority, upon receiving the documents and notice aforesaid, shall make the documents available for a period of not less than two weeks for inspection by the public during reasonable hours at the offices of the authority or at such other place, being a place within their area, as they may consider appropriate, and shall cause to be published in each week of that period in one or more local newspapers circulating in their area notice of the receipt of those documents stating—

(a) the place at which and the hours during which the documents may be inspected; and

(b) in accordance with the notice sent to the local authority, the time within which, and the manner in which, representations may be made to the commission with respect to the draft directions.

(3) Where any such representations are duly made, the commission shall, after giving not less than fourteen days' notice by advertisement in such local newspapers as appear to them to be appropriate, hold a public inquiry (or, if they think fit, two or more public inquiries) into those representations, and shall make such alterations, if any, in the draft directions as they may think fit having regard to those representations and to the results of any such inquiry.

(4) Not later than four months before the beginning of the manœuvres period, the commission shall transmit the draft directions with any alterations made under the last foregoing subsection to the *Secretary of State for War*.

(5) Where any draft directions transmitted to the *Secretary of State* under this section include any such provisions as are mentioned in subsection (3) of section 5 of this Act, and the *Secretary of State* is satisfied that any of those provisions would be likely to have the effect of frustrating all or some of the purposes of the manœuvres Order, the *Secretary of State* may not later than three months before the beginning of the manœuvres period by notice in writing to the commission (a copy of which he shall cause to be laid before each House of Parliament require the draft directions to be varied by deleting those provisions or by modifying them in such manner as may be specified in the notice:

Provided that any variation required by the *Secretary of State* by virtue of this subsection shall be the minimum which in his opinion is necessary to prevent any of the purposes of the Order from being frustrated.

(6) Where the *Secretary of State* determines that no variation of the draft directions is required, he shall as soon as may be give notice to the commission of that determination.

(7) As soon as may be after receipt of a notice under either of the two last foregoing subsections or, if by the date falling three months before the beginning of the manœuvres period no such notice has been received, as soon as may be after that date, the commission shall issue the directions in the form of the draft transmitted to the *Secretary of*

State with any variations required by the *Secretary of State* under subsection (5) of this section; and where any directions are issued with any such variation the directions shall indicate the nature and extent of the variation.

(8) On the issue of the directions the commission shall publish them in such manner as they may consider most suitable for giving notice of the directions to all persons likely to be affected by them.

(9) Where, in a case to which subsection (5) of section 5 of this Act applies, directions fall to be issued separately for different parts of the manœuvres area, the reference to that area in subsection (1) of this section shall be construed as a reference to the part of that area in relation to which the functions of the commission in question fall to be exercised.

7. **Compensation** (1) Where a manœuvres Order has been made, full compensation shall be paid out of moneys provided by Parliament for any damage to person or property or any interference with rights or privileges arising from any of the provisions of this Act, whether or not occasioned by the acts or defaults of the authorised forces, including compensation in re-spect of any expenses reasonably incurred in protecting person, property, rights and privileges and in respect of any damage by reason of excessive weight or extraordinary traffic caused to any highway for the repair of which any public body or any individual is responsible.

(2) The manœuvres commission or commissions formed in connection with the Order shall, with the concurrence of the Treasury, appoint one or more compensation officers to determine as speedily as possible any claim for compensation under this section and settle the amount payable.

(3) The said commission or commissions may make regulations with respect to the procedure for making and determining claims for compensation, for limiting the time within which claims must be made, and for regulating the mode in which compensation is to be paid.

(4) If any claim for compensation under this section is not settled by agreement between a compensation officer appointed under this section and the claimant, the difference between them shall be referred to arbi-tration; . . .

Town and Country Planning Act, 1959

PART II

24. Adjustment of accounts on appropriation of land (1) On an appropriation of land for any purpose by an authority to whom this Part of this Act applies, other than an appropriation falling within the next follow-ing subsection, such adjustment shall be made in the accounts of the authority as may be requisite in the circumstances.

(2) Where land is appropriated for any purpose by an authority to whom this Part of this Act applies, and—

(a) either the land was immediately before the appropriation held by the authority for the purposes of a grant-aided function, or it is appropriated by the authority for the purposes of such a function, and

(b) apart from this section, a Minister would by virtue of any enactment have power to direct an adjust-ment to be made in the accounts of the authority in connection with that appropriation,

such adjustment shall be made in the accounts of the authority as the Minister of Housing and Local Government may direct.

28. Appropriation of land by parish councils and parish meet-ings (1) Any land belonging to a parish council which is not required for the purposes for which it was acquired or has since been appropriated may, subject to the following provisions of this section, be appropriated by the council for any other purpose approved by the Minister of Housing and Local Government and the parish meeting.

(2) In the case of a rural parish not having a separate parish council, any land belonging to the parish meeting which is not required for the purposes for which it was acquired or has since been appropriated may, subject to the following provisions of this section, be appropriated by the parish meeting for any other purpose approved by the Minister of Housing and Local Government.

(3) A parish council or parish meeting shall not create or permit any nuisance on land appropriated by them under this section.

(4) The appropriation of land by a parish council or parish meeting under this section shall be without prejudice to any covenant or restriction affecting the use of the land in their hands.

(5) In the case of an appropriation under this section of land acquired under any enactment or order incorporating the Lands Clauses Acts, any work executed on the land after the appropriation has been effected shall, for the purposes of *Section 68 of the Lands Clauses Consolidation Act*, 1845, be deemed to have been authorised by the enactment or order under which the land was acquired.

(6) Where, by virtue of any enactment other than this section, a parish council have power, with or without the consent of a Minister, or may be authorised, to appropriate land for any purpose, the power conferred by subsection (1) of this section shall not be exercisable by the council for that purpose in relation to that land.

(7) The power conferred by subsection (2) of this section shall not be exercisable by a parish meeting in relation to any land for any purpose for which the parish meeting are or could be empowered (subject to the requisite consents) to appropriate that land under section 22 of the Land Settlement (Facilities) Act, 1919, or for which they

may be authorised to appropriate that land under section 42 of the Act of 1947.

(8) Subsections (1) and (2) of section 24 of this Act shall apply in relation to an appropriation of land by virtue of this section, as if parish councils and parish meetings were authorities to whom this Part of this Act applies.

30. General provisions relating to Part II (1) Any reference in this Part of this Act to a provision that a power is not to be exercised except with the consent of a Minister is a reference to a provision which either—

(a) requires such consent generally in respect of any exercise of the power, or

(b) requires such consent in respect of the exercise of the power in such circumstances as may be specified therein.

(2) For the purposes of this Part of this Act any provision whereby a power is to be exercised only if a Minister specified therein is satisfied as to any matters so specified shall be taken to be a provision that the power shall not be exercised except with the consent of that Minister.

(3) Any reference in this Part of this Act to an enactment whereby a power is conferred on an authority to whom this Part of this Act applies, or on a class of such authorities,—

(a) shall be taken to include any enactment whereby the power in question is conferred on local authorities generally, or on a class of local authorities which includes a class of authorities to whom this Part of this Act applies, or is conferred on a class of authorities to whom this Part of this Act applies together with any other class of local authorities, but

(b) shall not be taken to include any enactment whereby (without particular reference to local authorities, or to bodies of any description specified in the Fourth Schedule to this Act) a power is conferred generally on persons of a description specified in the enactment, notwithstanding that one or more authorities to whom this Part of this Act applies may fall within the description specified in the enactment.

(4) For the purposes of any provision of this Part of this Act whereby the consent of a Minister is required, or directions may be given by a Minister, for any purpose therein mentioned, the consent or directions may be given by that Minister either generally to all authorities to whom the provision relates, or to any class of such authorities, or may be given specifically in any particular case, and (whether given generally or otherwise) may be given either unconditionally or subject to such conditions as the Minister giving

the consent or directions may consider appropriate.

(5) For the purposes of this Part of this Act land shall be taken to have been acquired by an authority in the exercise (directly or indirectly) of compulsory powers if it was acquired by them compulsorily or was acquired by them by agreement at a time when they were authorised by or under an enactment to acquire the land compulsorily:

Provided that land shall not be taken to have been acquired by an authority in the exercise (directly or indirectly) of compulsory powers if it was acquired by them (whether compulsorily or by agreement) in consequence of the service in pursuance of any enactment (including any enactment contained in this Act) of a notice requiring the authority to purchase the land.

Highways Act, 1959

[30 April 1959]

Part III

33. Dedication of highway by agreement with parish council (1) The council of a parish shall have power to enter into an agreement with any person having the necessary power in that behalf for the dedication by that person of a highway over land in the parish or an adjoining parish in any case where such a dedication would in the opinion of the council be beneficial to the inhabitants of the parish or any part thereof.

(2) Where the council of a parish have entered into an agreement under the foregoing subsection for the dedication of a highway they shall have power to carry out any works (including works of maintenance or improvement) incidental to or consequential on the making of the agreement or to contribute towards the expense of carrying out such works, and may agree or combine with the council of any other parish to carry out such works or to make such a contribution.

Part IV

Maintenance of Highways

Highways maintainable at public expense

38. Highways maintainable at public expense (1) After the commencement of this Act no duty with respect to the maintenance of highways shall lie on the inhabitants at large of any area.

(2) Without prejudice to any other enactment (whether contained in this Act or not) whereby a highway may become for the purposes of this Act a highway maintainable at the public expense, and subject to the provisions of this section and of subsection (6) of section 206 of this Act, and to any order of a magistrates' court made under section 50 of this Act, the following highways shall for the purposes of this Act be highways maintainable at the public expense, that is to say—

(a) a highway which immediately before the commencement of this Act was maintainable by the inhabitants at large of any area or maintainable by a highway authority;

(*b*) a highway constructed by a highway authority after the commencement of this Act, otherwise than on behalf of some other person not being a highway authority;

(*c*) a highway constructed by the council of a borough or urban district, the Greater London Council, or the Common Council within their own area under Part V of the Housing Act, 1957, and a highway constructed by a local authority outside their own area under the said Part V, being, in the latter case, a highway the liability to maintain which is, by virtue of the said Part V, vested in the council of the county, borough or district in which the highway is situated;

(*d*) a highway being a trunk road or a special road; and

(*e*) a highway, being a footpath or bridleway, created after the commencement of this Act in consequence of a public path creation order or a public path diversion order or in consequence of an order made by the Minister of Transport or the Minister of Housing and Local Government under section 153 of the Town and Country Planning Act, 1962, or by a competent authority under section 94 of the Town and Country Planning Act, 1968 or dedicated after the said commencement in pursuance of a public path creation agreement.

(3) Paragraph (*a*) of the last foregoing subsection shall not be construed as referring to a highway maintainable by the council of a county, borough or urban district under a contract or otherwise than in their capacity as a highway authority.

(4) Paragraph (*d*) of subsection (2) of this section shall not be construed as referring to a part of a trunk road or special road being a bridge or other part which a person is liable to maintain under a charter or special enactment, or by reason of tenure, enclosure or prescription.

(5) Where, under any rule of law relating to the duty of maintaining a highway by reason of tenure, enclosure or prescription, and apart from any enactment (whether contained in this Act or not), a highway would, on the happening of any event after the commencement of this Act, become, or cease to be, maintainable by the inhabitants at large of any area, the highway shall become, or cease to be, a highway which for the purposes of this Act is a highway maintainable at the public expense:

Provided that a highway shall not by virtue of this subsection become a highway which for the purpose of this Act is a highway maintainable at the public expense unless either—

(*a*) it was a highway before the 31st day of August, 1835; or

(*b*) it became a highway after that date and has at some time been maintainable by the inhabitants at large of any area or a highway maintainable at the public expense;

and a highway shall not by virtue of this subsection cease to be a highway maintainable at the public expense if it is a highway which under any rule of law would become a highway maintainable by reason of enclosure but is prevented from becoming such a highway by section 54 of this Act.

Maintenance of highways maintainable at public expense

44. Duty to maintain highways maintainable at public expense (1) The authority who are for the time being the highway authority for a highway maintainable at the public expense shall, subject to the following subsection, be under a duty to maintain the highway.

(2) An order made by the Minister under section 7 of this Act directing that a highway proposed to be constructed by him shall become a trunk road may direct that—

HIGHWAYS ACT, 1959 451

(*a*) a part of a highway maintainable at the public expense by some other highway authority being a part which crosses the route of the highway to be so constructed, or

(*b*) any highway so maintainable which becomes a trunk road by virtue of the order,

shall, notwithstanding anything in the foregoing provisions of this section, be maintained by that authority until such date, not being later than the date on which the new route is opened for the purposes of through traffic, as may be specified in a notice given by the Minister to that authority.

46. Right of parish councils to maintain footpaths and bridleways The council of a parish shall have power, subject to the restrictions for the time being imposed by any enactment on their expenditure, to undertake the maintenance of any footpath or bridleway within the parish, being in either case a highway maintainable at the public expense:

Provided that nothing in this section shall affect the duty of any highway authority or other person to maintain the footpath or bridleway.

50. Power of magistrates' court to declare unnecessary highway to be not maintainable at public expense (1) Where a highway authority are of opinion that a highway maintainable at the public expense by them is unnecessary for public use and therefore ought not to be maintained at the public expense, they may, subject to the two next following subsections, apply to a magistrates' court for an order declaring that the highway shall cease to be so maintained.

(2) No application shall be made under this section for an order relating to a trunk road, special road, . . . footpath or bridleway.

(3) If a highway authority propose to make an application under this section for an order relating to a highway situated in a rural parish they shall give notice of the proposal to the parish council or, in the case of a parish not having a separate parish council, to the

chairman of the parish meeting, and the application shall not be made if, within two months from the date of service of the notice by the highway authority, notice is given to the highway authority by the parish council or the chairman of the parish meeting, as the case may be, that the council or meeting have refused to consent to the making of the application.

(4) Where an application is made to a magistrates' court under this section, two or more justices of the peace acting for the petty sessions area for which the court acts shall together view the highway to which the application relates, and no further proceedings shall be taken on the application unless they are of opinion, after viewing the highway, that there was ground for making the application.

(5) The clerk to the justices who view a highway in accordance with the provisions of the last foregoing subsection shall, as soon as practicable after the view, notify the highway authority by whom an application under this section relating to the highway was made of the decision of the justices, and, if the justices decide that there was ground for making the application, of the time, not being less than six weeks from the date of the notice, and place, at which the application is to be heard by a magistrates' court.

(6) A magistrates' court shall not hear an application under this section unless it is satisfied that the highway authority making the application have—

(*a*) not less than one month before the date on which the application is to be heard by the court, given notice to the owners and occupiers of all lands adjoining the highway to which the application relates of the making of the application, and the purpose thereof, and of the time and place at which the application is to be heard by the court, and

(*b*) given public notice in the terms and manner required by the next following subsection.

(7) A highway authority making an application under this section shall publish, once at least in each of the four weeks immediately preceding the week in which the application is to be heard, in a local newspaper circulating in the area in which the highway to which the application relates is situated, a notice—

(a) stating that an application has been made to a magistrates' court under this section and the purpose of the application,
(b) describing the highway, and
(c) specifying the time and place at which the application is to be heard,

and shall cause a copy of the notice to be fixed, at least fourteen days before the date on which the application is to be heard by the court, to the principal doors of every church and chapel in the parish in which the highway is situated, or in some conspicuous position near the highway.

(8) On the hearing of an application for an order under this section, a magistrates' court shall hear any person who objects to the order being made and may either dismiss the application or make an order declaring that the highway to which the application relates shall cease to be maintained at the public expense.

(9) Where an order is made under this section the highway to which the order relates shall cease to be a highway maintainable at the public expense.

(10) The highway authority on whose application an order is made under this section shall give notice of the making of the order to any public utility undertakers having apparatus under, in, upon, over, along or across the highway to which the order relates.

53. Maintenance of privately maintainable footpaths and bridleways (1) Where apart from section 44 of this Act a person would under a special enactment or by reason of tenure, enclosure or prescription be under an obligation to maintain a footpath or bridleway, the operation of subsection (1) of the said section 44

shall not release him from the obligation.

(2) The council of a parish shall have power, subject to the restrictions for the time being imposed by any enactment on their expenditure, to undertake by virtue of this subsection the maintenance of any footpath or bridleway within the parish (other than a footpath or bridleway the maintenance of which they have power to undertake under section 46 of this Act) whether or not any other person is under a duty to maintain the footpath or bridleway:

Provided that nothing in this subsection shall affect the duty of any other person to maintain the footpath or bridleway.

Enforcement of liability for maintenance

59. Enforcement of liability to maintain highway (1) No indictment shall be preferred in respect of neglect to maintain a highway.

(2) A person (in this and the next following section referred to as 'the complainant') who alleges that a way or bridge—

(a) is a highway maintainable at the public expense or a highway which a person is liable to maintain under a special enactment or by reason of tenure, enclosure or prescription, and
(b) is out of repair,

may serve a notice on the highway authority or other person alleged to be liable to maintain the way or bridge (in this and the next following section referred to as 'the respondent') requiring the respondent to state whether he admits that the way or bridge is a highway and that he is liable to maintain it.

(3) If, within one month from the date of service on him of a notice under the last foregoing subsection, the respondent does not serve on the complainant a notice admitting both that the way or bridge in question is a highway and that the respondent is liable to maintain it, the complainant may apply to a court of quarter sessions

for an order requiring the respondent, if the court finds that the way or bridge is a highway which the respondent is liable to maintain and is out of repair, to put it in proper repair within such reasonable period as may be specified in the order.

(4) If, within one month from the date of service on him of a notice under subsection (2) of this section, the respondent serves on the complainant a notice admitting both that the way or bridge in question is a highway and that the respondent is liable to maintain it, the complainant may, within six months from the date of service on him of that notice, apply to a magistrates' court for an order requiring the respondent, if the court finds that the highway is out of repair, to put it in proper repair within such reasonable period as may be specified in the order.

(5) A court, in determining under this section whether a highway is out of repair, shall not be required to view the highway unless it thinks fit, and such a view may be made by any two or more of the members of the court.

(6) Where an application under this section relates to a footpath or bridleway in respect of which a highway authority have made a certificate under *section thirty* of this Act, the court by whom the application is heard shall, in deciding whether the footpath or bridleway is out of repair, have regard to the provisions of subsection (3) of that section.

(7) If at the expiration of the period specified in an order made under subsection (3) or subsection (4) of this section a magistrates' court is satisfied that the highway to which the order relates has not been put in proper repair, then, unless the court thinks fit to extend the period, it shall by order authorise the complainant (if he has not the necessary power in that behalf) to carry out such works as may be necessary to put the highway in proper repair.

(8) Any expenses which a complainant reasonably incurs in carrying out works authorised by an order under the last foregoing subsection shall be re-coverable from the respondent summarily as a civil debt.

(9) Where any expenses authorised by an order under subsection (7) of this section to be incurred in carrying out the works necessary to put a highway in proper repair are recovered from the respondent, then, if the respondent would have been entitled to recover from some other person the whole or part of the expenses of repairing the highway in question if he had repaired it himself, he shall be entitled to recover from that other person the whole or the like part, as the case may be, of the expenses recovered from him.

(10) Where an application is made under this section for an order requiring the respondent to put a highway maintainable at the public expense, being a footpath or bridleway, in proper repair and some other person is liable to maintain the highway under a special enactment or by reason of tenure, enclosure or prescription, that other person shall have a right to be heard by the court which hears the application, but only on the question whether the highway is in proper repair.

60. Applications to quarter sessions under s. 59 (1) An application to a court of quarter sessions for an order under the last foregoing section shall be made to a court of quarter sessions having jurisdiction in the county or borough in which the way or bridge to which the application relates is situated.

(2) The complainant for the order shall give notice in writing of the application to the clerk of the peace and the notice shall specify—

   (*a*) the situation of the way or bridge to which the application relates,
   (*b*) the name of the respondent,
   (*c*) the part of the way or bridge which is alleged to be out of repair, and
   (*d*) the nature of the alleged disrepair;

and the complainant shall serve a copy of the notice on the respondent.

(3) The clerk of the peace shall enter the application and shall in due course give notice to the complainant and to the respondent of the date, time and place fixed for the hearing of the application.

(4) A court of quarter sessions may from time to time adjourn the hearing of any such application and may make such order as to costs to be paid by either party to the application as it thinks fit.

61. Further provisions for enforcement of liability to maintain privately maintainable highways (1) Where a person is liable under a special enactment or by reason of tenure, enclosure or prescription to maintain a footpath or bridleway, being in either case a highway maintainable at the public expense, and the highway authority for the highway repair it in performance of their duty to maintain it, they may, subject to subsection (3) of this section, recover the necessary expenses of doing so from that person in any court of competent jurisdiction.

(3) The right of recovery conferred by the foregoing provisions of this section shall not be exercisable—

(*a*) in a case where a highway authority repair a footpath or bridleway in obedience to an order of a court made under section 59 of this Act unless not less than twenty-one days before the date on which the application was heard by the court the authority gave notice to the person liable to maintain the path or way of the making of an application with respect to it and of the time and place at which the application was to be heard by the court, so however that the obligation to give notice to him imposed by this paragraph shall not operate if he was the person on whose application the order of the court was made;

(*b*) in any other case, unless the highway authority, before repairing the highway, have given notice to

the person liable to maintain it that the highway is not in proper repair, specifying a reasonable time within which he may repair it, and he has failed to repair it within that time.

(4) Where a highway authority exercise a right of recovery under the foregoing provisions of this section from the person liable to maintain the highway in question, then, if that person would have been entitled to recover from some other person the whole or part of the expenses of repairing the highway if he had repaired it himself, he shall be entitled to recover from that other person the whole or the like part, as the case may be, of the expenses recovered from him by the highway authority.

Trees, shrubs and verges

82. Powers of highway and local authorities to plant trees, lay out grass verges, etc. (1) Subject to the provisions of this section, a highway authority may, in a highway maintainable at the public expense by them, *plant trees and shrubs* and lay out grass verges, and may erect and maintain guards or fences and otherwise do anything expedient for the maintenance or protection of *trees, shrubs* and grass verges planted or laid out, whether or not by them, in such a highway.

A highway authority may alter or remove any grass verge, whether or not by them, in such a highway, and any guard, fence or other thing provided, whether or not by them for the maintenance or protection of any tree, shrub or verge in such a highway.

(2) Subject to the following provisions of this section, a highway authority may exercise the like powers as are conferred by the foregoing subsection on any land acquired in exercise of powers conferred on them by subsection (2), subsection (5), or subsection (6) of section 214 of this Act, or by section 215 thereof, notwithstanding that the land does not form part of a highway.

(3) A local authority, if they are not

the highway authority for a highway maintainable at the public expense in their area, may, with the consent of the highway authority therefor, exercise with respect to that highway any of the powers conferred by subsection (1) of this section on the highway authority.

(4) Subject to the restrictions for the time being imposed by any enactment on their expenditure, the council of a parish may, with the consent of the highway authority for a highway maintainable at the public expense in the parish, exercise with respect to that highway any of the powers conferred by subsection (1) of this section on the highway authority.

(5) No tree, shrub, grass verge, guard or fence shall be planted, laid out or erected under this section, or, if planted, laid out or erected thereunder, allowed to remain, in such a situation as to hinder the reasonable use of the highway by any person entitled to the use thereof, or so as to be a nuisance or injurious to the owner or occupier of premises adjacent to the highway.

(6) If damage is caused to the property of any person by anything done in exercise of the powers conferred by this section, that person shall, unless his negligence caused the damage, be entitled to recover compensation therefor from the authority or parish council by whom the powers were exercised:

Provided that if that person by his negligence contributed to the damage the compensation shall be reduced accordingly.

(8) References in this section to trees or shrubs shall be construed as including references to plants of any description.

PART VI

STOPPING UP AND DIVERSION OF HIGHWAYS

108. Power of magistrates' court to authorise the stopping up or diversion of a highway (1) Subject to the provisions of this section, if it appears to a magistrates' court, after a view, if the court thinks fit, by any two or more of the justices composing the court, that a highway (not being a trunk road or a special road) as respects which the appropriate authority have made an application under this section—

(a) is unnecessary, or
(b) can be diverted so as to make it nearer or more commodious to the public,

the court may by order authorise it to be stopped up, or, as the case may be, to be so diverted.

(2) If an authority propose to make an application under this section for an order relating to a highway situated in a rural parish (not being a classified road) they shall give notice of the proposal to the council of the rural district which comprises the parish and to the parish council or, in the case of a parish not having a separate parish council, to the chairman of the parish meeting, and the application shall not be made if, within two months from the date of service of the notice by the authority, notice is given to the authority either by the council of the rural district or by the parish council or the chairman of the parish meeting, as the case may be, that the council or meeting have refused to consent to the making of the application.

(3) An application under this section may be made, and an order thereunder may provide, for the stopping up or diversion of a highway for the purposes of all traffic, or subject to the reservation of a footpath or bridleway.

(4) An application or order made under this section may include two or more highways which are connected with each other.

(5) A magistrates' court shall not make an order under this section unless it is satisfied that the applicant authority have given the notices required by Part I of the Twelfth Schedule to this Act.

(6) On the hearing of an application under this section the applicant authority, any person to whom notice is

required to be given under paragraph 1 of the said Twelfth Schedule, any person who uses the highway and any other person who would be aggrieved by the making of the order applied for, shall have a right to be heard.

(7) An order under this section authorising the diversion of a highway—

(a) shall not be made unless the written consent of the local planning authority (if not the applicants), and of every person having a legal interest in the land over which the highway is to be diverted, is produced to and deposited with the court; and

(b) except in so far as the carrying out of the diversion may necessitate temporary interference with the highway, shall not authorise the stopping up of any part of the highway until the new part to be substituted for the part to be stopped up (including, where a diversion falls to be carried out under orders of two different courts, any necessary continuation of the new part in the area of the other court) has been completed to the satisfaction of two justices of the peace acting for the same petty sessions area as the court by whom the order was made and a certificate to that effect signed by them has been transmitted to the clerk of the peace.

(8) Every order under this section shall have annexed thereto a plan signed by the chairman of the court and shall be transmitted by the clerk of the court to the clerk of the peace, together with any written consents produced to the court under subsection (7) of this section; and the clerk of the peace shall enrol any documents so transmitted to him, and any certificates transmitted to him under that subsection, among the records of quarter sessions.

(9) Part II of the Twelfth Schedule to this Act shall apply where, in pursuance of an order made under this section, a highway is stopped up or diverted, and, immediately before the order is made, there is under, in, upon, over, along or across the highway any apparatus belonging to or used by any statutory undertakers for the purpose of their undertaking.

(10) In this section 'the appropriate authority' means—

(a) in relation to a highway which is situated in a non-county borough or in an urban district and for which a county council are the highway authority, the council of the borough or district, as the case may be, acting with the consent of the county council; and . . .

(b) in relation to any other highway, the highway authority for the highway.

A consent required by this subsection shall not be unreasonably withheld and any question arising under this subsection whether the withholding of a consent is unreasonable shall be determined by the Minister.

109. Application for order under s. 108 by highway or local authority on behalf of other person A person who desires a highway to be stopped up or diverted, but who is not authorised to make an application under the last foregoing section for an order authorising the stopping up or, as the case may be, diversion of the highway, may request the highway authority or local authority who, by virtue of that section, are the appropriate authority in relation to the highway to make such an application as aforesaid, and if the authority grant the request they may, as a condition of making such an application, require him to make such provision for any costs to be incurred by them in connection with the matter as they deem reasonable.

110. Stopping up of footpaths and bridleways (1) Where it appears to a *local authority* as respects a footpath or bridleway in their area (not being a trunk road or a special road) that it is expedient that the path or way should be stopped up on the ground that the path or way is not needed for public use, the *authority* may by order (in this Act referred to as a 'public path extinguishment order') made by them and submitted to and confirmed by the Minister of Housing and Local Government or confirmed as an unopposed order extinguish the public right of way over the path or way.

(2) The Minister of Housing and Local Government shall not confirm a public path extinguishment order unless he is satisfied that it is expedient so to do having regard to the extent (if any) to which it appears to him that the path or way would, apart from the order, be likely to be used by the public, and having regard to the effect which the extinguishment of the right of way would have as respects land served by the path or way, account being taken of the provisions as to compensation contained in section 31 of this Act as applied by subsection (2) of section 113 thereof.

(3) A public path extinguishment order shall be in such form as may be prescribed by regulations made by the Minister of Housing and Local Government, and shall contain a map, on such scale as may be so prescribed, defining the land over which the public right of way is thereby extinguished.

(4) The Seventh Schedule to this Act shall have effect as to the making, confirmation, validity and date of operation of public path extinguishment orders.

(5) Where in accordance with regulations made under paragraph 3 of the said Seventh Schedule proceedings preliminary to the confirmation of a public path extinguishment order are taken concurrently with proceedings preliminary to the confirmation of a public path creation order or of a public path diversion order made under the next following section then, in considering—

(a) under subsection (1) of this section whether the path or way to which the public path extinguishment order relates is needed for

public use, or

(b) under subsection (2) of this section to what extent (if any) that path or way would apart from the order be likely to be used by the public,

the *local authority* or the Minister of Housing and Local Government, as the case may be, may have regard to the extent to which the public path creation order or the public path diversion order would provide an alternative path or way.

(6) For the purposes of subsections (1) and (2) of this section, any temporary circumstances preventing or diminishing the use of a path or way by the public shall be disregarded.

NOTE. *See note to s. 111.*

111. Diversion of footpaths and bridleways (1) Where an owner, lessee or occupier of land crossed by a footpath or bridleway (not being a trunk road or a special road) satisfies the *local authority* in whose area the land is situated that for securing the efficient use of the land or of other land held therewith or providing a shorter or more commodious path or way it is expedient that the line of the path or way across his land, or part of that line, should be diverted (whether on to other land of his or on to land of another owner, lessee or occupier), the *authority* may by order (in this Act referred to as a 'public path diversion order') made by them and submitted to and confirmed by the Minister of Housing and Local Government or confirmed as an unopposed order—

(a) create, as from such date as may be specified in the order, any such new footpath or bridleway as appears to the *authority* requisite for effecting the diversion, and

(b) extinguish, as from such date as may be so specified in accordance with the provisions of the next following subsection, the public right of way over so much of the path or way as appears to the *authority* requisite as aforesaid:

Provided that—

(i) the order shall not alter a point of termination of the path or way if that point is not on a highway, and

(ii) the order shall not alter a point of termination of the path or way, being a point on a highway, otherwise than to another point on the same highway or a highway connected therewith, being a point substantially as convenient to the public.

(2) Where it appears to the *authority* that work requires to be done to provide necessary facilities for the convenient exercise of any such new public right of way as is mentioned in paragraph (a) of the foregoing subsection, the date specified under paragraph (b) of that subsection shall be later than the date specified under paragraph (a) thereof by such time as appears to the *authority* requisite for enabling the work to be carried out.

(3) A right of way created by a public path diversion order may either be unconditional or may (whether or not the right of way extinguished by the order was subject to limitations or conditions of any description) be subject to such limitations or conditions as may be specified in the order.

(4) Before determining to make a public path diversion order on the representation of an owner, lessee or occupier, the *authority* may require him to enter into an agreement with them to defray, or to make such contribution as may be specified in the agreement towards—

(a) any compensation which may become payable under section 31 of this Act as applied by subsection (2) of section 113 thereof, or

(b) where the *authority* are the highway authority for the path or way in question, any expenses which they may incur in bringing the new site of the path or way into a fit condition for use by the public, or

(c) where the *authority* are not the highway authority, any expenses which may become recoverable from them by the highway authority under the provisions of subsection (4) of section 30 of this Act as applied by subsection (8) of this section.

(5) The Minister of Housing and Local Government shall not confirm a public path diversion order unless he is satisfied that the diversion to be effected thereby is expedient as mentioned in subsection (1) of this section, and further that the path or way will not be substantially less convenient to the public in consequence of the diversion and that it is expedient to confirm the order having regard to the effect which—

(a) the diversion would have on public enjoyment of the path or way as a whole,

(b) the coming into operation of the order would have as respects other land served by the existing public right of way, and

(c) any new public right of way created by the order would have as respects the land over which the right is so created and any land held therewith,

so, however, that for the purposes of paragraphs (b) and (c) of this subsection the said Minister shall take into account the provisions as to compensation referred to in paragraph (a) of the last foregoing subsection.

(6) A public path diversion order shall be in such form as may be prescribed by regulations made by the Minister of Housing and Local Government, and shall contain a map, on such scale as may be so prescribed, showing the existing site of so much of the line of the path or way as is to be diverted by the order and the new site to which it is to be diverted, and indicating whether a new right of way is created by the order over the whole of the new site or whether some part thereof is already comprised in a footpath or bridleway and, in the latter case, defining the part thereof so comprised.

(7) The Seventh Schedule to this Act shall have effect as to the making, confirmation, validity and date of operation of public path diversion orders.

(8) The provisions of section 30 of this Act shall apply to a footpath or bridleway created by a public path diversion order with the substitution, for references to a public path creation order, of references to a public path diversion order, and, for references to subsection (3) of section 29 of this Act, of references to subsection (5) of the next following section.

NOTE. *'Local authority', as a result of the Countryside Act, 1968, includes a county council and a National Park Joint Planning Board, but these must consult the council of the county district or county borough before exercising the powers. This change does not however affect s. 112(3) and (7).*

112. Exercise of powers of making public path extinguishment and diversion orders (1) Subject to the following provisions of this section, the powers of making public path extinguishment orders and public path diversion orders conferred by the two last foregoing sections shall not be exercisable—

(a) by the council of a rural district except with the consent of the council of the county comprising the district and, if the county council are not the local planning authority, the consent of that authority,

(b) by the council of any other county district, except with the consent of the local planning authority,

(c) by the council of a county borough, not being the local planning authority, except with the consent of that authority, and

(d) by a council as respects a footpath or bridleway in a National Park, except after consultation with the National Parks Commission.

(2) Where a footpath or bridleway lies partly within and partly outside the area of a local authority, the powers conferred by the two last foregoing sections on the local authority shall extend to the whole of the path or way as if it lay wholly within their area.

Provided that, in relation to so much of the path or way as lies outside the area of the authority, the said powers shall not be exercisable—

(a) as respects any part thereof in a rural district, except with the consent of the council of that district and of the council of the county comprising that district, and, if that county council are not the local planning authority, the consent of that authority,

(b) as respects any part thereof in any other county district, except with the consent of the council of that district and the consent of the local planning authority, and

(c) as respects any part thereof in a county borough, except with the consent of the council of the county borough and, if that council are not the local planning authority, the consent of that authority.

(3) The Minister of Housing and Local Government, on the application of the council of a county, may direct, either generally or as respects the stopping up or diversion of a particular footpath or bridleway, that the powers conferred by the two last foregoing sections or either of them (including those powers as extended by the last foregoing subsection) on the council of a county district specified in the direction, being a district in the county in question, shall be exercisable by the county council and shall not be exercisable by the council of the county district.

(4) A county council exercising a power by virtue of a direction under the last foregoing subsection shall consult the local planning authority, where that authority is a joint board, but shall not be required to obtain the consent of the board to the exercise of the power:

Provided that a county council shall not exercise any such power as aforesaid as respects so much of a footpath or bridleway as lies in another county except with the consent of the council of that county and, if the last mentioned council are not the local planning authority, the consent of that authority.

(5) Where it appears to the Minister of Housing and Local Government as respects a footpath or bridleway that it is expedient as mentioned in subsection (1) of section 110 of this Act that the path or way should be stopped up, or where an owner, lessee or occupier of land crossed by a footpath or bridleway satisfies the said Minister that a diversion thereof is expedient as mentioned in subsection (1) of the last foregoing section, then if—

(a) the appropriate authority have not made and submitted to him a public path extinguishment order or a public path diversion order, as the case may be, and

(b) the said Minister is satisfied that, if such an order were made and submitted to him, he would have power to confirm the order in accordance with the provisions in that behalf of the two last foregoing sections,

the said Minister, after consultation with the said authority, may *direct the authority* to make and submit to him a public path extinguishment order or a public path diversion order, as the case may be, or *may himself make* the order; and where the said Minister gives a direction under this subsection, the restrictions on the making of such an order imposed by the relevant provisions of this section, that is to say, subsection (1), or that subsection and the proviso to subsection (2), or the proviso to the last foregoing subsection, as the case may be, shall not apply.

(6) A council proposing to make a public path diversion order such that the authority who will be the highway authority for a part of the path or way after the diversion will be a different body from the authority who before the diversion are the highway authority for it shall, before making the order, notify the first mentioned authority.

(7) In this section 'the appropriate authority', in relation to the making of a public path extinguishment order or a

public path diversion order, means the authority upon whom power to make the order (whether the power is exercisable with the consent of any other authority or not) is conferred by or under the relevant provisions of the two last foregoing sections and of subsections (2) and (3) of this section.

113. Supplementary provisions as to public path extinguishment and diversion orders (4) The Minister of Housing and Local Government shall not make or confirm a public path extinguishment order or a public path diversion order which extinguishes a right of way over land under, in, upon, over, along or across which there is any apparatus belonging to or used by any statutory undertakers for the purpose of their undertaking unless the undertakers have consented to the making or confirmation of the order, as the case may be; and any such consent may be given subject to the condition that there are included in the order such provisions for the protection of the undertakers as they may reasonably require.

The consent of statutory undertakers to any such order shall not be unreasonably withheld, and any question arising under this subsection whether the withholding of a consent is unreasonable or whether any requirement is reasonable shall be determined by the appropriate Minister.

(5) In the last foregoing subsection the 'appropriate Minister' means—

(a) in relation to statutory undertakers carrying on an undertaking for the supply of electricity, gas or hydraulic power, the Minister of Power;

(b) in relation to statutory undertakers carrying on an undertaking for the supply of water, the Minister of Housing and Local Government; and

(c) in relation to any other statutory undertakers, the Minister.

114. Power to make temporary diversion where highway about to be repaired or widened (1) A highway authority who are about to repair or widen a highway, and a person who is about to repair or widen a highway maintainable by him by reason of tenure, enclosure or prescription, may, subject to the provisions of this section, construct on adjoining land a temporary highway for use while the work is in progress.

(2) Where any damage is sustained by the owner or occupier of any land in consequence of the construction of a highway on that land in exercise of a power conferred by this section the owner or occupier of the land may recover compensation in respect of that damage from the authority or other person by whom the highway was constructed.

(3) Nothing in this section shall authorise interference with land which is part of the site of a house, or is a garden, lawn, yard, court, park, paddock, plantation, planted walk or avenue to a house, or is inclosed land set apart for building or as a nursery for trees.

115. Saving and interpretation (1) The provisions of any enactment contained in this part of this Act shall not prejudice any power conferred by any other enactment (whether contained in this Part of this Act or not) to stop up or divert a highway, and shall not otherwise affect the operation of any enactment not contained in this Part of this Act relating to the extinguishment, suspension, diversion or variation of public rights of way.

(2) Unless the context otherwise requires, expressions in this Part of this Act, other than expressions to which meanings are assigned by sections 294 and 295 of this Act, have the same meanings respectively as in the *Town and Country Planning Act*, 1947.

Part VII

Lawful and Unlawful Interference with Highways and Streets

Protection of public rights

116. Protection of Public rights
(1) The Minister may assert and protect

the rights of the public to the use and enjoyment of any trunk road, including any roadside waste which forms part of it.

(2) The council of a county as respects any county road in the county . . . may assert and protect the rights of the public to the use and enjoyment of any such road, including any roadside waste which forms part thereof.

(3) Without prejudice to subsections (1) and (2) of this section, it shall be the duty of the council of a county district to assert and protect the rights of the public to the use and enjoyment of all highways in their district and to prevent, as far as possible, the stopping up or obstruction of those highways, and the duty imposed by this subsection on the council of a county district shall extend to a highway in an adjoining county district in the county in which their district is situated if in the opinion of the council, the stopping up or obstruction of that highway would be prejudicial to the interests of their district.

(4) Without prejudice to the foregoing provisions of this section, it shall be the duty of the council of a county district to prevent any unlawful encroachment on any roadside waste comprised in a highway within their district.

(5) Without prejudice to their powers under section 276 of the Local Government Act, 1933, a council may, in the performance of their functions under the foregoing provisions of this section, institute or defend any legal proceedings and generally take such steps as the deem expedient.

(6) If the council of a parish, or, in the case of a rural parish not having a separate parish council, the parish meeting of the parish, represent to the council of the county district within which the parish is situated—

(a) that a highway, being one as to which the council of the county distict have the duty imposed by subsection (3) of this section, has been unlawfully stopped up or obstructed, or

(b) that an unlawful encroachment has taken place on a roadside waste comprised in a highway within the county district,

it shall be the duty of the council of that district, unless satisfied that the allegations are incorrect, to take proper proceedings accordingly.

(7) Where a parish council or a parish meeting have made representations under the last foregoing subsection to the council of a county district, and the council of that district refuse or fail to take proper proceedings in consequence of those representations, the parish council or parish meeting by whom the representations were made may petition the council of the county in which the highway to which the representations relate is situated, and, if that council so resolve, the functions of the district council under this section, as respects the highway in connection with which the representations were made, shall be transferred to the county council.

(8) The provisions of subsection (1) of section 63 of the Local Government Act, 1894 (which makes provision for the case where the powers of a district council are by virtue of a resolution under that Act transferred to a county council), shall apply in relation to a resolution passed under the last foregoing subsection as if it were a resolution passed under that Act.

(9) Any proceedings or steps taken by a council in relation to an alleged right of way shall not be treated as unauthorised by reason only that the alleged right is found not to exist.

(10) The functions of the council of a county district under this section shall, in the case of the area of the Isle of Wight constituting a rural district, be exercised by the council of the county of the Isle of Wight and not by the council of the rural district.

Damage to highways, streets, etc.

117. Penalty for damaging highway, etc. (1) If a person, without lawful authority or excuse,—

(a) makes a ditch or excavation in a highway which consists of or comprises a carriageway, or

(b) removes any soil or turf from any part of a highway, except for the purpose of improving the highway and with the consent of the highway authority for the highway, or

(c) deposits anything whatsoever on a highway so as to damage the highway, or

(cc) paints or otherwise inscribes or affixes upon the surface of a highway or upon any tree structure or works on or in a highway any picture letter sign or other mark, or

(d) lights any fire, or discharges any firearm or firework, within fifty feet from the centre of a highway which consists of or comprises a carriageway, and in consequence thereof the highway is damaged, or

(e) in any other manner wilfully damages a highway, any part of an embankment supporting a highway, any part of a bank which flanks a highway or any retaining wall or flank wall belonging to a highway,

he shall be guilty of an offence.

(2) If a person, without lawful authority or excuse,—

(a) wilfully damages a post, rail, wall or fence erected on or by the side of a highway, or a tree, hedge or shrub, or grass, planted or laid out in a highway, or

(b) wilfully destroys or damages a cattle-grid provided under this Act, a gate or other works on a highway for use in connection with such a cattle-grid, or a gate or other works or the proper control of traffic passing over a by-pass for use in connection with such a cattle-grid, or

(c) pulls down, damages or obliterates a *traffic sign* placed on or near a highway, or a milestone or direction post (not being a traffic sign) so placed,

he shall be guilty of an offence:

Provided that it shall be a defence in any proceedings brought under paragraph (c) of this subsection to show that the traffic sign, milestone or post was not lawfully so placed.

(3) A person guilty of an offence under this section shall be liable in respect thereof to a fine not exceeding £20 for the first offence and £50 for a second or subsequent offence.

NOTE. This section now applies to signposts for footpaths and bridleways.

119. Ploughing of footpath or bridleway (1) Where a footpath or bridleway crosses agricultural land or land which is being brought into use for agriculture, then, if—

(a) it is proposed in accordance with the rules of good husbandry to plough the land, and

(b) it is convenient, in so ploughing the land, to plough the path or way together with the rest of the land,

the public right of way shall be subject to the condition that the occupier shall have the right, subject to the following provisions of this section, to plough the path or way as well as the rest of the land.

(2) Before ploughing a footpath or bridleway in the exercise of the right conferred by the foregoing subsection the occupier shall give to the highway authority for the path or way not less than seven days' notice of his intention to plough it.

(3) Where a footpath or bridleway is ploughed in the exercise of the said right the occupier of the land shall *as soon as may be* after the ploughing is completed make good the surface of the path or way so as to make it reasonably convenient for the exercise of the public right of way.

(4) A person who fails to comply with the foregoing provisions of this section shall be guilty of an offence and shall be liable in respect thereof—

(a) in the case of a failure to comply with the provisions of subsection (2) of this section, to a fine not exceeding £10;

(b) in the case of a failure to comply with the provisions of the last foregoing subsection, to a fine not exceeding £50;

and where a person is convicted of the offence of failing to comply with the provisions of the last foregoing subsection and the offence in respect of which he was convicted is continued after the conviction he shall be guilty of a further offence and shall be liable in respect thereof to a fine not exceeding twenty shillings for each day on which the offence is so continued.

(5) It shall be the duty of a highway authority to enforce the provisions of subsections (2) to (4) of this section as respects any footpath or bridleway for which they are the highway authority; and no proceedings in respect of an offence under those provisions shall be brought except by the authority required by this subsection to enforce those provisions as respects the path or way in question.

(6) Nothing in the provisions of this section shall prejudice any limitation or condition having effect apart from those provisions.

Note. See Countryside Act, 1968, s. 29.

PART XII

271. Restriction on institution of proceedings (1) Proceedings for an offence under any provision of this Act to which this section applies or under byelaws made under any such provision, shall not, without the written consent of the Attorney General, be taken by any person other than a person aggrieved, or a highway authority or council having an interest in the enforcement of the provision or byelaws in question.

(2) This section applies to the provisions of this Act which are specified in the Seventeenth Schedule thereto, being provisions which re-enact with or without modifications public health enactments.

275. Appeals to quarter sessions from decisions of magistrates' courts (1) Where a person aggrieved by an order, determination or other decision of a magistrates' court under this Act is not by any other enactment authorised to appeal to a court of quarter sessions he may appeal to such a court.

(2) The applicant for an order under section 108 of this Act or any person who was entitled under subsection (6) of that section to be, and was, or claimed to be, heard on the application may appeal to a court of quarter sessions against the decision made by the magistrates' court on the application.

(3) Where an applicant for an order under the said section 108 appeals against the refusal of a magistrates' court to make the order applied for and more than two persons were, or claimed to be, heard on the application for the order, it shall be sufficient for the purposes of subsection (1) of section 84 of the Magistrates' Courts Act, 1952 (which relates to notices of appeal) if the appellant gives notice of appeal to any two of those persons in addition to the clerk of the magistrates' court:

Provided that this subsection shall not affect the right of any of those persons to appear as respondent to the appeal.

289. Amendment of s. 303 of Public Health Act, 1875 In section 303 of the Public Health Act, 1875 (which relates to the power of the Minister of Housing and Local Government to repeal and alter local Acts by means of orders subject to special parliamentary procedure), the reference to any local Act which relates to the same subject matters as that Act shall be construed as including a reference to any local Act which relates to the same subject matters as the following provisions of this Act, that is to say, sections 244, 253, 256, 261, 271, 307, and 308 and the other provisions thereof which are specified in the Seventeenth Schedule thereto, being provisions which re-enact with or without modifications public health enactments.

Interpretation

294. Meaning of 'highway' (1) In this Act, except where the context

otherwise requires, 'highway' means the whole or a part of a highway other than a ferry or waterway.

(2) Where a highway passes over a bridge or through a tunnel, that bridge or tunnel shall be taken for the purposes of this Act to be a part of the highway.

(3) In this Act, 'highway maintainable at the public expense' and any other expression defined by reference to a highway shall be construed in accordance with the foregoing provisions of this section.

295. Further provisions as to interpretation (1) In this Act, except where the context otherwise requires, the following expressions have the meanings hereby assigned to them respectively, that is to say—

'bridleway' means a highway over which the public have the following, but no other rights of way, that is to say, a right of way on foot and a right of way on horseback or leading a horse, with or without a right to drive animals of any description along the highway;

'carriageway' means a way constituting or comprised in a highway, being a way (other than a cycle track) over which the public have a right of way for the passage of vehicles.

'classified road' means a highway classified by the Minister under the Ministry of Transport Act, 1919, in Class I or Class II or any class declared by him to be not inferior to those classes for the purposes of this Act;

'council' means a county council . . . or a local authority.

'cycle track' means a way constituting or comprised in a highway, being a way over which the public have the following, but no other, rights of way, that is to say, a right of way on pedal cycles with or without a right of way on foot;

'footpath' means a highway over which the public have a right of way on foot only, not being a footway;

'footway' means a way comprised in a highway which also comprises a carriageway, being a way over which the public have a right of way on foot only;

'highway maintainable at the public expense' means a highway which by virtue of section 38 of this Act or of any other enactment (whether contained in this Act or not) is a highway which for the purposes of this Act is a highway maintainable at the public expense;

'horse' includes pony, ass and mule, and 'horseback' shall be construed accordingly;

'local authority' means the council of a county borough or county district;

'local highway authority' means a highway authority other than the Minister;

'owner', in relation to any premises, means a person, other than a mortgagee not in possession, who, whether in his own right or as trustee or agent for any other person, is entitled to receive the rack rent of the premises or, where the premises are not let at a rack rent, would be so entitled if the premises were so let;

'public path creation agreement' means an agreement made under section 27 of this Act;

'public path creation order' has the meaning assigned to it by section 28 of this Act;

'public path diversion order' has the meaning assigned to it by section 111 of this Act;

'public path extinguishment order' has the meaning assigned to it by section 110 of this Act;

'street' includes any highway and any road, lane, footpath, square, court, alley or passage, whether a thoroughfare or not, and includes any part of a street;

(2) A highway at the side of a river, canal or other inland navigation shall not be excluded from either of the following definitions contained in the foregoing subsection, that is to say, 'bridleway' and 'footpath', by reason only that the public have a right to use the highway for purposes of navigation, if the highway would fall within that definition if the public had no such right thereover.

(4) References in this Act to a parish, a parish council and the chairman of a parish council shall be construed as including references to a borough which has been included in a rural district, the council of such a borough and the mayor of such a borough respectively and, in a case where two or more parishes are grouped under a common parish council, references in this Act to a parish shall be construed as references to those parishes.

307. Saving for works, etc. of dock, harbour and canal undertakers (1) Subject to the provisions of this section, nothing in any of the provisions of this Act to which this section applies shall authorise a highway authority or council, without the consent of the dock, harbour or canal undertakers concerned—

(a) to execute any works in, across or under any dock, harbour, basin, wharf, quay or lock; or

(b) to execute any works which will interfere with the improvement of, or the access to, any river, canal, dock, harbour, basin, lock, reservoir or towing path, or with any works appurtenant thereto or any land necessary for the enjoyment or improvement thereof.

(2) A consent required for the purposes of the foregoing subsection shall not be unreasonably withheld, and if any question arises whether the withholding of a consent is unreasonable either party may require that it shall be referred to an arbitrator to be appointed, in default of agreement, by the President of the Institution of Civil Engineers.

(3) On an arbitration under this section, the arbitrator shall determine—

(a) whether any works which the highway authority or council propose to execute are such works as under subsection (1) of this section they are not entitled to execute without the consent of the undertakers concerned; and

(b) if they are such works, whether the injury, if any, to the undertakers will be of such a nature as to admit of being fully compensated by money; and

(c) if the works are of such a nature, the conditions subject to which the authority or council may execute the works, including the amount of the compensation, if any, to be paid by them to the undertakers.

If the arbitrator determines that the proposed works are such works as the highway authority or council are not entitled to execute without the consent of the undertakers and that the works would cause injury to the undertakers of such a nature as not to admit of being fully compensated by money, the authority or council shall not proceed to execute the works, but in any other case they may execute the works subject to compliance with such conditions, including the payment of such compensation, as the arbitrator determines.

(4) For the purposes of this section, dock, harbour and canal undertakers shall be deemed to be concerned with any river, canal, dock, harbour, basin, lock, reservoir, towing path, wharf, quay or land if it belongs to them and forms part of their undertaking, or if they have statutory rights of navigating on or using it, or of demanding tolls or dues in respect of navigation thereon or the use thereof.

(5) This section applies to section 256 of this Act and to the other provisions thereof which are specified in the Seventeenth Schedule thereto, being provisions which re-enact with or without modifications public health enactments.

(6) In this section 'canal' includes inland navigation.

308. Saving for works, etc. of land drainage authorities (1) Subject to the provisions of this section, nothing in any of the provisions of this Act to which this section applies shall authorise a highway authority or council to use or interfere with any watercourse (including the banks thereof), or any drainage or other works, vested in or under the control of a river board or other drainage authority within the meaning of the *Land Drainage Act*, 1930, without the consent of that board or that authority, as the case may be.

(2) A consent required for the purposes of the foregoing subsection shall not be unreasonably withheld, and if any question arises whether the withholding of a consent is unreasonable either party may require that it shall be referred to an arbitrator to be appointed, in default of agreement, by the President of the Institution of Civil Engineers.

(3) This section applies to [the provisions of this Act] . . . which are specified in the Seventeenth Schedule thereto, being provisions which re-enact with or without modifications public health enactments.

FIRST SCHEDULE

PROCEDURE FOR MAKING OR CONFIRMING CERTAIN ORDERS AND SCHEMES UNDER PART II OF THIS ACT

PART I

ORDERS

1. Where the Minister proposes to make an order under any of the following provisions of this Act, that is to say, section 7, section 9, section 13 or section 20 he shall prepare a draft of the order and shall publish in at least one local newspaper circulating in the area in which any highway, or any proposed highway, to which the order relates is situated, and in the London Gazette, a notice—

(a) stating the general effect of the proposed order;

(b) naming a place in the said area where a copy of the draft order and of any map or plan referred to therein may be inspected by any person free of charge at all reasonable hours during a period of three months from the date of the publication of the notice; and

(c) stating that, within the said period, any person may by notice to the Minister object to the making of the order.

2. Where an order is submitted to the Minister under the said section 13 by a local highway authority, that authority shall publish, in the manner specified in the foregoing paragraph, the notice referred to therein, and that paragraph shall have effect in relation to a notice published by any such authority as if, for the references to the draft order and the making of the order, there were substituted references to the order as submitted to the Minister and the confirmation of the order respectively.

3. Not later than the day on which the said notice is published or, if it is published on two or more days, the day on which it is first published, the Minister or the local highway authority, as the case may be, shall serve on each person specified in such head or heads of the Table set out at the end of this paragraph as apply in the case of the order in question—

(a) a copy of the said notice;
(b) a copy of the draft order or of the order, as the case may be; and
(c) a copy of any map or plan referred to in the draft order or the order relating to a matter which, in the opinion of the Minister or of the local highway authority, as the case may be, is likely to affect the said person.

TABLE

Persons to be served with copies of the documents specified in paragraph 3 of this Schedule

(i) In the case of every order proposed to be made under section 7, section 9, or section 20 of this Act—

Every council (other than the council of a county district) in whose area any highway or proposed highway to which the proposed order relates is situated and, in the case of a highway or proposed highway situated in a non-county borough or in an urban district, the council of that borough or district.

(ii) In the case of an order proposed to be made under section 7 of this Act which provides for the construction as part of a trunk road of a bridge over or tunnel under any navigable waters and in the case of every order proposed to be made under section 20 of this Act—

Every navigation authority and river board concerned with or having jurisdiction over the waters affected or the area comprising those waters.

(iii) In the case of an order proposed to be made under section 13 of this Act which authorises the carrying out of any works—

Every council in whose area any works authorised by the proposed order are to be carried out.

(iv) In the case of an order proposed to be made under section 13 of this Act which provides for transferring any highway from one highway authority to another—

The highway authorities to and from whom the highway is to be transferred.

(v) In the case of an order proposed to be made under section 13 of this Act which authorises the stopping up of any private means of access to any premises—

The owner (within the meaning of section 16 of this Act) and the occupier of those premises.

(vi) In the case of an order proposed to be made under section 13 of this Act which provides for entry by the special road authority on any land—

The occupier of that land.

(vii) In the case of an order proposed to be made under section 9 or section 13 of this Act which authorises the stopping up or diversion of any high-way—

The parish council (or, in the case of a rural parish not having a separate parish council, the parish meeting) of every rural parish in which the high-way is situated.

Any public utility undertakers having apparatus under, in, upon, over, along or across the highway.

4. Where the proposed order author-ises the stopping up or diversion of a highway, the Minister or the local high-way authority, as the case may be, shall, not later than the day on which the said notice is published or, if it is published on two or more days, the day on which it is first published, cause a copy thereof to be displayed in a promi-nent position at the ends of so much of any highway as is proposed to be stopped up or diverted under the order.

5. If any objection to the proposed order is received by the Minister from any person on whom a copy of the notice is required to be served under paragraph 3 of this Schedule within three months from the date of his being served therewith, or is received by the Minister from any other person appear-ing to him to be affected within three months from the day on which the notice of the proposed order is published, or, if it is published on two or more days, from the later or latest of them, and the objection is not withdrawn, the Minister shall cause a local inquiry to be held:

Provided that, except where the objection is made by a person entitled to receive a copy of the notice relating to the order in question by virtue of the said paragraph 3 and such one or more of the following heads of the Table set out at the end of that paragraph, that is to say, heads (i), (ii), (iii) and (iv), as apply in the case of that order, the Minister may dispense with such an inquiry if he is satisfied that in the cir-cumstances of the case the holding of such an inquiry is unnecessary.

6. After considering any objections to the proposed order which are not with-drawn, and, where a local inquiry is held, the report of the person who held

the inquiry, the Minister may make or confirm the order either without modi-fication or subject to such modifications as he thinks fit.

SECOND SCHEDULE

VALIDITY AND DATE OF

OPERATION OF CERTAIN SCHEMES

AND ORDERS

1. As soon as may be after a scheme or order to which this Schedule applies has been made or confirmed by the Minister, the Minister shall publish in the London Gazette, and in such other manner as he thinks best adapted for informing persons affected, a notice stating that the scheme or order has been made or confirmed, and naming a place where a copy thereof may be inspected free of charge at all reason-able hours.

2. If a person aggrieved by a scheme or order to which this Schedule applies desires to question the validity thereof, or of any provision contained therein, on the ground that it is not within the powers of this Act or on the ground that any requirement of this Act or of regu-lations made thereunder has not been complied with in relation thereto, he may, within six weeks from the date on which the notice required by the fore-going paragraph is first published, make an application for the purpose to the High Court.

3. On any such application as afore-said, the Court—

(a) may by interim order suspend the operation of the scheme or order, or of any provision contained therein, either generally, or in so far as it affects any property of the applicant, until the final determination of the proceedings; and

(*b*) if satisfied that the scheme or order, or any provision contained therein, is not within the powers of this Act or that the interests of the applicant have been substantially prejudiced by failure to comply with any such requirement as aforesaid, may quash the scheme or order or any provision contained therein, either generally or in so far as it affects any property of the applicant.

4. Subject to the provisions of the last foregoing paragraph, a scheme or order to which this Schedule applies shall not, either before or after it has been made or confirmed, be questioned in any legal proceedings whatever, and shall become operative on the date on which the notice required by paragraph 1 of this Schedule is first published, or on such later date, if any, as may be specified in the scheme or order.

5. In relation to any scheme or order to which this Schedule applies, being a scheme or order which is subject to special parliamentary procedure, the foregoing provisions of this Schedule shall have effect subject to the following modifications—

(*a*) if the scheme or order is confirmed by Act of Parliament under section 6 of the Statutory Orders (Special Procedure) Act, 1945, paragraphs 2 to 4 shall not apply; and

(*b*) in any other case, paragraph 2 shall have effect as if, for the reference therein to the date on which the notice required by paragraph 1 is first published, there were substituted a reference to the date on which the scheme or order becomes operative under the said Act of 1945, and paragraph 4 shall have effect as if the words from 'and shall become operative' to the end of the paragraph were omitted.

SEVENTH SCHEDULE

PROVISIONS AS TO MAKING, CONFIRMATION, VALIDITY AND DATE OF OPERATION OF CERTAIN ORDERS RELATING TO FOOTPATHS AND BRIDLEWAYS

PART I

PROCEDURE FOR MAKING AND CONFIRMING CERTAIN ORDERS RELATING TO FOOTPATHS AND BRIDLEWAYS

1.—(1) Before a public path creation order, a public path extinguishment order or a public path diversion order is submitted to the Minister of Housing and Local Government for confirmation or confirmed as an unopposed order the authority by whom the order was made shall give notice in the prescribed form—

(*a*) stating the general effect of the order and that it has been made and is about to be submitted for confirmation or to be confirmed as an unopposed order.

(*b*) naming a place in the area in which the land to which the order relates is situated where a copy of the order and of the map referred to therein may be inspected free of charge at all reasonable hours, and

(*c*) specifying the time (not being less than twenty-eight days from the date of the first publication of the notice) within which, and the manner in which, representations or objections with respect to the order may be made.

(2) Before the Minister of Housing and Local Government makes a public path creation order, a public path extinguishment order or a public path diversion order, he shall prepare a draft of the order and shall give notice—

(*a*) stating that he proposes to make the order and the general effect thereof, (*b*) naming a place in the area in which the land to which the draft order relates is situated where a copy of the draft order and of the map referred to therein may be inspected free of charge at all reasonable hours, and

(*c*) specifying the time (not being less than twenty-eight days from the date of the first publication of the notice) within which, and the manner in which, representations or objections with respect to the draft order may be made.

(3) The notices to be given under either of the two foregoing sub-paragraphs shall be given—

(*a*) in the case of a public path creation order, by publication in the London Gazette and in at least one local newspaper circulating in the area in which the land to which the order relates is situated, and by serving a like notice on every owner, occupier and lessee (except tenants for a month or any period less than a month and statutory tenants within the meaning of Part II of the Housing Repairs and Rents Act, 1954) of any of that land, so however that—

(i) except in the case of an owner, occupier or lessee being a local authority or statutory undertakers, the Minister of Housing and Local Government may in any particular case direct that it shall not be necessary to serve notice as aforesaid, but

(ii) if the said Minister so directs in the case of any land, then in addition to publication the notice shall be addressed to 'the owners and any occupiers' of the land (describing it) and a copy or copies of it shall be affixed to some conspicuous object or objects on the land;

(*b*) in the case of a public path extinguishment order or a public path diversion order, by publication and the service of notices as mentioned in head (*a*) of this sub-paragraph and also—

(i) by serving such a notice as is therein mentioned on every council, the council of every rural parish, and the parish meeting of every rural parish not having a separate parish council, being a council or parish whose area includes any of the land to which the order relates, and

(ii) by causing a copy of the notice to be displayed in a prominent position at the ends of so much of any footpath or bridleway as is to be stopped up or diverted by virtue of the order.

(4) Where under this paragraph a notice is required to be served on an owner of land and the land belongs to an ecclesiastical benefice, a like notice shall be served on the Church Commissioners.

2.—(1) If no representations or objections are duly made, or if any so made are withdrawn, the Minister of Housing and Local Government may, if he thinks fit, confirm or make the order, as the case may be, with or without modifications.

(2) If any representation or objection duly made is not withdrawn, the said Minister shall, before confirming or making the order, as the case may be, if the objection is made by a local authority cause a local inquiry to be held, and in any other case either—

(*a*) cause a local inquiry to be held, or

(*b*) afford to any person by whom any representation or objection has been duly made and not withdrawn an opportunity of being heard by a person appointed by him for the purpose,

and, after considering the report of the person appointed to hold the inquiry or to hear representations or objections, may confirm or make the order, as the case may be, with or without modifications:

Provided that in the case of a public path creation order or a public path diversion order, if objection is made by statutory undertakers on the ground that the order provides for the creation of a public right of way over land covered by works used for the purposes of their undertaking or the curtilage of such land, and the objection is not withdrawn, the order shall be subject to special parliamentary procedure.

(3) Notwithstanding anything in the foregoing provisions of this paragraph, the said Minister shall not confirm or make an order so as to affect land not affected by the order as submitted to him or the draft order prepared by him, as the case may be, except after—

(a) giving such notice as appears to him requisite of his proposal so to modify the order, specifying the time (not being less than twenty-eight days from the date of the first publication of the notice) within which, and the manner in which, representations or objections with respect to the proposal may be made,

(b) holding a local inquiry or affording to any person by whom any representation or objection has been duly made and not withdrawn an opportunity of being heard by a person appointed by him for the purpose, and

(c) considering the report of the person appointed to hold the inquiry or to hear representations or objections, as the case may be,

and, in the case of a public path creation order or a public path diversion order, if objection is made by statutory undertakers on the ground that the order as modified would provide for the creation of a public right of way over land covered by works used for the purposes of their undertaking or the curtilage of such land, and the objection is not withdrawn, the order shall be subject to special parliamentary procedure.

NOTE. See the Countryside Act, 1968.

3.—(1) The Minister of Housing and Local Government may, subject to the provisions of this Part of this Schedule, by regulations make such provision as to the procedure on the making submission and confirmation of orders to which this Schedule applies as appears to him to be expedient.

(2) Provision may be made by regulations of the said Minister for enabling proceedings preliminary to the confirmation of a public path extinguishment order to be taken concurrently with proceedings preliminary to the confirmation of a public path creation order or a public path diversion order.

(3) In this Part of this Schedule—

(a) 'local authority' means any council and any other authority being a local authority within the meaning of the Local Loans Act, 1875, and includes any drainage board and any joint board or joint committee if all the constituent authorities are such local authorities as aforesaid;

(b) 'prescribed' means prescribed by regulations made by the said Minister.

Part II

Validity and Date of Operation of certain Orders relating to Footpaths and Bridleways

4. As soon as may be after an order to which this Schedule applies has been confirmed or made by the Minister of Housing and Local Government or confirmed as an unopposed order, the authority by whom the order was made, or, in the case of an order made by the said Minister, the said Minister, shall publish, in the manner required in relation to the class of order in question by sub-paragraph (3) of paragraph 1 of this Schedule, a notice in the prescribed

form describing the general effect of the order, stating that it has been confirmed or made, and naming a place where a copy thereof as confirmed or made may be inspected free of charge at all reasonable hours, and—

(a) where under the said sub-paragraph (3) notice was required to be served, shall serve a like notice and a copy of the order as confirmed or made on any persons on whom notices were required to be served under that sub-paragraph or under sub-paragraph (4) of paragraph 1 of this Schedule; and

(b) where under the said sub-paragraph (3) a notice was required to be displayed, shall cause a like notice to be displayed in the like manner as the notice required to be displayed under that sub-paragraph:

Provided that no such notice or copy need be served on a person unless he has sent to the authority or the said Minister (according as the notice or copy would require to be served by an authority or by the said Minister) a request in that behalf specifying an address for service.

5. The Second Schedule to this Act (except paragraph 1 thereof) shall apply in relation to an order to which this Schedule applies as it applies in relation to a scheme or order to which that Schedule applies, but with the following modifications, that is to say—

(a) for references to a scheme or order to which that Schedule applies there shall be substituted references to an order to which this Schedule applies;

(b) for the references in paragraphs 2, 4 and 5 thereof to the date on which the notice required by paragraph 1 thereof is first published there shall be substituted references to the date on which the notice required by the last foregoing paragraph is first published; and

(c) the said paragraph 4 shall have effect as if the words 'or on such

later date, if any, as may be specified in the scheme or order' were omitted.

6. In this Part of this Schedule 'prescribed' means prescribed by regulations made by the Minister of Housing and Local Government.

TWELFTH SCHEDULE

Provisions as to Orders under Section 108 of this Act

Part I

Notices to be Given by Applicant for Order

1. At least twenty-eight days before the day on which an application for an order under section 108 of this Act is made in relation to a highway the applicant authority shall give notice of their intention to apply for the order, specifying the time and place at which the application is to be made and the terms of the order applied for (embodying a plan showing what will be the effect thereof)—

(a) to the local planning authority, unless that authority are the applicants;

(b) to the owners and occupiers of all lands adjoining the highway;

(c) to any statutory undertakers having apparatus under, in, upon, over, along or across the highway;

(d) if the highway is a classified road, to the Minister;

(e) if the highway is a classified road in, or partly in, a rural parish, to the council of the rural district which comprises the parish and to the parish council or, in the case of a parish not having a separate parish council, to the chairman of the parish meeting.

2. Not later than twenty-eight days before the day on which the application is made the applicant authority shall cause a copy of the said notice to be

displayed in a prominent position at the ends of the highway.

3. Once at least in each of two successive weeks the applicant authority shall publish in the London Gazette and in a local newspaper circulating in the area in which the highway is situated a notice containing the particulars specified in paragraph 1 of this Schedule, except that there may be substituted for the plan a statement of a place in the said area where the plan may be inspected free of charge at all reasonable hours.

PART II

APPARATUS OF STATUTORY UNDERTAKERS

4. Where this Part of this Schedule applies in relation to a highway, the statutory undertakers whose apparatus is under, in, upon, over, along or across the highway shall, subject to the provisions of this Part of this Schedule, have the same powers and rights in respect of that apparatus as if the order authorising the highway to be stopped up or, as the case may be, diverted, had not been made.

5. Where a highway is stopped up or diverted in pursuance of an order under section 108 of this Act, the statutory undertakers whose apparatus is under, in, upon, over, along or across the highway may, and, if reasonably requested so to do by the authority on whose application the order was made, shall—

(a) remove the apparatus and place it or other appratus provided in substitution for it in such other position as they may reasonably determine and have power to place it; or

(b) provide other apparatus in substitution for the existing apparatus and place it in such position as aforesaid.

Any works executed under this paragraph (including the provision of apparatus thereunder) are hereafter in this Part of this Schedule referred to as 'undertakers' works'.

6. Subject to the following provisions of this Part of this Schedule, the authority on whose application an order under the said section 108 stopping up or diverting a highway was made shall pay to any statutory undertakers an amount equal to the cost reasonably incurred by them in or in connection with—

(a) the execution of undertakers' works required in consequence of the stopping up or diversion of that highway, and

(b) the doing of any other work or thing rendered necessary by the execution of undertakers' works.

7. If in the course of the execution of undertakers' works under paragraph 5 of this Schedule—

(a) apparatus of better type, of greater dimensions or of greater capacity is placed in substitution for existing apparatus of worse type, of smaller dimensions or of smaller capacity, or

(b) apparatus (whether existing apparatus or apparatus substituted for existing apparatus) is placed at a depth greater than the depth at which the existing apparatus was,

and the placing of apparatus of that type, dimensions or capacity or the placing of apparatus at that depth, as the case may be, is not agreed by the authority concerned, or, in default of agreement, is not determined by arbitration to be necessary, then, if it involves cost in the execution of the undertakers' works exceeding that would have been involved if the apparatus placed had been of the existing type, dimensions or capacity, or at the existing depth, as the case may be, the amount which apart from this paragraph would be payable to the undertakers by virtue of the last foregoing paragraph shall be reduced by the amount of that excess.

Q*

8. For the purposes of the last foregoing paragraph—

(a) an extension of apparatus to a length greater than the length of existing apparatus shall not be treated as a placing of apparatus of greater dimensions than those of the existing apparatus;

(b) where the provision of a joint in a cable is agreed, or is determined to be necessary, the consequential provision of a jointing chamber or of a manhole shall be treated as if it also had been agreed or had been so determined.

9. An amount which apart from this paragraph would be payable to undertakers in respect of works of theirs by virtue of paragraph 6 of this Schedule (and having regard, where relevant, to paragraph 7 of this Schedule) shall, if the works include the placing of apparatus provided in substitution for apparatus placed more than seven-and-a-half years earlier so as to confer on the undertakers any financial benefit by deferment of the time for renewal of the apparatus in the ordinary course, be reduced by the amount which represents that benefit.

10. Any question arising under this Part of this Schedule shall, in default of agreement between the parties concerned, be determined by arbitration.

SEVENTEENTH SCHEDULE

PROVISIONS OF THIS ACT TO WHICH SECTIONS 244, 253, 256, 261, 271, 289, 307 and 308 THEREOF APPLY

3. *Provisions contained in Part V*

Subsections (2) to (6) of section 67, sections 72, 74, 75 and 78, and subsections (3) and (4) of section 82.

Road Traffic Act, 1960

Restrictions on Use of motor Vehicles off Roadway

17. Control of use of footpaths and bridleways for motor vehicle trials (1) No person shall promote or take part in a trial of any description between motor vehicles on a footpath or bridleway unless the holding of the trial has been authorised under this section by the local authority.

(2) A local authority shall not give an authorisation under this section unless satisfied that consent in writing to the use of any length of footpath or bridleway for the purposes of the trial has been given by the owner and by the occupier of the land over which that length of footpath or bridleway runs, and any such authorisation may be given subject to compliance with such conditions as the authority think fit.

(3) A person who contravenes subsection (1) of this section, or fails to comply with any conditions subject to which an authorisation under this section has been granted, shall be liable on summary conviction to a fine not exceeding £50.

(4) No statutory provision prohibiting or restricting the use of footpaths or bridleways or a specified footpath or bridleway shall affect the holding of a trial authorised under this section; but this section shall not prejudice any right or remedy of a person as having an interest in any land.

(5) In this section 'local authority'—

(a) as respects England and Wales, means the council of a county . . .

18. Prohibition of driving motor vehicles elsewhere than on roads (1) Subject to the provisions of this section, if without lawful authority a person drives a motor vehicle on to or upon any common land, moorland or other land of whatsoever description, not being land forming part of a road, or on any road being a footpath or bridleway, he shall be liable on summary conviction to a fine not exceeding £10.

(2) It shall not be an offence under this section to drive a motor vehicle on any land within fifteen yards of a road, being a road on which a motor vehicle may lawfully be driven, for the purpose only of parking the vehicle on that land.

(3) A person shall not be convicted of an offence under this section with respect to a vehicle if he proves to the satisfaction of the court that it was driven in contravention of this section for the purpose of saving life or extinguishing fire or meeting any other like emergency.

(4) It is hereby declared that nothing in this section prejudices the operation of section 193 of the Law of Property Act, 1925 (which relates to the rights of the public over commons and waste lands), or of any byelaws applying to any land or affects the law of trespass to land or any right or remedy to which a person may by law be entitled in respect of any such trespass or in particular confers a right to park a vehicle no any land.

Charities Act, 1960

PART II

PROVISIONS FOR INQUIRING INTO, MAKING KNOWN AND CO-ORDINATING CHARITABLE ACTIVITIES

Registration of charities

4. Register of charities (1) There shall be a register of charities which shall be established and maintained by the *Commissioners* and in which there shall be entered such particulars as the *Commissioners* may from time to time determine of any charity there registered.

(2) There shall be entered in the register every charity not excepted by subsection (4) below; and a charity so excepted may be entered in the register at the request of the charity, but (whether or not it was excepted at the time of registration) may at any time, and shall at the request of the charity, be removed from the register.

(3) Any institution which no longer appears to the *Commissioners* to be a charity shall be removed from the register, with effect, where the removal is due to any change in its purposes or trusts, from the date of that change; and there shall also be removed from the register any charity which ceases to exist or does not operate.

(4) The following charities are not required to be registered, that is to say,— . . .

(c) any charity having neither any permanent endowment, nor any income from property amounting to more than fifteen pounds a year, nor the use and occupation of any land; . . .

(5) With any application for a charity to be registered there shall be supplied to the *Commissioners* copies of its trusts (or, if they are not set out in any extant document, particulars of them), and such other documents or information as may be prescribed or as the *Commissioners* may require for the purpose of the application.

(6) It shall be the duty—

(a) of the charity trustees of any charity which is not registered nor excepted from registration to apply for it to be registered, and to supply the documents and information required by subsection (5) above; and

(b) of the charity trustees (or last charity trustees) of any institution which is for the time being registered to notify the *Commissioners* if it ceases to exist, or if there is any change in its trusts, or in the particulars of it entered in the register, and to supply to the *Commissioners* particulars of any such change and copies of any new trusts or alterations of the trusts;

and any person who makes default in carrying out any of the duties imposed by this subsection may be required by order of the *Commissioners* to make good that default.

(7) The register (including the entries cancelled when institutions are removed from the register) shall be open to the public inspection at all reasonable times; and copies (or particulars) of the trusts of any registered charity as supplied to the *Commissioners* under this section shall, so long as it remains on the register, be kept by them and be open to public inspection at all reasonable times, except in so far as regulations otherwise provide.

(8) Nothing in the foregoing subsections shall require any person to supply the *Commissioners* with copies of schemes for the administration of a charity made otherwise than by the court, or to notify the *Commissioners* of any change made with respect to a registered charity by such a scheme, or require a person, if he refers the *Commissioners* to a document or copy already in the possession of the *Commissioners* or of the *Minister* of Education, to supply a further copy of the document; but where by virtue of this subsection a copy of any document need not be supplied to the *Commissioners*, a copy of it, if it relates to a registered charity, shall be open to inspection under subsection (7) above as if supplied to the *Commissioners* under this section.

5. **Effect of, and claims and objections to, registration** (1) A institution shall for all purposes other than rectification of the register be conclusively presumed to be or have been a charity at any time when it is or was on the register of charities.

(2) Any person who is or may be affected by the registration of an institution as a charity may, on the ground that it is not a charity, object to its being entered by the *Commissioners* in the register, or apply to them for it to be removed from the register; and provision may be made by regulations as to the manner in which any such objection or application is to be made, prosecuted or dealt with.

(3) An appeal against any decision of the *Commissioners* to enter or not to enter an institution in the register of charities, or to remove or not to remove an institution from the register, may be brought in the High Court by the Attorney General, or by the persons who are or claim to be the charity trustees of the institution, or by any person whose objection or application under subsection (2) above is disallowed by the decision.

(4) If there is an appeal to the High Court against any decision of the *Commissioners* to enter an institution in the register, or not to remove an institution from the register, then until the *Commissioners* are satisfied whether the decision of the *Commissioners* is or is not to stand, the entry in the register shall be maintained, but shall be in suspense and marked to indicate that it is in suspense; and for the purposes of subsection (1) above an institution shall be deemed not to be on the register during any period when the entry relating to it is in suspense under this subsection.

(5) Any question affecting the registration or removal from the register of an institution may, notwithstanding that it has been determined by a decision on appeal under subsection (3) above, be considered afresh by the *Commissioners* and shall not be concluded by that decision, if it appears to the *Commissioners* that there has been a change of circumstances or that the decision is inconsistent with a later judicial decision, whether given on such an appeal or not.

8. **Receipt and audit of accounts of charities** (1) Statements of account giving the prescribed information about the affairs of a charity shall be transmitted to the *Commissioners* by the charity trustees on request; and, in the case of a charity having a permanent endowment, such a statement relating to the

permanent endowment shall be transmitted yearly without any request, unless the charity is excepted by order or regulations.

(2) Any statement of account transmitted to the *Commissioners* in pursuance of subsection (1) above shall be kept by them for such period as they think fit; and during that period it shall be open to public inspection at all reasonable times.

(3) The *Commissioners* may by order require that the condition and accounts of a charity for such period as they think fit shall be investigated and audited by an auditor appointed by them, . . .

(4) An auditor acting under subsection (3) above—

(a) shall have a right of access to all books, accounts and documents relating to the charity which are in the possession or control of the charity trustees or to which the charity trustees have access;

(b) shall be entitled to require from any charity trustee, past or present, and from any past or present officer or servant of the charity such information and explanation as he thinks necessary for the performance of his duties;

(c) shall at the conclusion or during the progress of the audit make such reports to the *Commissioners* about the audit or about the accounts or affairs of the charity as he thinks the case requires, and shall send a copy of any such report to the charity trustees.

(5) The expenses of any audit under subsection (3) above, including the remuneration of the auditor, shall be paid by the *Commissioners*.

(6) If any person—

(a) fails to transmit to the *Commissioners* any statement of account required by subsection (1) above; or

(b) fails to afford an auditor any facility to which he is entitled under subsection (4) above;

the *Commissioners* may by order give to that person or to the charity trustees for the time being such directions as the *Commissioners* think appropriate for securing that the default is made good.

9. Exchange of information, etc.
(1) The *Commissioners* may furnish the Commissioners of Inland Revenue and other government departments and local authorities, and the Commissioners of Inland Revenue and other government departments and local authorities may furnish the *Commissioners*, with the names and addresses of institutions which have for any purpose been treated by the person furnishing the information as established for charitable purposes or, in order to give or obtain assistance in determining whether an institution ought to be treated as so established, with information as to the purposes of the institution and the trusts under which it is established or regulated.

(2) The *Commissioners* shall supply any person, on payment of such fee as they think reasonable, with copies of or extracts from any document in their possession which is for the time being open to public inspection under this Act.

Powers of local authorities and of charity trustees

10. Local authority's index of local charities (1) The council of a county or of a borough may maintain an index of local charities or of any class of local charities in the council's area, and may publish information contained in the index, or summaries or extracts taken from it.

(2) A council proposing to establish or maintaining under this section an index of local charities or of any class of local charities shall, on request, be supplied by the *Commissioners* free of charge with copies of such entries in the register of charities as are relevant to the index or with particulars of any changes in the entries of which copies have been supplied before; and the Commissioners may arrange that they will without further request supply a council with particulars of any such changes.

(3) An index maintained under this section shall be open to public inspection at all reasonable times.

(4) A council may employ any voluntary organisation, and the council of a county may employ the council of any county district in the county, or the divisional executive (within the meaning of Part III of the First Schedule to the Education Act, 1944) for any part of the county, as their agent for the purposes of this section, on such terms and within such limits (if any) or in such cases as they may agree; and for this purpose 'voluntary organisation' means any body of which the activities are carried on otherwise than for profit, not being a public or local authority.

(5) A joint board discharging any of a council's functions shall have the same powers under this section as the council as respects local charities in the council's area which are established for purposes similar or complementary to any services provided by the board.

(6) . . .

(7) In this section the expression 'borough' shall extend to a borough included in a rural district, . . .

11. Reviews of local charities by local authority (1) The council of a county or of a borough may, subject to the following provisions of this section, initiate, and carry out in co-operation with the charity trustees, a review of the working of any group of local charities with the same or similar purposes in the council's area, and may make to the *Commissioners* such report on the review and such recommendations arising from it as the council after consultation with the trustees think fit.

(2) A council having power to initiate reviews under this section may co-operate with other persons in any review by them of the working of local charities in the council's area (with or without other charities), or may join with other persons in initiating and carrying out such a review.

(3) No review initiated by a council under this section shall extend to any charity without the consent of the charity trustees, nor to any ecclesiastical charity.

(4) No review initiated under this section by the council of a borough shall extend to the working in any county of a local charity established for purposes similar or complementary to any services provided by county councils, unless the review so extends with the consent of the council of that county or the council initiating it provides those services in its area under delegated powers.

(5) Subsections (4) to (7) of the last foregoing section shall apply for the purposes of this section as they apply for the purposes of that.

12. Co-operation between charities, and between charities and local authorities (1) Any local council and any joint board discharging any functions of such a council may make, with any charity established for purposes similar or complementary to services provided by the council or board, arrangements for co-ordinating the activities of the council or board and those of the charity in the interests of persons who may benefit from those services or from the charity, and shall be at liberty to disclose to any such charity in the interests of those persons any information obtained in connection with the services provided by the council or board, whether or not arrangements have been made with the charity under this subsection.

In this subsection 'local council' means the council of a county, of a county borough, of a metropolitan borough, of a county district, of a borough included in a rural district or of a rural parish . . .

(2) Charity trustees shall, notwithstanding anything in the trusts of the charity, have power by virtue of this subsection to do all or any of the following things, where it appears to them likely to promote or make more effective the work of the charity, and may defray the expense of so doing out of any income or moneys applicable as income of the charity, that is to say,—

(a) they may co-operate in any review undertaken under the last foregoing section or otherwise of the working of charities or any class of charities;

(b) they may make arrangements with an authority acting under subsection (1) above or with another charity for co-ordinating their activities and those of the authority or of the other charity;

(c) they may publish information of other charities with a view to bringing them to the notice of those for whose benefit they are intended.

PART III

APPLICATION OF PROPERTY CY-PRÈS, AND ASSISTANCE AND SUPERVISION OF CHARITIES BY COURT AND CENTRAL AUTHORITIES

Extended powers of court, and variation of charters

13. Occasions for applying property cy-près (1) Subject to subsection (2) below, the circumstances in which the original purposes of a charitable gift can be altered to allow the property given or part of it to be applied cy-près shall be as follows:—

(a) where the original purposes, in whole or in part,—

(i) have been as far as may be fulfilled; or

(ii) cannot be carried out, or not according to the directions given and to the spirit of the gift; or

(b) where the original purposes provide a use for part only of the property available by virtue of the gift; or

(c) where the property available by virtue of the gift and other property applicable for similar purposes can be more effectively used in conjunction, and to that end can suitably, regard being had to the spirit of the gift, be made applicable to common purposes; or

(d) where the original purposes were laid down by reference to an area which then was but has since

ceased to be a unit for some other purpose, or by reference to a class of person or to an area which has for any reason since ceased to be suitable, regard being had to the spirit of the gift, or to be practical in administering the gift; or

(e) where the original purposes, in whole or in parts, have, since they were laid down,—

(i) been adequately provided for by other means; or

(ii) ceased, as being useless or harmful to the community or for other reasons, to be in law charitable; or

(iii) ceased in any other way to provide a suitable and effective method of using the property available by virtue of the gift, regard being had to the spirit of the gift.

(2) Subsection (1) above shall not affect the conditions which must be satisfied in order that property given for charitable purposes may be applied cy-près, except in so far as those conditions require a failure of the original purposes.

(3) References in the foregoing subsections to the original purposes of a gift shall be construed, where the application of the property given has been altered or regulated by a scheme or otherwise, as referring to the purposes for which the property is for the time being applicable.

(4) Without prejudice to the power to make schemes in circumstances falling within subsection (1) above, the court may by scheme made under the court's jurisdiction with respect to charities, in any case where the purposes for which the property is held are laid down by reference to any such area as is mentioned in the first column in the Third Schedule to this Act, provide for enlarging the area to any such area as is mentioned in the second column in the same entry in that Schedule.

(5) It is hereby declared that a trust for charitable purposes places a trustee under a duty, where the case permits and requires the property or some part

of it to be applied cy-près, to secure its effective use for charity by taking steps to enable it to be so applied.

14. Application cy-près of gifts of donors unknown or disclaiming (1) Property given for specific charitable purposes which fail shall be applicable cy-près as if given for charitable purposes generally, where it belongs—

(a) to a donor who, after such advertisements and inquiries as are reasonable, cannot be identified or cannot be found; or

(b) to a donor who has executed a written disclaimer of his right to have the property returned.

(2) For the purposes of this section property shall be conclusively presumed (without any advertisement or inquiry) to belong to donors who cannot be identified, in so far as it consists—

(a) of the proceeds of cash collections made by means of collecting boxes or by other means not adapted for distinguishing one gift from another; or

(b) of the proceeds of any lottery, competition, entertainment, sale or similar money-raising activity, after allowing for property given to provide prizes or articles for sale or otherwise to enable the activity to be undertaken.

(3) The court may by order direct that property not falling within subsection (2) above shall for the purposes of this section be treated (without any advertisement or inquiry) as belonging to donors who cannot be identified, where it appears to the court either—

(a) that it would be unreasonable, having regard to the amounts likely to be returned to the donors, to incur expense with a view to returning the property; or

(b) that it would be unreasonable, having regard to the nature, circumstances and amount of the gifts, and to the lapse of time since the gifts were made, for the donors to expect the property to be returned.

(4) Where property is applied cy-près by virtue of this section, the donor shall be deemed to have parted with all his interest at the time when the gift was made; but where property is so applied as belonging to donors who cannot be identified or cannot be found, and is not so applied by virtue of subsection (2) or (3) above—

(a) the scheme shall specify the total amount of that property; and

(b) the donor of any part of that amount shall be entitled, if he makes a claim not later than twelve months after the date on which the scheme is made, to recover from the charity for which the property is applied a sum equal to that part, less any expenses properly incurred by the charity trustees after that date in connection with claims relating to his gift; and

(c) the scheme may include directions as to the provision to be made for meeting any such claim.

(5) For the purposes of this section, charitable purposes shall be deemed to 'fail' where any difficulty in applying property to those purposes makes that property or the part not applicable cy-près available to be returned to the donors.

(6) In this section, except in so far as the context otherwise requires, references to a donor include persons claiming through or under the original donor, and references to property given include the property for the time being representing the property originally given or property derived from it.

(7) This section shall apply to property given for charitable purposes, notwithstanding that it was so given before the commencement of this Act.

Powers of Commissioners and Minister to make schemes, etc.

18. Concurrent jurisdiction with High Court for certain purposes (1) Subject to the provisions of this Act, the *Commissioners* may by order exercise the same jurisdiction and powers as are exercisable by the High Court in charity proceedings for the following purposes, that is to say:--

(a) establishing a scheme for the administration of a charity;

(b) appointing, discharging or removing a charity trustee or trustee for a charity, or removing an officer or servant;

(c) vesting or transferring property, or requiring or entitling any person to call for or make any transfer of property or any payment.

(2) Where the court directs a scheme for the administration of a charity to be established, the court may by order refer the matter to the *Commissioners* for them to prepare or settle a scheme in accordance with such directions (if any) as the court sees fit to give, and any such order may provide for the scheme to be put into effect by order of the *Commissioners* as if prepared under subsection (1) above and without any further order of the court.

(3) The *Commissioners* shall not have jurisdiction under this section to try or determine the title at law or in equity to any property as between a charity or trustee for a charity and a person holding or claiming the property or an interest in it adversely to the charity, or to try or determine any question as to the existence or extent of any charge or trust.

(4) Subject to the following subsections, the *Commissioners* shall not exercise their jurisdiction under this section as respects any charity, except—

(a) on the application of the charity; or

(b) on an order of the court under subsection (2) above.

(5) In the case of a charity not having any income from property amounting to more than £50 a year, and not being an exempt charity, the *Commissioners* may exercise their jurisdiction under this section on the application—

(a) of the Attorney General; or

(b) of any one or more of the charity trustees, or of any person inter-

ested in the charity, or of any two or more inhabitants of the area of the charity, if it is a local charity.

(6) Where in the case of a charity, other than an exempt charity, the *Commissioners* are satisfied that the charity trustees ought in the interests of the charity to apply for a scheme, but have unreasonably refused or neglected to do so, the *Commissioners may apply to the Secretary of State for him to refer the case to them with a view to a scheme, and if, after giving the charity trustees an opportunity to make representations to him, the Secretary of State does so, the Commissioners* may proceed accordingly without the application required by subsection (4) or (5) above:

Provided that the *Commissioners* shall not have power in a case where they act by virtue of this subsection to alter the purposes of a charity, unless forty years have elapsed from the date of its foundation.

(7) The *Commissioners* may on the application of any charity trustee or trustee for a charity exercise their jurisdiction under this section for the purpose of discharging him from his trusteeship.

(8) Before exercising any jurisdiction under this section otherwise than on an order of the court, the *Commissioners* shall give notice of their intention to do so to each of the charity trustees, except any that cannot be found or has no known address in the United Kingdom or who is party or privy to an application for the exercise of the jurisdiction; and any such notice may be given by post, may be addressed to the recipient's last known address in the United Kingdom.

(9) The *Commissioners* shall not exercise their jurisdiction under this section in any case (not referred to them by order of the court) which, by reason of its contentious character, or of any special question of law or of fact which it may involve, or for other reasons, the *Commissioners* may consider more fit to be adjudicated on by the court.

(10) An appeal against any order of the *Commissioners* under this section may

be brought in the High Court by the Attorney General.

(11) An appeal against any order of the *Commissioners* under this section may also, at any time within the three months beginning with the day following that on which the order is published, be brought in the High Court by the charity or any of the charity trustees, or by any person removed from any office or employment by the order (unless he is removed with the concurrence of the charity trustees or with the approval of the special visitor, if any, of the charity):

Provided that no appeal shall be brought under this subsection except with a certificate of the *Commissioners* that it is a proper case for an appeal or with the leave of one of the judges of the High Court attached to the Chancery Division.

(12) Where an order of the *Commissioners* under this section establishes a scheme for the administration of a charity, any person interested in the charity shall have the like right of appeal under subsection (11) above as a charity trustee, and so also, in the case of a charity which is a local charity in any area, shall any two or more inhabitants of the area and the parish council of any rural parish comprising the area or any part of it; but a parish council shall not exercise their right of appeal without the consent of the parish meeting.

(13) In the application of this section to the *Minister* of Education, subsection (6) shall have effect so as to authorise him to proceed with a view to a scheme in the circumstances in which it authorises the Commissioners to apply to the Secretary of State for him to refer a case to them.

20. Power to act for protection of charities (1) Where the *Commissioners* are satisfied as the result of an inquiry instituted by them under section 6 of this Act—

    (*a*) that there has been in the administration of a charity any misconduct or mismanagement; and

    (*b*) that it is necessary or desirable to act for the purpose of protecting the property of the charity or securing a proper application for the purposes of the charity of that property or of property coming to the charity;

then for that purpose the *Commissioners* may of their own motion do all or any of the following things:—

    (i) they may by order remove any trustee, charity trustee, officer, agent or servant of the charity who has been responsible for or privy to the misconduct or mismanagement or has by his conduct contributed to it or facilitated it;

    (ii) they may make any such order as is authorised by subsection (1) section 16 of this Act with respect to the vesting in or transfer to the official custodian for charities of property held by or in trust for the charity;

    (iii) they may order any bank or other person who holds money or securities on behalf of the charity or of any trustee for it not to part with the money or securities without the approval of the *Commissioners*;

    (iv) they may, notwithstanding anything in the trusts of the charity, by order restrict the transactions which may be entered into, or the nature or amount of the payments which may be made, in the administration of the charity without the approval of the *Commissioners*.

(2) The references in subsection (1) above to misconduct or mismanagement shall (notwithstanding anything in the trusts of the charity) extend to the employment for the remuneration or reward of persons acting in the affairs of the charity, or for other administrative purposes, of sums which are excessive in relation to the property which is or is likely to be applied or applicable for the purposes of the charity.

(3) The *Commissioners* may also re-

move a charity trustee by order made of their own motion—

(a) where the trustee is a bankrupt or a corporation in liquidation, or is incapable of acting by reason of mental disorder within the meaning of the Mental Health Act, 1959;

(b) where the trustee has not acted, and will not declare his willingness or unwillingness to act;

(c) where the trustee is outside England and Wales or cannot be found or does not act, and his absence or failure to act impedes the proper administration of the charity.

(4) The *Commissioners* may by order made of their own motion appoint a person to be a charity trustee—

(a) in place of a charity trustee removed by them under this section or otherwise;

(b) where there are no charity trustees, or where by reason of vacancies in their number or the absence or incapacity of any of their number the charity cannot apply for the appointment;

(c) where there is a single charity trustee, not being a corporation aggregate, and the *Commissioners* are of opinion that it is necessary to increase the number for the proper administration of the charity;

(d) where the *Commissioners* are of opinion that it is necessary for the proper administration of the charity to have an additional charity trustee, because one of the existing charity trustees who ought nevertheless to remain a charity trustee either cannot be found or does not act or is outside England and Wales.

(5) The powers of the *Commissioners* under this section to remove or appoint charity trustees of their own motion shall include power to make any such order with respect to the vesting in or transfer to the charity trustees of any property as the *Commissioners* could

make on the removal or appointment of a charity trustee by them under section 18 of this Act.

(6) Any order under this section for the removal or appointment of a charity trustee or trustee for a charity, or for the vesting or transfer of any property, shall be of the like effect as an order made under section 18 of this Act.

(7) Subsections (10) and (11) of section 18 of this Act shall apply to orders under this section as they apply to orders under that, save that where the *Commissioners* have by order removed a trustee, charity trustee, officer, agent, or servant of a charity under the power conferred by subsection (1) of this section, an appeal against such an order may be brought by any person so removed without a certificate of the *Commissioners* and without the leave of one of the judges of the High Court attached to the Chancery Division.

(8) The power of the *Commissioners* under subsection (1) above to remove a trustee, charity trustee, officer, agent or servant of a charity shall include power to suspend him from the exercise of his office or employment pending the consideration of his removal (but not for a period longer than three months), and to make provision as respects the period of the suspension for matters arising out of it, and in particular for enabling any person to execute any instrument in his name or otherwise act for him and, in the case of a charity trustee, for adjusting any rules governing the proceedings of the charity trustees to take account of the reduction in the number capable of acting.

(9) Before exercising any jurisdiction under this section, the *Commissioners* shall give notice of their intention to do so to each of the charity trustees, except any that cannot be found or has no known address in the United Kingdom; and any such notice may be given by post and, if given by post, may be addressed to the recipient's last known address in the United Kingdom.

(10) If any person contravenes an order under paragraph (iii) of subsection (1) above, he shall be liable on summary conviction to a fine not

exceeding £100, or to imprisonment for a term not exceeding six months, or to both; but no proceedings for an offence punishable under this subsection shall be instituted except by or with the consent of the *Commissioners*.

(11) Notwithstanding subsection (8) of section 3 of this Act, paragraph (ii) of subsection (1) above shall apply to the *Minister* of Education as well as to the Commissioners.

21. Publicity for proceedings under ss. 18 to 20 (1) The *Commissioners* shall not make any order under this Act to establish a scheme for the administration of a charity, or submit such a scheme to the court or the Secretary of State for an order giving it effect, unless not less than one month previously there has been given public notice of their proposals, inviting representations to be made to them within a time specified in the notice, being not less than one month from the date of such notice, and, in the case of a scheme relating to a local charity in a rural parish (other than an ecclesiastical charity), a draft of the scheme has been communicated to the parish council or, in the case of a parish not having a parish council, to the chairman of the parish meeting.

(2) The *Commissioners* shall not make any order under this Act to appoint, discharge or remove a charity trustee or trustee for a charity (other than the official custodian for charities), unless not less than one month previously there has been given the like public notice as is required by subsection (1) above for an order establishing a scheme:

Provided that this subsection shall not apply in the case of an order discharging or removing a trustee if the *Commissioners* are of opinion that it is unnecessary and not in his interest to give publicity to the proposal to discharge or remove him.

(3) Before the *Commissioners* make an order under this Act to remove without his consent a charity trustee or trustee for a charity, or an officer, agent or servant of a charity, the *Commissioners* shall, unless he cannot be found or has no known address in the United Kingdom, give him not less than one month's notice of their proposal, inviting representations to be made to them within a time specified in the notice.

(4) Where notice is given of any proposals as required by subsections (1) to (3) above, the *Commissioners* shall take into consideration any representations made to them about the proposals within the time specified in the notice, and may (without further notice) proceed with the proposals either without modification or with such modifications as appear to them to be desirable.

(5) Where the *Commissioners* make an order which is subject to appeal under subsection (11) of section 18 of this Act, the order shall be published either by giving public notice of it or by giving notice of it to all persons entitled to appeal against it under that subsection, as the *Commissioners* think fit.

(6) Where the *Commissioners* make an order under this Act to establish a scheme for the administration of a charity, a copy of the order shall, for not less than one month after the order is published, be available for public inspection at all reasonable times at the *Commissioners'* office and also at some convenient place in the area of the charity, if it is a local charity.

(7) Any notice to be given under this section of any proposals or order shall give such particulars of the proposals or order, or such directions for obtaining information about them, as the *Commissioners* think sufficient and appropriate, and any public notice shall be given in such manner as they think sufficient and appropriate.

(8) Any notice to be given under this section, other than a public notice, may be given by post and, if given by post, may be addressed to the recipient's last known address in the United Kingdom.

Establishment of common investment funds

22. Schemes to establish common investment funds (1) The court or the *Commissioners* may by order make and bring into effect schemes (in this section referred to as 'common investment schemes') for the establishment of common investment funds under trusts which provide—

  (*a*) for property transferred to the fund by or on behalf of a charity participating in the scheme to be invested under the control of trustees appointed to manage the fund; and

  (*b*) for the participating charities to be entitled (subject to the provisions of the scheme) to the capital and income of the fund in shares determined by reference to the amount or value of the property transferred to it by or on behalf of each of them and to the value of the fund at the time of the transfers.

(2) The court or the *Commissioners* may make a common investment scheme on the application of any two or more charities.

(8) The powers of investment of every charity shall include power to participate in common investment schemes, unless the power is excluded by a provision specifically referring to common investment schemes in the trusts of the charity.

(9) A common investment fund shall be deemed for all purposes to be a charity, and the assets of the fund shall be treated for the purposes of this Act as a permanent endowment, except that if the scheme establishing the fund admits to participation only charities not having a permanent endowment, the fund shall be treated as a charity not having a permanent endowment; and if the scheme admits only exempt charities, the fund shall be an exempt charity for the purposes of this Act.

(10) The person managing a common investment fund shall not be treated for the purposes of the Prevention of Fraud (Investments) Act, 1958, as carrying on the business of dealing in securities within the meaning of that Act, nor shall subsection (1) of section 14 of that Act (which restricts the distribution of circulars relating to investments) prohibit the distribution or possession of any document by reason only that it contains an invitation or

information relating to a common investment fund.

(11) Subsections (9) and (10) above shall apply not only to common investment funds established under the powers of this section, but also to any similar fund established for the exclusive benefit of charities by or under any enactment relating to any particular charities or class of charity.

Miscellaneous powers of Commissioners and Minister

23. Power to authorise dealings with charity property, etc. (1) Subject to the provisions of this section, where it appears to the *Commissioners* that any action proposed or contemplated in the administration of a charity is expedient in the interests of the charity, they may by order sanction that action, whether or not it would otherwise be within the powers exercisable by the charity trustees in the administration of the charity; and anything done under the authority of such an order shall be deemed to be properly done in the exercise of those powers.

(2) An order under this section may be made so as to authorise a particular transaction, compromise or the like, or a particular application of property, or so as to give a more general authority, and (without prejudice to the generality of subsection (1) above) may authorise a charity to use common premises, or employ a common staff, or otherwise combine for any purpose of administration, with any other charity.

(3) An order under this section may give directions as to the manner in which any expenditure is to be borne and as to other matters connected with or arising out of the action thereby authorised; and where anything is done in pursuance of an authority given by any such order, any directions given in connection therewith shall be binding on the charity trustees for the time being as if contained in the trusts of the charity:

Provided that any such directions may on the application of the charity be modified or superseded by a further order.

(4) Without prejudice to the generality of subsection (3) above, the directions which may be given by an order under this section shall in particular include directions for meeting any expenditure out of a specified fund, for charging any expenditure to capital or to income for requiring expenditure charged to capital to be recouped out of income within a specified period, for restricting the costs to be incurred at the expense of the charity, or for the investment of moneys arising from any transaction.

(5) An order under this section may authorise any act, notwithstanding that ... the trusts of the charity provide for the act to be done by or under the authority of the court; but no such order shall authorise the doing of any act expressly prohibited by Act of Parliament ... or by the trusts of the charity, ... or shall extend or alter the purposes of the charity.

31. Protection of expression 'common good' (1) It shall not be lawful, without the consent of the *Commissioners*, to invite gifts in money or in kind to the funds of, or to any fund managed by, an institution which has the words 'common good' in its name, other than a body corporate established by Royal charter, or to any fund described in or in connection with the invitation by a name which includes the words 'common good' otherwise than as part of the name of such a body corporate.

(2) The words 'common good' shall not, without the consent of the *Commissioners*, be used in the name of any institution established in England or Wales, other than a body corporate established by Royal charter.

(3) Any person contravening subsection (1) or (2) of this section shall be guilty of an offence and liable on summary conviction to a fine not exceeding fifty pounds.

PART IV

MISCELLANEOUS PROVISIONS AS TO CHARITIES AND THEIR AFFAIRS

32. General obligation to keep accounts (1) Charity trustees shall keep proper books of account with respect to the affairs of the charity, and charity trustees not required by or under the authority of any other Act to prepare periodical statements of account shall prepare consecutive statements of account consisting on each occasion of an income and expenditure account relating to a period of not more than fifteen months and a balance sheet relating to the end of that period.

(2) The books of account and statements of account relating to any charity shall be preserved for a period of seven years at least, unless the charity ceases to exist and the *Commissioners* permit them to be destroyed or otherwise disposed of.

(3) The statements of account relating to a parochial charity in a rural parish, other than an ecclesiastical charity, shall be sent annually to the parish council or, if there is no parish council, to the chairman of the parish meeting, and shall be presented by the council or chairman at the next parish meeting.

This subsection shall apply in relation to a borough included in a rural district as if the borough were a rural parish, except as regards the presentation of the accounts to the parish meeting.

33. Manner of giving notice of charity meetings, etc. (1) All notices which are required or authorised by the trusts of a charity to be given to a charity trustee, member or subscriber may be sent by post, and, if sent by post, may be addressed to any address given as his in the list of charity trustees, members or subscribers for the time being in use at the office or principal office of the charity.

(2) Where any such notice required to be given as aforesaid is given by post, it shall be deemed to have been given by the time at which the letter containing it would be delivered in the ordinary course of post.

(3) No notice required to be given as aforesaid of any meeting or election need be given to any charity trustee, member or subscriber, if in the list above mentioned he has no address in the United Kingdom.

37. Parochial charities (1) Where trustees hold any property for the purposes of a public recreation ground, or of allotments (whether under inclosure Acts or otherwise), for the benefit of inhabitants of a rural parish having a parish council, or for other charitable purposes connected with such a rural parish, except for an ecclesiastical charity, they may with the approval of the *Commissioners* and with the consent of the parish council transfer the property to the parish council or to persons appointed by the parish council; and the council or their appointees shall hold the property on the same trusts and subject to the same conditions as the trustees did.

This subsection shall apply to property held for any public purposes as it applies to property held for charitable purposes, and shall apply in relation to a borough included in a rural district as if the borough were a rural parish.

(2) Where the charity trustees of a parochial charity in a rural parish, not being an ecclesiastical charith nor a charity founded within the preceding forty years, do not include persons elected by the local government electors, ratepayers or inhabitants of the parish or appointed by the parish council or parish meeting, the parish council or parish meeting may appoint additional charity trustees, to such number as the *Commissioners* may allow; and if there is a sole charity trustee not elected or appointed as aforesaid of any such charity, the number of the charity trustees may, with the approval of the *Commissioners*, be increased to three of whom one may be nominated by the person holding the office of the sole trustee and one by the parish council or parish meeting.

This subsection shall apply in relation to a borough included in a rural district as if it were a rural parish (but with the omission of references to the parish meeting).

(3) Where, under the trusts of a charity other than an ecclesiastical charity, the inhabitants of a rural parish (whether in vestry or not) or a select vestry were formerly (in 1894) entitled to appoint charity trustees for, or trustees or beneficiaries of, the charity, then—

(a) in a parish having a parish council, the appointment shall be made by the parish council or, in the case of beneficiaries, by persons appointed by the parish council; and

(b) in a parish not having a parish council, the appointment shall be made by the parish meeting.

(4) Where overseers as such or, except in the case of an ecclesiastical charity, churchwardens as such were formerly (in 1894) charity trustees of or trustees for a parochial charity in a rural parish, either alone or jointly with other persons, then instead of the former overseer or churchwarden trustees there shall be trustees (to a number not greater than that of the former overseer, or churchwarden trustees) appointed by the parish council or, if there is no parish council, by the parish meeting.

(5) Where, . . . overseers of a parish as such were formerly (in 1927) charity trustees of or trustees for any charity, either alone or jointly with other persons, then instead of the former overseer trustees there shall be trustees (to a number not greater than that of the former overseer trustees) appointed—

(a) where the parish is a rural parish, by the parish council or, if there is no parish council, by the parish meeting; and

(b) where the parish is an urban parish, but is comprised in a borough included in a rural district by the borough council;
. . .

(6) Any appointment of a charity trustee or trustee for a charity which is made by virtue of this section shall be for a term of four years, but a retiring

trustee shall be eligible for re-appointment:

Provided that—

(a) on an appointment under subsection (2), where no previous appointments have been made by virtue of that subsection or of the corresponding provision of the Local Government Act, 1894, and more than one trustee is appointed, half of those appointed (or as nearly as may be) shall be appointed for a term of two years; and

(b) an appointment made to fill a casual vacancy shall be for the remainder of the term of the previous appointment.

(7) This section shall not affect the trusteeship, control or management of any voluntary school within the meaning of the Education Act, 1944.

(8) The provisions of this section . . . shall have effect subject to any order (including any future order) made under any enactment relating to local government with respect to local government areas or the powers of local authorities.

(9) In this section the expression 'formerly (in 1894)' relates to the period immediately before the passing of the Local Government Act, 1894, and the expression 'formerly (in 1927)' to the period immediately before the first day of April, 1927; and the word 'former' shall be construed accordingly.

SECTION 13

THIRD SCHEDULE

ENLARGEMENT OF AREAS OF LOCAL CHARITIES

Existing area	Permissible enlargement
1. Greater London	Any area comprising Greater London.
2. Any area in Greater London and not in, or partly in, the city of London	(i) Any area in Greater London and not in, or partly in, the city of London; (ii) the area of Greater London, exclusive of the city of London; (iii) any area comprising the area of Greater London, exclusive of the city of London; (iv) any area partly in Greater London and partly in any adjacent parish or parishes (civil or ecclesiastical), and not partly in the city of London.
3. A borough .. .. .. 4. Any area in a borough	Any area comprising the borough. (i) Any area in the borough (ii) the borough; (iii) any area comprising the borough (iv) any area partly in the borough and partly in any adjacent parish or parishes (civil or ecclesiastical).
5. A parish (civil or ecclesiastical), or two or more parishes, or an area in a parish, or partly in each of two or more parishes.	Any area not extending beyond the parish or parishes comprising or adjacent to the area in column 1.

FOURTH SCHEDULE

SECTION 15

COURT'S JURISDICTION OVER
CERTAIN CHARITIES GOVERNED
BY OR UNDER STATUTE

1. The court may by virtue of sub-section (3) of section 15 of this Act exercise its jurisdiction with respect to charities— . . .

(e) in relation to allotments regulated by sections 3 to 9 of the Poor Allotments Management Act, 1873;

(d) in relation to fuel allotments, that is to say, land which, by any enactment relating to inclosure or any instrument having effect under such an enactment, is vested in trustees upon trust that the land or the rents and profits of the land shall be used for the purpose of providing poor persons with fuel;

(h) in relation to charities regulated by section 37 of this Act, or by any such order as is mentioned in that section.

2. Notwithstanding anything in section 19 of the Commons Act, 1876, a scheme for the administration of a fuel allotment (within the meaning of the foregoing paragraph) may provide—

(a) for the sale or letting of the allotment or any part thereof, for the discharge of the land sold or let from any restrictions as to the use thereof imposed by or under any enactment relating to inclosure and for the application of the sums payable to the trustees of the allotment in respect of the sale or lease; or

(b) for the exchange of the allotment or any part thereof for other land, for the discharge as aforesaid of the land given in exchange by the said trustees, and for the application of any money payable to the said trustees for equality of exchange; or

(c) for the use of the allotment or any part thereof for any purposes specified in the scheme.

The Public Bodies (Admission to Meetings) Act, 1960

1. Admission of public to meetings of local authorities and other bodies (1) Subject to subsection (2) below, any meeting of a local authority or other body exercising public functions, being an authority or other body to which this Act applies, shall be open to the public.

(2) A body may, by resolution, exclude the public from a meeting (whether during the whole or part of the proceedings) whenever publicity would be prejudicial to the public interest by reason of the confidential nature of the business to be transacted or for other special reasons stated in the resolution and arising from the nature of that business or of the proceedings and where such a resolution is passed, this Act shall not require the meeting to be open to the public during proceedings to which the resolution applies.

(3) A body may under subsection (2) above treat the need to receive or consider recommendations or advice from sources other than members, committees or sub-committees of the body as a special reason why publicity would be prejudicial to the public interest, without regard to the subject or purport of the recommendations or advice; but the making by this subsection of express provision for that case shall not be taken to restrict the generality of sub-section (2) above in relation to other cases (including in particular cases where the report of a committee or sub-committee of the body is of a confidential nature).

(4) Where a meeting of a body is re-

quired by this Act to be open to the public during the proceedings or any part of them, the following provisions shall apply, that is to say,—

(a) public notice of the time and place of the meeting shall be given by posting it at the offices of the body (or, if the body has no offices, then in some central and conspicuous place in the area with which it is concerned) three clear days at least before the meeting or, if the meeting is convened at shorter notice, then at the time it is convened;

(b) there shall, on request and on payment of postage or other necessary charge for transmission, be supplied for the benefit of any newspaper a copy of the agenda for the meeting as supplied to members of the body (but excluding, if thought fit, any item during which the meeting is likely not to be open to the public), together with such further statements or particulars, if any, as are necessary to indicate the nature of the items included or, if thought fit in the case of any item, with copies of any reports or other documents supplied to members of the body in connection with the item;

(c) while the meeting is open to the public, the body shall not have power to exclude members of the public from the meeting and duly accredited representatives of newspapers attending for the purpose of reporting the proceedings for those newspapers shall, so far as practicable, be afforded reasonable facilities for taking their report and, unless the meeting is held in premises not belonging to the body or not on the telephone, for telephoning the report at their own expense.

(5) Where a meeting of a body is required by this Act to be open to the public during the proceedings or any part of them, and there is supplied to a member of the public attending the meeting, or in pursuance of paragraph (b) of subsection (4) above there is supplied for the benefit of a newspaper, any such copy of the agenda as is mentioned in that paragraph, with or without further statements or particulars for the purpose of indicating the nature of any item included in the agenda, the publication thereby of any defamatory matter contained in the agenda or in the further statements or particulars shall be privileged, unless the publication is proved to be made with malice.

(6) When a body to which this Act applies resolves itself into committee, the proceedings in committee shall for the purposes of this Act be treated as forming part of the proceedings of the body at the meeting.

(7) Any reference in this section to a newspaper shall apply also to a news agency which systematically carries on the business of selling and supplying reports or information to newspapers, and to any organisation which is systematically engaged in collecting news for sound or television broadcasts; but nothing in this section shall require a body to permit the taking of photographs of any proceedings, or the use of any means to enable persons not present to see or hear any proceedings (whether at the time or later), or the making of any oral report on any proceedings as they take place.

(8) The provisions of this section shall be without prejudice to any power of exclusion to suppress or prevent disorderly conduct or other misbehaviour at a meeting.

2. Application of Act, and consequential provisions (1) This Act shall apply to the bodies specified in the Schedule to this Act, and to such bodies as may for the time being be added to that Schedule by order made under subsection (3) below; and where this Act applies to a body, the foregoing section shall apply in relation to any committee of the body whose members consist of or include all members of the body, as that section applies in relation to the body itself, but so that for the purposes of paragraph (c) of subsection (4) of that section premises belonging to the body shall be treated as belonging to the committee.

(2) In the Schedule to the Defamation Act, 1952 (by virtue of which, among other things, newspaper reports of all proceedings at meetings of local authorities and their committees are privileged unless admission to the meeting is denied to representatives of newspapers and other members of the public), in the definition of 'local authority' in paragraph 13 for the reference to the Local Authorities (Admission of the Press to Meetings) Act, 1908, there shall be substituted a reference to this Act.

(3) Any body established by or under any Act may be added to the Schedule to this Act, and any body so added may be removed from the Schedule, by order of the appropriate Minister made by statutory instrument, but a statutory instrument made by a Minister under this section shall be of no effect unless it is approved by resolution of each House of Parliament; and for this purpose the appropriate Minister is, in the case of any body, the Minister of the Crown in charge of the Government department concerned or primarily concerned with the matters dealt with by that body, but an order made under this subsection by any Minister of the Crown shall be effective, whether or not he is the appropriate Minister.

SCHEDULE

BODIES TO WHICH THIS ACT APPLIES

1. The bodies to which in England and Wales this Act applies are—

(a) local authorities within the meaning of the Local Government Act, 1933, ... the Common Council of the City of London ... , and joint boards or joint committees constituted to discharge functions of any two or more of those bodies;

(b) the parish meetings of rural parishes;

(c) ... joint boards and joint committees constituted by or under any Act for the purposes of water supply, and consisting of or including representatives of local authorities within the meaning of the Local Government Act, 1933;

(d) education committees (including joint education committees) constituted under Part II, and divisional executives constituted under Part III of the First Schedule to the Education Act, 1944;

(e) bodies constituted in accordance with regulations made under subsection (4) of section 22 of the National Health Service Act, 1946;

(f) regional hospital boards constituted under section 11 of the said Act of 1946;

(g) executive councils constituted under section 31 of the said Act of 1946, but only so far as regards the exercise of their executive functions;

(h) bodies not mentioned above but having, within the meaning of the Public Works Loans Act, 1875, power to levy a rate (other than police authorities).

Noise Abatement Act, 1960

2. Restriction of operation on highways, etc., of loudspeakers (1) Subject to the provisions of this section, a loudspeaker in a street shall not be operated—

(a) between the hours of nine in the evening and eight in the following morning, for any purpose;

(b) at any other time, for the purpose of advertising any entertainment, trade or business;

and any person who operates or permits the operation of a loudspeaker in contravention of this subsection shall be liable on summary conviction to a fine not exceeding £10.

In this subsection 'street' means a highway and any other road, footway, square or court which is for the time being open to the public.

(2) The foregoing subsection shall not apply to the operation of a loudspeaker—

(a) for police, fire brigade or ambulance purposes, or by a local authority within their area;

(b) for communicating with persons on a vessel for the purpose of directing the movement of that or any other vessel;

(c) if the loudspeaker forms part of a public telephone system;

(d) if the loudspeaker—

  (i) is in or fixed to a vehicle and

  (ii) is operated solely for the entertainment of or for communicating with the driver or a passenger of the vehicle or, where the loudspeaker is or forms part of the horn or similar warning instrument of the vehicle, solely for giving warning to other traffic, and

  (iii) is so operated as not to give reasonable cause for annoyance to persons in the vicinity;

(e) otherwise than on a highway, by persons employed in connection with transport undertaking used by the public in a case where the loudspeaker is operated solely for making announcements to passengers or prospective passengers or to other persons so employed;

(f) by a travelling showman on land which is being used for the purposes of a pleasure fair;

(g) in case of emergency.

(3) Paragraph (b) of subsection (1) of this section shall not apply to the operation of a loudspeaker between the hours of noon and seven o'clock in the evening on the same day if the loudspeaker—

(a) is fixed to a vehicle which is being used for the conveyance of a perishable commodity for human consumption; and

(b) is operated solely for informing members of the public (otherwise than by means of words) that the commodity is on sale from the vehicle; and

(c) is so operated as not to give reasonable cause for annoyance to persons in the vicinity.

(4) Proceedings for an offence under this section in England or Wales may, without prejudice to the powers of any other person to institute such proceedings, be instituted by any local authority within whose area the offence was committed. . . .

(5) In this section . . . 'local authority' means—

(a) as respects England and Wales, the council of a county, . . . or county district, . . . and for the purposes of subsection (4) of this section includes a parish council and the council of a borough included in a rural district;...

and in this section 'loudspeaker' includes a megaphone and any other device for amplifying sound.

Highways (Miscellaneous Provisions) Act, 1961

4. Contributions to expenditure of parish councils in maintaining footpaths etc. (1) The highway authority for any footpath or bridleway which a parish council have power to maintain under section 46 of the principal Act* may undertake to defray the whole or part of any expenditure in-

*i.e. The Highways Act, 1959.

curred by the council in maintaining the footpath or bridleway.

(2) For the purposes of any enactment restricting the expenditure of a parish council, their expenditure shall be deemed not to include any expenditure falling to be defrayed by a highway authority by virtue of the foregoing subsection.

Public Health Act, 1961

45. Attachment of street lamps to buildings—(1) Subject to the provisions of this section, a county council, local authority or parish council or parish meeting (hereafter in this section referred to as a 'street lighting authority') may affix to any building such lamps, brackets, pipes, electric lines and apparatus (hereafter in this section referred to as 'attachments') as may be required for the purposes of street lighting.

(2) A street lighting authority shall not under this section affix attachments to a building without the consent of the owner of the building:

Provided that, where in the opinion of the street lighting authority any consent required under this subsection is unreasonably withheld, they may apply to the appropriate authority, who may either allow the attachments subject to such conditions, if any, as to rent or otherwise as the appropriate authority thinks fit, or disallow the attachments.

(3) Where any attachments have been affixed to a building under this section and the person who gave his consent under subsection (2) of this section, or who was the owner of the building when the attachments were allowed by the appropriate authority, ceases to be the owner of the building, the subsequent owner may give to the street lighting authority notice requiring them to remove the attachments; and, subject to the provisions of this subsection, the street lighting authority shall comply with the requirements within three months after the service of the notice:

Provided that, where in the opinion of the street lighting authority any such requirement is unreasonable, they may apply to the appropriate authority, who may either annul the notice subject to such conditions, if any, as to rent or otherwise as the appropriate authority thinks fit or confirm the notice subject to such extension, if any, of the said period of three months as the appropriate authority thinks fit.

(4) Where any attachments have been affixed to a building under this section, the owner of the building may give the street lighting authority by whom they were affixed not less than fourteen days notice requiring them at their own expense temporarily to remove the attachments where necessary during any reconstruction or repair of the building.

(5) Where attachments are affixed to a building under this section, the street lighting authority shall have the right as against any person having an interest in the building to alter or remove them, or to repair or maintain them.

(6) If the owner of a building suffers damage by, or in consequence of, the affixing to the building of any attachments under this section, or by or in consequence of the exercise of the rights conferred by subsection (5) of this section, he shall be entitled to be paid by the street lighting authority compensation to be determined in case of dispute by the Lands Tribunal, and, so far as the compensation is properly to be calculated by reference to the depreciation of the value of his interest in the building, Rules 2 to 4 of the Rules set out in section five of the Land Compensation Act, 1961, shall apply.

(7) A street lighting authority shall not do anything under this section which would, to their knowledge, be in contravention of a building preservation order under section twenty-nine of the Town and Country Planning Act, 1947.

(8) In this section 'appropriate authority' means a magistrates' court, except that in relation to buildings of the descriptions in the Fourth Schedule to this Act it has the meaning there given.

(9) In this section—

'building' includes a structure and a bridge or aqueduct over a street; 'owner'—

(a) in relation to a building occupied under a tenancy for a term of years whereof five years or more remain unexpired, means the occupier of the building, and

(b) in relation to any other building, has the same meaning as in the Public Health Act, 1936, and 'owned' shall be construed accordingly;

'street lighting' includes the lighting of markets and public buildings under section one hundred and sixty-one of the Public Health Act, 1875, (which relates to the powers conferred on urban authorities within the meaning of that Act), and the lighting of public places under section three of the Parish Councils Act, 1957,

and the definitions in this section shall apply for the purposes of the Fourth Schedule to this Act.

(10) Section five of the Parish Councils Act, 1957 (which contains provisions as to the consents required for the exercise of the powers of street lighting conferred by that Act), shall not apply in relation to the affixing after the commencement of this Act of any attachments to a building within the meaning of this section but those powers shall not be taken to authorise anything to be done without consent for which consent is required by this section.

49. **Use by local authorities of vehicles and appliances on footways and bridleways** (1) No statutory provision prohibiting or restricting the use of footpaths, footways or bridleways shall affect the use by a county council, local authority, parish council or parish meeting of appliances or vehicles, whether mechanically operated or propelled or not, for cleansing or maintaining footpaths, footways or bridleways or their verges.

(2) The Minister of Transport and the Minister of Power acting jointly may make regulations* prescribing the conditions under which the rights conferred by this section may be exercised, and such regulations may in particular make provision as to—

(a) the construction of any appliances or vehicles used under this section,

(b) the maximum weight of any such appliances or vehicles, or the maximum weight borne by any wheel or axle,

(c) the maximum speed of any such appliances or vehicles,

(d) the hours during which the appliances or vehicles may be used, and

(e) the giving by the Minister of Transport or the Minister of Power of directions dispensing with or relaxing any requirement of the regulations as it applies to a particular authority or in any particular case.

The power of making regulations under this subsection shall be exercisable by statutory instrument which shall be subject to annulment in pursuance of a resolution of either House of Parliament.

(3) In this section 'statutory provision' means a provision contained in, or having effect under, any enactment.

54. **Boating pools and lakes** (1) Subject to the provisions of this section, a local authority or parish council may

*See SI. 1963 No. 2126.

in any park or pleasure-ground provided by them, or under their management and control, provide a boating pool.

(2) The local authority or parish council may provide such buildings and execute such work as may be necessary or expedient in connection with the provision of a boating pool under this section, and may also provide boats for the boating pool and such other equipment as may be reasonably required in connection with the use of the boating pool and buildings.

References in this section to a boating pool so provided shall include references to anything else provided under this subsection.

(3) The local authority or parish council may either—

(a) themselves manage a boating pool provided under this section, making such reasonable charges for its use, or for admission, as they think fit, or

(b) let it, or any part of it, for such consideration, and on such terms and conditions, as they think fit.

(4) Where the existence of a boating pool is likely to interfere with any water flowing directly or indirectly out of or into any watercourse which is vested in or controlled by a river board, catchment board or internal drainage board, the local authority or parish council shall before providing a boating pool under this section consult with the board.

(5) No power given by this section shall be exercised in such a manner as to contravene any covenant or condition subject to which a gift or lease of a park or pleasure-ground has been accepted or made without the consent of the donor, grantor, lessor or other person or persons entitled in law to the benefit of the covenant or condition.

(6) Subsection (2) of section 44 of the Public Health Acts Amendment Act, 1890 (which gives a local authority certain powers as regards lakes and water in parks and pleasure-grounds)—

(a) shall apply in relation to a park or pleasure-ground under the management and control of a local authority as it applies in relation to a park or pleasure-ground provided by them, and

(b) shall be in force throughout the district of every local authority;

and sections 3 and 5 of the said Act shall not apply to that subsection.

(7) Section 278 of the Public Health Act, 1936 (under which compensation may be paid for damage incurred in consequence of the exercise by the local authority of their powers under that Act), shall apply as if this section were contained in that Act.

(8) *Amends the First Schedule of the Parish Councils Act, 1957.*

(9) Sections 331 and 334 of the Public Health Act, 1936 (which contain savings for water rights and for the works of land drainage authorities), shall apply as if this section were contained in that Act and as if references in those sections to a local authority included references to a parish council.

(10) It is hereby declared that this section does not authorise a local authority or parish council to do anything in contravention of byelaws made under *section 47 of the Land Drainage Act*, 1930 (under which byelaws may be made, among other things, for regulating the use of watercourses).

81. Summary recovery of damages for negligence Damages recoverable by a county council, local authority or parish council or parish meeting . . . for damage caused by negligence to any lamp, lamp-post, notice board, fence, rail, post, shelter or other apparatus or equipment provided by them in a street or public place shall, if the amount thereof does not exceed twenty pounds, be recoverable summarily as a civil debt.

Trustee Investments Act, 1961

[3rd August 1961]

1. New powers of investment of trustees (1) A trustee may invest any property in his hands, whether at the time in a state of investment or not, in any manner specified in Part I or II of the First Schedule to this Act or, *subject to the next following section*, in any manner specified in Part III of that Schedule, and may also from time to time vary any such investments.

(2) The supplemental provisions contained in Part IV of that Schedule shall have effect for the interpretation and for restricting the operation of the said Parts I to III.

(3) No provision relating to the powers of the trustee contained in any instrument (not being an enactment or an instrument made under an enactment) made before the passing of this Act shall limit the powers conferred by this section, but those powers are exercisable only in so far as a contrary intention is not expressed in any Act or instrument made under an enactment, whenever passed or made, and so relating or in any other instrument so relating which is made after the passing of this Act. . . .

(4) In this Act 'narrower-range investment' means an investment falling within Part I or II of the First Schedule to this Act and 'wider-range investment' means an investment falling within Part III of that Schedule.

2. Restrictions on wider-range investment (1) A trustee shall not have power by virtue of the foregoing section to make or retain any wider-range investment unless the trust fund has been divided into two parts (hereinafter referred to as the narrower-range part and the wider-range part), the parts being, subject to the provisions of this Act, equal in value at the time of the division; and where such a division has been made no subsequent division of the same fund shall be made for the purposes of this section, and no property shall be transferred from one part of the fund to the other unless either—

(a) the transfer is authorised or required by the following provisions of this Act, or

(b) a compensating transfer is made at the same time.

In this section 'compensating transfer', in relation to any transferred property, means a transfer in the opposite direction of property of equal value.

(2) Property belonging to the narrower-range part of a trust fund shall not by virtue of the foregoing section be invested except in narrower-range investments, and any property invested in any other manner which is or becomes comprised in hat part of the trust fund shall either be transferred to the wider-range part of the fund, with a compensating transfer, or be reinvested in narrower-range investments as soon as may be.

(3) Where any property accrues to a trust fund after the fund has been divided in pursuance of subsection (1) of this section, then—

(a) if the property accrues to the trustee as owner or former owner of property comprised in either part of the fund, it shall be treated as belonging to that part of the fund;

(b) in any other case, the trustee shall secure, by apportionment of the accruing property or the transfer of property from one part of the fund to the other, or both, that the value of each part of the fund is increased by the same amount.

Where a trustee acquires property in consideration of a money payment the acquisition of the property shall be treated for the purposes of this section as investment and not as the accrual of property to the trust fund, notwithstanding that the amount of the consideration is less than the value of property acquired; and paragraph (a) of this subsection shall not include the case of a dividend or interest becoming part of a trust fund.

(4) Where in the exercise of any power or duty of a trustee property falls to be taken out of the trust fund, nothing in this section shall restrict his discretion as to the choice of property to be taken out.

3. Relationship between Act and other powers of investment (1) The powers conferred by section 1 of this Act are in addition to and not in derogation from any power conferred otherwise than by this Act of investment or postponing conversion exercisable by a trustee (hereinafter referred to as a 'special power').

(2) Any special power (however expressed) to invest property in any investment for the time being authorised by law for the investment of trust property, being a power conferred on a trustee before the passing of this Act or conferred on him under any enactment passed before the passing of this Act, shall have effect as a power to invest property in like manner and subject to the like provisions as under the foregoing provisions of this Act.

(3) In relation to property, including wider-range but not including narrower-range investments,—

(a) where a trustee is authorised to apart from—

(i) the provisions of section 1 of this Act or any of the provisions of Part I of the Trustee Act, 1925, . . . or

(ii) any such power to invest in authorised investments as is mentioned in the foregoing subsection, or

(b) which became part of a trust fund in consequence of the exercise by the trustee, as owner of property falling within this subsection, of any power conferred by subsection (3) or (4) of section 10 of the Trustee Act, 1925, . . .

the foregoing section shall have effect subject to the modifications set out in the Second Schedule to this Act.

(4) The foregoing subsection shall not apply where the powers of the trustee to invest or postpone conversion have been conferred or varied—

(a) by an order of any court made within the period of ten years ending with the passing of this Act, or

(b) by any enactment passed, or instrument having effect under an enactment made, within that period, being an enactment or instrument relating specifically to the trusts in question; or

(c) by an enactment contained in a local Act of the present Session;

but the provisions of the Third Schedule to this Act shall have effect in a case falling within this subsection.

4. Interpretation of references to trust property and trust funds (1) In this Act 'property' includes real or personal property of any description, including money and things in action:

Provided that it does not include an interest in expectancy, but the falling into possession of such an interest, or the receipt of proceeds of the sale thereof, shall be treated for the purposes of this Act as an accrual of property to the trust fund.

(2) So much of the property in the hands of a trustee shall for the purposes of this Act constitute one trust fund as is held on trusts which (as respects the beneficiaries or their respective interests or the purposes of the trust or as respects the powers of the trustee) are not identical with those on which any other property in his hands is held.

(3) Where property is taken out of a trust fund by way of appropriation so as to form a separate fund, and at the time of the appropriation the trust fund had (as to the whole or a part thereof) been divided in pursuance of subsection (1) of section 2 of this Act, or that subsection as modified by the Second Schedule to this Act, then if the separate fund is so divided the narrower-range and wider-range parts of the separate fund may be constituted so as either to be equal, or to bear to each other the same proportion as the two corresponding parts of the fund out of which it was so appropriated (the values of those parts of those funds being ascertained as at the time of appro-

priation), or some intermediate proportion.

5. Certain valuations to be conclusive for purposes of division of trust fund (1) If for the purposes section 2 or 4 of this Act or the Second Schedule thereto a trustee obtains, from a person reasonably believed by the trustee to be qualified to make it, a valuation in writing of any property, the valuation shall be conclusive in determining whether the division of the trust fund in pursuance of subsection (1) of the said section 2, or any transfer or apportionment of property under that section or the said Second Schedule, has been duly made.

(2) The foregoing subsection applies to any such valuation notwithstanding that it is made by a person in the course of his employment as an officer or servant.

6. Duty of trustees in choosing investments (1) In the exercise of his powers of investment a trustee shall have regard—

- (a) to the need for diversification of investments of the trust, in so far as is appropriate to the circumstances of the trust;
- (b) to the suitability to the trust of investments of the description of investment proposed and of the investment proposed as an investment of that description.

(2) Before exercising any power conferred by section 1 of this Act to invest in a manner specified in Part II or III of the First Schedule to this Act, or before investing in any such manner in the exercise of a power falling within subsection (2) of section 3 of this Act, a trustee shall obtain and consider proper advice on the question whether the investment is satisfactory having regard to the matters mentioned in paragraphs (a) and (b) of the foregoing subsection.

(3) A trustee retaining any investment made in the exercise of such a power and in such a manner as aforesaid shall determine at what intervals the circumstances, and in particular the nature of the investment, make it desirable to obtain such advice as aforesaid, and shall obtain and consider such advice accordingly.

(4) For the purposes of the two foregoing subsections, proper advice is the advice of a person who is reasonably believed by the trustee to be qualified by his ability in and practical experience of financial matters; and such advice may be given by a person notwithstanding that he gives it in the course of his employment as an officer or servant.

(5) A trustee shall not be treated as having complied with subsection (2) or (3) of this section unless the advice was given or has been subsequently confirmed in writing.

(6) Subsections (2) and (3) of this section shall not apply to one of two or more trustees where he is the person giving the advice required by this section to his co-trustee or co-trustees, and shall not apply where powers of a trustee are lawfully exercised by an officer or servant competent under subsection (4) of this section to give proper advice.

(7) Without prejudice to section 8 of the Trustee Act, 1925, . . . (which relate to valuation, and the proportion of the value to be lent, where a trustee lends on the security of property) the advice required by this section shall not include, in the case of a loan on the security of freehold or leasehold property in England and Wales . . . advice on the suitability of the particular loan.

7. Application of ss. 1–6 to persons, other than trustees, having trustee investment powers (1) Where any persons, not being trustees, have a statutory power of making investments which is or includes power—

- (a) to make the like investments as are authorised by section 1 of the Trustee Act, 1925, . . . or
- (b) to make the like investments as trustees are for the time being by law authorised to make,

however the power is expressed, the foregoing provisions of this Act shall with the necessary modifications apply in relation to them as if they were trustees:

Provided that property belonging to ... any ... fund applicable wholly or partly for the redemption of debt shall not by virtue of the foregoing provisions of this Act be invested or held invested in any manner specified in paragraph 6 of Part II of the First Schedule to this Act or in wider-range investments.

(2) Where, in the exercise of powers conferred by any enactment, an authority to which paragraph 9 of Part II of the First Schedule to this Act applies uses money belonging to any fund for a purpose for which the authority has power to borrow, the foregoing provisions of this Act, as applied by the foregoing subsection, shall apply as if there were comprised in the fund (in addition to the actual content thereof) property, being narrower-range investments, having a value equal to so much of the said money as for the time being has not been repaid to the fund, and accordingly any repayment of such money to the fund shall not be treated for the said purposes as the accrual of property to the fund:

Provided that nothing in this subsection shall be taken to require compliance with any of the provisions of section 6 of this Act in relation to the exercise of such powers as aforesaid.

(3) In this section ... 'statutory power' means a power conferred by an enactment passed before the passing of this Act or by any instrument made under any such enactment.

8. Application of ss. 1–6 in special cases (1) In relation to persons to whom this section applies—

  (a) notwithstanding anything in subsection (3) of section 1 of this Act, no provision of any enactment passed, or instrument having effect under an enactment and made, before the passing of this Act shall limit the powers conferred by the said section 1;

  (b) subsection (1) of the foregoing section shall apply where the power of making investments therein mentioned is or includes a power to make some only of the investments mentioned in para-

graph (a) or (b) of that subsection.

11. Local Authority investment Schemes (1) Without prejudice to powers conferred by or under any other enactment, any authority to which this section applies may invest property held by the authority in accordance with a scheme submitted to the Treasury by any association of local authorities ... and approved by the Treasury as enabling investments to be made collectively without in substance extending the scope of powers of investment.

(2) A scheme under this section may apply to a specified authority or to a specified class of authorities, may make different provisions as respects different descriptions of property or property held for different purposes, and may impose restrictions on the extent to which the power conferred by the foregoing subsection shall be exercisable.

(3) In approving a scheme under this section, the Treasury may direct that the Prevention of Fraud (Investments) Act, 1958, or the Prevention of Fraud (Investments) Act (Northern Ireland), 1940, shall not apply to dealings undertaken or documents issued for the purposes of the scheme, or to such dealings or documents of such descriptions as may be specified in the direction.

(4) The authorities to which this section applies are—

  (a) in England and Wales, the council of a ... borough (including a borough which has been included in a rural district) ... or a parish, ...

  (c) in any part of Great Britain, a joint board or joint committee constituted to discharge or advise on the discharge of the functions of any two or more of ... authorities ...

12. Power to confer additional powers of investment (1) Her Majesty may by Order in Council extend the powers of investment conferred by section 1 of this Act by adding to Part I, Part II or Part III of the First Schedule to this Act any manner of investment specified in the Order.

(2) Any Order under this section shall be subject to annulment in pursuance of a resolution of either House of Parliament.

13. Power to modify provisions as to division of trust fund (1) The Treasury may by order made by statutory instrument direct that, subject to subsection (3) of section 4 of this Act, any division of a trust fund made in pursuance of subsection (1) of section 2 of this Act during the continuance in force of the order shall be made so that the value of the wider-range part at the time of the division bears to the then value of the narrower-range part such proportion, greater than one but not greater than three to one, as may be prescribed by the order; and in this Act 'the prescribed proportion' means the proportion for the time being prescribed under this subsection.

(2) A fund which has been divided in pursuance of subsection (1) of section 2 of this Act before the coming into operation of an order under the foregoing subsection may notwithstanding anything in that subsection be again divided (once only) in pursuance of the said subsection (1) during the continuance in force of the order.

(3) If an order is made under subsection (1) of this section, then as from the coming into operation of the order—

(a) paragraph (b) of subsection (3) of section 2 of this Act and subparagraph (b) of paragraph 3 of the Second Schedule thereto shall have effect with the substitution, for the words from 'each' to the end, of the words 'the wider-range part of the fund is increased by an amount which bears the prescribed proportion to the amount by which the value of the narrower-range part of the fund is increased';

(b) subsection (3) of section 4 of this Act shall have effect as if for the words 'so as either' to 'each other' there were substituted the words 'so as to bear to each other either the prescribed proportion or'.

(4) An order under this section may be revoked by a subsequent order thereunder prescribing a greater proportion.

(5) An order under this section shall not have effect unless approved by a resolution of each House of Parliament.

15. Saving for powers of court The enlargement of the investment powers of trustees by this Act shall not lessen any power of a court to confer wider powers of investment on trustees, or affect the extent to which any such power is to be exercised.

SECTION 1

SCHEDULES

FIRST SCHEDULE

Manner of Investment

Part I

Narrower-Range Investments not Requiring Advice

1. In Defence Bonds, National Savings Certificates, Ulster Savings Certificates, Ulster Development Bonds and National Development Bonds.

2. In deposits in the Post Office Savings Bank, ordinary deposits in a trustee savings bank and deposits in a bank or department thereof certified under subsection (3) of section 9 of the Finance Act, 1956.

Part II

Narrower-Range Investments Requiring Advice

1. In securities issued by Her Majesty's Government in the United Kingdom, the Government of Northern Ireland or the Government of the Isle of Man, not being securities falling within Part I of this Schedule and being fixed-interest securities registered in the United Kingdom or the Isle of Man, Treasury Bills or Tax Reserve Certificates.

2. In any securities the payment of interest on which is guaranteed by Her Majesty's Government in the United Kingdom or the Government of Northern Ireland.

3. In fixed-interest securities issued in the United Kingdom by any public authority or nationalised industry or undertaking in the United Kingdom.

4. In fixed-interest securities issued in the United Kingdom by the government of any overseas territory within the Commonwealth or by any public or local authority within such a territory, being securities registered in the United Kingdom.

References in this paragraph to an overseas territory or to the government of such a territory shall be construed as if they occurred in the Overseas Service Act, 1958.

5. In fixed-interest securities issued in the United Kingdom by the International Bank for Reconstruction and Development, being securities registered in the United Kingdom. In fixed interest securities issued in the United Kingdom by the Inter-American Development Bank.

6. In debentures issued in the United Kingdom by a company incorporated in the United Kingdom, being debentures registered in the United Kingdom.

7. In stock of the Bank of Ireland.

8. In debentures issued by the Agricultural Mortgage Corporation Limited or the Scottish Agricultural Securities Corporation Limited.

9. In loans to any authority to which this paragraph applies charged on all or any of the revenues of the authority or on a fund into which all or any of those revenues are payable, in any fixed-interest securities issued in the United Kingdom by any such authority for the purpose of borrowing money so charged, and in deposits with any such authority by way of temporary loan made on the giving of a receipt for the loan by the treasurer or other similar officer of the authority and on the giving of an undertaking by the authority that, if requested to charge the loan as aforesaid, it will either comply with the request or repay the loan.

This paragraph applies to the following authorities, that is to say—

(a) any local authority in the United Kingdom;

(b) any authority all the members of which are appointed or elected by one or more local authorities in the United Kingdom;

(c) any authority the majority of the members of which are appointed or elected by one or more local authorities in the United Kingdom, being an authority which by virtue of any enactment has power to issue a precept to a local authority in England and Wales, or a requisition to a local authority in Scotland, or to the expenses of which, by virtue of any enactment, a local authority in the United Kingdom is or can be required to contribute;

(d) the Receiver for the Metropolitan Police District or a combined police authority (within the meaning of the Police Act, 1946);

(e) the Belfast City and District Water Commissioners.

(f) The Great Ouse Water Authority.

10. In debentures or in the guaranteed or preference stock of any incorporated company, being statutory water undertakers within the meaning of the Water Act, 1945, or any corresponding enactment in force in Northern Ireland, and having during each of the ten years immediately preceding the calendar year in which the investment was made paid a dividend of not less than five per cent. on its ordinary shares.

11. In deposits by way of special investment in a trustee savings bank or in a department (not being a department certified under subsection (3) of section 9 of the Finance Act, 1956) of a bank any other department of which is so certified.

12. In deposits in a building society designated under section 1 of the House Purchase and Housing Act, 1959.

13. In mortgages of freehold property in England and Wales or Northern

Ireland and of leasehold property in those countries of which the unexpired term at the time of investment is not less than sixty years, and in loans on heritable security in Scotland.

14. In perpetual rent-charges charged on land in England and Wales or Northern Ireland and fee-farm rents (not being rent-charges) issuing out of such land, and in feu-duties or ground annuals in Scotland

PART III

WIDER-RANGE INVESTMENTS

1. In any securities issued in the United Kingdom by a company incorporated in the United Kingdom, being securities registered in the United Kingdom and not being securities falling within Part II of this Schedule.

2. In shares in any building society designated under section 1 of the House Purchase and Housing Act, 1959.

3. In any units, or other shares of the investments subject to the trusts, of a unit trust scheme in the case of which there is in force at the time of investment an order of the Board of Trade under section 17 of the Prevention of Fraud (Investments) Act, 1958, or of the Ministry of Commerce for Northern Ireland under section 16 of the Prevention of Fraud (Investments) Act (Northern Ireland), 1940.

PART IV

SUPPLEMENTAL

1. The securities mentioned in Parts I to III of this Schedule do not include any securities where the holder can be required to accept repayment of the principal, or the payment of any interest, otherwise than in sterling.

2. The securities mentioned in paragraphs 1 to 8 of Part II, other than Treasury Bills or Tax Reserve Certificates, securities issued before the passing of this Act by the Government of the Isle of Man, securities falling within paragraph 4 of the said Part II issued before the passing of this Act or securities falling within paragraph 9 of that Part, and the securities mentioned in paragraph 1 of Part III of this Schedule, do not include—

(a) securities the price of which is not quoted on a recognised stock exchange within the meaning of the Prevention of Fraud (Investments) Act, 1958, or the Belfast stock exchange;

(b) shares or debenture stock not fully paid up (except shares or debenture stock which by the terms of issue are required to be fully paid up within nine months of the date of issue).

3. The securities mentioned in paragraph 6 of Part II and paragraph 1 of Part III of this Schedule do not include—

(a) shares or debentures of an incorporated company of which the total issued and paid up share capital is less than one million pounds;

(b) shares or debentures of an incorporated company which has not in each of the five years immediately preceding the calendar year in which the investment is made paid a dividend on all the shares issued by the company, excluding any shares which by their terms of issue did not rank for the dividend for that year.

For the purposes of sub-paragraph (b) of this paragraph a company formed—

(i) to take over the business of another company or other companies, or

(ii) to acquire the securities of, or control of, another company or other companies,

or for either of those purposes and for other purposes shall be deemed to have paid a dividend as mentioned in that sub-paragraph in any year in which such a dividend has been paid by the other company or all the other companies, as the case may be.

4. In this Schedule, unless the context otherwise requires, the following expressions have the meanings hereby respectively assigned to them, that is to say—

'debenture' includes debenture stock and bonds, whether constituting a charge on assets or not, and loan stock or notes;

'enactment' includes an enactment of the Parliament of Northern Ireland;

'fixed-interest securities' means securities which under their terms of issue bear a fixed rate of interest;

'local authority' in relation to the United Kingdom, means any of the following authorities—

(a) in England and Wales, the council of a county, a county, metropolitan or other borough (including a borough which has been included in a rural district), an urban or rural district or a parish, the Common Council of the City of London and the Council of the Isles of Scilly;

(b) in Scotland, a local authority within the meaning of the Local Government (Scotland) Act, 1947;

(c) in Northern Ireland, the council of a county, a county or other borough, or an urban or rural district;

'ordinary deposits' and 'special investment' have the same meanings respectively as in the Trustee Savings Banks Act, 1954;

'securities' includes shares, debentures, Treasury Bills and Tax Reserve Certificates;

'share' includes stock;

'Treasury Bills' includes bills issued by Her Majesty's Government in the United Kingdom and Northern Ireland Treasury Bills.

5. It is hereby declared that in this Schedule 'mortgage', in relation to freehold or leasehold property in Northern Ireland, includes a registered charge which, by virtue of subsection (4) of section 40 of the Local Registration of Title (Ireland) Act, 1891, or any other enactment, operates as a mortgage by deed.

6. References in this Schedule to an incorporated company are references to a company incorporated by or under any enactment and include references to a body of persons established for the purpose of trading for profit and incorporated by Royal Charter.

7. The references in paragraph 12 of Part II and paragraph 2 of Part III of this Schedule to a building society designated under section 1 of the House Purchase and Housing Act, 1959, include references to a permanent society incorporated under the Building Societies Acts (Northern Ireland) 1874 to 1940 for the time being designated by the Registrar for Northern Ireland under subsection (2) of that section (which enables such a society to be so designated for the purpose of trustees' powers of investment specified in paragraph (a) of subsection (1) of that section).

SECTION 3

SECOND SCHEDULE

MODIFICATION OF S. 2 IN
RELATION TO PROPERTY
FALLING WITHIN S. 3(3)

1. In this Schedule 'special-range property' means property falling within subsection (3) of section 3 of this Act.

2.—(1) Where a trust fund includes special-range property, subsection (1) of section 2 of this Act shall have effect as if references to the trust fund were references to so much thereof as does not consist of special-range property, and the special-range property shall be carried to a separate part of the fund.

(2) Any property which—

(a) being property belonging to the narrower-range or wider-range part of a trust fund, is converted into special-range property, or

(*b*) being special-range property, accrues to a trust fund after the division of the fund or part thereof in pursuance of subsection (1) of section 2 of this Act or of that subsection as modified by subparagraph (1) of this paragraph,

shall be carried to such a separate part of the fund as aforesaid; and subsections (2) and (3) of the said section 2 shall have effect subject to this sub-paragraph.

3. Where property carried to such a separate part as aforesaid is converted into property other than special-range property,—

(*a*) it shall be transferred to the narrower-range part of the fund or the wider-range part of the fund or apportioned between them, and

(*b*) any transfer of property from one of those parts to the other shall be made which is necessary to secure that the value of each of those parts of the fund is increased by the same amount.

SECTION 3

THIRD SCHEDULE

PROVISIONS SUPPLEMENTARY TO S. 3(4)

1. Where in a case falling within subsection (4) of section 3 of this Act, property belonging to the narrower-range part of a trust fund—

(*a*) is invested otherwise than in a narrower-range investment, or

(*b*) being so invested, is retained and not transferred or as soon as may be reinvested as mentioned in subsection (2) of section 2 of this Act,

then, so long as the property continues so invested and comprised in the narrower-range part of the fund, section 1 of this Act shall not authorise the making or retention of any wider-range investment.

2. Section 4 of the Trustee Act, 1925, or section 33 of the Trusts (Scotland) Act, 1921 (which relieve a trustee from liability for retaining an investment which has ceased to be authorised), shall not apply where an investment ceases to be authorised in consequence of the foregoing paragraph.

Town and Country Planning Act, 1962

190. Recovery from acquiring authorities of sums paid by way of compensation (1) Where an interest in land is compulsorily acquired, or is sold to an authority possessing compulsory purchase powers, and any of the land comprised in the acquisition or sale is land in respect of which a notice to which this section applies is registered (whether before or after the completion of the acquisition or sale) in respect of a planning decision or order made before the service of the notice to treat, or the making of the contract, in pursuance of which the acquisition or sale is effected, the Minister shall, subject to the following provisions of this section, be entitled to recover from the

acquiring authority a sum equal to so much of the amount of the compensation specified in the notice as (in accordance with subsection (6) of section 112 of this Act) is to be treated as attributable to that land.

(2) This section applies to notices registered under subsection (5) of section 112 of this Act and to notices registered under the provisions of that subsection as applied by subsection (5) of section 120 of this Act.

(3) If, immediately after the completion of the acquisition or sale, there is outstanding some interest in the land comprised therein to which a person other than the acquiring authority is entitled, the sum referred to in sub-

section (1) of this section shall not accrue due until that interest either ceases to exist or becomes vested in the acquiring authority.

(4) No sum shall be recoverable under this section in the case of a compulsory acquisition or sale where the Minister is satisfied that the interest in question is being acquired for the purposes of the use of the land as a public open space.

(6) In this and the next following section 'interest' (where the reference is to an interest in land) means the fee simple or a tenancy of the land, and does not include any other interest therein.

The Local Government (Records) Act, 1962

1. Power to promote adequate use of records (1) A local authority may do all such things as appear to it necessary or expedient for enabling adequate use to be made of records under its control, and in relation to such records may in particular—

(a) make provision for enabling persons, with or without charge and subject to such conditions as the authority may determine, to inspect the records and to make or obtain copies thereof;

(b) prepare, or procure or assist in the preparation of, indexes and guides to and calendars and summaries of the records;

(c) publish, or procure or assist in the publication of, the records or any index or guide to or calendar or summary of the records;

(d) hold exhibitions of the records and arrange for the delivery of explanatory lectures, with or without charging for admission to such exhibitions or lectures;

(e) direct that the records be temporarily entrusted to other persons for exhibition or study.

(2) Nothing in subsection (1) above shall be taken to authorise the doing of any act which infringes copyright or contravenes conditions subject to which records are under the control of a local authority.

2. Acquisition and deposit of records (1) A local authority to which this subsection applies may—

(a) by agreement acquire by way of purchase records which, or (in the case of a collection) the majority of which, appear to the authority to be of local interest;

(b) accept the gift of records which, or (in the case of a collection) the majority of which, appear to the authority to be of general or local interest.

(2) A local authority to which this subsection applies may accept the deposit of records—

(a) which appear to the authority to be of general or local interest; or

(b) which are the subject of an arrangement made under subsection (4) below.

(3) A local authority may accept the deposit of records authorised to be deposited with it by any enactment other than this section.

(4) A local authority other than a parish council or parish meeting may arrange to deposit any records under its control with an authority to which subsections (1) and (2) above apply or, if the Minister of Housing and Local Government consents, with any other person.

(5) Where by virtue of this section records are under the control of a local authority in relation to which a provision of . . . section 279 of the Local Government Act, 1933, ... that provision shall apply as respects those records notwithstanding that apart from this subsection it would not so apply.

(6) Subsections (1) and (2) above apply to the council of every county or

R*

county borough and to the council of any county district . . . specified in an order made in that behalf by the Minister of Housing and Local Government.

3. Power to appoint sub-committees A committee appointed under section 85 or 91 of the Local Government Act, 1933, . . . and having functions relating to records may appoint a sub-committee and delegate to it any of those functions:

Provided that if fewer than two-thirds of the members of the sub-committee are members of the local authority which appointed the main committee, or, where that is a joint committee, of one or other of the local authorities which appointed it, the sub-committee shall be advisory only.

4. Financial (1) A local authority may contribute a sum equal to the whole or a part of any such expenses as the following, that is to say—

(*a*) as respects records under the authority's control, expenses which have been incurred by any person in doing, by arrangement with the authority, anything relating to the records which the authority itself was empowered to do;

(*b*) as respects records not under the authority's control, being records which in the opinion of the authority are nevertheless of local interest,—

(i) expenses which have been incurred by any person in doing any such thing relating to the records as the authority is empowered by subsection (1) of section 1 above to do in relation to records under its control;

(ii) expenses which have been incurred by any person in looking after the records in a case where the authority are of opinion that reasonable provision is made for enabling persons to inspect and make copies of them.

6. Orders by Minister (1) Any power to make orders conferred by this Act shall be exercisable by statutory instrument; . . .

(2) Any order made under subsection (6) of section 2 of this Act may be varied or revoked by a subsequent order made thereunder.

7. Minor amendments (1) Subsection (4) of section 144 A of the Law of Property Act, 1922, and subsection (2) of section 36 of the Tithe Act, 1936 (which respectively empower the Master of the Rolls to direct the transfer to the Public Record Office, or to a public library or museum or historical or antiquarian society, of manorial documents and copies of instruments of apportionment) shall apply in relation to a local authority as they apply in relation to a public library and the governing body of a public library.

8. Interpretation (1) In this Act—
'local authority' means . . . the council of a borough included in a rural district, or a parish council or parish meeting . . .
'records' means materials in written or other form setting out facts or events or otherwise recording information.

(2) For the purposes of this Act records shall be treated as being under the control of a local authority if they are in the possession of the authority by virtue of section 2 of this Act or otherwise, or if the authority has power to give directions as to their custody.

Local Government (*Financial Provisions*) Act, 1963

1. Extension of local authority powers to pay expenses incurred in attending conferences and meetings (1) Section 267 of the Act of 1933 . . . shall have effect as if the references to a conference or meeting included references to—

(*a*) a conference or meeting convened by any person or body (other than a person or body convening it in the course of his or their trade or business or a body of which the objects are wholly or partly political) for the purpose of discussing matters relating to the discharge of the functions of the local authority or to the development of trade, industry or commerce in the area of the local authority;

(b) a conference or meeting convened by any government department or local authority, or by any other body exercising functions conferred by or under any enactment or Royal Charter, being a conference or meeting convened for the purpose of discussing any matter affecting the area of the local authority or its inhabitants.

(2) In the foregoing subsection 'the local authority' means the local authority whose powers under the said section 267 . . . are in question.

(3) For the purposes of the said section 267 . . . a loss of earnings necessarily suffered by a member of a local authority or a committee of a local authority for the purpose of enabling him to attend a conference or meeting, being earnings which he would otherwise have made, shall be treated as an expense incurred by him in attending that conference or meeting.

(4) [*Section* 114 (3) *of the Act of* 1948] . . . (3) shall have effect as if any reference therein to expenses incurred included a reference to any loss of earnings suffered which, by virtue of the last foregoing subsection is to be treated as an expense incurred and, in relation to the powers to defray expenses conferred by subsection (1) of this section, as if any such conference or meeting as aforesaid were included in paragraph (c) of the definition of 'approved duty' in section 115 of the Act of 1948.

5. Payment of expenses to local authority officers Nothing in any enactment, including an enactment contained in this Act, providing for the payment by a local authority of expenses of their members shall be taken to limit the power of the local authority to defray expenses properly incurred by an officer of the authority as such.

6. Power of local authority to incur expenditure in the interests of their area or its inhabitants but not otherwise authorised (1) A local authority may, subject to the provisions of this section, incur expenditure for any purpose which in their opinion is in the interests of their area or its inhabitants, but shall not, by virtue of this subsection, incur any expenditure for a purpose for which they are, either unconditionally or subject to any limitation or to the satisfaction of any condition, authorised or required by or by virtue of any enactment other than this section to make any payment.

(2) Expenditure of a local authority under this section in any financial year shall not exceed, in the case of a local authority other than a parish council, the product of a rate of *one penny* (·**4p**) in the pound for their area for that year, or, in the case of a parish council, that of a rate of *one-fifth of a penny* (·**1p**) in the pound for their area for that year.

(3) No expenditure shall be incurred under this section by a local authority in respect of any matter except in pursuance of a resolution of the authority authorising the incurring of the expenditure in respect of that matter.

(4) The accounts of a local authority by whom expenditure is incurred under this section shall include a separate account of that expenditure, and section 283 (4), (6) and (7) of the Act of 1933 . . . (which provide for the inspection by a local government elector of the abstract of accounts of the local authority and the making of copies thereof or extracts therefrom, and penalise failure to provide facilities for such inspection, or making of copies or extracts) shall have effect as if any reference to the abstract of the accounts of the local authority included a reference to any such separate account as aforesaid.

(5) The reference in this section to the product of a rate of any amount in the pound for an area shall, where there is more than one rating area within the area, be construed as a reference to the aggregate of the product of a rate of that amount for all the rating areas within the area.

(6) The product of a rate of *one penny* (·**4p**) in the pound for a rating area, shall, for the purposes of this section, be taken to be the product of a rate of that amount for that area ascertained, in the case of an area other than a county borough, in accordance with rules made for the purposes of section 9 (2) of the Rating and Valuation Act, 1925, . . . and the product of a rate of *one-fifth of a penny* (·**1p**) in the pound for a parish shall be taken to be the product of a rate of that amount for the parish ascertained in accordance with rules made for the purposes of the said section 9 (2).

(7) In this section—

'financial year' has the same meaning as in the Act of 1933;

'local authority' means . . . the council of a county, the council of a . . . county district, . . . , and the council of a rural parish.

8. Power to suspend annual provision for repayment of, and to borrow for payment of interest on, certain borrowed moneys (1) Where a sum is borrowed after the commencement of this Act by a local authority for any of the following purposes, that is to say,—

(*a*) meeting expenditure on the construction of new, or the extension or alteration of existing, works forming or to form part of an undertaking of a revenue-producing character;

(*b*) carrying out on land any other operations, being operations of such kind as may be prescribed or operations specified in relation to that land by direction of the Minister;

(*c*) acquiring land for the purpose of the construction thereon of new, or the extension or alteration of existing, works forming or to form part of an undertaking of a revenue-producing character, or for the purpose of the carrying out thereon of operations of a kind prescribed by virtue of the last foregoing paragraph, or operations specified in relation to that land by direction of the Minister;

it shall be lawful for the authority in respect of such one period as they may determine, not being longer than five years nor beginning five years or less before the expiration of the fixed period relevant to the sum borrowed, to do either or both of the following things, namely,—

(i) to suspend, in whole or in part, any annual provision required to be made during the first-mentioned period for the repayment of the sum borrowed;

(ii) to borrow money for the payment of all or any of the interest due in respect of the first-mentioned period on the sum borrowed.

(2) Where—

(*a*) land is acquired after the commencement of this Act by a local authority; and

(*b*) a sum is borrowed by the authority for the purpose of the acquisition; and

(*c*) the acquisition is not for the purpose of the construction on the land of new, or the extension or alteration of existing, works forming or to form part of an undertaking of a revenue-producing character, or for the purpose of carrying out on the land operations of a kind prescribed by virtue of subsection (1) (*b*) above or operations specified in relation to the land by direction of the Minister; and

(*d*) the land is subsequently appropriated for a purpose mentioned in the last foregoing paragraph;

it shall be lawful for the authority in respect of such one period as they may determine, not being longer than five years nor beginning five years or less before the expiration of the fixed period relevant to the sum borrowed, to do either or both of the following things, namely,—

(i) to suspend, in whole or in part, any annual provision required to be made during the first-mentioned period for the repayment of the sum borrowed;

(ii) to borrow money for the payment of all or any of the interest due in respect of the first-mentioned period on the sum borrowed.

(3) Where land has, before the commencement of this Act, been acquired by a local authority, and a sum was borrowed by the authority for the purpose of the acquisition, and either—

(a) the land was acquired for a purpose mentioned in subsection (2) (c) above, or (not having been so acquired) was, before the commencement of this Act, appropriated for such a purpose, but the construction, extension or alteration of the works or the carrying out of the operations that constitutes the purpose for which the land was acquired or appropriated is not begun till after that commencement, or was begun but not completed before that commencement; or

(b) the land is, after that commencement, appropriated for a purpose mentioned in the said subsection (2) (c);

it shall be lawful for the authority, in respect of such one period as they may determine, not being longer than five years nor beginning five years or less before the expiration of the fixed period relevant to the sum borrowed, to do either or both of the following things, namely,—

(i) to suspend, in whole or in part, any annual provision required to be made during the first-mentioned period for the repayment of the sum borrowed;

(ii) to borrow money for the payment of all or any of the interest due in respect of the first-mentioned period on the sum borrowed.

(4) A sum borrowed by virtue of paragraph (ii) of subsection (1), (2) or (3) above for the payment of interest on a sum borrowed must be repaid within the fixed period relevant to the last-mentioned sum.

(5) In any enactment, other than section 212 of the Act of 1933, passed before this Act, a reference to Part IX or section 198 of the Act of 1933 shall be construed as including a reference to the foregoing provisions of this section . . .

(6) In section 212 (2) of the Act of 1933 (which provides that, subject to the provisions of section 198 (2) of that Act, the first of the instalments of principal or of principal and interest combined by means of which a sum borrowed by a local authority is to be paid off, or the first payment to a sinking fund by means of which a sum so borrowed is to be paid off, shall be made within twelve months, or where the sum is repayable by half-yearly instalments, six months from the date of borrowing) the reference to the said section 198 (2) shall be construed as including a reference to this section . . .

(7) In this section—

'fixed period' has the same meaning as in Part IX of the Act of 1933;

'local authority' means a local authority within the meaning of the Act of 1933 . . .

'prescribed' means prescribed by the Minister by regulations made by statutory instrument;

'undertaking' has the same meaning as in the Act of 1933.

(8) Subsection (1) of this section shall, to the following extent, have effect in place of the following enactments, namely,—

(a) as regards sums borrowed after the commencement of this Act by authorities to whom section 198 (2) of the Act of 1933 applies, being sums borrowed for the purpose of meeting such expenditure as is mentioned in that subsection, in place of the said section 198 (2); and . . .

accordingly the said section 198 (2), as originally enacted and as applied by or by virtue of any other enactment, . . . shall cease to have effect except as respects sums borrowed before that commencement.

10. Application of unexpended portions of borrowed money (1) The balance of any money borrowed (whether before or after the commencement of this Act) by a local authority and not required for the purposes for which the money was borrowed (other than a balance to the application of which consent has been given under section 202 of the Act of 1933 . . . before that commencement) may be applied,—

(*a*) at the discretion of the authority, to either or both of the following purposes, namely,—

(i) in or towards the repayment of a sum borrowed by the authority in pursuance of the sanction of a Minister or the authority of a local enactment;

(ii) for a purpose for which the authority have obtained the sanction of a Minister, or have been authorised by a local enactment, to borrow money; or

(*b*) with the consent of the Minister, to any other purpose to which capital money may be applied.

(2) Where a sum is, by virtue of the foregoing subsection, applied for such a purpose as is mentioned in paragraph (*a*) (i) thereof, it shall thenceforward be treated as if, on the day when it was so applied, it had been duly borrowed for the purpose for which the sum re-

paid was borrowed, and in pursuance of the sanction or authority in question, and where a sum is, by virtue of the foregoing subsection, applied for such a purpose as is mentioned in paragraph (*a*) (ii) thereof, it shall thenceforward be treated as if, on the day on which it was so applied, it had been duly borrowed for that purpose in pursuance of the sanction or authority in question.

(3) Where money borrowed by a local authority of which a balance is applied by virtue of this section was borrowed for the purposes of a function of theirs other than that to which the balance is applied, there shall . . .

(*b*) . . . be made in those accounts such adjustments as may be requisite in the circumstances.

(4) In the foregoing provisions of this section—

(*a*) 'function' means a power or a duty; . . .

(*c*) 'local authority' means a local authority within the meaning of the Act of 1933 . . .

(5) In any enactment passed before this Act, a reference to Part IX or section 202 of the Act of 1933 . . . shall be construed as including a reference to the foregoing provisions of this section.

(6) The following enactments shall cease to have effect to the following extent, namely,—

(*a*) section 202 of the Act of 1933, except in relation to balances of moneys borrowed by authorities to whom that section applies, being balances to the application of which consent has been given before the commencement of this Act;

and in this subsection the reference to the said section 202 is to that section as originally enacted and as applied by or by virtue of any other enactment.

Public Works Loans Act, 1964

6. Re-borrowing powers of public authorities (1) The provisions of this section shall have effect notwithstanding anything in . . . the following enactments (which relate to the re-borrowing powers of local authorities), that is to say, section 216(1) of the Local Government Act, 1933, . . . (including any of those enactments as applied by or under any other enactment), or any other enactment with respect to the re-borrowing powers of any other public authority.

(2) Where a local authority or other public authority have borrowed moneys in pursuance of powers conferred by or under any Act and the loan is repayable by instalments or annual payments, any power of the authority to borrow under any of the enactments referred to in subsection (1) of this section shall be exercisable in connection with the repayment of that loan, but, subject to subsection (4) of this section, shall be so exercisable only—

(a) for the purpose of repaying forthwith, and before they would otherwise become due for repayment, all sums for the time being outstanding by way of principal on the loan; or

(b) where the authority borrowed the moneys for a period less than the maximum period for which they were authorised so to do, for the purpose of the payment of any amount by which any instalment or annual payment exceeds what

it would have been if it had been calculated by reference to that maximum period.

(3) Where a local authority or other public authority have borrowed moneys in pursuance of powers conferred by or under any Act, not being a loan repayable by instalments or annual payments, and payments towards the repayment of the loan have been made by the authority into any sinking or other fund maintained by the authority wholly or partly for the purpose of that repayment, any power of the authority to borrow under any of the enactments referred to in subsection (1) of this section shall be exercisable with respect to that loan, but, subject to subsection (4) of this section, shall be so exercisable only for the purpose of the repayment of the amount, if any, by which the principal of the loan exceeds the aggregate amount of those payments.

(4) Any power of a local authority or other public authority to borrow under any of the enactments referred to in subsection (1) of this section shall be exercisable for the purpose of replacing moneys, which, during the preceding twelve months, have been temporarily applied from other moneys of the authority in making such a repayment or payment as is authorised by subsection (2) or (3) of this section, and which at the time of that repayment or payment it was intended to replace by borrowed moneys.

Public Libraries and Museums Act, 1964

10. Default powers of Secretary of State (1) If

(a) a complaint is made to the Secretary of State that any library authority has failed to carry out duties relating to the public library service imposed on it by or under this Act; or

(b) the Secretary of State is of opinion that an investigation should be

made as to whether any such failure by a library authority has occurred,

and, after causing a local inquiry to be held into the matter, the Secretary of State is satisfied that there has been such a failure by the library authority, he may make an order declaring it to be in default and directing it for the purpose of removing the default to carry out such of its duties, in such manner and within such time, as may be specified in the order.

Museums and art galleries

12. Provision and maintenance of museums and galleries (1) A local authority may provide and maintain museums and art galleries within its administrative area or elsewhere in England or Wales, and may do all such things as may be necessary or expedient for or in connection with the provision or maintenance thereof:

Provided that a local authority not being a library authority and not already maintaining a museum or art gallery under this section shall not provide a museum or art gallery thereunder without the consent of the Secretary of State; and that consent may be given subject to such conditions as the Secretary of State thinks fit, and he may at any time vary or revoke any of the conditions.

(2) A local authority maintaining a museum or art gallery under this section may with the consent of the Secretary of State enter into an agreement with any other local authority empowered to maintain it for the transfer of the museum or gallery and its collections to that authority.

13. Charges for admission to museums and galleries (1) A local authority may make a charge for admission to a museum or art gallery maintained by it under section 12 of this Act.

(2) In determining whether, and in what manner, to exercise its powers under this section in relation to a museum or gallery, a local authority shall take into account the need to secure that the museum or gallery plays its full part in the promotion of education in the area, and shall have particular regard to the interests of children and students.

14. Contributions to expenses of museums and galleries A local authority being a library authority or maintaining a museum or art gallery under section 12 above may make contributions towards expense incurred by any person—

(a) in providing or maintaining a museum or art gallery in any place within England or Wales, or

(b) in providing advisory or other services or financial assistance for the benefit of a museum or art gallery in any such place.

19. Byelaws (1) A local authority may make byelaws regulating the use of facilities provided by the authority under this Act and the conduct of persons in premises where those facilities are provided, and the Secretary of State shall be the person by whom byelaws so made are to be confirmed.

(2) Without prejudice to section 251 of the Local Government Act, 1933 (under which byelaws may include provisions for imposing fines), byelaws made under this section may include provisions for enabling officers of the local authority to exclude or remove from premises maintained by the authority under this Act any person who contravenes the byelaws.

(3) As well as complying with section 250(7) of the said Act of 1933 (which requires byelaws, when confirmed, to be made available to the public), a local authority shall cause a copy of byelaws made by it and in force under this section to be displayed in any premises maintained by the authority under this Act to which the public have access.

20. Use of premises for educational or cultural events A local authority maintaining premises under this Act may use the premises, or allow them to be used (whether in return for payment or not), for the holding of meetings and exhibitions, the showing of films and slides, the giving of musical performances, and the holding of other events of an educational or cultural nature, and in connection therewith may, notwithstanding anything in section 8 above, make or authorise the making of a charge for admission.

21. Expenses of county councils

(1) expenses of a county council relating to the provision or maintenance of a museum or art gallery under this Act or in respect of contributions by the council under section 14 above shall be charged on the administrative area of any local authority maintaining a museum or art gallery under section 12 above only with the consent of that local authority.

(2) A condition imposed in relation to a local authority under the proviso to section 12(1) above may require the authority to give consent under the preceding subsection.

(3) Where a county council is comprised in a joint board established under section 5 of this Act—

(a) references in subsection (1) above to the library area of the council shall be construed as references to the area which would be its library area if the joint board did not exist and each authority comprised in it were a library authority; and

(b) references therein to a local authority maintaining a museum or art gallery under section 12 above shall not include the county council.

25. Interpretation In this Act—

'library authority' means a library authority under this Act or, in relation to a time before the commencement of this Act, under the Public Libraries Acts, 1892 to 1919;

'local authority' means the council of a county, county borough, London borough, county district or parish, or the Common Council of the City of London, or the council of a borough included in a rural district, or a joint board established under section 5 of this Act;

'officer' includes a servant.

Local Government (Pecuniary Interests) Act, 1964

1. Pecuniary interests of members

(1) For the purposes of section 76 of the Local Government Act, 1933 (duty of members of authorities to disclose pecuniary interests and abstain from voting etc.) a member shall not be treated as having a pecuniary interest in any contract or other matter by reason only of any interest—

(a) of that member, or

(b) of any company, body or person connected with him as mentioned in subsection (2) of that section,

which is so remote or insignificant that it cannot reasonably be regarded as likely to influence a member in the consideration or discussion of, or in voting on, any question with respect to that contract or matter.

(2) In proviso (i) to the said subsection (2) (connection with public bodies to be disregarded) the expression 'public body' shall include, and be deemed always to have included, any body established for the purpose of carrying on under national ownership any industry or part of an industry or undertaking, the governing body of any university, university college, college in a university or college of advanced technology, and the National Trust for Places of Historic Interest or Natural Beauty incorporated by the National Trust Act, 1907.

(3) *Amends s.* 76(4).

(4) *Amends s.* 76(6).

(5) The power of a county council and of the Minister under subsection (8) of that section to remove any disability imposed by that section shall include power to remove, either indefinitely or for any period, any such disability which would otherwise attach to any member (or, in the case of the power of the Minister, any member or any class or description of member) by reason of such interests, and in respect of such

matters, as may be specified by the county council or, as the case may be, the Minister.

(6) Nothing in that section shall preclude any person from taking part in the consideration or discussion of, or voting on, any question whether an application should be made to a county council or the Minister for the exercise of the powers conferred by the said subsection (8).

2. Pecuniary interests of officers and servants (1) For the purposes of section 123 of the said Act of 1933 (duty of officers and servants of authorities to disclose pecuniary interests in contracts) an officer or servant shall not be treated as having a pecuniary interest in any contract by reason only of any interest—

(a) of that officer or servant, or

(b) of any company, body or person connected with him as mentioned in subsection (2) of section 76 of that Act,

which is so remote or insignificant that it cannot reasonably be regarded as likely to influence an officer or servant in discharging his duties.

Commons Registration Act, 1965

1. Registration of commons and town or village greens and ownership of and rights over them (1) There shall be registered, in accordance with the provisions of this Act and subject to the exceptions mentioned therein,—

(a) land in England or Wales which is common land or a town or village green;

(b) rights of common over such land; and

(c) persons claiming to be or found to be owners of such land or becoming the owners thereof by virtue of this Act;

and no rights of common over land which is capable of being registered under this Act shall be registered under the Land Registration Acts, 1925 and 1936.

(2) After the end of 1969—

(a) no land capable of being registered under this Act shall be deemed to be common land or a town or village green unless it is so registered; and

(b) no rights of common shall be exercisable over any such land unless they are registered either under this Act or under the Land Registration Acts, 1925 and 1936.

(3) Where any land is registered under this Act but no person is registered as the owner thereof under this Act or under the Land Registration Acts, 1925 and 1936, it shall—

(a) if it is a town or village green, be vested in accordance with the following provisions of this Act; and

(b) if it is common land, be vested as Parliament may hereafter determine.

2. Registration authorities (1) The registration authority for the purposes of this Act shall be—

(a) in relation to any land situated in any county . . . , the council of that county . . .

(2) Where part of any land is in the area of one registration authority and part in that of another the authorities may by agreement provide for one of them to be the registration authority in relation to the whole of the land.

3. The registers (1) For the purpose of registering such land as is mentioned in section 1(1) of this Act and rights of common over and ownership of such land every registration authority shall maintain—

(a) a register of common land; and

(b) a register of town or village greens;

and regulations under this Act may require or authorise a registration authority to note on those registers such other information as may be prescribed.

(2) Any register maintained under this Act shall be open to inspection by the public at all reasonable times.

4. Provisional registration (1) Subject to the provisions of this section, a registration authority shall register any land as common land or a town or village green or, as the case may be, any rights of common over or ownership of such land, on application duly made to it and accompanied by such declaration and such other documents (if any) as may be prescribed for the purpose of verification or of proving compliance with any prescribed conditions.

(2) An application for the registration of any land as common land or as a town or village green may be made by any person, and a registration authority—

  (*a*) may so register any land notwithstanding that no application for that registration has been made, and

  (*b*) shall so register any land in any case where it registers any rights over it under this section.

(3) No person shall be registered under this section as the owner of any land which is registered under the Land Registration Acts, 1925 and 1936, and no person shall be registered under this section as the owner of any other land unless the land itself is registered under this section.

(4) Where, in pursuance of an application under this section, any land would fall to be registered as common land or as a town or village green, but the land is already so registered, the registration authority shall not register it again but shall note the application in the register.

(5) A registration under this section shall be provisional only until it has become final under the following provisions of this Act.

(6) An application for registration under this section shall not be entertained if made after *the end of the year* 1969.

(7) Every local authority shall take such steps as may be prescribed for informing the public of the period within which and the manner in which applications for registration under this section may be made.

5. Notification of, and objections to, registration (1) A registration authority shall give such notices and take such other steps as may be prescribed for informing the public of any registration made by it under section 4 of this Act, of the times and places where copies of the relevant entries in the register may be inspected and of the period during which and the manner in which objections to the registration may be made to the authority.

(2) The period during which objections to any registration under section 4 of this Act may be made shall be such period, ending not less than two years after the date of the registration, as may be prescribed.

(3) Where any land or rights over land are registered under section 4 of this Act but no person is so registered as the owner of the land the registration authority may, if it thinks fit, make an objection to the registration notwithstanding that it has no interest in the land.

(4) Where an objection to a registration under section 4 of this Act is made, the registration authority shall note the objection on the register and shall give such notice as may be prescribed to the person (if any) on whose application the registration was made and to any person whose application is noted under section 4 (4) of this Act.

(5) Where a person to whom notice has been given under subsection (4) of this section so requests or where the registration was made otherwise than on the application of any person, the registration authority may, if it thinks fit, cancel or modify a registration to which objection is made under this section.

(6) Where such an objection is made, then, unless the objection is withdrawn or the registration cancelled before the end of such period as may be prescribed, the registration authority shall refer the matter to a Commons Commissioner.

(7) An objection to the registration of any land as common land or as a town or village green shall be treated for the purposes of this Act as being also an objection to any registration (whenever made) under section 4 of this Act of any rights over the land.

(8) A registration authority shall take such steps as may be prescribed for informing the public of any objection which they have noted on the register under this section and of the times and places where copies of the relevant entries in the register may be inspected.

(9) Where regulations under this Act require copies of any entries in a register to be sent by the registration authority to another local authority they may require that other authority to make the copies available for inspection in such manner as may be prescribed.

6. Disposal of disputed claims (1) The Commons Commissioner to whom any matter has been referred under section 5 of this Act shall inquire into it and shall either confirm the registration, with or without modifications, or refuse to confirm it; and the registration shall, if it is confirmed, become final, and, if the confirmation is refused, become void—

(a) if no appeal is brought against the confirmation or refusal, at the end of the period during which such an appeal could have been brought;

(b) if such an appeal is brought, when it is finally disposed of.

(2) On being informed in the prescribed manner that a registration has become final (with or without modifications) or has become void a registration authority shall indicate that fact in the prescribed manner in the register and, if it has become void, cancel the registration.

(3) Where the registration of any land as common land or as a town or village green is cancelled (whether under this section or under section 5(5) of this Act) the registration authority shall also cancel the registration of any person as the owner thereof.

7. Finality of undisputed registrations (1) If no objection is made to a registration under section 4 of this Act or if all objections made to such a registration are withdrawn the registration shall become final at the end of the period during which such objections could have been made under section 5 of this Act or, if an objection made during that period is withdrawn after the end thereof, at the date of the withdrawal.

8. Vesting of unclaimed land (1) Where the registration under section 4 of this Act of any land as common land or as a town or village green has become final but no person is registered under that section as the owner of the land, then, unless the land is registered under the Land Registration Acts, 1925 and 1936, the registration authority shall refer the question of the ownership of the land to a Commons Commissioner.

(2) After the registration authority has given such notices as may be prescribed, the Commons Commissioner shall inquire into the matter and shall, if satisfied that any person is the owner of the land, direct the registration authority to register that person accordingly; and the registration authority shall comply with the direction.

(3) If the Commons Commissioner is not so satisfied and the land is a town or village green he shall direct the registration authority to register as the owner of the land the local authority specified in subsection (5) of this section; and the registration authority shall comply with the direction.

(4) On the registration under this section of a local authority as the owner of any land the land shall vest in that local authority and, if the land is not regulated by a scheme under the Commons Act, 1899, sections 10 and 15 of the Open Spaces Act, 1906 (power

to manage and make byelaws) shall apply in relation to it as if that local authority had acquired the ownership under the said Act of 1906.

(5) The local authority in which any land is to be vested under this section is—

(b) if the land is in a rural district, the council of the district, except in a case falling within paragraph (c) of this subsection;

(c) if the land is in a rural parish which has a parish council, that council, but, if the land is regulated by a scheme under the Commons Act, 1899, only if the powers of management under Part I of that Act have been delegated to the parish council.

9. Protection of unclaimed common land Where the registration under section 4 of this Act of any land as common land has become final but no person is registered under this Act or the Land Registration Acts, 1925 and 1936, as the owner of the land, then, until the land is vested under any provision hereafter made by Parliament, any local authority in whose area the land or part of the land is situated may take such steps for the protection of the land against unlawful interference as could be taken by an owner in possession of the land, and may (without prejudice to any power exercisable apart from this section) institute proceedings for any offence committed in respect of the land.

10. Effect of registration The registration under this Act of any land as common land or as a town or village green, or of any rights of common over any such land, shall be conclusive evidence of the matters registered, as at the date of registration, except where the registration is provisional only.

11. Exemption from registration (1) The foregoing provisions of this Act shall not apply to the New Forest or Epping Forest nor to any land exempted from those provisions by an order of the Minister, and shall not be taken to apply to the Forest of Dean.

(2) The Minister shall not make an order under this section except on an application made to him before 1st October 1966.

(5) If any question arises under this Act whether any land is part of the forests mentioned in subsection (1) of this section it shall be referred to and decided by the Minister.

12. Subsequent registration under Land Registration Acts, 1925 and 1936 The following provisions shall have effect with respect to the registration under the Land Registration Acts, 1925 and 1936, of any land after the ownership of the land has been registered under this Act, that is to say—

(a) section 123 of the Land Registration Act, 1925 (compulsory registration of title on sale) shall have effect in relation to the land whether or not the land is situated in an area in which an Order in Council under section 120 of that Act is for the time being in force, unless the registration under this Act is provisional only; and

(b) if the registration authority is notified by the Chief Land Registrar that the land has been registered under the Land Registration Acts, 1925 and 1936, the authority shall delete the registration of the ownership under this Act and indicate in the register in the prescribed manner that it has been registered under those Acts.

13. Amendment of registers Regulations under this Act shall provide for the amendment of the registers maintained under this Act where—

(a) any land registered under this Act ceases to be common land or a town or village green; or

(b) any land becomes common land or a town or village green; or

(c) any rights registered under this Act are apportioned, extinguished or released, or are varied or transferred in such circumstances as may be prescribed;

and may exclude or modify the application of section 14 of the Yorkshire Registries Act, 1884 (priority of assurances) with respect to matters capable of being registered under this Act.

14. Rectification of registers The High Court may order a register maintained under this Act to be amended if—

(*a*) the registration under this Act of any land or rights of common has become final and the court is satisfied that any person was induced by fraud to withdraw an objection to the registration or to refrain from making such an objection; or

(*b*) the register has been amended in pursuance of section 13 of this Act and it appears to the court that no amendment or a different amendment ought to have been made and that the error cannot be corrected in pursuance of regulations made under this Act;

and, in either case, the court deems it just to rectify the register.

15 Quantification of certain grazing rights (1) Where a right of common consists of or includes a right, not limited by number, to graze animals or animals of any class, it shall for the purposes of registration under this Act be treated as exercisable in relation to no more animals, or animals of that class, than a definite number.

(2) Any application for the registration of such a right shall state the number of animals to be entered in the register or, as the case may be, the numbers of animals of different classes to be so entered.

(3) When the registration of such a right has become final the right shall accordingly be exercisable in relation to animals not exceeding the number or numbers registered or such other number or numbers as Parliament may hereafter determine.

16. *Provides for the disregard of interruptions in prescriptive claims to rights of common caused by wartime requisition and prohibition or restriction of animal movements for reasons of animal health.*

18. *Provides for appeals on points of law from the Commons Commissioner to the High Court by way of case stated.*

21. Savings (1) Section 1(2) of this Act shall not affect the application to any land registered under this Act of section 193 or section 194 of the Law of Property Act, 1925 (rights of access to, and restriction on inclosure of, land over which rights of common are exercisable).

(2) Section 10 of this Act shall not apply for the purpose of deciding whether any land forms part of a highway.

22. Interpretation (1) In this Act, unless the context otherwise requires,—

'common land' means—

(*a*) land subject to rights of common (as defined in this Act) whether those rights are exercisable at all times or only during limited periods;

(*b*) waste land of a manor not subject to rights of common;
but does not include a town or village green or any land which forms part of a highway;

'land' includes land covered with water;

'local authority' means the Greater London Council, the council of a county, county borough, London borough or county district, the council of a parish or the council of a borough included in a rural district;

'the Minister' means the Minister of *Land and Natural Resources;*

'prescribed' means prescribed by regulations under this Act;

'registration' includes an entry in the register made in pursuance of section 13 of this Act;

'rights of common' includes cattlegates or beastgates (by whatever name known) and rights of sole or several vesture or herbage or of sole or several pasture, but does not include rights held for a term of years or from year to year;

'town or village green' means land which has been allotted by or under any Act for the exercise or recreation of the inhabitants of any locality or on which the inhabitants of any locality have a customary right to indulge in lawful sports and pastimes or on which the inhabitants of any locality have indulged in such sports and pastimes as of right for not less than twenty years.

(2) References in this Act to the ownership and the owner of any land are references to the ownership of a legal estate in fee simple in any land and to the person holding that estate, and references to land registered under the Land Registration Acts, 1925 and 1936, are references to land the fee simple of which is so registered.

23. Application to Crown (1) This Act shall apply in relation to land in which there is a Crown or Duchy interest as it applies in relation to land in which there is no such interest.

(2) In this section 'Crown or Duchy interest' means an interest belonging to Her Majesty in right of the Crown or of the Duchy of Lancaster, or belonging to the Duchy of Cornwall, or belonging to a Government department, or held in trust for Her Majesty for the purposes of a Government department.

Finance Act, 1965

66. (1) A local authority in the United Kingdom shall after the year 1965–66 be exempt from all charge to income tax in respect of its income, and shall be exempt from corporation tax and capital gains tax, and is not included in the expression 'company' as used in this Part of this Act; and this subsection shall apply to a local authority association as it applies to a local authority.

(2) In this section 'local authority' means—

(a) in relation to England and Wales, any authority being, within the meaning of the Local Loans Act, 1875, an authority having power to levy a rate, and includes a joint board or joint committee of such authorities; ...

(3) In subsection (2)(a) . . . above any reference to a joint board or joint committee of such authorities as are there mentioned applies, and applies only, to a joint board or joint committee of which all the constituent members are such authorities or which, having such authorities and other bodies corporate as its constituent members, is authorised by or under any enactment to require from those authorities, but not from other constituent members, the payment of sums to meet or towards meeting the amount or estimated amount by which its revenue for any period falls short or may fall short of its expenditure for that period; and for this purpose, if a member of a joint board or joint committee is a representative of or appointed by any authority or body, that authority or body (and not he) is to be treated as a constituent member of the board or committee.

(4) In this section 'local authority association' means any incorporated or unincorporated association of which all the constituent members are local authorities, groups of local authorities or local authority associations and which has for its object or primary object the protection and furtherance of the interests in general of local authorities or any description of local authorities; and for this purpose, if a member of an association is a representative of or appointed by any authority, group of authorities or association, that authority, group or association (and not he) is to be treated as a constituent member of the association.

Local Government Act, 1966

Specific grants

7. Grants for development and redevelopment (1) The Minister may, with the consent of the Treasury and after consultation with such associations of local authorities as appear to the Minister to be concerned and with any local authority with whom consultation appears to him to be desirable, make regulations providing for the payment to local authorities, for the year 1967–68 and subsequent years, of grants of such amounts, and payable over such periods and subject to such conditions, as may be determined by or under the regulations in respect of expenditure incurred by those authorities (whether before or after the passing of this Act) in or in connection with the acquisition of land approved for the purposes of the regulations, being land required for or in connection with—

(a) the development or redevelopment as a whole of any area (whether or not defined in a development plan as an area of comprehensive development); or

(b) the relocation of population or industry, or the replacement of open space, in the course or in consequence of such development or redevelopment,

or in respect of expenditure so incurred in or in connection with the clearing or preliminary development of such land.

(2) For the purposes of regulations under this section land appropriated by a local authority (whether before or after the passing of this Act) for use for purposes described in subsection (1) of this section may be treated as acquired by that authority for those purposes at a cost of such amount, and defrayed in such manner, as may be determined by or under the regulations.

(3) Provision may be made by regulations under this section—

(a) for the inclusion, in the expenditure incurred by local authorities in the acquisition of land approved for the purposes of the regulations, of any sums or part of sums paid by those authorities in connection with any restriction imposed on the development or use of the land by or under any enactment (whether by way of compensation or by way of contribution towards damage or expense incurred in consequence of the restriction);

(b) for the calculation of grants payable under the regulations by reference to the amount of the annual costs incurred or treated as being incurred by local authorities in respect of the borrowing of money to defray the expenditure in respect of which the grants are made, or by reference to the excess of such annual costs over receipts of those authorities which are attributable to such expenditure, or over the annual value of such receipts, or by reference to such other considerations as may be prescribed by the regulations;

(c) for the payment of capital sums in substitution for any periodical grants payable under the regulations in respect of such annual costs;

and for the purposes of this section 'clearing' and 'preliminary development' mean the carrying out of such works as may be prescribed by or determined under the regulations.

(4) Any grants to be paid or approval given under or for the purposes of regulations under this section shall be paid or given—

(a) in the case of local authorities in England excluding Monmouthshire, by the Minister;

(b) in the case of local authorities in Wales or Monmouthshire, by the Secretary of State.

(5) In this section 'enactment' and 'local authority' have the meanings assigned by subsection (1) of section 221 of the Town and Country Planning Act 1962; and references in this section to the relocation of population or industry and the replacement of open space shall be construed in accordance with that subsection, but as if for references in the definitions of those expressions to an area of extensive war damage or an area of bad lay-out or obsolete development there were substituted references to any area.

8. Grants for public open spaces

(1) Subject to the provisions of this section the Minister may, with the consent of the Treasury, pay to local authorities for the year 1967–68 and subsequent years grants of such amounts and payable at such times and subject to such conditions as he may from time to time determine, either generally or in the case of any particular authority, in respect of expenditure incurred by those authorities on and after 1st April, 1969 in or in connection with the acquisition for use as a public open space of land approved by the Minister for the purposes of this section.

(2) Grants under this section may be made either as periodical grants in respect of the costs from time to time incurred or treated as incurred by a local authority in respect of the borrowing of money to defray expenditure qualifying for such grants, or as capital grants in respect of such expenditure or in substitution for such periodical grants.

(3) The amount of the grant which may be paid to a local authority under this section in respect of any expenditure shall not exceed one-half of the amount of that expenditure, or of the costs incurred or treated as incurred as aforesaid on account of that expenditure, as approved by the Minister for the purposes of this section.

(4) For the purposes of this section any land appropriated by a local authority for use as a public open space may be treated as acquired by that authority for the purpose at a cost

of such amount, and defrayed in such manner, as the Minister may determine.

(5) In this section 'the Minister' in relation to local authorities in Wales and Monmouthshire means the Secretary of State; and 'local authority' means a local authority within the meaning of the Town and Country Planning Act, 1962.

9. Grants for reclamation of derelict land (1) Subject to the provisions of this section the Minister may, with the consent of the Treasury, pay to local authorities for the year 1967–68 and subsequent years grants of such amounts and payable at such times and subject to such conditions as he may from time to time determine, either generally or in the case of any particular authority, in respect of expenditure incurred by those authorities in or in connection with the acquisition at any time of land approved by the Minister for the purposes of this section, being—

   (a) derelict, neglected or unsightly land requiring reclamation or improvement; or

   (b) land required for purposes connected with the reclamation or improvement of such land as aforesaid,

or in or in connection with the carrying out on or after 1st April, 1967 of works approved as aforesaid for the reclamation or improvement of any such land.

(2) Grants under this section may be made either as periodical grants in respect of the costs from time to time incurred or treated as incurred by a local authority in respect of the borrowing of money to defray expenditure qualifying for such grants, or as capital grants in respect of such expenditure or in substitution for such periodical grants.

(3) The amount of the grant which may be paid to a local authority under this section in respect of any land shall not exceed one-half of the expenditure incurred in acquiring the land and in

carrying out any works for its reclamation or improvement, as approved by the Minister for the purposes of this section, reduced, unless the Minister otherwise determines, by the value of the land after carrying out those works, or one-half of the costs incurred or treated as incurred as aforesaid on account of that expenditure as so reduced.

(4) In this section 'the Minister' in relation to local authorities in Wales and Monmouthshire means the Secretary of State; and 'local authority' means a local authority within the meaning of the Town and Country Planning Act, 1962.

Lighting of highways

28. Provision of lighting by highway authorities (1) The Minister and every local highway authority shall have power to provide lighting for the purposes of any highway or proposed highway for which they are or will be the highway authority, and may for that purpose—

(a) contract with any persons for the supply of gas, electricity or other means of lighting; and

(b) construct and maintain such lamps, posts and other works as they consider necessary.

(2) A highway authority may alter or remove any works constructed by them under this section or vested in them under the following provisions of this Part of this Act.

(3) A highway authority shall pay compensation to any person who sustains damage by reason of the execution of works authorised by this section.

(4) Section 45 of the Public Health Act, 1961 (attachment of street lamps to buildings) and section 81 of that Act (summary recovery of damages for negligence) shall apply to a highway authority not being such a council as therein mentioned as they apply to such a council.

(5) For the purposes of the definition of 'improvement' in section 295 of the Highways Act, 1959, this section shall be treated as included in Part V of that Act.

29. Powers of existing lighting authorities (1) Subject to subsection (2) of this section, the powers of a lighting authority shall not be exercised, after the commencement of this Part of this Act, for purposes of the lighting of any highway for which they are not the highway authority except with the consent of the highway authority (which consent may be given either generally or in respect of any particular highway or length of highway, and either without conditions or subject to such conditions as the highway authority think fit).

(2) Subsection (1) of this section does not apply to the exercise of powers for the purpose only of the operation or maintenance of a lighting system which is not transferred to the highway authority under the following provisions of this Part of this Act.

(3) If a lighting authority are aggrieved by the refusal of a local highway authority to give their consent for the purposes of this section, or by any conditions subject to which such consent is given, they may appeal to the Minister, who may give such directions in the matter as he thinks fit.

(4) In this Part of this Act 'lighting authority' means a council or other body authorised to provide lighting . . . under section 3 of the Parish Councils Act, 1957 or any corresponding local enactment and includes (in relation only to the transfer of property, rights and liabilities) the representative body of a rural parish not having a parish council; and references to the powers of a lighting authority are references to their powers under the said enactments.

30. Delegation of lighting functions of highway authority (1) A highway authority may agree with the lighting authority for the delegation to the lighting authority of any of the functions of the highway authority with respect to the lighting of any highway or part of a highway within the area of the lighting authority.

(2) A lighting authority shall, for the

discharge of any functions delegated to them under subsection (1) of this section, act as agents for the highway authority; and it shall be a condition of the delegation—

(a) that any works to be executed or expenditure to be incurred by the lighting authority in the discharge of the delegated functions shall be subject to the approval of the highway authority;

(b) that the lighting authority shall comply with any requirements of the highway authority as to the manner in which any such works are to be carried out, and with any directions of the highway authority as to the terms of contracts to be entered into for the purposes of the discharge of the delegated functions; and

(c) that any such works shall be completed to the satisfaction of the highway authority.

(3) If at any time the highway authority are satisfied that a lighting system in respect of which the functions of that authority are delegated under this section is not in proper repair or condition, they may give notice to the lighting authority requiring them to place it in proper repair or condition, and if the notice is not complied with within a reasonable time may themselves do anything which seems to them necessary to place the system in proper repair or condition.

(4) A highway authority may agree with a lighting authority for the carrying out by the lighting authority of any works in connection with a lighting system provided or to be provided by the highway authority within the area of the lighting authority; and subsections (2) and (3) of this section shall apply to the conditions to be included in and to the discharge of functions pursuant to any such agreement, as they apply to the conditions to be attached to a delegation of functions under subsection (1) of this section and the discharge of functions so delegated.

(5) A delegation to a lighting authority under this section may be determined by notice given to that authority by the highway authority, and functions delegated to a lighting authority under this section may be relinquished by notice given by that authority to the highway authority; but a notice under this subsection shall not take effect until 1st April in the calendar year following that in which it is given, and shall not be given during the last three months of a calendar year.

31. Transfer of road lighting systems (1) On the *1st April, 1967* there shall be transferred to the highway authority for any highway for which a road lighting system was then provided by a lighting authority other than the highway authority—

(a) all lamps, lamp-posts and other apparatus which, immediately before that date, were vested in the lighting authority as part of that system;

(b) except as provided by subsection (2) of this section, all other property or rights which, immediately before that date, were vested in the lighting authority for the purposes of that system, and all liabilities incurred by that authority for those purposes and not discharged before that date.

(2) There shall not be transferred to a highway authority by virtue of this section any right or liability of a lighting authority in respect of work done, services rendered, goods (including gas and electricity) supplied or money due for payment before the said date, and there shall not be transferred to the Minister by virtue of this section any liability of a lighting authority in respect of loans or loan charges.

(3) A highway authority and a lighting authority, or any two or more highway authorities, may make agreements with respect to the transfer of property, rights and liabilities under this section, including agreements for defining the property, rights and liabilities thereby transferred to the

highway authority or any of those authorities, and for the transfer or retention of property, rights or liabilities held or incurred for the purposes of two or more road lighting systems, or partly for the purposes of such a lighting system and partly for other purposes; and any dispute between the authorities concerned as to the property, rights or liabilities transferred by this section shall be determined—

(a) where the Minister is one of those authorities, by arbitration;

(b) in any other case, by the Minister.

(4) If at any time after the *1st April, 1967* a road lighting system is provided by a lighting authority for the purposes of a highway for which they are not the highway authority, the foregoing provisions of this section shall apply as if for references to the *1st April, 1967* there were substituted a reference to such date as may be determined by agreement between the lighting authority or, in default of such agreement, as the Minister may direct.

(5) In this Part of this Act 'road lighting system' means a lighting system which is not a footway lighting system.

32. Special provisions as to footway lighting systems (1) In this Part of this Act 'footway lighting system' means a system of lighting, provided for a highway, which satisfies the following conditions, that is to say that either—

(a) no lamp is mounted more than 13 feet above ground level; or

(b) no lamp is mounted more than 20 feet above ground level and there is at least one interval of more than 50 yards between adjacent lamps in the system,

or such other conditions as may be prescribed by order of the Minister in substitution for the said conditions.

(2) Where a footway lighting system maintained by a lighting authority other than the highway authority becomes a road lighting system—

(a) in consequence of any order made by the Minister under subsection (1) of this section; or

(b) in consequence of any alterations effected by the lighting authority, section 31 of this Act shall apply in relation to that system as if for references in subsections (1) and (2) to the date of the commencement of this Part of this Act there were substituted references to such date as may be agreed upon between the lighting authority and the highway authority or, in default of such agreement, as the Minister may direct.

(3) If in the case of a road or part of a road in which a footway lighting system is maintained by a lighting authority other than the highway authority the highway authority propose to provide a road lighting system (either as a separate system or by means of alterations of the footway lighting system), they may give notice to that effect to the lighting authority; and where such notice is given section 31 of this Act shall apply in relation to the footway lighting system as if for references in subsections (1) and (2) to the date of the commencement of this Part of this Act there were substituted references to such date as may be specified for the purpose in the notice.

Supplemental

34. Construction and commencement of Part III (1) This Part of this Act shall be construed as one with the Highways Act, 1959; and without prejudice to the generality of this provision—

(a) 'the Minister' means, in relation to England exclusive of Monmouthshire the Minister of Transport, and in relation to Wales and Monmouthshire the Secretary of State;

(b) any reference in the said Act to that Act includes (unless the context otherwise requires) a reference to this Part of this Act.

Road Traffic Regulation Act, 1967.

Parish Parking Places for Bicycles and Motor Cycles

46. Power of parish councils to provide parking places for bicycles and motor cycles (1) Where for the purpose of relieving or preventing congestion of traffic or preserving local amenities it appears to a parish council in England or Wales to be necessary to provide within the parish suitable parking places for bicycles and motor cycles, the parish council may provide and maintain such parking places in accordance with the provisions of this section, and for that purpose (or for the purpose of providing means of entrance to and egress from any parking place provided under this section) may—

(*a*) utilise and adapt any land purchased by the council for the purpose or appropriated for the purpose under subsection (2) of this section; or

(*b*) subject to the provisions of the next following section, adapt and by order authorise the use of any part of a road within the parish;

and the power under this subsection to provide and maintain parking places shall include power to provide and maintain structures for use as parking places.

(2) Notwithstanding anything in any other enactment, a parish council may, with the consent of the Minister of Housing and Local Government, appropriate for the purpose of providing a parking place under this section—

(*a*) any part of a recreation ground provided or maintained by the council under section 8 of the Local Government Act, 1894;

(*b*) any part of an open space controlled or maintained by the council under the Open Spaces Act, 1906, other than a part which has been consecrated as a burial ground or in which burials have taken place;

(*c*) any part of any land provided by the council as a playing field or for any other purpose under section 4 of the Physical Training and Recreation Act, 1937:

Provided that any part so appropriated shall not exceed one-eighth of the total area of the recreation ground, open space or land concerned, or 800 square feet, whichever is the less.

(3) No order under subsection (1) of this section shall authorise the use of any part of a road as a parking place under this section so as unreasonably to prevent access to any premises adjoining the road, or the use of the road by any person entitled to use it, or so as to be a nuisance.

(4) A parish council may employ with or without remuneration such persons as may be necessary for the superintendence of parking places provided by the council under this section.

(5) A parish council may make byelaws (subject to confirmation by the Minister of Transport) as to the use of parking places provided under this section, and in particular as to the conditions upon which any such parking place may be used and as to the charges to be paid to the council in connection with the use of any parking place not being part of a road; and a copy of any byelaws made under this subsection shall be exhibited on or near every parking place to which they relate.

(6) A parish council may let for use as a parking place any parking place provided by them (not being part of a road) under this section; but (without prejudice to any power of a parish council under any other enactment to let a playing field or other land of which a parking place forms part) no single letting under this subsection shall be for a longer period than seven days.

(7) The exercise by a parish council of their powers under this section with respect to the use as a parking place of any part of a road shall not render them subject to any liability in respect of loss or damage to any vehicle or the fittings

or contents of any vehicle parked in such a parking place.

(8) An order made under this section may be varied or revoked by a subsequent order made in like manner.

(9) In the application of this section to Wales and Monmouthshire subsection (2) shall have effect as if for the reference to the Minister of Housing and Local Government these were substituted a reference to the Secretary of State.

47. Provisions as to consents for purposes of section 91 (1) A parish council shall not have power by virtue of the last foregoing section to provide a parking place—

(*a*) in a position obstructing or interfering with any existing access to any land or premises not forming part of a road, except with the consent of the owner and the occupier of the land or premises; or

(*b*) in a road which is not a highway or in a public path, except with the consent of the owner and the occupier of the land over which the road or path runs; or

(*c*) in any such situation or position as is described in the first column of the following Table, except with the consent of the persons described in relation thereto in the second column of that Table.

TABLE

In a trunk road or any other road maintained by the Minister or on land abutting on any such road.	The Minister.
In a road which is a highway (other than a trunk road or a road maintained as aforesaid or a public path) or on land abutting on any such road.	The county council.
In a road which is a highway belonging to and repairable by any railway, dock, harbour, canal, inland navigation or passenger road transport undertakers and forming the approach to any station, dock, wharf or depot of those undertakers.	The undertakers concerned.
On a bridge carrying a highway over a railway, dock, harbour, canal or inland navigation, or on the approaches to any such bridge or under a bridge carrying a railway, canal or inland navigation over a highway.	The railway, dock, harbour, canal or inland navigation undertakers concerned.

(2) Any consent required by paragraph (*c*) of subsection (1) of this section shall not unreasonably be withheld, but may be given subject to any reasonable conditions, including a condition that the parish council shall remove any thing to the provision of which the consent relates either at any time or at or after the expiration of a period if reasonably required so to do by the person giving the consent.

(3) A dispute between a parish council and a person whose consent is required under paragraph (*c*) of subsection (1) of this section whether that consent is unreasonably withheld or is given subject to reasonable conditions, or whether the removal of any thing to the provision of which the consent relates in accordance with any condition of the consent is reasonably required, shall—

(*a*) in the case of a dispute between the parish council and the Minister, be referred to and determined by an arbitrator to be appointed in default of agreement by the President of the Institution of Civil Engineers; and

(*b*) in any other case, be referred to and determined by the Minister, who may cause a public inquiry to be held for the purpose.

(4) Section 6 of the Local Government (Miscellaneous Provisions) Act, 1953 (which makes provision as to access to telegraphic lines, sewers, pipe-subways, pipes, wires and other apparatus) shall apply in relation to a parking place (including a structure for use as a parking place) provided by a parish council under section 46 of this Act, and to the council by which the parking place is so provided, as it applies in relation to a shelter or other accommodation provided, and to the local authority by which it is provided, under section 4 of that Act.

(5) In this section and in the said section 6 as they apply in relation to a parking place provided under section 46 of this Act which forms part of a road, references to removal shall be construed as including references to the suspension or revocation of the order authorising the use of that part of the road as a parking place.

48. Provisions ancillary to exercise of powers under section 46 (1) A parish council may contribute towards—

(*a*) the reasonable expenses incurred by any person in doing anything which by virtue of section 46 of this Act that council has power to do; and

(*b*) the expenses incurred by any other parish council in exercising their powers under that section.

(2) Where before 17th July, 1957, a parish council have provided anything which could be provided by them under section 46 of this Act or where, before the 1st September, 1960 (whether before or after the said 17th July) or on or after the 1st September, 1960 any other person has provided any such thing, the parish council shall have the like power to maintain that thing as if it had been provided by them under the said section 46.

(3) Without prejudice to any other power of combination, a parish council may by agreement combine with any other parish council for the purpose of exercising the powers conferred by the said section 46.

49. Application of sections 46 to 48 to boroughs included in rural districts. Sections 46, 47 and 48 of this Act shall apply to the council of a borough included in a rural district as they apply to a parish council, and in their application to the council of a borough so included references therein to the parish shall be construed as references to the borough.

50. Interpretation of sections 46 to 49 In the four last foregoing sections, except so far as the context otherwise requires,—

'in' in a context referring to things in a road includes a reference to things under, over, across, along or upon the road;

'owner' has the meaning assigned to it by section 343 of the Public Health Act, 1936;

'parish' in relation to a common parish council acting for two or more grouped parishes, means those parishes;

'public path' has the meaning assigned to it by section 27 of the National Parks and Access to the Countryside Act, 1949;

'road' means a highway (including a public path) and any other road, lane, footway, square, court, alley or passage (whether a thoroughfare or not) to which the public has access, but does not include a road provided or to be provided in pursuance of a scheme made or having effect as if made under section 11 of the Highways Act, 1959.

Civic Amenities Act, 1967

Removal and disposal of vehicles and other refuse

20. Removal of abandoned vehicles (1) Where it appears to a local authority that a motor vehicle in their area is abandoned without lawful authority on any land in the open air or on any other land forming part of a highway, it shall be the duty of the authority, subject to the following provisions of this section, to remove the vehicle.

(2) Where it appears to a local authority that the land on which a motor vehicle is abandoned as aforesaid is occupied by any person, the authority shall give him notice in the prescribed manner that they propose to remove the vehicle in pursuance of subsection (1) of this section but shall not be entitled to remove it if he objects to the proposal in the prescribed manner and within the prescribed period; and a local authority shall not be required by virtue of subsection (1) of this section to remove a vehicle situated otherwise than on a carriageway within the meaning of the Highways Act, 1959 if it appears to them that the cost of its removal to the nearest convenient carriageway within the meaning of that Act would be unreasonably high.

(3) Where in pursuance of this section a local authority propose to remove a vehicle which in their opinion is in such a condition that it ought to be destroyed they shall, not less than the prescribed period before removing it, cause to be affixed to the vehicle a notice stating that the authority propose to remove it for destruction on the expiration of that period.

(4) *applies to Greater London*

(5) While a vehicle, other than a vehicle to which a notice was affixed in accordance with subsection (3) of this section, is in the custody of a local authority . . . in pursuance of this section, it shall be the duty of the authority . . . to take such steps as are reasonably necessary for the safe custody of the vehicle.

(7) (*Applies to Scotland.*)

(8) The foregoing provisions of this section shall have effect during the period of six months beginning with the commencement of this Act as if for the words 'the duty of' in subsection (1) and 'but' in subsection (2) there were substituted respectively the words 'lawful for' and 'before doing so and' and as if in subsection (2) the words from 'and a' onwards and subsections (6) and (7) were omitted; and the Minister may, by order made before the expiration of the period of six months beginning with the commencement of this Act, provide that this subsection shall have effect in relation to any area specified by the order as if for the first reference to the period of six months there were substituted a reference to such longer period as may be specified by the order in relation to that area.

23. Removal and disposal etc. of other refuse (1) Where it appears to a local authority that any thing in their area, other than a motor vehicle, is abandoned without lawful authority on any land in the open air or on any other land forming part of a highway, the authority may if they think fit, subject to subsection (2) of this section, remove the thing.

(2) A local authority shall not be entitled to exercise their powers under subsection (1) of this section as respects a thing situated on land appearing to the authority to be occupied by any person unless the authority have given him notice in the prescribed manner that they propose to remove the thing and he has failed to object to the proposal in the prescribed manner and within the prescribed period.

In this subsection 'prescribed', in relation to England excluding Monmouthshire, means prescribed by regulations made by the Minister of Housing and Local Government.

(3) The following provisions (which

relate to the deposit and disposal of refuse), that is to say—

(a) section 76 of the Public Health Act, 1936 (except paragraph (a) of subsection (3));

(b) sub-paragraphs (3) and (4) of paragraph 15 of Part I of Schedule 11 to the London Government Act, 1963; and

(c) without prejudice to the generality of subsection (2) of section 30 of this Act, sub-paragraphs (1) and (2) of the said paragraph 15 so far as they relate to provisions of the said section 76,

shall apply to any thing removed in pursuance of subsection (1) of this section as those provisions apply to other refuse.

(4) A local authority by whom any thing is removed in pursuance of subsection (1) of this section shall be entitled to recover the cost of removing and disposing of it from any person by whom it was put in the place from which it was so removed or any person convicted of an offence under subsection (1) of section 19 of this Act in consequence of the putting of the thing in that place; . . .

General Rate Act, 1967

PART II

PROVISIONS AS TO PRECEPTS

11. Power and duty to make sufficient precepts Every authority having power to issue a precept to a rating authority shall from time to time issue such precepts as will be sufficient to provide for such part of the total estimated expenditure to be incurred by the authority during the period in respect of which the precept is issued as is to be met out of moneys raised by rates, together with such additional amount as is in the opinion of the authority required to cover expenditure previously incurred, or to meet contingencies, or to defray any expenditure which may fall to be defrayed before the date on which the moneys to be received in respect of the next subsequent precept will become available.

15. General power for securing payment of precepts (1) Where in pursuance of a precept issued to a rating authority by any other authority any amount is payable directly or indirectly by the rating authority to the precepting authority and, on an application for a certificate under this

section made by the precepting authority after 21 days' notice given to the rating authority, the Minister is satisfied that the rating authority have refused or through wilful neglect or wilful default failed to raise that amount by a rate, or that, having raised the amount by a rate, the rating authority have refused or through wilful neglect or wilful default failed to pay the amount due under the precept, the Minister may issue a certificate to that effect and thereupon—

(a) the precepting authority shall have the like power of applying for a receiver, and

(b) a receiver may on such an application be appointed in like manner, and when appointed shall have the like power,

as if—

(i) the precepting authority were a secured creditor of the rating authority for the amount due under the precept, with interest thereon at the rate of six per cent. per annum from the date when the amount became payable under the precept; and

S

(ii) the said amount and interest were due under a security issued under the *Local Loans Act, 1875,* charging them on the rates leviable by, and on all other property of, the rating authority; and

(iii) the conditions under which a receiver may in such a case be appointed under section 12 of the said Act of 1875 were fulfilled;

and the said section 12 shall apply accordingly.

(2) If the Minister so thinks fit an application under subsection (1) (*a*) of this section may be made by him instead of by the precepting authority.

(3) The powers conferred by this section shall be in addition to and not in derogation of any other powers for enforcing compliance with a precept issued to a rating authority.

40. Relief for charitable and other organisations (1) If notice in writing is given to the rating authority that—

(*a*) any hereditament occupied by, or by trustees for, a charity and wholly or mainly used for charitable purposes (whether of that charity or of that and other charities); or

(*b*) any other hereditament, being a hereditament held upon trust for use as an almshouse,

is one falling within this subsection, then, subject to the provisions of this section, the amount of any rates chargeable in respect of the hereditament for any period, during which the hereditament is one falling within either paragraph (*a*) or paragraph (*b*) of this subsection being a period beginning not earlier than the rate period in which the notice is given shall not exceed one-half of the amount which would be chargeable apart from the provisions of this subsection:

Provided that where a hereditament ceases to be one falling within the said paragraphs (*a*) and (*b*), a previous notice given for the purposes of this subsection shall not have effect as respects any subsequent period during which the hereditament falls within either of those paragraphs.

(5) Without prejudice to the powers conferred by section 53 of this Act, a rating authority shall have power to reduce or remit the payment of rates chargeable in respect of—

(*a*) any hereditament falling within subsection (1) (*a*) or (*b*) of this section;

(*b*) any other hereditament which is occupied for the purposes of one or more institutions or other organisations which are not established or conducted for profit and whose main objects are charitable or are otherwise philanthropic or religious or concerned with education, social welfare, science, literature or the fine arts;

(*c*) any other hereditament which is occupied for the purposes of a club, society or other organisation not established or conducted for profit and is wholly or mainly used for purposes of recreation,

for any such period as is mentioned in subsection (6) of this section:

Provided that any such reduction or remission shall cease to have effect on a change in the occupation of the hereditament in respect of which it was granted.

(6) Any reduction or remission of rates determined under (5) of this section may at the discretion of the rating authority be granted—

(*a*) for the year in which, or the year next following that in which, the determination to grant it is made; or

(*b*) for a specified term of years, not exceeding five, beginning not earlier than the year in which the determination was made nor more than twenty-four months after the date of the determination;

or

(*c*) for an indefinite period beginning not earlier than the last mentioned year subject, however, to the exercise by the rating authority of their powers under subsection (7) of this section.

(7) Where any such reduction or remission is granted for an indefinite period the rating authority may, by not less than twelve months' notice in writing given to the occupiers of the hereditament, terminate or modify the reduction or remission as from the end of a year specified in the notice.

(8) The foregoing provisions of this section shall not apply to any hereditament . . . occupied (otherwise than as trustee) by any authority having, within the meaning of the Local Loans Act, 1875, power to levy a rate.

(9) In this section 'charity' means an institution or other organisation established for charitable purposes only and 'organisation' includes any persons administering a trust . . .;

44. Exemption of parks, etc. (1) A park which has been provided by, or is under the management of, a local authority and is for the time being available for free and unrestricted use by members of the public shall, while so available, be treated for rating purposes as if it had been dedicated in perpetuity for such use.

(2) In this section—

(*a*) references to a park include references to a recreation or pleasure ground, a public walk, an open space within the meaning of the Open Spaces Act, 1906, or a playing field provided under the Physical Training and Recreation Act, 1937;

(*b*) 'local authority' means the council of a county, county borough, county district, London borough, or borough included in a rural district, a parish council or parish meeting, the Greater London Council, the Common Council of the City of London . . . or any two or more of them acting in combination.

Countryside Act, 1968

2. New functions of the Commission (1) The Commission* shall have the general duties imposed by this section, but nothing in this section shall be construed as modifying the effect of any provision of this Act or of the Act of 1949 whereby any general or specific power or duty is conferred or imposed on the Commission, or whereby an obligation is imposed on any other person to consult with the Commission.

(2) The Commission shall keep under review all matters relating to—

(*a*) the provision and improvement of facilities for the enjoyment of the countryside,

(*b*) the conservation and enhancement of the natural beauty and amenity of the countryside, and

(*c*) the need to secure public access to the countryside for the purposes of open-air recreation,

* The Countryside Commission.

and shall consult with such local planning authorities and other bodies as appear to the Commission to have an interest in those matters.

(3) The Commission shall encourage, assist, concert or promote the implementation of any proposals with respect to those matters made by any person or body, being proposals which the Commission consider to be suitable.

(4) The Commission shall advise any Minister having functions under this Act, or any other Minister or any public body, on such matters relating to the countryside as he or they may refer to the Commission, or as the Commission may think fit.

(5) Where it appears to the Commission that the provision and improvement of facilities for enjoyment of the countryside or the conservation and enhancement of the natural beauty and amenity of the countryside presents special problems or requires special

S*

professional or technical skill, the Commission—

(a) shall notify their opinion to the appropriate local planning authority or other public body, and

(b) on the application of any such authority or other body in any case where it appears to the Commission expedient having regard to the provisions of section 1 (2) of this Act, and to the provisions of section 5 (1) of the Act of 1949 (general provisions as respects National Parks), shall place the services of officers or servants of the Commission, or the services of consultants engaged by the Commission, at the disposal of the authority or other body for such period as may be agreed between them, and on such terms as to payment or otherwise, as may be so agreed with the approval of the Minister.

(6) The Commission shall make to local planning authorities and other public bodies, as respects the exercise of the powers of making byelaws conferred by this Act and the Act of 1949, recommendations as to the matters in respect of which byelaws should be made.

(7) The Commission shall carry out, or commission the carrying out of, such inquiries, investigations or researches, either on their own account or jointly with other persons, as the Commission may deem necessary or expedient for the purposes of any of their functions.

(8) The Commission shall provide, or assist in the provision of, publicity and information services relating to the countryside, to places of beauty or interest therein, or to the functions of the Commission, and shall take such steps as appear to them expedient for securing that suitable methods of publicity are used for the prevention of damage in the countryside and for encouraging a proper standard of behaviour on the part of persons resorting to the countryside.

(9) The Commission shall make to the Minister such recommendations as the Commission think proper in respect of applications by local authorities for Exchequer grants under this Act or the Act of 1949.

3. Exercise of functions of Commission in Wales and Monmouthshire (1) The commission shall, after consultation with the Secretary of State, appoint a Committee for Wales.

(3) The Commission may, after consulting the Secretary of State and subject to such conditions as they think appropriate, delegate any of their functions in Wales or Monmouthshire to the Committee for Wales . . .

4. Experimental projects or schemes (1) The Commission, after consultation with such local authorities and other bodies as appear to the Commission to have an interest, may from time to time prepare and submit to the Minister for his approval proposals with respect to any area for an experimental project or scheme designed to facilitate the enjoyment of the countryside, or to conserve or enhance its natural beauty or amenity, which—

(a) in relation to that area involves the application of new or developed methods, concepts or techniques, and

(b) is designed to illustrate the appropriateness of such a project or scheme to that area or other areas of a similar nature or which present similar problems to that area,

and the Minister may approve in whole or in part or with modifications any proposals so submitted to him, or may refuse to approve them.

(2) The Commission shall concert, promote, or undertake either by themselves or in conjunction with any other authority or person, measures to implement any proposals so approved.

(3) For the purpose of their functions under the foregoing provisions of this section the Commission may—

(a) with the approval of the Minister acquire land by agreement, or may be authorised by the Minister in a particular case to acquire land compulsorily,

(b) hold and manage land, and with the approval of the Minister and subject to the subsequent provisions of this section, dispose of or otherwise deal with land,

(c) erect buildings and carry out works or other operations on land,

(d) provide equipment, facilities and services on or in connection with land or with the use of land,

(e) hold, manage, maintain, hire, let or otherwise dispose of such works, equipment, facilities or services,

(f) exercise any powers to carry out work or to provide facilities or services conferred by this Act or the Act of 1949 on local authorities or local planning authorities,

(g) with the approval of the Minister and the Treasury, acquire by agreement and carry on or set up and carry on, directly or through an agent, or themselves carry on as agent, any business or undertaking relevant to the experimental project or scheme, and, subject to the approval of the Minister and the Treasury, may dispose of any such business or undertaking.

(4) The disposal of land under this section may be by way of sale or exchange, or by the letting of land or the granting of any interest in or right over land, but the Commission shall not under this section dispose of land by way of gift.

(5) The powers conferred by paragraphs (c) to (f) of subsection (3) above may be exercised by the Commission—

(a) on land belonging to them, or

(b) on such terms as may be agreed with the owners and any other persons whose authority is required for the purpose, on other land,

and an agreement under paragraph (b) above may provide for the making by the Commission of payments in consideration of the making of the agreement and payments by way of contribution towards expenditure incurred by the persons making the agreement in consequence thereof.

(6) The provisions of this section, except for that authorising compulsory purchase of land, shall have effect only for the purpose of removing any limitation imposed by law on the capacity of the Commission, and shall not authorise any act or omission on the part of the Commission which, apart from the said provisions of this section, would be actionable at the suit of any person on any ground other than such a limitation.

5. **Grants and loans to persons other than public bodies** (1) In accordance with arrangements approved by the Minister and the Treasury, the Commission shall have power to give financial assistance by way of grant or loan, or partly in the one way and partly in the other, to any person, other than a public body, carrying on or proposing to carry on any project approved by the Minister for the purposes of this section which in the opinion of the Commission is conducive to the attainment of any of the purposes of this Act or the Act of 1949.

(2) Financial assistance by way of grant under this section shall not exceed 75% of the expenditure in respect of which the grant is made.

(3) Before applying for the approval of the Minister under this section to any project the Commission shall satisfy themselves that in all the circumstances it is preferable that the project should be carried out by a person other than a public body.

(4) On making a grant or loan under this section the Commission may impose such conditions as they think fit, including (in the case of a grant) conditions for repayment in specified circumstances.

(5) In this section 'public body' does not include the National Trust.

New powers of local authorities

6. Country parks and commons: preliminary (1) The powers conferred by this and the three next following sections shall be exercisable for the purpose of providing, or improving, opportunities for the enjoyment of the countryside by the public, and a local authority in exercising those powers in any area in the countryside shall have regard—

  (*a*) to the location of that area in the countryside in relation to an urban or built-up area, and

  (*b*) to the availability and adequacy of existing facilities for the enjoyment of the countryside by the public.

(2) In this and the three next following sections 'local authority' means—

  (*a*) the council of a county, county borough or county district, or

  (*b*) the Greater London Council, the Common Council of the City of London or any London borough council, or

  (*c*) a National Park joint planning board, that is to say a joint planning board constituted under section 2 of the Town and Country Planning Act, 1962 for an area which consists of or includes any part of a National Park.

(3) A local authority may exercise the powers conferred by the three next following sections inside or outside their area,. . .

(4) Before a local authority exercise any of the powers conferred by the next following section as respects any land, or acquire any land, or any additional land, for the purpose of exercising those powers, they shall comply with the requirements in the following Table.

TABLE

Requirement	*Authority exercising powers*
Consult the council of any county district in the county which will comprise all or any part of the land.	A county council
Obtain the consent of the council of any other county which will comprise all or any part of the land.	
Obtain the consent of the county council, and of the council of any other county which will comprise all or any part of the land.	Council of a county district
Obtain the consent of the council of any county which will comprise all or any part of the land.	Council of a county borough, the Greater London Council, Common Council of the City of London, or any London borough council.
Consult the council of any county district which is wholly or partly in the area of the board and which will comprise all or any part of the land.	National Park joint planning board.
If any part of the land will be outside the area of the board, obtain the consent of the council of any county which will comprise any such part of the land.	
If any part of the land is within a National Park and also within the area of a National Park joint planning board, obtain the consent of the board	Any local authority

(in addition to any necessary consent of a county council).

If all or any part of the land is in a parish, inform the parish council or, in the case of a parish not having a parish council, the chairman of the parish meeting.

Any local authority

(5) Before a county council or National Park joint planning board give any consent so required they shall consult the council of any county district within, or partly within, their area which will comprise all or any part of the land.

(6) A local authority may apply to the Minister on the grounds that a county council or National Park joint planning board have unreasonably withheld any consent so required, and the Minister, after affording to the county council, or the board, an opportunity of making representations, may if he thinks fit direct the county council, or the board, to give the consent to which the application relates.

The county council or board shall comply with any direction given by the Minister under this subsection.

(7) Section 29 of the Town and Country Planning Act, 1959 (protection of persons deriving title under transactions requiring the consent of a Minister) shall apply as if any reference in that section to the consent of a Minister included a reference to a consent of a local authority required under this section.

7. Power to provide country parks (1) Subject to section 6 above, a local authority shall have power, on any site in the countryside appearing to them suitable or adaptable for the purpose set out in section 6 (1) above, to provide a country park, that is to say a park or pleasure ground to be used for that purpose.

(2) A local authority shall have power to extend, maintain and manage the country park and to do all other things appearing to them desirable for the said purpose in connection with the provision of a country park and in particular—

(a) to lay out, plant and improve the site, and to erect buildings and carry out works,

(b) to provide facilities and services for the enjoyment or convenience of the public, including meals and refreshments, parking places for vehicles, shelters and lavatory accommodation,

(c) to provide facilities and services for open-air recreation:

Provided that a local authority shall not under this section provide accommodation, meals or refreshments except in so far as it appears to them that the facilities therefor within the country park are inadequate or unsatisfactory, either generally or as respects any description of accommodation, meals or refreshments, as the case may be.

(3) The powers conferred by the foregoing provisions of this section and by the next following section may be exercised by the local authority—

(a) on land belonging to them, or

(b) on such terms as may be agreed with the owners and any other persons whose authority is required for the purpose, on other land,

and an agreement under paragraph (b) above may provide for the making by the local authority of payments in consideration of the making of the agreement and payments by way of contribution towards expenditure incurred by the persons making the agreement in consequence thereof.

(4) A local authority shall have power to acquire compulsorily any land required by them for the purpose of their functions under this and the next following section.

(5) If it appears to a local authority that a park or pleasure ground provided or acquired by the local authority before the coming into force of this section, or otherwise than under or for the purposes of this section, can suitably be used as a country park, that park or pleasure ground shall, from such date as the local authority may determine, be treated for all the purposes of this Act as a country park provided under this section, but—

(a) this subsection shall not affect any trust, covenant or other restriction to which the park or pleasure ground is subject, and

(b) no grant shall be payable under this Act in respect of expenditure incurred before the date so determined.

(6) If it appears to a local authority that land provided or acquired by them before the coming into force of this section, as open country to be used for the purposes of Part V of the Act of 1949, can suitably be used as a country park, that land, or any part of it, shall, from such date as the local authority may determine, be treated for all the purposes of this Act as a country park provided under this section; and, if the land was acquired under section 76 of the Act of 1949 (compulsory acquisition for public access), the land so treated shall cease to be subject to that section, but—

(a) this subsection shall not affect any trust, covenant or other restriction to which the land is subject; and

(b) no grant shall be payable under this Act in respect of expenditure incurred before the date so determined.

(7) A country park provided under this section shall not be subject to any of the following enactments (which relate to parks and pleasure grounds):

Section 164 of the Public Health Act, 1875.

Section 44 of the Public Health Acts Amendment Act, 1890.

Sections 76 and 77 of the Public Health Acts Amendment Act, 1907.

Section 56 (5) of the Public Health Act, 1925.

Section 132 of the Local Government Act, 1948.

8. Country parks: sailing, boating, bathing and fishing (1) Without prejudice to the generality of section 7 (2) of this Act, where a country park comprises any waterway the kinds of open-air recreation for which the local authority may provide facilities and services under that subsection shall include sailing, boating, bathing and fishing.

(2) If a country park is bounded by the sea, or by any waterway which is not part of the sea, the local authority providing the country park shall have power to carry out such work and do such things as may appear to them necessary or expedient for facilitating the use of the waters so adjoining the country park by the public for sailing, boating, bathing and fishing and other forms of recreation.

(3) The powers conferred by subsections (1) and (2) above include power to erect buildings or carry out works on land adjoining the sea or other waters but outside the country park, and to construct jetties or other works wholly or partly in the sea or other waters.

(4) The local authority, before acting under the foregoing provisions of this section, shall consult with, and seek the consent of, any river authority having functions relating to the sea or other waters in question, and of such other authorities, being authorities which under any enactment have functions relating to the sea or other waters in question, as the Minister may either generally or in particular case direct, and Schedule 1 to this Act shall have effect where any authority so consulted withhold their consent.

(5) A local authority may make bye-laws regulating the use of works carried out by them pursuant to this section and of any facilities or services provided in connection with the works, but before making any such byelaws the

local authority shall consult the Commission:

Provided that byelaws made under this subsection shall not interfere with the exercise of any functions relating to the waters or land to which the byelaws apply which are exercisable by any authority under any enactment.

Section 106 of the Act of 1949 (supplementary provisions as to byelaws) shall have effect as if byelaws under this subsection were byelaws under that Act.

(6) Nothing in this section shall authorise the carrying out of any operation in contravention of section 34 of the Coast Protection Act, 1949 (works detrimental to navigation) or section 9 of the Harbours Act, 1964 (control of habour development).

9. Powers exercisable over or near common land (1) This section has effect as respects any common land to which the public have rights of access, and the powers conferred by this section are to be exercised in the interests of persons resorting to the common land for open-air recreation.

(2) Subject to the provisions of section 6 above, a local authority may exercise the powers conferred by this section on land taken out of the common land in accordance with this section and Schedule 2 to this Act, or on other land in the neighbourhood of the common land.

(3) A local authority shall have power to do anything appearing to the local authority to be desirable for the purpose set out in section 6 (1) above, and in the interests of persons resorting to the common land, and in particular—

- (a) to provide facilities and services for the enjoyment or convenience of the public, including meals and refreshments, parking places for vehicles, shelters and lavatory accommodation,
- (b) to erect buildings and carry out works:

Provided that a local authority shall not under this section provide accommodation, meals or refreshments except in so far as it appears to them that the facilities therefor in the neighbourhood of the common land are inadequate or unsatisfactory, either generally or as respects any description of accommodation, meals or refreshments, as the case may be.

(4) Schedule 2 to this Act shall have effect for the purposes of this section, and in that Schedule 'the principal section' means this section.

(5) A local authority shall have power to acquire compulsorily any land in the neighbourhood of the common land which is required by them for the purposes of their functions under this section and which is not common land.

(6) In this section—

'common land' has the meaning given by section 22 (1) of the Commons Registration Act, 1965;
'common land to which the public have rights of access' means—
- (a) land to which section 193 of the Law of Property Act, 1925 for the time being applies, other than land to which that section applies by virtue of a revocable instrument, or
- (b) common land comprised in an access agreement or access order under Part V of the Act of 1949, other than a revocable access agreement or an access agreement expressed to have effect only for a period specified in the agreement, or
- (c) any other common land to which the public have rights of access permanently or for an indefinite period.

Public rights of way

27. Signposting of footpaths and bridleways (1) A highway authority, after consultation with the owner or occupier of the land concerned, shall have power to erect and maintain signposts along any footpath or bridleway for which they are the highway authority.

(2) Subject to subsection (3) below, at every point where a footpath or bridleway leaves a metalled road the highway authority shall in exercise of

their power under subsection (1) above erect and maintain a signpost—

(a) indicating that the footpath or bridleway is a public footpath or bridleway, and

(b) showing, so far as the highway authority consider convenient and appropriate, where the footpath or bridleway leads, and the distance to any place or places named on the signpost.

(3) A highway authority need not erect a signpost in accordance with subsection (2) above at a particular site if the highway authority, after consulting the council of the parish in which the site is situated, or as the case may be the chairman of the parish meeting for the parish, not having a parish council, in which the site is situated, are satisfied that it is not necessary, and if the parish council, or as the case may be the chairman of the parish meeting, agree.

(4) It shall also be the duty of a highway authority in exercise of their powers under subsection (1) above to erect such signposts as may in the opinion of the highway authority be required to assist persons unfamiliar with the locality to follow the course of a footpath or bridleway.

(5) With the consent of the highway authority, any other person may erect and maintain signposts along a footpath or bridleway.

(6) *Amends the Highways Act, 1959, s. 117 (2) (c).*

(7) In this section (and in the amendments made by this section in other enactments) references to signposts shall include references to other signs or notices serving the same purpose and references to the erection of a signpost shall include references to positioning any such other sign or notice.

28. Duty to maintain stiles, etc., on footpaths and bridleways (1) Any stile, gate or other similar structure across a footpath or bridleway shall be maintained by the owner of the land in a safe condition, and to the standard of repair required to prevent unreason-

able interference with the rights of the persons using the footpath or bridleway.

(2) If it appears to the highway authority for the footpath or bridleway that the duty imposed by subsection (1) above is not being complied with, the highway authority, after giving to the owner and occupier not less than 14 days' notice of their intention, may take all necessary steps for repairing and making good the stile, gate or other works, and may recover from the owner of the land the amount of any expenses reasonably incurred by the highway authority in and in connection with the exercise of their powers under this subsection, or such part of those expenses as the highway authority think fit.

(3) The highway authority shall contribute not less than a quarter of any expenses shown to their satisfaction to have been reasonably incurred in compliance with subsection (1) above, and shall have power to make further contributions of such amount in each case as they shall, having regard to all the circumstances, consider reasonable.

(4) Subsection (1) above shall not apply to any structure if and so long as the highway authority are, under an agreement in writing with any other person, liable to maintain the structure, or if any conditions for the maintenance of the structure are for the time being in force under section 126 of the Highways Act, 1959 (authority for erection of stiles, etc.).

(5) This section shall be construed as one with the Highways Act, 1959.

29. Ploughing of footpath or bridleway (1) Subject to subsection (2) of this section, the duty to make good the surface of a footpath or bridleway imposed by section 119 (3) the Highways Act, 1959 (ploughing of footpath or bridleway) shall be carried out not later than six weeks from the date of the giving of the notice of intention to plough required by subsection (2) of the said section 119, or if, in contravention of the said subsection (2), no such notice was given, not later than three weeks from the time when the occupier began to plough the footpath or bridleway in pursuance of the said section 119.

(2) If on the application of the occupier the highway authority are satisfied that it is expedient in the interests of good farming that the period of six or three weeks mentioned in subsection (1) of this section should be extended the highway authority may—

(a) order the temporary diversion of the path or way until such date as may be specified in the order being a date not more than three months after the time when the occupier began to plough the footpath or bridleway, and

(b) by the order extend the period of six weeks or three weeks mentioned in subsection (1) of this section so as to expire on that date.

(3) On the making of the order the highway authority shall forthwith cause a copy of the order to be displayed in a prominent position at the ends of the diversion.

(4) In deciding whether to make an order under subsection (2) of this section a highway authority shall take into account the interests of the users of the path or way, and the highway authority shall before refusing to make an order under subsection (2) of this section consult the Minister of Agriculture, Fisheries and Food.

(5) An order under this section diverting a path or way—

(a) shall not affect the line of the path or way on land not occupied by the applicant,

(b) shall not divert any part of the path or way on to land not occupied by the applicant, unless written consent to the making of the order has been given by the occupier of that land, and by any other person whose consent is needed to obtain access to the land,

(c) may require as a condition of the taking effect of the order the provision of any necessary facilities for the convenient use of the diversion,

and the highway authority may enter into an agreement with the applicant for the provision of any such facilities by the highway authority at the expense of the applicant.

(6) The said section 119 shall not apply to so much of a footpath or bridleway as follows what are for the time being the headlands or sides of a field or enclosure.

(7) If a footpath or bridleway is ploughed, and the occupier has no right to plough it, or if there is a failure to comply with subsection (3) of the said section 119, the highway authority, after giving to the occupier not less than 14 days' notice of their intention, may take all necessary steps for making good the surface of the path or way so as to make it reasonably convenient for the exercise of the public right of way, and may recover from the occupier the amount of any expenses reasonably incurred by the highway authority in and in connection with the exercise of their powers under this subsection.

(8) Subsection (1) of this section shall bind the Crown.

(9) This section shall be construed as one with the Highways Act, 1959.

30. Riding of pedal bicycles on bridleways (1) Any member of the public shall have, as a right of way, the right to ride a bicycle, not being a motor vehicle, on any bridleway, but in exercising that right cyclists shall give way to pedestrians and persons on horseback.

(2) Subsection (1) above has effect subject to any orders made by a local authority, and to any byelaws.

(3) The rights conferred by this section shall not affect the obligations of the highway authority, or of any other person, as respects the maintenance of the bridleway, and this section shall not create any obligation to do anything to facilitate the use of the bridleway by cyclists.

(4) Subsection (1) above shall not affect any definition of 'bridleway' in this or any other Act.

(5) In this section 'motor vehicle' has the same meaning as in the Road Traffic Act, 1960.

(6) It is hereby declared that sections 9, 10, 11 and 13 of the said Act of 1960 (offences connected with riding of bicycles) apply to bridleways as being highways which are 'roads' within the meaning of that Act.

(7) Section 12 (1) of the said Act (prohibition of cycle racing on highways) shall have effect as if the expression 'public highway' included a bridleway, but without the exception for a race or trial authorised by regulations under that section.

49. Interpretation (1) Section 114 of the Act of 1949 shall apply for the construction of this Act.

(2) In this Act, unless the context otherwise requires—

'the Act of 1949' means the National Parks and Access to the Countryside Act, 1949;

'boat' includes any hover vehicle or craft being a vehicle or craft designed to be supported on a cushion of air and which is used on or over water;

'bridleway' and 'footpath' have the meanings given by section 295 (1) of the Highways Act, 1959;

'land' includes any interest in or right over land;

'the Minister', as respects Wales and Monmouthshire, means the Secretary of State, and otherwise means the Minister of Housing and Local Government;

'public body' includes any local authority or statutory undertaker, and any trustees, commissioners, board or other persons, who, as a public body and not for their own profit, act under any enactment for the improvement of any place or the production or supply of any commodity or service;

'river authority' means a river authority constituted by or under the Water Resources Act, 1963

and the Conservators of the River Thames, the Lee Conservancy Catchment Board and the Isle of Wight River and Water Authority; 'statutory water undertakers' has the same meaning as in the provisions of the Water Act, 1945, other than Part II of that Act.

(3) In this Act 'parish' means a rural parish and references to a parish and parish council shall be construed as including references to a borough which has been included in a rural district and the council of such a borough respectively.

(4) References in this Act to the conservation of the natural beauty of an area shall be construed as including references to the conservation of its flora, fauna and geological and physiographical features.

SCHEDULE 1

PROPOSALS SUBMITTED TO STATUTORY UNDERTAKERS AND OTHER AUTHORITIES

1. This Schedule has effect where any authority are consulted in accordance with section 8, section 12 (4) or section 16 (7) of this Act.

2.—(1) If the authority withhold their consent to the proposals about which they are consulted, the proposals shall not be proceeded with unless, on an application in that behalf specifying the proposals and the grounds for withholding consent, the Minister so directs, and subject to any conditions or modifications specified in the direction.

(2) Before giving a direction under this paragraph the Minister shall afford to the objecting authority, and the authority by whom the proposals are made, an opportunity of being heard by a person appointed by him for the purpose, and shall consider that person's report.

(3) This Schedule shall apply with the necessary modifications where the Minister in accordance with section 16 (8) of this Act consults any authority

as respects an access order to be made
by him.

SCHEDULE 2

PROCEDURE FOR TAKING COMMON LAND

1.—(1) For the purpose of enabling a
local authority to exercise their powers
under the principal section on land
taken out of the common land the
Minister may in accordance with this
Schedule authorise a local authority to
acquire any part of the common land,
including all commonable and other
rights in or over the land, and, where
the local authority already hold the
land, to appropriate that land for the
purposes of the principal section.

(2) Where the local authority already
hold the land, but subject to any commonable or other rights in or over the
land, they shall not appropriate the
land until they have, under sub-
paragraph (1) above, acquired all those
rights.

(3) Land acquired or appropriated
as authorised under this paragraph
shall be held by the local authority free
from the public right of access, but shall
be used for the benefit of the public
resorting to the common land.

(4) The Minister shall not give his
authority under this paragraph unless
he is satisfied—

(a) that there has been or will be
given in exchange for the land
other land, not being less in area
and being equally advantageous
to the persons, if any, entitled to
commonable and other rights,
and to the public, and that the
land given in exchange has been
or will be vested in the persons in
whom the land taken was
vested, and subject to the like
rights, trusts and incidents as
attached to the land taken, or

(b) that the giving in exchange of
such other land is unnecessary,
whether in the interests of the
persons, if any, entitled to
commonable or other rights or in
the interests of the public.

Preliminary notices

2.—(1) Before a local authority
apply to the Minister for authority
under paragraph 1 above as respects
any part of the common land, they
shall in two successive weeks publish
in one or more newspapers circulating
in the locality of the land a notice—

(a) stating that the local authority
propose to make the application;
(b) giving particulars of the land
which it is proposed to take out
of the common land;
(c) stating whether land has been or
is to be given in exchange, and,
if so, giving particulars of that
land, and stating the respective
areas of the land to be taken and
of the land given or to be given
in exchange.

(2) If all or any part of the land to be
taken is in a parish, the local authority
shall, not later than the time of first
publication of the notice, serve a copy
of the notice on the parish council or, in
the case of a parish not having a parish
council, on the chairman of the parish
meeting.

(3) The notice shall name a place
within the locality where a map
showing the said land, and any land
given or to be given in exchange, may
be inspected, and shall specify the time
not being less than 28 days from first
publication of the notice) within which
and the manner in which representations with respect to the proposals in the
notice may be made to the Minister.

(4) The Minister shall before giving
his decision on the application take into
consideration every representation
which has been duly made and which
has not been withdrawn, and may if he
thinks fit either afford to each person
making such a representation an
opportunity of appearing before and
being heard by a person appointed by
the Minister for the purpose, or cause a
public inquiry to be held.

Compulsory purchase

3.—(1) A local authority shall have
power to acquire compulsorily any land

which is required by them for the purposes of their functions under the principal section, and which is part of the common land (or any commonable or other rights in or over that land), but the Minister shall not confirm a compulsory purchase order made in pursuance of this section except after giving his authority under paragraph 1 above as respects the land.

(2) Any notice which relates to a compulsory purchase order made in pursuance of this paragraph and which is published or served under paragraph 3 of Schedule 1 to the Acquisition of Land (Authorisation Procedure) Act, 1946 shall refer to the provisions of this Schedule and shall state whether land has been, or is to be, given in exchange.

(3) The notice to be published under paragraph 2 of this Schedule may be combined with a notice to be published under the said paragraph 3 in the Act of 1946 in the same newspaper and relating to the same land.

(4) If land has been, or is to be, given in exchange—

(a) the notice to be published and served under the said paragraph 3 in the Act of 1946 shall give particulars of that land and state the respective areas of the land to be taken and of the land given or to be given in exchange,

(b) the map in the compulsory purchase order shall show that land,

(c) the compulsory purchase order may provide for vesting any land to be given in exchange in the persons, and subject to the rights, trusts and incidents, mentioned in paragraph 1 (4) above.

(5) A compulsory purchase order made in pursuance of this paragraph may provide for discharging the land purchased from all rights, trusts and incidents to which it was previously subject.

(6) Paragraph 11 of Schedule 1 to the Acquisition of Land (Authorisation Procedure) Act, 1946 (special provisions for acquisition of common land) shall not apply to a compulsory purchase order made in pursuance of this paragraph, and section 22 of the Commons Act, 1899 (consent of Minister required for purchase of common land) shall not apply to the acquisition of land in pursuance of such a compulsory purchase order.

Acquisition by agreement and appropriation

4.—(1) A local authority shall not acquire by agreement, or appropriate, any common land for the purposes of the principal section except as authorised under paragraph 1 of this Schedule.

(2) Subject to sub-paragraph (1) above, a local authority may appropriate any common land for the purposes of the principal section without compliance with the provisions of section 163 of the Local Government Act, 1933 or section 104 of the Act of 1949 as amended by section 23 of the Town and Country Planning Act, 1959 (under which the approval of the Minister is required).

(3) On an appropriation of land under this paragraph such adjustment shall be made in the accounts of the local authority as the Minister may direct.

Power to override restrictions affecting common land

5. No restrictions applying to commons generally, or to any particular common, contained in or having effect under any enactment, and no trust subject to which the common land is held, shall prevent a local authority from taking part of common land in accordance with this Schedule.

Protection for statutory undertakers

6. References in this Schedule to commonable and other rights in or over common land shall not be taken as including references to any right vested in statutory undertakers for the purpose of the carrying on of their undertaking.

Interpretation

7. In this Schedule 'common land' has the meaning given by section 22 (1) of the Commons Registration Act, 1965.

SCHEDULES

PUBLIC RIGHTS OF WAY

PART 1

MISCELLANEOUS ENACTMENTS

HIGHWAYS ACT 1959

Section112 (5) (public path diversion order made at instance of Minister)

Where under section 112 (5) the Minister directs an authority to make a public path diversion order or decides himself to make a public path diversion order, the local authority, or as the case may be the Minister, may require the owner, lessee or occupier on whose representations the Minister is acting to enter into an agreement with the local authority (that is to say, both where the local authority are directed to make the order and where the Minister himself is to make the order, the 'appropriate authority' as defined in section 112 (7)) for the owner, lessee or occupier to defray, or to make such contribution as may be specified in the agreement towards, any such compensation or expenses as are specified in paragraphs (a), (b) and (c) or section 111 (4) of the Act of 1959.

Section 126 (authority for erection of stiles etc. in footpath or bridleway)

In section 126 references to agricultural land, and to land being brought into use for agriculture, shall include references to land used, or as the case may be land being brought into use, for forestry.

Schedule 7 (Orders for creation, extinguishment or diversion of public paths)

1. Paragraph 2 of the Schedule shall have effect as respects any order not made by the Minister, as defined in this Act, subject as follows.

2. If no representations or objections are duly made, or if any so made are withdrawn, the authority by whom the order was made may, instead of submitting the order to the Minister, themselves confirm the order (but without any modification).

3. The authority shall not confirm a public path extinguishment order or a public path diversion order unless satisfied on all the matters on which the Minister must, under section 110 (2), or as the case may be section 111 (5), of the Act be satisfied when it is the Minister who is confirming the order.

4. *Makes consequential verbal amendments*

5. Section 286 (2) of the Act of 1959 (variation or revocation of orders) shall apply to a public path creation order, a public path extinguishment order, or a public path diversion order, confirmed as an unopposed order as it applies to such an order confirmed by the Minister, but so that an order confirmed in either way may be revoked or varied by a subsequent order confirmed in the other way.

6. In paragraph 3 (1) of the said Schedule 7 (regulations about procedure) the word 'making' shall be inserted before 'submission and confirmation'.

7. These amendments of the Act of 1959 shall not affect an order made before the coming into force of this Act.

PART II

REVISION OF MAPS AND STATEMENTS

1. Any review of further begun under section 33 of the Act of 1949 after the coming into force of this Act shall be carried out in accordance with this Part of this Schedule, and subsections (1) and (2) of section 34 of the Act of 1949 shall not apply to it.

2.—(1) Before carrying out the review the authority shall consult with the councils of county districts and parishes in the area of the authority as to the arrangements to be made for the provision by the councils of information for the purposes of the review, and subsections (2), (3) and (4) of section 28 of the Act of 1949 shall apply to the arrangements.

(2) If the authority is a joint planning board the reference in subparagraph (1) above to the councils of county districts and parishes shall include a reference to the council of every county or county borough wholly or partly comprised in the area of the board.

3. The review shall include the preparation of a revised map and statement in draft.

4.—(1) On completing the preparation of the draft map and statement (hereafter called the 'draft revision') the authority shall notify the Minister and shall publish in the London Gazette and in one or more newspapers circulating in the area of the authority a notice of the preparation of the draft revision stating—

    (a) the places where copies of the draft revision can be inspected at all reasonable hours,

    (b) the time (not being less than 28 days) within which, and the manner in which, representations or objections with respect to alterations effected by the draft revision, or to anything omitted therefrom, may be made to the Minister.

(2) If the alterations effected by the draft revision include a new item showing a public path, or a road used as a public path, or any alteration of the particulars concerning a public path, or road used as a public path, section 29 (2) of the Act of 1949 (right of owner and other interested persons to require the authority to give information about documents taken into account by the authority) shall apply with any necessary modifications.

(3) If any representation or objection is duly made in respect of alterations effected by the draft revision, or of anything omitted therefrom, and is not withdrawn, the Minister shall cause a local inquiry to be held.

(4) If any such representation or objection is duly made, and is not withdrawn, the Minister shall, subject to the following provisions of this paragraph, and after taking into consideration any report by the person appointed to hold the local inquiry, take a decision on the objection or representation, and if he considers that the draft revision should be modified to give effect to his decision he shall give to the authority such directions as appear to him necessary for the purpose.

(5) If it appears to the Minister that any modification which he proposes to make under sub-paragraph (4) above may adversely affect any persons other than the person who made the representation or objection, he shall, before giving any direction to the authority, afford to those persons an opportunity of being heard by a person appointed by the Minister.

5.—(1) This paragraph has effect as respects the revised map and statement, if any, to be prepared under subsection (4) or proviso (d) of subsection (5) of section 33 of the Act of 1949 (map and statement to be prepared on completion of the review except where there is no change).

(2) The map and statement shall be prepared as soon as may be after the time prescribed by the notice under paragraph 4 (1) (b) above, and after any representations or objections duly made, and not withdrawn, have been dealt with by the Minister.

(3) The authority shall publish in the London Gazette and in one or more newspapers circulating in the area of the authority notice of the preparation of the map and statement, and of places where copies of the map and statement may be inspected at all reasonable hours.

(4) The particulars to be contained in the map and statement shall be those contained in the draft revision, subject to such modifications as may be required for giving effect to any direction given by the Minister under paragraph 4 (4) above.

(5) The authority shall furnish to the Minister such number of copies of the revised map and statement, as prepared in definitive form, as he may require.

(6) Subsections (4), (5) and (6) of section 32 of the Act of 1949 (effect of definitive maps and statements) shall apply to the said revised map and statement as they apply to an (unrevised) definitive map and statement.

6. This Part of this Schedule shall be construed as one with section 33 of the Act of 1949.

PART III

ROADS USED AS PUBLIC PATHS

The special review

7. In this Part of this Schedule the 'special review' carried out by any authority means the first review begun by that authority after the coming into force of this Act.

8.—(1) Subject to the provisions of this paragraph, the draft revision in the special review shall be published not later than three years after the date of the coming into force of this Act.

(2) If on the said date the authority have not completed a survey or revision begun earlier—

(a) the draft revision in the special review shall be published not later than three years after the date of the coming into force of this Act, or one year after notice is published of the completion of the survey or earlier review, whichever is the later,

(b) the special review (hereafter in this Schedule called a 'limited special review') shall be confined to a review of roads used as public paths in accordance with this Part of this Schedule:

Provided that if on a review begun before the date of the coming into force of this Act no revised map and statement has been published in draft before that date, the review shall be abandoned, and shall be begun again under Part II of this Schedule as the special review.

(3) If it appears to the Minister that any stage of a special review has been or is likely to be unduly delayed, he may give to the authority such directions as appear to the Minister appropriate for expediting the review, and it shall be the duty of the authority to comply with the directions.

Reclassification of roads used as public paths

9.—(1) In the special review the draft revision, and the definitive map and statement, shall show every road used as a public path by one of the three following descriptions—

(a) a 'byway open to all traffic',
(b) a 'bridleway',
(c) a 'footpath',

and shall not employ the expression 'road used as a public path' to describe any way.

(2) As from the date of publication of the definitive map and statement in the special review—

(a) each way shown in the map in pursuance of this paragraph by any of the three descriptions shall be a highway maintainable at the public expense,

(b) subject to paragraph (c) below, any entry in the map describing a way as a 'byway open to all traffic' shall be conclusive evidence of the existence on the date of publication of a public right of way for vehicular and all other kinds of traffic,

(c) section 32 (4) (c) of the Act of 1949 (position and width, and limitations or conditions affecting the public right of way, as shown in the statement) shall apply to any byway so shown as it applies to a footpath or bridleway.

(3) In this paragraph 'road used as a public path' means—

(a) a way which is shown as a 'road used as a public path' in the last definitive map and statement, or

(b) a way which is shown as a 'bridleway' or as a 'footpath' in the last definitive map and statement, and which in the opinion of the authority ought to have been there shown as a road used as a public path, or

(c) where the special review is not a limited special review, a way which in the opinion of the authority would, but for the provisions of this Part of this Schedule, have fallen to be shown, in the definitive map and statement resulting from the special review, as a road used as a public path.

(4) In subsection (2) (*a*) and in subsection (5) of section 51 of the Act of 1949 (long distance routes) references to roads used as public paths shall include references to any way shown on a definitive map and statement as a 'byway open to all traffic'.

(5) Nothing in this paragraph shall limit the operation of road traffic orders under the Road Traffic Regulation Act, 1967 or oblige a highway authority to provide, on a way shown on a definitive map as a 'byway open to all traffic', a metalled carriageway, or a carriageway which is by any other means provided with a surface suitable for the passage of vehicles.

Test for reclassification

10. The considerations to be taken into account in deciding in which class a road used as a public path is to be put shall be—

- (*a*) whether any vehicular right of way has been shown to exist,
- (*b*) whether the way is suitable for vehicular traffic having regard to the position and width of the existing right of way, the condition and state of repair of the way, and the nature of the soil,
- (*c*) where the way has been used by vehicular traffic, whether the extinguishment of vehicular rights of way would cause any undue hardship.

Procedure on special review

11.—(1) Part II of this Schedule shall apply to a special review subject as follows.

(2) The published notices shall state that the review reclassifies roads used as public paths.

(3) The representations or objections referred to in paragraph 4 in Part II shall include representations or objections with respect to the reclassification of any road used as a public path.

(4) The time, as stated in the published notice of the draft revision, within which any representation or objection (of any description) may be made to the draft revision shall not be less than four months.

Survey begun after commencement of Act

12.—(1) Subject to the provisions of this paragraph, paragraphs 9 and 10 above shall apply to an initial survey begun after the coming into force of this Act as if it were the first review so begun.

(2) In paragraph 9 (1), as applied to the survey, for references to the draft revision and the definitive map and statement there shall be substituted references to the map and statement in drift, provisional and definitive form, and in paragraphs 9 and 10, as applied to the survey, 'road used as a public path' shall mean a way which in the opinion of the authority would, but for the provisions of this Part of this Schedule, have fallen to be shown, in the definitive map and statement resulting from the survey, as a road used as a public path.

Interpretation and construction

13.—(1) In this Part of this Schedule references to a definitive map and statement include references to a revised map and statement prepared in definitive form.

(2) This Part, and Part IV, of this Schedule shall be construed as one with Part IV of the Act of 1949.

Town and Country Planning Act, 1968

Stopping-up and diversion of highways
89. Transfer of Ministerial functions as to stopping up etc. of footpaths and bridleways (1)

Section 153 of the principal Act (power of Minister of Transport to make orders authorising the stopping-up or diversion of highways in order to enable development to be carried out) shall be amended in accordance with this section.

(2) The power conferred on the Minister of Transport by section 153 (1) of the principal Act to make an order authorising the stopping-up or diversion of a highway, where he is satisfied that it is necessary to do so in order to enable development to be carried out as mentioned in that subsection, shall, in the case of a footpath or bridleway, be exercisable also by the Minister of Housing and Local Government where that Minister is so satisfied; and the Minister of Transport shall not make an order under that subsection in the case of a footpath or bridleway unless, at the time when he first publishes notice of the order in accordance with section 154 (1) of the principal Act, it appears to him to be necessary for the said purpose also to authorise the topping-up or diversion of some others highway, not being a footpath or bridleway.

(3) Subsection (2) of the said section 153 shall not apply to an order made thereunder by the Minister of Housing and Local Government; but an order so made may make such provision as appears to the Minister to be necessary or expedient for the creation of an alternative highway for use as a replacement for the one authorised by the order to be stopped-up or diverted, or for the improvement of an existing highway for such use.

(4) In relation to an order made by the Minister of Housing and Local Government under section 153 of the principal Act, subsection (3) of that section and section 154 of the Act (procedure and publicity for orders under section 153) shall apply with the substitution of references to that Minister for references to the Minister of Transport; and in subsections (4) and (5) of section 153 references to the latter shall be construed as including references to the former.

(5) In section 32 of the Mineral Workings Act, 1951 (power of Minister of Transport to make temporary stopping-up or diversion order in connection with surface working of minerals),—

(a) in subsection (1), after the words 'Minister of Transport' there shall be inserted the words 'or the Minister of Housing and Local Government'; and

(b) in subsection (2), after the words 'Minister of Transport' there shall be inserted the words 'or the Minister of Housing and Local Government, as the case may be'.

(6) In this Act, 'footpath' and 'bridleway' have the same meanings as in the Highways Act, 1959.

(7) Nothing in this section applies to or affects an order made by the Minister of Transport before the commencement of this section, or an order with respect to which he has, before that commencement, published in the London Gazette the notice required by section 154 (1) of the principal Act.

(8) This section shall not apply to Wales.

90. Procedure for making orders for stopping-up and diverting highways (1) Where the responsible Minister would, if planning permission for any development had been granted under Part III of the principal Act, have power to make an order under section 153 (1) of that Act authorising the stopping-up or diversion of a highway in order to enable that development to be carried out, then, notwithstanding that such permission has not been granted, that Minister may, in the circumstances specified in subsections (2) to (4) below, publish notice of the draft of such an order in accordance with section 154 of that Act (procedure in relation to orders under section 153).

(2) The responsible Minister may publish such a notice as aforesaid where the relevant development is the subject of an application for planning permission and either—

(a) that application is made by a local authority or statutory undertakers or the National Coal Board; or

(b) that application stands referred to the Minister of Housing and Local Government or the Secretary of State in pursuance of a direction under section 22 of the principal Act; or

(c) the applicant has appealed to the Minister of Housing and Local Government or the Secretary of State under section 23 of that Act against a refusal of planning permission or of approval required under a development order, or against a condition of any such permission or approval.

(3) The responsible Minister may publish such a notice as aforesaid where—

(a) the relevant development is to be carried out by a local authority, statutory undertakers or the National Coal Board and requires, by virtue of an enactment, the authorisation of a government department; and

(b) the developers have made application to the department for that authorisation and also requested a direction under section 41 of the principal Act or, in the case of the National Coal Board, under section 2 of the Opencast Coal Act, 1958, that planning permission be deemed to be granted for that development.

(4) The responsible Minister may publish such a notice as aforesaid where the council of a county . . . certify that they have begun to take such steps, in accordance with regulations made by virtue of section 42 of the principal Act (application of planning control to local planning authorities), as are requisite in order to enable them to obtain planning permission for the relevant development.

(5) Section 154 (4) of that Act (power of responsible Minister to make an order under section 153 after considering any relevant objections and report) shall not be construed as authorising the responsible Minister to make an order under section 153 (1) of that Act of which notice has been published by virtue of subsection (1) above until planning permission is granted for the development which occasions the making of the order.

(6) In this section 'the responsible Minister' means, except in relation to Wales,—

(a) in relation to an order authorising the stopping-up or diversion of a footpath or bridleway only, the Minister of Housing and Local Government; and

(b) otherwise the Minister of Transport;

and, in relation to Wales, means the Secretary of State.

91. New powers to authorise stopping-up and diversion of highways (1) If planning permission is granted under Part III of the principal Act for constructing or improving, or the responsible Minister proposes to construct or improve, a highway (hereafter in this section referred to as 'the main highway'), that Minister may by order authorise the stopping-up or diversion of any other highway which crosses or enters the route of the main highway or which is, or will be, otherwise affected by the construction or improvement of the main highway, if it appears to that Minister expedient to do so—

(a) in the interests of the safety of users of the main highway; or

(b) to facilitate the movement of traffic on the main highway.

(2) In this section, 'the responsible Minister' means, except in relation to Wales, the Minister of Transport and, in relation to Wales, the Secretary of State.

(3) Sections 153 (2) to (5), 154, 156, 157 and 158 of the principal Act (ancillary provisions, provisions as to compulsory acquisition of land in connection with highways and provisions as to telegraphic lines) and section 90 above shall apply in relation

to an order under this section as they apply in relation to an order made by the Minister of Transport under section 153 (1) of that Act with the substitution in the said sections of the principal Act for references to that Minister and the said section 153 (1) of references to the responsible Minister (as defined by subsection (2) above) and this section.

(4) In section 32 (3) of the Mineral Workings Act, 1951 (rights of statutory undertakers in respect of their apparatus where order made under section 153 of principal Act), after the reference to the said section 153 there shall be inserted an alternative reference to this section.

92. Conversion of highway into footpath or bridleway (1) The provisions of this section shall have effect where a local planning authority by resolution adopt a proposal for improving the amenity of part of their area, being a proposal which involves a highway in that area (being a highway over which the public have a right of way with vehicles, but not a trunk road or a road classified as a principal road for the purposes of advances under section 235 of the Highways Act, 1959) being changed to a footpath or bridleway.

(2) The responsible Minister may, on an application made by the local planning authority after consultation with the highway authority (if different), by order provide for the extinguishment of any right which persons may have to use vehicles on that highway.

(3) An order made under subsection (2) of this section may include such provision as the responsible Minister (after consultation with the highway authority) thinks fit for permitting the use on the highway of vehicles (whether mechanically propelled or not) in such cases as may be specified in the order, notwithstanding the extinguishment of any such right as is mentioned in that subsection; and any such provision may be framed by reference to particular descriptions of vehicles, or to particular persons by whom, or on

whose authority, vehicles may be used, or to the circumstances in which, or the times at which, vehicles may be used for particular purposes.

(4) No statutory provision prohibiting or restricting the use of footpaths, footways or bridleways shall affect any use of a vehicle on a highway in relation to which an order made under subsection (2) above has effect, where the use is permitted in accordance with provisions of the order included by virtue of subsection (3) above.

(5) Any person who, at the time of an order under subsection (2) of this section coming into force, has an interest in land having lawful access to a highway to which the order relates shall be entitled to be compensated by the local planning authority in respect of any depreciation in the value of his interest which is directly attributable to the order and of any other loss or damage which is so attributable.

In this subsection 'lawful access' means access authorised by planning permission granted under the principal Act or the Town and Country Planning Act, 1947, or access in respect of which no such permission is necessary.

(6) A claim for compensation under subsection (5) above shall be made to the local planning authority within the time and in the manner prescribed by regulations under the principal Act.

(7) Sections 153 (2), (3) and (5), 154 156, 157 and 158 of the principal Act (provisions ancillary to section 153 (1), provisions as to compulsory acquisition of land in connection with highways, and provisions as to telegraphic lines) shall apply in relation to an order under this section, as they apply in relation to an order under section 153 (1) of that Act, with the substitution for references to the Minister of Transport and that section of references to the responsible Minister and this section.

(8) The responsible Minister may, on an application made by the local planning authority after consultation with the highway authority (if different) by order revoke an order made by him

T

in relation to a highway under subsection (2) above; and the effect of the order shall be to reinstate any right to use vehicles on the highway, being a right which was extinguished by virtue of the order under the said subsection.

(9) Subsection (8) above shall not be taken as prejudicing any provision of the principal Act enabling orders to be varied or revoked.

(10) In this section—

(a) 'the responsible Minister' means, except in relation to Wales, the Minister of Transport and, in relation to Wales, the Secretary of State; and

(b) 'statutory provision' means a provision contained in, or having effect under, any enactment.

93. Provision of amenity for highway reserved to pedestrians
(1) Where in relation to a highway an order has been made under subsection (2) of section 92 of this Act, a competent authority may carry out and maintain any such works on or in the highway, or place on or in it any such objects or structures, as appear to them to be expedient for the purposes of giving effect to the order or of enhancing the amenity of the highway and its immediate surroundings or to be otherwise desirable for a purpose beneficial to the public.

(2) The powers exercisable by a competent authority under this section shall extend to laying out any part of the highway with lawns, trees, shrubs and flower-beds and to providing facilities for recreation or freshment.

(3) A competent authority may so exercise their powers under this section, as to restrict the access of the public to any part of the highway, but shall not so exercise them as—

(a) to prevent persons from entering the highway at any place where they could enter it before the order under section 92 was made; or

(b) to prevent the passage of the public along the highway; or

(c) to prevent normal access by pedestrians to premises adjoining the highway; or

(d) to prevent any use of vehicles which is permitted by an order made under the said section 92 and applying to the highway; or

(e) to prevent statutory undertakers from having access to any works of theirs under, in, on, over, along or across the highway.

(4) An order under subsection (8) of the said section 92 may make provision requiring the removal of any obstruction of the highway resulting from the exercise by a competent authority of their powers under this section.

(5) The competent authorities for the purposes of this section are—

(a) the councils of counties, county boroughs and county districts;... but such an authority shall not exercise any powers conferred by this section unless they have obtained the consent of the local planning authority and the highway authority (in a case where they are themselves not that authority).

94. Powers for local authorities analogous to s. 153 of principal Act
(1) Subject to section 96 below, a competent authority may by order authorise the stopping-up or diversion of any footpath or bridleway if they are satisfied that it is necessary to do so in order to enable development to be carried out—

(a) in accordance with planning permission granted under Part III of the principal Act or the enactments replaced by that Part of the Act; or

(b) by a government department.

(2) The competent authorities for the purposes of this section are—

(a) the local planning authority; and

(b) in relation to development for which planning permission was granted by another authority to whom had been delegated the power of granting it, that other authority.

(3) An order under this section may, if the competent authority are satisfied that it should do so, provide—

(a) for the creation of an alternative highway for use as a replacement for the one authorised by the order to be stopped up or diverted, or for the improvement of an existing highway for such use;

(b) for authorising or requiring works to be carried out in relation to any footpath or bridleway for whose stopping-up or diversion, creation or improvement, provision is made by the order;

(c) for the preservation of any rights of statutory undertakers in respect of apparatus of theirs which immediately before the date of the order is under, in, on, over, along or across any such footpath or bridleway;

(d) for requiring any person named in the order to pay, or make contributions in respect of, the cost of carrying out any such works.

(4) The powers of a competent authority under this section shall include power to make an order authorising the stopping-up or diversion of a footpath or bridleway which is temporarily stopped up or diverted under any other enactment.

(5) Section 32 (1) and (2) of the Mineral Workings Act, 1951 (power of Ministers to make temporary order for stopping-up or diversion of highway in connection with working of surface minerals) shall apply to an order made by a competent authority under this section as it applies to an order made by a Minister under section 153 of the principal Act, with the substitution—

(a) for references to Ministers, of references to a competent authority for the purposes of this section; and

(b) for the reference in subsection (2) to section 153 (3) of the principal Act, of a reference to subsection (3) of this section.

95. Extinguishment of footpaths etc. over land held for planning purposes (1) Subject to section 96 below, where any land has been acquired or appropriated for planning purposes and is for the time being held by a local authority for the purposes for which it was acquired or appropriated, the authority may by order extinguish any public right of way over the land, being a footpath or bridleway, if they are satisfied that an alternative right of way has been or will be provided, or that the provision of an alternative right of way is not required.

(2) Any reference in subsection (1) above to the acquisition of land for planning purposes is a reference to the acquisition thereof under section 68 or 71 of the principal Act or section 28 of this Act; and any reference to the appropriation thereof for purposes for which land can, or could have been, acquired under those sections.

96. Confirmation, validity, etc. of orders under ss. 94 and 95 (1) An order under section 94 or 95 of this Act shall not take effect unless confirmed by the Minister, or unless confirmed, as an unopposed order, by the authority who made it.

(2) The Minister shall confirm any such order unless satisfied as to every matter of which the authority making the order are required under section 94 or 95 (as the case may be) to be satisfied.

(3) The time specified—

(a) in an order under section 94 above as the time from which a footpath or bridleway is to be stopped up or diverted; or

(b) in an order under section 95 above as the time from which a right of way is to be extinguished.

shall not be earlier than confirmation of the order.

(4) Schedule 7 to this Act shall have effect with respect to the confirmation

of orders under section 94 or 95 of this Act and the publicity for such orders after they are confirmed.

97. Miscellaneous amendments of Part IX of principal Act (1) It is hereby declared for the avoidance of doubt that the incidental and consequential provisions which may be included in an order under section 153 of the principal Act or section 91 or 92 above by virtue of section 153 (3) of that Act shall include provisions providing for the preservation of any rights of statutory undertakers in respect of any apparatus of theirs which immediately before the date of the order is under, in, on, over, along or across the highway to which the order relates.

(2) In section 154 (1) (*b*) and (3) of the principal Act (periods for inspecting and objecting to a draft order under section 153) for the words 'three months' there shall be substituted the words 'twenty-eight days'.

(3) Subsections (2) to (5) of section 290 of the Local Government Act, 1933 (evidence and costs at local inquiries shall apply in relation to any inquiry caused to be held by any Minister of the Crown under the said section 154 (3) as they apply in relation to an inquiry caused to be held by a department under subsection (1) of the said section 290, with the substitution for the references to a department of references to the Minister.

SCHEDULE 7

Section 96

Procedure in Connection with Orders relating to Footpaths and Bridleways

Part I

Confirmation of Orders

1.—(1) Before an order under section 94 or 95 of this Act is submitted to the Minister for confirmation or confirmed as an unopposed order, the authority by whom the order was made shall give notice in the prescribed form—

(*a*) stating the general effect of the order and that it has been made and is about to be submitted for confirmation or to be confirmed as an unopposed order;

(*b*) naming a place in the area in which the land to which the order relates is situated where a copy of the order may be inspected free of charge at all reasonable hours; and

(*c*) specifying the time (not being less than twenty-eight days from the date of the first publication of the notice) within which, and the manner in which, representations or objections with respect to the order may be made.

(2) Subject to sub-paragraph (4) below, the notice to be given under sub-paragraph (1) above shall be given—

(*a*) by publication in the London Gazette and in at least one local newspaper circulating in the area in which the land to which the order relates is situated; and

(*b*) by serving a like notice on—

(i) every owner, occupier and lessee (except tenants for a month or a period less than a month and statutory tenants within the meaning of the Rent Act, 1968) of any of that land,

(ii) every council, the council of every rural parish and the parish meeting of every rural parish not having a separate parish council, being a council or parish whose area includes any of that land; and

(iii) any statutory undertakers to whom there belongs, or by whom there is used, for the purposes of their undertaking, any apparatus under, in, on, over, along or across that land; and

(*c*) by causing a copy of the notice to be displayed in a prominent position at the ends of so much of any footpath or bridleway as is to be stopped up, diverted or extinguished by virtue of the order.

(3) In the foregoing sub-paragraph 'council' means a county council, a county borough council, a county district council, the Greater London Council or a London borough council.

(4) Except in the case of an owner, occupier or lessee being a local authority or statutory undertakers, the Minister may in any particular case direct that it shall not be necessary to comply with sub-paragraph (2) (b) (i) above; but if he so directs in the case of any land, then in addition to publication the notice shall be addressed to 'the owners and any occupiers' of the land (describing it) and a copy or copies of the notice shall be affixed to some conspicuous object or objects on the land.

(5) Where under this paragraph a notice is required to be served on an owner of land and the land belongs to an ecclesiastical benefice, a like notice shall be served on the Church Commissioners.

2. If no representations or objections are duly made, or if any so made are withdrawn, the authority by whom the order was made may, instead of submitting the order to the Minister, themselves confirm the order (but without any modification).

3.—(1) If any representation duly made in not withdrawn, the Minister shall, before confirming the order, if the objection is made by a local authority cause a local inquiry to be held, and in any other case either—

    (a) cause a local inquiry to be held; or

    (b) afford to any person by whom any representation or objection has been duly made and not withdrawn an opportunity of being heard by a person appointed by the Minister for the purpose,

and, after considering the report of the person appointed to hold the inquiry or to hear representations or objections, may confirm the order, with or without modifications:

Provided that in the case of an order under section 94 of this Act, if objection is made by statutory undertakers on the ground that the order provides for the creation of a public right of way over land covered by works used for the purpose of their undertaking, or over the curtilage of such land, and the objection is not withdrawn, the order shall be subject to special parliamentary procedure.

(2) Notwithstanding anything in the foregoing provisions of this paragraph, the Minister shall not confirm an order so as to affect land not affected by the order as submitted to him, except after—

    (a) giving such notice as appears to him requisite of his proposal so to modify the order, specifying the time (not being less than twenty-eight days from the date of the first publication of the notice) within which, and the manner in which, representations or objections with respect to the proposal may be made;

    (b) holding a local inquiry or affording to any person by whom any representation or objection has been duly made and not withdrawn an opportunity of being heard by a person appointed by the Minister for the purpose; and

    (c) considering the report of the person appointed to hold the inquiry or to hear representations or objections as the case may be;

and, in the case of an order under section 94 of this Act, if objection is made by statutory undertakers on the ground that the order as modified would provide for the creation of a public right of way over land covered by works used for the purposes of their undertaking, or over the curtilage of such land, and the objection is not withdrawn, the order shall be subject to special parliamentary procedure.

4.—(1) The Minister shall not confirm an order under section 94 of this Act which extinguishes a right of way over land under, in, on, over, along or across which there is any apparatus belonging to or used by statutory undertakers for the purpose of their undertaking, unless the undertakers have consented to the confirmation of the order; and any such consent may be given subject to the condition that there are included in the order such provisions for the protection of the undertakers as they may reasonably require.

(2) The consent of statutory undertakers to any such order shall not be unreasonably withheld; and any question arising under this paragraph whether the withholding of consent is unreasonable, or whether any requirement is reasonable, shall be determined by whichever Minister is the appropriate Minister in relation to the statutory undertakers concerned.

5. Regulations under this Act may, subject to this Part of this Schedule, make such provision as the Minister thinks expedient as to the procedure on the making, submission and confirmation of orders under sections 94 and 95 of this Act.

Parish Councils and Burial Authorities (Miscellaneous Provisions) Act, 1970
[29th May, 1970]

1. Maintenance of private graves (1) A burial authority or a local authority may agree with any person in consideration of the payment of a sum by him, to maintain—

(a) a grave, vault, tombstone, or other memorial in a burial ground or crematorium provided or maintained by the authority;

(b) a monument or other memorial to any person situated in any place within the area of the authority to which the authority have a right of access;

so, however, that no agreement or, as the case may be, none of the agreements made under this subsection by any authority with respect to a particular grave, vault, tombstone, monument or other memorial, may impose on the authority an obligation with respect to maintenance for a period exceeding 99 years from the date of that agreement.

(2) On the transfer of a burial ground or crematorium or of responsibility for the maintenance of a burial ground to a burial authority or local authority, any person who was responsible before the transfer for the maintenance of the burial ground or crematorium may transfer to the

authority any assets held by him for the general purpose of the maintenance of the burial ground or crematorium, other than any such assets the devolution of which is affected by any condition of a trust, being a condition relating to the maintenance of a particular grave, vault, tombstone or other memorial.

(3) If assets are transferred to an authority by any person under subsection (2) of this section, any agreement binding on that person and made with a third party for the maintenance of any grave, vault, tombstone or other memorial in the burial ground or crematorium to which those assets relate shall also be binding on the authority.

(4) In this section, the expression "local authority" shall be construed as if contained in the Local Government Act 1933, but it shall also be deemed, for the purposes of this section, to include the Council of the Isles of Scilly.

2. Form of grants Where a burial authority has power under any enactment (whether local or general) to grant, with respect to a burial ground, any right relating to burial, the construction and use of a vault or other place of burial, or the placing of any tombstone or other memorial therein, that right may be granted under the hand of the town clerk, clerk, or other authorised officer of the burial authority.

3. Signs etc (1) In this section references to "highway authority", "traffic sign", "road", "public service vehicles", "footpaths" and "bridleway" shall be construed in like manner as if they were contained in the Road Traffic Regulation Act 1967 and section 67 of that Act shall have effect in relation to references in this section to a highway authority as it has effect in relation to references thereto in sections 55, 56, 56A, 61, 62 and 63 of that Act.

(2) A parish council may with the permission of the highway authority and subject to any conditions imposed by that authority provide on or near any road (other than a footpath or bridleway), or may contribute either wholly or in part towards the cost of providing on or near any road (other than a footpath or bridleway), traffic signs indicating—

(a) a stopping place for public service vehicles;
(b) a warning of the existence of any danger; or
(c) the name of the parish or of any place therein.

(3) A parish council may provide or contribute either wholly or in part towards the cost of providing, on or near any footpath or bridleway any object or device not being a traffic sign for conveying to users of that footpath or bridleway warnings of the existence of danger.

(4) No traffic sign, object or device provided by a parish council in pursuance of this section shall be placed on any land (not being a road or part thereof) without the consent of the owner and occupier thereof.

(5) Nothing in this section shall prejudice the exercise by the highway authority or the appropriate Minister of their powers under section 61 of the Road Traffic Regulation Act 1967

(Removal of traffic signs, etc.), but in the case of any such object or device as is mentioned in subsection (1) of that section, being such an object or device provided by a parish council in pursuance of this section on land which the council neither owns nor occupies, the powers conferred on the highway authority by the said subsection (1) shall be exercisable in relation to the parish council instead of in relation to the owner or occupier of the land; but, for the purpose of complying with a notice under that subsection which, by virtue of this subsection, requires a parish council to remove any such object or device, the council may enter any land and exercise such other powers as may be necessary for that purpose.

(6) A parish council may warn the public of any danger in or apprehended in their area, subject, however, in the case of a warning given by providing any traffic sign, object or device, to the provisions of subsections (2) to (4) of this section.

4. Power to amend local Acts Subsections (1), (2), (4) and (5) of section 82 of the Public Health Act 1961 shall apply for the purpose of conferring power on the Minister of Housing and Local Government to repeal or amend any such provision as is mentioned in subsection (1) of that section, being a provision appearing to him to be inconsistent with, or unnecessary in consequence of, any provision of this Act, as if references in those subsections to that Act were references to this Act.

5. Interpretation (1) In this Act references to a parish council shall be construed as including references to the council or corporation of a borough included in a rural district.

(2) In this Act "burial authority" means any body or authority exercising powers under the Burial Acts 1852 to 1906, the Public Health (Interments) Act 1879, the Cremation Acts 1902 and 1952, or any local Act relating to the provision or maintenance of a burial ground, and "burial ground" has the same meaning as in the Open Spaces Act 1906.

Index

Page references to principal entries are set in **bold** numerals; text references are set in ordinary figures, and references to the statutes are given in *italic* figures.

INSURANCE
industrial injuries, 171
litigation costs, 199
national, 171
various types, **167–8**, *414–15*, *430*
INTEREST PECUNIARY, 51
book, 52
committees, 66, *361*
declaration of, 74
disclosure of, 51
Interest
loans, short periods, 156
reborrowing, 157
sinking funds, 152, *377–8*
INTERPRETATION ACT, 1889, 193, *304*
INVESTMENTS, 105, 115
sinking funds, 152
Trustee Act, *501*

J

JOINT BOARDS
burial authorities, 284
returns, **98**
JOINT COMMITTEES, **67**
compulsory, 67, *550*
discretionary, 68, *360*
finance, 68
income tax, **161**
returns, **98**
JUSTICES' LICENCE, INNS, 266

K

KENT
land registration, 100
local acts, 209
KERBING, 215

L

LAMPLIGHTERS
national insurance, 171
LAMP-POSTS
design, 241
LANCASHIRE
local acts, 209
LANCASTER CHANCERY COURT, 24
LAND
access, **232**
accretion, **110**
allotments, adaptation, 253
appropriation by council, 116, *333*
burial grounds, 285
compulsory purchase, 286
byelaws, 232, **300**
charitable,
allotments, 115
compulsory acquisition, 231
for new towns, 198
letting, 115, *371*

compulsory acquisition, procedure, 111–2, *323*
parliamentary procedure, 202
consecrated, management, 228, *315–16*
corporate, 103, 131, 135
drainage, *see* Drainage
exchange, **114**, *371*
necessary consents, 114, *371*
grants for purchase as open spaces, 139
Inclosure Act, 1845, *295*
letting, **115**, *371*
with consent, 115, *408–9*
without consent, 115, *371*
literary institutes, **236**
local rights, 103
management by parish council, 230, *408–9*
playing fields, 230–1
Powers (Defence) Act, 1958, *431–3*
recovery, operation of time, 113
registration, 117
compulsory areas, 118
sale of, **114, 140**, *371*
application for, 212
contracts, 190
National Trust, 114
necessary consents, 114, *371*
schools, 236
scientific institutes, 236
Settlement (Facilities) Act, 1919, *331–4*
transfer, council powers, 227, *312–16*, *318*
LANES
lighting, 249
seats, 277, *426–30*
shelters, 277, *426–30*
LAUNDERETTES, 263, *405–7*
LAVATORIES, PUBLIC
provision, 215
turnstiles, **266**
LEASES
documents, 101
LEGAL BUSINESS, **199–206**
preparation of cases, 199
LEGAL PROCEEDINGS
briefs, 200
general rules, 199
representation of parish council, 200
retainers, 200
LIABILITIES
definition, *304*
miscellaneous, 161–72
LIBEL, 60
LIBRARY, 217
LICENSED PREMISES
illegal hiring, 40
meetings, 47
use of, 39
LICENCES
bodies, removal after burial, *555*
entertainments in parish hall, 162
innkeepers', **266**
meeting, **266**